THE *Virgin* ENCYCLOPEDIA OF

REGGAE

COLIN LARKIN

IN ASSOCIATION WITH MUZE UK LTD.

Dedicated to Lee Perry

First published in Great Britain in 1998 by
VIRGIN BOOKS
an imprint of Virgin Publishing Ltd
332 Ladbroke Grove, London W10 5AH
This work is Copyright © Muze UK Ltd. 1998

A catalogue record for this book is available from the British Library

ISBN 0 7535 0242 9

Written, edited and produced by
MUZE UK Ltd
to whom all editorial enquiries should be sent
Iron Bridge House, 3 Bridge Approach, Chalk Farm, London NW1 8BD

Editor In Chief: Colin Larkin
Production Editor: Susan Pipe
Editorial and Research Assistant: Nic Oliver
Copy Editor: Sarah Lavelle
Typographic Design Consultant: Roger Kohn
Special thanks to Trev Huxley, Tony Laudico, Paul Zullo
and all the Klugettes at Muze Inc.,
and to Rob Shreeve of Virgin Publishing.
Typeset by Concrete Jungle Studio
Printed and bound in Great Britain by Butler & Tanner Ltd, Frome and London

INTRODUCTION

Of all the books we have issued based on the *Encyclopedia Of Popular Music*, the original Reggae volume provoked the most congratulatory letters, probably because we were among the first to recognize this genre as being worthy of its own book. Along the way we had one or two dissenters. One male reviewer who has a name like an old tape recorder gave us a deliberately dud review. Others seemed more interested in the colour of the skin of the people who had contributed to it. One or two of the past contributors I had only met over the telephone: I didn't care whether their skin was blue or green. If they knew and loved Reggae and could follow our style sheet, that was my only requirement. This is still true today. Any person of any sex of any colour from any planet can be a contributor, if they can write.

Recently, I am flattered to see other similar books attempting to share shelf space with ours in the bookstore. We are also pleased to see some of our original contributors gain further exposure by being involved in other publications. Ultimately that is good for Reggae and for an ever evolving body of contributors.

When I went to Jamaica in 1973, I got so sunburnt I swear it altered the pigmentation of my whiter-than-white skin to not quite so white. Since that time I have never suffered from sunburn and unfortunately I like the sun too much. Similarly, the music of that time radically altered and broadened my musical taste like a cultural revolution. It was quite different from anything I had heard in the past. Can you really mix bass that high to sound as smooth as cotton wool? And can you really play on the off-beat throughout and talk over the top? Well, yes you can, and it sounds pretty amazing.

Twenty-five years on, with rap, ragga and trip-hop metamorphosing Reggae, the basic foundation is still there, growing and flourishing with a strong debt to the past. My apprenticeship in Jamaica taught me a lot and I am eternally grateful to Mark, the Lime Squash King, and Chris for my induction course in Scotty, U Roy, I Roy and for me, the master, Big Youth.

The Virgin Encyclopedia Of Reggae is one in the major series of books taken from the *Encyclopedia Of Popular Music*. Other titles already available are:

The Virgin Encyclopedia Of Fifties Music
The Virgin Encyclopedia Of Sixties Music
The Virgin Encyclopedia Of Seventies Music
The Virgin Encyclopedia Of Eighties Music
The Virgin Encyclopedia Of Popular Music
The Virgin Encyclopedia Of Indie & New Wave
The Virgin Encyclopedia Of The Blues
The Virgin Encyclopedia Of Country Music
The Virgin Encyclopedia Of Soul And R&B

ENTRY STYLE

Albums, EPs (extended play 45s), newspapers, magazines, television programmes, films and stage musicals are referred to in italics. All song titles appear in single quotes. We spell rock 'n' roll like this. There are two main reasons for spelling rock 'n' roll with 'n' as opposed to 'n'. First, historical precedent: when the term was first coined in the 50s, the popular spelling was 'n'. Second, the 'n' is not simply an abbreviation of 'and' (in which case 'n' would apply) but a phonetic representation of n as a sound. The ' ', therefore, serve as inverted commas rather than as apostrophes. The further reading section at the end of each entry has been expanded to give the reader a much wider choice of available books. These are not necessarily recommended titles but we have attempted to leave out any publication that has little or no merit.

We have also started to add videos at the ends of the entries. Again, this is an area that is expanding faster than we can easily cope with, but there are many items in the videography and further items in the filmography, which is another new section we have decided to include. Release dates in keeping with albums attempt to show the release date in the country of origin. We have also tried to include both US and UK titles where applicable.

ALBUM RATING

Due to many requests from our readers we have now decided to rate all albums. All new releases are reviewed either by myself or by our team of contributors. We also take into consideration the review ratings of the leading music journals and critics' opinions.

Our system is slightly different to most 5 Star ratings in that we rate according to the artist in question's work. Therefore, a 4 Star album from Bob Marley may have the overall edge over a 4 Star album by the Cimarons.

Our ratings are carefully made, and consequently you

will find we are very sparing with 5 Star and 1 Star albums.

Outstanding in every way. A classic and therefore strongly recommended. No comprehensive record collection should be without this album.

Excellent. A high standard album from this artist and therefore highly recommended.

Good. By the artist's usual standards and therefore recommended.

Disappointing. Flawed or lacking in some way.

Poor. An album to avoid unless you are a completist.

PLAGIARISM

In maintaining the largest text database of popular music in the world we are naturally protective of its content. We license to approved licensees only. It is both flattering and irritating to see our work reproduced without credit. Time and time again over the past few years I have read an obituary, when suddenly: hang on, I wrote that line. Secondly, it has come to our notice that other companies attempting to produce their own rock or pop encyclopedias use our material as a core. Flattering this might also be, but highly illegal. We have therefore dropped a few more textual 'depth charges' in addition to the original ones. Be warned.

ACKNOWLEDGEMENTS

Our in-house editorial team is lean and efficient. Our Database is now a fully grown child and needs only regular food, attention and love. Thanks to my team for carrying out their task with great responsibility and humour: Susan Pipe, Nic Oliver and Sarah Lavelle are simply the best. Our outside contributors are further reduced in number, as we now write most of and amend all our existing text. However, we could not function without the continuing efforts and dedication of 'Oor' Alex Ogg. Mike Kaye is still our Database doctor, and he is currently performing some major surgery on the MUZE EPM Database. Jon Staines came back to us for about ten minutes, Charlie Furniss is with us full-time at present and the Hoboken bundle Dawn Eden joined for the long haul, in between her duties as president of the Curt Boettcher appreciation society.

We almost had David Katz as a contributor but circumstances and our respective schedules did not coincide. I hope we can use his vast knowledge next time. We do, however, have our own secret weapon, Salsri Nyah. She approached us with some important corrections and

is now a valuable freelance contributor.

Other past contributors' work appears in this volume and I acknowledge once again with great thanks; Harry Hawke, Ian McC, Lol Bell-Brown, Jean Scrivener and John Masouri. Occasional entries may appear from Mike Atherton, Gavin Badderley, Alan Balfour, Michael Barnett, Johnny Black, Chris Blackford, Keith Briggs, Michael Ian Burgess, Paul M. Brown, Tony Burke, John Child, Rick Christian, Alan Clayson, Paul Cross, Norman Darwen, Roy Davenport, Peter Doggett, Kevin Eden, John Eley, Lars Fahlin, Ian Garlinge, Mike Gavin, Andy Hamilton, Mike Hughes, Arthur Jackson, Mark Jones, Simon Jones, Dave Laing, Steve Lake, Paul Lewis, Graham Lock, Chris May, Dave McAleer, Greg Moffitt, Nick Morgan, Michael Newman, Pete Nickols, Lyndon Noon, Zbigniew Nowara, James Nye, Ken Orton, Ian Peel, Dave Penny, Lionel Robinson, Johnny Rogan, Alan Rowett, Dave Sissons, Neil Slaven, Chris Smith, Steve Smith, Mitch Solomons, Mike Stephenson, Jeff Tamarkin, Ray Templeton, Gerard Tierney, John Tobler, Pete Wadeson, Pete Watson, Dave Wilson and Barry Witherden.

Record company press offices are often bombarded with my requests for biogs and review copies. Theirs is a thankless task, but thanks anyway.

Thanks for the continuing enthusiasm and co-operation of all our new colleagues at Virgin Publishing under the guidance of Rolling Stones groupie Rob Shreeve, in particular to the common-sense glamour of Roz Scott who is so sensible and glamorous. To the quite great Pete Bassett who handles our press and radio publicity, for giving clear and concise instructions, like when and where.

To our colleagues at Muze Inc., who are the business partners I always knew I wanted but never knew where to ask, and many of them are becoming good friends.

To everyone at the offices on 304 Hudson Street in New York. A new wind of change has swept through those offices in recent months and there are a lot of happy faces about. In particular to the popular new CEO Tony Laudico, the elegantly groomed Paul Zullo, Steve 'cheque's in the post' Figard, Marc 'The Ox' Miller, sensible Mike Nevins, the timid Gary Geller, Sylvia and all the other Klugettes, and of course, the consistently entertaining Trev Huxley. And lastly to my indispensable and rewarding tin lids: 'Well though you ride like lightnin', cos' man if you ride like lightnin' then you'll crash like tunda'.

Colin Larkin, April 1998

ABYSSINIANS

Formed in 1968 in Jamaica, the Abyssinians consisted of lead singer Bernard Collins, along with the brothers Lynford and Donald Manning, who had both previously been members of their brother Carlton's group, Carlton And His Shoes. The latter's 1968 recording, 'Happy Land', strongly influenced the Abyssinians' first record, 'Satta Massa Gana', a Rastafarian hymn sung partly in the ancient Ethiopian Amharic language, and recorded at Coxsone Dodd's Studio One in March 1969. 'Satta', which has been covered by dozens of artists, is a classic reggae roots song, its plangent, understated rhythm and the group's cool harmonies providing the template for the roots music that dominated the following decade. Dodd apparently saw little potential in the song at the time, however, and 'parked' it. Eventually the group saved enough money to buy the tape and release it on their own Clinch label in 1971, and the song became a huge Jamaican hit. In the wake of the song's success, Dodd released his own DJ and instrumental versions. The Abyssinians' second hit record, 'Declaration Of Rights', which featured Leroy Sibbles on backing vocals, is similarly notable for its militant lyrics, close harmony vocals and hard, rootsy rhythms. In 1972 the trio released two more singles on Clinch, 'Let My Days Be Long' and 'Poor Jason White', both recorded at Dynamic Studios, as well as a version of 'Satta', retitled 'Mabrak', which featured the group reciting passages from the Bible. Their next release, 'Yim Mas Gan' (1973), was recorded for producer Lloyd Daley and was released in the UK on the Harry J label. The group continued releasing tunes on their own label throughout the 70s, including 'Leggo Beast', Bernard Collins' solo on the 'Satta' rhythm track, 'Satta Me No Born Yah', Big Youth's DJ version of 'Satta' called 'I Pray Thee'/'Dreader Dan Dread', Dillinger's 'I Saw Esaw', and Bernard, solo again on 'Crashie Sweep Them Clean', backed with Dillinger's 'Crashie First Socialist'. Records for other producers during the same period included 'Reason Time' (c.1974) for Federal Records, 'Love Comes And Goes' (1975) for Tommy Cowan's Arab label and the Amharic 'Tenayistillin Wandimae' (1975) for Geoffrey Chung. *Forward On To Zion* was released in 1976 after being pirated in the UK, and further singles appeared on Clinch, including 'Prophecy' (1977) and 'This Land Is For Everyone' (1979). However, internal rivalries threatened the group's stability, and *Arise* was recorded under stressful conditions. Eventually, relations worsened and the members went their separate ways. Little was heard from any of them throughout the next decade, although Donald Manning, as Donald Abyssinians, released an excellent single, 'Peculiar Number', in the early 80s on his own Dahna Dimps label, and an American record company, Alligator Records, released the *Forward* compilation. By the 90s, however, the members reunited to release two excellent singles, 'African Princess' and 'Swing Low', as well as making available much of their classic back catalogue.

● ALBUMS: *Forward On To Zion* (Different 1976)★★★★, *Arise* (Tuff Gong/Clinch 1978)★★★.

● COMPILATIONS: *Forward* (Alligator/Clinch 1980)★★★, *Satta Massa Gana* (Heartbeat 1993)★★★.

ACES

The Aces were initially known as the Four Aces featuring Carl, Patrick, Clive and Barry Howard. Legend has it that the foursome were playing cricket, when Clive began strumming on a guitar and the others began singing. Their impromptu harmonies led to an association with Desmond Dekker, who, on hearing them in 1965, supported the group in an audition at Beverley's studio with Leslie Kong. The producer arranged for the group to provide backing vocals for Dekker, initially on the classic 'Get Up Adinah', credited to Desmond Dekker And The Four Aces. They provided backing on many hits, including 'The King Of Ska', which featured the group under the curious guise of Desmond And His Cherry Pies. The group's successful association with Beverley's and Dekker resulted in a number of pop and reggae hits, including '007 (Shanty Town)', 'Israelites', 'Shing A Ling', 'Pretty Africa', and the winner of the 1968 Jamaican Song Festival, 'Music Like Dirt'. By 1967 the Aces' line-up had been reduced to Barry, performing alongside James Samuels. In 1969 the success of 'Israelites' in the UK and USA led to further promotional touring, although Dekker elected to travel without the group. However, in 1970 they recorded 'Mademoiselle Ninette', which reached the reggae charts and established the group in their own right. By 1971 the modified line-up settled as a duo featuring Carl, who had returned from the USA, and Barry. In 1972 they released a version of the Little Eva classic, 'Locomotion', retitled 'Reggae Motion', which led to wry suggestions that the duo were on the wrong track. In spite of the criticism a series of hits followed, including 'Take A Look', 'Oh I Miss You', 'Call Me Number One', 'Be My Baby' and 'Sad Sad Song'. In 1973 the group released 'Working On It Night And Day' through Trojan Records, which almost crossed over into the pop chart amid accusations that the duo had abandoned their roots. Undeterred, the duo signed a short-lived partnership with EMI Records in 1975, releasing 'She's A Gypsy' and an album. By the 80s the Aces languished in obscurity, although they resurfaced briefly in 1982 with the release of 'One Way Street'.

● ALBUMS: *The World Is On Fire* (EMI 1975)★, with Desmond Dekker *The Original Reggae Hitsound* (Trojan 1985)★★★★.

ADAMS, GLEN

b. c.1950, Jamaica, West Indies. Reggae organist and vocalist Glen Adams first came to prominence in the late 60s as a solo singer and a member of the Reggae Boys/Hippy Boys, although he had spent time earlier in the decade as part of the Pioneers. His noisy, but varied, organ style made him a favourite in the studio bands of Lee Perry and Bunny Lee, and Adams was first choice for Perry's band on the UK tour that followed his 1969 hit, 'Return Of Django'. Perry was unlucky when 'A Live Injection', the most likely follow-up to 'Django', failed to chart, as Adams' playing on the record was astonishingly exciting. As part of Perry's Upsetters,

Adams backed the Wailers, and when Bob Marley took Perry's rhythm section, the Barrett Brothers, with him to Island Records, Adams remained loyally with Perry. However, by 1973-74 a new life was beckoning in the USA, and Adams began to spend more and more time in Brooklyn, issuing records on his own Capo label. He finally moved to New York permanently in 1975, working on the Clocktower and Bullwackie labels, his material betraying the new influences of soul and funk. In the early 80s he worked with rapper T Ski Valley, meeting with limited success, and appears to have retired from the business since that time.

ADMIRAL BAILEY

b. Glendon Bailey, Kingston, Jamaica, West Indies. The good-humoured Admiral, with his burly, hook-laden dancehall anthems and a taste for military uniforms, gained his break in 1986 when fellow DJ Josey Wales took him from U-Roy's King Sturgav Hi-Fi to King Jammy's. With Steely And Clevie building the new digital rhythms and a prodigious line-up of artists to cater for, the Waterhouse studio was a hub of activity; Bailey promptly broke through the ranks with a run of hit tunes beginning with 'One Scotch', duetted with Chaka Demus. Then came 'Politician', 'Chatty Chatty Mouth', 'Ballot Box' (with Josey Wales) and in 1987, 'Punany', which fell foul of an airplay ban and necessitated a 'clean' version retitled 'Healthy Body'. Further singles 'Big Belly Man', 'Jump Up', 'Top Celebrity Man' and 'Cater For Woman' continued the winning sequence throughout that year as Jammys released his debut album, *Kill Them With It*. There was work for other producers too; 'Neighbourhood Living' and 'Newsflash Time' for DJ Papa Biggy, and in 1988 tunes for Donovan Germain and Jah Life. Hits including 'No Way No Better Than Yard', 'Don't Have Me Up', 'Original Dela Move' and 'Science' maintained Jammy's presence but found him flagging in the wake of Shabba Ranks' success, prompting the assertive 'Think Me Did Done'. Sadly, *Ram Up You Party* failed to live up to expectations and he slipped into a relative decline, despite the occasional flurry of activity for Penthouse ('Help') in 1990 and Bobby Digital ('Ah Nuh Sin') a year later.

In 1993 he returned to King Jammy, the only

producer with whom he has enjoyed a consistent run of success.

● ALBUMS: *Kill Them With It* (Jammys/Live & Love 1987)★★★★, *Undisputed* (Dynamic 1988)★★★, *Ram Up You Party* (Powerhouse 1989)★★, *Born Champion* (Jammys/Live & Love 1991)★★★.

ADMIRAL TIBET

Among the more 'correct' or 'cultural' of the new dancehall singers, Tibet enshrined his approach with the title track of his Bobby Digital-produced album, *Reality Time*, which featured the lyric: 'Reality time, culture time, We want no slackness'. In the process, Tibet accomplished one of the happier compromises between the dancehall era and the Rasta/roots fundamentals inspired by Bob Marley, Burning Spear *et al*. He also recorded excellent tracks with Winston Riley and King Jammy.

● ALBUMS: *Come Into The Light* (Live & Love 1987)★★★, *The Time Is Going To Come* (Greedy Puppy 1988)★★★, *War In A Babylon* (RAS 1988)★★★★, with Thriller U *Two Good To Be True* (Blue Mountain 1990)★★★, *Reality Time* (Digital B 1991)★★★.

AFARI, YUSUS

b. J. Sinclair, *c*.1968, Jamaica, West Indies. There has been a myriad of dub poets in Jamaica, with Oku Onuora and Mutabaruka having carved a considerable niche in this particular market. Yusus Afari's recitals are comparable in both articulation and pronunciation to that of Mutabaruka. His earliest recording was produced by Courtney Cole and Barry O'Hare at the Grove Studios in Ocho Rios in the north of the island. Cole was proving to be a serious contender in the reggae field with his Roof International label, which introduced a number of new performers to the arena, including Mikey Spice and Garnett Silk. It was in combination with Silk that Afari's debut appeared; the duo covered Johnny Nash's 'I Can See Clearly Now', interspersed with verses from Afari. In 1993 Afari had recorded an album's worth of material with assistance from Maxi Priest for the track 'Work' and again with Silk for 'People Dancing'. Appearing in traditional African dress, Afari was proclaimed to be the Afromantic Honour Dread. In the spring of 1996 he accompanied fellow dub poet Mutabaruka, Tony Rebel and Uton Green on a tour of Ethiopia.

● ALBUMS: *Dancehall Baptism* (Ras 1993)★★★, *Mental Assassin* (1995)★★★.

AGGROVATORS

This was the name given by Jamaican producer Bunny Lee to whichever team of session musicians he happened to be using at any given time. Lee had named his reggae shop and record label 'Agro Sounds' in the late 60s, after hearing about the UK skinheads' adoption of the word to mean a fight or problem, and he passed on the name to his musicians. These included many artists of varying quality, but on their few long-playing releases the Aggrovators included Robbie Shakespeare (bass), Carlton 'Santa' Davis (drums), Earl 'Chinna' Smith (lead guitar), Ansel Collins (piano), Bernard 'Touter' Harvey (organ), Tony Chin (guitar), Bobby Ellis (trumpet), Vin Gordon (trombone), Tommy McCook (tenor saxophone) and Lennox Brown (alto saxophone). Lee's work came to the fore during the rocksteady period, but he achieved real prominence in the mid-70s when his 'flying cymbals' sound, originally a reaction to the then-popular American 'disco beat', was ubiquitous. Rivalling the popularity of the vocal sides of the flying-cymbal releases, were the instrumental b-side 'versions', credited to the Aggrovators and mixed by King Tubby, and it was through these Jackpot and Justice record label releases that the Aggrovators achieved fame.

● ALBUMS: *Bunny Lee Presents The Roots of Dub*, *Bunny Lee Presents Dub From The Roots*, with Tommy McCook *Brass Rockers* (Total Sounds 1975)★★★, with King Tubby *King Tubby Meets the Aggrovators At Dub Station* (Live & Love 1975)★★★★, *Meets The Revolutionaries* (Third World 1977)★★★★, *Kaya Dub* (Third World 1978)★★★, *Jammies In Lion Dub Style* (Live & Love 1978)★★★★, *Johnny In The Echo Chamber* (Attack 1989)★★★, *Dub Jackpot* (Attack 1990)★★★, *Dub Justice* (Attack 1990)★★★.

AISHA

b. Pamela Ross, *c*.1967, Wolverhampton, England. Assuming a name meaning 'life', and occasionally referred to as 'Sister Aisha', Aisha began singing at the age of eight, and through her live performances built a significant following in and around the Midlands. Demonstrating her individualism, she followed in the direction of roots music as opposed to singing sweet, soulful cover versions of R&B hits, the latter usually being the most frequent route for reggae divas. In the late 80s Aisha began recording with the Mad Professor and released 'Prophecy' on his Ariwa Sounds label. This success led to other recording sessions with female vocalists, performing conscientious lyrics and culminating with the *Roots Daughters* series, in which Aisha featured alongside the revitalized Fabian, Kofi and Sandra Cross. In 1996 Aisha released 'Hail H.I.M.', which resulted in her appearance at the Essential Music Festival in that year. This salute to Haile Selassie was followed by 'Don't Tell Me No Lies' and 'Raise Your Voice', both of which achieved acceptable placings among the ragga hits that dominated the reggae chart. Aisha's work with Norman Grant of the Twinkle Brothers led to her featuring as part of the Twinkle Showcase alongside Princess Sharifa, Kid Livi and Steve Santana.

Aisha has been showered with accolades for her accomplished performances, captivating audiences wherever she appears, and she continues to pursue a career based on her assertion that 'music comes from the root of love'.

● ALBUMS: *High Priestess* (Ariwa 1988)★★★, *Daughters Of Zion* (Twinkle 1993)★★★, *True Roots* (Ariwa 1994)★★, *Raise Your Voice* (Twinkle 1996)★★★★.

AITKEN, LAUREL

b. 1927, Cuba. Of mixed Cuban and Jamaican descent, Laurel, with his five brothers (including the veteran guitarist Bobby Aitken) and sisters, settled in his father's homeland, Jamaica, in 1938. In the 40s he earned a living singing calypso for the Jamaican Tourist Board, as visitors alighted at Kingston Harbour. By the age of 15 Aitken, like many of the early Jamaican R&B and ska singers, including Owen Gray and Jackie Edwards, entered Vere John's 'Opportunity Hour', an amateur talent contest held on Friday nights at Kingston's Ambassador Theatre. He won the show for several weeks running, and his success there led to his estab-

lishment as one of the island's most popular club entertainers.

His first sessions were for Stanley Motta's Caribbean Recording Company, where he recorded some calypso songs, the spiritual 'Roll Jordan Roll' and 'Boogie Rock'. The latter was one of the first ever Jamaican R&B/shuffle recordings. In 1958 he recorded 'Little Sheila'/'Boogie In My Bones', one of the first records produced by future Island Records boss Chris Blackwell, using a Jamaican saxophonist and a white Canadian backing band. It emerged on Blackwell's R&B label (where it spent over 12 months in the Jamaican chart), and in the UK on Starlite and, some years later, Island. Between 1958 and 1960, Aitken made a number of recordings in the pre-ska shuffle mode, including 'Bartender' and 'Brother David' for Ken Khouri, 'Judgement Day', 'More Whisky', 'Mighty Redeemer' and 'Zion' for Duke Reid, and 'Remember My Darling', 'The Saint', 'I Shall Remove', 'What A Weeping'/'Zion City Wall' and 'In My Soul' for Leslie Kong. On the strength of the popularity of these records in the UK, Aitken came to London in 1960, where he recorded a number of songs including 'Sixty Days & Sixty Nights', 'Marylee' and 'Lucille'. These were released on the entrepreneur Emile Shalett's new Blue Beat label, created to handle Jamaican music exclusively in the UK, one of its first releases being Aitken's 'Boogie Rock'. Aitken returned to Jamaica in 1963 and recorded 'Weary Wanderer' and 'Zion' for Duke Reid: these, too, were released on Blue Beat.

Back in London, he recorded for Graeme Goodall's Rio Records, which released around 20 titles by Aitken between 1964 and 1966, including 'Adam & Eve', 'Bad Minded Woman', 'Leave Me Standing' and 'We Shall Overcome', other titles appearing on the Ska Beat and Dice labels. In 1969 he enjoyed great success on Nu Beat, a subsidiary of the Palmer brothers' Pama group of labels, writing songs for other artists, including 'Souls Of Africa' for the Classics. He also recorded 'Guilty' by Tiger (which was Aitken under a different name), and enjoyed great success with his own exuberant reggae songs such as 'Woppi King', 'Haile Selassie', 'Landlords & Tenants', 'Jesse James', 'Skinhead Train', 'Rise & Fall', 'Fire In Me Wire', and the notorious 'Pussy Price', in which he bemoaned the rising cost of personal services. During this period Aitken's popularity among Britain's West Indian population was matched only by his patronage by white skinhead youths, and it is mainly with successive skinhead and mod revivals that his name and music have been preserved.

The emerging trend towards cultural and religious (i.e., Rasta) themes among a new generation of young British (and Jamaican) blacks in the early 70s sharply contrasted with Aitken's brand of simple knees-up. It was probably not to his advantage that he spent so long away from Jamaica's rapidly changing music scene, where producers such as Lee Perry and Bunny Lee were coming up with new rhythms and ideas in production almost monthly. Aitken spent the 70s in semi-retirement, gave up regular recording and moved to Leicester, performing the occasional club date, his show-stopping act undiminished despite his advancing years. He has recorded intermittently since, almost achieving a Top 40 hit with 'Rudi Got Married' for Arista in 1981, and riding for all he was worth on the 2-Tone bandwagon. UB40's *Labour Of Love* featured a cover version of 'Guilty', but since then Aitken has largely disappeared from public notice.

● ALBUMS: *Ska With Laurel* (Rio 1965)★★★, *High Priest Of Reggae* (Nu Beat 1969)★★★, with Potato 5 *Potato 5 Meet Laurel Aitken* (Gaz's 1987)★★, *Early Days Of Blue Beat, Ska And Reggae* (Bold Reprive 1988)★★★, *It's Too Late* (Unicorn 1989)★★, *Rise And Fall* (Unicorn 1989)★★, *Sally Brown* (Unicorn 1989)★★.
● VIDEOS: *Live At Gaz's Rockin' Blues* (Unicorn 1989).

ALCAPONE, DENNIS

b. Dennis Smith, 6 August 1947, Clarendon, Jamaica, West Indies. Initially inspired by U-Roy, Alcapone began DJing for El Paso Hi-Fi in 1969. He was the first DJ to enjoy success on record after U-Roy, and likewise the first to challenge his dominance. His initial records were made for youth producer and sometime ghetto dentist Keith Hudson, with titles including 'Shades Of Hudson' (1970), 'Spanish Omega' (1970), 'Revelation Version' (1970), 'Maca Version' (1970) and 'The Sky's The Limit' (1970). From 1970 to 1972 Dennis had big hits with Duke Reid, toasting his witty, half-sung, half-spoken lyrics over classic Treasure Isle rhythms and coasting to the top of the Jamaican chart with regularity. Tunes such as 'Number One Station' (1971), 'Mosquito One' (1971), 'Rock To The Beat' (1972), 'Love Is Not A Gamble' (1972), 'Wake Up Jamaica' (1972), 'The Great Woggie' (1972), 'Teach The Children' (1972) and 'Musical Alphabet' (1972), all of which were recorded at Treasure Isle, and 'Ripe Cherry' (1971) and 'Guns Don't Argue' (1971) for producer Bunny Lee, put Alcapone in the front rank of Jamaican DJs.

In the period from 1970 until he left for the UK in 1973, Alcapone's services were continually in demand. He made over 100 singles in this time and released three albums, in the process working with such producers as Coxsone Dodd, Lee Perry, Sir JJ, Winston Riley, Joe Gibbs, Prince Buster, Randy's and others. He toured Guyana in 1970 and the UK in 1972 and 1973, after having won the cup presented to the best DJ by *Swing* magazine in Jamaica. He also began production work, issuing music by himself, Dennis Brown, Augustus Pablo and Delroy Wilson. Since the mid-70s he has been less active, still finding time to record albums for Sidney Crooks, Bunny Lee and Count Shelly. In the late 80s he returned to live performance, appearing at the WOMAD festival in Cornwall and Helsinki in 1989. In 1990 he made more club appearances in the UK. Later in the year he returned to Jamaica for three months and recorded over digital rhythms for Bunny Lee. Alcapone remains the classic Jamaican toaster, on his best form capable of transforming and adding to any song he DJs, in the great toasting tradition pioneered in Jamaican dancehalls.

● ALBUMS: *Forever Version* (Studio One 1971)★★★, *Guns Don't Argue* (Attack/Trojan 1971)★★★, with Lizzy *Soul To Soul DJ's Choice* (Treasure Isle/Trojan 1973)★★★, *King Of The Track* (Magnet 1974)★★★★, *Belch It Off* (Attack 1974)★★★★, *Dread Capone* (Third World 1976)★★★, *Investigator Rock* (Third World 1977)★★★, *Six Million Dollar Man* (Third World 1977)★★★.
● COMPILATIONS: *My Voice Is Insured For Half A Million Dollars* (Trojan 1989)★★★, *Universal Rockers* (RAS 1992)★★★.

ALLEN, LILLIAN

b. 1952, Jamaica, West Indies. Arguably the finest female exponent of dub poetry, Toronto, Canada-based Allen has crafted a significant niche in the reggae market with her mastery of language, underpinned by a capable and capacious backing band. It is a music that neatly distils Allen's two principal influences, dub poet Oku Onuora and folk-singer Ferron. Her patois tales of struggle and emancipation have built a strong following in her adopted home, and she has been awarded the prestigious Juno Award.
● ALBUMS: *Revolutionary Tea Party* (Redwood 1986)★★★, *Conditions Critical* (1988)★★.

ALPHA AND OMEGA

This post-digital roots dub duo, consisting of Christine Woodbridge and John Sproson, began making music together in the mid-80s in their respective home-towns of London and Plymouth. Both had experience of reggae groups before the formation of Alpha And Omega, and Sproson had also appeared as part of the Roaring Lion sound system. They marketed their first home-recorded cassette album in 1988. Their debut album was accompanied by the 'Gather Together' single, and their second album reflected the growing reawakening of interest in roots music in general, and dub in particular. Subsequent albums built on and refined the formula, the band attracting strong press and securing sound system slots with the like-minded Jah Shaka. There was also an appearance on indie-dance band Flowered Up's 'The Reggae Song'. Finally, in 1992, they signed to Greensleeves, keeping their own A&O label as part of the contract.
● ALBUMS: *Daniel In The Lion's Den* (A&O 1990)★★★★, *King & Queen* (A&O 1991)★★★, *Overstanding* (A&O 1991)★★★, *Watch And Pray* (A&O/Greensleeves 1992)★★★, *Safe In The Ark* (A&O/Greensleeves 1993)★★★.

ALPHONSO, ROLAND

b. *c.*1936, Clarendon, Jamaica, West Indies. Alphonso attended the Alpha Catholic School For Boys where he learned tenor saxophone, flute and music theory. In 1959, he joined the studio group Clue J And His Blues Blasters, who recorded several instrumentals including 'Shuffling Jug', which many hail as the first ska record. Other members of the group included Cluett Johnson (bass), Ernest Ranglin (guitar), Theophilus Beckford (piano) and Rico Rodriguez (trombone). In 1963, he became a founding member of the Skatalites, and was featured on hits such as 'Phoenix City' and 'El Pussy Cat'. After the Skatalites split up, he became the leader of the newly founded Soul Brothers, whose hits included 'Dr Ring A Ding' and 'Miss Ska-Culation', many of which were credited to Rolando Al and the Soul Brothers. In 1967 he became a member of the Soul Vendors, led by Jackie Mittoo (organ, piano and arrangements). Alphonso was a featured soloist on many of the group's instrumentals, such as 'Death In The Arena' and 'Ringo Rock', and can be heard on many other recordings made at Coxsone Dodd's Studio One. Dodd also released two excellent solo albums by Alphonso, *The Best Of Roland Alphonso* and *King Of Sax*. During the mid- to late 70s, he recorded as a session musician for Bunny Lee, and an album of solo recordings from this period, *Brighter Shade Of Roots*, was later issued.
In the early 80s he spent some time in New York recording for Lloyd Barnes' Wackies label. In 1984, a solo album from these sessions, *Roll On*, was issued.
● ALBUMS: *The Best Of Roland Alphonso* (Studio One 1973)★★★★, *King Of Sax* (Studio One 1975)★★★★, *Brighter Shade Of Roots* 1977-78 recordings (Imperial 1982)★★★, *Roll On* (Wackies 1984)★★★, with various artists *Plays Ska Strictly For You.*, with Jerry Johnson *Reggae Sax.*, with Don Drummond *I Cover The Waterfront.*

ALTHEA AND DONNA

Jamaican schoolgirls Althea Forest and Donna Reid were 17 and 18 years old, respectively, when their irritatingly catchy novelty hit, 'Uptown Top Ranking', hit the top of the charts in their home country. Their producer Joe Gibbs had supplied the tune for his own label (Lightning in the UK) and the girls were responsible for the patois lyrics, complete with girlish yelps in the background. The infectious tune and lyrics also caught the attention of the British record-buying public in 1978 and the record went to number 1. This was a highly unusual event, made doubly so by the fact that 'Uptown

Top Ranking' was actually an answer record to Trinity's 'Three Piece Suit'. Despite the backing of major record company Virgin, the duo found it impossible to produce an equally effective follow-up and went into the annals of pop history as chart-topping one-hit-wonders.
● ALBUMS: *Uptown Top Ranking* (Front Line 1978)★★★.

ANDERSON, AL

b. Albert Anderson, 1950, Jersey, New York, USA. Anderson learnt to play the trombone prior to his expulsion from the Mount Clairidge High School. He later enrolled at the Berklee College Of Music where he took ensembles rather than registering for full-time education. He devoted his spare time to practising and playing bass guitar, which led to his performing with the Centurions. While playing with the band he impressed Chris Wood from Traffic. Wood invited Anderson to play on his band's projected album, to be recorded in the UK; however, the Traffic project faltered, but it led to Anderson becoming an Island Records employee. In 1972, while an apprentice at Island, Anderson was recruited to play lead guitar with Bob Marley And The Wailers for the *Natty Dread* sessions. With the Wailers, he also provided lead guitar on 'Crazy Baldhead' as well as appearing on *Live*, which featured the distinguished 'No Woman No Cry'. Anderson remained with Bob Marley until 1976 when he joined Word Sound And Power alongside Sly And Robbie as the driving force behind Peter Tosh. Anderson played on the sessions for the singer's pivotal albums *Legalise It* and *Equal Rights*. By 1979 Anderson was back with Bob Marley, performing alongside lead guitarist Junior Murvin on *Survival* and *Uprising*. Following Marley's death in 1981, the Wailers continued to perform, covering Marley's hits and introducing their own compositions. The band toured Europe alongside the revamped Black Uhuru, featuring the original line-up of Don Carlos, Derrick 'Ducky' Simpson and Garth Dennis with DJ Lieutenant Stitchie. Following the tour, Anderson returned to his native New York where he began working with a number of session musicians, including the legendary Nile Rodgers at the Power Station. He continued to work as a session musician into the 90s, particularly with Jamaica Papa Curvin, notably contributing to the latter's *Heavy Load*.

ANDY, BOB

b. Keith Anderson, 1944, Jamaica, West Indies. A former member of the original Paragons, Andy's late 60s work with Coxsone Dodd has become almost common property in reggae, and his rhythms and lyrics are still recycled time after time. All of his legendary Studio One output is conveniently collected on *Bob Andy's Song Book*. He has continually maintained that he is neither a great singer nor a great songwriter, and it is probably this self-effacement that has led to his lack of recognition outside reggae circles, despite national chart success in the UK with Marcia Griffiths, recording as Bob And Marcia. Two duets (versions of 'Young, Gifted And Black' and 'Pied Piper') made the charts in the UK and led to extensive touring but little financial reward. Best known for his intelligent, thoughtful lyrics set within memorable song structures, Andy continued to work through the 70s and 80s with varying degrees of success, at times returning to his acting career. He has, however, produced more time-honoured tracks than many more prolific artists, and songs such as 'You Don't Know', 'Feel The Feeling', 'The Ghetto Stays In The Mind' and 'Sun Shines For Me' are regarded as classics, serving only to enhance his reputation as one of the most important figures in Jamaican music.
● ALBUMS: *Bob Andy's Songbook* (Studio One 1972)★★★, *The Music Inside Me* (Sound Tracks 1975)★★★, *Lots Of Love And I* (High Note 1978)★★★, *Friends* (I-Anka 1983)★★★, *Freely* (I-Anka 1988)★★★, *Bob Andy's Dub Book As Revealed To Mad Professor* (I-Anka 1989)★★★, *Bob Andy's Dub Rock* (I-Anka 1992)★★★.
● COMPILATIONS: *Retrospective* (I-Anka 1986)★★★★, *Andy Work* (I-Anka 1994)★★★★.

ANDY, HORACE

b. Horace Hinds, 1951, Kingston, Jamaica, West Indies. This artist was affectionately renamed Andy as a tribute to Bob Andy, in respect of their mutual songwriting abilities, by Coxsone Dodd. Horace, also known as Sleepy, has always been a favoured vocalist among reggae fans and his eerie, haunting style has been imitated endlessly by scores of lesser talents over the years.

It was his work with Dodd that established his reputation. His career at Studio One began with the single 'Something On My Mind', and eventually resulted in the classic 'Skylarking', one of reggae's most popular songs. From the mid-70s onwards, after leaving Studio One, Andy has worked with many important reggae producers in Jamaica, America and England. In the process he has recorded literally hundreds of records, most of which are now only available on rare 45s, although some of the high points of his work with Dodd, Bunny Lee and Wackies are still available on the listed albums. In the late 70s Andy moved to his new home in Hartford, Connecticut. His influence on reggae music in general, and reggae singers in particular, is incalculable, yet he remains a diffident figure among many other brasher, yet less talented, reggae 'stars'. *Skylarking: The Best Of Horace Andy*, released in 1996, is an excellent compilation of the artist's work.

● ALBUMS: *Skylarking* (Studio One 1972)★★★, *You Are My Angel* (Trojan 1973)★★★, *In The Light* (Hungry Town 1977)★★★, with Bim Sherman *Bim Sherman Meets Horace Andy And U Black* (Yard International 1980)★★★, with Errol Scorcher *Unity Showcase* (Pre 1981)★★★, *Dance Hall Style* (Wackies 1982) released in the UK as *Exclusively* (Solid Groove 1982)★★★, *Showcase* (Vista Sounds 1983)★★★, *Sings For You And I* (Striker Lee 1985)★★★, *Confusion* (Music Hawk 1985)★★★, with Patrick Andy *Clash Of The Andys* (Thunderbolt 1985)★★★, *Elementary* (Rough Trade 1985)★★★, with Dennis Brown *Reggae Superstars Meet* (Striker Lee 1986)★★★, with John Holt *From One Extreme To Another* (Beta 1986)★★★, *Big Bad Man* (Rockers Forever 1987)★★★, *Haul And Jack Up* (Live & Love 1987)★★★, *Fresh* (Island In The Sun 1988)★★★, *Shame And Scandal* (1988)★★★, *Everyday People* (Wackies 1988)★★★.

● COMPILATIONS: *Best Of Horace Andy* (Coxsone 1974)★★★, *Best Of Horace Andy* (Culture Press 1985)★★★, *Skylarking: The Best Of Horace Andy* (Melankolic 1996)★★★★, *Good Vibes* (Blood & Fire 1997)★★★.

ANDY, PATRICK

b. *c*.1965, Clarendon, Jamaica, West Indies. Andy began singing while still at school and also in church. In the mid-70s he recorded with Yabby You and covered a number of Horace Andy's tunes. In 1978, accompanied by Ranking Barnabus, he found success with 'Woman, Woman, Woman' and also had a solo hit with 'My Angel'. Andy's initial output resulted in a reputation as Horace Andy's understudy, which proved a hindrance to his career. By the early 80s Andy began recording with Joseph 'Joe Joe' Hookim at Channel One where he enjoyed hits with 'Tired Fe Lick Inna Bush' and 'Pretty Me'. The label also released a clash album with Wayne Smith. In 1984 Andy released the popular hits 'Get Up Stand Up' and 'Smiling'. His biggest success came in 1985 when he recorded 'Sting Me A Sting, Shock Me A Shock' with King Jammy, which emulated Sugar Minott riding the Sleng Teng rhythm, made popular by Andy's old sparring partner Wayne Smith. Sleng Teng is noted for bringing about the digital revolution in reggae, although Andy's version used real musicians as opposed to a computer for the accompaniment. The success of the song led to a number of hits including 'Life Is So Funny', 'Speak Your Mind', 'Cow Horn Skank', 'Music Market', 'Cooling Out' and 'What A Hell'. The latter also demonstrated the similarities between his and Minott's vocal phrasing, particularly when he sang, 'Oh what a hell when the rice can't swell - Can't get me water outa the well'. Andy's success also led to a number of clash albums with Half Pint, Frankie Jones and, paradoxically, Horace Andy.

● ALBUMS: with Wayne Smith *Showdown* (Channel One 1984)★★★, with Frankie Jones *Two New Superstars* (Burning Sounds 1985)★★★, with Horace Andy *Clash Of The Andys* (Thunderbolt 1985)★★★.

ANTHONY, MIKE

The UK Saxon sound system from Lewisham, London, has spawned a number of revered performers, including Phillip Papa Levi, Daddy Colonel, Maxi Priest and Tippa Irie. Priest enjoyed initial hits with Barry Boom, who nurtured Anthony's recording career in the late 80s. Anthony performed in the lovers rock style and enjoyed a reggae Top 10 hit with 'Crash Crash',

swiftly following that success with 'Glide Gently', which showcased his smooth vocals. Numerous hits ensued, including 'Cruising In Love', 'Open Your Heart' and, with the illustrious Fashion label producer Gussie Prento, 'Still Your Number One'. In 1991 Anthony topped the reggae chart for an extensive period with his cover version of David Ruffin's 'Walk Away From Love'. The song had been a reggae hit in the 70s for Ken Boothe, which inspired Anthony to emulate the Studio One veteran (producer Lloyd Charmers, motivated by Anthony's unprecedented success, eventually re-released Boothe's version). Anthony followed this success with 'No Halfway Love', which reaffirmed his popularity. Throughout the 90s he has consistently enjoyed Top 10 placings in the UK reggae charts, with notable hits including 'Spread Love', 'Don't Play Games', 'Sexy Eyes', 'Call Me' and Top Cat's 'rude boy mix', 'This Time I Know', which was released as part of an innovative joint venture between Gussie P and Nine Lives.
● ALBUMS: *Short Of Nothing* (Merger 1992)★★, *Back 4 More* (Gussie P 1996)★★★★.

APACHE INDIAN

The 'Don Raja' of British Asian raggamuffin, Apache Indian (b. Steve Kapur, 11 May 1967, Birmingham, England) has come to represent a cross-cultural fusion of musics that has both baffled and excited pundits and punters alike in the mid-90s. Apache Indian grew up in Handsworth, Birmingham, in the 70s - an era when the city was being celebrated as a kind of UK reggae melting pot through the efforts of Steel Pulse, and others, whose *Handsworth Revolution* album first put it on the musical map. Although he was of Indian parentage, Apache associated with reggae sound systems in the early 80s, sporting dreadlocks and an abiding love of Bob Marley. By the mid-80s, locks trimmed to a sharp fade, he was known locally on the mic as a dancehall rapper, and in 1990 he cut his first single, 'Movie Over India', as a white label, later picked up by British reggae distributors Jet Star. A compelling, catchy ragga tune, with a few elements of bhangra, the preferred music of many UK Asian kids, the record was a huge hit in both the reggae and bhangra markets. Two more cult hits followed, 'Chok There' and 'Don Raja', before

the majors became interested in him.
Island Records finally lured him into a contract, and 1993's *No Reservations* was cut in Jamaica and included Sly Dunbar, Bobby Digital and Robert Livingstone producing. Critically acclaimed, it saw Apache move away from the frothier elements of his distinctive ragga-reggae and towards a role as social commentator and Anglo-Asian representative. This approach was exemplified in the three crossover hits, 'Arranged Marriage', 'Boom Shack A Lack' and 'Moving On (Special)', the latter a cry of resistance against the election of a BNP member to a council seat in Tower Hamlets, London. Apache's assimilation into the mainstream music business continued apace, although he drew some flak from the more traditional elements in the reggae business, who may have been displeased at the apparent ease with which Apache conquered the pop charts, and he subsequently began to lose his ragga audience. His propensity for winning awards ('Best Newcomer' in the British Reggae Industry Awards 1990, a shortlist entry for the Mercury Prize in 1993 and a nomination for four BRIT awards in 1994) and his open, friendly personality made him a media favourite throughout 1993. Subsequent albums were artistically disappointing, and commercial success had also began to elude Apache Indian. By 1997's *Real People* he had been dropped by Island.
● ALBUMS: *No Reservations* (Island 1993)★★★★, *Make Way For The Indian* (Island 1995)★★★, *Real People* (Coalition 1997)★★.

ARIWA SOUNDS

One of only two studio-owning reggae labels to survive in the UK for any length of time (the other is Fashion), the success of Ariwa Sounds can be attributed to the determination of one man, Neil Fraser. Guyana-born Fraser started Ariwa as a four-track operation in his living room in Thornton Heath, south London, in 1979, prompted by a lifelong love of electronics and reggae, plus an interest in Philly soul and the related sweet sounds of lovers rock. Those first recordings, including the debut of the late lovers legend Deborahe Glasgow, can be found on *The Early Sessions* album. By 1982 Fraser had moved premises to Peckham, working on at first eight-track, and subsequently, 16-track equipment. Styling himself as the Mad Professor, and calling his band the Sane Inmates, Fraser rapidly acquired a reputation for eccentric, attention-grabbing records. Though his influences could clearly be discerned, his mixes soon revealed a highly unique quality, to the point where an Ariwa recording could be easily differentiated from all others. His 'Dub Me Crazy' series, eventually running into double figures, won him a reputation on the alternative rock scene, and disc jockey John Peel was an early champion, frequently spinning his productions. Early albums with Tony Benjamin, Sergeant Pepper and Ranking Ann did not sell especially well in the reggae market, but were always distinctive or noteworthy. By 1984 Fraser had teamed up with Sandra Cross, a lovers rock singer and sister of Victor Cross, an early Ariwa sessioneer. The siblings had worked together as the Wild Bunch, an Ariwa album act, before Sandra, a sweet-voiced, confident singer, proved capable of delivering Ariwa the hits it was seeking. Her *Country Life* (1985), built around a string of hits including a cover version of the Stylistics' 'Country Living' (previously covered in the reggae idiom by the Diamonds), was something of a commercial breakthrough. Other albums from Jamaican singer Johnny Clarke and DJs Peter Culture and Pato Banton brought further acclaim, and the open-minded Fraser began to work with acts as diverse as UK indie bands and sound system legend Jah Shaka.

Wolverhampton-based DJ Macka B's debut album, *Sign Of the Times* (1986), was the strongest Ariwa release yet, and remains perhaps the most effective roots statement ever recorded in the UK. A move to West Norwood found Fraser the boss of the largest black-owned studio complex in the UK, with two consoles, one a powerful, outboard-littered 24-track. It was here that he fashioned some of his most wonderful lovers rock records, including John Mclean's 'If I Give My Heart To You' (actually produced by Captain Sinbad at Ariwa in 1988), Sandra Cross's 'My Best Friend's Man' and Kofi's revival of her own earlier hit, 'I'm In Love With A Dreadlocks' (both 1989). Fraser also attracted some heavyweight Jamaican names to his premises, including Bob Andy, Lee Perry and Faybiene Miranda. He did not neglect his eccentric side, however, cutting strange tunes such as

Professor Doppler's 'Doppler Effect', and 'Echoes Of Deaf Journalists', an attack on the writers at *Echoes* newspaper. Although recent times have seen less frequent appearances from the Mad Professor in the UK reggae charts (Fraser has always shied away from the g, you's'n'sex sound of ragga), he retains huge respect and a loyal following worldwide. Regular Ariwa jaunts from New York to Holland, Australia to Poland, and elsewhere, have ensured strong export sales for his unique talents.

● ALBUMS: *Dub Me Crazy* (Ariwa 1982)★★★★, *Mad Professor: The African Connection* (Ariwa 1984)★★★, *Jah Shaka Meets Mad Professor At Ariwa Sounds* (Ariwa 1984)★★★, *Negus Roots Meets The Mad Professor* (Negus Roots 1984)★★★★, *Dub Me Crazy Part 5* (Ariwa 1985)★★★, *Professor Captures Pato Banton* (Ariwa 1985)★★★★, *Schizophrenic Dub* (Ariwa 1986)★★★, *Stepping In Dub Wise Country* (Ariwa 1987)★★★, *The Adventures Of A Dub Sampler* (Ariwa 1987)★★★★, *Dub Me Crazy Party* (Ariwa 1987)★★★, *Roots Daughters* (Ariwa 1988)★★★, with Lee Perry *Lee Scratch Perry Meets The Mad Professor, Volumes 1 & 2* (Ariwa 1990)★★★, with Perry *Lee 'Scratch' Perry Meets The Mad Professor In Dub, Volumes 1 & 2* (Angella 1991)★★★ *Dub Tek The Voodoo* (Ariwa 1996)★★★★, and Jah Shaka *A New Decade Of Dub* (RAS 1996)★★★.

Productions: Macka B *Sign Of The Times* (Ariwa 1986)★★★; Sandra Cross *Comet In The Sky* (Ariwa 1988)★★★; Kofi *Black With Sugar* (Ariwa 1989)★★★; Various *Roots Daughters* (Ariwa 1988)★★★, *Ariwa Hits '89* (Ariwa 1989)★★★.

ARROW

b. Alphonsus Cassell, Montserrat, West Indies. Soca artist Arrow leaned heavily on traditional Trinidadian calypso music, but expanded its commercial possibilities by acknowledging a variety of other styles in his compositions. Cassell began singing at school and by 1971 had been crowned the Calypso Monarch of Montserrat. A series of hits followed, as he built his reputation within the Leeward Islands calypso fraternity, including 'On Target' (1974), 'Instant Knockout' (1983) and 'Double Trouble' (1983). Combining R&B and salsa, he enjoyed his first Caribbean hit in 1983 with 'Hot Hot Hot', its popularity later translating into international sales when it became the official theme tune to the Mexico World Cup football tournament. Since that time he has continued to experiment, embracing urban north American rhythms from hip-hop, as well as those associated with African and world cultures, and writing lyrics that, in a traditional Trinidadian fashion, invite the audience to an ever-higher degree of physical rapture. It is a combination that requires a deft hand and yet is accomplished with a natural, easy feel. The best examples are the Latin fusion of 'Party Mix' (1984), the Guadeloupe-influenced 'Zouk Me' (1990) and even a rock-tinged set, in 1988's *Knock Dem Dead* (with guitar provided by Chris Newland). The fact that he is the most easily available soca artist in the USA (the result of his late 80s contract with Island Records subsidiary Mango) has certainly not hindered his progress. *Zombie Soca* saw him take a rare detour into social commentary, though he had previously composed the occasional politically motivated lyric, such as 'Bills' from the late 70s. The album's stand-out track, however, was the frantic 'Wine Yuh Body'.

● ALBUMS: *Instant Knockout* (Charlie's 1980)★★★★, *Hot Hot Hot* (Arrow/Chrysalis 1983)★★★, *Soca Savage* (Arrow 1984)★★★, *Deadly* (Deadly Arrow 1986)★★, *Heavy Energy* (Arrow 1987)★★★, *Knock Dem Dead* (Mango 1988)★★★★, *O'la Soca* (Mango 1989)★★, *Massive* (Arrow 1989)★★★, *Soca Dance Party* (Mango 1990)★★★, *Zombie Soca* (Arrow 1992)★★.

● COMPILATIONS: *Best Of* (Red Bullet 1988)★★★★, *Hot Soca Hot* (Arrow 1990)★★★.

ASWAD

Formed in west London, England, in 1975, this premier UK reggae group featured Brinsley 'Dan' Forde (b. 1952, Guyana; vocals, guitar), George Oban (bass), Angus Gaye (b. 1959, London; drums) and Donald Griffiths (b. 1954, Jamaica, West Indies; vocals). Additional musicians include Vin Gordon, Courtney Hemmings, Bongo Levi, Karl Pitterson and Mike Rose. Taking their name from the Arabic word for black, they attempted a fusion of Rastafarianism with social issues more pertinent to their London climate. Their self-titled debut was well

received, and highlighted the plight of the immigrant Jamaican in an unfamiliar and often hostile environment. A more ethnic approach was evident on the superior follow-up, *Hulet*, which placed the group squarely in the roots tradition only partially visited on their debut. Their instrumentation impressed, with imaginative song structures filled out by a dextrous horn section. The departure of Oban, who was replaced by Tony 'Gad' Robinson (the former keyboard player) did little to diminish their fortunes. Forde, meanwhile, was featured in the film *Babylon*, which featured Aswad's 'Warrior Charge' on its soundtrack.

A brief change of label saw them record two albums for CBS before they returned to Island Records for *Live And Direct*, recorded at London's Notting Hill Carnival in 1982. By early 1984 they were at last making a small impression on the UK charts with 'Chasing The Breeze', and a cover version of Toots Hibbert's '54-46 (Was My Number)'. *To The Top* in 1986 represented arguably the definitive Aswad studio album, replete with a strength of composition that was by now of considerable power. While they consolidated their reputation as a live act, they used *Distant Thunder* as the launching pad for a significant stylistic overhaul. The shift to lightweight funk and soul, although their music maintained a strong reggae undertow, made them national chart stars. The album bore a 1988 UK number 1 hit in 'Don't Turn Around'. Since then, Aswad have remained a major draw in concert, although their attempts to plot a crossover path have come unstuck in more recent times, despite the appearance of artists such as Shabba Ranks on their 1990 set, *Too Wicked*. Although they have not always appealed to the purists, Aswad are one of the most successful reggae-influenced groups operating in the UK, thoroughly earning all the accolades that have come their way, particulary with their riveting live act.

● ALBUMS: *Aswad* (Mango/Island 1975)★★★, *Hulet* (Grove Music 1978)★★★★, *New Chapter* (Columbia 1981)★★★, *Not Satisfied* (Columbia 1982)★★★, *A New Chapter Of Dub* (Mango/Island 1982)★★★, *Live And Direct* (Mango/Island 1983)★★★, *Rebel Souls* (Mango/Island 1984)★★★, *Jah Shaka Meets Aswad In Addis Ababa Studio* (Jah Shaka

1985)★★★, *To The Top* (Simba 1986)★★★★, *Distant Thunder* (Mango/Island 1988)★★★, *Too Wicked* (Mango/Island 1990)★★, *Rise And Shine* (Bubblin 1994)★★.
● COMPILATIONS: *Showcase* (Grove Music 1981)★★★, *Renaissance* (Stylus 1988)★★★, *Crucial Tracks - The Best Of Aswad* (Mango/Island 1989)★★★★, *Don't Turn Around* (Mango/Island 1993)★★★, *Firesticks* (Mango/Island 1993)★★★, *Roots Rocking: The Island Anthology* (Island Jamaica 1998)★★★.
● VIDEOS: *Distant Thunder Concert* (Island Visual Arts 1989), *Always Wicked* (Island Visual Arts 1990).

AUDIO ACTIVE

From Japan, and led by singer Masa, Audio Active are one of the premier bands from Asia to have reinterpreted that continent's recent fascination with Jamaican reggae. Masa began listening to reggae when he was a teenager, forming the band with like-minded friends in the early 90s. With a preference for dub and roots over other reggae forms, their first international release came when they were heard by British reggae pioneer Adrian Sherwood, who produced and released *Happy Hoppers* on his On-U-Sound label at the end of 1995. It featured contributions from New York comedian and busker Laraaji. In keeping with the best traditions of reggae, 'happy hoppers' actually translates as 'happy smoke/weed'.
● ALBUMS: *Happy Hoppers* (On-U-Sound 1995)★★.

AURA

b. Aura Lewis, *c*.1958, Johannesburg, South Africa. Lewis has worked with a variety of musicians in her varied career, including making extraordinary recordings with her fellow expatriots and exponents of township jive, the Malopoets. In 1976 she went to Jamaica where she formed an allegiance with *Rockers* star Kiddus I, who performed as a soloist and occasionally alongside the Sons Of Negus. His connections led to an introduction to Jimmy Cliff, who invited Aura to perform backing vocals on his forthcoming tour, which was filmed and subsequently released on video as *Bongo Man*. While working with Cliff she met Lee Perry, who brought her into the recording studio where she was initially employed as a backing vocalist. Her ambitions to record as a soloist were fulfilled when she recorded 'Midnight', 'Full Experience' and a version of Nina Simone's 'Young Gifted And Black'. Aura left Jamaica and embarked on a career with the Malopoets and a South African jazz group featuring Louis Moholo. In the late 80s rumours about experimental recording sessions with Lee Perry and two West African vocalists were curtailed when the master tapes of Aura's work emerged. The Upsetter recordings survived the events relating to the destruction of the Black Ark studio in Washington Gardens, and were eventually licensed to Blue Moon.
● ALBUMS: with Lee Perry *Full Experience* (Blue Moon/Mesa 1990)★★★.

B

B., ANTHONY

b. Anthony Blair, c.1976, Trelawny, Jamaica, West Indies. Anthony B. shot to fame in 1996 when his hugely controversial single, 'Fire Pon Rome', became one of the biggest hits of the year, in spite of the presence of a blanket radio ban. When he followed its success with further hits, 'Raid The Barn' and 'Hurt The Heart', it was clear that a major new dancehall star had been born. The artist, who wisely decided against issuing his records under the name 'Tony Blair', had grown up in rural Jamaica, weeding canefields as part of a poor family. There he memorized songs from the radio, his greatest influences being Peter Tosh and Bob Marley. A large number of critics, in fact, suggested comparisons with Tosh when Anthony B. broke through in the 90s. He moved to Kingston in his teens at the height of dancehall reggae's popularity, but while appreciating the musical vitality of the scene, he was disappointed by the 'slack' lyrics and lack of 'positivity'. His efforts to launch a solo career temporarily thwarted, he eventually returned to his village. However, his perseverance was rewarded when he came to the attention of producer/writer Richard 'Bello' Bell, owner of the Startrail studio complex and label in Miami. The label had moved to Kingston in the early 90s after enjoying commercial success with Beres Hammond and Cutty Ranks, and Anthony B. became their second major project there, following the breakthrough of Everton Blender. He later recorded a successful single, 'I'm Gonna Tell You', with the Mystic Revealers.
● ALBUMS: *So Many Things ...* (Greensleeves 1996, Startrail/VP 1997)★★★, *Universal Struggle* (Charm 1998)★★★★.

BABY WAYNE

b. c.1973, St. Catherine, Jamaica, West Indies. Baby Wayne specialized in conscientious lyrics, designed to teach villainous members of Jamaican society that crime does not pay. To appease the dancehall fans, he was drawn into the fashionable slackness style, but remains more generally noted for his individual stand against the glorification of violent fantasy lyrics. With producers Steely And Clevie, he enjoyed a hit in 1991 with 'Mama'. Baby Wayne also recorded for Paul 'Jah Screw' Love and Mixing Lab, producing hits including 'Road Mi Waan Come' and 'Warder'. By 1993 Baby Wayne had recorded 'Money Friend' with Leroy Smart, which earned a Top 10 placing in both Jamaican charts. The single was produced by Winston 'Niney' Holness, who had revitalized Baby Wayne's career following a lull and secured a contract with the US-based Heartbeat label for the release of *Ram DJ*. The album featured the hit single along with guest vocals from Sugar Minott and Dennis Brown. Baby Wayne also maintained a high profile in the dancehall with a notable appearance at the Killamanjaro vs. Conquering Lion sound clash. In 1995 he found success recording with producer Lloyd Dennis, and his campaign for rational behaviour continued with 'Tongue Make Not'. He also recorded 'See War' and 'Wha' Dem Defend' with Wee Pow of the Stone Love crew.
● ALBUMS: *Ram DJ* (Heartbeat 1994)★★★, *Move With The Crowd* (VP 1995)★★★.

BANTON, BUJU

b. Mark Myrie, 1973, Kingston, Jamaica, West Indies. Raised in Denham Town, Buju began his DJ apprenticeship at the age of 13 with the Rambo Mango and Sweet Love sound systems. Fellow DJ Clement Irie took him to producer Robert Ffrench for his debut release, 'The Ruler', in 1986. The following year he sang for Red Dragon, Bunny Lee and Winston Riley, who later remixed his tracks with a notable degree of success. By 1990 his voice had ripened to a warm, deep growl that drew comparisons with Shabba Ranks. He was then introduced to Dave Kelly, resident engineer at Donovan Germain's Penthouse Studio. Together they wrote many of the hits that established Buju as the most exciting newcomer of 1991, courting controversy with lyrics revealing his preference for light-skinned girls on 'Love Mi Browning', and defining dancehall fashions with tunes such as 'Women Nuh Fret', 'Batty Rider', 'Bogle Dance' and 'Big It Up', the debut release on Kelly's own Mad House label. Penthouse released the *Mr. Mention* album just as a wave of hits for themselves, Soljie, Shocking Vibes, Bobby Digital and Exterminator began to underline Buju's rapid rise to prominence. Most notorious of these projects was the violently homophobic 'Boom Bye Bye' for Shang. Receiving national TV exposure in the UK, it created a storm of media protest. By this time, his records were dominating the reggae charts, often in combination with fellow Penthouse artists including Wayne Wonder, Beres Hammond, Marcia Griffiths and Carol Gonzales. Mercury Records signed him to a major-label US contract later that year. By 1993 his lyrics dealt increasingly with cultural issues. 'Tribal War', featuring an all-star ensemble, was voiced in response to Jamaica's warring political factions; 'Operation Ardent' railed against Kingston's curfew laws; and 'Murderer' was provoked by the shooting of his friend and fellow DJ, Pan Head. It is this streak of hard-edged reality - offset by his typically coarse, melodic romancing of the ladies - that has established him as an artist of international repute. *'Til Shiloh* remains his strongest collection to date.

● ALBUMS: *Stamina Daddy* (Techniques 1991)★★★, *Mr. Mention* (Penthouse 1991)★★★★, *Voice Of Jamaica* (Mercury 1993)★★★, *'Til Shiloh* (Loose Cannon 1995)★★★★, *Inna Heights* (Jet Star 1997)★★★.

BANTON, BURO

b. *c*.1960, Western Kingston, Jamaica, West Indies. The nickname Buro has been with him from his schooldays and Banton was the title given to a lyrics champion. His early influences included Dillinger, Trinity, U. Brown and Ranking Trevor. He would frequent dances where his heroes performed and emulate their gestures and phrasings, which eventually evolved into his own presentation. In 1976, persuaded by his friends, he made his debut as a DJ at the renowned Skateland discotheque in Kingston when he entered a talent contest. Banton began his career in earnest on the Roots Unlimited sound system alongside Josey Wales. His success led to him becoming the resident DJ for the Gemini sound system, which resulted in his association with Henry 'Junjo' Lawes' Volcano sound. Performing alongside Peter

Metro, Little John, Billy Boyo and Ranking Toyan, the sound clashed with People's Choice, where Banton battled with his old sparring partner, Josey Wales. Volcano won the contest and shortly after the event Wales joined the Volcano posse. In the early 80s, Banton's distinctive voice, which sounded similar to Prince Jazzbo, had only been heard on yard tapes. Throughout 1980-82 Henry 'Junjo' Lawes had proved to be a successful producer with Barrington Levy, Yellowman, Eek A Mouse and the aforementioned DJs. Having served his apprenticeship on the sound system, Banton went into the studio with Junjo for his vinyl debut, *Buro*. Notable inclusions were 'Better Than The Rest', 'Tell Me What You Want' and the sublime 'Tenement'. The album was overshadowed by the phenomenal success of Yellowman, which resulted in a vast number of distinguished DJs being disregarded by the media. He recorded 'Out A Hand' with references to the albino star, 'Seh, when I was a yout' dem a call me Buro - But now that I'm a man what I can't understand - Dey change fe mi name into the lyrics Banton - Me sing more church song than Yellowman', as part of a traditional dancehall confrontation. A similar encounter in 1983 with Peter Metro resulted in Banton winning the honours, although Metro maintained foul play. In 1984 Banton recorded 'Non Stop' with Junjo, toured Canada with DJ John Wayne and nurtured his protégé Little Buro. Banton continued to maintain his popularity in Jamaica where his perpetual chanting at the mike has become legendary. After leaving Volcano he was employed on the Stereo Mars system alongside Tenor Saw, Cocoa Tea, Major Worries, Supercat and Nicodemus. By the early 90s Banton was in New York and voiced the legality of his US residency on a remix of Shinehead's hit, 'Jamaican In New York'. In 1994 he was recording for the Brooklyn-based Massive B label, who specialized in both reggae and hip-hop. His initial output, including 'Boom Wha Dis' and 'Sensi Come From', was greeted with enthusiasm, leading to an album release in the summer of 1995.

● ALBUMS: *Buro* (CSA 1983)★★★, *Original Banton* (Massive B 1995)★★★★.

BANTON, MEGA

b. Garth Williams, c.1973, Kingston, Jamaica, West Indies. In the history of Jamaican music there are many cases of similarly named performers, for example, U-Roy, I. Roy, Nu Roy and U. Roy Jnr. Mega Banton continued with the theme of Banton initiated by Buro Banton, who in turn inspired Buju and Pato Banton. Mega's vocals were similar to Buju's gruff style, which had brought the latter unprecedented success, and producers were keen to emulate his accomplishments with the young contender. Fulfilling the demand for this style, Mega soon achieved international success. Initial hits include 'Decision' and 'Sound Boy Killing' produced by Jack Scorpio. The latter tune bore a remarkable resemblance to Buju Banton's 'Red Rose', in which Buju remarked, 'I have never seen a girl so pretty and so fair' (on his release, Mega stated, 'I have never heard a sound play so heavy and so clear'). In 1993 the tune was remixed in an effort to penetrate other dance markets. Also with Scorpio, a duet, 'Mr Want All', with the original don, Leroy Smart, was unable to achieve the success it deserved, but was featured in the popular *Just Ragga* series. Another Black Scorpio release, 'Mr Mention', was frequently mistaken for a Buju Banton release, and even more confusingly, the tune was also the title of Buju's first Penthouse album. In 1994 Mega courted controversy when he recorded 'Money First', produced by Mafia And Fluxy. The lyrics advised, 'Mek sure you get the money first before you lie down inna bed and start do the wuk', leading to criticism that Mega was encouraging girls into a life of prostitution. The song was licensed to RCA Records and the promotional wheels were set in motion. A rare television appearance found Mega rendering the song, but his performance was marred due to problems with the sound system. Following the untimely demise of Garnett Silk, Banton recorded 'A Tribute To Garnett Silk' with Sattalite, whose voice was uncannily similar to that of the late singer. A combination with Barrington Levy, reworking his 1988 hit 'She's Mine', produced by Jack Scorpio, continued to maintain Banton's profile into 1995 when included on the compilation *D. J. Counteraction*. He also enjoyed hits with Ricky General, including 'Combination Mix Part 2', as well as 'Good Ganja' for Shocking Vibes and 'Hot Stepper'. A new breed of DJ has overshadowed his output in recent times but he still maintains a following. In 1995 Banton joined the ranks of DJs signed up by the major record companies *1,000,000 Megawatts*.

● ALBUMS: *First Position* (Black Scorpio 1992)★★★, with Ricky General *Showcase* (VP 1993)★★★, *New Year New Style* (Black Scorpio 1995)★★★★, *1,000,000 Megawatts* (Relativity 1995)★★★.

BANTON, PATO

b. Patrick Murray, Birmingham, England. Banton first came to the public's attention in 1982 on the Beat's *Special Beat Service* album, duelling with Ranking Roger on 'Pato And Roger A Go Talk', before releases on the Fashion Records and Don Christie labels. His debut single, 'Hello Tosh', was a novelty take on the Toshiba advertising campaign of 1985. His first long-playing effort saw him paired with the wizardry of the Mad Professor, a combination to which he would return four years later for the *Recaptured* set. On his solo debut Banton was backed by the Birmingham-based Studio 2 house band. Throughout, he coloured his Rasta toasting/dub with comic impersonations of the characters populating his songs. Since then, his records have leaned progressively towards pop and soul, blurring the dividing lines between Jamaican toasting and American rap. For *Wize Up!*, which contained an unlikely alternative radio hit in his cover version of the Police's 'Spirits In The Material World', Banton was joined by David Hinds of Steel Pulse. In the 90s Banton began to attract a large US following, where he was signed to IRS Records. However, his tremendous live popularity was not translated into record sales, and in 1994 IRS persuaded him to release a pop cover version. Backed by Robin and Ali Campbell of UB40 and written by Eddy Grant, 'Baby Come Back' became a worldwide success, selling one and a half million copies in Europe and Australasia. In its wake, Sting invited Banton to chat over his 'Cowboy Song' single, which became another major chart success.

● ALBUMS: *Mad Professor Captures Pato Banton* (Ariwa 1985)★★★, *Never Give In* (Greensleeves 1987)★★★, *Visions Of The World* (IRS

1989)★★★, *Recaptured* (Ariwa 1989)★★★, *Wize Up! (No Compromize)* (IRS 1990)★★★, *Collections* (IRS 1995)★★★.

BANTON, STARKEY

b. David Murray, 15 November 1962, Hammersmith, London, England. Banton began his career on the sound system circuit in and around west London during the mid-70s, performing under the name Starkey Super. He eventually changed his name to Banton in acknowledgment of the Jamaican patois term for a DJ 'full of lyrics'. Initially, he maintained a low profile, working with many of the UK's top DJs, including Sweetie Irie, Chuckie Star and General Levy. In 1993 he released his debut, 'Lover Dread', a conscientious recording at a time when slackness and gun lyrics were in fashion. The sessions led to further releases, including the authoritative 'Blackman Memories' and an ode to marijuana, 'Ganja Baby'. By 1994 he had joined the One Love crew, who released the favoured 'Wicked Man', leading to combination hits with Sweetie Irie and Horace Andy. With the advent and popularity of jungle music in the UK Starkey caused a major controversy when he released 'Jungle Bungle' through Fashion Records; the song became a summer anthem and, along with his subsequent releases, fuelled the jungle versus ragga debate. Banton maintained a high profile with the release of 'Fire The Gal', 'Don't Diss The Rass', and a guest appearance on Danny Dread's 'Rolling Stone'. He also appeared at the 1995 Jamaican Reggae Sunsplash Festival. Banton's partnership with Fashion led to further hits, including the contentious 'Nah Wear Nuh Versace' (the song was inauspiciously released on the day the designer was killed, somewhat eclipsing the essence of the tune). In 1997 he released a well-received mini-album, which featured Mykal Rose ('Love King Selassie'), with whom he also appeared on 'Release Me' and 'Another Day In Babywrong'. Banton later embarked on session work for the eagerly anticipated *Ancient Spirit*.

● ALBUMS: *Powers Youth - Starkey Banton Meets The Dub Organiser* (Fashion 1997)★★★★.

BARKER, DAVE

b. David Collins, *c*.1952, Kingston, Jamaica, West Indies. Barker began his career as part of Winston Riley's vocal group the Techniques alongside Bruce Ruffin and Pat Kelly. After leaving the group he became a session vocalist at Lee Perry's Black Ark Recording Studio. Recording there under his own name, he enjoyed an instant hit with 'Shocks Of A Mighty'. In 1970 *Prisoner Of Love* featured the single and the title track, along with cover versions of 'Blowing In The Wind' and 'Runaway Child'. The DJ style of his hit led to the release of 'Shocks 71', a toast over the Wailers' 'Small Axe', with references to his original hit. This included a cameo appearance from Charlie Ace who contributes the line: 'Come on Dave, do it like you did in "Shocks Of A Mighty" - you remember'. Barker's reply was, 'That ol' thing', as he proceeded to mimic his first hit. He enjoyed international acclaim in March 1971 with his brother Ansell Collins when the duo achieved a UK number 1 hit with 'Double Barrel', produced by Winston Riley, and featuring Sly Dunbar playing drums on his first session. This was followed by the number 7-peaking 'Monkey Spanner' in June 1971, as *Double Barrel* also made a brief appearance in the UK album chart. The two hits were featured on the latter, along with ten other tracks showing a return to the singing style of *Prisoner Of Love*. In an effort to capitalize on the duo's success, 'Shocks Of A Mighty' was reissued, credited to Dave and Ansell, but it failed to complete a chart hat-trick. A new recording, 'Ton Up Kids', followed, but in spite of national airplay, it also flopped. Ansell returned to Jamaica, while as a soloist, Dave recorded 'Ride Your Pony' and 'Hot Line', produced by Larry Lawrence. In 1976 he released *In The Ghetto*, credited to Dave and Ansell Collins, although the cover featured a photograph of only Dave, and the contents, too, featured his solo output. The same year he joined a vocal group, Chain Reaction, with Bruce Ruffin and Bobby Davis. The outcome of these sessions was *Never Lose Never Win*, an ill-fated attempt to cross over to the soul market. Persevering with soul he recorded an album's worth of material with songstress Jaqui Jones; it prefaced 'Good Lovin' and 'Love Tonight' in 1989. 'Double Barrel' has been frequently sampled, notably on the

remixed Chaka Demus And Pliers hit 'Gal Wine', which resulted in the tune returning to the UK charts in 1994.
● ALBUMS: with Lee Perry *Prisoner Of Love* (Trojan 1970)★★★★, *Double Barrel* (Techniques 1971)★★★, *In The Ghetto* (Trojan 1976)★★, *Roadblock* (Bushranger 1979)★★★, with Chain Reaction *Never Lose Never Win* (Gull 1976)★★, *Change Of Action* (Vista 1983)★★, *Chase A Miracle* (Vista 1983)★★★, with the Techniques *Classics* (Techniques 1991)★★★★.
● COMPILATIONS: *Run Come Celebrate -Their Greatest Hits* (Heartbeat 1993)★★★★.

BARNES, LLOYD

b. *c.*1948, Jamaica, West Indies. In the early 70s Barnes emigrated to New York where he commenced his career as a producer and recording engineer, having previously recorded as a singer for Prince Buster in the mid-60s. Originally working in partnership with Munchie Jackson, he established one of the first reggae studios in the USA, and developed his own roots sound. Using the Reckless Breed as his house band, his recordings with local and established talent were released on a bewildering array of labels including Hamma, Rawse, Bullwackie, City Line, Senrab (Barnes backwards), Senta (his mother's name) and Wackies, the latter becoming his main outlet. By the late 70s he had developed a magical and intoxicating sound and issued outstanding recordings by artists such as Horace Andy, Junior Delahaye, Jerry Harris, Milton Henry, Jah Batta, Wayne Jarrett, Jezzreel, the Lovejoys, Maxine Miller, Sugar Minott and Audley Rollins. He also issued his own vocal recordings as the Chosen Brothers, as well as a series of dub albums featuring his skills as an engineer. He issued streams of music until the mid-80s, after which his output became more erratic, but he was still capable of releasing such fine works as Chris Wayne's *Freedom Street* (1988), and Jackie Mittoo's *Wild Jockey* (1989).
● ALBUMS: As the Chosen Brothers *Sing And Shout* (Wackies 1985)★★. Dub albums: *Creation Dub* (Wackies 1977)★★★★, *Tribesman Assault* (Wackies 1977)★★★★, *Blackworld Dubwise* (1979)★★★, *Nature's Dub* (1980)★★★★, *African Roots Act 1* (Wackies 1980)★★★★, *African Roots Act 2* (Wackies 1980)★★★,

African Roots Act 3 (Wackies 1983)★★★, *Jamaica Super Dub* (Wackies 1983)★★★★, *African Roots Act 4* (Wackies 1984)★★★, *African Roots Act 5* (Wackies 1985)★★★. Productions: Various *Selective Showcase* (Wackies 1980)★★★, *Jah Son Invasion* (Wackies 1982)★★★, *Jah Children Invasion* (Wackies 1983)★★★, *Dance Hall Collection* (Tachyon 1987)★★, *Free South Africa* (Wackies 1987)★★, *Dance Hall Reality* (Wackies 1987)★★★; Roland Alphonso *Roll On* (Wackies 1984)★★★; Horace Andy *Dance Hall Style* (Wackies 1982)★★★★, *Everyday People* (Wackies 1988)★★★; John Clarke *Visions Of John Clarke* (Wackies 1979)★★★; Junior Delahaye *Reggae* (Wackies 1982); Tyrone Evans *Sings Bullwackie Style* (Wackies 1984)★★; Jerry Harris *I'm For You* (Wackies 1982)★★; Milton Henry *Who Do You Think I Am?* (Wackies 1985)★★, *Babylon Loot* (Wackies 1988)★★; Jah Batta *Argument* (Wackies 1984)★★★; Wayne Jarrett *Bubble Up* (Wackies 1982)★★; Jezzreel *Great Jah Jah Showcase* (Wackies 1980)★★★, *Rockers* (Wackies 1982)★★★; Jerry Johnson *For All Seasons* (Wackies 1985)★★★, *The Score* (Wackies 1988)★★★; The Lovejoys *Lovers Rock Showcase* (Wackies 1981)★★★; Maxine Miller *Showcase* (Wackies 1980)★★★; Sugar Minott *Wicked A Go Feel It* (Wackies 1984)★★★, *Jamming In The Street* (Wackies 1987)★★★; Jackie Mittoo *Wild Jockey* (Wackies 1989)★★★★; Audley Rollins *Role Model* (Wackies 1985)★★★; Chris Wayne *Freedom Street* (Wackies 1988)★★★.

BAYETTE

In some African tongues, Bayette means 'between god and man', an ennobled state bestowed upon the chosen few. The band revolves around the iconic Jabu Khanyile (b. 1959, South Africa). Khanyile endured a long hard struggle to achieve his fame. At 14 he was forced to abandon his education to earn money from hard labour, the only available option at a time when the harsh apartheid regime was still in force. Khanyile came from a musical background: his father, a miner, performed traditional a cappella and his brother John played in a band covering reggae and soul. Influenced by his brother, Khanyile joined the Editions as drummer, although he later emerged as the lead singer. The band released a number of singles, including their debut, 'Cheeky Mama', followed by 'Izinyembizi (My Tears)' and 'Inhlonipho', the latter two songs featured Khanyile on lead. By 1984, Khanyile had joined Bayette as drummer, playing a unique style of Afro-jazz and reggae. The band gradually built up a following within the townships, and in 1994 Khanyile moved to lead vocals. He also reorganized the band, recruiting a Zimbabwean drum 'n' bass team alongside keyboardist Thapelo Khomo and two female backing singers, Khanyo Maphumelo and Khululiwe Sithole. The reformed band released a series of popular hits and in 1996 became internationally renowned following an appearance at the Royal Gala evening for Nelson Mandela in the UK.

● ALBUMS: *Mmalo-We* (Teal/Island 1993)★★★, *Africa Unite* (Mango 1997)★★★★.

BECKFORD, THEOPHILUS

b. 1935, Kingston, Jamaica, West Indies. One of the pioneers of indigenous Jamaican music, Theo Beckford's piano playing was one of the factors that determined and defined the feel and sound of ska music (as opposed to Jamaican rhythm and blues) in the late 50s and early 60s. Having purchased a piano in 1955 Beckford conquered the instrument and was playing professionally two years later. His 'Easy Snapping', on Coxsone Dodd's Worldisc label, was a huge hit, and its incredibly laid-back feel, with the emphasis firmly on the off-beat, was widely imitated. Beckford had a further hit with Dodd with 'Jack & Jill Shuffle', and he then formed his own label, King Pioneer, but it is his session work with Clue J And His Blues Blasters, and countless other studio/session bands, that forms the bulk of his recorded work. He was employed by Dodd in this capacity as well as by Duke Reid, Beverley's, Prince Buster and Clancy Eccles. Beckford reappeared in 1991 as part of Studio One's *The Beat Goes On: 35 Years In The Business* shows at Kingston's National Arena, and in 1992 'Easy Snapping' enjoyed something of a revival when it was used as background music for a television jeans advert - further proof of its timeless appeal.

● ALBUMS: various *Oldies But Goodies (Volume 1)* (Studio One 1968)★★★★.

BEENIE MAN

b. Anthony Moses Davis, 22 August 1973, Waterhouse, Kingston, Jamaica, West Indies. Davis started his musical career toasting at the age of five. His uncle Sydney Wolf was a musician playing drums for Jimmy Cliff, and encouraged the young DJ. After winning the Teeny Talent show at eight years old, radio DJ Barry G introduced him to King Jammy's, Volcano and other sound systems, where he soon established notoriety. His popularity inspired Bunny Lee to invite him into the studio, resulting in the release of *The Ten Year Old DJ Wonder*. An early example of his style can be heard on the live session set *Junjo Presents Two Big Sound*, alongside Dillinger, U. Brown, Toyan and Early B, among others. He also enjoyed a hit single produced by Winston 'Niney' Holness, 'Too Fancy'/ 'Over The Sea', which was followed by a lengthy silence. In the 90s he returned with a number of singles, beginning with 'Wicked Man'. After this, the hits kept coming, with Beenie holding the top chart positions in Jamaica. As is often the case when a DJ becomes popular, an obligatory clash with an equally popular DJ - in his case, Bounty Killer - was arranged, with the event taking place at Sting '93. Following the clash, the release of *Guns Out* featured both DJs, further fuelling support for the individual toasters. Working with Sly Dunbar and Robbie Shakespeare, Beenie covered two of Bob Marley's hits, 'No Mama (Sic) No Cry' and 'Crazy Baldhead', the latter in a combination with Luciano. Beenie's version of 'No Woman No Cry' represented a condemnation of the ghetto violence that had claimed the lives of some of the island's top performers. He toured the UK in 1994 and featured a celebrated cameo appearance from Shabba Ranks at one of the shows. While in the UK, Beenie recorded a jungle tune, and also his earlier ragga hit with Barrington Levy was remixed as 'Under Mi Sensi X Project Jungle Spliff', which reached the lower end of the UK chart. Still courting controversy, Beenie Man released 'Slam', the lyrics of which suggested that downtown girls were better lovers than those who lived uptown. His success led many to believe that Beenie had taken the crown from Buju Banton as the top Jamaican DJ. In 1995 Beenie was romantically linked with Carlene The Dancehall Queen, and the photogenic couple became Jamaica's equivalent to royalty. He also formed a pact with Bounty Killer through the arbitrating skills of Jamaican radio disc jockey Richard Burgess. In 1996 Beenie Man embarked on a highly acclaimed international tour with the Shocking Vibes crew. *Many Moods Of Moses* was another acclaimed set, with the single 'Who Am I' breaking the singer into the UK Top 10.

● ALBUMS: *The Ten Year Old DJ Wonder* (Bunny Lee 1981)★★★, *Gold* (Charm 1993)★★★, *Cool Cool Rider* (VP 1993)★★★★, *Best Of* (VP 1993)★★★★, *Rough And Rugged Strictly Ragga* (Rhino 1994)★★★★, *Live Contact* (VP 1994)★★★, with Bounty Killer *Guns Out* (Greensleeves 1994)★★★, *Dis Unu Fi Hear* (High Tone 1995)★★, with Dennis Brown, Triston Palma *Three Against War* (VP 1995)★★★★, with Mad Cobra, Lieutenant Stitchie *Mad Cobra Meets Lt Stitchie And Beenie Man* (VP 1995)★★★★, *Maestro* (Greensleeves 1996)★★★, *Many Moods Of Moses* (Greensleeves 1998)★★★★.

BELL, NYANKA

b. 1954, Touba, Côte d'Ivoire. Like her fellow Ivoirean vocalist Alpha Blondy, Bell has looked overseas for much of her inspiration. While Blondy turned to Jamaican reggae, Bell found a stylistic home in the faster and more effervescent rhythms of the Francophone Caribbean. Her 1984 debut album, *Amio*, embraced funk, disco and ballads. Two years later the follow-up, *If You Came To Go*, moved towards the Antilles. One track, 'Emotion', was written by Jacob Desarieux of the Antillean band Kassav, who also arranged 'Chogologo'. Despite a strong international repertoire - she speaks French but sings in English - Bell remains largely unknown outside of the Caribbean. In 1988 she contributed to an album by Eboa Lottin which also featured James Brown as a guest.

● ALBUMS: *Amio* (Celluloid 1984)★★★, *If You Came To Go* (Celluloid 1986)★★, *Djama* (Celluloid 1989)★★★.

BENNETT, LORNA

b. 1954, Kingston, Jamaica, West Indies. Bennett began her musical career singing in nightclubs. Prior to Geoffrey Chung's personal involvement in promoting Sharon Forrester, he recom-

mended that Bennett should embark on a recording career. Inspired by her performance at the Epiphany nightclub, they recorded a version of 'Morning Has Broken'. The single failed to generate a hit but impressed producer Harry J., who in 1972 commissioned Chung to record Bennett's rendition of 'Breakfast In Bed', originally a soul hit for Baby Washington. The song was an instant success throughout the West Indies and made a significant impression with both the US and UK audiences. The single appeared through the Island Records-affiliated Blue Mountain label, initially pressed with 'Remember When' on the b-side, followed by the DJ version, 'Skank In Bed', by Scotty, on later pressings. Prior to Bennett's achievement, no female performer had topped the Jamaican chart in five years. Her follow-up was a version of the Dixie Cups' 'Chapel Of Love', which successfully emulated her previous hit by reaching number 1. In 1976 Harry J. licensed 'Run Johnny' and 'Reverend Lee' to Trojan Records, although neither single was able to recapture past glories. Bennett also recorded her own composition, 'Other Woman'. Inspired by his earlier success with 'Breakfast In Bed', Harry J. recorded Sheila Hylton's version of the song, which entered the UK pop chart in 1979. In 1988 UB40 recorded their own version with Chrissie Hynde, which provided the alliance with a Top 10 hit. By this time Bennett had left the music business to study at university and has since pursued a successful career as a lawyer.

BENZ, SPRAGGA

b. Carlton Errington Grant, c.1975, Kingston, Jamaica, West Indies. Among the fast-rising stars of 1993 were Chuckleberry, General Pecus, Bounty Killer and Spragga Benz. His title was inspired by the prevailing trend for a fusion of hip-hop and ragga, and the fact that Spragga frequently appeared with a Mercedes Benz insignia dangling from his gold chain. Early hits included the Sly And Robbie-produced 'No Cater' and, with Steely And Clevie, 'Girls Hooray'. By 1994 he was recording with many of Jamaica's top producers, including Bobby Digital on 'The Wuk' and 'Sweet Sugar Pie', while King Jammy's son John John produced 'Bad Man No Beg No Friend', along with 'Born Good Looking'. In 1995 his prolific output encompassed the renowned

'W', a combination tune with Tamma Hawk, 'Flex Insane', as well as 'Car Crash', 'She Wrong' and 'Plan B', which were all dancehall favourites. His reputation grew when, in combination with Bounty Killer and General Degree, 'More Gal Book Book' appeared on the UK reggae Top 10. Many reggae performers have set up their own labels and Benz was no exception, releasing 'A1 Lover' on his Spragga Speculous imprint. The single featured vocals from Chevelle Franklin, who enjoyed an international hit when she accompanied Shabba Ranks on his Sony remake of 'Mr Loverman'. Conceivably induced by reggae's flourishing acceptance, Capitol Records signed Benz, releasing the single that featured on *Uncommonly Smooth*. The outcome of previous major label reggae releases had often been disappointing, but with this release, Benz was able to maintain artistic control and a fine collection of his work ensued.

● ALBUMS: *Jack It Up* (VP 1995)★★, *Uncommonly Smooth* (Capitol 1995)★★★★.

BEVERLEY'S

Beverley's was the name of a record shop based at 135 Orange Street, Kingston, Jamaica. The shop was run by three Chinese Jamaican brothers. One of the family, Leslie Kong, was lured into the recording business by a young Jimmy Cliff, who persuaded him to produce 'Hurricane Hattie' with 'Dearest Beverley' on the b-side (the title of the latter track might have influenced the family's decision to finance the recording session). Kong knew nothing about record producing, but through his funding of the session the pair were able to hire the cream of Jamaica's musicians. With names such as Lloyd Brevett, Theophilus Beckford, Jah Jerry and Drumbago supporting the venture, success was assured. Kong continued working with Jimmy Cliff, and production credits included the notable hit 'Miss Jamaica' and the album *Jimmy Cliff*. In 1962 Kong also launched the career of Robert Nesta Marley, with the singles 'Judge Not' and 'One Cup Of Coffee', both of which appeared on the Beverley's label. The second of the singles was credited to Bobby Martell And Beverley's All Stars, as Kong felt that a name change would ameliorate Marley's career. In 1963 Desmond Dekker embarked on a partnership with Kong; they initially recorded 'Honour Your Mother And Father', followed by a selection of Beverley's hits. From 1963-65 Beverley's productions were licensed to the Black Swan label in the UK, featuring recordings from Laurel Aitken, Jackie Edwards, Stranger Cole and top instrumentalists including Baba Brooks and Don Drummond. By the mid-60s Beverley's productions were licensed to the Pyramid label in the UK and in 1969 Dekker topped the UK chart with 'The Israelites'. He was no stranger to the chart as in 1967 his rendition of '007' also became a Top 20 hit. Other Beverley's hits for Dekker included 'It Mek' and 'Pickney Gal'. By 1970 Beverley's international achievements included hits for the Pioneers ('Long Shot Kick De Bucket'), the Melodians ('Sweet Sensation'), and the Maytals ('Monkey Man'). Bob Marley also returned to Beverley's accompanied by Peter Tosh and Bunny Wailer, recording 'Caution', 'Soul Shakedown Party' and 'Cheer Up', among others. Tosh had also recorded solo outings at Beverley's, notably 'Stop The Train' and 'Soon Come'. Other artists of note who passed through Beverley's included Derrick Morgan ('Forward March'), Derrick And Patsy ('Housewives Choice'), Ken Boothe ('Freedom Street'), Bruce Ruffin ('Bitterness Of Life'), the Gaylads ('There's A Fire') and Delroy Wilson ('Gave You My Love'). In 1971, at the age of 38, Kong died of a heart attack and the demise of Beverley's followed.

● ALBUMS: *King Sized Reggae* (Trojan 1971)★★★.

● COMPILATIONS: *The Best Of Beverley's Records Or Masterpieces From The Works Of Leslie Kong* (Trojan 1981)★★★★, *The King Kong Compilation* (Island 1981)★★★★.

BIG JOE

b. Joseph Spalding, *c*.1955, Kingston, Jamaica, West Indies. Big Spalding began his recording career in the early 70s. His initial sessions were with Harry Mudie, when he cut 'Run Girl', 'Woodcutter Skank' and 'Black Stick Rock'. In 1973, with Lloyd Daley, he recorded 'Glitter Not Gold', relating the aphorism to everyday life in Jamaica. With producer Winston Edwards he recorded 'Weed Specialist', 'Hog Inna Minty' and 'Selassie Skank'. The latter was released in the UK through Dennis Harris's DIP label and resulted in his biggest hit. The song recalled the celebrations generated by the visit to Jamaica of Haile Selassie, utilizing Roman Stewart's 'Try Me' rhythm. Following his sessions with Winston Edwards, Big Joe moved to Studio One, where he recorded 'Get Out Baldhead', 'Red Rob' and a DJ version of Larry Marshall's 'Nanny Goat' titled 'Nanny Version'. Further hits surfaced, reuniting him with Daley and Jackie Brown, before Big Joe set up his own productions and label. He also ran his own Small Axe Hi Fi sound system, playing venues such as Chocomo's Lawn and Jubilee Lawn. He continued recording through to the early 80s, enjoying hits with 'Dignity And Principal' and the Bunny Lee-produced 'Out Of Sight Out Of Mind'.

● ALBUMS: *Keep Rocking And Swinging* (Third World 1976)★★★★, *At The Control* (Third World 1977)★★★, *African Princess* (Trojan 1979)★★★.

BIG MOUNTAIN

Big Mountain evolved from a Californian reggae band, the Rainbow Warriors, in the mid-80s. They toured the USA playing gigs to the uninitiated, introducing a diluted form of reggae to American ears. The multicultural line-up featured Quino (vocals), Lance Rhodes (drums, percussion), Billy Stoll (keyboards), Lynn Copeland (bass), James McWhinney (vocals) and Jamaican Tony Chin (lead guitar). The group released a version of Peter Frampton's 'Baby I Love Your Way', which when featured in the film *Reality Bites* became an international top-seller, peaking at number 2 in the UK pop chart in 1994. The single also featured a Spanish version, enabling the group to enjoy successful sales in the South American market. The hit was followed by 'Sweet Sensual Love', performed in both English and Spanish, although it only reached number 51 in the UK pop chart. *Unity* followed, selling over a million copies worldwide. The group's accomplishment led to successful appearances at Jamaica's 1994 and 1995 Reggae Sunsplash festivals. They have since been unable to match the success of their first hit, but have continued to record with a number of Jamaica's top sessionmen, including Sly And Robbie and Handel Tucker. In 1995 the single 'Caribbean Blue' failed to make an impression in either the reggae or pop charts. *Free Up* featured singer-songwriter Sheryl Crow on co-writing credits.

● ALBUMS: *Wake Up* (Giant 1993)★★★★, *Unity* (Giant 1994)★★★★, *Resistance* (Giant 1995)★★★★, *Free Up* (Giant 1997)★★★.

BIG YOUTH

b. Manley Augustus Buchanan, February 1955, Jamaica, West Indies. A stylistic and artistic innovator of the highest order, Big Youth started adult life, following a youth of extreme poverty, as a cab driver. He subsequently found employment as a mechanic working in the Skyline and Sheraton hotels in Kingston. He practised while at work, listening to his voice echo around the empty rooms, and would sometimes be allowed to take the microphone at dances and thereby gain some experience. His popularity grew steadily until Big Youth became the resident DJ for the Lord Tippertone sound system (one of the top Kingston sounds in the early 70s), where he clashed regularly with other top DJs and gradually built a reputation. It was not long before he was approached by record producers. Unfortunately, his early attempts, notably the debut cut 'Movie Man', released on Gregory Isaacs' and Errol Dunkley's African Museum label, failed to capture his live magic. Further sides such as 'The Best Big Youth', 'Tell It Black' and 'Phil Pratt Thing' gradually helped to enhance his reputation. However, his first recording for Keith Hudson in 1972 changed everything. Hudson was a producer who understood DJs and knew how to present them properly, and was one of the first to record U-Roy and Dennis Alcapone. Big Youth's memorable 'S.90 Skank' stayed at number 1 in Jamaica for many weeks. Celebrating the West Kingston cult of the motorbike (the S.90 was a Japanese model), it opened with the sounds of an actual bike being revved up in the studio, and continued with Youth proclaiming, 'Don't you ride like lightning or you'll crash like thunder'. For the next few years he did ride like lightning and Bob Marley was the only artist to approach his popularity. Even the latter could not lay claim to Youth's unique distinguishing feature, front teeth inlaid with red, green and gold jewels. Representing the authentic sound of the ghetto, Big Youth set new standards for DJs to say something constructive on record as well as exhort dancers to greater heights. The stories he told offered penetrating insights into the downtown Kingston ghettoes and the minds of the Rastafarian youth. His debut set featured rhythms from previous Dennis Brown and Gregory Isaacs recordings, though by *Hit The Road Jack*, Youth had moved on to covering soul standards in his distinctive style. Hit followed hit and while he always gave his best for other producers, his self-produced records were even better. He formed his Negusa Nagast (Amharic for King of Kings) and Augustus Buchanan labels in 1973 for greater artistic and financial control of his career, and many of these records' stark, proud lyrics, set against jagged, heavy rhythms, sound just as stunning over 20 years after their initial release. He held little appeal outside of the Jamaican market, perhaps because he was too raw and uncompromising, but his innovations continue to reverberate through reggae and rap. Though his records and live appearances are now few and far between, Youth has remained at the top for longer than any other DJ apart from U-Roy, and he is still respected and revered by the reggae cognoscenti.

● ALBUMS: *Screaming Target* (Trojan 1973)★★★★★, *Reggae Phenomenon* (Negusa Nagast 1974)★★★, *Dreadlocks Dread* (Klik 1975)★★★★, *Natty Cultural Dread* (Trojan 1976)★★★, *Hit The Road Jack* (Trojan 1976)★★★, *Isaiah First Prophet Of Old* (Front Line 1978)★★★, *The Chanting Dread Inna Fine Style* (Heartbeat 1983)★★★, *Live At Reggae Sunsplash* (Sunsplash 1984)★★★, *A Luta Continua* (Heartbeat 1985)★★★, *Manifestation* (Heartbeat 1988)★★★.

● COMPILATIONS: *Everyday Skank - The Best Of Big Youth* (Trojan 1980)★★★★, *Some Great Big Youth* (Heartbeat 1981)★★★, *Jamming In The House Of Dread* (ROIR 1991)★★★.

BIGGS, BARRY

b. 1953, St Andrews, Jamaica, West Indies. Biggs is a lovers rock specialist, who started his professional career in 1968 with a version of Stevie Wonder's 'My Cheri Amour' for his producer Harry J. Previously, he had worked as a backing singer on mid-60s Coxsone Dodd productions at Studio One, and with Duke Reid at Treasure Isle.

He also spent six months working with the Crystalites. Biggs subsequently made the local Jamaican charts with 'One Bad Apple' for the Dynamic Sounds label, where he also worked as a producer and engineer. However, it took a recording originally completed in 1972, 'Work All Day', to break him internationally. From then on, he was closely identified with the blend of sweet reggae and high-pitched soul vocals the single introduced. Although he amassed a total of six UK chart entries between 1976 and 1981, he only broke the UK Top 20 once, with the release of 'Sideshow', distinguished by its low-key, distant production, which reached number 3 in December 1976. There were also two albums cut with Bunny Lee that were destined never to see the light of day. However, both 'Wide Awake In A Dream' (1980) and 'A Promise Is A Comfort To A Fool' (1982) topped the reggae listings.

● ALBUMS: *What's Your Sign Girl?* (Dynamic 1980)★★★, *Barry Biggs & The Inner Circle* (Trojan 1983)★★★, *Mr Biggs* (Trojan 1983)★★, *So In Love* (Starlight 1989)★★, *Sideshow* (Qualiton 1995)★★★.

BINGI BUNNY

b. Eric Lamont, *c.*1956, Kingston, Jamaica, West Indies, d. January 1994. Lamont began his career working with Bongo Herman as 'Bunny', recording 'Know For I' with producer Derrick Harriott. In 1973 he joined forces with Maurice Wellington in the Morwells, who in 1974 released 'Mafia Boss' and 'You Got To Be Happy'. While remaining a member of the band, he was also employed as a session musician playing rhythm guitar with other artists, including Errol Holt who joined the Morwells. As members of the group they continued to enjoy hits with 'Crab Race' and 'Proverbs'. In the late 70s they recorded 'Kingston 12 Tuffy' which was a big sound system hit and still enjoys cult status. They were associated with the Sir Jesus Sound Of Shepherds Bush and a number of their recordings would debut on the sound exclusives. The duo of Eric and Maurice also worked as the Morwell production team; notable releases came from the Jah Lloyd The Black Lion (*The Humble One*) and Prince Hammer (*Bible*). In 1981 when the Morwells disbanded, Lamont and Holt joined forces with Lincoln Valentine 'Style'

Scott and Noel 'Sowell' Bailey to form the Roots Radics. The band became the island's most in-demand session group, providing backing for Michael 'Dread' Campbell, Gregory Isaacs and Bunny Wailer, as well as a number of sessions for producers Henry Lawes and Linval Thompson. With Gregory Isaacs they were the featured musicians on *More Gregory*, *Night Nurse* and *Out Deh*. With Bunny Wailer they provided backing on *Rock And Groove*, which found the singer in a change of style, winning over new supporters. With Henry Lawes they featured on Barrington Levy's debut, *Bounty Hunter*, heralding the arrival of a new sound that remained popular through to the mid-80s, by which time they faced competition from the Sagittarius Band. As well as playing guitar, Lamont had provided vocals with the Morwells, and in the spring of 1982 he returned to singing as a soloist. He released 'Young Lover', which had been included on the compilation *The Best Of The Morwells*. The b-side featured 'Him A Natty Dread' with DJ Nicodemus. Other singles followed, including 'Me And Jane' and 'Street Lover'. Lamont died of prostate cancer in January 1994. The posthumous 1995 release of *Live At Channel One* included the track 'Tribute To Bingi Bunny'.

● ALBUMS: *Me And Jane* (Cha Cha 1982)★★★. With the Morwells: *Presenting The Morwells* (Morwells 1975)★★★, *Dub Me* (1975)★★★★, *Crab Race* (Burning Sounds 1978)★★★, *Cool Runnings* (Bushays 1979)★★★★, *Kingston 12 Toughies* (Carib Gems 1980)★★★, *The Best Of The Morwells* (Night Hawk 1981)★★★★. With the Roots Radics *Roots Radics Dub Session* (Solid Groove 1982)★★★★, *Radification* (Cha Cha 1982)★★★, *Live At Channel One* (Live And Love 1995)★★★.

BLACK REBELS

The multicultural US-based reggae band Black Rebels features the line-up of Manou (rhythm guitar, lead vocals), Jeanotte (vocals), Ras Toph (bass guitar), Chris Smith (drums), Rui Santos (keyboards), Dave Boatwright (lead guitar) and Kalpana Devi (vocals). The band were initially formed by Manou and his brother Jeanotte, who originally came from Portugal. Although raised in Europe, the brothers shared a direct lineage from the Portuguese African colony Cape Verde,

home to Rui Santos. The band's cosmopolitan feel was heightened by the inclusion of Jamaican, Senegalese and US performers. The Black Rebels enjoyed cult status in the USA, especially among world music devotees who enjoyed the band's merging of reggae with traditional African and Caribbean rhythms, including merengue and mbalakh. By the mid-90s the band settled in Massachusetts where, in addition to hectic touring schedules, Manou and Jeanotte also taught soccer skills to young Americans. In addition to touring, the band recorded *Thank You Jah*, which showcased their unique, multilingual, multi-sound fusions.

● ALBUMS: *Thank You Jah* (1997)★★.

BLACK ROOTS (UK)

Black Roots, not to be confused with Sugar Minott's project of the same name, formed in Bristol, England in the early 80s. The line-up comprised Errol Brown (vocals), Delroy Ogilvie (vocals), Kondwani Ngozi (congas, vocals), Jabulani Ngozi (rhythm guitar), Cordell Francis (lead guitar), Carlton Roots (keyboard, vocals), Trevor Seivwright (drums) and Derrick King (bass). The group soon established an ardent clique of local supporters following a series of live appearances where they demonstrated their awesome talent. They gained wider exposure when they appeared on the first televised edition of *Rockers Roadshow*, a showcase of British black music screened in the early days of Channel 4. The group, introduced by Mikey Dread, performed the popular hits 'Move On', 'Survival Time', 'Africa' and opened the show with a tribute to one of the UK's first immigrant slaves, Scipio Africanus, buried in Whiteladies Road on Blackboy Hill in the St. Pauls district of Bristol. They established themselves as a powerful and potent force in reggae and initiated an exhaustive touring programme promoting *Black Roots*. The collection appeared on their own Nubian label and was met with much acclaim from the reggae media, and even crossed into the mainstream when reviewed in *The Guardian*. The growing interest in the band inspired the BBC to commission the group to provide the theme tune to *The Front Line*, a situation comedy featuring two black brothers, one a streetwise dreadlocked rasta and the other a policeman. The opening sequence of the show featured the band performing the song and led to an album of the same name. In the same year the group released 'Juvenile Delinquent', which bubbled under the national chart when licensed to the Kick label. The group accompanied Linton Kwesi Johnson and Eek A Mouse on European tours, attracting favourable reviews. In 1985 the group maintained their profile, performing at the WOMAD festival in Essex alongside Toots And The Maytals and Thomas Mapfumo. Deemed as a conscientious roots outfit, the group enrolled the production skills of the Mad Professor to produce their third album, which also featured accompaniment from Vin Gordon and Michael 'Bammi' Rose. The compilation included a remarkable lovers rock track, 'Seeing Your Face', with Carlton Roots on lead vocals, which was sadly overlooked for a single release, as was a cover version of the Fat Larry's Band hit, 'Zoom'. In 1988 the group released 'Start Afresh', which was moderately successful, and demonstrated their versatility with the appropriately titled *In A Different Style*. Further sessions with the Mad Professor followed in the late 80s when the depleted band enrolled the multi-talented Black Steel to amplify the sound, resulting in the enchanting 'Guide Us', 'Voice Of The People' and 'Natural Reaction'.

● ALBUMS: *Black Roots* (Nubian 1982)★★★, *The Front Line* (BBC 1984)★★, *All Day All Night* (Nubian 1985)★★★, *In A Different Style* (Nubian 1988)★★★, *Live Power* (Nubian 1989)★★★, *Natural Reaction* (Nubian 1990)★★.

● VIDEOS: *Celebration* (Nubian 1989).

BLACK SLATE

A large roots reggae ensemble consisting of members drawn from both Jamaica and the UK, Black Slate originally comprised George Brightly aka Sir George (b. 1960, London, England, d. 1995, Jamaica, West Indies; keyboards), Desmond Mahoney (b. 1955, St. Thomas, Jamaica, West Indies; drums), Keith Drummond (b. 1955, Mandeville, Jamaica, West Indies; lead vocals), Chris Hanson (b. 1956, Kingston, Jamaica, West Indies; lead guitar), Cledwyn Rogers (b. 1955, Anguilla; rhythm guitar) and Ras Elroy (b. Elroy Bailey, 1958, London, England; bass and vocals). Subsequent members included Henschell Holder, Rudy Holmes, Ray

Carness and Nicky Ridguard. Formed in 1974, they found their first employment as backing band to Dennis Brown, Delroy Wilson, Ken Boothe and many other visiting Jamaican musicians. After gigging heavily on the London reggae circuit, their first hit under their own steam came with the anti-mugging 'Sticks Man' in 1976. They embarked on their first nationwide tour in 1978, launching their own TCD label and going on to their debut chart appearance with 'Mind Your Motion'. The band's watershed year was 1980: a simple Rastafarian rallying call, 'Amigo', was picked up by Ensign, and with the extra corporate muscle, the single rose to number 7 in the UK charts. It became their signature tune, and although follow-ups brushed the charts, notably 'Boom Boom', the band's initial impact was never repeated. George Brightly was fatally shot in Jamaica during the spring of 1995.

● ALBUMS: *Black Slate* (TCD 1979)★★★, *Sirens In The City* (Ensign 1981)★★, *Six Plus One* (Top Ranking 1982)★★, *Black Slate* (Sierra 1985)★★★.

BLACK UHURU

Formed in Jamaica by Garth Dennis, Derrick 'Ducky' Simpson and Don McCarlos in the early 70s, Black Uhuru first recorded a version of Curtis Mayfield's 'Romancing To The Folk Song' for Dynamic's Top Cat label as Uhuru (the Swahili word for 'freedom'), which met with limited success. Dennis then joined the Wailing Souls and McCarlos (as Don Carlos) went on to a solo career. Simpson then enlisted Michael Rose (b. Jamaica, West Indies) as lead singer, who himself had previously recorded as a solo artist for Yabby You (on the excellent 'Born Free') and for Winston 'Niney' Holness, including the first recording of 'Guess Who's Coming To Dinner', inspired by the Sidney Poitier film. Errol Nelson, from the Jayes, was used for harmonies. This line-up sang on an album for Prince Jammy in 1977 entitled *Love Crisis*, later reissued and retitled *Black Sounds Of Freedom*, after the group had found success. Nelson returned to the Jayes soon afterwards and Puma Jones (b. Sandra Jones, 5 October 1953, Columbia, South Carolina, USA, d. 28 January 1990, New York, USA) took over. Formerly a social worker, she had worked with

Ras Michael And The Sons Of Negus as a dancer in a bid to retrace her African ancestry via Jamaica. This combination began work for Sly Dunbar and Robbie Shakespeare's Taxi label in 1980, and Black Uhuru mania gripped the Jamaican reggae audience. The solid bedrock of Sly And Robbie's rhythms with Jones's and Simpson's eerie harmonies provided a perfect counterpoint to Rose's tortured vocals, as his songs wove tales of the hardships of Jamaican life that managed to convey a far wider relevance. Their first album for Taxi, *Showcase*, later reissued as *Vital Selection*, gave equal prominence to the vocal and instrumental versions of songs such as 'General Penitentiary', 'Shine Eye Gal' and 'Abortion', and was a massive reggae seller.

Island Records signed the group and they became a hot property throughout the musical world over the next few years. Their albums for Mango/Island continued in the same militant vein, and *Anthem* was remixed for the American market and earned a Grammy for the band. They toured the globe with the powerhouse rhythm section of Sly And Robbie, in addition to a full complement of top Jamaican session musicians. For a time they were widely touted as the only reggae band with the potential to achieve international superstar status, but although their popularity never waned after their initial breakthrough, it sadly never seemed to grow either. Michael Rose left the band in the mid-80s for a solo career that always promised more than it has actually delivered, although his 1990 album *Proud* was very strong. Junior Reid took over on lead vocals, but in retrospect, his approach was too deeply rooted in the Jamaican dancehalls at the time for Black Uhuru's international approach, and after a couple of moderately well-received albums, he also left for a solo career, which to date has been remarkably successful. For *Now*, Don Carlos returned to his former position as lead singer, reuniting the original triumvirate of himself, Simpson and Dennis, and the group still tour and release records, which are particularly popular in America. Tragically, Puma Jones died of cancer in 1990. She had left the band after *Brutal*, replaced by soundalike Olafunke.

Black Uhuru will always remain one of *the* great reggae acts, despite the fact that the interna-tional status that they deserved proved elusive.

● ALBUMS: *Love Crisis* (Prince Jammys/Third World 1977)★★★, *Showcase* (Taxi/Heartbeat 1979)★★★, *Sinsemilla* (Mango/Island 1980)★★★, *Red* (Mango/ Island 1981)★★★★, *Black Uhuru* (Virgin 1981)★★★, *Chill Out* (Mango/Island 1982)★★★, *Tear It Up - Live* (Mango/Island 1982)★★★, *Guess Who's Coming To Dinner* (Heartbeat 1983)★★★, *The Dub Factor* (Mango/Island 1983)★★★, *Anthem* (Mango/ Island 1984)★★★, *Uhuru In Dub* (CSA 1985)★★★, *Brutal* (RAS 1986)★★★★, *Brutal Dub* (RAS 1986)★★★, *Positive* (RAS 1987)★★★, *Positive Dub* (RAS 1987)★★★, *Live In New York City* (Rohit 1988)★★★, *Now* (Mesa 1990)★★★, *Now Dub* (Mesa 1990)★★★, *Iron Storm* (Mesa 1991)★★★, *Mystical Touch* (Mesa 1993)★★★.

● COMPILATIONS: *Reggae Greats* (Mango/Island 1985)★★★★, *Liberation: The Island Anthology* 2-CD box set (Mango/Island 1993)★★★★.

● VIDEOS: *Tear It Up* (Channel 5 1988), *Black Uhuru Live* (Polygram Music Video 1991).

BLACKSTONES

The Blackstones were a UK-based vocal trio featuring Leon Leiffer alongside his brothers Byron and Neville. The singers began performing in the mid-70s, releasing their debut, 'We Nah Go Suffer', for Daddy Kool, which topped the reggae charts and led to sessions with producer Phil Pratt. The rhythms were initially recorded at Channel One and the master tapes were shipped to the UK; the group added their vocals at Chalk Farm studios, followed by an eventual remix in Jamaica. These sessions resulted in the eagerly awaited *Insight*, which met with critical acclaim when it was eventually released. Inspired by Bob Marley, in 1978 the group released 'Punk Rockers', through Phil Pratt's Channan Jah, a pairing of reggae and punk that proved unable to match the superstar's success. The talented trio continued to release excellent tracks, including the popular 'Sweet Feeling'. By 1983, their fortunes improved with a new line-up of Leiffer alongside Tony Douglas (brother of Keith Douglas) and Ken Kendricks. The band topped the reggae album chart with *Take Another Look At Love*, which took its title from the trio's chart-topping single. During the mid-80s the group enjoyed a high profile in the charts with the hits

'Aint She Looking Fine', 'Created By One', 'Jealousy', 'Revolution Time', 'Fighting To The Top' and Leon's solo, 'Rockers Medley'. However, this success was marred by the 1985 release of a somewhat misguided disco collaboration, 'Nothing You Can Do About Love'. The group were enrolled to perform as the Blackstones featuring Lance Ellington, and enjoyed major label promotion; however, despite the new formula, they again failed to secure crossover success. Nevertheless, the band continued to maintain a flourishing career solely within the reggae market and are highly popular in Jamaica.

● ALBUMS: *Insight* (Burning Rockers 1979)★★★★, *Take Another Look At Love* (Pressure 1983)★★★, *Silhouettes* (Jah Larry 1995)★★★, *Outburst* (Prestige 1995)★★★, *Riding High* (Prestige 1996)★★★, *Somebody Ought To Write About It* (Prestige 1997)★★★.

BLACKWELL, CHRIS

b. 22 June 1937, London, England. The son of Middleton Joseph Blackwell, a distant relative of the power behind the Crosse & Blackwell food empire, Chris moved to Jamaica at the age of six months with his family, who settled in the affluent area of Terra Nova. Three years later he returned to England to attend prep school and subsequently enrolled at Harrow public school. A mediocre scholar, he failed to gain entrance to university and spent the late 50s commuting between London and Kingston, uncertain of his career plans. During the summer of 1958 he was stranded on a coral reef near the Hellshire Beaches. Dehydrated and sunburnt, he was rescued by members of a small Rastafarian community, and this formative incident influenced in later life his willingness to deal directly with Rasta musicians and to introduce their philosophy and culture to European and American audiences. Blackwell was one of the first to record Jamaican rhythm and blues for his R&B and Island labels, and he achieved the very first number 1 hit in Jamaica with Laurel Aitken's 'Little Sheila'/'Boogie In My Bones'.

Through his mother's friendship with writer Ian Fleming, Blackwell entered the film business during the early 60s, and worked with producer Harry Saltzman on the set of *Dr No*. Although he was offered the opportunity of working on further Bond films, Blackwell instead moved towards music (he has since purchased Ian Fleming's former mansion in Jamaica). In May 1962 he founded Island Records in London, borrowing the name from Alec Waugh's 50s novel, *Island In the Sun*. One of his early successes was with the Spencer Davis Group and he looked after Steve Winwood's interests for many years with Traffic and his solo work. After leasing master recordings from Jamaican producers such as Leslie Kong, Coxsone Dodd and King Edwards, he issued them in the UK through Island. The company boasted a number of subsidiaries, including Jump Up, Black Swan and, most notably, Sue, co-managed by producer Guy Stevens. Blackwell bought and promoted his own records, delivering them in his Mini Cooper. Early signings included a host of Jamaican talent: Owen Gray, Jimmy Cliff, Derrick Morgan, Lord Creator and Bob Morley (aka Bob Marley). However, it was 14-year-old Millie Small who provided Blackwell with his first UK breakthrough outside the exclusively West Indian and mod audiences. The infectious 'My Boy Lollipop' sold six million copies, and precipitated Blackwell's move into the mainstream UK pop/R&B market.

Blackwell continued to build up Island Records during the 60s and 70s simply by having a remarkably 'good ear'. He knew his own preferences and chose well from a slew of 'progressive' groups and, it seemed, largely lost interest in Jamaican music - Island's catalogue was now handled by Trojan Records. Important artists and groups signed and nurtured by Blackwell included Spooky Tooth, Free, John Martyn, Cat Stevens and Fairport Convention. However, he signed up and promoted Bob Marley And The Wailers in 1972 as if they were one of his rock bands, and because of Island's huge influence (and the eye-catching Zippo sleeve for *Catch A Fire*), the rock audience was forced to accept reggae on its own terms - and they liked what they heard. Island continued to promote reggae music throughout the 70s, 80s and 90s, always giving the music and its performers the type of promotion and profile that they so rarely received elsewhere. Such attention was almost invariably deserved and nearly all of the first-division Jamaican (and UK) reggae artists have worked with Island Records at one time or another. Blackwell sold Island records to

PolyGram in 1989 for £300 million and pocketed a sizeable fortune (approximately £100 million). Blackwell's reputation for nurturing talent and persevering with his artists has long been legendary and his contribution to exposing reggae music to a wider audience is inestimable.
● COMPILATIONS: Various *Pressure Drop* 7-LP box set (Mango/Island 1987)★★★, *Tougher Than Tough - The Story Of Jamaican Music* 4-CD box set (Mango/Island 1993)★★★★★.

BLONDY, ALPHA

b. Seydou Kone, 1953, Dimbokoro, Ivory Coast. During the mid-80s, reggae vocalist Blondy, whose name translates as First Bandit, became one of West Africa's most successful bandleaders, his songs widely covered by other local reggae artists. Adopting not only the rhythms and instrumental arrangements of Jamaican reggae, Blondy also followed its tradition of militant protest lyrics. After releasing his searing *Apartheid Is Nazism* album, he took the logical next step of flying to Jamaica to record the follow-up, *Jerusalem*, with the Wailers. Blondy's embracing of reggae and rasta was not without its problems; after he returned in 1981 from two years' study at Columbia University in the USA, his parents committed him to a psychiatric hospital for eighteen months because of his Rasta beliefs. There is certainly some evidence to support their view: although he dresses as a Rasta, Blondy travels everywhere with the Star of David, a copy of the bible, and one of the Koran. He also speaks Arabic in Israel, and Hebrew in the Arab world.
● ALBUMS: *Jah Glory* (Celluloid 1983)★★★, *Cocody Rock* (Shanachie 1984)★★★, *Apartheid Is Nazism* (Shanachie 1985)★★★★, *Jerusalem* (Shanachie 1986)★★, *Jah Jah Seh* (1989)★★, *Masada* (EMI 1992)★★★.
● COMPILATIONS: *Best Of Alpha Blondy* (Shanachie 1990)★★★

BLOODFIRE POSSE

The Bloodfire Posse featured Paul Emerson Blake, Donovan 'Benjie' Belnavis, Carl 'Teddy P' Ayton, Alden 'Trapper John' Stewart and Haldane 'Danny' Brown. Blake began singing while still at school, followed by a stint playing to the tourists on the north coast of Jamaica. The group had performed individually and gleaned professional experience playing in other bands. Notable contributions were made with the Caribs, the In Crowd, the Sagittarius Band, Natural Mystics and 7th Extension. The band members also played on a number of recording sessions before combining their talents. As a group, they recorded 'Rub A Dub Soldier', 'Get Flat' and 'Are You Ready', all of which topped the Jamaican charts. They toured the island playing concerts for students, which often resulted in the school gates being mobbed. Bloodfire Posse quickly gained international notoriety and in 1985 made their UK debut at the second Reggae Sunsplash Festival held in Selhurst Park, which led to a tour of Europe. While in the UK the group performed at a young offenders prison. The inmates prepared the backdrop, which featured the Pink Panther cartoon character, a reference to the group's instrumental interpretation of the theme tune, and the project was televised in the UK. The group's success generated interest from CBS Records and they secured a contract for the release of *Are You Ready*, featuring the hit singles. By 1986 Trevor 'Skatta' Bonnick replaced Blake as lead singer, initially voicing the hits 'Do You Feel Like Dancing', 'Can't Stop Rocking Tonight' and a version of the Four Tops' 'Aint No Woman (Like The One I Got)'. In June 1990 the band were shocked by the death of founding member Alden Stewart, which resulted in a lapse of work for about a year. By 1991 the group were back on the live circuit, and in the studio recording the hits 'Dance All Night' and 'Rude Boys'.
● ALBUMS: *Rough* (1985)★★★, *Are You Ready* (Columbia 1985)★★★★, *Bloodfire Posse* (1989)★★★, *Primo* (Ras 1993)★★.

BLUE BEAT RECORDS

Blue Beat was the record label that not only gave Jamaican ska a home in the UK, but also temporarily gave its name to the frenetic early form of reggae so beloved of British mods and skinheads. Between 1960 and 1967 Blue Beat issued some 400 singles and over a dozen albums as one of the many subsidiaries of Emile E. Shalit's Melodisc Records. Shalit, born of Serbo-Croatian stock, was a multilingual entrepreneur, though his interest in music was purely as a business concern. When Laurel Aitken emigrated to England in 1960, Melodisc issued his 'Lonesome

Lover' single, and the response in inner cities prompted Shalit to found a label devoted specifically to ska. However, he also had the wisdom to find someone to run the label for him, Sigimund 'Siggy' Jackson, who knew more about the new music than he did. The name Blue Beat was chosen by Jackson from an adaptation of blues beat, a then generic term for Jamaican blues. Aitken was retained to pilot Blue Beat's first release, 'Boogie Rock', leased from Coxsone Dodd's Downbeat label. A second single, 'Dumplins', was offered by the long-established Lee Byron And The Dragonaires. However, the label's distinctive blue artwork with silver logo was not unveiled until its third release, Higgs And Wilson's 'Manny Oh'. Shalit journeyed back and forth from Jamaica, making agreements with all the major production houses of the day, including Dodd's and those of Edward Seaga and Duke Reid. These licensing activities allowed Blue Beat to build up an impressive roster of artists, with Aitken joined by Joe Higgs, Delroy Wilson, Derrick Morgan and Dodd's house band, Clue J And The Blues Blasters. In the wake of this success Siggy Jackson established his own Blue Beat night at the Marquee in London, and fashion accessories with Blue Beat's logo began to sell almost as well as the records. At first the audience was composed almost entirely of expatriate West Indians in Britain's larger urban centres (particularly London), but eventually the native mod movement took the rhythms of ska to their hearts. Fundamental to this conversion was the arrival of Blue Beat's premier act, Prince Buster. After having made his debut on the b-side of a Rico Rodriguez instrumental in 1961, Buster went on to release a steady flow of high-quality 45s, including 'Al Capone' and 'Madness' (which the highly successful 80s UK pop group took as its name), which engendered Blue Beat's golden period. Other classic records, including the Folks Brothers' 'Oh Carolina', the Maytals' 'Dog War' and Roland Alphonso's 'Just A Closer Walk', all emerged in England on Blue Beat, though the label was now facing competition from Chris Blackwell's Island Records. However, as Blue Beat was still almost exclusively dependent on Jamaica's musical culture for its releases, it was forced to change tempo when the hot summer of 1966 provoked the more comfortable pace of rocksteady, a ska derivant

that quickly eclipsed the parent form. Melodisc decided a new label was needed, FAB Records, and Blue Beat fell by the wayside. After disagreements with Shalit, Jackson moved over to EMI Records to form Columbia Blue Beat. However, the original Blue Beat Records continued to sell its existing catalogue, and the label was revived again in 1972 for John Holt's 'OK Fred'.

Shalit persevered with FAB until 1977, before his death five years later. Despite his oft-repeated assertion that to him selling records was 'the same as selling potatoes', he nevertheless made a huge contribution to the development of Jamaican music in the UK.

● COMPILATIONS: various artists *All Stars - Jamaican Blues* (Blue Beat 1961)★★★★.

BLUES BUSTERS

The Jamaican vocal duo Philip James and Lloyd Campbell formed the Blues Busters in 1962. They began by performing in cabaret shows in Kingston and on the north coast to the tourists with their interpretations of then current R&B favourites. Their lucky break came when the duo was invited to accompany the soul legend Sam Cooke on his Jamaican tour. Naturally curious, they scrutinized his performance and were inspired by him. On returning to the cabaret circuit they emulated his soulful harmonies and were soon recording a number of cover versions of popular soul and reggae tunes. They enjoyed minor hits with the singles 'Thinking' and 'Privileged', although they relished greater commercial success with their hit compilations. The group also attempted to write and produce their own material with songs such as 'Baby I'm Sorry' and 'Keep On Doing It'. In the late 70s, acknowledging their support on the inspirational Jamaican tour with Sam Cooke, the duo recorded a tribute to the star. They recorded together for almost 25 years including productions with Byron Lee, Lloyd Charmers and Neville Hinds.

● ALBUMS: *Philip And Lloyd* (Creole 1976)★★★, *Truth* (Sarge/Blue Inc. 1979)★★★, *Tribute To Sam Cooke* (Orbitone 1980)★★, *Top Of The Pops* (Echo 1982/Vista 1983)★★★★.

BOB AND MARCIA

Bob Andy (b. Keith Anderson, 1944, Jamaica, West Indies) and Marcia Griffiths (b. 1954, Kingston, Jamaica, West Indies) had two UK chart entries at the turn of the 70s - the first, a version of Nina Simone's 'Young, Gifted And Black', was a UK Top 5 hit in 1970 on reggae producer Harry J's self-titled label, and the follow-up, 'Pied Piper', reached number 11 on the Trojan label. Both Andy and Griffiths were hugely popular artists in Jamaica in their own right before and after their pop crossover success, but neither felt that this particular interlude was successful for them, especially in financial terms. It is sad that these two hits have become the only records for which they are known outside of reggae music circles. It is sadder still, that their best duet of the period, the timeless 'Always Together', which they recorded for Coxsone Dodd, failed to make any impression outside Jamaica.

● ALBUMS: *Young, Gifted And Black* (Harry J 1970)★★★, *Pied Piper* (Harry J 1971)★★★, *Really Together* (I-Anka 1987)★★★.

BOLO, YAMMIE

b. Rolando Ephraim McClean, 1970, Kingston, Jamaica, West Indies. Bolo entered the music business as a youngster, singing on Sugar Minott's Youth Promotion sound system. He cut his first record, 'When A Man's In Love' (1985), for producer Winston Riley. Several other 45s followed, including 'Jah Made Them All' (1986) for Riley, 'Roots Pon Mi Corner' (1986) for Minott, and 'Free Mandela' (1987) for Miami-based Skeng Don. Afterwards, he linked up with Junior Delgado and Augustus Pablo to record a number of excellent singles exploring social and cultural issues, including 'Ransom Of A Man's Life' (1987), 'Tell Me Why Is This Fussing & Fighting' (1988), 'Love Me With Feeling' (1989), 'Poverty & Brutality' (1989), 'Poor Man's Cry' (1990) and 'Struggle In Babylon' (1990). In 1989 Junior Delgado produced *Ransom*, and later that year Pablo issued *Jah Made Them All*, a vocal/dub set. More singles for other producers followed: 'Turbo Charge' (1991) for Winston 'Niney' Holness, 'Blood A Run' and 'Iniquity Worker' (both 1991) for Trevor Douglas, 'Jah Jah Loving' (1991), a co-production between Bolo and Neville Thompson, 'It's Not Surprising' (1992) for Barry O'Hare, 'Joe The Boss', 'Be Still' (both 1992) and 'Revolution' for Tapper Zukie, and 'Bowl Must Full' for Augustus Pablo. He made his best album, *Up Life Street*, for Trevor Douglas's Leggo label, and *Who Knows It Feels It* for Holness. The same year also saw the inauguration of Bolo's own Yam Euphony label, with a version of Madonna's 'La Isla Bonita', and the fiery anti-gunman title, 'The Glock War, Gun War'. In 1994 he successfully collaborated with Japanese star Miya (Kazafumi Miyazawa), and has recently recorded for Sly And Robbie's Taxi label. Bolo's vocal delivery is similar to that of the so-called Waterhouse style of Junior Reid, Don Carlos and Michael Rose (Black Uhuru). Nevertheless, Bolo is an exciting and original young artist in his own right.

● ALBUMS: *Ransom* (Greensleeves 1989)★★★, *Jah Made Them All* (Greensleeves 1989), *Who Knows It Feels It* (Holness 1991)★★★, *Up Life Street* (Leggo 1992)★★★★, *Cool And Easy* (Tappa 1993)★★, with Lloyd Hemmings *Meets Lloyd Hemmings* (Message/Jamaica 1993)★★★, *Born Again* (Ras 1996)★★★.

BOOM, BARRY

Barry Boom is the pseudonym Paul Robinson first employed to mask his musical backroom duties. These activities were many; he helped to write and produce Maxi Priest's debut album, and Phillip Papa Levi's groundbreaking 'Mi God Mi King' single. He had also been part of the hotly tipped One Blood with other family members, until his brother and fellow band member, Errol, died. Robinson briefly worked with Sly And Robbie before electing to pursue a solo career under the name Barry Boom, which he had previously only used in a production capacity. He kicked off his career on the Fashion subsidiary Fine Style in 1989, cutting a number of hit singles, including the reggae number ones 'Making Love and 'Number One Girl', and 'Hurry Over'. His debut album was a consistent, polished affair that mixed lovers rock lyrics with more cultural concerns, all conducted over an understated, rootsy backing. Boom is still striving for the kind of mainstream success his talents deserve, and 1994 saw him reunited with Fashion once more.

● ALBUMS: *The Living Boom* (Fine Style 1990)★★★.

BOOTHE, KEN

b. 1948, Kingston, Jamaica, West Indies. Boothe began his recording career with Stranger Cole in the duo Stranger And Ken, releasing titles including 'World's Fair', 'Hush', 'Artibella' and 'All Your Friends' from 1963-65. When the rocksteady rhythm began to evolve during 1966, Boothe recorded 'Feel Good'. He released a series of titles for Coxsone Dodd's Studio One label that revealed him to be an impassioned, fiery vocalist, with an occasionally mannered style ultimately derived from US soul. During this period he was often referred to as the Wilson Pickett of Jamaican music. He continued recording with Dodd until 1970, releasing some of his best and biggest local hits. He made records for other producers at the same time, including Sonia Pottinger's Gayfeet label, for which he recorded the local hit 'Say You' in 1968. By the following year he had switched again, this time to Leslie Kong's Beverley's label, where he stayed until 1971, notching up two more local hits with 'Freedom Street' and 'Why Baby Why', as well as several other singles and an album.

He then freelanced during the early 70s for various producers, including Keith Hudson, Herman Chin-Loy, Randy's and George 'Phil' Pratt. During the same period he began an association with former Gaylad, B.B. Seaton, which resulted in an album in 1971. At this point in time he was hugely popular with Jamaican audiences, particularly teenage girls, who loved his emotive voice and good looks. When he started working with the pianist/vocalist/ producer Lloyd Charmers in 1971 it was not long before the hits started to flow again, first in Jamaica and then in the UK charts. 'Everything I Own', a David Gates composition, topped the UK chart in November 1974. The follow-up, 'Crying Over You', also charted, reaching the number 11 position in February 1975. Pop singer Boy George covered Charmers and Boothe's version of 'Everything I Own', reaching the UK chart with the song in 1987. Boothe sadly failed to capitalize on this success, having continued to record for a variety of Jamaican producers throughout the late 70s and 80s. He has also produced his own material with occasional commercial success. He regularly appears on Jamaican oldies shows, usually singing his classic 60s and 70s material, and remains one of the great Jamaican soul voices.

● ALBUMS: *Mr. Rock Steady* (Studio One 1968)★★★, *More Of Ken Boothe* (Studio One 1968)★★★, *A Man And His Hits* (Studio One 1970)★★★, *Freedom Street* (Beverley's 1971)★★★, *The Great Ken Boothe Meets B.B. Seaton And The Gaylads* (Jaguar 1971)★★★, *Black Gold And Green* (Trojan 1973)★★★, *Everything I Own* (Trojan 1974)★★★, *Let's Get It On* (Trojan 1974)★★★, *Blood Brothers* (Trojan 1975)★★★, *Live Good* (Liberty 1978)★★★, *Who Gets Your Love* (Trojan 1978)★★★, *I'm Just A Man* (Bunny Lee 1979)★★★, *Showcase* (Justice 1979)★★★, *Reggae For Lovers* (Mountain 1980)★★★, *Imagine* (Park Heights 1986)★★, *Don't You Know* (Tappa 1988)★★, *Power Of Love* (1993)★★.

● COMPILATIONS: *Ken Boothe Collection* (Trojan 1987)★★★, *Everything I Own* (Trojan 1997)★★★.

BORN JAMERICANS

Born Jamericans are a Washington, USA-based singer/DJ combination who successfully fuse hip-hop with dancehall. The duo comprises Notch Howell (b. 11 May 1974, Hartford, Connecticut, USA) and Edley Payne (b. 1 August 1973, Washington, DC, USA). They met and combined their talents in the early 90s, their unique style attracting the attention of producer Chucki Thompson, who supported the duo in recording their debut. The record label Delicious Vinyl broke with their exclusively hip-hop tradition by taking on the duo's unique fusion of reggae and hip-hop. Commercial success quickly followed with the release of 'Boom Shak Attack', which topped the reggae charts, and led to the release of the debut album, *Kids From Foreign*. In 1996 the pair contributed to the soundtrack of the movie *Klash* and released 'Nastee', 'Why Do Girls', Warning Sign' and 'Informer Fe Dead'. The combination built a solid foundation, playing to an international audience on a tour of Japan with Shinehead and the Mad Lion. The association with the two DJs resulted in a recording session alongside Sleepy Wonder for the track 'Gotta Get Mine', which featured on their second album. Other associations include work with producer Salaam Remi (who produced Ini Kamoze's 'Here Comes The

Hot Stepper'), Johnny Osbourne ('Roadblock', which provided the foundation to 'State Of Shock') and Merciless on the assertive 'Cyaan Done'.

In the summer of 1997 the group embarked on a promotional tour, featuring an acclaimed appearance at The Reggae On The River Festival; they are celebrated as the 'prodigal kids from foreign'.

● ALBUMS: *Kids From Foreign* (Delicious Vinyl 1993)★★, *Yardcore* (Delicious Vinyl 1997)★★★.

BOUNTY KILLER

b. Rodney Pryce, June 1972, Riverton City, Jamaica, West Indies. Coming from a dancehall background, Pryce's father ran the Black Scorpio Sound System, and it was not long before he picked up the microphone himself. He soon became known performing on other sound systems, including Stereo Two and Metromedia. His first recording session was in the spring of 1992 at King Jammy's studio when he sang 'Watch The Gun', produced by Uncle T. After singing a number of other rhythms, Uncle T's brother King Jammy recognized Bounty Killer's potential and 'Fat And Sexy' was the resulting hit. Many ragga hits related to guns and Killer's contribution to the list is considerable: 'New Gun', 'Cop A Shot', 'Kill Fe Fun' and 'New Gun Gal Say Yes'. The flurry of gun-related hits continued unabashed and in 1993 the inevitable clash took place with his main rival, Beenie Man. In 1994 Killer recorded a number of singles away from gun lyrics, including, with Chuck Turner, 'Run Around Girl' and 'Roots Reality And Culture'. His big hit 'Down In The Ghetto' described how guns and drugs reached the ghettos sanctioned by corrupt government officials: 'Down in the ghetto where the gun have a ting - and the politician is the guns them a bring - hey - and the crack and the coke them a support the killing - me check it out the whole a dem ah the same ting'. With Colin Roach and Junior Reid, his vocals enhanced 'I'll Be Back' and 'This World's Too Haunted', respectively. Seasoned Studio One performer Dawn Penn returned to Jamaica and re-recorded her classic 'You Don't Love Me (No No No)', produced by Steely And Clevie, who took their version into the UK Top 10. She also recorded the same song with King Jammy producing, and enjoyed a

reggae hit with 'No No No (World A Respect)', featuring fellow Studio One veterans Dennis Brown and Ken Boothe, along with Bounty Killer. His popularity and unique vocal style led to a tour of the UK and in the spring of 1995 his single with Sanchez, 'Searching', enjoyed a long stay on the reggae chart.

Bounty Killer continued to record many hits throughout 1995, including 'Book Book', 'Cellular Phone', 'Smoke The Herb', 'Mama', 'No Argument' and 'Fear No Evil'. By the end of 1995 the continuing feud with Beenie Man was resolved through RJR's disc jockey Richard Burgess, who invited the two to the station where a truce was announced. In the summer of 1996 Bounty's inimitable style enhanced the dancehall mix of the Fugees' chartbusting version of Roberta Flack's 'Killing Me Softly'.

● ALBUMS: *Jamaica's Most Wanted* (Greensleeves 1993)★★★★, *Down In The Ghetto* (Jammys 1994)★★★★, with Beenie Man *Guns Out* (Greensleeves 1994)★★★, *No Argument* (Greensleeves 1995)★★★, *My Xperience* (Blunt/Virgin 1996)★★, *Ghetto Gramma* (Greensleeves 1997)★★.

BOVELL, DENNIS

b. 1953, St. Peter, Barbados, West Indies. Guitarist who, as co-founder of Matumbi, one of the UK's first and best indigenous bands, has had a long apprenticeship in reggae music. Though born in the West Indies, Bovell grew up in south London. There he fell in love with Jamaican dub music and its ethos, setting up an early British sound system, Jah Sufferer, in north London. It brought him his first clash with the establishment: he was imprisoned for six months on remand after one event, only to be released on appeal.

Like many reggae musicians operating in the UK in the late 70s, Bovell discovered common ground with the punk/new wave movement. He was friends at school with keyboard player Nick Straker and producer Tony Mansfield (New Musik, Captain Sensible), and this pair and others would help spice up his solo releases. In turn Bovell became embroiled in the early recordings of bands such as the Pop Group and the Slits. Bovell's own efforts, particularly his first two sets, offered an impressive collection of experimental dubs. Indeed, at one point his

name was linked in one way or another to no fewer than 18 singles in the UK Reggae Top 20.
● ALBUMS: As Blackbeard: *Strictly Dub Wize* (Tempus 1978)★★★★, *I Wah Dub* (More Cut/EMI 1980)★★★★. As Dennis Bovell: *Brain Damage* (Fontana 1981)★★★. As Dennis Bovell And The Dub Band: *Audio Active* (Moving Target 1986)★★★.

BREEZE, JEAN 'BINTA'

Jean 'Binta' Breeze is a poet and performer of international status. She was born and raised in rural Jamaica before moving to Kingston to study at the Jamaican School Of Drama, where the pivotal dub poets Oku Onuora and Michael Smith also studied. While at the academy she was also instrumental in the formation of the renowned women's theatre company, Sistren, in addition to developing her poetic skills. The virtuosity of Jamaican sound system DJs of the early 70s, including Big Youth and U-Roy, inspired the birth of dub poetry and the basis of Breeze's career. The technique is widely regarded as being initiated by Linton Kwesi Johnson, who, after hearing her perform, encouraged Breeze to join him in the UK. Through Johnson and the 'devil's advocate', Darcus Howe, her first book of poetry, *Ryddim Ravings*, was published in 1988 by the Race Today co-operative and led to her being commissioned to write the script and screenplay for *Hallelujah Anyhow*, a production for the British Film Institute and Channel 4. Breeze also performed 'Mr Cool' on the channel's *Club X* programme, and her career was examined in the series *The Bandung File* for a documentary entitled 'Mood And Moments'. In 1986 her admonition of indiscriminate foreign relief workers, 'Aid Travel With A Bomb', was greeted with fervour ('They buy your land - To dump their nuclear waste - You sell it for the food - That your children taste'). In 1991 she recorded *Tracks* with Dennis Bovell's Dub Band. Her second book of poetry, *Spring Cleaning*, was published in 1992, and she was also involved in the direction of a number of theatrical productions, including *Moon Dance Night* and *In And Out Of The Window*, while as a performer she took the lead in *The Love Space Demands*. She continues to divide her time between Jamaica and London, recently being involved in *Rude Girls*

for the Irie Dance Company, and she has been commissioned to write a screenplay for the proposed *Brixton*. She is one of only a few female dub poets alongside such notables as 'Miss Lou' Bennett and Sister Farika, and is also widely admired for her ability to maintain her commitment to a diverse career while raising her son and two daughters.
● ALBUMS: with others *Woman Talk* (Heartbeat 1986)★★★, *Tracks* (LKJ 1991)★★★★, *Riding On De Riddym* (57 Productions 1997)★★.
● FURTHER READING: *Ryddim Ravings*, *Spring Cleaning*.

BRIGADIER JERRY

b. Robert Russell, Kingston, Jamaica, West Indies. Brigadier Jerry was one of the most influential Jamaican DJs of the 80s, but his impact was achieved almost entirely through sound tapes (i.e., live recordings of sound system dances). As a spontaneous lyricist, he is unsurpassed, despite a scarcity of recordings throughout his career. He was born in the Papine area of eastern Kingston, and his sister Nancy also became a DJ. An early interest in music took him to King Strugav Hi-Fi, owned by the legendary U-Roy, whom he acknowledges as his principal influence and mentor. By 1978 he had joined the Twelve Tribes of Israel organization, spreading their message on the affiliated Jah Love sound system, and occasionally recording with other members such as Fred Locks. Encouraged by Freddie McGregor and Judah Eskender Tafari, he sang three sides for Studio One, before Delroy Stansbury released 'Pain' and 'Gwan A School' in 1982 on the Jwyanza label. Outside of Jah Love he had made regular appearances on a number of other sound systems, including Supreme Love, Wha Dat and Black Star, and while in the US Downbeat International, accumulating a growing band of younger DJ admirers who frequently recorded his lyrics, although his own trips to the studio remained rare.
In 1985 Jah Love Musik released his debut album proper, *Jamaica Jamaica*, which remains one of his best works, and contains a definitive cut of Bunny Wailer's 'Armagideon'. A follow-up single, 'Roots Girl', proved less successful, but by 1986 it seemed as though he was finally ready to

grasp the challenge of transferring his skills to vinyl, singing several inspired sides for the Supreme label, Techniques and George Phang. Apart from 'Hard Drugs' for Pioneer, however, there was little until his second album, *On The Road*, in early 1991. In 1992 he recorded the *Hail Him* set for Tapper Zukie.

● ALBUMS: *Live At The Controls* (Vista Sounds 1983)★★★, *Jamaica Jamaica* (RAS 1985)★★★★, *On The Road* (RAS 1989)★★, *Hail Him* (Tappa 1992)★★★.

BRIMSTONE

Ladbroke Grove, London-based Michael Campbell and King Sounds formed Grove Music, which was responsible for promoting the careers of Aswad, Sons Of Jah and Brimstone. Brimstone were formed in 1977 by Sam Jones (b. Samson Jones, 1945, Dominican Republic; rhythm guitar) and Gus Phillips (b. 1957, Sierra Leone; vocals). The line-up also included Peter Harris (b. 1955, Jamaica, West Indies; lead guitar), Leo Charles (b. 1959, Dominican Republic; drums), John Thomas (b. 1948, Trinidad, West Indies; percussion), Wayne Griffiths (b. 1951, Trinidad, West Indies; bass) and Vivienne Clark (b. 1958, England; vocals). The line-up expanded to include Tony 'Gad' Robinson, who later joined Aswad, Angela Francis and Grace Reid. They toured as part of the 'Grove package' alongside King Sounds and Sons Of Jah, and following the success of their debut single, 'Final Judgement', in 1978, the band became the headline act. They had built up a distinctive catalogue, which later grew to include 'Malcolm X', 'Praise Jah' and 'Solomon's Day'. In 1979 they followed their debut hit with 'Release Me', which provided the band with a Top 20 hit in the reggae chart. In common with a number of UK-based reggae bands, the group found greater success in Europe, becoming particularly popular in Belgium. In 1982 the band released their debut, *Jah See And Know*, which featured a version of Bob Marley's 'Craven Choke Puppy' alongside seven original tracks. The album was recorded by the revised line-up of founder-members Gus Phillips, Leo Charles with Vivienne Clark, alongside Stephen Rene, Tony Clarke, George Joseph and Lynford Odum.

● ALBUMS: *Jah See And Know* (Lark 1982)★★★.

BRISSET, ANNETTE

b. Jamaica, West Indies. Brisset grew up singing in church, learning the drums from her brother, and moved to New York, USA, at the age of 12. She began her career in the early 70s as a drummer in the studio, and supported a number of Jamaican superstars passing through New York. As a soloist Brisset worked with Lloyd Barnes, who released her debut, 'What A Feeling'.

While working at Wackies she encountered several Studio One legends, including the Heptones, Alton Ellis, Sugar Minott, Horace Andy, Jackie Mittoo and Marcia Griffiths. Inspired by Griffiths and her association with the I-Threes, Brisset formed Sistren. The all-female line-up was only ever acknowledged by their first names, a move interpreted by the media as an attempt to negate any possible slave-master lineage. Alice, Annette, Cori, Donna, Lori, Pamela, Phylis and Rebecca launched their musical career in the mid-80s. The women performed in and around New York where they built a solid fanbase and continued supporting visiting reggae names including Marcia Griffiths, Dennis Brown and Steel Pulse. Her first solo album flopped because of inadequate promotion, and she relocated to Miami in 1987 in time for the second. She maintained a version of Sistren, who continued to strive for recognition, and in 1988 the group, recording as Annette Brisset And Sistren, released *Gun Shooting Raw*, which included the tracks 'In The Country' and 'Half A Mile'.

In addition to providing lead vocals, the multi-talented Brisset played drums, keyboards and synthesizer, while the other members contributed steadfast backing vocals. In 1989 Brisset gained further prominence with the release of 'Kiss What I Miss' and a series of critically acclaimed performances showcasing her fine, soulful voice and neat arrangements. In the 90s she has attempted to consolidate her position with further recordings.

● ALBUMS: *Love Power* (Wackies 1986)★★★, as Annette Brisset And Sistren *Gun Shooting Raw* (Sastan 1987)★★★, *Get Up And Dance* (Zodiac/VP 1991)★★★, *Annette* (Imp 1993)★★.

BROOKS, BABA

b. Oswald Brooks, *c*.1935, Kingston, Jamaica, West Indies. When there was a shortage of R&B sounds coming from the USA in the late 50s, the sound system men enrolled the services of musicians who would record their own tunes. Many of these recordings were jazz-orientated and featured a horn section to complement the shuffling beat. Baba Brooks played trumpet and in the early 60s had his own band, whose recordings included the celebratory 'Independence Ska', commemorating Jamaica's break from colonialism in 1962. Both 'Bus Strike' and 'Musical Workshop' were hits in 1964. His band were also noted for their rendition of 'Distant Drums', which had the distinction of being the debut release for Philip and Justin Yap's newly formed Top Deck label. As well as providing backing on a number of early ska hits, including 'Run Joe' with Stranger Cole and 'Penny Reel' with Eric Morris, the band released the classic 'Guns Fever', recorded at Studio One in Brentford Road in 1965. His 1966 instrumental hit 'King Size' appeared to be a ska interpretation of 'Making Whoopee' and originally surfaced as the b-side to the Saints' 'Brown Eyes'. In 1967 he returned to the frantic pace of his 1965 hit with 'One Eyed Giant', which featured a 'chika chika' vocal sound and on which each player performed a jazzy solo. Other hits included 'Teenage Ska', 'River To The Bank' and 'Ball Of Fire'. His recording of 'Chang Kai Check' provided the foundation of many reggae hits. His band continued to play on sessions until the early 70s.

● ALBUMS: with others *The Birth Of Ska* (Trojan 1990)★★★.

BROOKS, CEDRIC 'IM'

b. 1943, Kingston, Jamaica, West Indies. At the age of 11 Brooks became a pupil at the Alpha Catholic School for Boys, where he learned clarinet and music theory, and in his late teens studied tenor saxophone and flute. In the early 60s he was a member of several groups including the Vagabonds and Granville Williams Band. He teamed up with trumpeter David Madden during 1968 for an excellent series of instrumentals for Coxsone Dodd, released under the name Im And David. Some of the best of these singles, such as 'Candid Eye', 'Black Is

Black' and 'Soul Brother', were included on the various artists album *Money Maker*. Brooks also played on many sessions for Dodd, and had several solo singles released in the early 70s.

In 1970 Brooks commenced his association with Count Ossie, the first fruits of which were 'So Long Rastafari Calling' and 'Give Me Back Me Language And Me Culture', released under the name Im And Count Ossie. Shortly after this, the two formed the Mystic Revelation of Rastafari, which combined the forces of Count Ossie's hand-drummers with a brass section arranged by Brooks. Together they recorded the groundbreaking *Grounation* album. In 1974 Brooks left Count Ossie to form the Light Of Saba, taking some members of the Mystic Revelation Of Rastafari with him. The Light Of Saba retained the brass and Rasta drums that had characterized the previous group, added guitars, and incorporated a more pronounced reggae element. Around 1974, after recording a single for Randys, 'Demauungwani', they recorded their first album for the Institute Of Jamaica, *From Mento To Reggae To Third World Music*, under the name Cedric Brooks And The Divine Light. It offers a history of the development of Jamaican music, and includes beautifully performed pieces in the mento, junkunoo, ska, rocksteady and reggae styles, plus one forward-looking Pan-Caribbean piece. Their superb *The Light Of Saba* included reworkings of 'Peanut Vendor' and Horace Silver's 'Song To My Father', but consisted mostly of original Rastafarian songs and instrumentals. *The Light Of Saba In Reggae* was an even stronger collection of original material. Shortly after this, Brooks left, although the Light Of Saba continued for one further album, the mediocre *Sabebe*.

In 1977 Studio One issued an exceptional solo album by Brooks, *Im Flash Forward*. This material may have been recorded in the early 70s, as it uses rhythm tracks from that period, but it is more likely that it was recorded shortly before its release. Regardless of this, Brooks' tenor playing on the album is beautifully restrained, and has a meditative quality that evokes a sublime, spiritual atmosphere. It has become firmly established as one of the greatest Jamaican instrumental albums. In 1978 Brooks assembled a large ensemble featuring a host of percussionists and horn players for *United Africa*, an album that not only utilized Jamaican musical forms such as reggae and nyahbinghi, but also incorporated African and Caribbean forms. It was a highly successful enterprise, and sadly, has never been followed up. Since then, Brooks has recorded widely as a session musician, but his only solo recordings have been some singles for Studio One. His thorough understanding of Jamaica's musical heritage, and the innovative and organic way in which he has built on that foundation to extend its scope, ensures the longevity of his music. It seems inconceivable that others will not continue with the work that he has started.

● ALBUMS: As Cedric Brooks And The Divine Light *From Mento To Reggae To Third World Music* (Institute Of Jamaica 1975)★★. As Cedric Brooks And The Divine Light Of Saba *The Light Of Saba* (Total Sounds 1976)★★★★, *The Light Of Saba In Reggae* (Total Sounds 1977)★★★★. As Cedric Brooks: *Im Flash Forward* (Studio One 1977)★★★★, *United Africa* (Water Lily 1978)★★★.

BROOKS, MIKE

b. Edmund Brooks, 1953, Westmoreland, Jamaica, West Indies. Brooks initially entered the recording industry in 1972, performing with an obscure band called the Tots. Their debut, 'Earth Is The Fullness', warranted limited attention and the members of the ensemble left to pursue solo careers. Recording as Mike Brooks, his solo career was the most distinguished. In 1977 with producer Alvin 'GG' Ranglin, he released 'Guiding Star', which led to a series of hits within the Jamaican community at home and abroad. Biding his time, he continued intermittently to release high-quality hits throughout the 70s and 80s, including 'Who Have Eyes To See' in combination with Prince Far I, alongside the solo hits 'Come Sister Love', 'Grooving', 'Open The Door' and the celebratory 'What A Gathering'; the latter song utilized Leroy Smart's 'Ballistic Affair' rhythm. This modicum of success led Brooks to the UK, where he joined the British Reggae Artists Famine Appeal as a featured vocalist on the charity single 'Let's Make Africa Green Again'. He continued recording while in the UK, notably with the Instigators for the lovers rock theme 'Beyond The Hills'. In 1990 he teamed up with producer Glen Brown for an ill-advised project with Norwegian producers Otto and Frank Hestness. The Nordic team recorded digital rhythms that were overdubbed in London, unfortunately resulting in an incomprehensible mess. His 1995 release, *Hardcore Lover*, resulted in his exoneration, largely owing to notable combination tunes with Delroy Wilson and Pat Kelly.

● ALBUMS: *True Love* (Harvest 1977)★★★, *What A Gathering* (Burning Sounds 1979)★★★★, *One Love* (Vista Sounds 1983)★★, *Respect Due* (Good Times 1985)★★★, with Glen Brown *Mike Brooks And Glen Brown Meet Rhythm Foundation* (Rhythm Foundation 1990)★★, *Hardcore Lover* (Pre 1995)★★★.

BROWN SUGAR

Brown Sugar was a female lovers rock trio consisting of Caron Wheeler, Carol Simms and Pauline Catilin. The group began recording with Dennis Harris at Eve Studios in Brockley Rise, south London, England. With Harris they topped the reggae charts in 1977 with the exhilarating 'Black Pride', a version of the Barbara Lewis 1963 *Billboard* chart-topper 'Hello Stranger', and the defiant 'I'm In Love With A Dreadlocks'. The singles were released on the newly formed Lovers Rock label, a name that has since become the specific nomenclature for the genre. Following the group's departure from the label, Harris ironically released 'Free', followed by 'Forever My Darling' and 'Do You Really Need Me'. The tracks were scheduled for inclusion on *Brown Sugar*. With Studio 16 producer Winston Edwards, and inspired by Pat Kelly's hit 'I Am So Proud', the trio released their own version of the Impressions' classic. The single was credited to Pauline And Brown Sugar as it was primarily a solo outing for Catilin. In the autumn of 1978 the group released 'Confession Hurts', and at the 1979 *Echoes* Awards Show, the backing band, Well Pack, swapped roles with the group halfway through their performance - Wheeler, Simms and Catilin proved adept at providing the musical accompaniment. They also collected an award as Best Vocal Group by the weekly magazine's readers. Further hits with Edwards followed, including 'You And Your Smiling Face', 'Suddenly He's Gone' and 'Runaway Love'. By 1983 their output had dwindled, although 'Go Now' for El Jay proved a minor hit. In 1984 Wheeler and Catilin returned to studio work providing backing vocals, notably with Keith Douglas's 'Cool Down Amina'. In the late 80s the members concentrated on their solo careers; Wheeler joined the Funki Dred sound system with Soul II Soul and in 1988 topped the UK chart with 'Back To Life (However D'You Want Me)' and 'Keep On Moving'. Simms recorded prolifically as Kofi, often re-recording former Brown Sugar hits. In 1996 the name Brown Sugar re-emerged with the exceptional 'Sensimillia Babe', produced by Anthony Malvo and Anthony Red Rose in Jamaica, although it was considered to be an alias for Chevelle Franklin.

● ALBUMS: *Brown Sugar* (Eve 1977)★★★★.

BROWN, AL

b. Kingston, Jamaica, West Indies. A smooth reggae artist, and ex-member of Skin, Flesh And Bones, whose first recording was for Coxsone Dodd, Brown subsequently teamed up with the Volcanoes, but enjoyed a UK solo hit with his version of Al Green's 'Here I Am Baby' for Trojan Records. Later singles included 'Caribbean Queen' and 'No Soul Today', but he proved unable to repeat the success, despite working with the Seventh Extension band and others.

● ALBUMS: *Dying Love* (Studio One 1970)★★★, *Here I Am Baby* (Trojan 1978)★★.

BROWN, BARRY

b. c.1962, Kingston, Jamaica, West Indies. Brown's first release was 'Girl You're Always On My Mind' (produced by Bunny Lee) which had little impact. However, his militant roots-style vocals, similar to Linval Thompson, soon earned him international acclaim. In 1979 he had a hit with 'Step It Up Youthman', which led to an album of the same name. His success led to much Barry Brown material becoming available, including 'Put Down Your Guns', 'We Can't Live Like This', 'Big Big Pollution', 'Politician' and 'Conscious Girl'. By 1980 Brown's vocals appeared on disco-mix releases with notable DJs including Jah Thomas ('Jealous Lover'), Ranking Joe ('Don't Take No Steps') and Ranking Toyan ('Peace And Love'). Having worked with Linval Thompson on 'Separation' and Sugar

Minott on 'Things And Time', Brown decided to go into self-production. His initial release, 'Cool Pon Your Corner', preceded an album that featured the classic 'Jah Jah Fire'. In 1981 his self-produced 'Problems Get You Down' and 'Physical Fitness' were not successful. In 1983 he recorded at the legendary Studio One, resulting in the release of a 10-inch disco-mix, 'Give Love', and 'Far East'. The tune revived interest in the singer and other releases followed, including 'Dreadful Day' and 'Serious Man'. In 1984 Brown was riding on the wave of the current dance trend with 'Belly Move', accompanied by DJ Charlie Chaplin. Though he no longer set the charts ablaze, Brown continued to release high-quality tunes.

● ALBUMS: *Step It Up Youthman* (Third World 1979)★★★, *Cool Pon Your Corner* (Trojan 1980)★★★, *Superstar* (Micron 1980)★★, *Showcase* (Jammys 1980)★★★, *Not So Lucky* (Black Roots 1981)★★★, *Barry* (Starlight 1982)★★, with Little John *Showdown* (Empire 1983)★★★, with Willie Williams *Roots & Culture* (VP 1983)★★★, *Far East* (Hit Bound/Channel One 1983)★★★, *Right Now* (Time 1984)★★★, *Same Sound* (VP 1984)★★, with Johnny Clarke *Sings Roots And Culture* (Roots 1992)★★, *Mr Moneyman* (Esoludon 1993)★★★.

BROWN, DENNIS

b. Dennis Emanuel Brown, 1957, Kingston, Jamaica, West Indies. Now regularly billed as 'The Crown Prince Of Reggae', it is only Brown's self-effacing nature that has denied him advancement to the office of king. He is loved in reggae music like no other singer and has been regularly courted by the major record labels, and even enjoyed a couple of token chart hits in Britain. More to the point, he has produced more reggae classics than just about anyone else. He began his career at the age of 11 as one of the Studio One label's many child stars. His first hit, 'No Man Is An Island' (1969), found him singing in much the same style he now uses, only with a far less croaky voice. 'If I Follow My Heart', his other chief hit at Studio One, was every bit as good. He spent the early 70s freelancing between studios, recording for Lloyd Daley, Impact, Joe Gibbs and Aquarius, before recording his third collection, *Super Reggae And*

Soul Hits, a mature, classic record, full of Derrick Harriott's soulful arrangements and Brown's rich tones. A move to Winston 'Niney' Holness's label was no less profitable, with the two albums he made there, *Just Dennis* and *Wolf & Leopards*, recorded with a three-year gap between them, yet with a seamless rootsy artistry making them clearly part of one body of work. Many regard the latter album as his best. A long, fruitful liaison with Joe Gibbs and Errol Thompson resulted in a further series of classic albums, among them *Visions*, *Joseph's Coat Of Many Colours*, *Spellbound* and *Yesterday, Today & Tomorrow*.

While the rock critics were latching on to dub in the mid-70s, it was Brown who was drawing a mass audience almost unnoticed outside reggae's heartlands. His combination of serious, 'message' songs and soul-wailing love melodies was irresistible. His stage shows, too, were genuine 'events', and always packed a punch. 'Money In My Pocket' (1979) was the first of three incursions into chart territory, with Brown eventually signing with A&M Records in the early 80s. Simultaneously, he became co-owner of the DEB label, successfully producing Junior Delgado and female lovers rock trio 15-16-17. Brown gradually spent more time in London as a consequence, eventually settling there for much of the 80s. His Joe Gibbs connection was terminated in 1982, marking the *de facto* end of Gibbs's prominence as a producer. Brown's series of reggae hits, including 'To The Foundation' for Gussie Clarke, 'Revolution' for Taxi or cuts on his own Yvonne's Special label (named after his wife), saw him become one of the few established singers to ride the early dancehall boom unscathed. However, when digital music exploded onto reggae in 1985-86, Brown faltered for the first time in his career, seemingly unsure of his next move. Eventually, he settled into the new style, recording *The Exit* for King Jammy's in the digital mode. A move to Gussie Clarke's Music Works Studio in 1989 gave him more kudos with the youth market, particularly on the duet with Gregory Isaacs, 'Big All Around'. Once again, Dennis Brown was in demand in Jamaica, back at the roots of the music, and rolling once again, recording everywhere and anywhere for a few months. In 1995 he recorded with Beenie Man and Triston Palma

for the hit compilation *Three Against War*. Clearly he has the ability and energy to do whatever he wants.

● ALBUMS: *No Man Is An Island* (Studio One 1970)★★, *If I Follow My Heart* (Studio One 1971)★★, *Super Reggae & Soul Hits* (Trojan 1972)★★★★, *Just Dennis* (Observer/Trojan 1975)★★★★, *West Bound Train* (Third World 1977)★★★, *Visions* (Joe Gibbs 1977)★★★★, *Wolf & Leopards* (Weed-Beat/DEB-EMI 1978)★★★★, *Words Of Wisdom* (Laser 1979)★★★★, *So Long Rastafari* (Harry J 1979)★★★, *Joseph's Coat Of Many Colours* (Laser 1979)★★★★, *20th Century Dubwise* (DEB 1979)★★★, *Yesterday, Today & Tomorrow* (JGM 1982)★★★★, *Satisfaction Feeling* (Tads 1983)★★★, *The Prophet Rides Again* (A&M 1983)★★★, *Love's Gotta Hold On Me* (JGM 1984)★★★, *Dennis* (Vista Sounds 1984)★★★, *Time And Place* (Clock Tower 1984)★★★, with Gregory Isaacs *Two Bad Superstars Meet* (Burning Sounds 1984)★★★, with Isaacs *Judge Not* (Greensleeves 1984)★★★, *Live At Montreux* (Blue Moon 1984)★★★, *Slow Down* (Greensleeves 1985)★★★, *Revolution* (Yvonne's Special 1985)★★★, *Spellbound* (Blue Moon 1985)★★★, *Wake Up* (Natty Congo 1985)★★★, *The Exit* aka *History* (Jammys/Trojan 1986)★★★, *Money In My Pocket* (Trojan 1986)★★★, *Hold Tight* (Live & Love 1986)★★★, with Enos McLeod *Baalgad* (Goodies 1986)★★★, *Brown Sugar* (Taxi 1986)★★★, *Smile Like An Angel* (Blue Moon 1986)★★★, with Horace Andy *Reggae Superstars Meet* (Striker Lee 1986)★★★, with John Holt *Wild Fire* (Natty Congo 1986)★★★, with Janet Kay *So Amazing* (Body Work 1987)★★★, *In Concert* (Ayeola 1987)★★★, *Love Has Found Its Way* (A&M 1988)★★★, *Inseparable* (J&W 1988)★★★, *More* (Black Scorpio 1988)★★★, *My Time* (Rohit 1989)★★★, with Isaacs *No Contest* (Greensleeves 1989)★★★, with Isaacs *Big All Around* (Greensleeves 1989)★★★, *Unchallenged* (Greensleeves 1990)★★★, *Overproof* (Greensleeves 1990)★★★, *Good Tonight* (Greensleeves 1990)★★★, *Go Now* (Rohit 1991)★★★, *Victory Is Mine* (Blue Moon 1991)★★★, *Friends For Life* (1992)★★★, *Some Like It Hot* (1992)★★★, *Limited Edition* (1992)★★★, *Blazing* (Greensleeves 1992)★★★,

Beautiful Morning (1992)★★★, *Cosmic Force* (1993)★★★, *Unforgettable* (Charm 1993)★★★, *Light My Fire* (Heartbeat 1994)★★★, *Temperature Rising* (Trojan 1995)★★★, with Beenie Man, Triston Palma *Three Against War* (VP 1995)★★★★.

● COMPILATIONS: *Best Of* (Joe Gibbs 1975)★★★, *Best Of Volume 2* (Joe Gibbs 1982)★★★, *Super Hits* (Trojan 1983)★★★, *Collection* (Dennis Ting 1985)★★★, *20 Classic Reggae Tracks* (Meteor 1985)★★★, *Good Vibrations* (Chartsounds 1989)★★★, *Classic Hits* (Sonic Sounds 1992)★★★, *20 Magnificent Hits* (1993)★★★, *Musical Heatwave* (Trojan 1993)★★★, *The Prime Of Dennis Brown* (Music Club 1993)★★★.

● VIDEOS: *Dennis Brown Live At Montreux* (MMG Video 1987), *The Living Legend* (Keeling 1992).

BROWN, FOXY

b. Jeniffer Hylton, Jamaica, West Indies. Foxy Brown's version of Tracy Chapman's 'Baby Can I Hold You Tonight', produced by Steely And Clevie, topped the reggae charts and in 1989 secured a placing on the *Billboard* Top 100 Black Singles chart. She followed her debut with another of Chapman's hits, 'Fast Car', which paralleled its predecessor. Although the songs were a commercial success, Brown was regarded as Jamaica's Tracy Chapman, which hindered her burgeoning career. She proved her competence in songwriting with 'Let's Celebrate', 'Try' and 'Baby It's You', all featured on *Foxy*. In 1990 her popularity continued with the release of the dancehall hit 'Always For Me', which demonstrated her versatility. Since the release of her second album she has maintained a low profile, although in the mid-90s the media were inaccurately hailing her return. The misconception related to US rapper Inga Marchand who also performed as Foxy Brown, and whose *ill na na* spawned the crossover hit 'Get Me Home', with BLACKstreet.

● ALBUMS: *Foxy* (Ras 1989)★★★, *My Kind Of Girl* (Ras 1990)★★.

BROWN, GLEN

b. Glenmore Lloyd Brown, Jamaica, West Indies. Brown started in the music business in the mid-60s as a singer, recording duets with Lloyd Robinson and Dave Barker (see Dave And Ansell Collins) for various producers, including Duke Reid and Coxsone Dodd. However, it was in the early 70s that he found his true vocation as a producer, and his legendary Pantomine label became home to dozens of unique and often eccentric records. He enjoyed a big hit in 1972 with 'Merry Up', a melodica instrumental much in the vein of Augustus Pablo, who had popularized the instrument some months earlier with his hit 'Java'. Brown was adept at recycling his rhythms in new and interesting ways. If one of his backing tracks proved particularly popular, he would go on to cut a number of versions of it using different singers, instrumentalists and DJs, thereby prolonging its life and recouping the maximum profit for his outlay. He worked with many of the best DJs of the time, including Big Youth ('Come Into My Parlour', 'Opportunity Rock'), Prince Jazzbo ('Meaning Of One', 'Mr Harry Skank', 'Mr Want All'), I. Roy ('Brother Toby Is A Movie From London'), Berry 'Prince Hammer' Simpson ('Whole Lot of Sugar') and U-Roy ('No 1 In The World').

As well as providing fine vocal renditions himself on sides such as 'Realize' (with Richie MacDonald), 'Tell It Like It Is', 'Boat To Progress' and 'Away With The Bad', Brown recorded the likes of Roman Stewart, Keith Poppin, Johnny Clarke, Lloyd Parks ('Slaving') and Gregory Isaacs, the latter's 'One One Cocoa' being among that singer's finest vinyl moments. However, perhaps the real grist to Brown's mill were the many instrumental sides his various labels carried, cuts such as 'Dirty Harry' by Tommy McCook and Richard Hall, 'More Music' by McCook and trombonist Ron Wilson, and the melodica sides by the man himself - 'Pantomine Rock', 'Crisp As A Ball' and '2 Wedden Skank'. Brown's highly individual approach, coupled with the God Sons' tough bass and drum rhythms, has ensured these records a special place in the hearts of many reggae fans. In the latter half of the 70s the hits were fewer, but records such as his own 'Father For The Living' and 'Lambs Bread Collie Man', Wayne Jarrett's 'Youthman' and a run of Sylford Walker gems like 'Lambs Bread', 'Eternal Day' and 'Chant Down Babylon', maintained his profile and reputation. During the 80s Brown became less vis-

ible on the reggae scene as he divided his time between Jamaica, New York and the UK. He recorded a melodica instrumental album for London's Fashion Records in 1990 that captured much of his charm. Brown's productions for Sylford Walker were *Chant Down Babylon* (1989), *Dubble Attack* (Greensleeves 1989), *Boat To Progress* (Greensleeves 1989), *Dub From The South East* (Pantomine 1991), and for various artists, *Check The Winner* (Greensleeves 1990).
● ALBUMS: *Horny Dub* (Grounation 1989)★★★★, *Number One Sound* (Pantomine 1989)★★★, *Glen Brown Plays Music From The East* (Fashion 1990)★★, with Mike Brooks *Mike Brooks And Glen Brown Meet Rhythm Foundation* (Rhythm Foundation 1990)★★, *The Rhythm Master* (Pantomine 1991)★★★, *The Way To Mt. Zion* (ROIR 1995)★★★.

BROWN, JUNIOR

b. 14 March 1957, Hammersmith, London, England. In his youth Brown studied for an apprenticeship in mechanics but was preoccupied with his love of music. He linked up with a variety of reggae performers in London, including Ijahman Levi, who allowed him to sit in on recording sessions at the Island Records Basing Street Studios. A chance meeting at the studio with Stephen 'Cat' Coore of Third World influenced Brown to strive towards a recording career. In 1975 he recorded his debut with Dennis Harris; the single was not a success, although Brown was undeterred and began working with Sam Jones of Brimstone. The partnership was short-lived and Brown pursued a more independent path. Throughout the latter half of the 70s he recorded with a variety of producers, including Alton Ellis for 'Rosemary' and 'Girly Come On', while John Francis produced the rootsy 'Jah Find Babylon Guilty'. By the early 80s Brown had carved a niche with roots devotees, resulting in the reggae chart-toppers 'Jah Find Babylon Guilty', 'Warrior' and 'Fly Me Away' for the mighty Jah Shaka. Many hits followed for an assortment of producers, including the equally popular 'Rockers' for Solid Groove, 'Reggae Melody' for Roots Music, 'Show The Youth The Way' for Kingdom and 'My Devotion', released as an a-side for CSA while appearing on the b-side of the Solid Groove release. Reunited with Brimstone, Brown recorded 'Knock Knock' and maintained a high profile with Oak Sound for the dancehall hit 'Time Is Getting Hot'.
● ALBUMS: *Fly Me Away Home* (Shaka 1981)★★★★, *Rockers Delight* (Solid Groove 1982)★★★.

BROWN, PREZIDENT

b. Fitzroy Cotterell, Ocho Rios, Jamaica, West Indies. The towering figure of Fitz (hence the 'z' in his title) built a solid foundation in the dancehall performing on local sound systems, before embarking on his recording career in the early 90s as a DJ. His initial sessions were with producers Barry O'Hare and Courtney Cole at the Ocho Rios, based at Grove Recording Studio and Roof International, respectively. As a soloist he recorded 'Tears' in combination with Jack Radics and as Professor Frisky he covered Inner Circle's 'Everything Is Great', retitled 'Everything Is Right'. Brown's notoriety led to him being featured on the popular Jamaican festival dancehall nights, which resulted in outstanding performances at the 1995 Reggae Sumfest in Montego Bay and an equally acclaimed appearance at Reggae Sunsplash in St. Ann's. With Everton Blender he recorded the anti-drug hit 'Blow Your Nose Part Two', advising that it was better to 'blow your nose and not your brain'. While Brown was establishing his reputation, Red Dragon, alongside Brian and Tony Gold, recorded 'Compliments On Your Kiss', produced by Sly Dunbar and Robbie Shakespeare. Brown's vocal style was similar to that of Red Dragon, resulting in his being employed by One World productions to record in a similar style alongside Sabre; 'Wrong Or Right' was greeted with enthusiasm and achieved international daytime radio play. An association with Anthony Red Rose and Anthony Malvo found Brown guesting on the popular 'Swell Headed' rhythm for 'Red Alert', which topped the Jamaican charts throughout the summer. He maintained a high profile when he returned to Grove Studios, where he recorded the equally popular 'Bun Down Rome' over a reggae version of the jazz hit 'Bongo Chant', originally performed by Kenny Graham And The Afro-Cubists. Sessions with Bobby Digital led to the release of 'Mr. Want All', 'Poor People Cry' and the controversial 'Parable'. A reunion with producer O'Hare led to the release of *Prezident Selection*; the compilation including guest vocal contributions from Don Yute, Third World's vocalist Bunny Rugs, veteran DJ U. Brown and the popular lovers rock singer Mikey Spice. Brown's increasing popularity led to his combination hit with Foundation, 'Beverley Hills', and he joined the increasing number of artists to sign with Chris Blackwell's newly formed Island Jamaica label.

● ALBUMS: *Big Bad And Talented* (X Rated 1995)★★★, *Original Blue Print* (Digital B 1996)★★, *Prezident Selection* (Runnetherlands 1996)★★★.

BROWN, U.

b. Huford Brown, *c*.1958, Waterhouse, Kingston, Jamaica, West Indies. Brown began his career djing on the Silver Bullet Sound System in the early 70s. His performance was heavily influenced by the 'dee jay daddy' U-Roy, who, following his departure from King Tubby's Hi Fi, was replaced by U. Brown. His vocals bore an uncanny resemblance to his hero and no other DJ on the island was able to mimic the originator as convincingly. Brown continued exciting the crowds with his parody and by the mid-70s began a prolific recording career. He enjoyed a hit in 1976 with 'Starsky And Hutch', and a series of albums followed produced by Bunny Lee. The producers Joe Gibbs and Errol Thompson were enjoying a run of big hits in the mid-70s and employed the young DJ to perform 'This Old Man' on the discomix version of Jacob Miller's 'Keep On Knocking'. The song had also been recorded in a different style by Miller for Augustus Pablo and it was this version that was preferred by the record-buying public, resulting in less exposure for the DJ. Although the single was not a big success, Virgin Records in the UK decided to build up an extensive catalogue of Jamaican music and U. Brown was one of many reggae performers signed to the label. In 1978 he released 'Black Star Liner'/'River John Mountain', and this was successfully followed by 'Front Line' (graphically exhibiting a fist gripping barbed wire with blood flowing down the forearm) from *Mr Brown Something*, a self-production with the assistance of the Mighty Fatman. Brown chanted in the style of U-Roy over old rhythms, notably on 'Natty Dread Upon

A Mountain Top', where he used Black Uhuru's 'I Love King Selassie' as a backing tune, before the group achieved notoriety. The Virgin contract enabled U. Brown to visit the UK frequently and his regular appearances on the Unity Hi Power sound system were met with fervour, which he acknowledged on 'Tottenham Rock'. His final set for the label appeared in 1979 and featured further cover versions of reggae standards including 'Row Mr. Fisherman', 'Natty Step It Inna Greenwich Farm' and 'Step It In A Freedom Street'. Although he recorded with Jah Thomas ('Things A Come Up A Go Bump') and Sly And Robbie ('Out Of Hand'), little was heard from U. Brown following the end of his Virgin contract. It was not until 1981 that he enjoyed a triumphant resurgence with a cover version of Dennis Brown's 'If This World Were Mine', retitled 'Tu-Sheng-Peng', which became a firm favourite in the dancehalls. A compilation, *Tu Sheng Peng*, was swiftly released including earlier cuts, but was not considered to be the official release by the performer. It followed that producers who had worked with U. Brown were quick to dust off any master tapes and the wave of enthusiasm for his recorded work was thwarted by a glut of available material, including *Jam It Tonight*, which was the official album accompanying his hit.

● ALBUMS: *Satta Dread* (Klik 1976)★★★★, *London Rock* (Third World 1977)★★★, *Revelation Time* (Live & Love 1977)★★★, *Mr Brown Something* (Front Line 1978)★★★, *Repatriation* (Hit Sound 1979)★★, *Can't Keep A Good Man Down* (Front Line 1979)★★★, *Ravers Party* (Trojan 1982)★★★, *Jam It Tonight* (CSA 1983)★★★, *Superstar* (Vista 1984)★★.

● COMPILATIONS: *Tu Sheng Peng* (Vista 1982)★★★, *Train To Zion (1975-1979)* (Blood & Fire 1997)★★★★.

BUCCANEER

b. Andrew Bradford, *c*.1974, Jamaica, West Indies. In the days of slavery Jamaica was considered to be a pirates' haven, and the notorious smuggler Henry Morgan was elevated to the position of Jamaica's Governor General in the then capital, Port Royal. The island's dubious past was acknowledged by the DJ known as Buccaneer, whose appearance was enhanced with an eye-patch and a bizarre hairstyle featuring a bleach ring. His jocose demeanour was complemented by his unique style, and recording sessions throughout the mid-90s have been copious. With Patrick Roberts' Shocking Vibes crew, Buccaneer enjoyed enormous success when he performed 'Hey Yah, Hey Yah' over the rhythm utilized by Beenie Man for his 'Press Button'. The hits continued with 'Chatty Chatty Mouth', 'Yu Nah Beg', 'Call Me', 'Yu Nuh Care', 'Disaster', 'Ganja Pipe', 'Unity' and 'Good Director'. With the mellifluous-voiced Wayne Wonder, he featured on 'Sensi Ride' and 'Trust'. In January 1995 Buccaneer's debut album was met with enthusiasm; it featured production credits from Patrick Roberts, Dave Kelly, Danny Brownie and Bobby Digital. At the Reggae Sumfest '95 Festival, held in the grounds of Catherine Hall, Montego Bay, Buccaneer demonstrated his appeal when he won approval with an exuberant performance on dancehall night. In the summer of 1996 he released 'Skettel Concerto', a unique combination of light opera and ragga; 'You love sket-tel - You love sket-tel - You love sket-tel' emulated 'The Marriage Of Figaro'. Also included on the discomix were the popular 'Punky Brewster' and 'Vintage Old Bruk'. By the end of that summer he consolidated his popularity when he evoked the memory of Dirtsman with 'Hotter This Year'. ● ALBUMS: *There Goes The Neighbourhood* (VP 1995)★★★, *Classic* (Greensleeves 1997)★★★.

BURNING SPEAR

b. Winston Rodney, 1948, St. Ann's Bay, Jamaica, West Indies. Burning Spear, who appropriated the name from former Mau Mau leader Jomo Kenyatta, then president of Kenya, entered the music business in 1969 after fellow St. Ann's artist Bob Marley organized an audition for him with his erstwhile producer Coxsone Dodd. The three songs Spear sang for Dodd that Sunday afternoon included his eventual debut, 'Door Peep', a sombre, spiritual chant quite unlike anything that had previously emerged in the music, although a reference point may perhaps be found in the Ethiopians and Joe Higgs. 'Door Peep' and other early Spear recordings such as 'We Are Free' and 'Zion Higher' emerged in the UK on the Bamboo and Banana labels. Rodney continued to make records for Dodd until 1974, including

'Ethiopians Live It Out', 'This Population' and 'New Civilisation', nearly all in a serious, cultural style, mostly without any commercial success, although 'Joe Frazier' (aka 'He Prayed') did make the Jamaican Top 5 in 1972. Most of these songs can be found on the two albums Spear completed for Dodd. In 1975 Ocho Rios sound system owner Jack Ruby (real name Laurence Lindo) approached the singer, and the two, along with pick-up backing vocalists Rupert Wellington and Delroy Hines, began working on the material that eventually emerged as *Marcus Garvey* (1975), in honour of the great St. Ann's-born pan-Africanist. 'Marcus Garvey' and 'Slavery Days' were released as singles, perfectly capturing the mood of the times and becoming huge local hits. The public were at last ready for Burning Spear and when the album finally emerged it was hailed as an instant classic. Spear became recognized as the most likely candidate for the kind of international success Bob Marley And The Wailers were beginning to enjoy, and soon *Marcus Garvey* had been snapped up by Island Records who released it in the UK with an added track and in remixed form. This tampering with the mix, including the speeding-up of several tracks, presumably in order to make the album more palatable to white ears, raised the hackles of many critics and fans. Its popularity caused Island to release a dubwise companion set entitled *Garvey's Ghost*. Rodney began to release music on his own Spear label at the end of 1975, the first issue being another classic, 'Travelling' (actually a revision of the earlier Studio One album track 'Journey'), followed by 'Spear Burning' (1976), 'The Youth' (1976), 'Throw Down Your Arms' (1977), the 12-inch 'Institution' (1977), 'Dry And Heavy' (1977), 'Free' (1977) and 'Nyah Keith' (1979). He also produced 'On That Day' by youth singer Burning Junior, and 'Love Everyone' by Phillip Fullwood, both in 1976. That same year Jack Ruby released 'Man In The Hills', followed by the album of the same name, again on Island, which marked the end of their collaboration. Rodney also dropped Wellington and Hines. In 1977 *Dry & Heavy* was released, recorded at Harry J's Studio, which satisfyingly reworked many of his Studio One classics, including 'Swell Headed', 'Creation Rebel', 'This Race' and 'Free Again'. In October that year he made an electrifying appearance at London's Rainbow Theatre, backed by veteran trumpeter Bobby Ellis and the UK reggae band Aswad. Island released an album of the performance that inexplicably failed to capture the excitement generated.

In 1978 Rodney parted with Island and issued *Marcus Children*, arguably his best album since *Marcus Garvey*, released in the UK on Island Records' subsidiary One Stop as *Social Living*, again using members of Aswad alongside the usual Kingston sessionmen. In 1980 he signed to EMI who issued his next album, the stunning *Hail H.I.M.*, produced by Rodney and Family Man Barrett at Bob Marley's Tuff Gong studio, on his own Burning Spear subsidiary. Two excellent dubs of *Social Living* and *Hail H.I.M.* also appeared as *Living Dub Vols. 1* and *2*, mixed by engineer Sylvan Morris. Throughout the following years to the present day, Burning Spear has continued to release albums regularly, as well as touring the USA and elsewhere. *Resistance*, nominated for a Grammy in 1984, was a particularly strong set, highlighting Spear's impressive, soulful patois against a muscular rhythmic backdrop. *People Of The World* similarly saw his backing group, the Burning Band, which now encompassed an all-female horn section, shine. His 1988 set, *Mistress Music*, added rock musicians, including former members of Jefferson Airplane, though artistically it was his least successful album. *Mek We Dweet*, recorded at Tuff Gong studios, was a return to his unique, intense style. His lyrical concerns - black culture and history, Garveyism and Rasta beliefs, and universal love - have been consistently and powerfully expressed during his recording career.

● ALBUMS: *Studio One Presents Burning Spear* (Studio One 1973)★★★, *Rocking Time* (Studio One 1974)★★★, *Marcus Garvey* (Mango/Island 1975)★★★★★, *Man In The Hills* (Fox-Wolf/Island 1976)★★★★, *Garvey's Ghost* (Mango/Island 1976)★★★★, *Dry & Heavy* (Mango/Island 1977)★★★★, *Burning Spear Live* (Island 1977)★★, *Marcus Children* aka *Social Living* (Burning Spear/One Stop 1978)★★★★, *Living Dub* (Burning Spear/Heartbeat 1979)★★★★, *Hail H.I.M.* (Burning Spear/EMI 1980)★★★★, *Living Dub Volume 2* (Burning Spear 1981)★★★★, *Farover* (Burning Spear/ Heartbeat 1982)★★★, *Fittest Of The Fittest* (Burning Spear/Heartbeat 1983)★★★, *Resistance* (Heartbeat 1985)★★★★, *People Of The World* (Slash/Greensleeves 1986)★★★, *Mistress Music* (Slash/Greensleeves 1988)★★, *Live In Paris: Zenith '88* (Slash/Greensleeves 1989)★★★, *Mek We Dweet* (Mango/Island 1990)★★★, *Jah Kingdom* (Mango/Island 1992)★★★, *The World Should Know* (Mango/Island 1993)★★★, *Rasta Business* (Heartbeat 1996)★★★, *Appointment With His Majesty* (Heartbeat 1997)★★★.

● COMPILATIONS: *Reggae Greats* (Island 1985)★★★★, *Selection* (EMI 1987)★★★★, *100th Anniversary Marcus Garvey* and *Garvey's Ghost* (Mango/Island 1990)★★★★, *Chant Down Babylon: The Island Anthology* (Island 1996)★★★★.

BURRELL, PHILIP 'FATIS'
(see Exterminator)

BUSHAY, CLEMENT
Bushay's earliest reggae productions surfaced through Trojan Records, notably his work with Owen Gray and Louisa Mark. Mark's initial hit with Bushay, 'Keep It Like It Is', established a successful partnership and the producer was keen to promote the new lovers rock genre. He ventured into a commitment with the Burning Sounds label. His own productions surfaced, alongside those of Linval Thompson, the Morwells, Leroy Smart, Alvin 'GG' Ranglin and Gussie Clarke. His production skills were utilized by many UK-based reggae performers including Junior English ('Got To Come Back') and Jackie Robinson ('Don't Leave Me This Way'). Emulating Jamaican producers, Bushay used the rhythms to provide the foundation to the vocal sparring of Trinity and Dillinger for the release of *Clash*. Owen Gray's 'Rizla' became 'Rizla Skank', Jackie Robinson's 'Don't Leave Me This Way' became 'Spike Heeled Shoes' and Louisa Mark's 'Keep It Like It Is', 'Step It Brother Clem'. Bushay's success with Mark continued when his production of 'Six Sixth Street' reached the top of the reggae chart. By the late 70s the Burning Sounds label went into liquidation and he set up his Bushays label as an outlet for his productions. He paired Mark with Kevin for a version of 'Re-United', but it was unable to main-

tain the success of her earlier hits. Other lovers rock performers passed through his studio, including Janet Kay and Rico, Al Campbell, Paulette Walker and Dave Barker. He also set up the Bushranger label from which came Owen Gray's version of 'The Greatest Love Of All'. In the early 80s Louisa Mark felt that Bushay had released *Markswoman* before it had been properly mixed, resulting in what appeared to be the end of their partnership. After a year they resolved their differences and continued working together. The Bushays label continued to prosper with releases from the Morwells, Prince Jazzbo, Gregory Isaacs, Tony Tuff, Barrington Levy and Jah Thomas.

BUSHMAN

b. Dwight Duncan, 1973, Prospect Beach, Jamaica, West Indies. Duncan was raised in the Rastafarian faith in his early years, and he later attended drama school and sang in the local church choir where his idiosyncratic vocals were nurtured. He began work as a DJ under the name Junior Melody at the Black Star Line sound system in St. Thomas, and later hitch-hiked the 70 miles to Kingston where he met Wycliffe 'Steely' Johnson at the Arrows Dub Plate Studio. Duncan was invited to record at Studio 2000, performing 'Grow Your Natty', followed by 'Call The Hearse' over Steely And Clevie's popular 'Skettel' rhythm. Steely decided to release the single under the pseudonym of Bushman, and although initially Duncan felt this was a derogatory title, it was in fact an African term for 'medicine man'. 'Call The Hearse' was a success in Jamaica, and led to the equally popular 'Rude Boy Life', and his debut album *Nyah Man Chant*. The songs on the latter proclaimed his spiritual beliefs: he maintains a strict ital diet, bathes in the hot water springs of his parish and takes to the hills with his bible.

● ALBUMS: *Nyah Man Chant* (Greensleeves 1997)★★★.

BYLES, JUNIOR

b. Keith Byles, 1948, Kingston, Jamaica, West Indies. Growing up in the Jonestown district of Kingston, Byles started work as a fireman in his late teens. By 1967 he had formed the Versatiles with Louis Davis and a youth named Dudley. The trio recorded a series of titles for producer Joe Gibbs during 1968/9, including 'Just Can't Win', 'Trust The Book' and 'Push It In'. By 1970 Byles was recording solo for producer Lee Perry as King Chubby. In 1972 Byles had two hits, the dread anthem 'Beat Down Babylon', which was also the title of his first album released the following year, and the Jamaican Song Festival competition winner, 'Da Da'. He continued working with Perry, recording both militant roots material and intense love songs, nearly scraping into the UK charts with 'Curly Locks' (1975). That same year he had a hit in Jamaica with 'Fade Away' for Joseph 'Joe Joe' Hookim at Channel One, one of the best early rockers' tunes. He also recorded for the Ja-Man label, and producers Winston 'Niney' Holness and Pete Weston. In 1976, he entered Bellevue Hospital, retiring from music until 1978, when he wrote two songs for Joe Gibbs. He became less active as the 80s began, recording sessions for Maurice 'Blacka' Wellington (of the Morwells) in 1982 that were finally released in 1986 as *Rasta No Pickpocket*. He has recorded some of the most powerful reggae of the 70s, militant and deeply moving by turns, yet remains relatively unknown.

● ALBUMS: *Beat Down Babylon* (Trojan 1973)★★★, *Jordan* (1976)★★★★, *Rasta No Pickpocket* (Night Hawk 1986)★★★, *Beat Down Babylon: The Upsetter Years* (Trojan 1987)★★★★, *When Will Better Come* (Trojan 1988)★★★.

CABLES

The Cables recorded one classic album and a handful of tracks for various producers. Fronted by the fragile yet assertive voice of Keble (sometimes Keeble) Drummond, the Cables arrived at Studio One in the late 60s. It was a terrifically fertile time for the label, and the producer Coxsone Dodd already had his hands full with the Heptones, Delroy Wilson, the Termites and a number of other acts. However, Drummond, whose first name provided the group with its name, supported by harmony singers Elbert Stewart (baritone) and Vince Stoddart (tenor), recorded a string of excellent singles for the label, including 'Be A Man', 'Love Is A Pleasure', 'Baby Why' and 'What Kind Of World'. Dodd later collected them on the frustratingly short, but still excellent, *What Kind Of World*. The rhythm tracks were classics, later reused by Dodd for a slew of 'versions' with other artists. However, the original cuts remain much prized by reggae enthusiasts today. By 1970 the Cables and Dodd had parted, and despite a few singles for other producers (J.J. Johnson, Harry J.), they failed to recapture their hit-making touch. Drummond went solo in 1972, but his career petered out within a few years.
● ALBUMS: *What Kind Of World* (Studio One 1970)★★★★.

CADOGAN, SUSAN

b. Alison Susan Cadogan, *c*.1959, Kingston, Jamaica, West Indies. Cadogan studied to be and qualified as a librarian, but her singing prompted the Jamaican Broadcasting DJ Jerry Lewis to introduce her to Lee Perry. Cadogan recorded at the Black Ark Studios a version of Millie Jackson's soul hit 'Hurts So Good'. In 1974 the single appeared through Dennis Harris's DIP International label and topped the reggae chart in the UK. The success of the single led to the Magnet label licensing the tune and taking the

song into the Top 5 of the pop chart in April 1975. While Cadogan enjoyed the benefit of her success the Black Wax label released 'Love My Life', which failed to match the achievements of her debut. The Magnet label released the official follow-up, 'Love Me Baby', which, although a Top 20 hit, marked the end of Cadogan's foray into the UK pop charts. Trojan Records signed her and released a compilation of cover versions including 'Fever', 'Don't You Burn Your Bridges', 'Congratulations' and 'In The Ghetto'. The production was in a similar vein to John Holt's *1000 Volts* series and proved a commercial success. The single 'How Do You Feel The Morning After' intensified her reputation but was followed by intermittent output. By 1982 she successfully recorded cover versions of the soul classics 'Piece Of My Heart' and 'Tracks Of My Tears'. In 1983, with Hawkeye producing, she recorded 'Love Me' and, in combination with Ruddy Thomas, the chart-topping, '(You Know How To Make Me) Feel So Good'. After nearly a decade away, she returned in fine style with the Mad Professor, who in 1992 recorded an album hailing her comeback. The Professor also utilized her re-recording of 'Hurts So Good' for U-Roy's 'The Hurt Is Good', from his Ariwa Records *Smile A While*. It was Cadogan's rendition of the song that inspired a successful cover version in 1995 by UK pop singer Jimmy Somerville and in turn regenerated interest in the original.
● ALBUMS: *Doing It Her Way* (Magnet 1975)★★★, *Hurt So Good* (Trojan 1976)★★★, *Soulful Reggae* (Ariwa 1992)★★★, *Chemistry Of Love* (Imp 1995)★★★.

CAMPBELL, AL

b. 31 August 1954, Kingston, Jamaica, West Indies. Campbell first recorded as one of the Thrillers for Studio One in the late 60s. Though he provided backing vocals on many sessions for Coxsone Dodd, he is not the Al Campbell who sang the well-known 'Take A Ride' for Dodd. Throughout the 70s, 80s and 90s, Campbell has recorded successfully in just about all of the many styles through which reggae music has passed, the excellent 'roots' records that he made for Joe Gibbs and Phil Pratt providing but one example of his talents. However, his greatest popularity was achieved when he covered lovers rock material for Phil Pratt again - with 'Gee Baby' in particular, which was a huge hit in 1975, both in Jamaica and the UK. From then on, he flitted between the two countries and his recording of 'Late Night Blues', for London-based JB Records, formed part of the soundtrack of 1980, and has been in constant demand ever since. He made many more records in a similar vein, several of which are collected on his *Mr Lovers Rock* set. He has retained his position as one of the music's foremost vocalists in the 90s, while his most recent recordings have been for King Jammy's Kingston II label. He is still out there, despite the fickle nature of the traditional reggae audience, largely due to his smooth, relaxed, accomplished style, coupled with his ability to move with the times and give the public what they want.

● ALBUMS: *Rainy Days* (Hawkeye 1978)★★★, *Mr Lovers Rock* (Sonic Sounds 1980)★★★★, *Other Side Of Love* (Greensleeves 1981)★★★, *Bad Boy* (CSA 1984)★★, *Freedom Street* (Londisc 1984)★★★, *Forward Natty* (Move 1985)★★★, *Reggae '85* (Blue Mountain 1985)★★★, *Fence Too Tall* (Live & Love 1987)★★, *Ain't That Loving You* (Vista 1989)★★★, *Shaggy Raggy* (Sampalau 1989)★★.

● COMPILATIONS: *Revival Selection* (Kickin' 1998)★★★.

CAMPBELL, CORNELL

b. *c*.1948, Jamaica, West Indies. One of Jamaica's most distinctive falsetto voices, Cornell Campbell has been a reggae hitmaker for years, but has somehow never been bigger than his last record. He first recorded for Studio One in the ska era during the early 60s, both solo and as part of a duo with Alan Martin. After a three-year gap he re-emerged in 1967 as a member of the Uniques, a popular but short-lived vocal group that also featured the exceptional falsetto of Slim Smith.

By 1969 Cornell was leading his own group, the Eternals, and was back at Studio One recording hits with 'Queen Of The Minstrels' and 'Stars'. In 1971 he began a long association with producer Bunny Lee, re-recording his Eternals hits solo and sounding better than ever. By 1974 Campbell was second only to Johnny Clarke in Lee's large stable, singing largely in the lovers rock style. His debut, *Cornell Campbell* (1973), was a shoddy affair despite the excellence of the music; the front cover featured an ice-cream cone (no picture of the singer was available) and Campbell did not even hear of its existence until 1977. In 1975 he changed his approach, becoming a rasta singer as befitted his appearance, and immediately Campbell's stock increased: 'Natty Dread In A Greenwich Farm', the superb 'Natural Fact' and 'Dance In A Greenwich Farm' were all considerable Jamaican hits. The latter formed the title of his second album. A series of 'gorgon' records, with Campbell declaring himself 'the gorgon (ruler) of dis yah dance' set up another string of hits, as did 'Boxing', a brutal and much-covered record for Joe Gibbs. He also intermittently returned to Studio One for one-off singles. When his popularity began to wane in 1977, Campbell returned to love songs with 'The Investigator', a consummate piece of lovers rock.

By 1980, however, the joint creativity of Campbell and Lee had run its course and the duo parted company, reputedly acrimoniously. Campbell drifted from producer to producer until the mid-80s, when he became only an occasional visitor to Kingston's studios, occasionally arriving at Waterhouse to make records with King Jammy or King Tubby. Since that time, only sporadic releases have increased the Campbell catalogue.

● ALBUMS: *Cornell Campbell* (Trojan 1973)★★★★, *Dance In A Greenwich Farm* (Grounation 1975)★★★★, *Gorgon* (Klik 1976)★★★, *Turn Back The Hands Of Time* (Third World 1977)★★★, *Stalowatt* (Third World 1978)★★, *Sweet Baby* (Burning Sounds 1978)★★★, *Yes I Will* (Micron 1979)★★★, *The Inspector General* (Imperial 1979)★★, *Reggae Sun* (AMO 1980)★★, *Boxing* (Starlight 1982)★★, with Johnny Clarke *Johnny Clarke Meets Cornell Campbell In New Style* (Vista Sounds 1983)★★★, *Fight Against Corruption* (Vista Sounds 1983)★★★, *Follow Instructions* (Mobiliser 1983)★★★, with the Gaylads *Cornell Campbell Meets The Gaylads* (Culture Press 1985)★★★.

● COMPILATIONS: *The Cornell Campbell Collection* (Striker Lee 1985)★★★★.

CAMPBELL, DON

Don Campbell was the biggest breakthrough in the UK reggae market of 1993, when his first three singles (beginning with 'See It In Your Eyes') and debut album went to the top of the reggae charts. Campbell was subsequently awarded six prizes at the British Reggae Industry Awards of 1994. Afterwards he took a break from his solo work, when DJ and producer General Saint was looking for a new collaborator. Saint had already recorded several tracks in early 1993 with studio master and Ruff Cut band member Jazwad. It was Jazwad who brought Campbell to Saint's attention, having worked with him both on his solo material and when Campbell was part of Undivided Roots. Campbell was drafted in to provide vocals to material that included a sensuous cover version of Neil Sedaka's 1959 hit 'Oh Carol'. This peaked just outside the UK Top 50 when released as a single in April 1994. The duo also released 'Save The Last Dance' and 'Stop That Train'. The full contents of their sessions together were eventually released by Copasetic in 1995. Campbell then joined up with Steely (of Steely And Clevie).

● ALBUMS: *Don Campbell* (Juggling 1994)★★★, with General Saint *Time On The Move* (Copasetic 1995)★★★.

CANDY, ICHO

b. Winston Evans, *c.*1964, Jamaica, West Indies. The sound system in Jamaica is known to be the place where many DJs have served their apprenticeships, but in the late 70s a number of singers were also found performing on the sound systems, including Candy. His initial appearance was with the late Jack Ruby on his Jack Ruby Hi Fi Sound System. Ruby had produced a number of top artists, notably Burning Spear following his departure from Studio One. Ruby produced Candy's debut, 'Little Children No Cry', which failed to generate interest in further recordings. Candy then went to Joe Gibbs' studio in Retirement Crescent, where he recorded 'Bandulu', which also failed to make a significant impression. UK television's Channel 4 series *Deep Roots Music* featured a performance on Jack Ruby's Hi Fi, which sparked interest in his work from the UK audience. He eventually found success working with Prince Jazzbo, who had set up his own Ujama label. The label specialized in producing acts that other producers overlooked, often with surprising results. The recording session resulted in 'Mr User' and 'Blood Sucker', both of which became roots hits, increasing Prince Jazzbo's confidence. As with many Jamaican performers, he worked with a number of producers, including Augustus Pablo and Tesfa Macdonald. In 1989 he voiced some rhythms with Jah Shaka at King Tubby's, alongside other notable Jamaican performers. In 1993 Jah Shaka released an album of Candy's work but still retains specials that can only be heard on his sound system. Candy is regarded as a spiritual performer and, with reggae turning full circle, much of his unreleased material is destined to surface.

● ALBUMS: *Devils High* (Black Star 1990)★★★, *Glory To The King* (Shaka 1993)★★★★, *Dub Salute 2 (Featuring Icho Candy)* (Shaka 1994)★★.

CAPLETON

b. Clifton Bailey, 1974, Kingston, Jamaica, West Indies. The reggae artist Capleton quickly captured the imagination of the dancehall audience with his first big hit, 'Number One (On The Good Look Chart)', for Jah Life in 1990. Many of his recordings over the next 12 months, for producers such as Philip 'Fatis' Burrell ('Bumbo Red'/'Bible Fi Dem'), King Jammy ('The Red'), Roof International ('Dem No Like Me'), Peterkins ('We No Lotion Man') and Black Scorpio ('Ghetto Youth'/'Somebody'), were compiled on the *Capleton Gold* album in 1991. That year he voiced half an album for Gussie P ('Double Trouble'), combined with Johnny Osbourne on the highly successful 'Special Guest' for Outernational, and released several fine sides for African Star, as well as dueting with Bobby Zarro on 'Young, Fresh And Green'. In December he visited the UK with the late Pan Head, courting controversy over a shooting incident at one London venue, and recording 'Dance Can't Done' for Brixton label Jungle Rock. Back in Jamaica Capleton began to record for Burrell's Exterminator label. 'Almshouse' (1992) was a stirring call for unification within the music and, like 'Prophet' for Penthouse, revealed that he could handle cultural and reality issues with the same formidable insight

and power as his trademark slackness (of which 'Good Hole', in combination with Buju Banton for Stone Love, was an obvious example). The singles 'F.C.T', 'Matey A Dead', 'Make Hay' and 'Unno Hear' preceded an album for Burrell, while he continued a winning streak throughout 1992. The following year he released 'Everybody Needs Somebody' and 'Mankind' for Colin Fat, 'Good Love' and Stampede' for Mad House, 'Cold Blooded Murderer' for Black Scorpio and the rabid 'Buggering' for African Star (also 'Good So'/'Bad So'), maintaining his growing reputation. In 1994 he recorded combinations with Brian and Tony Gold and Nadine Sutherland, and worked with Gussie Clarke, and looked poised to become one of the most radical cultural DJs of his era with his work for African Star (including the best-selling 'Tour'). The US success of a hip-hop mix of 'Tour' led to Capleton being signed by Def Jam, who released the exceptional *Prophecy*. The long-awaited *I-Testament* was a strident and powerful follow-up.
● ALBUMS: with Tony Rebel, Ninjaman *Real Rough* (1990)★★★, *We No Lotion Man* (Charm 1991)★★★, *Capleton Gold* (Charm 1991)★★★★, with General Levy *Double Trouble* (Gussie P. 1991)★★★, with Cutty Ranks, Reggie Stepper *Three The Hard Way* (Techniques 1991)★★★, *Almshouse* (Exterminator 1993)★★★, *Prophecy* (Def Jam/African Star 1995)★★★★, *I-Testament* (Def Jam/Mercury 1998)★★★★.

CAPP, ANDY

b. Lynford Anderson, *c.*1948, Kingston, Jamaica, West Indies. Anderson worked on various recording sessions for a variety of performers in Jamaica. An early production of George Penny's 'Win Your Love' confirmed his ability as a studio engineer. In 1969 he co-produced Derrick Morgan's remake of his 1961 hit 'Fat Man'. Following on from the success of his work with Morgan in 1970 Anderson teamed up with Clancy Eccles, and engineered 'Herbsman Shuffle', a hit for the DJ King Stitt. It was while with Clancy that Anderson crossed the studio floor, demonstrating that he was also a competent artist. Adopting the name of the disagreeable strip-cartoon character Andy Capp, he performed 'Pop A To p'. The tune featured a 'chugga chugga' organ riff interspersed with comments from Andy Capp: 'Ah -The monkey speaks his

mind - Pop a top - Pop a top - Sip a sup - Sip a sup - taste the tits -taste the tits'. In the UK, Radio 1 disc jockey John Peel featured the tune on his radio show, which resulted in a number of complaints. He was quoted in *The Sunday Times A - Z Of Reggae* as commenting 'any music which agitates the listener might be worth persevering with', and he continues to play reggae alongside his usual mix. The tune was also utilized by Canada Dry's marketing department for their promotional campaign in the 70s. In 1971 Anderson returned to the microphone where, with Byron Lee, he recorded 'The Law', which was a dancehall smash and featured a continuing version on the b-side. When U-Roy performed over the classic rocksteady hits of Treasure Isle, the DJ style almost changed overnight and Andy Capp's style was no longer fashionable; he soon returned to the mixing desk. His engineering skills were featured on many recording sessions, including Bob Marley And The Wailers when they recorded at Dynamics Studios.

CAPTAIN SINBAD

b. Carl Dwyer, Kingston, Jamaica, West Indies. Now known as a producer, Dwyer began his career as DJ Captain Sinbad on the sound system Sound Of Silence alongside Sugar Minott in the mid-70s. Minott took him to Studio One, where he recorded two songs, both unreleased. In 1978 Henry 'Junjo' Lawes produced the first of two albums and he teamed up with Little John for '61 Storm'. Sinbad's own debut as a producer was with Little John's 'A1 Sound'. He also guested on Minott's own 'Hard Time Pressure' and recorded unreleased albums for Black Roots and Linval Thompson. His next effort was for Dillinger's Oak Sound label in 1982, the year he moved to England. There he recorded 'Sister Myrtle' live on the Saxon sound system for Rusty International (which later appeared on Studio One), and began recording UK artists on his own Rockfort label. John McLean's 'If I Give My Heart To You' was a notable success, although issued on the Mad Professor's Ariwa label. By 1989 he was back in Jamaica, 'Wickedest Thing In Life' by Gospel Fish being the debut release on a new Sinbad label. Singles by Nerious Joseph, Capleton ('Two Minute Man'), Mike Ninja, Cobra ('Merciless Bad Boy'),

O'Neil Shines, Daddy Woody and General T.K. followed, with Frankie Paul's 'Heart Attack' becoming a big hit in 1991. Working closely with both Fashion and Penthouse, he began experimenting with hip-hop remixes and released first *Sin Badda Than Them* and then *Gangster*, both 'version' albums of his popular rhythms. Meanwhile, the roster of artists increased, established names such as Anthony Red Rose, Glen Ricks and Prilly Hamilton sharing the credits alongside newcomers Sugar Black, Fragga Ranks and Poison Chang. In 1993 he started the *Romantic Ragga* series and introduced DJ Glamour Murphy. With his wide experience of working with both Jamaican and UK acts, Sinbad is well placed for future success.

● ALBUMS: various *Sin Badda Than Them* (Sinbad 1992)★★★, *Gangster* (Sinbad 1992)★★, *Romantic Ragga Volume 1* (Sinbad 1993)★★★, *Ambush* (Sinbad 1993)★★★★, *Romantic Ragga Volume 2* (Sinbad 1994)★★★.

CARLTON AND HIS SHOES

Carlton, Donald and Lynford Manning (and sometimes Alexander Henry of 'Please Be True' fame) made up the harmony group known as Carlton And His Shoes. Carlton Manning, probably the purest singer of love songs ever to come out of Jamaica, originally named the group Carlton And His Shades, but a printer's misspelling on their debut release for Sonia Pottinger remained with them for their entire career. Their debut single vanished but their subsequent work for Coxsone Dodd at Studio One established them as a seminal force in Jamaican music. 'Love Me Forever', for Dodd's Supreme label, was a massive rocksteady hit in the late 60s and has been re-released and interpreted countless times since its original recording. The b-side, 'Happy Land', formed the basis for 'Satta Amassa Ganna', one of the most covered tunes in the history of reggae and its most enduring anthem, first performed by the Abyssinians - Donald and Lynford with the addition of Bernard Collins. Carlton, who had by now trademarked the double and treble tracking of his own sweet, aching lead vocals, continued to make fine records at Studio One (he was also working at their Brentford Road Studios as a session guitarist). The last, 'Let Me Love You', was released on 12-inch in Jamaica in 1979 and showcased one of his finest-ever performances. He has also occasionally worked for other producers and released some excellent self-produced tracks since the halcyon days of the late 60s. Unfortunately, he has never been able to repeat his original success but remains a legendary figure in the development of Jamaican music.

● ALBUMS: *Love Me Forever* (Studio One 1978)★★★, *This Heart Of Mine* (1980)★★★.

CHAKA DEMUS AND PLIERS

The list of DJ/singer combinations in reggae is endless. None have been as commercially successful - and deservedly so - as Chaka Demus And Pliers. Chaka Demus (b. John Taylor, 1965, West Kingston, Jamaica, West Indies), the rapping half of the pairing, began his career chatting on a variety of sound systems, the most famous of these being Supreme and Jammy's, as Nicodemus Jnr. In 1985 a name change provoked a shift of fortunes, and Chaka, whose gruff but avuncular tones made him a stand-out in any DJ company, cut his first single, 'Increase Your Knowledge', soon afterwards. A string of 45s bearing his name arrived, 'One Scotch, One Bourbon, One Beer', an adaptation of the old Amos Milburn R&B chestnut, and '2 Foot Walk', among them. However, chiefly associated with Jammy's studio, Chaka's mild manner perhaps held him back in what was then the biggest recording stable in Jamaica. A move to Penthouse Studio for 'Chaka On The Move' (1987) improved matters, and it was here that Chaka first became friendly with Pliers, a singer who, like Chaka, had not yet made the fullest impact on reggae's landscape.

Pliers (b. Everton Banner, 1965, Kingston, Jamaica) first found fame cutting sides with Black Scorpio (Maurice Johnson). Influenced by his brother, Spanner Banner, and fellow tool/tunesmith Pinchers, Pliers cut sides for a variety of labels, among them Pickout, Pioneer Musik ('Murder We Wrote', a song to which he would later return), Jammys, Harry J. and Studio One. Successful though he was, Pliers always seemed to trail in the wake of more celebrated, if faddish, singers such as Wayne Wonder and Sanchez. While playing shows together in Miami in 1991, Chaka and Pliers decided to team up. 'Gal Wine' for Ossie Hibbert was their first 45 together, which led to a slew of reggae chart successes, 'Rough This Year', 'Love Up The Gal', 'Without Love', 'Winning Machine' and 'Worl' A Girls', among them. A collaboration with producers Sly Dunbar and Robbie Shakespeare created a new model of 'Murder She Wrote', which hit number 1 in the specialist charts worldwide. Having evidently developed a successful formula, they secured a contract with Mango Records, Island's reggae division, and hit the charts with 'Tease Me', a fine, bright ragga-pop record. 'She Don't Let Nobody', the follow-up, also went into the UK Top 10, and a version of 'Twist & Shout', with extra vocal support from Jack Radics, became a UK number 1. All these titles were included on the *Tease Me* album. For a long time, it seemed that Chaka and Pliers would not make it as big as their peers - now those same rivals can only gape in amazement and envy.

● ALBUMS: *Gal Wine* (Greensleeves 1992)★★★, *Ruff This Year* (RAS 1992)★★★, *Chaka Demus And Pliers* (Charm 1992)★★★★, *Tease Me* (Mango/Island 1993)★★★★, *For Every Kinda People* (Island 1996)★★★★. Solo: Chaka Demus *Rough & Rugged* (with Shabba Ranks) (Jammys 1988)★★★, *Everybody Loves The Chaka* (Black Scorpio 1988)★★, with Shabba Ranks *Best Baby Father* (John John/Blue Mountain 1989)★★★, *The Original Chaka* (Witty 1989)★★★. Pliers (with Pinchers) *Pinchers With Pliers* (Black Scorpio 1988)★★★.

● VIDEOS: *Chaka Demus And Pliers* (PolyGram Video 1994), *Tease Me* (Island Video 1994).

CHALICE

In the mid-60s Wayne Armond and Richard Daley, later of Third World, formed a band known as the Hells Angels. The group performed locally in a number of live shows. Succumbing to peer pressure, the duo split and Armond pursued a career in advertising. He devoted his spare time to performing with another band, Time. During his time with the band, they recorded two singles but failed to make any impact. His obvious talents prompted Byron Lee to approach and enrol Armond as part of his band the Dragonaires. A chance meeting with Robi Peart led to a musical partnership and Chalice was formed. The line-up featured Keith Francis, Desi Jones, Trevor

Roper, Michael Wallace and Ervin Lloyd. With a diversity of musical talent, each member contributed a different sound, and they notched up a hit initially in a reggae style, 'Don't Call Me No Nigger Now'. The follow-up single, 'I Still Love You', recorded in a soul style, topped the Jamaican charts for 14 weeks. In 1981 they were earmarked as the most spectacular live act in Jamaica following their first appearance at Sunsplash. The group's popularity escalated when they began recording exclusively in a reggae style; 'I'm Trying', 'Good To Be There' and 'Stew Peas' all became massive sellers. Their professionalism and reputation as an experienced live act led to their being frequently selected to support major performers in Jamaica, including the Commodores, the Detroit Spinners and the Four Tops. The group's electric live performances resulted in appearances at the 1982 Reggae Superjam and Reggae Sunsplash. In 1983 international exposure was assured when they stole the show with their third manifestation at the annual Reggae Sunsplash Festival, transmitted globally courtesy of Synergy. The exposure resulted in the band signing to Ariola and undertaking international touring, culminating in a critically acclaimed performance at The Lyceum following in Bob Marley's footsteps. In 1986 they returned to the top of the Jamaican chart with 'Revival Time', and three years later, 'Pocomania Day' completed the hat-trick. In 1991 the group combined classical music and DJ-style for the hit 'Dance Hall Manic', featuring guest appearances from Tiger, Lovindeer and Papa San.

● ALBUMS: *Blasted* (Sonic 1982)★★★, *Standard Procedure* (Sonic 1983)★★, *Good To Be There* (Ariola 1984)★★★, *Live At Reggae Sunsplash* (Sunsplash/Vista 1984)★★, *Stand Up* (CSA 1985)★★★, *Crossfire* (1986)★★★, *Up Till Now* (Ras 1988)★★★, *Catch It* (Rohit 1990)★★, *Si Mi Ya* (VP 1991)★★.

CHANNEL ONE RECORDS

(see Hookim, Joseph 'Joe Joe')

CHARLIE CHAPLIN

b. Richard Bennett. The tradition of adopting pseudonyms from the film industry is a long-established practice among the sound system DJs of Jamaica. Westerns have provided the inspiration for Trinity, his brother Clint Eastwood, Lee Van Cliff and the Lone Ranger, to name but a few. Silent movies had been ignored until the arrival of Charlie Chaplin, who had been nicknamed such from his schooldays. He began his career toasting on the revived King Sturgav sound system operated by DJ daddy U-Roy. His popularity on the live circuit led to recording sessions with Roy Cousins who, while pursuing his career with the Jamaican Post Office, was the leading light behind vocal group the Royals. He enjoyed a number of hits followed by the release of *Presenting Charlie Chaplin*, which included distinctive material such as 'Mother In Law', 'Leave Me Chalawah', 'Chaplin's Chant' and 'Jamaican Collie'. In the same year he released *One Of A Kind*, which featured the title track and a tribute to the Sturgav system. The UK-based CSA label secured the release of *Unity Is Strength*, an early example of the popular singer/DJ combination style, which saw him partnered by Don Carlos, one of the founding members of Black Uhuru. He continued performing on the sound system, and in 1984 'International Robbery' told the fantasy tale of a bank robbery carried out by the Sturgav Posse, including U-Roy, Josey Wales and Inspector Willie.

At the 1984 Reggae Sunsplash festival held in Jamaica, he came close to claiming the DJ crown from Yellowman, appearing on stage emulating Michael Jackson and wooing the crowd. Shortly after the show, Yellowman and Charlie joined forces for *Slackness Vs Pure Culture*, with lewd numbers from the albino star and more conscientious lyrics from Charlie. In the 90s he continued to release the occasional single, notably 'Do Good', with his sparring partner Josey Wales, in combination with Yammie Bolo and Jack Radics.

● ALBUMS: *Presenting Charlie Chaplin* (Kingdom 1982)★★★, *One Of A Kind* (Trojan 1982)★★★, with Josey Wales *Sturgav Vs. Atuaras Live* (Rusty 1983)★★★★, with Yellowman *Slackness Vs Pure Culture* (Arrival 1984)★★★★, *Sound System* (Arrival 1985)★★★, *Que Dem* (Powerhouse 1985)★★, with Yellowman *The Negril Chill* (ROIR 1988)★★★, *Portrait* (Ras 1997)★★★.

CHARMERS, LLOYD

b. Lloyd Tyrell, 1938, Kingston, Jamaica, West Indies. In 1962 Tyrell entered the Vere Johns Talent Hour with Roy Willis as one half of a duo, the Charmers. With encouragement from Alton Ellis, who taught them harmonies, they soon began recording. Their first sessions were at Studio One where Coxsone Dodd produced 'Splish Splash', 'Crying Over You' and 'Jeanie Girl'. A film documentary, *This Is Ska*, recorded in the early 60s, includes footage of the duo performing in such circumstances. With Prince Buster producing, the duo enjoyed their biggest hit with 'Time After Time', but by the late 60s the partnership dissolved. Charmers had already recorded a solo outing in 1964, 'Loneliest Boy In Town', which was a minor hit in Jamaica. After the duo dissolved, he joined forces with Slim Smith and Jimmy Riley, who became collectively known as the Uniques. They enjoyed an instant hit with 'Watch This Sound' and in 1969 they released *Absolutely The Uniques*, including the classic 'My Conversation' and a cover version of Curtis Mayfield's 'Gypsy Woman'. The group stayed together for a year before disbanding to concentrate on solo careers.

In 1970 the release of *Reggae Charm* and *Reggae Is Tight* included tracks recorded during Charmers' time with the Uniques. During this prolific period he also released work using his real name, notably the risqué 'Bang Bang Lulu' and 'Birth Control'. The latter tune inspired the Coventry-based ska revival group the Specials to record 'Too Much Too Young', which reached number 1 in the UK charts in 1980. In 1972 Charmers released *Censored*, credited to Lloydie And The Lowbites, which saw him continuing in the style of 'Bang Bang Lulu' and 'Birth Control', both of which were re-recorded for this release. He once claimed that Trojan Records declined the offer of further volumes in this vein, considering them to be too crude. After the limited-pressing release of *Too Hot To Handle* in Jamaica, his next venture was as part of the Messengers, whose line-up included Ken Boothe, B.B. Seaton and Busty Brown. They are best remembered for 'Crowded City'. This song, a reggae chart hit, was an early plea for the environment, although with lyrics asking 'What are we gonna do about pollution?', countered with 'I think we should move the factories to the countryside', no genuine solutions seemed to be on offer.

It was as a producer in 1974 that Charmers enjoyed his biggest commercial success with Ken Boothe's number 1 hit, a cover version of David Gates' 'Everything I Own'. He also produced three albums with Boothe, *Black, Gold And Green* (1973), *Let's Get It On* (1974) and *Everything I Own* (1974). In Jamaica his productions surfaced through the Wildflower label, including Bob Andy's classic hit, 'Fire Burning', while his own performances included 'Run Joe' and 'Judgement'. An early 80s cover version of Phil Collins' plea, 'If Leaving Me Is Easy', almost made the pop charts.

● ALBUMS: *Reggae Charm* (Trojan 1970)★★★★, *Reggae Is Tight* (Trojan 1970)★★★★, *Censored* (Lowbite 1972)★★★, *Charmers In Session* (Trojan 1973)★★★, *Wildflower Original Reggae Hits* (Trojan 1974)★★★, *Too Hot To Handle* (Wildflower 1975)★★★, *Golden Days* (Sarge 1980)★★★, *Sweet Memories* (Echo 1982)★★★.

● COMPILATIONS: *Best Of Lloyd Charmers* (Trojan 1974)★★★★, *The Best Of ...* covers 1967-69 (1994)★★★.

CHICKEN CHEST

b. Alton O'Reilly, 28 November 1962, St. Thomas, Jamaica, West Indies. Demonstrating his skills as a wordsmith during his formative years, O'Reilly won several awards for drama, speech and poetry. On leaving school he was employed at his brother's Fried Chicken restaurant in downtown Kingston, and would often entertain the customers by chanting in a DJ style, which led to his pseudonym. He performed on the sound system circuit whenever the opportunity arose, and eventually released his debut, 'Ragamuffin Selector'. The song brought him national fame in Jamaica and in 1988 he was invited to tour Africa and Europe alongside Gregory Isaacs and Edi Fitzroy. Although he had only one hit, audiences were entertained by his strutting and chest-beating, interspersed with the occasional crowing. Following the successful tour, Chicken Chest was invited to perform at the Jamaican Nelson Mandela birthday celebration, followed by an equally successful appearance at the annual

Reggae Sunsplash Festival. His follow-up, 'Negative Can't Conquer Positive', pre-empted his rivals' accusations that he was a one-hit-wonder. He maintained his dancehall credibility by performing on the Arrows sound system in Jamaica, where he introduced Leslie Thunder to the dancehall massive. His popularity in the dancehall lasted only briefly, and he has since returned to anonymity.

● ALBUMS: *Action Packed* (Danceteria 1990)★★.

CHIN, CLIVE

Record producer based at Randy's Studio 17, situated above the famous record shop of the same name in North Parade, Kingston, Jamaica. His first successful production came with the instrumental 'Java' in 1971, featuring the melodica playing of his old schoolfriend, Augustus Pablo. He went on to achieve several more local hits in 1972 with releases including Dennis Brown's 'Cheater', its accompanying horns cut, 'Harvest In The East' by Tommy McCook, and Junior Byles' 'King of Babylon'. He also produced Pablo's classic debut, *This Is*, in 1974, and two dub albums, one based around the 'Java' track, which was mixed by resident Randy's engineer, Errol 'T' Thompson.

In 1975 he produced Carl Malcolm's 'Miss Wire Waist', a sizeable hit on the local market, in the wake of Malcolm's popular 'No Jestering' for fellow producer Leonard 'Santic' Chin (no relation). Clive Chin followed this with the ribald 'Fattie Bum Bum', whose inane catchy refrain appealed to the pop sensibilities of the British entrepreneur Jonathan King. He leased it to his UK label and hyped it into the British charts, where it rose to number 8 in October 1975. Despite appearances to the contrary, this proved to be a less than satisfactory financial venture, and Chin concentrated once more on the grass roots audience with records such as the stalking 'Guns In The Ghetto' and Jah Woosh's 'Shine Eye Gal'.

Eventually he emigrated to America - settling in the Bronx district of New York - to run the J & C Kitchen, serving Jamaican food to the local expatriate population. His family had established the VP record distribution company in the same locale. Over the last few years, he has made tentative steps towards the music business again, but so far no new productions have been forthcoming.

● ALBUMS: *Java Java Dub* (White label 1973)★★★, *Randys Dub* (Randys 1974)★★★★.

CHIN, TONY

b. Albert Valentine Chin, Kingston, Jamaica, West Indies. Chin began his musical career playing drums and the bugle as a member of various youth groups. As lead guitarist he later joined forces with bassist George 'Fully' Fullwood in the Rhythm Raiders, who evolved into the Soul Syndicate. The Soul Syndicate proved a highly popular session band, also featuring the talents of Earl 'Chinna' Smith, Carlton 'Santa' Davis and Bernard 'Touter' Harvey, later replaced by Keith Sterling. The group played on sessions for Winston 'Niney' Holness, Keith Hudson and Bunny Lee, who named them the Aggrovators. The celebrated 'Observer Station' featured Chin's characteristic bottleneck guitar playing. The band also played live support to a number of Jamaica's finest lead vocalists, including Freddie McGregor, Dennis Brown, Cynthia Richards and Earl Zero. During the 70s the group supported U-Roy, the Mighty Diamonds and Big Youth on the international circuit before being enrolled to support Peter Tosh, replacing Sly And Robbie in the second manifestation of Word Sound And Power. Following Tosh's untimely death, the group performed at a tribute concert where they formed an allegiance with the deceased's son, Andrew Tosh. By the early 90s the group had retired from the business, and Chin remained in Florida, where he was approached to join the multicultural band Big Mountain, following a brief spell with the Reggae All Stars. The band have the distinction of being the pre-eminent US reggae band, having crossed over into the pop chart with a version of 'Baby I Love Your Way'. In addition to playing rhythm guitar in the group, Chin also became involved in songwriting and had an opportunity to sing vocals.

CHIN-LOY, HERMAN

Of Chinese-Jamaican extraction, Herman Chin-Loy's earliest involvement in the music business came when he worked for his famous record-producing cousin, Leslie Kong, in his Beverley's record shop in the 60s. In 1969 he opened up his own Aquarius Record Store in Half Way Tree and moved into record production via instrumentals such as 'African Zulu' and 'Shang I'. To this end he utilized the talents of Lloyd Charmers and the Hippy Boys, featuring future Wailers (see Bob Marley) rhythm section Carlton And Family Man Barrett. On his later productions he is credited with being the first to use the highly influential Now Generation Band. He was also responsible for the debut recordings of Augustus Pablo: it was Chin-Loy, in fact, who gave Pablo his name. Chin-Loy had been releasing instrumentals, mainly organ-led affairs by Upsetter acolyte Glen Adams, and crediting them to an invented name, Augustus Pablo. When the young Horace Swaby (Pablo's real name) arrived on the scene, Chin-Loy saw no reason to change the credit, and so Horace Swaby became Augustus Pablo. In return, Pablo made a number of records for the producer between 1971 and 1973, including 'Higgi Higgi', 'East Of The River Nile', 'Song Of The East' and 'The Red Sea'. Chin-Loy worked with a number of other artists in the early 70s, including Dennis Brown ('Song My Mother Used To Sing', 'It's Too Late') and Alton Ellis ('Alton's Official Daughter').

In May 1971 his production of Bruce Ruffin's 'Rain' became a crossover hit and secured the number 19 position in the UK pop charts. According to his own testimony, *Aquarius Dub*, one of the first ever dub albums, emerged from a half-hour mix-and-go session at Dynamics studio with Chin-Loy himself at the controls. He built his own 24-track studio, the first in Jamaica, in the mid-70s, which was used primarily for the recording of non-reggae music. In fact, Chin-Loy's own productions were largely absent from the reggae scene until 1979. It was then that he began to score local hits once more with a number of 12-inch mixes on the cusp of the burgeoning dancehall style, including material by Little Roy ('Long Time Rock Steady', 'Skanking On The Banking') and Ernest Wilson ('Truth & Rights'). Largely absent from the scene throughout the 80s, there were hints of activity in the 90s but nothing concrete has emerged as yet.

● ALBUMS: *Aquarius Dub* (Aquarius 1973)★★★★, *Aquarius Dub Part 2* (Aquarius 1974)★★★.

CHOSEN FEW

In 1968 the Federals, a vocal trio featuring Franklin Spence and David Scott (known as Scotty), performed regularly at the Sombrero club in Kingston, Jamaica. It was at this club that Derrick Harriott spotted the group and took them into the recording studio, producing a number of minor hits, notably 'Penny For Your Song'. By 1969 the group had evolved into the Chosen Few when the third member left and was replaced by Noel Brown. The addition of Richard McDonald completed the line-up as they began recording reggae versions of hits by Blue Mink and the Delphonics. Scotty soon left the group to pursue his solo career and was replaced by Busty Brown after the demise of his former studio group, the Messengers. Scotty went on to enjoy a number of DJ hits, including 'Draw Your Brakes', 'Clean Race' and 'Skank In Bed', the latter a toast to Lorna Bennett's 'Breakfast In Bed', which when covered by UB40 and Chrissie Hynde (Pretenders), later became a number 1 hit in the UK. The line-up of the Chosen Few finally settled with McDonald being replaced by Errol Brown. Brown had been performing with various soul groups in New York and his influence led to the soulful reggae tunes that followed. Cover versions of the Stylistics' 'People Make The World Go Round' (credited to Errol Brown And The Chosen Few), 'You're A Big Girl Now' and the Main Ingredients' 'Everybody Plays The Fool' were big hits in the reggae charts. In 1973 they released *Hit After Hit* which included the singles along with cover versions as diverse as 'Stranger On The Shore' and 'Mexican Divorce'. The group went on to record with Jamaican-born King Sporty in Miami, resulting in *Night And Day* - one side being reggae and the other being soul tunes. Guest musicians included KC And The Sunshine Band on 'Funky Buttercup', 'Hit Me With Music' and 'Wandering' (the release of *The Chosen Few In Miami* in the UK was simply a repackaged version of *Night And Day*).

In the 80s the group's line-up featured Brown, Michael Deslandes and founding member Franklin Spence. They had set up their own label, Kufe, and continued to record soul-influenced selections, notably 'On The Right Tracks'. Scotty revived his career in 1989 with a cover version of Carl Malcolm's 'Miss Wire Waist', in a return to the singing style of his early career.

● ALBUMS: *Hit After Hit* (Trojan 1973)★★, *Night And Day* aka *The Chosen Few In Miami* (Trojan 1975)★★.

CHUKKI STAR

b. Harlesden, London, England. Chukki began his career when he formed his own Echo Tone Hi Fi sound system, performing as Chukki Brown. The DJ's debut, 'Goodas Gal', was produced by Stonehead of the UK-based Volcano sound and signalled Chukki's emergence from the UK dancehall scene. His distinctive style led to recording sessions, primarily with Everton Samuels of the Ruff Cut Band. In 1994 he released a series of hits as Chukki Star, including 'Career Time', 'Evilous System', 'Who Dem Fi Rate', 'Almighty Father', and in combination with Don Campbell, 'Reggae Music So Sweet'. In 1995 he performed DJ lyrics for Aswad on one of the numerous remixes of 'Warrior Charge'. In 1996 Chukki performed in western Kingston on the sound system circuit, followed by sessions with some of Jamaica's top producers. He initially recorded in combination with Edi Fitzroy at Bobby Digital's studio, which led to sessions with African Star, Black Scorpio and Yard Face Productions. Some of his best chants included 'The Most High', an anthem to Haile Selassie, 'Time To Go', and the popular combination with Gregory Isaacs, 'The Look Of Love'. By 1997 Chukki was considered to be one of the UK's top DJs following the success of his own Makiel label release, 'Forever I Shall Praise', and the combination hit with Aisha, 'Hard Times'. Chukki maintained a high profile in 1998 and worked with the Mad Professor for his debut album release.

● ALBUMS: *Ghetto Youth Livity* (Ariwa 1998)★★★.

CHUNG, GEOFFREY

b. *c*.1950, Kingston, Jamaica, West Indies, d. November 1995. Chung began his career in the Peter Ashbourn Affair playing middle-of-the-road reggae tunes. In the early 70s he formed the Now Generation session band with his brother Mikey Chung, Val Douglas, Mikey 'Boo' Richards, Earl 'Wire' Lindo and Robert Lynn. He was also responsible for Sharon Forrester's debut, 'Silly Wasn't I', backed by the Now

Generation. The group released a number of reggae cover versions, including a rendering of 'Alone Again Naturally' released in 1973. His synthesizer skills were demonstrated on the Harry J. release 'U.F.O.', credited to Geffrey Chang Allstars. In 1974 Chung concentrated on Forrester's career, playing virtually all of the instruments, producing, arranging and composing tracks for her debut, *Sharon*, notably 'Words With No Meaning'. The collection was named best reggae album of the year by *Melody Maker*. His diverse skills enabled him to set up his own Edge Productions, where he enjoyed notable hits with the Heptones and Marcia Griffiths. Both hits were cover versions of popular Philly Sound releases - Harold Melvin And The Bluenotes' 'I Miss You' from the Heptones and the Three Degrees' 'When Will I See You Again', which maintained Griffiths' chart profile. So popular was the latter hit that Ken Boothe recorded a reply, 'Now You Can See Me Again'. In 1975 Chung performed with the Rastafarian group Ras Michael And The Sons Of Negus. The group recorded an album, *Rastafari*, which won critical acclaim by successfully integrating reggae rhythms with traditional burra drumming. At Dynamics studio Chung played keyboards alongside such luminaries as Peter Tosh (guitar and clavinet), Robbie Shakespeare (bass guitar), Earl 'Chinna' Smith (lead guitar), Carlton 'Santa' Davis (drums) and Tommy McCook (flute). The album surfaced in the UK with a gatefold sleeve, something quite unusual in reggae circles, and soon topped the charts. When Inner Circle signed the rights to *Reggae Thing* with Capitol Records, Chung played keyboards and provided backing vocals, notably on '80,000 Careless Ethiopians'. In the early 80s Chung became the resident engineer at Byron Lee's Dynamics Sound Studio. His engineering skills were employed by Peter Tosh following his contribution on *Bush Doctor*. Chung mixed the recordings at Dynamics in Kingston and flew to Sound Mixers and A&R in New York to remix the follow-ups *Mystic Man* and *Wanted Dread And Alive*. The projects resulted in Chung being assisted by his brother Mikey who had become a member of Word Sound And Power. As well as his high international profile, Chung also played on sessions with melodica maestro Augustus Pablo, notably on *Africa Must Be Free By 1983*,

Hugh Mundell's masterpiece. With Freddie McGregor, Chung co-produced a hit in 1985 for Frankie Paul, 'Inferiority Complex', which was one of the first of the singer's numerous international hits. By the late 80s Chung set up home in Miami where he was a successful producer and engineer. In November 1995, Chung died of kidney failure, and to mark his contribution to reggae a tribute concert was held featuring a number of artists with whom he had worked, including Sly And Robbie, Lieutenant Stitchie, Chalice and Pablo Moses.

● ALBUMS: with Now Generation *For The Good Times* (Trojan 1974)★★★★, with Ras Michael And The Sons Of Negus *Rastafari* (Vulcan 1975)★★★, with Ras Michael And The Sons Of Negus *Freedom Sounds* (Dynamic 1976)★★★.

CHUNG, MIKEY

b. Michael Chung, 1954, Kingston, Jamaica, West Indies. Affectionately known as 'Mao', an acknowledgement of his Chinese ancestry, Chung played lead guitar on recording sessions as part of the Now Generation band, where he backed a number of artists including Bob Marley, following Peter Tosh's and Bunny Wailer's decisions to pursue solo careers. In 1976 Chung appeared with the heavyweight trio of Jacob Miller, Ian 'Munty' Lewis and Roger Lewis on stage, attracting a good deal of attention as Chung, like the others, was not slim. His musical skills were utilized on the trio's *Reggae Thing*, a fine major label debut that was unfairly criticized by the purists. He appeared with the group in what was only the fourth television documentary concerning reggae aired in the UK. The programme, *Roots Rock Reggae*, ended with Chung and the group giving a performance of 'Love Is The Drug', which he co-wrote, and 'All Night 'Til Daylight'. In 1978 Chung joined Word, Sound And Power, Tosh's backing band following the departure of Al Anderson. The group consisted of Sly Dunbar, Robbie Shakespeare and a seasoned associate from his Now Generation days, Robert Lynn, supported by other sessionmen. Chung was a proficient lead guitarist and had mastered the synthesizer, and both skills were initially applied on Tosh's third album, *Bush Doctor*. His brother, Geoffrey Chung, engineered the tracks, recorded at Dynamics Sound Studio in Kingston. To promote the album, Tosh, along with Word, Sound And Power, toured Europe and the USA, playing in stadiums where the audience figures were comparable to those drawn by pop supergroups. Though still part of Tosh's backing group Sly Dunbar signed to Virgin Records in 1979 and it was Chung, along with Sly And Robbie, who penned 'Oriental Taxi', the name later used by the 'rhythm twins' for their production company. His association with Sly And Robbie led to the release of 'Hold Me Tight' and 'Brand New Day', credited to Robbie And Mao on Delroy Witter's Niagara label. The embryonic Taxi Gang returned to Jamaica and the sessions for *Mystic Man* commenced with Chung and his brother taking more responsibility for the sessions. While Mikey supervised the horn arrangements, Geoffrey supervised the recording and remixing.

In 1981 following the sessions for *Wanted Dread And Alive*, Mikey joined Sly And Robbie on the Black Uhuru sessions for *Red* and *Chill Out*. He returned to Europe with the band and a live album and video, *Tear It Up - Live*, recorded the event. Chung was last seen performing with Pluto And Co., a Miami-based group consisting of Jamaican expatriates, led by Pluto Shervington.

CIMARONS

The Cimarons' main claim to fame is the honour of being the UK's first indigenous reggae band. Like many later British outfits, the Cimarons, who formed in 1967 at a north London Methodist youth club, eked out a living in their early days supporting visiting Jamaican musicians on club dates, and they proved so adept that they were later invited to tour Africa. On their return they recorded their debut single, 'Mammy Blue', released on Downtown Records. By this time, they had built themselves sufficient standing to make touring in their own right viable. These engagements paved the way for two album releases, the first of which, *In Time*, predominantly comprised soul standards given the reggae treatment. The second, *On The Rock*, was recorded in Jamaica.

Riding on the crest of the reggae boom, they were picked up by Polydor in the late 70s. By recording *Reggaebility*, which included takes on several Beatles songs, they certainly helped to

bring the genre mainstream attention. They also backed a record by Australian songwriter Gary Shearston. Members of the band have included Sonny Binns (keyboards), Franklyn Dunn (bass), Locksley Gichie (guitars) and Winston Reid (vocals). In the 80s they were joined by former Matumbi drummer, Jah 'Bunny' Donaldson.

● ALBUMS: *In Time* (Trojan 1977)★★★, *On The Rock* (Vulcan 1977)★★★, *Maka* (Polydor 1978)★★, *Live* (Polydor 1979)★★, *Reggaebility* (Hallmark 1982)★★★.

CLARENDONIANS

While Jamaican music is packed with child prodigies, to find three in one group is unusual even by reggae standards. The Clarendonians, originally Fitzroy 'Ernest' Wilson and Peter Austin, formed during 1965 in their home parish of Clarendon in rural Jamaica, and after several talent competition victories, they came to the attention of producer Coxsone Dodd, owner of the Studio One label, while they were in their early teens. Dodd liked their feisty approach and soon put the pair in the studio, where they helped to define the 'rude boy' era of ska alongside Dodd's other youthful protégés, Bob Marley And The Wailers. If anything, the Clarendonians were more successful than Marley's group at the time, finding great success with brash, loud singles such as 'You Can't Be Happy', 'You Can't Keep A Good Man Down', 'Sho Be Do Be', 'Rudie Gone A Jail', 'Be Bop Boy', and their anthem, 'Rudie Bam Bam'. As young as their audience and the music they worked with, the Clarendonians were briefly the perfect ska vocal group. Somewhere along the line, Dodd added another member, Freddie McGregor, who at the age of seven had to stand on a box to reach the microphone, and Dodd permutated the members as Freddie And Fitzie, Freddie And Peter, or simply recorded them solo. Ernest Wilson was the first member to really strike out as a solo act with a cover version of Billy Vera's 'Storybook Children' and Tim Hardin's 'If I Were A Carpenter', as well as recording under the unlikely moniker of King Shark. He is still something of a star in Jamaica today, if only sporadically successful. McGregor was not as immediately successful, but after a series of excellent records with Studio One lasting right into the

early 70s, he finally hit with 'Bobby Babylon'. Austin's attempt at a solo career sadly faltered.
● COMPILATIONS: *The Best Of The Clarendonians* (Studio One 1968)★★★.

CLARKE, ERIC

b. Eric Clarke, *c.*1960, Kingston, Jamaica, West Indies. Clarke, popularly known as 'Fish', followed in the footsteps of his brother Johnny Clarke into the Jamaican music business. While Johnny established himself as a popular vocalist, Eric found his vocation playing drums. In 1978 he toured the UK with the late Prince Far I as part of his backing band the Arabs. The line-up of the group included Errol Holt on bass, Earl 'Chinna' Smith on lead guitar and Winston 'Bo Peep' Bowen on keyboards. He contributed his percussion skills on a number of tracks on the Front Line release *Message From A King*, notably 'Foggy Road' and the title track. Whilst in the UK he also played drums on the first of a series of dub albums with the DJ. When he returned to Jamaica he was replaced by Lincoln 'Style Scott' in the Arabs - he later joined the Roots Radics alongside Errol Holt, Bingi Bunny and Noel 'Sowell Radics' Bailey. Clarke had, in the meantime, formed an allegiance with Maurice 'Blacka' Wellington, having performed with the Roots Radics, and fulfilled his ambition as a soloist for the single 'Nice Inna Jamaica', on which he emulated his brother's vocal phrasing.
● ALBUMS: *Cry Tuff Dub Encounter Chapter One* (Hit Run 1978)★★★.

CLARKE, GUSSIE

b. Augustus Clarke, *c.*1953, Kingston, Jamaica, West Indies. Clarke started in the reggae business by cutting dub plates. He grew up alongside reggae DJ Big Youth, and Clarke was an early pioneer of the new DJ style. His first production was U-Roy's 'The Higher The Mountain' in 1972, which became an instant classic. His initial album productions, Big Youth's *Screaming Target* and I. Roy's *Presenting*, are among the best DJ albums of all time. Clarke was not one to push his own name at the expense of his acts, however, and unlike many of his contemporaries, he preferred a low-key, crafted approach, reflected in the name of his 'house band', Simplicity People. During the 70s he recorded many of the greatest names in reggae, including Augustus Pablo, Dennis Brown, Gregory Isaacs and Leroy Smart, and his Gussie and Puppy labels became synonymous with high-quality reggae. Clarke kept production almost as a sideline to his main business of dub cutting and record export. Unlike other producers in the grab-and-flee reggae business, he paid royalties and maintained a publishing company. By the early 80s Clarke's activities as a producer were restricted to the occasional outing with reggae superstars such as Dennis Brown (*To The Foundation*), Gregory Isaacs (*Private Beach Party*) and vocal groups Cultural Roots (*Whole Heap A Daughters*) and the Mighty Diamonds (*The Roots Is There* and *The Real Enemy*). The announcement that Clarke had recorded some of the Diamonds' *Real Enemy* at his own studio was met with indifference, but the first single to emerge from his Music Works Studio, Isaacs' 'Rumours', could not be ignored. Clarke had abandoned his solid, rather traditional sound and had 'gone digital', using computers and synthesizers to create an entirely new, dub-centred sound. The record was a massive hit, and another version of it, 'Telephone Love', from female singer JC Lodge, was the biggest reggae hit of 1988 in the USA. Suddenly, Clarke appeared to be way ahead of the pack, and he spent 1989 and the start of 1990 with everyone queueing to record at his hi-tech studio, among them, Aswad, Maxi Priest and jazz musician Courtney Pine. His 'Pirates Anthem' single with Home T, Cocoa Tea and Shabba Ranks was a huge underground hit in London, but then Clarke started work on another project - a bigger, more 'international' studio. Once again, his production work took a back seat as he block-booked Music Works to other producers and concentrated on his new baby. Towards the end of 1991 he issued a few singles, but it remains to be seen whether Clarke can once again deliver a shock to reggae, this time from his new premises.
● COMPILATIONS: *Black Foundation* (Burning Sounds 1976)★★★, *Gussie Presents The Right Tracks* (1977)★★★, *Music Works Showcase* (Music Works 1984)★★★, *Music Works Showcase '88* (Greensleeves 1988)★★★, *Music Works Showcase '89* (Greensleeves 1989)★★★, *Ram Dancehall* (Mango/Island 1988)★★★★, *Hardcore Ragga* (Greensleeves 1990)★★★★.

CLARKE, JOHNNY

b. January 1955, Jamaica, West Indies. After winning a talent contest at Bull Bay on the south-western coast of Jamaica, Johnny Clarke made his first record, 'God Made The Sea And Sun', which flopped. His next two releases for producer Rupie Edwards, 'Everyday Wandering' and 'Julie', both enjoyed considerable sales in Jamaica and among expatriate communities in the UK, USA and Canada. By 1974 Clarke was working with Bunny Lee in the studios of Treasure Isle, Randy's and Harry J., while voicing the finished instrumental tracks at King Tubby's studio in Kingston's Waterhouse district. Under Lee's tutelage during 1975-76, Clarke became the most exciting new singer in Jamaica. His repertoire, an astute mix of militant 'dread' tunes and love songs, given a contemporary gloss or 'style' by the Aggrovators studio band, found immediate favour with the discerning dancehall patrons of Jamaica and elsewhere. His hits in those two years included 'None Shall Escape The Judgement', 'Move Out Of Babylon', 'Rock With Me Baby', 'Enter Into His Gates With Praise' and 'Joshua's Word', all new songs, while Lee encouraged him to cover classic Jamaican standards by artists such as John Holt. Holt's canon supplied further local hits for Clarke, including 'Fancy Make-Up', 'Stranger In Love', 'Left With A Broken Heart' and 'So Much Pain', all backed by the then current 'flying cymbal sound' of Lee's Aggrovators. Following this period, Clarke continued to record for Lee and other producers as diverse as Errol Thompson and Prince Jammy. He has continued to produce high-quality reggae material to the present day, after a period of inactivity in the mid-80s. Most recently, he has recorded for Fashion Records and Jah Shaka in the UK, and the 90s hitmaking production duo of Steely And Clevie.
● ALBUMS: *None Shall Escape* (1974)★★★, *Enter Into His Gates With Praise* (Attack 1974)★★, *Put It On* (Vulcan 1975)★★★, *Authorised Version* (Virgin 1976)★★★, *Rocker's Time Now* (Virgin 1976)★★★, *Girl I Love You* (Justice 1977)★★, *I Man Come Again* (Black Music 1982)★★★, *Yard Style* (Ariwa 1983)★★★, with Cornell Campbell *Johnny Clarke Meets Cornell Campbell In New Style* (Vista Sounds 1983)★★★, *Reggae Party* (Vista Sounds 1984)★★★, with Sly And Robbie *Sly & Robbie Present The Best Of Johnnie Clarke* (Vista Sounds 1985)★★★★, *Give Thanks* (Ariwa 1985)★★★, *Don't Trouble Trouble* (Attack/Trojan 1989)★★★.
● COMPILATIONS: *20 Massive Hits* (Striker Lee 1985)★★★, *Reggae Archives* (Gong Sounds 1991)★★★★, *Authorised Rockers* compiled from *Rockers Time Now* and *Authorised Version* (Front Line 1991)★★★★, *Originally Mr Clarke* (Clocktower 1995)★★★.

CLIFF, JIMMY

b. James Chambers, 1948, St. Catherine, Jamaica, West Indies. One of the great popularizers of reggae music, Jimmy Cliff blazed a trail into rock that Bob Marley later followed, but without ever capitalizing on his great advantages as a singer-songwriter, nascent film star and interpreter of other people's material. Raised by his father, Cliff first moved to Kingston in 1962 after the dream of a musical career seduced him from his studies. An early brace of singles, 'Daisy Got Me Crazy', with Count Boysie, and 'I'm Sorry', for sound system operator Sir Cavalier, did little to bring him to the public's attention. His career began in earnest when a song he had written himself, 'Hurricane Hattie', describing the recent arrival in South America of the self-same meteorological disaster, became a local hit. He was still only 14 years old.
Cliff subsequently emerged as a ska singer for producer Leslie Kong in 1963, singing 'King Of Kings' and 'Dearest Beverly' in a hoarse, raucous voice to considerable local acclaim. He can be seen in this fledgling role on the video *This Is Ska*, shot in 1964. The same year Cliff joined a tour promoted by politician Eward Seaga and headlined by Byron Lee And The Dragonaires, with the intention of exporting reggae music to the wider world. Though it later collapsed in acrimony, the jaunt at least brought Cliff to the attention of Island Records' boss Chris Blackwell, and in the mid-60s the young singer moved to London. By 1968 Cliff was being groomed as a solo star for the underground rock market. Musicians teamed with him included Mott The Hoople's Ian Hunter and vocalists including Madeline Bell and P.P. Arnold. The shift away from the conventional reggae audience was confirmed by a cover version of Procul

Harum's 'Whiter Shade of Pale' and appearances alongside the Incredible String Band and Jethro Tull on Island samplers. In 1968 Cliff chanced his arm in Brazil, representing Jamaica in the International Song Festival. His entry, 'Waterfall' (a flop in England), earned him a considerable following in South America. More importantly, the sojourn gave him the chance to take stock and write new material. He finally broke through in 1969 with 'Wonderful World, Beautiful People', a somewhat over-produced single typical of the era, which he had written in Brazil. 'Vietnam' was a small hit the following year, and was described by Bob Dylan as not only the best record about the war, but the best protest song he had heard. Paul Simon went one step further in his praises; after hearing the song he travelled to Kingston and booked the same rhythm section, studio and engineer to record 'Mother And Child Reunion' - arguably the first US reggae song. In local terms, however, its success was outstripped by 'Wild World', a cover version of the Cat Stevens song, the link between the two singers perhaps strengthened by a shared Muslim faith.

While the albums *Jimmy Cliff*, *Hard Road To Travel* and particularly *Another Cycle* were short on roots credibility, his next move, as the gun-toting, reggae-singing star of *The Harder They Come* (1972), was short on nothing. Cliff, with his ever-present five-point star T-shirt, was suddenly Jamaica's most marketable property. *The Harder They Come* was the island's best home-grown film, and its soundtrack one of the biggest-selling reggae records of all time. Cliff seemed set for superstardom. Somehow, it never happened: his relationship with Island soured and contracts with EMI, Reprise and CBS failed to deliver him to his rightful place. In fact, his star began to wane directly as Bob Marley signed to Island. The company executed the same marketing process for both artists - rebellion, great songwriting, hipness - but it was Marley who embodied the new spirit of reggae and reaped the rewards. Cliff's artistic fortunes were revived, ironically enough, by the recruitment of Wailers producer Joe Higgs as his bandleader. Despite their merits, Cliff's excellent records for his own Sunpower label did not really connect. To many outside the reggae world he remains best known for writing the beautiful tear-jerker 'Many Rivers To Cross', a massive hit for UB40. However, his popularity on the African continent is enormous, arguably greater than that of any other reggae artist, Marley included. He is similarly venerated in South America, whose samba rhythms have helped to inform and enrich his latter-day material. Jimmy Cliff's most recent studio albums highlight, as ever, his plaintive, gospel-tinged delivery, offering ample evidence to dispel the widely held belief (particularly in the West) that he is a perennial underachiever.

● ALBUMS: *Jimmy Cliff* (Trojan 1969)★★★, *Wonderful World, Beautiful People* (A&M 1970)★★★★, *Hard Road To Travel* (Trojan/A&M 1970)★★★, *Another Cycle* (Island 1971)★★★, *The Harder They Come* film soundtrack (Mango/Island 1972)★★★★★, *Unlimited* (EMI 1973, Trojan 1990)★★★, *Struggling Man* (Island 1974)★★★, *Brave Warrior* (EMI 1975)★★★, *Follow My Mind* (Reprise 1976)★★, *Give Thanx* (Warners 1978)★★, *Oh Jamaica* (EMI 1979)★★, *I Am The Living* (Warners 1980)★★, *Give The People What They Want* (Oneness/Warners 1981)★★, *House Of Exile* (1981)★★, *Special* (Columbia 1982)★★, *The Power And The Glory* (Columbia 1983)★★★, *Can't Get Enough Of It* (Veep 1984)★★★, *Cliff Hanger* (Dynamic/Columbia 1985)★★, *Sense Of Direction* (Sire 1985)★★★, *Hang Fire* (Dynamic/Columbia 1987)★★★, *Images* (Cliff Sounds 1989)★★★, *Save Our Planet Earth* (Musidisc 1990)★★, *Breakout* (Cliff Sounds 1993)★★★, *The Cool Runner Live In London* (More Music 1995)★★.

● COMPILATIONS: *The Best Of Jimmy Cliff* (Island 1974)★★★★, *The Best Of Jimmy Cliff In Concert* (Reprise 1977)★★★, *The Collection* (EMI 1983)★★★, *Jimmy Cliff* (Trojan 1983)★★★, *Reggae Greats* (Island 1985)★★★, *Fundamental Reggae* (See For Miles 1987)★★★, *The Best Of Jimmy Cliff* (Mango/Island 1988)★★★★.

● VIDEOS: *Bongo Man* (Hendring Video 1989).

● FILMS: *The Harder They Come* (1972)

CLINT EASTWOOD AND GENERAL SAINT

b. Robert Brammer. Jamaican-born Eastwood (Trinity's younger brother) came to prominence with British reggae fans in the late 70s with a series of big-selling singles recorded in his home country, and albums such as *African Youth*, *Death In The Arena* and *Sex Education*. In the early 80s he teamed up with General Saint (b. Winston Hislop), who had already established a devoted following working in London's Front Line International sound system, and the pair formed a talented pop-reggae duo. Their first release, a tribute to the late General Echo, topped the reggae charts, and the follow-up, 'Another One Bites The Dust', repeated the feat in 1981, reaching as far as the lower rungs of the national chart. Their subsequent records and live appearances enhanced their reputation further and they were instrumental in the Jamaican DJ style crossing over to the early 80s pop audience.

● ALBUMS: Clint Eastwood: *African Youth* (Third World 1978)★★★, *Death In The Arena* (Cha Cha 1978)★★★, *Love & Happiness* (Burning Sounds 1979)★★★, *Sex Education* (Greensleeves 1980)★★★. Clint Eastwood And General Saint *Jah Lights Shining* (Vista Sounds 1984)★★★.

● COMPILATIONS: Clint Eastwood *Best Of Clint Eastwood* (Culture Press 1984)★★★★. Clint Eastwood And General Saint: *Two Bad DJ* (Greensleeves 1981)★★★, *Stop That Train* (Greensleeves 1983)★★★.

CLUE J AND HIS BLUES BLASTERS

Double-bassist Cluett Johnson's most lasting contribution to the history of music happened by accident. From 1959, Jamaican-born Johnson led the first band to make records in Jamaica; the Blues Blasters' line-up included Ernest Ranglin (guitar), Emmanuel 'Rico' Rodriguez (trombone), Roland Alphonso (tenor saxophone), Theophilius Beckford (piano) and Arkland 'Drumbago' Parks (drums). Their early recordings, such as 'Shuffling Jug' (1959), were in a calypso or R&B vein and were promoted on producer Coxsone Dodd's Downbeat sound system, which played in and around Kingston. Having thus created a demand, Dodd would release their records on his Worldisc label. Rehearsing in the studio, Johnson reportedly instructed Ranglin to 'Play it like ska, ska', thus unwittingly coining the name of his island's predominant music of the 1962-66 period. By that time, the Blues Blasters had evolved into the Skatalites and Johnson had slipped from view.

● COMPILATIONS: various *All Star Top Hits* (Studio One 1961)★★★, with the Cecil Lloyd Trio *Live At The Penthouse*.

COBRA

b. Ewart Everton Brown, 1968, Kingston, Jamaica, West Indies. Brown grew up in St. Mary's and was nicknamed Cobra after a character in the G.I. Joe comic books. Early experience on the Mighty Ruler, Climax, Stereo One and Inner City sound systems led to his first record, 'Respect Woman', in 1989. The producer was his uncle, Delroy 'Spiderman' Thompson, then engineer at Tuff Gong. His first local hit was 'Nah Go Work', a duet with Tricia McKay, produced by Carl Mitchell in 1990. Carl 'Banton' Nelson and Captain Sinbad were quick to follow their example in early 1991, encouraging him to voice titles including 'Ze Taurus' and 'Merciless Bad Boy', as a wave of gun lyrics - influenced by the Gulf War and championed by the DJ Ninjaman - began to gain popularity in the Jamaican dancehalls.

The next stop was Donovan Germain's Penthouse studio, where he immediately struck up a successful partnership with resident engineer Dave Kelly. Singles such as 'Yush', 'Bad Boy Talk' and 'Gundelero' sealed his burgeoning reputation as an uncompromising lyricist, and were crowned by the bestselling *Bad Boy Talk* album. His most prolific and rewarding year was 1991, with a glut of releases from King Jammy, Bobby Digital ('Tek Him' almost attained crossover status), Sly And Robbie, John John and Penthouse dominating the reggae charts, especially in the UK where he enjoyed no less than five number 1 hits. UK producers played their part in helping to widen his appeal; so too Montego Bay label Top Rank who had followed the *Spotlight* album with Cobra's haunting 'Love Forever'. The latter was evidence of a shift towards romantic lyrics and softer, more R&B-orientated rhythms, as also exemplified by 'Flex', which he had voiced for Shang. It was this song that persuaded Columbia to sign him and by the end of 1992 he was number 1 on the US Billboard Chart. In 1993, after an impressive major label album debut with *Easy To Wet Hard To Dry* - complete with guest US rappers - he unexpectedly returned to the dancehall market, working with several of his former producers, including King Jammy.

● ALBUMS: *Bad Boy Talk* (Penthouse 1991)★★★, *Spotlight* (Top Rank 1992)★★★, *Merciless Bad Boy* (Sinbad 1992)★★★, *Easy To Wet Hard To Dry* (Columbia 1993)★★★★.

COCOA TEA

b. Calvin Scott, 1960, Kingston, Jamaica, West Indies. Cocoa Tea began his career while still a child in Kingston in 1974, singing on a couple of obscure records for an equally obscure producer, Willie Francis; 'Searching In The Hills' was issued under the name of Calvin Scott. He vanished again until 1983, when, sporting dreadlocks and his new nickname, he began to carve a niche in dancehall reggae with producer Henry 'Junjo' Lawes, hitting with 'Rockin' Dolly', and 'I Lost My Sonia'. Unlike other dancehall singers, he did not find it necessary to attempt to dominate a song with energy, instead preferring a subtler, more melodic approach. His 1985 album debut, *Wha Them A Go Do, Can't Stop Cocoa Tea*, suggested a great future, which proved to be correct as *The Marshall, Sweet Sweet Cocoa Tea, Come Again* and *Cocoa Tea* established him further. A collaboration with producer Gussie Clarke led to the formation of a group alongside the trio Home T and DJ Shabba Ranks. Their *Holding On* and the single 'Pirate's Anthem' were huge Jamaican hits in 1989. As a solo artist, *Riker's Island* established that he had more to say than most. The 'No Blood For Oil' single was a lucid comment on the Gulf war, and was also to be found on *Another One For The Road* (1991), recorded with Home T after Cutty Ranks had replaced Shabba in the group. In 1997 he successfully revived the King Sporty hit, 'I'm Not A King'. The only thing currently preventing Cocoa Tea from becoming a major musical star is his apparent reluctance to travel.

● ALBUMS: *Wha Them A Go Do, Can't Stop Cocoa Tea* (Volcano 1985)★★★★, *Sweet Sweet Cocoa Tea* (Blue Mountain 1986)★★★, *The Marshall* (Jammys 1986)★★★, *Cocoa Tea* (Firehouse 1986)★★★★, with Tenor Saw *Clash* (Witty 1987)★★★, *Come Again* (Super Power 1987)★★★, with Shabba Ranks, Home T *Holding On* (Greensleeves 1989)★★★, *Rikers Island* (Greensleeves 1991)★★★, with Cutty Ranks, Home T *Another One For The Road* (Greensleeves 1991)★★★, *Authorized* (Greensleeves 1992)★★★, *I Am The Toughest* (King Jammys 1992)★★★, *Kingston Hot* (Greensleeves 1992)★★★, *One Up* (Exterminator/ Greensleeves 1993)★★★, *Tune In* (Greensleeves 1994)★★★.

COLE, STRANGER

b. Winston Cole, c.1945, Kingston, Jamaica, West Indies. In 1962 Cole made his recording debut with Duke Reid, topping the local hit parade with 'Rough And Tough' and 'When You Call My Name', the latter a duet with Patsy Todd. His understated, laconic delivery could be heard on further hits for Reid including 'Stranger At The Door' (1963), 'We Are Rolling' (1964), and 'Run Joe' (1965). During this period, he also worked with other producers, including a duet with Ken Boothe, 'Worlds Fair', for Coxsone Dodd, and he sang harmony on Eric Morris's huge hit 'Penny Reel', a Prince Buster production. By the late 60s his voice had developed into a much more powerful, soulful instrument. He recorded for several producers, including another duet with Patsy Todd, 'Down By The Tramline' (1967) for Sonia Pottinger, a duet with Gladstone Anderson, 'Just Like A River' (1968) for Joe Gibbs, 'Crying Every Night' (1970) for Byron Smith, and 'Lift Your Head Up High' (1970), a self-production. In 1971 he emigrated to England where he toured extensively, before relocating to Canada in 1973, settling in Toronto. He released his first album, *Forward In The Land Of Sunshine*, in 1976. In the late 70s he produced two songs, 'Capture Land' and 'The Time Is Now', for the New York-based Wackies label. Three albums were also issued on his own label, *The First Ten Years Of Stranger Cole, Capture Land* and *The Patriot*. He was less fortunate when working for other producers, as albums he recorded for Coxsone Dodd and Chinna Smith in the early 80s were not issued. His most recent album was *No More Fussing And Fighting*, his first to be released in the USA. Sadly, Stranger's rich back-catalogue has never been reissued.

● ALBUMS: *Forward In The Land Of Sunshine* (1976)★★★★, *The First Ten Years Of Stranger Cole* (1978)★★★★, *Capture Land* (1980)★★★, *The Patriot* (1982)★★★, *No More Fussing And Fighting* (1986)★★★★.

COLOURMAN

b. Fidel Hugh Henry, c.1965, Manchester, Jamaica, West Indies. Henry initially demonstrated his DJ skills on the Clarendon-based Cosmic Force sound system. Performing as the Bible Man, he played on other little-known sound systems, including Ghetto International, Masterblaster and Cadett Hi Power. In 1984 he moved to Kingston where he was coached by Snagga Puss, who at the time was performing as Dickie Ranking, then the principal DJ on the Gemini sound system. Henry's popularity grew, prompting an invitation from Henry 'Junjo' Lawes to perform alongside Buro Banton, Billy Boyo, Little Harry and Danny Dread on the Volcano Hi Power sound. The sound was set up in 1983 and Colourman had access to dub plates from Jamaica's finest, including Cocoa Tea, Frankie Paul, Johnny Osbourne and Barrington Levy. In 1985 Lawes invited Colourman to join him when he decided to take the sound to New York. Colourman resisted the offer, preferring to perform 'a yard', and joined Sugar Minott's Youth Promotion posse. In 1985 Youth Promotion released his DJ debut, 'Skin It A Go Peel', followed by 'Vibes Up A Sound'. Although the releases were hits on the sound system he was unable to emulate his accomplishment on record.

His debut, however, resulted in him being enrolled by I. Roy to voice a track at Channel One, although it only surfaced on *Adam & Eve*. His significant achievement in the history of Jamaican music came when he was joined by Jackie Knockshot for the release of the aptly titled 'Kick Up Rumpus'. The song was banned by both RJR and JBC, as certain lines within the tune were considered blasphemous; this prompted sufficient sales to take the song to the top of both charts. Colourman was unable to capitalize on his hit and subsequently languished in obscurity.
● ALBUMS: *Kick Up Rumpus* (Creation 1985)★★★.

CONGO ASHANTI ROY

b. Roy Johnson, 1943, Hanover, Jamaica, West Indies. Johnson began his career performing with Ras Michael And The Sons Of Negus, as well as the lesser-known Rightful Brothers. He was introduced to the former vocalist with the Tartans, Cedric Myton, through the DJ Big Youth and producer Trevor 'Leggo Beast' Douglas. The combination of Myton's falsetto vocals and Johnson's tenor led to the duo forging a perfect vocal partnership. In 1975 the duo began recording as the Congos; Lee Perry produced their debut, 'At The Feast'. The song led to sessions for the pivotal *Heart Of The Congos*, which featured Watty Burnett's distinctive baritone. Various singles were released, including 'Ark Of The Covenant' and 'Congo Man', which surfaced in the UK through Island Records. The hearsay regarding the non-release of the album through Island is inconsistent and has become the stuff of legend. The album has, however, continuously resurfaced in various formats and mixes since its initial Black Art release in 1977. Disenchanted with the lack of promotion, the group decided to produce their own follow-up, curiously released through CBS Records in France. The terms of the agreement also included an obligation for the group to perform in a film entitled *Jamdown*, but both projects faltered and by 1980 the individual members were pursuing solo careers. Myton continued to perform as the Congos, releasing *Face The Music* through the English Beat's Go Feet label, while Johnson began performing under the name of Congo Ashanti Roy. He initially released *Sign Of The Star* through Pre, the label responsible for Gregory Isaacs' classic *Lonely Lover*. The album featured love songs delivered in a style similar to Isaacs, although the collection failed to generate equivalent enthusiasm. The release was accompanied by a suitably lauded promotional concert alongside Prince Far I, who had produced Johnson's solo debut. Encouraged by the critical acclaim, Johnson began sessions for his follow-up, which was recorded in Jamaica and the UK with the Roots Radics and Undivided Roots, respectively. Notable tracks included 'Road Block', 'Give It To The Postman' and the emotional 'Sweet Love'. Although still involved in the music he has maintained a low profile within the industry through to the present day. In the mid-90s Myton re-formed the Congos with Burnett and Lindburgh Lewis.
● ALBUMS: *Sign Of The Star* (Pre 1981)★★★, with various *Dub X Perience* (On U Sound 1981)★★★, *Level Vibes* (Sonic Boom 1985)★★★, *Big City* (Jah Power 1994)★★, with

Jah Power Band *Light Up The City* (Jah Power 1995)★★, with various *Dub X Perience* reissue (Cleopatra 1996)★★★.

CONGOS

Jamaican vocal group comprising Cedric Myton (b. 1947, St. Catherine, Jamaica, West Indies; falsetto), Roy Johnson (b. 1943, Hanover, Jamaica, West Indies; tenor) plus Watty Burnett (baritone). Little is known about the formation of the Congos (sometimes spelt Congoes) and even less about their demise. However, for a brief period they recorded some of the most alluring and exciting roots reggae of all time. Myton and Johnson, both serious rasta artists from Jamaica, first emerged as the Congos on a single, 'At The Feast', for producer Lee Perry (1976). Before teaming with Johnson, Myton had been a member of the Tartans alongside Lloyd Robinson and had also sung with Ras Michael and recorded with Prince Lincoln And the Royal Rasses. Perry had been auditioning vocal groups at his Black Ark Studio in Kingston for a project he had in mind: a roots vocal album featuring a classic falsetto-tenor-baritone line-up. However, the Congos proved to be more than he had expected, although they did not feature a baritone. Early singles 'Ark Of The Covenant' and 'Congo Man' confirmed the prospect of something special, even by Perry's own high standards. Perry added Black Ark regular Watty Burnett to the group to handle deeper chores, and an album was completed. Unfortunately, Perry was in dispute with Island Records, the label handling his international releases at the time, and hence did not offer the Congos' *Heart Of The Congos* to the company, preferring instead to press it on his own Black Art label. This caused a row with the group, who felt they were being sold short, and the album only reached the specialist shops in small quantities.

The group split from Perry, arranging another limited pressing of the album themselves, and they eventually signed to CBS in France. In 1980 UK label Go-Feet released *Heart Of The Congos*. However, it made their current efforts seem lacklustre by comparison and subsequent records flopped, with Burnett quitting the group. Johnson was the next to go solo, although Myton continued to perform as the Congos. The group's story is one typical of reggae: they had plenty of talent, but the business dealings were unsatisfactory. Whether in different circumstances they could have equalled *Heart Of The Congos* remains a moot point. In the mid-90s Myton re-formed the Congos with Burnett and Lindburgh Lewis.

● ALBUMS: *Heart Of The Congos* (Black Art 1977)★★★★, *Image Of Africa* (Epic 1979)★★, *Congo Ashanti* (Columbia 1980)★★.

COOL NOTES

The Cool Notes initially embarked on their recording career in the lovers rock style, and featured Lauraine and Heather on lead vocals. The full line-up consisted of Joseph Charles, Peter Lee Gordon, Peter Rowlands and Ian Dunstan. In 1978 the group recorded for Pat Rhoden's Jama group; the success of the single 'My Tune' resulted in Rhoden's licensing the song to the major record companies in 1979, as the song was expected to cross over into the mainstream. Jama also released the ineffectual 'Just Girls' and 'Sweet Vibes', which signalled a change of direction. The band continued to record into the early 80s when they released 'I Forgot How To Love You', 'Morning Child' and *Down To Earth*, which demonstrated the group's adaptability. The album cover featured the band dressed as astronauts, and despite this lamentable marketing ploy, the debut was well received.

By 1984 the band felt the need for a further transformation, which led to the formation of the Abstract Dance label and the release of 'Never Too Young', aimed at the club scene, and which entered the lower regions of the pop chart. The release was met with enthusiasm in the clubs and the band followed the hit with the excusable 'I Forgot', striving for a profile on the radio playlists. The single failed to impress disc jockeys and followed its predecessor by scraping a Top 75 position. A discerning decision resulted in the group returning to the club sound for the release of 'Spend The Night', which peaked at number 11 in the UK pop chart in spite of the indifference shown towards the band by radio stations. They enjoyed a run of hits with 'In Your Car', 'Have A Good Forever', and culminating with 'Into The Motion'. Their songs continued to have a reggae vibe, contradicting their assertions that they wished to be regarded as a UK soul band.

● ALBUMS: *Down To Earth* (Mass Media Music 1982)★★★, *Have A Good Forever* (Abstract Dance 1985)★★, *Flashback* (Jama 1998)★★★.

COTTON, JOSEPH

b. Silbert Walton, 1957, St. Ann, Jamaica, West Indies. Prior to his success in the music industry Walton spent a year in the Jamaican Police Force before recording as Jah Walton for Joe Gibbs in 1976. By 1977 he recorded a number of tracks for producer Harry Mudie, including the popular combination hit with Prince Heron, 'Stay A Yard And Praise God', 'Touch Her Where She Want It Most' and the hilarious 'Married To A Bank Cashier'. With Sonia Pottinger he was enrolled to perform on the rehashed 'It's Raining' by the Techniques, made available in the disco mix format. In 1982 he released the dancehall stepper 'All Kinda People Come To The Dance' and the Nicodemus-influenced 'Senator Dee', which enhanced his credibility and led to a session at Channel One for the equally popular 'River To The Bank'. In the mid-80s he became known as Joseph Cotton, which led to a change of fortune when he recorded the chart-topping 'No Touch The Style' for Fashion Records in the UK, featuring the uncredited vocals of Janet Lee Davis. The release was coupled with a celebratory instrumental, 'Cotton Comes To Harlesdon', a pun relating to the 1970 blaxploitation movie starring Godfrey Cambridge. The success of the single resulted in a rare UK television appearance in 1987 on the Channel 4 *Club Mix* programme, where he performed his hit to an exuberant crowd. The single led to numerous hits including 'Things Running Slow', 'Pat Ha Fe Cook', 'Tutoring', 'Judge Cotton', and the combination with Janet Lee Davis (credited to her alter ego Shako Lee), 'What Is This'. In the late 80s Cotton teamed up with veteran producer Glen Brown, who had enjoyed a revival when he recorded the instrumental *Glen Brown Plays Music From The East*. In the early 90s he joined fellow expatriate Errol Dunkley, performing their interpretation of Ken Boothe's 'The Train Is Coming' as 'Bad Boy Train'. A surprise appearance at a concert headlined by Dunkley at the Podium in London's Vauxhall resulted in several false starts, a prac-

tice drawn from the dancehall phrase 'haul and pull', which denotes audience approval. In 1995 he released 'Smile Orange', taking its title from the classic Jamaican film, and in 1996 followed with the equally popular 'You Sexy Thing'. He also recorded in combination with Sylvia Tella the hit 'Warm And Tender Love'/'Rastaman'. In 1997 he appeared as Jah Walton at the Essential Festival Weekender alongside Dennis Alcapone, recreating the excitement of dancehall.

● ALBUMS: as Jah Walton *Touch Her Where She Want It Most* (Ital 1981)★★★, *Cotton Style* (South East Music 1990)★★★, *No Touch The Style* (Blue Mountain 1991)★★★★, *Talk Of The Town* (Imp 1994)★★★.

COUNT OSSIE

b. Oswald Williams, *c*.1928, Jamaica, d. 18 October 1976. As a boy, Williams became involved in the Rastafarian community where he learnt hand-drumming and the vocal chanting technique that reverberates back to pre-slavery days in Africa. By the late 50s, he had become a master-drummer and had formed a group of other percussionists around him, the Count Ossie Group. By the turn of the 60s Count Ossie was more of a cultural icon than pop star, and it was only the ingenuity of Prince Buster that made him a part of reggae. Buster, ever eager to gain advantage over his rivals, was looking for a sound that no one else in Jamaica had managed to put on a ska record. Buster was aware of Count Ossie, but had been informed that Ossie would never agree to work on a commercial record, particularly since Buster was a Muslim and Ossie a Rastafarian. However, Buster managed to secure the services of both Ossie and several drummers. The first and most famous record they made was 'Oh Carolina' and 'I Met A Man', featuring Ossie and ensemble, thundering away on funde and kette drums, with the vocals of the Folks Brothers at the fore. The record was a unique combination of ska, R&B and 'grounation', fundamentalist music that was highly popular both in Jamaica and on the London mod scene. Subsequent sessions for Coxsone Dodd followed, accompanying the Mellocats' 'Another Moses', Bunny And Skitter's 'Lumumbo' and Lascelles Perkins' 'Destiny'. They also made some records under their own name including 'Cassavubu' (for Prince Buster) and 'Babylon Gone' (for Harry Mudie). The group then refrained from recording until 1970, when they issued 'Whispering Drums' (for Mudie), 'Back To Africa Version One' (for Lloyd Daley), and 'Holy Mount Zion' and 'Meditation' (for Dodd). Around this time, Count Ossie's drummers were augmented by a bass player and a horn section led by Cedric Brooks, and the group took the name the Mystic Revelation Of Rastafari.

In 1973 they recorded a triple album set, *Grounation*, which remains a landmark recording in Jamaican music. The set included treatments of Charles Lloyd's 'Passin' Thru', the Jazz Crusaders' 'Way Back Home', Ethiopian melodies, improvisations, hymns and poetry. In 1975 the group recorded a follow-up album, the similarly excellent *Tales Of Mozambique*. Shortly after this, in 1976, Ossie died and left behind a unique legacy, to be carried on by Ras Michael And The Sons Of Negus and several other outfits. During the 80s, the Mystic Revelation Of Rastafari re-formed with several original members. Only two songs by the group have so far been released, 'Little Drummer Boy' and 'Hero Is He', the latter made for *A Tribute To Marcus Garvey*.

● ALBUMS: *Grounation* 3-LP set (Ashanti 1973)★★★★, *Tales Of Mozambique* (Dynamic 1975)★★★★.

COUSINS, ROY

b. *c*.1945, Cockburn Pen, Kingston, Jamaica, West Indies. In the early 60s Cousins formed a vocal quartet, the Royals, with a line-up that has featured a number of notable vocalists and began recording in 1966. He was also an early influence on the rudimentary talents of Nicky Thomas, Tinga Stewart, and the Tartans, with whom a dispute over the rights to a song arose. While recording with the Royals, he maintained a career with the Jamaican Post Office, a job he had held since leaving school in Molynes Road. A number of singles surfaced, including 'Pick Up The Pieces', produced by Coxsone Dodd, as well as 'Only For A Time', 'Never See Come See' and 'Never Gonna Give You Up', resulting in Cousins becoming a cult figure. Following bad experiences of acrimonious dealings with producers and UK-based record labels, he set up his own Tamoki label in 1972. His initial self-

financed productions met with little success, and the label quickly folded. However, his recorded work provided strong evidence of his love of the music, and it was clear that profits were less of a priority than quality. His position with the Post Office enabled him to support his wife and four children in Spanish Town, and he was able to save enough to finance studio time. One of his sessions as producer resulted in the track that is considered to have established Gregory Isaacs, 'Way Of Life'. In 1974 he returned with the Wambesi label, which survived and continued to release tracks. In June 1977 Cousins decided to concentrate on his first love and abandoned his job with the Post Office. In 1978 a compilation of the Royals' work, *Pick Up The Pieces*, surfaced. The album featured the vocal talents of the Jays on such hits as 'Ghetto Man', 'Sufferer Of The Ghetto', 'Peace And Love' and the title track. The success of this compilation led to a contract with Ballistic, which was licensed to United Artists Records, resulting in an international audience for Cousins' music. With new recruits Carl Green and Errol Davis providing backing vocals as the Royals, *Ten Years After* and *Freedom Fighters Dub* appeared. The success and critical acclaim that had previously eluded Cousins finally arrived with these releases. In the winter of 1978 he secured an agreement for the release of *Israel Be Wise*, which featured the vocal talents of Heptones lead singer Barry Lewellyn on the title track. Cousins was also instrumental in the re-formation of the Gaylads, producing four of the tracks on the showcase album, *Understanding*. In 1979 Cousins almost lost his sight when it was discovered that he had cataracts in both eyes. After months of specialist care, he steered his musical talents in another direction, and by the early 80s Cousins was concentrating on his production skills, nurturing the talents of Charlie Chaplin, Earl Sixteen, the Meditations, Prince Far I and Cornell Campbell. While maintaining a successful run of hits, he also found time to run a business supplying juke-boxes around the island.

● ALBUMS: *International Heroes Dub* (Pre 1990)★★★★, *Roy Cousins Presents Kings And Queens Of Dub* (Wambesi 1994)★★★.

● COMPILATIONS: *Visions Of Reggae* (Wambesi 1985)★★★, *Wambesi Showcase* (Heartbeat

1986)★★★★, *History Of Tamoki Wambesi* (Wambesi 1994)★★★, *Reggae Greatest Hits Volume Two* (Heartbeat 1993)★★★.

COWAN, TOMMY

b. *c*.1950, Kingston, Jamaica, West Indies. Tommy Cowan has been involved in the reggae industry for 30 years as a performer, producer, promoter and master of ceremonies. In 1966 he formed a group called the Merricoles and successfully entered an amateur talent contest. In 1967 the group changed their name to the Jamaicans and are remembered as winners of the celebrated Jamaican Song Festival, with 'Baba Boom'. The recording, produced by Duke Reid, topped the Jamaican charts and led to a series of hits, including 'Sing Freedom', 'Woman Go Home' and the re-release of their debut, a plaintive song relating to the inevitability of life, 'Things You Say You Love, You're Gonna Lose'. Following the group's demise, Cowan joined the Dynamic studio, where he was employed as the resident engineer. Having accumulated sufficient knowledge in studio work he went into record production, working with Jacob Miller and Inner Circle, Junior Tucker, Earl Zero, Ray I and Dean Stone, as well as recording the occasional single, notably a version of the Wailers' 'Lick Samba'.

Cowan formed the Top Ranking label and successfully managed Inner Circle, balancing their commercial career alongside hits solely for the roots market. While *Killer* and *Wanted* appeased the group's reggae fanbase, *Reggae Thing* and *Ready For The World* enjoyed international success. By the late 70s, Cowan had established a reputation for wooing the crowds as an MC, introducing a number of performers at the Reggae Sunsplash Festivals and the legendary One Love Peace Concert.

In 1980 he was invited to accompany Bob Marley on his tour of Zimbabwe when the reggae legend played at the independence ceremony. When he returned to Jamaica, Cowan concentrated on expanding his Talent Corporation. One of the artists affiliated to this company was his second wife Carlene Davis, who initially recorded reggae ballads. In 1988 she topped the Jamaican charts with 'Dial My Number', which led to greater exposure for Cowan's corporation. By the mid-90s his roster of performers included John Holt, Dobby Dobson, Ruddy Thomas, Toots Hibbert, Ernie Smith, General Degree, Scotty and Jack Radics.

COXSONE, LLOYD

b. Lloyd Blackwood. An influential figure in the growth of the UK reggae scene, Lloyd Coxsone left his home in Morant Bay, Jamaica, and arrived in the UK in 1962, settling in south-west London and setting up his first sound system, Lloyd The Matador. This venture floundered due to inexperience and Coxsone joined the UK-based Duke Reid sound, but he eventually left in 1969, taking some of that operation's personnel with him. He went on to form his own sound system, adopting the name of the biggest sound in Jamaica at the time, and also, pointedly, the main rival to Jamaica's Duke Reid, Sir Coxsone. Coxsone sound soon gained a strong following that eventually led to his residency at the famous London nightclub the Roaring Twenties, in Carnaby Street. Throughout the 70s Sir Coxsone Sound's success lay with maintaining the sound to rigorous standards, playing the most exclusive dub plates direct from Jamaica, and keeping abreast of trends within the music. Rather than specializing in one particular style, Coxsone Sound offered music for all tastes.

Coxsone, like other sound men, also expanded into the record business, licensing music from Jamaica at first, then trying his hand at his own productions using local UK artists. In 1975 he enjoyed huge success, and kickstarted the UK lovers rock phenomenon in the process, with his production of 'Caught You In A Lie' - originally a US soul hit by Robert Parker - featuring the vocal talents of 14-year-old south London schoolgirl Louisa Mark. That same year he issued one of the best dub albums of the era, *King Of The Dub Rock*, which featured dubwise versions of his own productions and those of Gussie Clarke, mixed in part at King Tubby's. Other notable records appeared on his Tribesman and Lloyd Coxsone Outernational labels and elsewhere during the late 70s and early 80s, including Faybiene Miranda's Jack Ruby-produced 'Prophecy', 'Love And Only Love' and 'Voice Of The Poor' by Fred Locks. Others included 'Stormy Night' and 'Homeward Bound' by the Creation Steppers, a version of the Commodores' 'Easy' by Jimmy Lindsay (many of which are available on *12 The Hard Way*) and many more. During the mid-80s Coxsone handed control of his sound over to the younger elements in his team, notably Blacker Dread, and a new breed of DJs. Blacker released his own productions by the likes of Fred Locks, Frankie Paul, Mikey General, Sugar Minott, Michael Palmer, Don Carlos, Earl Sixteen and Coxsone DJ, Jah Screechy.

Recently, as interest in the roots music of the 70s has increased, Coxsone has emerged from his semi-retirement to stand once again at the controls of his sound.

● ALBUMS: *King Of The Dub Rock* (Safari 1975)★★★★, *King Of The Dub Rock Part 2* (Tribesman 1982)★★★, *12 The Hard Way* (Tribesman 1989)★★★.

CROSS, SANDRA

b. *c.*1963, London, England. Cross's voice was cultivated, like so many great performers before her, through singing in church. In Jamaica many artists' careers started on the sound systems or through talent shows. Cross began her career by performing in a talent show as one half of the duo Love And Unity. In 1980 their first recording, 'I Adore You', topped the reggae chart and was produced by Winston Edwards of Studio 16. The hit was followed by a version of the Wailers' 'Put It On' and with the Itals' 'Glue On Paper'. In 1982, disillusioned with the industry, she pursued a career in commerce. Two years later she was encouraged back into the industry by her brother Garnett, who recorded as Sergeant Pepper and later as Slim Linton at Ariwa Sounds. Her earlier recordings were in the lovers rock style. Cross also joined forces with Sandra Sampson and Sandra Williams to perform as the Wild Bunch. As a soloist Cross won many accolades, and came to be regarded as the queen of lovers rock, performing on hits such as 'Fit And Ready', 'Blinded By Love', 'My Best Friend's Man' and 'Why Oh Why'. Most of her songs were self-compositions, although her 1985 interpretation of the Stylistics' 'Country Living', influenced by the Mighty Diamonds' rendition of the song, reinstated her at the top of the reggae chart. When U-Roy, who had toured with the Mighty Diamonds, heard her version of the song he covered it on his Ariwa-produced *True Born African*

set. By 1997, Cross was enjoying semi-retirement in the Caribbean.

● ALBUMS: with the Wild Bunch *The Wild Bunch* (Ariwa 1984)★★★, *Country Life* (Ariwa 1986)★★★, with the Wild Bunch *Stepping In Dub Wise Country* (Ariwa 1987)★★★, *Comet In The Sky* (Ariwa 1988)★★★, *Crossing Over* (Ariwa 1989)★★★, *This Is* (Ariwa 1990)★★★, *Foundation Of Love* (Ariwa 1992)★★★.

CULTURE

Culture became the runaway success of 1977 with their single 'Two Sevens Clash' for Joe Gibbs, and with an album of the same name, they came to dominate reggae with their stark prophecy and apocalyptic warnings. They even found a sympathetic ear in the emergent punk audience of the period. The group was led by songwriter Joseph Hill, who had started his career at Studio One as a member of the Soul Defenders, releasing one solo single, 'Behold The Land'. With Albert 'Ralph' Walker and Kenneth Paley (aka Kenneth Dayes) providing the harmonies, the trio came from the same school of style and lyrical content as Burning Spear. Largely through the groundwork of artists such as Bob Marley And The Wailers, the aforementioned Burning Spear and the Abyssinians, cultural or socio-political themes abounded in Jamaican music, and many new listeners were attracted to a genre they had previously dismissed. Culture were ready-made champions for this new-found reggae audience, and their popularity was further enhanced by electrifying live appearances, with Hill, in particular, proving himself to be an effusive showman. The strong level of interest attracted Virgin Records' Front Line label, who stepped in with the type of contract rarely offered to reggae acts. Culture had by that point finished working with Joe Gibbs, and their all-important follow-up album was produced by Sonia Pottinger. *Harder Than The Rest* confounded the critics, and the hugely popular single 'Stop The Fighting' was further proof of their standing. A strange release from America at the same time, titled *Africa Stand Alone*, featured a number of tracks from the Virgin album, although the versions were substantially different. If anything this second album stimulated interest in the 'official' release and each boosted the sales of the other for months, while at the same time consolidating Culture's reputation for militant lyrics set against raw roots rhythms. Culture have always remained rooted in the same lyrical preoccupations and, even if the rhythms have changed over the years, their beliefs have not. Joseph Hill split with his two backing singers in 1982, but continues to use the name Culture, and his records always sell well despite being far removed from any current reggae trends.

● ALBUMS: *Two Sevens Clash* (Joe Gibbs/Lightning 1977)★★★★, *Baldhead Bridge* (Joe Gibbs 1978)★★★, *Africa Stand Alone* (April Records 1978)★★★★, *Harder Than The Rest* (Front Line 1978)★★★, *Cumbolo* (Front Line 1979)★★★, *International Herb* (Front Line 1979)★★★★, *Lion Rock* (Sonic Sounds/Heartbeat 1981)★★★★, *Culture In Culture* (Blue Track 1986)★★★, *Culture At Work* (Shanachie 1986)★★, *Nuff Crisis!* (Blue Mountain 1988)★★, *Good Things* (RAS 1989)★★, *Wings Of A Dove* (Shanachie 1993)★★, *Trod On* (Heartbeat 1993)★★★, *One Stone* (RAS 1996)★★★, *Trust Me* (RAS 1997)★★★.

● COMPILATIONS: *Vital Selection* (Virgin 1981)★★★★, *Too Long In Slavery* (Front Line 1989)★★★★, *Strictly Culture - Best Of 1977-79* (Music Club 1994)★★★★.

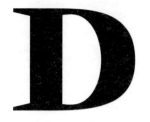

DADDY FREDDIE

b. Jamaica, West Indies. Though the holder of the *Guinness Book Of Records* World's Fastest Rapper title, Daddy Freddie emerged as more than a simple novelty act. Having enjoyed several hits in Jamaica, he emigrated to London in the mid-80s. Teaming up with Asher D he recorded 'Raggamuffin Hip Hop' for Music Of Life, which brought him to the wider public's attention for the first time, particularly in New York. While his patter blurred the distinction between ragga DJ and American-styled rap artist, Daddy Freddie's irreverent, quickfire mode enhanced the possibilities of both genres.

● ALBUMS: *Cater Fi She* (Exterminator 1989)★★★, *Stress* (Music Of Life 1991)★★.

DADDY RINGS

b. Everald Dwyer, 1972, Christiana, Manchester, Jamaica, West Indies. Dwyer became known as Daddy Rings as a reference to his love of flashy fingerwear. His initial experience as a DJ came from chanting on the Black Cat, Oneness and his uncle's Culture-Shanti sound systems. After relocating to Kingston and graduating, he began an apprenticeship as a welder. In his leisure time he practised his sing-jay skills, a term used to describe artists who chat their rhymes with melody. Once he had mastered his style he achieved a successful audition with King Jammy. Recording at Jammy's St. Lucia Road studio, Dwyer voiced his debut, the dancehall hit 'Politician', plus a number of tunes with Uncle T and John John. A brief spell with the Firehouse crew led to an encounter with Delroy Harrison. Harrison was impressed with Dwyer's style and persuaded him to record at Gussie Clarke's Anchor studio. In 1996 Clarke produced Freddie McGregor's 'Rumours' and asked Daddy Rings to perform alongside the youthful veteran. The single topped UK reggae charts, exposing the DJ to international acclaim. Daddy Rings'

European success led to the release of his mixed debut album, *Stand Out*. The compilation demonstrated his singing style alongside the preferred DJ arrangements. In late 1996 he embarked on a tour of Europe, which incorporated an appearance at the MIDEM gala in Paris on the 'New Artists' stage alongside Anthony B. Daddy Rings followed his successful European debut supporting the Mighty Diamonds to rave reviews. His debut album was remixed with a slight variation in the track-listing for its UK release.
● ALBUMS: *Stand Out* (Greensleeves 1996)★★★.

DALEY, LLOYD

b. 1942, Kingston, Jamaica, West Indies. A reggae producer whose work is distinguished by the motto of quality over quantity, Daley's interest in music grew out of his work as an electrician, running his own shop, Lloyd's Radio & Television Service, in Waltham Park, Kingston. During the late 50s he started a sound system, Lloyd The Matador, and from there it was an almost inevitable step to production work. His early productions for his Matador (later Mystic) label were ska-based, but it was not until 1968 that he began to make an impact, his first big success being the Scorchers' 'Uglyman'. Hits with Little Roy ('Bongo Nyah', 'Scrooge'), the Heptones ('Righteous Man'), the Viceroys, and the Ethiopians were notable for their spare, unfussy quality, and his works with Little Roy were among the first explicitly Rasta-themed reggae releases. He also recorded one of Dennis Brown's best early singles ('Baby Don't Do It'), a couple of Alton Ellis's most powerful 45s ('Back To Africa', 'Deliver Us'), one Abyssinians classic ('Yim Mas Gan'), and was a pioneer in the DJ field, issuing records from U-Roy and Big Joe. Perhaps because he was not dependent on music for an income, he faded from the scene in the early 70s, returning only to reissue his classic singles on two essential albums in 1992.
● ALBUMS: *Scandal* (Matador 1992)★★★, *Way Back When* (Matador 1992)★★★.
● COMPILATIONS: *Lloyd Daley's Matador Productions 1968-72* (Heartbeat 1992)★★★★.

DAN, MICHAEL

b. Michael Dorane, 1948, Newmarket, St. Elizabeth, Jamaica, West Indies. Dorane was raised in California until his eighth birthday when his family moved to London. He mastered a number of instruments and at 15 he formed Soul Funk, performing in an R&B style. Carving a niche in Europe, the band embarked on a tour of the Continent and enjoyed two Top 10 hits in Germany. By the early 70s the band returned to the UK where Dorane decided to embark on a career within the reggae industry, initially as a session musician for Pama Records. He ploughed his earnings into establishing a collection of his own recordings and produced the debut singles of newcomers Fitzroy Henry and Carol Williams. He secured a distribution agreement with Island Records, who allocated his work exclusively on the newly formed Rockers label. The release of Fitzroy Henry's 'Can't Take My Eyes Off You' and Carol Williams' 'You've Gotta Save All Your Love' signalled the new label's arrival, although neither made a significant impression on the chart. As a vocalist, Dorane recorded a version of the Supremes' 'Stop In The Name Of Love', which, although heavily promoted by Island, subsequently remained in obscurity. Having failed to achieve his ambition to establish reggae's equivalent of Motown Records in the UK, Dorane returned to session work, where, as Michael Dan, he established a reputation as an exemplary sound engineer, having notable success with Virgin Records' Front Line enterprise. Enrolled to mix the Twinkle Brothers' classic *Praise Jah*, he built a solid reputation following the success of the discomix version of 'Jahoviah', which was lifted from the album. His unique mixing style was a feature of Front Line releases, including the bizarre *Live At The Lyceum* EP featuring U-Roy. Since his halcyon days with Front Line he has maintained a low profile within the industry, although examples of his work resurfaced through various reissue programmes.
● ALBUMS: *Reggae Time* (Rockers 1976)★★.

DANCEHALL

Dancehall, a particularly spare, uncluttered form of reggae, first emerged at the start of the 80s and was so-called because it began in the dances that have always been the lifeblood of

Jamaican music. Essentially, a sound system would play a song, usually specially recorded on a dub plate, and a singer or DJ would extemporize over the top of it live. Drawing its lead from the empty, slow rhythms of Roots Radics, and, to a lesser extent, Sly And Robbie, dancehall was the least fanciful genre of reggae to date, offering the rhythm, a voice, the dancers' energy and little else. By 1982, various acts had emerged who recorded predominantly dancehall music, among them Yellowman, an albino MC with a witty, if rude, way with a lyric, Barrington Levy, a ferocious singer who never gave less than 100 per cent, and General Echo, another rudely talented chatter. Sound systems such as Jammy's, Volcano and Black Scorpio kept the public thirsting for more material, which they then began to supply on their own labels, with the sound bosses King Jammy, Henry 'Junjo' Lawes and Scorpio creating new stars such as Junior Reid, Michael Palmer and Josey Wales. A similar process occurred in the UK, with the sounds of Saxon Studio, Wassifa Hi-Fi and Unity all offering something different to their Jamaican counterparts. Dancehall never 'finished' as such. Instead, Jammy's released a record in 1985 featuring singer Wayne Smith, 'Under Me Sleng Teng', which single-handedly created the 'digital' style of dancehall, and subsequently, raggamuffin.

● COMPILATIONS: various *Best Of Reggae Dance Hall Volume 1* (Rohit 1984)★★★★, *Best Of Reggae Dance Hall Volume 2* (Rohit 1985)★★★, *Dance Hall Session* (RAS 1986)★★★.

DANCEHALL QUEEN

Dancehall Queen is a modern-day Cinderella tale set in Kingston, Jamaica, and features the celebrated veteran reggae film star Carl Bradshaw. Audrey Reid made her film debut, starring alongside Paul Campbell, Carl Davis and Pauline Stone-Myrie. The film also includes cameos from Beenie Man, Chevelle Franklin, Anthony B. and Lady Saw. The story revolves around Marcia, a humble street vendor who leads a double life. By day she sells her wares on the streets of the Jamaican capital, while at night she becomes 'The Mystery Lady', the new star of the dancehall. Marcia hopes that her success will give her the means to escape from the

clutches of the wicked 'Uncle Larry', who supports the family, but in return, expects sexual favours from Marcia's daughter Tanya. Marcia's problems increase when Priest, a homicidal charlatan, tries to set up shop on her territory. As the problems mount, Marcia enters a dancehall contest in the hope of winning enough money to escape from the ghetto with her family. The soundtrack features Sharon and Cedella Marley performing in an R&B style, alongside tracks from Black Uhuru, Third World, Bounty Killer, Junior Demus, Beenie Man, Buccaneer, Chaka Demus, Sugar Minott, and Chevelle Franklin. The film was directed by Carl Bradshaw, with Don Letts (noted for the Bob Marley And The Wailers *Legend* video) also involved in writing and directing. The film premiered in Jamaica on 5 August 1997, followed by the release of the theme tune, which Franklin and Beenie Man performed to an ecstatic audience at the Notting Hill Carnival prior to the film's UK premiere in Brixton.

● ALBUMS: *Dancehall Queen Soundtrack* (Island Jamaica 1997)★★★.

● VIDEOS: *Dancehall Queen* (Manga 1997).

DAVE AND ANSELL COLLINS

A Jamaican duo who topped the UK charts in 1971 with 'Double Barrel', which was written and produced by Winston Riley. The duo comprised Dave Barker, a session vocalist and sometime pioneering DJ, and keyboard player Ansell Collins. Both had worked for Lee Perry in the late 60s before joining forces. 'Double Barrel' was one of the first reggae hits in the USA. The follow-up, 'Monkey Spanner', was also a UK Top 10 hit. However, they split shortly after the release of their sole album. Ansell, who had previously worked solo in the late 60s, continued to record for small reggae labels throughout the 80s, principally as a session musician. Barker became a UK resident and fronted several short-lived soul bands. The duo briefly reunited as Dave And Ansell Collins in 1981 but to little effect.

● ALBUMS: *Double Barrel* (Techniques/Trojan 1972)★★★, *In The Ghetto* (Trojan 1975)★★★.

● COMPILATIONS: *Classic Tracks* (Classic Tracks 1988)★★★.

DAVIS, CARLENE

Popular modern reggae singer whose career was carefully orchestrated by renowned producer/promoter Tommy Cowan. Her musical output was characterized by slick, professional standards, addressing a wide variety of styles both in and outside of the reggae idiom.
● ALBUMS: *No Bias* (Silveredge 1991)★★★.

DAVIS, RONNIE

b. *c.*1950, Savannah La Mar, Jamaica, West Indies. Davis began his musical career by winning local talent contests in the early 60s. In 1967 the bright lights of Kingston beckoned, and Davis was enrolled to perform as part of the Tennors by the group's director, Clive Murphy. With the group Davis recorded his debut, 'The Whole World Is A Stage', which led to a slew of singles through to the early 70s. During his time with the group, Davis aspired towards a solo career, which eventually came to fruition with the classic 'Won't You Come Home' and 'Stop Yu Loafing'. He subsequently enjoyed a number of hits through to the mid-70s, including 'Jah Jah Jehovah', 'Forget Me Now', 'On And On', 'Babylon Falling', 'Fancy Make Up', 'Won't You Come Home', and 'Pretend', alongside the discomix featuring Nu Roy, 'It's Raining'. In 1976 he abandoned his solo career when he joined Keith Porter and Roy Smith in the Itals. The band became Jamaica's premier vocal group following the success of 'Brutal'. Davis remained with the Itals until 1994 when he inaugurated his own vocal group, Ronnie Davis And Idren, and enrolled his one-time schoolfriend and singing partner, Roy Smith, along with Lloyd Ricketts and Robert Doctor. The group initially recorded at Black Scorpio with a host of top Jamaican musicians, including Earl 'Chinna' Smith, Errol Holt, and the late Bingi Bunny. The resulting album was critically acclaimed and confirmed Davis as one of reggae music's finest ambassadors.
● ALBUMS: *Gregory Isaacs Meets Ronnie Davis* (Plant 1970)★★★, *Beautiful People* (Pre 1977)★★★, *How Can I Leave* (Paradise 1979)★★★, *Wheel Of Life* (Upstairs Music 1997)★★★, *Come Straight* (Nighthawk 1997)★★★.
● COMPILATIONS: *The Hits From Studio One* (Bunny Lee 1998)★★★.

DEAN, NORA

b. *c.*1952, Jamaica, West Indies. From the ska days to the present, there have been numerous female reggae performers who have recorded erotic songs, including the Soul Sisters, Patra, Lady G and Lady Saw. Dean began her recording career in 1970 with producer Byron Smith at Treasure Isle's rooftop studios in Bond Street. Her initial hit was a ribald version of the Techniques' rocksteady hit 'You Don't Care', retitled 'Barbwire'. The song was an instant hit, proving especially popular in the dancehall. The follow-up, with the suggestive title 'Night Food Reggae', proved equally popular. The song was also a success for Des' All Stars, although altered to reflect the male perspective. With producer Bunny Lee she recorded a version of Doris Day's 'Que Sera Sera (Whatever Will Be)' as 'Kay Sarah', succeeded by 'How Could You Do This'. In the 50s the Cordells, the Fontaine Sisters and originally the Teen Queens all had hits in the US Top 20 with 'Eddie My Love', which inspired a cover version by Dean in 1974. The song was later recorded by Hortense Ellis with Bunny Lee for inclusion on *Jamaica's First Lady Of Songs*. Also released that year was the easily forgettable 'Judge Dread Is My Lover', which surfaced on the Magnet label in the UK. In the mid-70s she enjoyed success with 'Scorpion' and 'What's Your Plan', which was followed by a lean period. Her output over the years has been sparse, although in 1980 she resurfaced performing in a lovers rock style.
● ALBUMS: *Play Me A Love Song* (Ital 1981)★★★.

DEKKER, DESMOND

b. Desmond Dacres, 16 July 1942, Kingston, Jamaica, West Indies. Dacres spent much of his orphaned childhood near Seaforth in St. Thomas before returning to Kingston, where he worked as a welder. His workmates encouraged him to seek a recording audition and, after receiving rejections from leading producers Clement Dodd and Duke Reid, he found a mentor in the influential Leslie Kong. In 1963, the newly named Dekker released his first single, 'Honour Your Father And Mother', which was also issued in the UK courtesy of Chris Blackwell's Island label. During the same period, Dekker teamed up with his backing group, the Aces. Together, they enjoyed enormous success in Jamaica during the mid- to late 60s with a formidable run of 20 number 1 hits to their credit. The emergence of rocksteady in the latter half of 1966 propelled his *James Bond*-inspired '007 (Shanty Town)' into the UK charts the following year. A catchy, rhythmically infectious articulation of the 'rude boy' street gang shenanigans, the single presaged Dekker's emergence as an internationally famous artist. In 1967, Dekker came second in the Jamaican Song Festival with 'Unity' and continued his chart-topping run in his home country with such titles as 'Hey Grandma', 'Music Like Dirt', 'Rudie Got Soul', 'Rude Boy Train' and 'Sabotage'. In 1969 Dekker achieved his greatest international success. 'Get up in the morning, slaving for bread, sir, so that every mouth can be fed', was a patois-sung opening line that entranced and confused pop listeners on both sides of the Atlantic. The intriguing 'Israelites' had been a club hit the previous year, and by the spring of 1969 had become the first reggae song to top the UK charts, a considerable achievement for the period. Even more astonishing was its Top 10 success in the USA, a country that had previously proved commercially out of bounds to Jamaican performers.

Back in Britain, Dekker's follow-up was the Top 10 hit 'It Mek'. It was originally recorded the previous year under the title 'A It Mek', which roughly translates as 'That's Why It Happened'. 'It Mek' was inspired by Desmond's sister Elaine, who fell off a wall at her home and cried 'like ice water'. Dekker enjoyed translating everyday observations into sharp, incisive lines. 'Israelites' similarly articulated the plight of the downtrodden working man, while 'Problems' was a rousing protest number featuring the refrain '*everyday* is problems'. Dekker's success in the UK, buoyed by consistent touring, spearheaded the arrival of a number of Jamaican chart singles by such artists as the Harry J's All Stars, the Upsetters and the Pioneers. Until the arrival of Bob Marley, Dekker remained the most famous reggae artist on the international scene.

Dekker took up residence in the UK in 1969, where he was a regular club performer and continued to lay down his vocals over rhythm tracks recorded in Jamaica. A further minor success with 'Pickney Gal' was followed by a massive number 2 hit with the Jimmy Cliff composition 'You Can Get It If You Really Want', from the film *The Harder They Come*. When Dekker's long-term manager/producer Kong died from heart failure in 1971, the artist joined the Cactus label. A reissue of 'Israelites' restored him to the UK Top 10 in 1975 and was followed by the pop/reggae 'Sing A Little Song', which reached number 16. During the 2-Tone ska/mod revival in 1980, Dekker recorded *Black And Dekker* with Graham Parker's Rumour, but the experiment was not commercially successful. A follow-up, also on Stiff Records, *Compass Point*, was his last major attempt at chart action, though he remained a perennial performer of old hit material and has frequently been featured on compilation albums. In 1984 he was found bankrupt by a British court, and publicly complained that he had failed to receive funds from his former manager. It was a sad moment for one of reggae's best-known personalities. In 1993, during another 2-Tone revival, Dekker released *King Of Kings* with four original members of the Specials. His unmistakable falsetto vocal remains one of reggae's most memorable, while his pioneering importance as the first major reggae artist to achieve international success deserves wider acknowledgement.

● ALBUMS: *007 (Shanty Town)* (Beverley's 1967)★★★★, *Action!* (Beverley's 1968)★★★, *The Israelites* (Beverley's 1969)★★★★, *This Is Desmond Dekker* (Trojan 1969)★★★★, *You Can Get It If You Really Want* (Trojan 1970)★★★★, *Black And Dekker* (Stiff 1980)★★★, *Compass Point* (Stiff 1981)★★★, *Officially Live And Rare* (Trojan 1987)★★, *Music Like Dirt* (Trojan 1992)★★, with the Specials *King Of Kings* (Trojan 1993)★★★.

● COMPILATIONS: *Double Dekker* (Trojan 1974)★★★★, *Sweet 16 Hits* (Trojan 1978)★★★★, *The Original Reggae Hitsound* (Trojan 1985)★★★★, *20 Golden Pieces* (Bulldog 1987)★★★★, *Best Of And The Rest Of* (Action Replay/Trojan 1989)★★★, *King Of Ska* (Trojan 1991)★★★★, *20 Greatest Hits* (Point 2 1992)★★★★, *Crucial Cuts - The Best Of Desmond Dekker* (1993)★★★★, *First Time For Long Time* (Trojan 1997)★★★.

DELGADO, JUNIOR

b. Oscar Hibbert, c.1958, Kingston, Jamaica, West Indies. Junior 'Jux' Delgado started singing as a schoolboy, winning prizes at school concerts and local talent contests. His first recordings, 'Reaction' and 'The Twenty Third Psalm', were produced by Lee Perry in 1973 with the band Time Unlimited, alongside Orville Smith and Glasford Manning, later of the Jewels. In 1974 Delgado recorded two solo sides for Rupie Edwards - 'Rasta Dreadlocks', on the producer's popular 'Skanga' rhythm, issued under the name the Heaven Singers, and, under his own name, 'Run Baldhead'. Sessions with Total Sounds and Tommy Cowan and Warwick Lyn's Talent Corp, however, failed to emerge and Delgado left Time Unlimited for a solo career. During 1975 he recorded sides for producers Larry Lawrence and Winston 'Niney' Holness - a version of Ken Boothe/Garnett Mimm's 'Thinking' betraying the debt Delgado owed to that great singer, and 'Every Natty', before linking up with his friend Dennis Brown who released 'Tition', produced by Soul Syndicate/Aggrovators guitarist Earl 'Chinna' Smith, on his DEB label. 'Tition' (1975), short for politician, was a big reggae hit both in Jamaica and the UK, and the raw bass, drum and piano rhythm, topped with Delgado's heartfelt, gritty moan and the hard-hitting social commentary of the lyrics, set the tone for much of his subsequent output, and marked the beginning of a long musical collaboration between the two singers that lasted throughout the decade.

From 1976-79, Delgado recorded numerous sides for DEB including 'Devils Throne', a version of the Heptones' 'Love Won't Come Easy', the ever popular 'Trickster', 'She Gonna Marry Me', 'Warrior' and 'Famine', as well as completing an excellent album, Taste Of The Young Heart. Other tunes for different producers during this period included the storming 'Sons Of Slaves' for Lee Perry, 'Armed Robbery' and 'United Dreadlocks' for Joe Gibbs, 'Away With Your Fussing And Fighting' and 'Blackmans Heart Cries Out' for Augustus Pablo, and two self-productions, 'Fisherman Row' and 'Jah Stay', utilizing the 'Tition' rhythm, the latter appearing on his own Incredible Jux label in Jamaica. All this activity served to forge a reputation as one of the most exciting roots singers on the 70s reggae scene. In the early 80s he spent much of his time commuting between Jamaica and the UK, maintaining his reputation with further searing cuts including 'Fort Augustus' for Sly And Robbie. However, in 1983, disaster struck in the form of an 18-month prison sentence. On his release, his astonishing 'Broadwater Farm' 12-inch (1985), for London production outfit Maccabees, prophesied the riots in that troubled area of north London, and was banned as soon as they took place. Nevertheless, it proved that his enforced hiatus had done nothing to diminish his productivity, and he soon immersed himself in a flurry of recordings for Skengdon ('Nine Fence' 1985), Mikey Carrol's Creative Sounds ('Poverty' 1986), King Jammy ('Illegal Gun' 1987), and his own 'Bus I Skull' (1988), released on London's Fashion Records and recorded at their A Class Studio.

His biggest hit during this period, however, was the epochal 'Raggamuffin Year' (1986) which saw him paired back with Augustus Pablo. More singles followed: 'Forward Revolution', the superb comment on events in South Africa; 'Hanging Tree', 'Riot Inna Juvenile Prison' and 'Dub School', all for Pablo; and 'We A Blood' for Fashion. He appeared with Pablo in concert at London's Astoria Theatre in 1986 and thrilled the crowd with a superb show-stopping performance, and somehow still found the time to nurture the talents of two upcoming youngsters, Yammie Bolo and White Mice. Though he has been a little quiet in the early 90s, it is surely only a matter of time before reggae fans are once more treated to the generous talents of the Incredible Jux.

● ALBUMS: Taste Of the Young Heart (DEB-EMI 1978)★★★, Effort (DEB-EMI 1979)★★★, Dance A Dub (Jux 1980)★★★★, More She Love It (Yvonne's Special 1981)★★★, Disco Style Showcase (Yvonne's Special 1981)★★★, Bushmaster Connection (Jux 1982)★★★★, Classics (Maccabees 1985)★★★, Sisters And Brothers (Blue Moon 1985)★★★, In Griechenland (Arcade 1986)★★, Raggamuffin Year (Mango/Island 1986)★★★, Stranger (Skengdon 1987)★★★, Moving Down The Road (Live & Love 1987)★★, Roadblock (Blue Trac 1987)★★★, It Takes Two To Tango (Fashion 1987)★★★, One Step More (Mango/Island

1988)★★, *Taste Of The Young Heart* (Incredible 1989)★★★, *Dub School* (Buffalo 1990)★★★, with Augustus Pablo *Raggamuffin Dub* (Rockers International 1990)★★★, *Showcase* (Rockers International 1993)★★★.

DELTONES

This UK ska/R&B group was formed in 1985 and comprised mainly an all-women personnel with the line-up fluctuating variously during their existence - sometimes amounting to as many as 11 members. Early musicians included Jacqui Callis (vocals, ex-Delta 5 and later the Renees) and Sara McGuinness (keyboards). As contemporaries of the ska group the Potato 5, they often appeared on the same bill, becoming mainstays on the London ska scene. The group often drew praise from luminaries such as Lloyd Coxsone and were popular on the European continent, leading eventually to the release of *Nana Choc Choc In Paris* on the Unicorn (UK)/Boucherie (France) label. The line-up on the album comprised Penny Leyton (trumpet, ex-Bodysnatchers and the Belle Stars), Serena Parsons (guitar), Anna Keegan (saxophone), Nicky Ford (saxophone), Julie Liggett (keyboards), Anna Risler (bass), Jeremy Brill (drums) and Amanda Fenn, Dill Hammond and Verona Davis (all vocals). In later years the Deltones have pursued a less hard-line ska attitude, opening up to other styles, and although the group's profile has been low during the 90s, the Deltones survive as a unit and perform whenever commitments allow.

● ALBUMS: *Nana Choc Choc In Paris* (Unicorn 1989)★★★.

DETERMINE

b. Rohan Bennett, *c.*1972, Jamaica, West Indies. Bennett began his career performing on the Jamaican sound system circuit. In 1995 his popularity led to him being nominated and winning the Rockers award for best new DJ. A series of singles followed, including the blistering 'Burn Up', 'Dem No Know Love' and a combination with Brian And Tony Gold, 'Bulls Eye Part Two'. Alongside the top-ranking DJ Beenie Man, he enjoyed international notoriety when the duo recorded the popular 'Kette Drum', produced by Bobby Digital. The song was originally intended as a solo venture, but Beenie Man was so impressed with the rhythm that he invited Determine to record it as a duet. The record affirmed the revival of Nyahbingi drumming, a form not heard on record since the 70s. The success of the rhythm led to a profusion of versions, with notable inclusions from Shabba Ranks And Cocoa Tea ('Flag Flown High'), Bounty Killer ('Seek God') and Garnett Silk ('Silk Chant'). In 1996, as part of the trend of reviving Bob Marley rhythms in the dancehall, Determine was enrolled by producer Barry O'Hare and his X-Rated crew to perform 'Heathen Chant'. He reinforced his high profile with a succession of hits, including a striking combination with Yogi, 'No One Cares', and with Turbo Belly, 'What Dem A Tink', as well as solo hits that included 'Welcome Shaka Zulu', 'I Shall Not', 'Born Pressurizer', 'Nuh Duh Nuttin', 'Wuk Out Yu Body' and 'If A Nevah Jah'.

● ALBUMS: with Daddy Rings, African and Dandymite *Four The Hard Way* (Jammys 1995)★★★, *Rock The World* (Digital B 1996)★★★.

DIGITAL

A term used to describe reggae music from the mid-80s onwards, when computer-generated music took over. The first example of this type of music (although, notably, Lee Perry, Augustus Pablo and Sly And Robbie, among others, had all previously experimented with drum machines) was released by Prince (later King) Jammy by Wayne Smith, utilizing a Casio 'music box'. The resulting 'Under Me Sleng Teng' spawned over 200 different versions during the next couple of months and the computer became ubiquitous. Jammys was at the forefront of this musical revolution and former employees, producer Bobby Digital and musicians Steely And Clevie, went on to become top names in their own right. Jammys' former employer King Tubby also proved adept at this music and many more famous names from reggae's illustrious past soon allied themselves to the new beat. Once again, the music was opened up to all sorts of newcomers and possibilities as expensive studio time and costly session musicians were no longer a prerequisite for making records. Like all new forms, it has had its share of detractors, but digital reggae has proved incredibly successful, and has become one of the most popular styles of the music outside of its immediate audience since the late 60s/early 70s.

DIGITAL B
(see Digital, Bobby)

DIGITAL, BOBBY

b. Robert Dixon, Kingston, Jamaica, West Indies. Dixon was named 'Digital' because his arrival at King Jammy's coincided with the rise of Steely And Clevie's computerized rhythm tracks in 1985. He quickly began to learn dub-cutting, voicing and mixing under Jammy's tuition, fulfilling a line of descendency that went back to the late dub pioneer King Tubby. Soon, he was to play a pivotal role in the running of the studio, enhancing the careers of artists such as Cocoa Tea, Shabba Ranks, Chaka Demus, Admiral Bailey, Sanchez, Pinchers and many more. When he left in 1988 to form the Heatwave sound system and build his own studio, all those artists voiced for the new Digital B label. Hits for Shabba Ranks included 'Wicked Inna Bed' and 'Gal Yuh Good', which led to the *Just Reality* album in 1990. He, Ninjaman and Admiral Tibet joined forces for 'Serious Time', and by 1991 he had attracted new talent including Cobra ('Tek Him'), Tony Rebel, Penny Irie and Shaka Shamba ('Reggae Fight'), as well as established names such as Gregory Isaacs, Johnny Osbourne and Cornell Campbell. Whether cutting hardcore rhythms or recreating classics from the past, the quality of his productions reaped huge success throughout that year, including albums by Pinchers, Sanchez and Admiral Tibet, various 'version' sets and Half Pint's 'Substitute Lover'.

In 1992 Garnett Silk visited the studio, recording his debut album and several hit singles, which led to a major contract with Atlantic Records. By this time, Digital was producing tracks for the international market, Shabba Ranks, Buju Banton, Cobra and Tiger among them. By the end of 1993 he had released a staggering volume of music, most of it exceptional. There were albums from Glen Ricks and Leroy Smart, some fine performances by Gregory Isaacs ('Easy'), Cocoa Tea, Red Dragon, Sugar Minott, Josey Wales and Lieutenant Stitchie, all of whom revitalized their careers accordingly. Mafia And Fluxy, Sly And Robbie and Danny Browne also created new, exciting rhythms such as 'Mad Dog' and 'Top Ten', upon which a myriad of younger artists, such as Terror Fabulous, Daddy Screw, Roundhead, Jigsy King and Saaba Tooth, leapt with rapid results. As 1994 opened he was recording rhythms specifically to reintroduce Shabba to his dancehall audience. With his credentials as a fellow ghetto youth made good, an extensive array of gifted artists and a burgeoning reputation with a wider audience following his work with international acts, Bobby Digital is well placed to remain a leading producer for many years.

His productions include Shabba Ranks' *Just Reality*, Sanchez's *I Can't Wait*, Dirtsman's *Acid*, Admiral Tibet's *Separate Class*, Pinchers' *Hotter*, Leroy Smart's *Talk About Friend*, Garnett Silk's *It's Growing*.

● COMPILATIONS: Various *Wicked In Bed* (Blue Mountain 1989)★★★, *Gal Yuh Good* (Blue Mountain 1990)★★★, *Full House* (Digital B 1991)★★★, *Ripe Cherry* (Digital B 1991)★★, *Moving Away* (VP 1992)★★, *Top Ten* (VP 1993)★★★, *Mad Dog* (VP 1993)★★★, *Strictly Dancehall* (VP 1993)★★★, *Digital B Presents Kette Drum* (Digital B 1995)★★★.

DILLINGER

b. Lester Bullocks, 25 June 1953, Kingston, Jamaica, West Indies. In 1971, Dillinger commenced his career as a DJ, working on the sound systems of Prince Jackie and El Brasso, where he initially imitated U-Roy, Dennis Alcapone and Big Youth, before forging his own style. In 1974, he recorded the excellent 'Freshly' for Yabby You, and the following year had a glut of material released, including 'Brace A Boy' for Augustus Pablo, 'CB 200' for Joseph 'Joe Joe' Hookim and 'Killer Man Jaro' for Coxsone Dodd. It was Dodd who released Dillinger's stunning first album, *Ready Natty Dreadie*, on which he effortlessly delivered 10 strong toasts over a selection of Studio One's classic rocksteady and reggae rhythms. It is only the first pressing of the album that contains the brilliant title track, as it was subsequently replaced by 'Natty Kung Fu'. Hookim released Dillinger's second album, *CB 200*, which features several singles including the title track, 'Plantation Heights, 'Cocaine In My Brain' and

'Crank Face'. In late 1976, he made an album (*Clash*) in the UK with Trinity for producer Clement Bushay, which suffered from hurried recording sessions. Hookim released a further album, *Bionic Dread*, which was far less compelling than its predecessor. 'Cocaine In My Brain' had proven to be so popular in Europe and the USA that he recorded a follow-up, 'Marijuana In My Brain' (1979), which became a number 1 hit in Holland, and an album of the same name quickly followed. Unfortunately, most of his material from this time did not match his earlier work, although he was still brave enough to attempt one of the first reggae electro recordings with 1980's *Badder Than Them*. He was inactive for most of the 80s, but in 1990, he returned to the recording scene.

● ALBUMS: *Ready Natty Dreadie* (Studio One 1975)★★★★, *CB 200* (Island 1976)★★★★, *Bionic Dread* (Black Swan 1976)★★★, with Trinity *Clash* (Burning Sounds 1976)★★, *Talkin' Blues* (Magnum 1977)★★★, *Top Ranking* (Third World 1978)★★★, *Answer My Questions* (Third World 1979)★★★, *Marijuana In My Brain* (Jamaica Sound 1979)★★★, *Badder Than Them* (A&M 1980)★★★, *Corn Bread* (Vista Sounds 1983)★★★, with Clint Eastwood *Live At London* (Vista Sounds 1983)★★★, *King Pharaoh* (Blue Moon 1984)★★★, *Best Of Live* (Vista Sounds 1984)★★, *Cocaine* (New Cross 1984)★★★, *Tribal War* (New Cross 1986)★★★, *Say No To Drugs* (Lagoon 1993)★★★, *Funky Punk* (1993)★★★.

DILLON, PHYLIS

b. *c*.1948, Kingston, Jamaica, West Indies. Dillon was a greatly underrated vocalist who had been recording in Jamaica for a number of years before her first hit. In 1967 she released 'Perfidia' and 'Don't Stay Away' with Tommy McCook And The Supersonics, which was produced by Duke Reid at Treasure Isle studios in Bond Street. She emigrated to New York but periodically returned to Jamaica where she recorded at the Bond Street studio. In 1970 Reid produced 'The Right Track', a duet with Hopeton Lewis, which demonstrated her sweet vocals and impeccable talent. When rocksteady evolved into reggae, Dillon was able to adapt to the new beat with dexterity. The turning point in her career came on one of her reappearances

at Treasure Isle when the Duke Reid-produced 'One Life To Live, One Love To Give' reached the Jamaican Top 10. Reid licensed *One Life To Live* to Trojan Records in the UK, which featured her hits along with 'Long Time No Nice Time', 'The Love That A Woman Should Give A Man', 'Love The One You're With', 'I Can't Forget About You Baby' and 'Close To You'. A bizarre interpretation of the latter was used by Dennis Al Capone for a wedding ceremony, appropriately entitled 'The Wedding Song', on his album *DJ's Choice*. He also chanted over Dillon's 'Woman Of The Ghetto' and 'Picture On The Wall'. Trojan lifted her cover version of George Harrison's 'Something' from the album, which proved a moderate success. By the mid-70s Dillon devoted her time to raising a family, although she made a moderately successful comeback in the 90s.

● ALBUMS: *One Life To Live* (Trojan 1972)★★★.

● COMPILATIONS: *Love Is All I Had* (Treasure Isle 1995)★★★.

DIRTSMAN

b. Patrick Thompson, 1966, Spanish Town, Jamaica, West Indies, d. 21 December 1993. The brother of Papa San, Dirtsman was a similarly inclined dancehall DJ until his brutal death. His father was the owner of the Black Universe sound system, but he subsequently moved on to the Creation Rock Tower Sound, based in Willowdene. His first chart appearance came with 'Thank You' in 1990, preceding 'Borrow Man' on Steely And Clevie's label. Later, he teamed up with Phillip Smart in New York, achieving further success with 'Hot This Year'. On the cusp of mainstream success, he signed to BMG, but his career was cut short in 1993 when he was shot on his veranda by four gunmen, being pronounced dead on arrival at Spanish Town Hospital.

● ALBUMS: *Acid* (VP 1988)★★★.

DOBSON, DOBBY

b. Highland Dobson, 1942, Kingston, Jamaica, West Indies. 'The Loving Pauper', as he has been affectionately nicknamed, has crafted an impressively individual technique, built around a voice of rich, modular tone. Dobson began singing as part of a group known as the Deltas while at the Kingston College; the group also included Howard Barrett (later to form the Paragons). They recorded their first song for the Tip Top label - 'Cry A Little Cry', written by Dobson, and produced by Sonia Pottinger. Though it proved a radio hit, the group split and Dobson continued to record solo for Pottinger. His first recording session resulted in the release of a duet with Chuck Joseph, 'Baby How Can I'. Although the Tip Top release was greeted with indifference, Dobson's distinctive vocal style secured recording sessions with Coxsone Dodd and Duke Reid. With Reid, he recorded 'Loving Pauper', as well as cutting 'Seems To Me I'm Losing You' for Coxsone Dodd at roughly the same time. He enjoyed a succession of hits with both producers, although it was 'Loving Pauper' that garnered most attention and became his signature tune. He recorded it twice more after its initial release on Treasure Isle, and many other reggae stars (including Freddie McGregor and Ruddy Thomas) would also cover it.

Nevertheless, Dobson modestly maintained his jobs as a salesman and proof-reader for the *Jamaican Gleaner*. In his spare time he was enrolled to perform with various short-term local bands, including the Sheiks alongside Jackie Mittoo, and the Virtues, before establishing a fruitful partnership in 1971 with Rupie Edwards. His initial single, 'That Wonderful Sound', sold in excess of 40,000 copies in the Caribbean and was followed by his other distinguished opus, 'Endlessly'. The song was equally successful and signalled international fame when the independent Ashanti label took the song into the lower reaches of the UK pop chart. Despite his prolific past, it was not until Edwards compiled an album directly following the success of 'Wonderful Sound' that Dobson added a long-player to his canon. Unfortunately, it failed to sell in the quantities that both parties anticipated, and was followed shortly afterwards by *Sweet Dreams* for Federal Records. This comprised big 50s and 60s ballads, delivered in Dobson's smoothest lovers tones. His bad luck was compounded, however, when a third album, for a Miami label, failed to produce any royalties. He began working as a producer and relished a notable achievement with the Meditations' *Wake Up*, released through Count Shelley. In 1979 Dobson emigrated to New York where he pursued a career outside of the music industry, although he occasionally returned to the studio. Instead he worked in real estate and junior management (he had previously been a marketing student at the University of West Indies). In 1982, during one of his sporadic studio sessions, he recorded 'Sweetheart', produced by Inner Circle, which enjoyed another brush with the UK pop chart. While pursuing other interests, he occasionally performed live and is a favourite on the 'oldies night' section at both Reggae Sunsplash and Reggae Sumfest celebrations in Jamaica. His popularity as a 'big people's' performer prompted the release of a series of mellow lovers compilations, including *Love You Through It All*, *Sweet Dreams Again Volume Two*, *Love Your Woman*, *Nothing But Love Songs Volume Three*, *At Last* and *To Lovers Everywhere*.

● ALBUMS: *Wonderful Sound* (Success 1977)★★★, *Sweet Dreams* (Federal 1978)★★★★, *History For Lovers* (Shelley 1990)★★★, *Through The Years* (Studio One 1991)★★★.

● COMPILATIONS: *Best Of Dobby Dobson* (Super Power 1997)★★★★.

DOCTOR ALIMANTADO

The 'Ital Surgeon' Winston Thompson came to the record-buying public's attention with his DJ work for Lee Perry in Jamaica during the early 70s, but it was only when he started producing records for himself that he found his niche. His 'The Best Dressed Chicken In Town' (a version to 'Ain't No Sunshine'), released on Capo Records, leaned heavily on the production techniques of Lee Perry, but was an unmatched assault on the senses - later to be described as two and a half minutes of dub lyricism. His manic approach and choice of top rhythms assured his cult status in the UK where his records on the Ital Sounds and Vital Food labels were eagerly awaited and purchased by a cult following. He was nearly killed when a downtown Kingston bus knocked him over in 1977, and his subsequent comeback single for Channel One, 'Born For A Purpose', and the DJ version, 'Life All Over', brought him to the fore at the same time that the punk market discovered reggae. He moved to England not long afterwards, to capitalize on his new-found fame and has remained there, on and off, ever since.

He still releases records on his ISDA label, none of which have matched the quality of his early recordings. He is now resident in Holland.

● ALBUMS: *Best Dressed Chicken* (Greensleeves 1978)★★★★, *Born For A Purpose/Songs Of Thunder* (Greensleeves 1981)★★★, *Love Is* (Keyman 1983)★★★, *In The Mix Volumes 1-5* (Keyman 1985-1990)★★★, *King's Bread* (Ital Sounds 1986)★★★, *King's Bread Dub* (Keyman 1989)★★★, *The Privileged Few* (Keyman 1990)★★★.

● COMPILATIONS: *Reggae Revue Part 1* (Keyman 1988)★★.

DODD, COXSONE

It is an indisputable fact that without the vision and work of Clement Seymour Dodd, reggae music as we now understand it would not exist. Always interested in music, he was among the first in Jamaica to run his own sound system - Sir Coxsone The Down Beat ('Coxsone' was inspired by a popular Yorkshire cricketer of the 50s) - a forerunner to the mobile discos of the 60s. The power and amount of amplification equipment ensured that the listener could 'feel' the music, rather than merely hear it. Competition was fierce to be first with the latest and most exclusive discs. The music favoured was hard R&B, with Shirley And Lee, Amos Milburn and Lyn Hope being particular favourites. The 'sounds' would often play in competition with each other, drawing wild cheers and ecstatic reactions when certain tunes were played. Titles were scratched out on the records and songs were renamed to prevent rival sounds discovering their identity. For instance, 'Later For Gator' by Willis Jackson was known as 'Coxsone Hop' to Down Beat followers. Reportedly, Coxsone had been playing 'Later For Gator' for months and Dodd's closest rival, Duke Reid, had been unable to find its true identity. Later, Reid managed to acquire the record for himself, and played it against Dodd at one of their 'clashes'; Dodd apparently almost passed out with shock. Small fortunes were spent on record-buying sprees in America in order to keep on top.

In the mid-50s the supply of hard R&B records dried up as smoother productions began to find favour with the black American audience. These were not popular in Jamaica, however, and starved of American records, the sound system operators started to create their own music. Initially, these productions were intended solely for live use and were played as dub plates only, but their popularity proved overwhelming and the sound system owners began to offer them for sale to the public. Among the earliest sides to appear at the end of the 50s on Coxsone's Worldisc label were records by local artists such as Jackie Estick, Lascelles Perkins ('Destiny'), Bunny And Skitter ('Lumumba'), Basil Gabbidon And The Mellow Larks ('Time To Pray'), Clue J And His Blues Blasters ('Shufflin' Jug'), Aubrey Adams and the Dewdroppers ('Marjie') and Theophilius Beckford ('Easy Snappin'). Other artists recorded later included organist Monty Alexander And The Cyclones ('Stack Is Back'), the Jiving Juniors, featuring a young Derrick Harriott, Derrick Morgan, Clancy Eccles ('River Jordan' and 'Freedom'), Alton (Ellis) And Eddie ('Muriel'), the Charmers (featuring Lloyd Tyrell aka Lloyd Charmers), (Joe) Higgs And Wilson ('How Can I Be Sure'), Cornell Campbell, and Owen Gray ('On The Beach'), as well as the first sides by such legendary hornsmen as Don Drummond ('Don Cosmic') and Roland Alphonso. Some of these early recordings can be found on *All Star Top Hits*, and *Oldies But Goodies (Volumes 1 & 2)*. Although his empire was growing rapidly, Dodd shrugged off the attention with a typical: 'I didn't realize that this could be a business. I just did it for enjoyment!'. Dodd's productions caught the mood of the times, and as Jamaican R&B evolved into ska, with the accent firmly on the off-beat, he was always at the forefront with his teams of session musicians and raw young vocalists. Throughout the ska era he ruled with records such as 'Joe Liges' and 'Spit In The Sky' by Delroy Wilson, 'Six & Seven Books Of Moses' and 'Hallelujah' by the Maytals, 'Simmer Down', 'Hooligan', 'Rudie' and many more by the Wailers, 'Rude Boy Gone A Jail' and 'Shoo Be Do Be' by the Clarendonians, 'I've Got To Go Back Home' by Bob Andy, a brace of Lee Perry tunes including 'Rub & Squeeze' and 'Doctor Dick', as well as dozens of fiery instrumentals by the Skatalites (often released crediting only the lead instrumentalist), the crack ensemble who also provided the backing on all Coxsone recordings during this time. Dodd opened his own studio on Brentford Road in the early 60s, known as Studio One, which became the generic title for all Coxsone productions thereafter. The advantages were numerous: multiple 'takes' to ensure that the final one was right; the opportunity to experiment without having to worry about the high costs of studio time; and the capacity to attempt 'uncommercial' ventures. Dodd placed many of the island's top musicians on his payroll and the results were impressive. With accomplished arrangers and musicians supervising - such as Lee Perry, Jackie Mittoo, Leroy Sibbles and Larry Marshall - just about every top name in reggae music worked for Studio One at some stage in his or her career - usually at the beginning, because Dodd was always keen to develop new talent, holding regular Sunday auditions for aspiring artists.

During the 1967-70 period, the hits flowed out of Brentford Road in a veritable deluge of unparalleled creativity. By late 1966, ska's furious pace was beginning to give way to the slower rocksteady beat, the sparser instrumentation and the availability of multi-track recording equipment allowed for a greater emphasis on melody and subtlety, and although it is recognized that Duke Reid's Treasure Isle productions represent much of the finest rocksteady extant, Dodd's raw, almost organic productions from this period have since gone on to form what amounts to the foundation of reggae music in the following decades.

Much of this incredible output appeared on a number of labels in the UK, notably the Coxsone and Studio One imprints handled by Island's B&C group, and, later, on the Bamboo and Banana labels. Such artists as Ken Boothe (a cover of Kenny Lynch's/Garnet Mimms' 'Moving Away', 'Thinking', 'Without Love', 'Just Another Girl'), Bob Andy ('I've Got To Go Back Home', 'Too Experienced', 'Going Home', 'Unchained', 'Feeling Soul'), Alton Ellis ('I'm Just A Guy', 'I'm Still In Love With You', 'Can I Change My Mind', 'Still Trying'), the Heptones ('Fattie Fattie', 'Love Won't Come Easy', 'Heptones Gonna Fight', 'I Hold The Handle'', 'Pretty Looks', 'Give Me The Right', 'Sweet Talking'), Marcia Griffiths ('Truly', 'Feel Like Jumping'), John Holt ('Strange Things', 'Love I Can Feel', 'OK Fred'), Slim Smith ('Born To Love You', 'Never Let Go', 'Rougher Yet'), Delroy Wilson ('Never Conquer', 'I Don't Know Why'), Carlton And His Shoes ('Love Me Forever'), Jackie Mittoo ('Ram Jam', 'Hot Milk', 'One Step Beyond', 'Drum Song', 'Peanie Wallie', 'In Cold Blood'), Ernest Wilson ('Undying Love'), Larry (Marshall) And Alvin ('Nanny Goat', 'Throw Me Corn', 'Mean Girl'), Ken Parker ('My Whole World Is Falling Down'), Roland Alphonso ('Jah Shaky'), the Gaylads ('Africa', 'Love Me With All Your Heart'), the Eternals featuring Cornell Campbell ('Queen Of The Minstrels', 'Stars'), the Cables ('Baby Why', 'What Kind Of World', 'Be A Man') and dozens of instrumental sides by the in-house session band the Soul Vendors/Sound Dimension ('Full Up', 'Swing Easy', 'Psychedelic Rock', 'Frozen Soul', 'Real Rock', 'Mojo Rocksteady') and countless others made some of their finest records at Brentford Road. Many of these songs, arrangements and rhythm tracks in particular, are endlessly recycled by younger artists and producers. Indeed, one recent trend in the music was to sample snatches of Dodd's classic old rhythms and build new versions out of the sample. Other younger producers, some of whom - Lee Perry and Winston 'Niney' Holness, in particular - had learnt their trade while with Coxsone, began to take over in the early 70s, leaving Coxsone to take a less prominent role in the music's development. Nonetheless, throughout the decade Coxsone still produced a great deal of fine music including some of the earliest material from Horace Andy ('Skylarking', 'Just Say Who', 'Fever', 'Every Tongue Shall Tell'), Dennis Brown ('No Man Is An Island', 'If I Follow My Heart', 'Easy Take It Easy'), the Wailing Souls ('Mr Fire Coal Man', 'Back Out With It'), Burning Spear ('Door Peep', 'Joe Frazier', 'Swell Headed'), Dennis Alcapone ('Power Version', *Forever Version*), Dillinger (*Ready Natty Dreadie*) and Freddie McKay (*Picture On The Wall*). He also re-released much of his back catalogue through the 1974-79 period, which ensured his music was heard by a new generation of reggae music lovers.

As the dancehall style began to supersede the rockers and steppers forms, he was once more in full swing with artists such as Freddie McGregor, Sugar Minott, Johnny Osbourne, Judah Eskender Tafari, Willie Williams and DJs Michigan And Smiley and the Lone Ranger all recording fine singles and albums. This proved to be the final golden period for Studio One, however, and in the mid-80s Dodd closed his Brentford Road studio and relocated to New York.

Some of the pivotal albums in reggae history have been Coxsone Dodd productions, including The Skatalites' *Ska Authentic*, Dub Specialist's *Hi-Fashion Dub Top Ten*, Roland Alphonso and Jackie Mittoo's *Macka Fat*, Cedric Brooks' *Im Flash Forward*, Dennis Brown's *If I Follow My Heart*, Bob Andy's *Song Book*, Burning Spear's *Studio One Presents*, Carlton And His Shoes' *Love Me Forever*, Alton Ellis's *Sunday Coming*, Heptones' *On Top*, Freddie McGregor's *Bobby Babylon*, Bob Marley And The Wailers' *Wailing Wailers*, Johnny Osbourne's *Truths & Rights*, Maytals' *Never Grow Old*, Sugar Minott's *Live Loving*, Wailing Souls' *Studio One Presents* and Delroy Wilson's *Feel Good All Over*.

In 1991 Dodd celebrated 35 years in the business with two huge shows in Jamaica, featuring many of the people with whom he had worked over the years. He is reluctant to talk about past glories, however, preferring to look to the future. Sadly, with the exception of the occasional gem, his newer work rarely matches his previous high standards - he works more frequently in New York than in Brentford Road. He still presses hundreds of his old records and there is always a selection of his music available at specialist reggae shops - and, in a business controlled by the latest and the newest, they continue to sell. Despite rumours of financial and personal disagreements between Dodd and his recording artists, the majority have stated that their time was well spent at Coxsone's 'musical college'. His position as the guiding light of Jamaican music is beyond question and the true extent of his influence has yet to be fully realized.

● ALBUMS: various *All Star Top Hits* (Studio One 1961)★★★★, *Oldies But Goodies (Volumes 1 & 2)* (Studio One 1968)★★★★, *Best Of Studio One (Volumes 1, 2, & 3)* (Heartbeat 1983-87)★★★★, *Respect To Studio One* (Heartbeat 1995)★★★.

● FURTHER READING: *A Scorcha From Studio One/More Scorcha From Studio One*, Roger Dalke.

DON YUTE

b. Jason Andrew Williams, 9 May 1974, Kingston, Jamaica, West Indies. Don Yute is best remembered for his 1995 combination hit with Wayne Wonder, 'Sensi Ride'. He performed in a style reminiscent of Beenie Man and Bounty Killer. He also recorded in combination with Prezident Brown on the enlightening 'African Thing'. Don Yute's success led to him working with a number of producers, including Donovan Germain ('All That Glitters'), Bobby Digital ('Funny Funny') and Steely And Clevie ('Hard Core'), while Colin 'Bulby' York produced 'Click Click'. He maintained a high profile with the hits 'Gal It Wouldn't Easy', 'You Own Di Man', 'La La La', 'Golden Child' and 'Livin' In A Dream'. In 1997 he released his debut album, which included the cream of his hits. In the same year he appeared at Sting 97 with newcomer Sean Paul, who had enjoyed a combination hit, 'Ladies Night', with Spanner Banner. Don Yute is considered a 'name brand' DJ, but he has yet to repeat the success of 'Sensi Ride'. In the latter half of the 90s the studios in Jamaica were delivering literally thousands of dancehall releases, and much of Don Yute's later work was neglected as a result; some hope emerged, however, when the Jamaican Government asked the island's producers to limit the number of releases.

● ALBUMS: *Golden Child* (Nuff Tings 1997)★★★.

DONALDSON, ERIC

b. 11 June 1947, Jamaica, West Indies. Eric Donaldson, one of Jamaica's most accomplished falsetto voices, will forever be associated with the Jamaican Festival Song Competition, and in particular, with one of his five winning entries in that contest, 'Cherry Oh Baby', which won in 1971, and launched his career in reggae music. Donaldson attended school in Spanish Town before taking up a job as a house-painter, singing in his spare time. In 1964 he cut some unreleased sides for Studio One in Kingston, and in the mid-60s he formed vocal group the West Indians, alongside Leslie Burke and Hector Brooks. A collection of sides for producer J.J. Johnson produced one hit, 'Right On Time', in 1968. They also recorded for Lee Perry ('Oh Lord') the following year, to negligible reaction.

A name-change to the Killowatts and a succession of songs for J.J. Johnson and Lloyd Daley's Matador label ('Slot Machine', 'Real Cool Operator') failed to ignite the fire of fame and the group split.

In 1970 Donaldson cut some sides for Alvin Ranglin's GG's label, the best of which was 'Lonely Night', and a trip to Dynamic Sounds studio for 'Never Going To Give You Up' again led nowhere, although it did bode well for the future. In 1971, apparently as a last stand, he entered the Festival Song Competition with 'Cherry Oh Baby'. By the day of the festival, he had enrolled the astute Tommy Cowan as manager, and the disc eventually sold an extraordinary 50,000 copies on Dynamic Records. While it has not been a smooth ride from that point, Donaldson has been periodically successful, releasing albums sporadically and recording a clutch of songs that are fondly remembered by reggae aficionados, notably 'Miserable Woman' (1972), 'What A Festival' (1973) and 'Freedom Street' (1977). Donaldson apparently still loves the festival, winning in 1971, 1977, 1978, 1984 and 1993, and he always seems ready to give his career a shot in the arm by appearing there. He now lives in Kent Village, Jamaica, where he runs the 'Cherry Oh Baby Go-Go Bar'. The song itself is perennially popular, and both UB40 and the Rolling Stones have covered it. The rhythm remained popular in 1991, with over 30 new versions issued in Jamaica, including Donaldson's own update.

● ALBUMS: *Eric Donaldson* (Trojan 1971)★★★, *Keep On Riding* (Dynamic 1976)★★, *Kent Village* (Dynamic 1978)★★★, *Right On Time* (Dynamic 1985)★★★, *Trouble In Afrika* (Blue Mountain 1992)★★★, *Love Of The Common People* (1993)★★★.

DOUGLAS, KEITH

b. 7 December 1957, London, England. Douglas followed the local sounds in London, including Sir Coxsone's and the Mighty Frontline. He was inspired to perform as a DJ by his brother Tony, a member of the Blackstones, who topped the reggae album charts with *Take Another Look At Love*. Inspired by his love of music, Douglas embarked on a recording career, initially under the pseudonym Imperial Keith. He released his debut, 'Struggling In A Babylon', in 1976, which

was well received and led to sessions with Clement Bushay following an introduction by Pablo Gad for the masterful 'Teacher Never Taught Me'. The song enhanced his notoriety as a roots singer, although this classification proved inaccurate. While pursuing his career, he learned much from his contemporaries, a notable influence being King Sounds who taught Douglas basic guitar skills. The release of the classic 'Blessed Are The Meek' signalled a change of direction when he embarked on recording sessions with Fashion Records. Through the label he released 'I Specialise In Good Girls' and the chart-topping 'Cool Down Amina'. The success of the two singles led to him being described as Mr Lovers Rock, and in 1982 he released 'Try Love Again' with similar success. In 1983 he began working with Aswad, with backing vocals provided by Brown Sugar's Pauline Catilin and Caron Wheeler for the buoyant 'Angel', released on the band's own label. The Ladbroke Grove connection continued when he appeared with the Sons Of Jah for the dancehall favourite 'Boom', backed with the appropriately titled 'Explosive Dub'. While working with Trevor Bow and the Sons Of Jah he recorded his debut album, featuring melodies supplied by members of Aswad and the Wailers. Indicating a desire for independence he went into self-production for the release of 'You Move Me'. Douglas also appeared on the one rhythm *Front Line Reggae* compilation.

● ALBUMS: *What The World Needs* (Natty Congo 1984)★★.

DREAD, MIKEY

b. Michael Campbell, Port Antonio, Jamaica, West Indies. Dread achieved prominence in Jamaica in the late 70s as a DJ on the JBC station with his four-hour Saturday night *Dread At The Controls* show. Campbell's show played exclusively reggae (bizarrely, until the rise of IRIE FM, most official Jamaican radio stations played anything but reggae). His selections - many of them hot off the cutting lathe, dub plate specials - were punctuated by wild sound effects and suitably manic utterances. This made him a hero to the grassroots audience, but put him at odds with fellow broadcasters and the conservative JBC directorship, leading to his resignation in 1979. He had already entered the recording business with DJ sides such as 'Dread At The Controls' and 'Homeguard' for Lee Perry, and 'Rootsman Revival' for Sonia Pottinger's High Note label. After a brief spell as an engineer for Treasure Isle studio, he formed a working relationship with producer Carlton Patterson, for whom he cut 'Barber Saloon' and helped to produce Ray I's popular 'Weatherman Skank'. He inaugurated his own DATC label in 1979 and began releasing records by Earl Sixteen, Rod Taylor, Edi Fitzroy, Sugar Minott and others, as well as his own popular DJ titles such as 'Love The Dread', 'African Map' and 'Proper Education'; these were also sought after for the entertaining 'version' sides, mixed by Campbell and King Tubby. Perhaps his most enduring contributions are the two dubwise albums, *Dread At The Controls* and *African Anthem*, replete with many of the effects and jingles featured on his radio show. In 1982 he narrated Channel 4's six-part *Deep Roots* programme, and presented *The Rockers Road Show* for the same company the following year. He has also worked with UB40 and the Clash, toasting on the latter's 'Bank Robber'. He now resides in America where he continues to record, make stage appearances and host a music programme for television.

● ALBUMS: *Dread At The Controls* (DATC/Trojan 1979)★★★, *African Anthem* (DATC 1979)★★★★, *At The Control Dubwise* (DATC 1979)★★★★, *World War III* (DATC 1981)★★, *S.W.A.L.K.* (DATC 1982)★★, *Dub Merchant* (DATC 1982)★★★, *Pave The Way* (Heartbeat 1984)★★★, *Pave The Way Parts I & II* (DEP 1985)★★★, *Beyond World War III* (DATC 1986)★★, *Happy Family* (RAS 1989)★★★, *African Anthem Revisited* (RAS 1991)★★★, *Dub Party* (ROIR 1995)★★★.

DREAD ZONE

This UK trance-dub club team comprises Greg Roberts (ex-BAD; Screaming Target), Leo Williams and Tim Bran. Roberts is responsible for rhythms and sampling, and Bran for programming and other feats of technology. Part of Dread Zone's distinctive charm is drawn from Roberts' appetite for cult films, many of his samples being taken from this field; dialogue from b-movies (often to avoid the problems of copyright clearance) is a particular favourite. However, their dub credentials were ensured by

the arrival of the single 'House Of Dread'. This came complete with a 'Howard Marks' remix - the latter being among the world's most famous cannabis traffickers. 'Zion Youth' broached the UK Top 40 in 1995 and was followed by an excellent second album, *Second Light*.

● ALBUMS: *360°* (1993)★★★, *Second Light* (Virgin 1995)★★★★, *Biological Radio* (Virgin 1997)★★.

DRUMMOND, DON

b. 1943, Kingston, Jamaica, West Indies, d. 6 May 1969, Kingston, Jamaica, West Indies. One of the principal innovators in Jamaican music, Drummond tragically died before seeing the growth and success of the genre he helped to create. Don Drummond was educated at the famous Alpha Catholic Boys Home and School, in the heart of the Kingston ghetto, where he, like so many others, was allowed to develop and express his musical talents, first as a pupil and later as a teacher. By the early 50s he had established his reputation as one of the island's top jazz trombonists. His main inspiration at this stage was the American big-band sound, but as the decade wore on, the influence of R&B and sound systems began to be felt in Jamaica. When the sound system operators began to make their own records, they immediately turned to accomplished musicians such as Drummond, Roland Alphonso and Rico Rodriguez, who had consolidated their reputations throughout the decade with residencies at clubs such as the Glass Bucket and the Silver Slipper. Their musical knowledge and expertise were critical in determining the feel and direction of these early recordings, which were usually credited to the Skatalites. Drummond was also an early convert to the Rastafarian faith and his beliefs were reflected in records such as 'Addis Ababa', 'Far East' and countless uncredited recordings. His fragile mental condition was not helped by the lack both of financial rewards and recognition of his talents. Following the murder of Marguerita, his common-law wife, in 1965, he was committed to Belle Vue, Kingston's lunatic asylum, where he ended his days in 1969. Drummond's case was an early tragedy in Jamaican music and he was the precursor of much that was to follow. Since his death, his work has been assessed for its true worth, while one particularly perceptive critic stated that his music 'contained the hurt of his people'. Always a quiet, reserved and shy man, he let his music do the talking.

● COMPILATIONS: *Best Of* (Studio One)★★★★, *100 Years After* (Studio One)★★★, *Memorial* (Treasure Isle)★★★, *In Memory Of* (Studio One)★★★★, *Scattered Lights* (Top Deck 1985)★★★★.

DUB

Essentially reggae in the raw, this cultish, perennially popular form strips out the majority of the music's melody at the mixing desk, leaving behind the rhythm section ('drum 'n' bass' music in reggae parlance) and the residue of other instruments, often with massive layers of echo. Reggae records with crashing effects and decidedly eccentric arrangements date back to the ska era. By 1969-70 many producers, among them Lee Perry, Chin-Randy's, Joe Gibbs, Bunny Lee and Lynford 'Andy Capp' Anderson, were making largely instrumental music that was heavily dependent on the rhythm section (the Upsetters' 'Clint Eastwood' in 1970, for example), and it took only the addition of delay units such as the Copycat and Echoplex to create the dub boom.

In 1972, encouraged by Bunny Lee, King Tubby, an electronics engineer and sound system owner, began to mix records in four-track, and by late 1973 his name graced many b-side 'versions' (the name is a corruption of instrumental version, or 'Version 2') of other people's records, notably those of Bunny Lee and Lee Perry. At the same time, engineer Sylvan Morris at Harry J./Studio One, and Errol Thompson at Randy's, also experimented with the dub sound. Occasional, very limited-pressing dub albums began to appear in the shops, and quickly became collectors' items. Among the best-known of these were Perry/Tubby collaborations, including the ingenious stereo LP *Blackboard Jungle Dub*, which had three different mixes, one for each speaker and one for both, and *King Tubby Meets The Upsetter At The Grass Roots Of Dub*, a record that was *the* underground reggae album of 1974 in the UK. Tubby's uniquely precise, often stunningly heavy, mixes also graced numerous Bunny Lee productions on his Jackpot, Justice and Attack labels.

By the mid-70s virtually no reggae singles were released without a dub version on the flip-side, and artists such as Augustus Pablo and Glen Brown had created a career from instrumental music in dub form. New engineers such as Prince (later King) Jammy, Pat Kelly (also a singer) and Scientist gradually took over from the original dub mixers, but by 1982 the original boom was pretty much finished, save a few die-hards such as UK engineer-producers Mad Professor and Adrian Sherwood. However, by 1991 a new breed of dub-inspired musicians, such as Jah Shaka, Sound Iration and the Disciples, had founded the 'new roots' movement, and placed the music back on the map, albeit with digital equipment and modern intentions.

● COMPILATIONS: various *Blackboard Jungle Dub* (Upsetter 1974)★★★★, *King Tubby Meets The Upsetter At The Grass Roots Of Dub* (Fay Music 1974)★★★★, *Pick A Dub* (Atra 1975)★★★, *King Tubby Meets Rockers Uptown* (Clocktower 1976)★★★★, *King Tubby's Prophecy Of Dub* (Prophets 1976)★★★★ *Beware* (Grove Music 1978)★★★, *Dub Gone Crazy: The Evolution Of Dub At King Tubby's 1975-79* (Blood & Fire 1994)★★★★.

DUB PLATE

A dub plate is simply an acetate cut onto a plastic-coated metal disc, featuring an unusual mix of a well-known record, or a recording unavailable elsewhere, and used by a sound system to help to promote the exclusivity of the music it plays. 'Dubs' are highly prized by collectors, particularly those cut by King Tubby's or King Jammy's, or those that feature famous artists offering amended renditions of classics.

DUB POETRY

Dub poetry is a style of reggae in which poets recite their works over heavy 'dubbed' rhythms, influenced by 70s DJs such as U-Roy, I. Roy and Big Youth. One of the originators was Linton Kwesi Johnson, who was born in Jamaica in 1952 and moved to England in 1963. His early poetry was in the traditional European style until he began listening to DJs and decided to set his work to music. From early on, he had found the English language too restricting and austere, and he set to work in the heavy patois in which the DJs specialized. His first album, *Dread Beat & Blood*, was released in the late 70s and proved hugely influential. Almost single-handedly it gave birth to a whole sub-genre of reggae music, where poets such as Michael Smith, Benjamin Zephaniah, Jean Binta Breeze, Oku Onuora and Mutabaruka performed to the accompaniment of roots reggae rhythms. Probably the most successful of all has been the Jamaican-based Mutabaruka, whose debut album in 1982 for Earl 'Chinna' Smith's High Times label was something of a classic.

In reggae music the rhythm or backing track is never completely subservient to the vocal, instrumental or DJ's contribution, but in the case of some of the dub poets, their voices became the predominant factor. Although much of the DJ output is revered in Jamaica, its Kingston patois means little to the uninitiated, and in this respect, the dub poets' clearer diction was more successful, particularly in the USA and Europe, where many have large, committed followings outside of the usual reggae audience. Most poets are well aware of the irony of their position, and Mutabaruka summarized the situation thus: 'Revolutionary poets, Have become entertainers, Babblin' out angry words'.

● ALBUMS: Linton Kwesi Johnson: *Dread Beat An' Blood* originally credited to Poet And The Roots (Front Line 1977)★★★, *Forces of Victory* (Island 1979)★★★★, *Bass Culture* (Island 1980)★★★★, *In Concert With The Dub Band* (LKJ 1986)★★★; Mutabaruka: *Check It* (High Times 1982)★★★★, *The Mystery Unfolds* (Shanachie 1986)★★★, *Out Cry* (Shanachie 1987)★★★, *Any Which Way* (Greensleeves 1989)★★★; Jean Binta Breeze *Tracks*. (LKJ 1991)★★★★; Benjamin Zephaniah: *Dub Ranting* (Upright 1983)★★★★, *Rasta* (Upright/Helidon 1987)★★★, *Us And Dem* (Mango/Island 1990)★★★; Michael Smith *Mi Cyaan Believe It* (Island 1982)★★★.

● COMPILATIONS: Various *Dread Poets Society*.

DUBE, LUCKY

b. 1967, Ermelo, Eastern Transvaal, South Africa. The most successful African reggae artist of all time, Lucky Dube (pronounced Doobay) has taken his Peter Tosh-influenced music further than his hero himself managed. Guitarist-vocalist Dube formed his first group, a mbqanga combo entitled The Sky Way Band, while still at school. An interest in Rastafarianism complemented a musical predilection for reggae, although, as a member of the Love Brothers, his first album betrayed none of these influences. His first hit single, the 'Zulu soul' of 'Baxoleleni', arrived in 1983, from his debut solo set *Lengane Ngeyetha*. Several LPs later, he starred in a South African movie, *Getting Lucky*, and performed reggae tracks for its soundtrack. His first reggae LP, *Rastas Never Die*, was banned in South Africa on account of its militancy, and Dupe diversified into rap for *Help My Krap*. In 1986 his new band, the Slaves, recorded 'Think About The Children', and their second LP, *Slave*, sold 300,000 copies. In 1989 he toured France and the USA with the group and appeared in the movie *Voice In The Dark*. Two albums in that year, *Together As One* and *Prisoner*, sold heavily, the latter going double platinum in South Africa in five days.

In 1991 Dube became the first South African artist to play the Reggae Sunsplash festival in Jamaica, and again he issued two albums in one year, *Captured Live* (incidentally also the title of a Peter Tosh LP) and *House Of Exile*. Tours of Japan and Australia were also a success, and Dube additionally played WOMAD with Peter Gabriel. 1993's *Victims* again broke his own record for worldwide sales, shifting in excess of a million copies on various licensee imprints. Although Dube's style is probably too dated ever to achieve great success in Jamaica, he remains head and shoulders above his African reggae compatriots. Should he ever commit himself to a major label, he may eventually become the mainstream star he evidently wishes to be.

● ALBUMS: *Lengane Ngeyetha* (1983)★★★, *Rastas Never Die* (1985)★★★★, *Help My Krap* (1986)★★, *Slave* (Shanachie 1986)★★★, *Together As One* (1989)★★, *Prisoner* (Shanachie 1989)★★★★, *Captured Live* (Shanachie 1991)★★, *House Of Exile* (1991)★★★, *Victims* (Shanachie 1993)★★★, *Taxman* (Shanachie 1997)★★★.

DUNBAR, SLY

b. Lowell Charles Dunbar, 10 May 1952, Kingston, Jamaica, West Indies. In 1969 Dunbar commenced his recording career with Lee Perry, playing drums on 'Night Doctor' by the

Upsetters, which appears on both *The Upsetter* and *Return of Django*. The following year, he played on Dave Barker and Ansell Collins' massive hit 'Double Barrel'. Around this time he also joined the Youth Professionals who had a residency at the Tit For Tat Club on Red Hills Road, Kingston. He paid frequent visits to another club further up the same road, Evil People, where he struck up a friendship with bass player Robbie Shakespeare (b. 27 September 1953, Kingston, Jamaica, West Indies). Deciding to work together, their professional relationship as Sly And Robbie began.

In 1972/3, Dunbar joined Skin Flesh And Bones, backing Al Brown on his bestselling cover version of Al Green's 'Here I Am Baby'. The same year, Sly and Robbie became founder-members of the Revolutionaries, Channel One studio's house band. They recorded hit after hit, and the studio soon became the most in-demand on the island. Dunbar's technical proficiency and relentless inventiveness drove him constantly to develop original drum patterns, and while most of the island's other drummers were copying his latest innovations, he would move on and create something new. In this way, he had an enormous influence on the direction that reggae took from the mid-70s onwards. Dunbar's inventive and entertaining playing can be heard on dub and instrumental albums such as *Vital Dub*, *Satta Dub* and *Revolutionary Sounds*, as well as supporting the Mighty Diamonds on their classic *Right Time*. He also recorded extensively with the Professionals, Joe Gibbs' house band, playing on classics such as *Visions* by Dennis Brown, *Two Sevens Clash* by Culture and *African Dub Chapter 3*. Derrick Harriott went one step further and put him on the cover of *Go Deh Wid Riddim* (1977), which was credited to Sly And The Revolutionaries. He was then signed to Virgin Records, who released two disappointing solo albums, *Simple Sly Man* (1978) and *Sly Wicked And Slick* (1979). Around this time, Dunbar was the first drummer successfully to integrate synthesized drums into his playing, and a little later became the first reggae drummer to use a Simmons electronic drum kit. In 1979 Sly And Robbie moved into record production with their own Taxi label, finding success with Black Uhuru's bestselling *Showcase*. Further recordings included Gregory Isaacs'

Showcase and the various artists compilation *Presenting Taxi* (1981). They had their greatest commercial success with Black Uhuru, with whom they recorded four further albums. In 1984, they became official members of the group, but left later that year after the departure of Michael Rose. At the same time, they established Ini Kamoze as a major new reggae artist, released Dennis Brown's *Brown Sugar* and Sugar Minott's *Sugar And Spice*, plus three groundbreaking albums with Grace Jones that were hugely successful and introduced their talents to the world outside of reggae. They have since recorded widely with artists such as Mick Jagger, Carly Simon, Gwen Guthrie, Bob Dylan, Robert Palmer, James Brown, Manu Dibango and Herbie Hancock. They also teamed up with Bill Laswell for a series of innovative soul/funk/crossover albums including *Language Barrier*, *Rhythm Killers*, *Silent Assassin* and Material's *The Third Power*.

They have continued to develop their own reggae sound with recordings from their new discoveries 54-46 and Kotch, some of which are included on the compilations *Sound Of The 90s* and *Carib Soul*. They have already changed the musical world, and their restless creativity ensures that they will continue to do so.

● ALBUMS: *Go Deh Wid Riddim* (Crystal 1977)★★★, *Simple Sly Man* (Virgin 1978)★★, *Sly Wicked And Slick* (Virgin 1979)★★, *Sly-Go-Ville* (Mango/Island 1982)★★★.

DUNKLEY, ERROL

b. 1951, Kingston, Jamaica, West Indies. Dunkley had already cut his first records, a duet with Roy Shirley entitled 'Gypsy' for Lindel Pottinger's Gaydisc label, 'My Queen' with Junior English for Prince Buster, and 'Love Me Forever', issued on the Rio label in 1965, by the ripe old age of 14. Between 1967 and 1968, he recorded 'Please Stop Your Lying', 'I'm Going Home', 'I'm Not Your Man' and 'You're Gonna Need Me' for Joe Gibbs, before switching to Coxsone Dodd in 1969 where he cut 'Satisfaction' and 'Get Up Now', among others.

In 1971 he recorded a medley of his Joe Gibbs hits, entitled 'Three In One', 'Deep Meditation' and 'Darling Ooh' for Rupie Edwards. In an attempt to achieve musical and financial autonomy he teamed up with fellow singer

Gregory Isaacs to form the African Museum label, achieving a local success with a version of Delroy Wilson's 'I Don't Know Why', retitled 'Movie Star'. However, the partnership collapsed and Dunkley went on to form his own Silver Ring label, although no hits were forthcoming. In 1972 producer Jimmy Radway recorded him on two of his best sides: 'Keep The Pressure On' and the big hit, 'Black Cinderella'. An album also emerged produced by Sonia Pottinger, entitled *Presenting Errol Dunkley* (re-released in 1981 as *Darling Ooh*), an excellent selection of originals and cover versions, including the classic, self-penned 'A Little Way Different'.

Throughout the first half of the 70s Dunkley appeared on a variety of labels, recording a number of fine singles including 'Little Angel', 'Oh Lord', 'Where Must I Go', 'Down Below' and 'Act True To Your Man'. The second half of the decade saw Dunkley gaining successes among the UK reggae fraternity with tunes such as 'I'm Your Man' and 'Eunoch Power' for Winston 'Niney' Holness, 'Stop Your Gun Shooting' for Tapper Zukie, and a new version of 'A Little Way Different' for Dennis Bovell. His biggest success, however, came in 1979 with his rendition of John Holt's naggingly catchy 'OK Fred', which appealed to the pop sensibilities of Britain's wider record-buying public, rising to number 11 in the UK national charts in September of that year, and leading to unforgettable performances on great British television institutions such as *Top Of The Pops* and *Basil Brush*. Further forays into pop chart success proved elusive and Dunkley, now resident in the UK, had to be satisfied with the continued grassroots popularity of records such as 'Happiness Forgets', 'Rush Me No Badness', 'If I Can't Have You', 'Come Natural' and a version of the Stylistics' 'Betcha By Golly Wow'.

● ALBUMS: *Presenting Errol Dunkley* (Gay Feet 1972)★★★★, *OK Fred* (Third World 1979)★★★, *Profile* (Third World 1980)★★★, *Special Request* (1987)★★, *Aquarius* (1989)★★★.

DYNAMITES

The Jamaican house band for producer Clancy Eccles during the early reggae years of the late 60s and early 70s, the Dynamites backed numerous Clan Disc artists, such as Eccles himself, Cynthia Richards and pioneer DJ King Stitt. Their line-up fluctuated, though its nucleus was Winston Wright (organ, piano), Hux Brown (guitar), Jackie Jackson (bass), Gladstone Anderson (piano) and Paul Douglas (drums). This combo, with added saxophones, recorded *Fire Corner* in 1969, a unique set of moody reggae instrumentals that also included King Stitt on the title track and 'Vigorton 2'.

● ALBUMS: with King Stitt *Fire Corner* (Trojan/Clandisc 1969)★★★★, with Clancy Eccles *Herbsman Reggae* (Trojan 1970)★★★★.

● COMPILATIONS: *The Wild Reggae Bunch* (Jamaican Gold 1997)★★★.

EARL SIXTEEN

b. Earl Daley, 1958, Kingston, Jamaica, West Indies. After winning local talent shows, Daley joined the group Flaming Phonics as lead vocalist before voicing the self-penned 'Malcolm X' for Joe Gibbs in 1975, later covered by Dennis Brown. In 1977 Daley became a member of the Boris Gardiner Happening who introduced him to Lee Perry at the Black Ark. There he recorded four tracks in 1978/9 and met Earl Morgan of the Heptones, who produced his debut album, *Singing Star*. His next collection was for the radio disc jockey and DATC producer Mikey Dread, although there were singles for Augustus Pablo ('Changing World'), Linval Thompson, Derrick Harriott and others, released throughout the early 80s, including an excellent set for former Stur-Gav duo Ranking Joe and Jah Screw. By 1982/3 he was at Studio One where his third version of 'Love Is A Feeling' was recorded. The previous two versions were for Aston 'Family Man' Barrett and Stafford Douglas; to date, it remains Earl Sixteen's most popular song. The Brentford Road sessions resulted in Coxsone Dodd's *Showcase* album of 1985. Shortly afterwards, he switched allegiance to former Royals founder Roy Cousins, then Skengdon and Blacka Dread ('Batman And Robin') and Bert Douglas ('Problems'). In 1988 after a two-year break, he resurfaced in England, covering Simply Red's 'Holding Back The Years' and making a short-lived attempt to produce himself. During 1991/2 he was at Ariwa, recording *Babylon Walls* and several fine singles for the Mad Professor. Since then he has voiced for a growing number of UK producers with varying degrees of success, and appeared on tracks by Dread Zone and Leftfield. He made his major label debut in 1997 with *Steppin' Out* for WEA.
● ALBUMS: *Shining Star* (Vista 1980)★★★, *Reggae Sounds* (DATC 1981)★★★, *Julie* (Roy Cousins 1982)★★★, *Special Request* (Roy Cousins 1983)★★★, *Super Duper* (Time 1986)★★★, *Showcase* (Studio One 1985)★★★★, *Babylon Walls* (Ariwa 1991)★★★, *Boss Man* (Carib Sounds 1992)★★★, *Not For Sale* (Next Step 1993)★★, *Phoenix Of Peace* (1993)★★, *Steppin' Out* (Warners 1997)★★★.

EARTH MESSENGERS

Back in the mid-70s, Vincent 'Vinnie' Taylor (b. c.1960, St. Anns, Jamaica, West Indies) was a Rasta youth seeking an outlet for his singing talents. That outlet arrived in 1976 when Taylor formed Vinnie Taylor And The Revealers, a roots vocal trio modelled along the lines of local heroes Burning Spear. The Revealers went to Spear's producer, Jack Ruby, who recorded their single 'Hard Times'. When it flopped, Taylor returned to grass roots, changing the group's name to Earth Messengers and acting as a channel for frustrated Ocho Rios youth talent. Among those who passed through Earth Messengers were Donovan Francis, later to sign to Island as a solo singer, and Errol Douglas, who later appeared in Foundation. In 1988 Ruby picked up on Earth Messengers, now comprising Vinnie Taylor, his brother Milton, and Bedster Henry, and they recorded *Ivory Towers*, which was critically well received but commercially unsuccessful. Persistence did not pay off for Taylor: further recordings were stymied when Ruby died of a heart attack in the spring of 1989, and Earth Messengers' current activities are unknown. They remain yet another unlucky reggae act.
● ALBUMS: *Ivory Towers* (Mango/Island 1989)★★★.

ECCLES, CLANCY

b. c.1940, Jamaica, West Indies. One of the most loved and respected personalities in the history of Jamaican music, Clancy Eccles started making records for Coxsone Dodd in 1959, recording 'Freedom', initially as an acetate that was featured on Dodd's sound system for nearly two years before its official release in 1961. For the same producer he also recorded the local hits 'River Jordan' and 'Glory Hallelujah'. He then provided 'Judgement' for Leslie Kong's business mentor Charlie Moo in late 1962. By the mid-60s he had completed three other records, 'Roam Jerusalem'/'Sammy No Dead', and 'Miss Ida' for Sonia Pottinger and 'I'm The Greatest' for Mike Shadeen. By 1967 he had started his own label, his first release being Eric 'Monty' Morris's local hit, 'Say What You're Saying'. During the next few years Eccles was one of reggae's leading producers. He was instrumental in helping Lee Perry to set up his own operation when that producer left Coxsone, arranging Perry's huge local hit, 'People Funny Boy', in 1968.

From 1969 Trojan Records released Eccles's productions on UK Clandisc. Records such as 'Fire Corner' by DJ King Stitt and the bawdy 'Fatty Fatty' by Eccles were very popular, not only with audiences in Jamaica and the Afro-Caribbean communities in North America and the UK, but also appealing to the British skinheads who followed Jamaican music at that time. In this period, utilizing his studio band the Dynamites, Eccles produced records by such artists as Alton Ellis, Lord Creator, the Fabulous Flames, Lee Perry, Larry Marshall, Joe Higgs, the Beltones, Busty Brown, Carl Dawkins and Cynthia Richards. He issued many records featuring his own vocals, singing either heartfelt love songs or stinging social comment. A lifelong socialist, Eccles has continued to record material on this theme right up to 1985, when he issued 'Mash Up We Country', a song that takes its place alongside such classics as the pro-PNP (People's National Party) anthem 'Rod Of Correction' (1972) and 'Generation Belly' (1976). Eccles was also an adviser to Michael Manley's PNP Government from 1972 on matters relating to the music business. He continues to release compilations of oldies, as well as the occasional new production. Eccles is the quintessential Jamaican producer, particularly in the attention he pays to his craft and his awareness of his audience's tastes.

● ALBUMS: *Freedom* (Trojan 1969)★★★, with the Dynamites *Herbsman Reggae* (Trojan 1970)★★★★, *Top Of The Ladder* (Top Of The Ladder 1973)★★★.
● COMPILATIONS: *Jamaica Reggae Volume 1* (1986)★★★★, *Reggae Vintage Volume 2* (1987)★★★, *Fatty Fatty 1967-1970* (Trojan 1988)★★★★, *Joshua's Rod Of Correction* (Jamaican Gold 1997)★★★.

EDWARDS, JACKIE

b. Wilfred Edwards, 1938, Jamaica, d. 15 August 1992. The honeyed tones of Jackie Edwards graced hundreds of ska, R&B, soul, rocksteady, reggae and ballad recordings since he composed and sang 'Your Eyes Are Dreaming', a sentimental ballad, and the gentle Latin-beat 'Tell Me Darling', for future Island Records owner Chris Blackwell in 1959. Probably the most accomplished romantic singer and songwriter that Jamaica ever produced, he always had enough soul in his voice to escape the descent into schmaltz. In 1962, when Blackwell set up Island Records in London, Edwards made the trip to Britain with him. At Island in the early years, his duties included not only singing and songwriting, but also delivering boxes of ska records by bus to the capital's suburban shops. His persistence paid off when, in 1966, the Spencer Davis Group enjoyed two consecutive UK number 1 pop hits with his now classic compositions, 'Keep On Running' and 'Somebody Help Me'. In more recent years he continued to issue records whose standards of production were variable, but on which his crooning justified his sobriquet of 'the original cool ruler'.

● ALBUMS: *The Most Of ...* (Island 1963)★★★, *Stand Up For Jesus* (Island 1964)★★★, *Come On Home* (Island 1966)★★★★, *By Demand* (Island 1967)★★★, *Premature Golden Sands* (Island 1967)★★★, with Millie Small *Pledging My Love* (1967)★★★, *I Do Love You* (Trojan 1973)★★★, with Hortense Ellis *Let It Be Me* (Jamaica Sound 1978)★★★, *Sincerely* (Trojan 1978)★★, *King Of The Ghetto* (Black Music 1983)★★, *Original Cool Ruler* (Vista Sounds 1983)★★.
● COMPILATIONS: *The Best Of* (Island 1966)★★★, with Millie Small *The Best Of Jackie & Millie* (1968)★★★.

EDWARDS, RUPIE

b. 4 July 1945, Goshen, near Brownstown, St. Anns, Jamaica, West Indies. Edwards found his first musical inspiration while attending the Anglican church school in Sergeantville as a seven-year-old. In early 1958 he moved to Kingston, where he attended Kingston Senior School and, like others of similar musical inclination, he formed a band with home-made instruments, bamboo saxophone and thumb piano, and performed at school concerts. In

1962 he had appeared on Vere John's *Opportunity Hour* and the same year he made four records, for the Hi-Lite label based at the Hi-Lite Haberdashery, and for the Little Wonder Music Store in Kingston. One title, 'Guilty Convict', was released in the UK on the Blue Beat label. Edwards was paid £15 for the session. He made two more records for President Bell's sound system, and then two further titles with Junior Menz, 'Mother's Choice' and a cover version of the Impressions' 'Amen'. By the mid-60s, Edwards was a member of the Virtues, again with Menz and guitarist Eric Frater.From 1968, Edwards began to release his own productions; the first was 'Burning Love', recorded at Studio One and engineered by Coxsone Dodd and Graham Goodall. This and other early productions enabled him to devote himself full-time to music and give up his job at a local garage, where he repaired cars owned by Dodd and Duke Reid.

By the early 70s Edwards had produced hits by himself and other artists, including Bob Andy, Joe Higgs, the Ethiopians and the Tellers, and had been instrumental in bringing the talents of Johnny Clarke and Gregory Isaacs to the attention of the public. He also recorded DJs such as the late U-Roy Junior, Shorty the President and I. Roy, as well as scores of excellent instrumentals by Jamaica's finest session musicians.In December 1974 Edwards' single 'Ire Feelings (Skanga)' entered the UK charts and stayed there for the next 10 weeks, eventually reaching number 9. The follow-up, 'Leggo Skanga', charted for six weeks from February 1975. During this period Edwards issued an entire album on which all the tracks used the same backing track. This concept subsequently became an important feature of Jamaican music. The album, *Yamaha Skank*, utilized a rhythm given to Edwards by producer Bunny Lee, Slim Smith's 'My Conversation'. Following his UK chart success, Edwards took up residence in London, continuing his operations from there up to the present day. He released a series of his own oldies in both 12-inch and album form and also leased some material to Creole during the 70s, though there were no further hits. Edwards continued to record material for the religious and sentimental love song markets, enjoying steady sales, and operating his own retail outlet.

● ALBUMS: *Yamaha Skank* (Success 1974)★★★★, *Rupie Edwards Dub Basket* (Cactus 1976)★★★★, *Dub Basket Chapter 2* (Cactus 1976)★★★, *Jamaica Serenade* (Cactus 1976)★★★, *Dub Classic* (Success 1977)★★★★, *Hit Picks Volume 1* (Cactus 1977)★★★, *Ire Feelings: Chapter & Version* (Trojan 1990)★★★, *Let There Be Version* (Trojan 1990)★★★.

EEK A MOUSE
b. Ripton Joseph Hilton, 1957, Kingston, Jamaica, West Indies. One of the most individual talents to emerge from Jamaica, Eek A Mouse's unique phrasing and singing style became as instantly recognizable as his 6 feet 6 inches frame. (Eek A Mouse was the name of a racehorse on which Hilton frequently lost money at the races; the one occasion on which he refused to back it, the horse, naturally, won.) His first two releases, 'My Father's Land' and 'Creation', were made under his real name in the mid-70s. After spells with the Papa Roots, Black Ark, Gemini, Jah Life, Black Scorpio and Virgo sound systems, he began recording with Joe Gibbs in 1980. 'Once A Virgin', 'Modelling Queen' and 'Virgin Girl' became sizeable hits the following year, by which time he had joined forces with producer and Volcano sound owner Henry 'Junjo' Lawes. Utilizing the Roots Radics at Channel One, with Scientist invariably mixing the final results, Lawes and Linval Thompson coaxed from the idiosyncratic DJ a series of bestselling albums and numerous hit singles throughout the years 1980-84. In 1981, following his debut album *Wa Do Dem*, he became the unexpected star of that year's Reggae Sunsplash.

In 1982 singles such as 'Ganja Smuggling', 'For Hire And Removal' and 'Do You Remember' maintained his rocketing profile, as did the album *Skidip*. 'Terrorists In The City', 'Anarexol' and 'Operation Eradication' - voiced in response to the death of his friend Errol Scorcher - all sold well, and *The Mouse And The Man* and *Assassinator* albums (not to mention several appearances on live dancehall albums) quickly followed in 1983. However, there were already signs that his distinctive trademark 'biddy biddy bengs' were becoming all too familiar. After *Mouseketeer* - the last of his albums with Lawes - his popularity began to wane despite the occasional good record and a steady reputation as a performing artist. *U-Neek* heralded a comeback in 1991 with tracks produced by Gussie Clarke, Daddy O and Matt Robinson. That year he enjoyed a walk-on part in the movie *New Jack City*, and recorded for both Wild Apache and former Channel One engineer, Soljie.

● ALBUMS: *Wa Do Dem* (Greensleeves 1981)★★★, *Skidip* (Greensleeves 1982)★★★, with Michigan And Smiley *Live At Reggae Sunsplash* (Sunsplash 1982)★, *The Mouse And The Man* (Greensleeves 1983)★★★, *Assassinator* (RAS 1983)★★★, *Mouseketeer* (Greensleeves 1984)★★, *King And I* (RAS 1987)★★, *U-Neek* (Mango/Island 1991)★★★.
● COMPILATIONS: *The Very Best Of Eek A Mouse* (Greensleeves 1987)★★★.

ELLIS, ALTON

b. 1944, Kingston, Jamaica, West Indies. Ellis, Jamaica's most soulful singer, celebrated 30 years in the business several years ago and yet he is still making important records. In many ways he epitomizes the story of reggae vocalists: a start in the business at a very early age, massive popularity for a limited period, and a gradual decline in prominence while continuing to make excellent records. In addition to his songwriting abilities and voice, Ellis's particular gift was his ability to take R&B or soul songs and place them in a specifically Jamaican context, and so make them 'reggae songs' rather than mere cover versions. Ellis was born into a musical family, and he first recorded in the late 50s as part of a duo with singer Eddy Perkins for Randys and Studio One as Alton And Eddy. They enjoyed some success in the R&B style and 'Muriel' was a massive hit for them. Perkins departed soon afterwards for a solo career and Alton continued with Studio One at Brentford Road, as well as working with Coxsone Dodd's arch-rival in the business, Duke Reid, at his Treasure Isle Studio in Bond Street, initially as Alton Ellis And The Flames. He came to undisputed prominence with the rise of rocksteady in 1965-66, when the ska beat slowed down and instrumental records became less important. This 'cool' music gave singers far greater freedom to express themselves - they no longer had to battle against the frantic ska pace and 'noisiness', and Alton Ellis reigned supreme - his

'Get Ready - Rock Steady' was one of the first records actually to use the term. Both Dodd and Reid made many classic records with Ellis as he moved between Brentford Road and Bond Street, but he recorded the definitive rocksteady album for Treasure Isle - *Mr Soul Of Jamaica* - while his Studio One output is collected on three albums, all of which have their high points.

In the late 60s and early 70s he went on to record for some of Jamaica's finest producers and he achieved two huge hit records for Lloyd Daley - 'Deliver Us' and 'Back To Africa', while a cover version of 'Too Late To Turn Back Now' that he made for Randys in the early 70s, has remained a firm favourite with the reggae audience ever since. He toured the UK in the 60s as a vocalist for Studio One's Soul Vendors band, and he returned to England in 1972, where he has based himself (intermittently) ever since. However, he has now sadly admitted his disillusionment with the reggae business. He accepts its machinations with a dignified resignation, just as in the early days when his songs were covered and no royalties were forthcoming: 'I was just proud that, whoever, would do an Alton Ellis song.' He was involved in the beginnings of Janet Kay's career and a cover version of one of his greatest songs, 'I'm Still In Love With You', formed the basis for Althea And Donna's 'Uptown Top Ranking' - a UK number 1 in 1978 - but his records and live shows are now few and far between.

● ALBUMS: *Sunday Coming* (Studio One)★★★, *Best Of Alton Ellis* (Studio One)★★★, *Sings Rock & Soul* (Studio One 1966)★★★★, *Love To Share* (Third World 1979)★★★, *Showcase* (Studio One 1980)★★, *25th Silver Jubilee* (Skynote 1984)★★★, *Still In Love* (Horse 1985)★★★, *Continuation* (All Tone 1985)★★★, *Jubilee Volume 2* (Sky Note 1985)★★★, *Here I Am* (Angella Records 1988)★★, *My Time Is Right* (Trojan 1990)★★★, *Sunday Coming* (Heartbeat 1995)★★★.
● COMPILATIONS: with Hortense Ellis *At Studio One* (Heartbeat 1993)★★★★ *Mr Soul Of Jamaica* (Treasure Isle) reissued as *Cry Tough* (Heartbeat 1993)★★★★, *Reggae Max* (Jet Star 1997)★★★★.

ELLIS, HORTENSE

b. 1949, Trenchtown, Jamaica, West Indies. Ellis began her career performing on the Vere Johns Opportunity Hour, where she appeared in six semi-finals and four finals demonstrating her vocal skills. Her own success has been over-shadowed by her brother Alton Ellis, who has often been quoted as the godfather of reggae. In 1964 she was awarded the honour of Jamaica's best female vocalist. She began recording with Ken Lack where she enjoyed hits with 'I Shall Sing' and 'Brown Girl In The Ring'. With Coxsone Dodd she recorded 'I'll Come Softly' and an interpretation of Alton's hit, 'I'm Just A Girl', both of which were greeted with enthu-siasm. Byron Lee enrolled her services to per-form with his band the Dragonaires and in 1969 she was again awarded the silver cup as the island's top female vocalist. She continued to record throughout the 70s. Much of her output was with Bunny Lee and in response to Althea And Donna's international hit 'Up Town Top Ranking', he recorded her as Queen Tiney for 'Down Town Ting', followed by the popular 'Natty Dread Time'. She recorded a cover version of another song that her brother had recorded at Studio One, 'Sitting In The Park', and the pop-ular 'Mark My Word'. A duet with her brother, 'Since I Fell For You', and 'Superstar' maintained her profile. With Gussie Clarke, she recorded 'Unexpected Places', a classic cut that demon-strated her extensive vocal range. In combina-tion with Jackie Edwards she had a hit with 'Let It Be Me', while as a soloist she released 'Got To Make It' and 'Time After Time'. Ellis proved an erratic performer who had to balance a career while raising her family. In 1993 she appeared with Bunny Lee in the television documentary *Stir It Up*, where she complained that slackness and gun lyrics were detrimental to the music and were a bad influence on young people.

● ALBUMS: *Jamaica's First Lady Of Song* (Third World 1977)★★★★, *Reflections* (Ballistic 1979)★★★, with Jackie Edwards *Let It Be Me* (Jamaica Sound 1978)★★★, with Johnny Clarke, Pat Kelly *Lover's Rock* (Third World 1979)★★★, *Feelings* (1989)★★.

● COMPILATIONS: with Alton Ellis *At Studio One* (Heartbeat 1993)★★★★.

ENGLISH, JUNIOR

b. Lindel Beresford English, 1951, Kingston, Jamaica, West Indies. English began performing in his teens and in 1965 he recorded 'Fay Is Gone' for Prince Buster. He arrived in the UK in the latter half of the 60s where he completed his education. He entered and won a talent contest run by the Palmer brothers, noted for their con-tribution to the UK reggae scene with Pama Records and later Jet Star, at the popular Club 31. His success led to him joining a band called the Magnets, with whom he recorded 'Somewhere'. The preference for Jamaican reggae thwarted his career and he spent the late 60s performing with the group on a European tour. On his return he joined another band, the Nighthawks, releasing 'Jasmine' and an obscure album. By 1970 he returned to the UK where he recorded 'Miss Playgirl', 'Daniel', 'I Don't Wanna Die' and the popular 'Back On The Scene'. He enjoyed a prolific run of hits with Clement Bushay, who produced 'Never Lose Never Win', which provided the backing to the combination hit for Trinity and Dillinger, 'Starsky & Hutch'. The song led to an album of the same name fea-turing accomplished versions of Delano Stewart's 'Stay A Little Bit Longer', the Chi-Lites' 'Bet You'll Never Be Sorry', Matumbi's 'After Tonight' and the Royal Rasses' 'Humanity'. With Bushay, he released the classic 'In Loving You', which, although released in October, had the distinction of being 1978's Christmas number 1 on the UK reggae charts. The success of the single was acknowledged when he won the Afro-Caribbean Post Golden Sunrise Award for best male vocalist in the same year. He maintained a high profile with 'Natural High', which was equally successful, lending its title to his second album for Bushay. The compilation was a self-production recorded at Channel One Studios with the Revolutionaries. In 1979 his credibility increased with the release of 'I'll Make It Up To You', securing a respectable position in the reggae charts alongside 'Love And Key' and 'I Am The One You Love'. He continued to release hit singles throughout the 80s, including 'Daddy's Home', 'Equal Love' and the popular 'Ready To Learn', which surfaced on his own International English label. In 1985 English was one of the many performers who featured on the British Reggae Artists Famine Appeal release

'Let's Make Africa Green Again'. In the 90s he maintained his profile, covering 'Queen Majesty', 'Cruising', 'Ready To Learn' and other popular standards.

● ALBUMS: with the Nighthawks *Man It's Reggae* (Saga 1969)★★★, *Back On The Scene* (Trojan 1975)★★★, *The Dynamic Junior English* (Cactus 1976)★★★, *Never Lose Never Win* (Burning Sounds 1977)★★★, *Naturally High* (Burning Sounds 1978)★★, *Lovers Key* (International English 1980)★★★, *Mr. Man* (International English 1990)★★★.

ENGLISHMAN

b. Erald Brisco. Raised in the UK, Englishman, despite his adopted name, has actually spent the majority of his years in Washington, DC, USA. He first recorded as a teenager with the London-based Revelation Reggae Band. By the time of his 18th birthday he was to be found touring Europe alongside Ras Michael. He has gone on to release a slew of albums, most backed by his own six-piece Roots Vibration Band, that have attracted a sizeable American audience. His rich delivery has often been compared to that of Nat 'King' Cole, while his bass guitar skills are credited to the influences of Robbie Shakespeare and Paul McCartney.

● ALBUMS: *My African Sister* (1988)★★★, *Check For The Youth* (1988)★★★.

● COMPILATIONS: *Check For The Best* comprises selections from *My African Sister* and *Check For The Youth* (Mad Dawg 1991)★★★★.

ETHIOPIANS

The Ethiopians were originally a trio comprising Leonard 'Sparrow' Dillon (b 1945, Portland, Jamaica, West Indies), Stephen Taylor (b. 1944, St. Mary, Jamaica, d. 1975) and Aston Morris. Prior to their formation in 1966, Dillon had recorded a series of ska/mento titles for the seminal Jamaican producer Coxsone Dodd under the name of Jack Sparrow, including 'Ice Water' and 'Suffering On The Land' (1965). In late 1966 Morris left, and the duo of Dillon and Taylor began recording for Dodd as the Ethiopians, mostly in a style that bridged ska and rocksteady. Titles recorded during late 1966 and early 1967 included 'Free Man', 'Live Good', 'Owe Me No Pay Me', 'I'm Gonna Take Over Now' and 'Dun Dead Already'. After leaving

Dodd they recorded at Dynamic Studios for the WIRL label, enjoying massive local hits with the rocksteady 'Train To Skaville' (1967), and the title track of their first album, *Engine 54*. In late 1967 they recorded for Sonia Pottinger's Gayfeet label including 'Stay Loose Mama', 'The Whip' and 'Train To Glory'. They also worked with Lee Perry and his fledgling company, releasing 'Cut Down' and 'Not Me'. By 1968 they had begun an association with producer J.J. Johnson that turned out to be their most consistent, comprising a series of quintessential Jamaican vocal records that remain emblematic of the then new beat of reggae's first phase. As well as being great dance tunes, their lyrics had begun to reflect and criticize ghetto life. Rasta themes also received an airing. Their first big hit for Johnson, 'Everything Crash', was an incisive look at the post-colonial legacy and a classic rhythm. Many further titles were recorded for Johnson during 1968-71, including 'What A Fire', 'Gun Man', 'Hong Kong Flu', 'Woman Capture Man', 'The Selah', and many others. From 1969 they began to work with other producers; in that same year they had success with 'Fire A Mus' Mus' Tail' and 'Reggae Hit The Town' for H. Robinson. In 1970 they made 'Satan Girl' for Lloyd Daley, titles for Derrick Harriott - 'Lot's Wife', 'No Baptism' and 'Good Ambition' - and sessions at Duke Reid's Treasure Isle Studios produced 'Mother's Tender Care', 'Condition Bad A Yard' and 'Pirate' (1971). They continued recording with many other label owners, including Randy's (1971), Winston Riley (1972), Alvin 'GG' Ranglin (1972), Joe Gibbs (1971, 1975), Rupie Edwards (1972-73), Harry J. (1972) and Lee Perry again (1973).

In 1975 Stephen Taylor died in a car crash, and Dillon continued alone, occasionally using session singers, including members of the Cordells. In 1977 Winston 'Niney' Holness produced a solid Rasta-based album entitled *Slave Call*. 'Open The Gate Of Zion' was recorded in 1978 at Channel One, with Sly Dunbar, Robbie Shakespeare and the Revolutionaries. Dillon returned to Dodd for the release of *Everything Crash*. This was a mature, rootsy set with new versions of the title song and 'No Baptism', and excellent new songs based on vintage Studio One rhythms. The late 70s saw the release of more 45s for Dodd, followed by a break until a lively self-produced reissue of 'Pirate' surfaced in 1986. Since then, Dillon has worked with new members Harold Bishop and former Burning Spear drummer, Neville Duncan.

● ALBUMS: *Engine 54* (WIRL 1968)★★★★, *Reggae Power* (Trojan 1969)★★★, *Woman Capture Man* (Trojan 1970)★★★, *Slave Call* (Third World 1977)★★★, *Open The Gate Of Zion* (GG's 1978)★★★, *Everything Crash* (Studio One 1979)★★★, *Dread Prophecy* (Night Hawk 1986)★★★, *The World Goes Ska* (1993)★★★.

● COMPILATIONS: *Original Reggae Hit Sound* (Trojan 1986)★★★, *Owner Fe De Yard* (Heartbeat 1995)★★★★.

EXTERMINATOR

Record label run by Philip 'Fatis' Burrell (b. Kingston, Jamaica, West Indies). It took Burrell a decade to become one of Jamaica's leading producers of the 90s. He was born in Trenchtown but spent part of his childhood in England before returning to Jamaica in his teens. George Phang and Robbie Shakespeare encouraged him to take up production, his first release being Sugar Minott's 'More Dogs To The Bone' in 1984, the year his short-lived Kings & Lions label made its appearance. *The Summit* was an early dub album featuring the rhythms of Sly And Robbie, although it was King Tubby's Firehouse Crew who played on most subsequent recordings at either Dynamics or Music Works. By 1987 he had founded the Vena label, and discovered Sanchez, Pinchers and Thriller U, all of whom featured on the label with some of their earliest works. Frankie Paul and Red Dragon both voiced hit tracks, and sampler albums from 1988 reveal established names such as Gregory Isaacs, Charlie Chaplin and General Trees rubbing shoulders with Burrell protégés such as Quench Aid, Lukie D, Conrad Crystal and Daddy Freddy, whose 1989 *Cater Fi She* album for Burrell was his debut. That same year saw the introduction of 'live' dancehall sets, and some seriously militant marketing of the Exterminator label, which mirrored the hard, driving rhythm tracks and often uncompromising material found on it.

Throughout 1990-91 artists of the calibre of Ninjaman, Ini Kamoze ('Hot Stepper'), Cocoa Tea, Admiral Tibet, Tony Rebel ('Real Rough'), Frankie Paul, Gregory Isaacs, Beres Hammond ('Emptiness Inside'), Johnny Osbourne and Tiger - whose *Ready Fi Dem* was released the following year - appeared as part of Burrell's roster. He also issued a similarly prolific number of exceptional releases in the following two years, beginning with Capleton's 'Armshouse' (which spawned two version albums) and culminating in long-players by Cocoa Tea, Sugar Minott, Pinchers, Sanchez, Luciano and Beres Hammond, whose *Full Attention* crowned a richly creative body of work for Burrell. Dennis Brown, Yammie Bolo, Nadine Sutherland, Cocoa Tea, Buju Banton, General Degree, Chaka Demus And Pliers, Singing Sweet, Marcia Griffiths and Brian and Tony Gold all voiced excellent tracks for Exterminator between 1993 and 1994, arguing that the long-term potential of the Exterminator empire remains huge. Whether creating classic rhythms from the past or breaking new ground with adventurous hardcore beats, Burrell's standards remain impeccable.

● COMPILATIONS: Various *Exterminator Volumes 1 & 2* (Exterminator 1988)★★★★, *Turn On The Heat* (Exterminator 1989)★★★★, *Exterminator Live Volumes 1 & 2* (Exterminator 1989)★★★★, *Exterminator Presents* (Exterminator 1990)★★★.

FABULOUS FIVE INC.

The Fabulous Five Inc. were initially a show-band supporting various singers in Jamaica. Lloyd Lovindeer and Glen Ricks both began their careers performing in the Fabulous Flames before enlisting in the group's line-up. The band formed in the late 60s and in the ensuing years received numerous awards in Jamaica, being voted the top band for three consecutive years by *Swing* magazine. They were the featured musicians on Johnny Nash's *I Can See Clearly Now*, which introduced authentic reggae rhythms to a global audience. In 1972 they recorded 'Come Back And Stay', which was a popular hit within the reggae community, with two cuts of the same song being available. The preferred version included an introduction from Scotty, who stated: 'Heartbreak in the first degree'. The success of the single led to the release of *Fabulous Five Inc.*, produced by John Templar and Junior Lincoln. The album featured the hit single along with versions of Bob Marley's 'Guava Jelly' and Lloyd Parks' 'Officially'. They also demonstrated their versatility with a version of the Skatalites hit, 'Lee Oswald', the DJ-styled 'Nanny Skank', and a calypso tune, 'That's The Time She Go Love You'. They were able to exhibit their musical talents when they toured the island backing performers in the 1975 Jamaican Song Festival. The winner was Roman Stewart with 'Hooray Festival', who toured alongside Freddie McKay, Johnny Clarke, Jackie Edwards and the Silvertones. In 1976 the group recorded the lewd 'Shaving Cream', which maintained their popularity. Following the release of 'My Jamaican Girl', little was heard of the group until 1982 when Island Records released the group's recording of 'Ooh Ah', backed with Lee Perry's 'Dreadlocks In The Moonlight' from the soundtrack *Countryman*. Through to the 90s, the group provided backing for a number of performers, often touring with the Jamaica Song Festival finalists; they also notched up a number of local awards and released sporadic output through their own Stage Records. Following his departure from the group, Lloyd recorded as Lovindeer and enjoyed many hits, notably 'Man Shortage', 'Wash Wash' and, with Shabba Ranks, 'Manhunt'. Lovindeer's career proved the most commercially successful with a string of releases, *Government Boops*, *Bad Boy Crew*, *Your Boss DJ*, *Dirty Dancing Dollar Winds* volumes one and two, and *Snookie Nookie Nookie Sayonara*. In 1995 Lovindeer responded to Beenie Man's popular 'Slam' with 'Slam Fashion' and 'Slam Of The Century'. He also wrote and produced a UK chart hit for Pam Hall, 'Dear Boopsie', in the 80s. Glen Ricks' solo career included *Ready For Love* and *Fall In Love*.

● ALBUMS: *Fabulous Five Inc.* (Ashanti 1973)★★★, *My Jamaican Girl* (Trojan 1975)★★★★, *Yu Safe* (Stage 1986)★★★, *All Night Party* (Stage 1989)★★.

● COMPILATIONS: *The Best Of Fab 5* (Stage 1996)★★★.

FABULOUS FLAMES

The Fabulous Flames were initially a dance troupe performing choreographed routines alongside Byron Lee And The Dragonaires on Jamaica's north coast. The group featured Lovindeer, Kirk Salmon and Oswald 'Dougie' Douglas. Their rhythmic cavorting led to deserved distinction, and they were enrolled to perform with Carlos Malcom And His Afro Caribs, accompanying the band on a tour of the West Indies. In 1969 they were invited to demonstrate their agility at the Caribana festival in Canada, which led to further engagements. The group secured a concert in Toronto's famed Yonge Street where they met and performed alongside Glen Ricks, who was persuaded to join the group. Ricks returned to Jamaica with the Flames, where, with producer Clancy Eccles, they recorded Neil Diamond's 'Holly Holy'. The organ-led song, driven by a creeping rhythm, was an instant hit and the band became the mainstay of the Clandisc label. The success of the single led Prince Buster to utilize an identical rhythm for his lewd interpretation, 'Holy Fishey'. When released in the UK the original song almost crossed into the pop chart and featured Lord Creator's 'Kingston Town' on the b-side. 'Kingston Town' was later included on UB40's multi-million-selling *Labour Of Love II* and topped the UK chart in 1990 when released as a single. Subsequent hits for the Flames included the melancholy 'Growing Up' and, conversely, the blithe 'Hi De High'. By the early 70s the members went their own separate ways. Lovindeer and Ricks joined the Fabulous Five Inc. before pursuing solo careers, and the remaining two members relocated to Canada. In the 80s Salmon returned to his musical career when he played guitar in a Canadian-based band, Livestock.

FASHEK, MAJEK

b. Majekodunmi Fasheke, Lagos, Nigeria. Fashek is one of the increasing number of African artists to be drawn to the music of the Caribbean, specifically reggae, rather than indigenous hybrids such as fuji, juju or highlife. Having grown up in a fervently religious and musical family, he was exposed to the imported sounds of Bob Marley at an early age, alongside the innovations of local stars such as Fela Kuti. After learning to play the guitar he made his first notable appearance on a television show in the early 80s, before spending the rest of the decade touring Nigeria with the Mandators. He left that group in 1987 and quickly fashioned a solo career that made him Nigeria's biggest reggae star. Following the receipt of no less than six awards at the annual PMAN ceremony, he was signed to CBS Nigeria in 1988. However, soon afterwards he transferred to Island Records' subsidiary Mango, a label more accustomed to marketing reggae internationally. His first album for the company included a cover version of Marley's 'Redemption Song'. It saw him begin to rival Alpha Blondy as Africa's foremost reggae star.
● ALBUMS: *I & I Experience* (CBS Nigeria 1989)★★★, *Prisoner Of Conscience* (Mango 1990)★★★★.

FASHION RECORDS

Founded in the summer of 1980, Fashion Records has been a rare success among UK-based reggae labels, and alongside rival Ariwa, remains the only studio-owning, domestic-producing company to have survived since the early 80s. The label is the brainchild of John MacGillivray and Chris Lane, two reggae devotees, and is essentially a spin-off from MacGillivray's Dub Vendor record store. The first Fashion release reached number 1 in the UK reggae charts in 1980 – Dee Sharp's 'Let's Dub It Up', with south London lovers rock band the Investigators supplying the rhythms (Lane had previously produced a couple of singles for the band as the Private I's). 'Let's Dub It Up' provided a benchmark in British reggae and set a standard that Fashion, incredibly, nearly always fulfilled: fine, classy harmonies, punchy rhythms, bright arrangements and, above all else, strong songs. In the next few years a veritable who's who of British reggae, and those passing through from Jamaica, appeared on the label: Keith Douglas, Carlton Manning (of Carlton And His Shoes), Alton Ellis and Carlton Lewis, among many others. In 1982 Fashion opened a four-track studio, A-Class, in the basement of the new Dub Vendor shop at Clapham Junction. By this time, the UK MC explosion had begun, and Fashion were at the centre of it with chatters Papa Face, Laurel And Hardy, Pato Banton, Bionic Rhona, Macka B and Asher Senator. A dub-cutting service saw Paul Robinson of One Blood and Maxi Priest's 'Caution' band (Lane was also a member, as was Priest himself) as regulars at the tiny subterranean studio. Robinson soon enjoyed hits with the label as 'Barry Boom', and the company was rarely out of the specialist charts. Chirpy, fast-talking MC Smiley Culture had one of the biggest reggae hits of 1984 on the label with 'Cockney Translation', but bettered it when 'Police Officer' went top 12 in the national charts, as several Fashion band regulars frightened Britain on *Top Of The Pops*. Their connection with the UK MC boom made the step into ragga in the mid-80s a comparatively natural one. Meanwhile, Fashion was also cutting lovers rock hits through Michael Gordon and the underrated Nerious Joseph, often coming out on another label, Fine Style. Two female acts were also recruited, Winsome and Shako Lee (Janet Lee Davis). Winsome's 'Am I The Same Girl', 'Born Free' and 'Super Woman' (with Tippa Irie) proved themselves classics of their type. Fashion also began to work with a variety of Jamaican acts, including Junior Delgado,

Joseph Cotton ('No Touch The Style'), Leroy Gibbon, Frankie Paul, Glen Brown and Augustus Pablo.

In 1988 the label opened the new A-Class Studio, a sixteen-track set-up in Forest Hill, and began to use tracks laid at Penthouse Studios in Jamaica, voicing and mixing them in London. In 1989/90 the label produced a string of reggae chart hits, with Shako Lee's 'Two Timing Lover' and Cutty Ranks' 'The Stopper' both hitting number 1. Fashion also became involved in distribution of other labels, such as Mafia And Fluxy's M&F, Paul Robinson's Merger, Captain Sinbad's Sinbad and Gussie Prento's Gussie P. The label now stands virtually alone in British reggae as an entity capable of working with almost all of the modern strands of the music. A long-awaited second pop chart success, Louchie Lou And Michie One's inspired ragga cover version of the Isley's 'Shout', licensed to ffrr, and the rise of General Levy, also leased to ffrr and perhaps the most accomplished UK ragga rapper yet, should ensure that the label's future remains secure into the next century.

● COMPILATIONS: various artists *Great British MCs* (Fashion 1985)★★★, *JA To UK MC Clash Volume 2 - Papa San Meets Tippa Irie* (Fashion 1988)★★★★, *Fashion Revives Classic Lovers* (Fashion 1989)★★★, *Fashion Revives Classic Lovers Volume 2* (Fashion 1988)★★, *Jamaica's Finest Volume 1* (Fashion 1990)★★★★, *Funky Punany* (Fashion 1990)★★★.

FFRENCH, ROBERT

Ffrench first achieved notoriety when he performed 'In My Heart There Is A Song' at the 1984 Jamaican Song Festival. In the same year he performed at the Reggae Sunsplash festival in Jarret Park, Montego Bay, where he wooed the crowds with his interpretation of the popular dance craze 'Shoulder Move'. His recording career gained momentum when he performed alongside the frequently extolled DJ Clement Irie for the hit 'Bun And Cheese'. The song proved internationally successful, leading to a one-rhythm album of the same name. Ffrench continued to record throughout the 90s, including a cover version of the R&B hit 'Earth Angel', 'Too Young' and 'Modern Girl'. Throughout the late 80s he endorsed his reputation as a writer and arranger with artists,

including Johnny P for the popular 'Stamina', Clement Irie with 'Stop It' as well as Pliers and Henkel Irie. Following on from the success of his 1994 hit, 'More Love', with rapper Heavy D, the duo signed with Doctor Dread's Washington-based RAS label for a one-album contract. By the end of 1995, Ffrench performed with Junior Reid on the highly acclaimed One Blood tour of the USA alongside Big Youth. A year later, inspired by his earlier celebrated collaboration, he teamed up with another rapper, Grand Puba, who had recorded with Shaggy, and Jeff Redd for the R&B-styled 'Cry No More'.

● ALBUMS: with Frankie Paul *Reggae For The World* (Sonic 1990)★★★, with various artists *Robert Ffrench, Heavy D And Friends* (RAS 1995)★★★.

15·16·17

15-16-17 were a female vocal trio formed in 1974 in the UK, although they came from Jamaica. The line-up consisted of Sonia Williams (b. 1959), Christine McNabb (b. 1958) and her sister Wraydette McNabb (b. 1957). They entered a talent contest at the Georgian club in Croydon, Surrey, England, performing as the Gorgon Sisters, but changed to 15-16-17 (the name reflecting the girls' ages) on the advice of the owner of the club, Castro Brown. They won the contest for two weeks in a row with a cover version of Lousia Mark's lovers rock track, 'Caught You In A Lie'. With Brown producing, the group recorded 'If You Love Me Smile' and 'Black Skin Boy', which featured Dennis Bovell. The singles surfaced on Castro Brown's Morpheus label which enjoyed considerable support from his patriarchal colleague Dennis Brown. When the label folded in 1976, the trio suffered a setback, but loyally remained with Castro Brown. In 1977 a partnership was formed with Dennis Brown and the D.E.B. (Dennis Emmanuel Brown) label was set up. Castro produced their cover version of the Temptations track 'Just My Imagination' as 'Girls Imagination'. The track was also featured on a DEB showcase compilation *Black Echoes*, promoted by the weekly music journal of the same name. The single was an instant hit in the reggae charts and was followed by the equally popular 'Suddenly Happiness'. In 1978 they released 'Emotions', 'Good Times' and 'Someone Special'. Following an association with

Pablo Black and Oneness the girls changed their style for the release of 'I'm Hurt', which was closer to roots than the lovers style for which they were renowned. They also undertook several live appearances touring Italy with the Wreckless Breed and supporting Gregory Isaacs on his UK tour. By the early 80s the group disbanded, although Christine went on to pursue a solo career and Castro Brown set up his New Name Music label. In 1984 'Girls Imagination' was re-released.

● ALBUMS: *Good Times* (DEB 1979)★★★.

FITZROY, EDI

b. 1958, Clarendon, Jamaica, West Indies. Fitzroy, like many teenagers, followed the sound systems, in particular, a sound called Anchio One. After leaving school he started a career with the Jamaican Broadcasting Corporation working as an accounts clerk. With a colleague, in his spare time he would often sing over dubs and play them back using the radio station's equipment. In 1975 Mikey Dread was the station's top disc jockey, playing reggae on his *Dread At The Controls Show*, and he heard Fitzroy's demos. Fitzroy's first hit, 'Miss Molly Colly', broke into the Jamaican Top 10 as the result of Dread's patronage, and the follow-up, 'Country Man', confirmed him as Dread's protégé. The hits kept coming, including 'African Religion', 'Gun' and 'Stylee', leading to a tour of the UK with Dread in 1980 supporting punk group The Clash. On returning to Jamaica Fitzroy began working with other producers, firstly Lloyd Norris, with whom he recorded 'Bad Boy', a minor hit when released in 1981. With Trevor Elliot of Musical Ambassador he recorded an album, and enjoyed a massive hit with 'Check For You Once', followed by 'Youth Man In Penitentiary' (when interviewed on the radio in Jamaica, he stated categorically that the song was not inspired by personal experience) and 'Have You Ever'. His success led to a performance at the 1984 Sunsplash Festival and his commitment to equality for women led to an appearance at Zinc Fence in Kingston on International Women's Day. His commitment was evident in the hit 'Princess Black', and he was also dubbed Jamaica's most socially conscious singer. His follow-up, a reworking of 'The Gun', enjoyed a prolonged stay on the chart,

breaking all previous records for longevity. In the series of charity records to help the starving in Ethiopia, Fitzroy performed on Jamaica's contribution, 'Land Of Africa'. He provided the vocals alongside Gregory Isaacs, Freddie McGregor, Mutabaruka, Triston Palmer, Bunny Rugs, David Hinds and the I Threes. The artists involved were determined to help to alleviate the situation and formed the Music Is Life organization to emphasize their commitment. However, the single alone was regarded by the collective as an insufficient gesture towards relieving Africa's dilemma. Fitzroy became a co-director alongside Rita Marley, Judy Mowatt, Ibo Cooper and Orville Tyson, and between them, they established other projects. His recordings and Music Is Life commitments were undertaken alongside his career at JBC.

● ALBUMS: *Check For You Once* (Alligator 1986)★★★, *Eclipse* (RAS 1987), *Coming Up Strong* (Musical Ambassador 1988)★★, *Pollution* (VP 1990)★★★.

FLOURGON

b. Michael May, Kingston, Jamaica, West Indies. May began his career on the sound system circuit, performing with Stone Love, Small Axe, Rambo Mango and his own Sweet Love set. He often performed alongside his DJ sibling, Red Dragon, with whom he nurtured the careers of Buju Banton and Terry Ganzie. May released a succession of combination hits, including 'How You So Hot' with Brian And Tony Gold, 'Girls Just Wanna Have Fun' with Thriller U, 'Go Sit Down' with Clement Irie, 'Dungle Lover' and 'Madly In Love' with Sanchez, 'Jump And Spread Out' and 'Turn And Stab' with Daddy Lizard, alongside the favoured 'Million And More' and the chart-topping 'Zig It Up', both of which featured the enigmatic Ninjaman. Following May's successful combination with the controversial DJ, Ninjaman curiously released the contemptuous 'Last Of The Flourgon'. The latter, however, had little impact on Flourgon's career and his distinctive gritty voice continued to grace a profusion of vinyl releases. He enjoyed a notable partnership with Mikey Bennett and Patrick Lindsay, primarily for his version of the 'Oil Thing' rhythm, 'Bow Ting'. Other solo hits included 'Tender Touch', 'Bounce', 'Fret And Worry', 'Trophy', 'Live Good',

'Bad Boy Tune' and 'Follow Me'. In 1994 Jamaican producers, inspired by the dancehall trend of mixing various DJs over the same rhythm, began recording various artist singles that often featured Flourgon, including 'Can't Stop The Dance', performed by the 'Yardcore collective', which incorporated the talents of General Degree, Tony Rebel, Papa San and Buju Banton, among others, while 'Informer' featured Snagga Puss, Anthony Malvo, Anthony Red Rose, Frankie Paul, Lizard and Flourgon's brother Red Dragon. By the late 90s his output was lost in the flood of dancehall releases, although his combination with Freddie McGregor, 'Bless My Soul', enjoyed some success. Although his career has been somewhat overtaken by the young contenders, Flourgon is regarded as an influential DJ who inspired a wave of sonorous vocalists.

● ALBUMS: *Red Dragon Vs Flourgon* (Techniques 1989)★★★.

FOLKS BROTHERS

To be labelled a one-hit-wonder is generally something of an insult, but to be a one-record-wonder is an accolade. The Jamaican artists who have made one perfect recording and then vanished, leaving a reputation forever untarnished by later lapses, could be counted on the fingers of one hand. The Folks Brothers are among that number: in 1961 or early 1962 they recorded 'Oh Carolina', a unique and perfect single, and never appeared again. The record has Count Ossie's Rastafarian drummers thundering out complex African cross-rhythms, Owen Gray contrastingly American-styled on piano, and the Brothers, a soulful lead singer and two lighter-voiced male accompanists, delivering the song. In 1993 an updated version of 'Oh Carolina' reached number 1 in the UK charts for Shaggy.

FONTAINE, CLAUDIA

b. 1961, London, England. Fontaine began her career in her early teens, initially providing backing vocals on various recording sessions. She joined a number of lovers rock trios, including Mellow Rose, One Love and True Harmony, before emerging as a soloist. In 1981 she recorded her version of Bloodstone's classic R&B ballad, 'Natural High', with producer Junior Boothe. The song became a popular lovers rock hit and was licensed to a major label, although with little success, and the follow-up, 'Not A Little Girl Any More', failed to make any impact. Fontaine continued in session work, providing backing vocals for Keith Douglas, Tony Tuff and King Sounds, and in 1982 she joined La Famile, singing lead vocals alongside Brown Sugar and Soul II Soul vocalist Caron Wheeler. The group recorded the 1982 disco hit 'Dancer', followed by the acclaimed 'All Night Long'. In 1983 she teamed up with Raymond Simpson as Raymond And Claudia, and the duo recorded versions of George Benson's 'Turn Your Love Around' and Jermaine Jackson's 'Paradise In Your Eyes'. The former was commercially successful, prompting a return to the studio for 'Is It Always Gonna Be Like This'. Fontaine maintained her connections with La Famile, provided backing vocals on the Jam's farewell tour, and pursued a career in journalism on *West Indian World*.

FORRESTER, SHARON

b. 1956, Kingston, Jamaica, West Indies. Forrester's vocals were nurtured by singing from the age of six in church choirs. She came from a musical background: her father played guitar and sang, her brother was a gospel singer based in the USA, and her sister was a vocalist in a group called the Peter Ashburn Affair. Following a performance at her school of the Supremes' 'Baby Love', she was inspired to embark on a musical career, performing to tourists on the north coast of Jamaica. Her performances led to a television appearance in Jamaica alongside Richard Ace, and an introduction to Geoffrey Chung of the Now Generation Band. Chung had performed alongside Forrester's sister in the Peter Ashburn Affair and she introduced him to Sharon. Impressed by her vocal range he took her into the studio in the spring of 1973, and they covered Valerie Simpson's 'Silly Wasn't I' with backing provided by the Now Generation. In November of the same year, Forrester appeared alongside the Wailers for The Ethiopian Benefit Concert - predating Live Aid by more than a decade. The single was not a big hit, but Chung remained undeterred and in 1974, because of the musicians strike in Jamaica, he took the young singer to the UK to complete the album *Sharon*. Tracks included a cover version of Smokey Robinson's 'Holly', 'Words With No Meaning' and 'Put A Little Love Away', which was lifted for release on the Vulcan label. While in the UK, she also appeared alongside Danny Ray in a film, *Moon Over The Alley*, made by the British Film Institute. Forrester's career was showing potential when in the autumn of 1974 she appeared alongside Al Brown, Cynthia Richards, Dennis Brown, the Maytals and Count Prince Miller as part of the blighted Jamaica Showcase tour. Junior Lincoln, the man behind Ashanti, and Chung were both enthusiastic about Forrester's capability, but but she failed to achieve the commercial success expected of her. She appeared in the UK television programme *Aquarius*, performing George Harrison's 'Here Comes The Sun' (her single at the time). Though the occasional recording surfaced, Forrester faded into obscurity. During this period she continued with studio session work, providing back-up vocals on a variety of productions. It was not until 1994 that she resurfaced performing 'Love Inside' over a jungle rhythm for the FFRR label, which bubbled under the UK Top 40 in the spring of 1995. Other releases emerged, 'Dreams' and 'Heaven', both of which were included on the appropriately titled *This Time*. In the spring of 1996 she was managed by the newly formed Sandosa group in Jamaica. A major label contract with Zomba/BMG resulted in the release of 'Red Rose' in combination with Papa San. The lyrics were penned by B.B. Seaton, and the melody was a version of 'Telstar', a 60s hit for the Tornadoes. Ernest Ranglin played guitar and the single was produced by Steely And Clevie. With all the credentials for a crossover hit, it was surprisingly still ignored by the mainstream media.

● ALBUMS: *Sharon* (Ashanti 1974)★★★, *This Time* (Steely And Clevie 1996)★★★.

FRANCIS, WINSTON

b. 1948, Kingston, Jamaica, West Indies. Francis attended school in Jamaica and began an apprenticeship in the printing trade before relocating to Miami at the age of 16. In Miami he attended a music school where his teacher, the impresario, writer and performer Chuck Bird, likened his vocals to those of Nat 'King' Cole. Bird arranged a performance at the Fountain Blue Hotel in Miami in 1965 with the Jackie Gleason Orchestra, witnessed by noted US politician Spiro Agnew. Francis began his career in earnest, performing with Carlos Malcom alongside Derrick Harriott and Boris Gardiner, touring the USA and Caribbean. His recording career began at Studio One where he made a number of classic rocksteady hits, including a version of Joe South's 'Games People Play', and the captivating 'Reggae And Cry', while in combination with Alton Ellis he covered Junior Walker's 'What Does It Take'. He had also recorded with producer Joe Gibbs as part of the Mellowtones, noted for their hit 'Feel Good'. In 1971 he relocated to the UK to promote his version of the Mamas And The Papas' 'California Dreaming', which was chosen as record of the week for two consecutive weeks on national radio. The b-side, 'Too Experienced', featured falsetto backing vocals from Bob Marley and Bunny Wailer. In 1972 Francis began touring the club circuit and recorded sessions for EMI Records, including 'Follow Your Star' and a version of 'Blue Moon'. Throughout the 70s he recorded a number of sessions in the UK, including a remake of 'California Dreaming' with Danny Ray. Between 1980 and 1986 he took a sabbatical from the music business and worked as a youth leader and social worker. He was coaxed back into the recording studio in 1987 when he sang backing vocals for the Melodians and performed for Trevor Star and the Skaticians, with whom he still sings. In 1993 Francis was approached by Dennis Bovell to record as a soul performer under the pseudonym of King Cool for the compilation *Jamaican Soul*. He became a prominent performer in France when his interpretation of Ben E. King's 'Stand By Me' was released as a single, selling in excess of 90,000 copies. Although a celebrity in Europe he remained in relative obscurity in the UK, remembered predominantly as a Studio One veteran. His European success resulted in collaborations with Sly And Robbie, albeit playing soul tunes for his King Cool album debut. In the 90s Francis was asked by Linton Kwesi Johnson to provide the vocals for a rocksteady revival project under the direction of the distinguished reggae guitarist John Kpiaye. Francis toured Europe and the USA performing rocksteady classics, including a notable performance at the Sierra Nevada Reggae Festival in San Francisco. The project led to a compilation of Jamaican classics, *Sweet Rock Steady*. The cover featured a photograph of the young Francis that originally appeared on the Studio One various artists compilation *Reggae In The Grass*, released in the late 60s.

● ALBUMS: *Mr Fix It* (Studio One 1970)★★★★, as King Cool *His Majesty Requests* (BMG France 1993)★★, *Sweet Rock Steady* (LKJ 1997)★★★.

FRANKLIN, CHEVELLE

b. 1976, Spanish Town, Jamaica, West Indies. Franklin came from a large family and left school at an early age. Franklin demonstrated her singing skills whenever the opportunity arose, and was eventually noticed by Winston Riley, who recorded her performing a cover version of Janet Jackson's 'Let's Wait A While'. Franklin's initial recording did not make a significant impression on the reggae charts but her determination led to an association with Brian And Tony Gold, and the result was a Jamaican number 1 hit with 'Here I Am'. It was through Brian and Tony that Franklin teamed up with Home T and Clifton 'Specialist' Dillon, where her international reputation grew. In 1992 Franklin was asked to record Deborahe Glasgow's 'Champion Lover', which was covered by Shabba Ranks as 'Mr Loverman'. Shabba's success led to a major label signing and a decision to re-record versions of his earlier hits. Franklin was drafted in for the challenging task of emulating Glasgow's fine vocals, which, despite the predictable opposition, she accomplished. The song was released in 1992 but found success two years later upon its re-release, when it featured in the film *Deep Cover*. A year later, Franklin released 'Ooh Aah', through Buju Banton's Cell Block 321 label. Franklin continues to record both as a soloist and in combination; she performed with Spragga Benz on his 'A1 Lover', with Daddy Lizard on 'Wait Until Tonight', and with Lady G on a series of classic songs, including 'Love And Hate', 'Thank You' and 'The Real Slam'. Her solo hits include 'Heart Of Mine', 'Wanna Be Down', 'Bending Knees' and the semi-autobiographical 'Mama Are You Proud'.

● ALBUMS: *Serious Girl* (Blue Moon 1996)★★★.

FRASER, DEAN

b. *c.*1955, Kingston, Jamaica, West Indies. The premier modern Jamaican reggae saxophonist, Dean Fraser has long been known among the reggae cognoscenti for his fulsome, warm-hearted tenor tone, a sound that matched both his size and demeanour. Fraser first emerged in the Jamaican music business in the mid-70s when horns were starting to diminish in importance within reggae bands. His own first musical experiments were as a clarinettist, at a youth club in Jonestown, as part of the National Volunteer programme. There he met fellow musicians Ronald 'Nambo' Robinson and Junior 'Chico' Chinn, who played trombone and trumpet, respectively. Together with Fraser on sax, they became the foremost horn section in Jamaica throughout the 80s. Initially, they played at old people's homes, covering jazz and R&B standards, until Fraser left to join Sonny Bradshaw's band, a large ensemble playing mainly jazz arrangements and offering much scope for young musicians keen to learn all aspects of the music business. In 1975 he played on his first recording session with Lloyd 'Gitsy' Willis, and two years later joined the We The People Band, led by singer, producer and bassist Lloyd Parks. Robinson and Chinn were enrolled shortly afterwards as the band achieved prominence backing Dennis Brown, and subsequently recording a string of successful records for producer Joe Gibbs.

It was Gibbs who produced Fraser's first album, *Black Horn Man*, in 1978, followed by *Revolutionary Dream* for Donovan Germain some two years later. Fraser's early singles included several vocal records rendered in a pure, gentle tone somewhat akin to that of Slim Smith. In the early 80s, known as 'Youth Sax', he would fire up the sessions of Sly And Robbie, and became a regular on both their world tours and in support of other acts such as Gregory Isaacs. An emotional instrumental version of Bob Marley's 'Redemption Song' at the 1981 Reggae Sunsplash, the first held since Marley's death, put Fraser uncharacteristically in the spotlight, and prompted Mango to commission the *Pumping Air* set. Ironically, as reggae was swept by 'computerized' music in the mid-80s, Fraser was suddenly in demand as the best-known human instrumentalist, and his saxophone tones sweetened literally dozens of pre-recorded 'digital' rhythms. He enjoyed a surprise hit with 'Girlfriend' for Dennis Star in 1987, encouraging him to rediscover his singing voice for the excellent *Sings And Blows* and *Dancehall Sax* for the same producer, which delivered several Jamaican vocal hits. From 1988 onwards he worked increasingly with Gussie Clarke at Music Works, first as a session musician and guest instrumentalist on Clarke's one-rhythm albums, then as an invaluable part of the production team, arranging and playing on a variety of albums by artists such as Cocoa Tea, Gregory Isaacs, Dennis Brown and Freddie McGregor. It is a role he also performs for the producers Carlton Hines and Philip 'Fatis' Burrell. Fraser remains as popular today as ever and forms part of a saxophone tradition that goes back to the likes of Tommy McCook and Roland Alphonso in reggae; his records, like those of R&B player Ace Cannon, will remain endlessly popular with the older Jamaican community. In recognition of his musical services, he was awarded the Musgrave Medal by the Jamaican government in 1993.

● ALBUMS: *Black Horn Man* (1978)★★★, *Revolutionary Dream* (1980)★★★, *A Touch Of Sax, Revolutionary Sounds* (1982)★★★, *Pure Horn* (1983)★★★, with Willie Lindo *Double Dynamite* (1983)★★★, *Pumping Air* (Island 1984)★★★, *Big Bad Sax* (Super Power 1988)★★, *Sings And Blows* (Greensleeves 1988)★★★★, *Dancehall Sax* (Greensleeves 1988)★★★, *Raw Sax* (Greensleeves 1989)★★★, *Call On Dean* (1991)★★★, *Moonlight* (Greensleeves 1991)★★★, *Taking Chances* (1993)★★★, *Big Up* (Island 1997)★★★★.

FRAZIER, PHILIP

b. Philip Fraser, c.1958, Kingston, Jamaica, West Indies. In 1975 Frazier improvised songs in Greenwich Town alongside his colleague Earl Zero. Earl had enjoyed previous hits produced by Al Campbell and Tommy Cowan and urged Frazier to pursue a recording career. The Freedom Sounds collective, founded by Bertram Brown, produced Frazier's debut, 'This Time Won't Be Like The Last Time'. His career went into overdrive with the releases of 'Breaking Up', 'Come Ethiopians', 'Single Man', 'Two Thousand Years' and 'Sentimental Feelings', a double a-

side backed with Prince Allah's 'Sun Is Shining'. Freedom Sounds was an ambitious project, designed to promote forthright dealings in the industry, and it enrolled top-class performers including Earl Zero, Michael Prophet, Sammy Dread, Prince Allah, Rod Taylor and the Soul Syndicate. Frazier's career enjoyed a boost when he recorded a version of 'Never Let Go' as a tribute to his neighbouring companion Slim Smith. His success continued with 'Ain't No Sunshine', 'Mr Wicked Man', 'Blood Of The Saint' and a tribute to his R&B idols, 'Special Request To The Manhattans'. By 1978 his reputation had extended to Europe and the USA, resulting in an international tour. While in Britain he linked up with the Silver Camel Sound System based at the 100 Club in London's Oxford Street. Like their Jamaican counterparts, the sound diversified into distribution and began releasing a number of roots hits. The label secured the release of Frazier's 'Blood Of The Saint' and a rare compilation, *Loving You*, before it dissolved. The label's demise prompted Frazier's return to Jamaica, recording with Henry 'Junjo' Lawes and Barry Clarke. The hits continued, including 'Please Stay' and 'When I Run Out', which both featured heavily on U-Roy's Stur Gav Sound System and resulted in Frazier becoming a cult hero. By the mid-80s he was working with Bunny Gemini and Triston Palma. His solo hits included 'Send Us Back Home', 'Sad And Blue' and 'Don't Ring My Doorbell'. Throughout the late 80s and early 90s he surfaced with sporadic hits, including a version of the Uniques' 'Watch This Sound', a variation of the Four Tops' hit 'If I Was A Carpenter', 'Coming On Strong' and in 1995, he released 'It's Magic' over the Wailers' 'Hypocrites' rhythm.

● ALBUMS: *Come Ethiopians* (Freedom Sounds 1976)★★★, *Loving You* (Silver Camel 1978)★★★, with Earl Zero, Prince Allah *Ethiopian Kings* (Love Child 1981)★★★★, with Triston Palma *I & I In Inity* (Black Solidarity 1985)★★★.

FREE I

b. Jeff Samuel Dixon, 31 March 1946, Davyton, Manchester, Jamaica, West Indies, d. 11 September 1987. In 1964 Dixon began working as a radio broadcaster on JBC where he built a strong following on his show, playing both local and American hits. His recording debut was at Studio One with Coxsone Dodd where he performed with Marcia Griffiths on 'Words' and released the solo hits 'Tickle Me' and 'The Rock'. A myriad of recordings followed under various guises as Soul Sam, Bigger D and Free I. With Treasure Isle he performed over John Holt's 'I'll Be Lonely' and as JD The Rock for 'Superbad'. By the late 60s Free I found work in the USA broadcasting the sounds of Jamaica to a new audience. He was a staunch advocate of black pride, which was clearly evident in his transmissions. While in America, he combined his radio career with a successful foray into artist management. As with many Jamaicans, the homeland beckoned and by the early 80s he had returned to JBC to pursue his promotional work. He formed an allegiance with Peter Tosh and was invited to be the road manager on the singer's 1987 US tour. On 11 September of that year, Free I and his wife Joy were at Tosh's house when an armed robbery took place. Alongside Free I were Tosh, Carlton 'Santa' Davis, Joy Dixon, Marlene Tosh, Doc Brown and Michael. All were robbed and Tosh, Brown and, three days after the felony, Free I joined the number of fatalities as a result of the shooting. After the tragic incident, Free I was nominated for a citation as a broadcaster in the Jamaican Music Hall Of Fame.

FRISCO KID

b. Stephen Wray, c.1970, Western Kingston, Jamaica, West Indies. Wray began to emulate the DJs while still at school and was eventually given a chance on the microphone at smaller dances. While working in a garage in Kingston, a chance meeting with the owner of the Exodus Nuclear sound system led to his performing as the Paro Kid. He became the resident DJ for Exodus and subsequently went to King Jammys' studio to record some specials, changing his name to Frisco Kid. As his career developed, he recorded 'Dance Again' at Donovan Germain's Penthouse studio. Frisco Kid's career prospects looked promising as a result of this release, but after the initial fervour died down, no further recordings surfaced. He returned to recording specials for the sound and it was at Black Scorpio in 1993 that his recording career took an upward turn. Confusion over studio time led Frisco Kid and DJ Terror Fabulous back to

Penthouse, where he recorded 'Big Speech'. His second break led to a number of hits, including 'Wakey News', 'Yuh And Yuh Man', 'Tribulation', 'Yuh A Boom', 'Step Up In Life' and 'Gal A Di Clothes'. His notoriety led to an appearance at the 1995 Reggae Sunsplash festival where he captivated the crowds with an exceptional performance. His success led to an alliance with Patrick Roberts, who enrolled Frisco Kid as part of the Shocking Vibes crew. The crew embarked on an international tour featuring Little Kirk, Silver Cat, Tanto Metro, Snagga Puss and Beenie Man; the tour represented the debut performances in Europe for Silver Cat and Frisco Kid. The shows received rave receptions from both the critics and audiences alike. In 1996 Frisco Kid joined Buju Banton's label, the newly formed Cell Block 321. The enterprise was designed to promote new talent and Frisco Kid's career advanced with the release of the phenomenal 'Video Light'. His success continued with 'If Looks' and the multi-combination hit 'Matey Anthem', alongside Mega Banton, Spragga Benz, Mad Cobra, General Degree, Gringo and Johnny P.

G

GARDINER, BORIS

b. 1954, Kingston, Jamaica, West Indies. Boris Gardiner, bass player, vocalist and musical director, has never been one of reggae's most celebrated names, but he has remained a permanent fixture in the music and has three major UK chart hits to his credit. His bass-playing skills first emerged in the late 60s, and the bands he graced included Byron Lee's Dragonaires, the Aggrovators, Crystalites and many more. His first brush with chart success was 'Elizabethan Reggae', recorded for Lee, which hit number 14 in January 1970. Gardiner toured the UK in support of his hit, which, at first, was incorrectly credited to its producer. His debut album, again produced by Lee, was released the same year. In its wake, Gardiner immersed himself in session work, regularly playing as part of the Now Generation band, and he later became a member of Lee Perry's Upsetters, following the Barrett brothers' defection to the Wailers. His solid, incisive basslines were seldom prominent, yet always effective.

In the 80s, as reggae was on the cusp of the digital era, an age likely to put paid to the careers of bass players, Gardiner's mellow, soulful voice came to the fore on a MOR reggae ballad, 'I Want To Wake Up With You', which reached number 1 in the UK charts in July 1986. Gardiner, who had been intermittently dogged by illness throughout the 80s, was finally receiving his due. His follow-up, 'You're Everything To Me', went to number 11, and the seasonal 'The Meaning Of Christmas' also scraped the charts.

● ALBUMS: *Reggae Happening* (Duke 1970)★★★★, *I Want To Wake Up With You* (Revue 1986)★★★, *Everything To Me* (Revue 1986)★★, *Its Nice To Be With You* (K&K 1986)★★★, *Soulful Experience* (Dynamic 1988)★★★, *Let's Take A Holiday* (WKS 1989)★★★.
● COMPILATIONS: *Classic Tracks* (Counterpoint 1988)★★★, *Reggae Happening* (Jamaican Gold 1994)★★★★.

GAYFEET RECORDS

(see Pottinger, Sonia)

GAYLADS

A vocal trio consisting of Winston Delano Stewart (b. 5 January 1947, Kingston, Jamaica, West Indies), Harris 'BB' Seaton (b. 3 September 1944, Kingston, Jamaica, West Indies), and Maurice Roberts (b. 2 July 1945, Kingston, Jamaica, West Indies). Together they began recording during the ska period but came to prominence during the rocksteady era in the mid- to late 60s. It is probable that at any other time and in any other place, their names would be highly revered, but such was the strength of the competition for three-part harmony vocal groups in Jamaica during the 60s that they are seldom remembered outside of reggae's cognoscenti. Most of their finest ska and rocksteady material was recorded for Coxsone Dodd's Studio One organization (where they also recorded in the calypso style), and the best of it is collected on two classic albums, *Soul Beat* and *The Best Of The Gaylads*, with Seaton writing most of their material.

As with most other Dodd singers, their talents were used extensively for harmony work for other Studio One artists such as Slim Smith and Peter Tosh. They also recorded some beautiful rocksteady sides for WIRL - 'Joy In The Morning' is one of their most enduring and much versioned songs - and 'ABC Rocksteady' and 'It's Hard To Confess', for Sonia Pottinger's Gayfeet label, are two all-time classics of the genre. Stewart and Seaton pursued solo careers in the 70s with varying degrees of success. Their legacy is a proud one, the Gaylads' name gracing some of the most beautiful three-part harmonies ever recorded.

● ALBUMS: *Sunshine Is Golden* (Studio One 1967)★★★, *Soul Beat* (Studio One 1969)★★★.
● COMPILATIONS: *The Best Of* (Studio One 1992)★★★★, *After Studio One* (Metronome 1992)★★★, *Over The Rainbow's End* (Trojan 1995)★★★.

GENERAL ECHO

d. 1980. Jamaican DJ Echo (aka Ranking Slackness) was one of the first to challenge the predominantly 'cultural' approach of the majority of mid- to late 70s DJs, and his influence on the new generation of DJs who made it in the 80s (in particular the UK MC school) was profound. He was one of the first DJs to be heard and fully appreciated on yard tapes, as he tore up Jamaica on his own Echo Tone Hi Fi set, and his preference for 'slack' or risqué lyrics, in particular his timing and tone of voice, was very popular and widely imitated. Echo felt no compunction about stopping the music altogether, if the vibes were right, in order to tell a joke or two - a facet that endeared him even more to his followers. His version of Winston Riley's 'Stalag' rhythm - 'Arleen' - was a number 1 hit in Jamaica and the future was looking very bright for Echo until he was shot dead by the police in Kingston in 1980, along with Flux and Big John (both from his sound system), in an incident that has never been fully explained.

● ALBUMS: as Ranking Slackness *The Slackest LP* (Techniques 1979)★★, *12-Inches Of Pleasure* (Greensleeves 1980)★★★.

GENERAL LEVY

b. Paul Levy, 1971, Park Royal, London, England. As ragga music finally made it into the mainstream in 1993 with Chaka Demus And Pliers, Shaggy, Shabba Ranks and others storming the UK national charts, it was left to just one home-grown DJ to fly the flag for British ragga music. A north London youth, Levy began his career DJing as General Levy, working his way through Vigilante, Java and Robbo Ranx's Tipatone sound systems. His first release was for Robbo's Muzik Street label in 1988, and 'New Cockatoo' proved to be something quite different, as Levy's freshness, youth and enthusiasm hiccuped out of every groove. His next move was to south London where Fashion Records' resident engineer, Gussie P, released his debut album, on which he shared the honours with Jamaican superstar DJ Capleton. Entitled *Double Trouble* the format (already tried and trusted) highlighted both Levy's and Capleton's different styles and approaches, spanning Jamaican and UK traditions. His popularity was boosted by numerous

'specials' for sound systems and he finally came to the public's attention in a big way with 'Original Length & Strength' on Fashion Records. His next trio of releases for Fashion, 'Heat', 'Breeze' and 'The Wig' established him as *the* British DJ. His lyrics ranged from serious culture to risqué 'slackness', with barely a pause for breath. His live shows had to be experienced to be believed, as he exploded all over the stage, arms and legs flailing to the accompaniment of non-stop, infectious, raucous rhyming. His branching out with Justice Records for some hip-hop-based recordings further broadened his appeal, and the late 1992 long-playing release for Fashion of *The Wickeder General* was an immediate runaway success. His burgeoning talent and personality was soon spotted by the majors (especially with all the frantic interest in ragga in the spring of 1993), and ffrr/London clinched the big contract. They retitled, repackaged and re-promoted *The Wickeder General* as *Wickedness Increase* and the strength of the added tracks ensured healthy sales - even to the reggae market where his fans had already purchased the original pressing.

● ALBUMS: with Capleton *Double Trouble* (Gussie P. 1991)★★★, *The Wickeder General* (Fashion 1992)★★★★, *Wickedness Increase* (ffrr/London 1993)★★★★, with Top Cat *Rumble In The Jungle* (Glamma 1995)★★★★.

GENERAL PUBLIC

When the Birmingham ska-influenced Beat disbanded, the band's two vocalists, Dave Wakeling and Ranking Roger, formed General Public with ex-Specials bassist Horace Panter (bass), Stoker (drums), Micky Billingham (keyboards) and Kevin White (guitar), plus veteran saxophonist Saxa. A self-titled debut single on Virgin Records combined a strong pop sound with an underlying dance feel and brushed the UK charts. 'Tenderness', in October, fared better in the USA (on IRS), coinciding with a fine debut album, . . . *All The Rage*. Without a British hit, the band's blend of musical influences, characterized by Roger's all-round skills, was largely ignored. General Public tried again in 1986 with *Hand To Mouth*, but despite aiming at the singles market with 'Faults And All', the world seemed oblivious and the band disappeared. Ranking Roger surfaced in a revitalized International Beat,

before a new album finally appeared in 1995, with the line-up consisting of Wakeling, Ranking Roger, Michael Railton (vocals, keyboards), Norman Jones (vocals, percussion), Wayne Lothian (bass) and Dan Chase (drums). Produced by Jerry Harrison, the album sounded fresh and energetic. In addition to invigorating originals such as 'It Must Be Tough' and 'Rainy Days', there was an interesting ska/reggae version of Van Morrison's 'Warm Love'.
● ALBUMS: . . . *All The Rage* (Virgin 1984)★★★, *Hand To Mouth* (Virgin 1986)★★★, *Rub It Better* (Epic 1995)★★★.

GEORGE, SOPHIA

b. *c*.1963, Jamaica, West Indies. In 1985 the reggae media were printing laudatory articles about a pre-release from Jamaica produced by Sangie Davis, entitled 'Girlie Girlie'. The song was a tale about a philandering juvenile manipulating the opposite sex. By December, the record was released in the UK and crossed over into the pop chart, peaking at number 7. George's appearance on the UK chart show *Top Of The Pops* was commended because she actually performed the song live. While in the UK she embarked on a tour, where her performances, including a version of Dire Straits' 'Walk Of Life' triumphed. In 1986 her follow-up, 'Lazy Body', originally a hit for Echo Minott, made a minor impression in the pop charts and proved a favourable hit within the reggae market. The single was released as a double a-side with the carefully crafted 'Can't Live Without You', which demonstrated her fine vocals. In 1987 George recorded 'Final Decision' with producer Willie Lindo, a warning to domineering males emulating the dancehall style of her debut. Other notable recordings included 'Aint No Meaning' with DJ Charlie Chaplin, 'It Burn Me Belly' and 'Maga Dog', loosely based around the Peter Tosh classic. Between her extensive touring, which included the 1989 Reggae Sunsplash Festival and supporting Yellowman on his 1990 US concerts, she returned to the recording studio with producer Home T and the Two Friends crew to cut *For Everyone*.
● ALBUMS: *Fresh* (Winner 1987)★★, *For Everyone* (Pow Wow 1989)★★★.

GERMAIN, DONOVAN

b. 7 March 1952. A producer whose involvement in 80s and 90s reggae music has helped to define and popularize the format, Germain started in the business with a record shop in New York, and he began producing his own work in 1972. From the outset his style was characterized by its dignified, musical approach and Germain soon proved that he could make lovers rock as adeptly as 'roots' records - his 'Mr Boss Man' with Cultural Roots was a huge underground hit in 1980. He made the UK national charts in the mid-80s with Audrey Hall's 'One Dance Won't Do' - strangely enough, an answer version to Beres Hammond's 'What One Dance Can Do', which was not a hit outside of the reggae sphere. He had many more hits throughout the 80s. However, everything came together towards the end of the decade when he opened his own Penthouse Studio on Slipe Road in Kingston in 1987. The quality and feel of the studio ensured that it was in constant demand for outside sessions and many classic recordings have been made there under the auspices of Germain and Dave 'Rude Boy' Kelly. It retains its position as one of the top Kingston studios - no mean feat in the hectic competition that abounds in this particular field, and Penthouse's clean, sophisticated sound and production work have ensured the popularity of the music with a much wider audience. Germain is a modest man who always prefers to let his music do the talking - a keen student of reggae, his involvement has always been imbued with a sense of, and sympathy for, the music's history and traditions. Now recognized as one of the very top reggae producers, he has proved himself many times over and there are few who would begrudge him the accolade. The discography lists just a small selection of the man's prolific output; all the releases demonstrate the clean, crisp sound that has become a byword for Penthouse productions, and Germain's ability to draw the best from both vocalists and DJs.
● COMPILATIONS: Various: *What One Rhythm Can Do* (Germain 1987)★★★, *Ninja Turtle (Volumes 1, 2 & 3)* (Penthouse 1989)★★★★, *Good Fellas* (Penthouse 1989)★★★, *Reggae Ambassadors (Volumes 1 & 2)* (Penthouse 1990)★★★, *Rhythm Exclusive* (Penthouse 1992)★★★, *Best Of Penthouse* (Penthouse

1993)★★★, *Dance Hall Hits (Volumes 1, 2 & 3)* (Penthouse 1993)★★, *Lovers Rock* (Penthouse 1993)★★★, *Penthouse Sampler* (Penthouse 1993)★★★★.

GIBBS, JOE

b. Joel Gibson, 1945, Montego Bay, Jamaica, West Indies. Gibbs started in the music business selling records in his television repair shop situated in Beeston Street, Kingston. In 1966 he moved into record production, releasing his material on the Jogib, Amalgamated, and Pressure Beat labels in Jamaica. He found instant success with Roy Shirley's 'Hold Them', one of the earliest records to introduce the new rocksteady beat, issued on the Doctor Bird label in the UK. By 1968 his productions were being released in the UK on Amalgamated, a subsidiary of Trojan Records set up exclusively for that purpose. The early issues were in the rocksteady format including 'Just Like A River' and 'Seeing Is Knowing' by Stranger (Cole) And Gladdy (Gladstone Anderson), and 'El Casino Royale' by guitarist Lynn Tait. Later came reggae sides by the Versatiles, who included Junior Byles in their number, Errol Dunkley, the Royals, the Reggae Boys, Ken Parker, the Immortals, the Slickers, Jimmy London, Ernest Wilson, Keith Blake (aka Prince Alla, also a member of the Leaders with Milton Henry), the Soulmates, and Nicky Thomas, whose 'Love Of The Common People' reached number 9 in the UK charts during July 1970. Other local hits came via the Pioneers, who recorded extensively for Gibbs before defecting to the Leslie Kong camp. Their hits included 'Give Me A Little Loving', 'Long Shot', 'Jackpot', 'Catch The Beat', and 'Mama Look Deh'. Many of these were written and produced by Lee Perry, who cut his own records, 'The Upsetter' and 'Kimble', for Gibbs before leaving to set up his own label. The parting was not exactly amicable, Perry's first self-production, 'People Funny Boy', being a vitriolic attack on Gibbs, who responded on record with the identical-sounding 'People Grudgeful'. Once Perry had departed, Gibbs enlisted Winston 'Niney' Holness to perform similar duties. With Holness at the helm, working the board alongside Errol 'ET' Thompson at Randy's, Gibbs' label entered into the nascent dub/version boom with instrumental sides such as

'Nevada Joe' and its version, 'Straight To The Head', and 'Franco Nero' by Joe Gibbs And The Destroyers. Other popular instrumentals such as 'Hi-Jacked' and 'Movements' were credited to the Joe Gibbs All Stars. In 1969 he installed a two-track studio at the back of his newly established Joe Gibbs Record Mart in West Parade, later moving to North Parade, and began producing successful records such as 'Jack Of My Trade' by veteran DJ Sir Lord Comic, 'Them A Fi Get A Beatin'', 'Maga Dog' and 'Arise Black Man' by Peter Tosh, the first cut of 'Money In My Pocket' by Dennis Brown, and its DJ version 'A So We Stay' by Big Youth, 'Warricka Hill' by the Versatiles, and 'Pretty Girl' by Delroy Wilson. These appeared on a variety of labels in Jamaica and, primarily, on the Pressure Beat imprint through Trojan in the UK. Gibbs also released several albums including *Best Of Dennis Brown*, *Heptones & Friends Vols. 1 & 2* and two of the earliest dub albums, the elusive *Dub Serial* and the first chapter of his classic *African Dub* series, both mixed by Thompson.

By 1975 Gibbs had opened his own 16-track studio and pressing plant in Retirement Crescent, Kingston. With Thompson installed at the controls, the hits soon flowed from artists such as Leo Graham, Sylford Walker ('Burn Babylon'), Junior Byles ('Heart And Soul'), Dillinger ('Production Plan'), George Washington ('Rockers No Crackers'), Dhaima ('Inna Jah Children'), Earl Sixteen ('Malcolm X'), Ruddy Thomas ('Every Day Is A Holiday'), Gregory Isaacs ('Babylon Too Rough'), Jah Berry aka Prince Hammer ('Dreadlocks Thing'), Naggo 'Dolphin' Morris ('Su Su Pon Rasta'), Trinity (*Three Piece Suit*), Prince Far I (*Under Heavy Manners*), and a brace of Revolutionaries-style instrumentals by Joe Gibbs And The Professionals. This was his studio band, incorporating the talents of Lloyd Parks, Sly And Robbie, Bingi Bunny and Bopeep on keyboards, Sticky and Ruddy Thomas on percussion, and a horn section comprising Bobby Ellis, Tommy McCook, Herman Marquis and Vin Gordon. Two further instalments of the *African Dub* series also emerged, with the notorious *Chapter 3*, which benefited (or suffered, depending on your point of view) from a particularly over-the-top mix from Thompson and Gibbs, achieving great popularity among the UK's punk adherents in 1977. These records appeared on a variety of Gibbs-affiliated labels, including Joe Gibbs, Town & Country, Errol T, Reflections and Heavy Duty. The late 70s/early 80s were a fruitful time for Gibbs, with two of his acts, Culture and Dennis Brown, breaking internationally. Gibbs gained two more UK chart entries, with teenage female DJ duo Althea And Donna's novelty 'Up Town Top Ranking' in 1977 and Dennis Brown's re-recording of 'Money In My Pocket' in 1979. Gibbs also produced popular sides by Eek A Mouse ('Virgin Girl'), Nigger Kojak And Liza ('Sky Juice'), and Junior Murvin ('Cool Out Son'). This activity continued on into the 80s, when, after moving to Miami, he temporarily ceased his operations following a lawsuit over copyright. He sold his old studio to Bunny Lee, but continues to lease and reissue his old material.

● COMPILATIONS: Various Artists: *Explosive Rock Steady* (1968)★★★★, *Jackpot Of Hits* (1968)★★★, *African Dub All-Mighty Chapters 1, 2 & 3* (Joe Gibbs 1975, 1976, Lightnight 1978)★★★★, *Top Ranking DJ Session Volume 1* (1980)★★★★, *Top Ranking Deejay Session Volume 2* (1982)★★★; Joe Gibbs And Friends *The Reggae Train 1968-1971* (1988)★★★. Joe Gibbs And Errol Thompson *The Mighty Two* (Heartbeat 1990)★★★.

GIBBY

b. Leebert Morrison, *c.*1959, Clarendon, Jamaica, West Indies. Morrison, known as Gibby, initially played lead guitar with the Solid Foundation band. His experience with the group led to him playing lead guitar for a number of reggae stars, including Jimmy Cliff, Peter Tosh, Dennis Brown, Gregory Isaacs, Bunny Wailer and dub poet Mutaburaka. Other prestigious performances include sessions with Earl 'Chinna' Smith's High Times band and with Dean Fraser's 809 band through to the 90s. Following the demise of the 809 band, Morrison performed his debut as a solo guitarist in Kingston at a theme night promoting rock music. He performed a heavy metal interpretation of the Troggs' 60s hit, 'Wild Thing', inspired by his guitar hero Jimi Hendrix. Although his performance was well received, heavy guitar sounds were not prevalent in Jamaica; nevertheless, Peter Blake of Kingston Muzik was suf-

ficiently inspired to sign him. Morrison ambitiously embarked on a mission to introduce this style to the dancehall and enrolled Junior 'Big Bird' Baille (drums), Lyndon 'Ace Bass' Webb (bass guitar) and Andrew 'Simmo' Simpson (guitar) to perform as Gibby. The band embarked on sessions for *Electric Avenue*, which showcased their unique style and the versatility of the reggae veteran Ruddy Thomas, who engineered the project. In 1997 Morrison performed at MIDEM in Cannes, France, illustrating the diversity of Jamaican music. Although his endeavours have been lauded by the media, the dancehall audience generally remains impervious to Gibby's unprecedented sound.

● ALBUMS: *Electric Avenue* (Kingston Muzik 1997)★★★.

GLADIATORS

Formed in Jamaica *c.*1965, the group originally comprised Albert Griffiths (vocals, guitar), Clinton Fearon (vocals, guitar) and David Webber (vocals). Griffiths adopted the group's name after a workmate suggested it. Their earliest recordings include 'The Train Is Coming Back' (1968) for Leeward Robinson, 'You Were To Be' (*c.*1969) for Duke Reid and 'Hello Carol' (1969) for Coxsone Dodd. During 1970, Webber was replaced by Dallimore Sutherland (bass, vocals). The group's focus became more roots-orientated, and good examples of this approach include two fine songs they recorded for Lloyd Daley in 1971, 'Rock A Man Soul' and 'Freedom Train'. Throughout the early 70s they recorded a stunning body of work for Dodd, including 'A Prayer To Thee', 'Bongo Red', 'Jah Jah Go Before Us', 'Roots Natty' and 'Serious Thing'. In 1976, they signed to Virgin Records. Their first album, *Trenchtown Mix-up*, was a strong collection of new songs and remakes, and this was followed by *Proverbial Reggae* and *Naturality*. Between 1977 and 1978, further singles appeared from Studio One, including 'Mr Baldwin' and 'Peace'. In 1979, Dodd finally released a collection of their singles as *Presenting The Gladiators*. Meanwhile, their Virgin contract concluded with *Sweet So Till* and *The Gladiators*, the latter being a misjudged crossover attempt. Further albums have all been consistent, although failing to reach the heights of their earlier recordings.

● ALBUMS: *Trenchtown Mix-up* (Virgin 1976)★★★, *Proverbial Reggae* (Front Line 1978)★★★★, *Naturality* (Front Line 1979)★★★, *Sweet So Till* (Front Line 1980)★★★, *The Gladiators* (Virgin 1980)★★, *Symbol Of Reality* (1982)★★★, *Serious Thing* (Night Hawk 1984)★★, *Country Living* (Heartbeat 1985)★★★, *In Store For You* (1988)★★★, *On The Right Track* (1989)★★★, *Dreadlocks The Time Is Now* (Front Line 1990)★★★, *Valley Of Decision* (1991)★★, *A True Rastaman* (1993)★★★.
● COMPILATIONS: *Presenting The Gladiators* 1969-78 recordings (Studio One 1979)★★★★, *Vital Selection* (Virgin 1987)★★★★.

GLAMMA KID

b. Iyael Constable, 14 March 1978, Hackney, London, England. Constable began his quest for stardom in his formative years by imitating Michael Jackson's dance steps and emulating his singing style. He attended acting classes at the Anna Shears Drama School where he secured a role on the television series *Corners*. In addition to pursuing his quest to be an all-round entertainer, he joined the Air Training Corps and in two years climbed to the rank of corporal. In 1989 he entered a talent competition and was pipped at the winning post by a DJ; this influenced his subsequent change of direction. In the next competition, he switched from dancing to performing as a DJ and came away with first prize. His success led to the formation of his own Glamma Guard sound system, playing in local blues and house parties in and around London. The system disbanded in 1994 with the members branching out in different musical directions. In the autumn of 1994 Constable, performing as Glamma Kid, met up with Mafia And Fluxy who both managed his career and produced his debut, 'Fashion Magazine'. The song led to a number of sessions and Glamma Kid became regarded as the UK's answer to Bounty Killer. He provided the DJ lyrics to a number of hits including 'Moschino', 'Girls Terminus', 'Nation Of Girls' and the anti-cocaine anthem, 'Outertain'. He was also notable for comments regarding the unhealthy obsession of some musicians with the gangster image, leading to the release of 'Eastwood Clint', where he warned against guns: 'Bwoy you could a bad like a Eastwood Clint - but you tink bad man gun fire flint'. He was also in demand for recording in a combination style, notably alongside Sylvia Tella, Peter Hunningale, Nerious Joseph and Robbie Valentine. In January 1997 he joined forces with Mafia And Fluxy, Hunningale and Joseph as part of the reggae supergroup Passion, for 'Share Your Love', which crossed over into the lower end of the UK pop chart. Glamma Kid was offered and accepted the role of supporting act to his Jamaican counterpart Bounty Killer on his 1997 UK tour, and continued working on his debut album.

GLASGOW, DEBORAHE

b. 1965, d. 25 January 1994. Glasgow's career began at the tender age of 12 when she first worked with the Mad Professor. Under the name Debbie G. she released 'Falling In Love' for his Ariwa label, which anticipated her powerful lovers rock style. She subsequently apprenticed herself to the London sound system circuit, mixing with the likes of Tippa Irie and Phillip Papa Levi, gaining a reputation for knowing her own mind and music. After meeting London producer Patrick Donegan, she signed to UK Bubblers, a Greensleeves subsidiary, making her debut for the label with 'You're My Sugar'. It became her first entry in the reggae charts. Other hits followed, including 'Knight In Shining Armour', 'Don't Stay Away' and 'When Somebody Loves You Back', a lovers rock standard. Later she travelled to Jamaica to work with Gussie Clarke, and these sessions would produce the best work of her tragically short life. A self-titled album emerged, which was strengthened by the presence of Shabba Ranks and the inclusion of the singles 'Champion Lover' and 'Don't Test Me'. Later, Shabba's version of 'Champion Lover', retitled 'Mr Lover Man', became a huge international hit. After this career peak, Glasgow kept her distance from the music business, concentrating instead on bringing up her family in Wandsworth, London. However, she did collaborate with General Lee for 'Weak' and 'Knocking The Boots'. Shortly afterwards, she was diagnosed as having cancer of the lymph gland, and died of a brain haemorrhage in January 1994.
● ALBUMS: *Deborahe Glasgow* (Greensleeves 1989)★★★.

GOLD, BRIAN AND TONY

During a trip to Jamaica, Anthony Anderson (b. 1968, Birmingham, West Midlands, England) entered a variety of talent shows on the island, frequently appearing on the same bill as Brian Thompson (b. 1967, Kingston, Jamaica, West Indies), and they eventually formed an illustrious partnership. They decided to perform together as Brian And Tony Gold and with the demise of vocal groups were in the fortunate position of being regarded as *the* unrivalled vocal duo in Jamaica. They embarked on recording sessions for King Jammy, Mikie Bennett, Donovan Germain, Philip 'Fatis' Burrell and Dave 'Rude Boy' Kelly. Although the duo were primarily considered to be session singers, they released the occasional hit, including the haunting, anti-apartheid 'Can You', in 1992. The song showcased their distinctive style, which inspired Sly And Robbie to enrol the singers to perform with DJ Red Dragon on 'Compliments On Your Kiss'. The relaxed rhythm and smooth singing, combined with the laid-back DJ, was destined to cross over. The formula proved successful and the single reached number 2 in the UK pop chart in 1994. Following their commercial success, the duo returned to Jamaica where they recorded a series of notable songs including 'If Loving Was A Crime' with Buju Banton, who later released the favoured 'Searching For The Light' on his own Cell Block 321 label. The duo continue to release sporadic hits, including 'Girls Can't Do', 'All I Want', 'Free At Last', 'Ram Dance', 'Bulls Eye', and the popular combination hits 'Private Property' (with Shabba Ranks), 'Saturday Night At The Movies' (with Lady Saw), 'S.L.A.' (with Junior Tucker) and 'You Give Me Your Love' (with Shaggy).
● ALBUMS: *Green Light* (Pow Wow 1993)★★, *Bulls Eye* (VP 1995)★★★.

GOOFY

b. Chad Simpson, 1 June 1974, Jamaica, West Indies. Simpson grew up within the reggae industry and drew help as well as inspiration in his burgeoning career from the likes of Big Youth, Yellowman, Beenie Man, Bounty Killer and General Degree. In 1996 he recorded the chart-topping 'Fudgie', which also featured Lady Saw and Hawkeye on the 12-inch disco mix. The hit led to a series of singles including 'Don't

Talk', 'How You Bless' and 'Dog Bark'. Goofy's association with Danny Brownie's Main Street Crew led to him recording in combination with Red Rat, initially on 'Big Man Little Yute' for Studio 2000, which topped the reggae charts worldwide. The duo followed their success with 'Cruise'. The Main Street Crew made their UK debut at the 1997 Notting Hill Carnival in London, featuring the trio of Red Rat, Goofy and Hawkeye. Scheduled to appear on both the Radio One and Kiss FM stages, the trio's arrival caused a crushing surge towards the stage, an incident grossly exaggerated in the national press. Goofy continued to produce hits, including 'Yu Brush Yu Tooth From Morning' and 'Bad Man Crew'.

GOPTHAL, LEE

b. 1 March 1939, Constant Spring, Kingston, Jamaica, West Indies, d. 29 August 1997. Gopthal is regarded as a pioneer in promoting Jamaican music. He moved to the UK in 1952 where he qualified as an accountant, and by the early 60s was representing producer Leslie Kong in the UK. Initially, Gopthal was involved in providing records for the West Indian population through his primary venture, Pyramid Records. By the early 60s Chris Blackwell had arrived in the UK and joined forces with Gopthal, who distributed Black Swan and Island Records pressings under the Beat And Commercial banner. The association led to the inauguration of the Muzik City chain, which sold Jamaican music within the Afro-Caribbean community. The shops were opened in and around London and included the legendary Desmond's Hip City in Brixton. In 1967 Gopthal's Pyramid label released Desmond Dekker's 'The Israelites', which topped the UK charts two years after its release and is acknowledged as the first reggae tune to conquer the US charts. Gopthal and Blackwell co-founded Trojan Records in 1967, releasing Jamaican hits and allocating labels to represent the growing number of producers, including Lee Perry, Joe Gibbs, Duke Reid, Clancy Eccles and, for a brief period, Coxsone Dodd. Gopthal also worked with UK-based performers, including Dandy Livingstone, whose production of Tony Tribe's version of Neil Diamond's 'Red Red Wine' gave the company its first reggae hit on the UK chart. Following his label's early chart success Gopthal also enjoyed mainstream hits with 'The Liquidator', by Harry J.'s Allstars, 'Long Shot Kick De Bucket' by the Pioneers, 'Wonderful World Beautiful People' by Jimmy Cliff, and the double a-side, 'Return Of Django'/'Dollar In The Teeth', by the Upsetters. The hits continued in abundance following the departure of Blackwell, who decided to concentrate on the lucrative rock market, although the Wailers later emerged as the label's most significant asset. By 1974, with increasing financial problems, Trojan were unable to compete with the major record companies, and the label was eventually sold to Saga Records. Gopthal maintained a low profile within the music industry until the late 70s when he decided to pursue a career in commerce.

GOSPEL FISH

b. Everald Thomas, Spanish Town, Jamaica, West Indies. Gospel Fish's quirkily inventive lyrics are invariably marked by a maturity and intelligence that sets him apart from many of his contemporaries. He was raised in Thompson Pen, learning hand drums from his Rasta father before fellow DJ Jimmy Crazy dubbed him Gospel Fish after watching him sing hymns in the local church choir. The pair duetted on their first ever release, 'Neighbourhood Cousin', in 1987, which Gospel - then working as a security guard - produced himself. 'Walk An' Wine', 'Ruff An' Tuff' and 'Cash Ready' followed, but his first two hits, 'Golden Rule' and 'Bandy Leg', did not arrive until a year later. His producer was now Dennis Star, who brought him to the UK in 1988 for his first shows outside Jamaica. Until then he had been a regular feature on the Happy Tone, Nite Flight, Lightning and Leo Taurus sound systems, inspired by DJs such as Lieutenant Stitchie, Tony Rebel and Professor Nuts. In 1990 he began voicing for Captain Sinbad, Fashion Records and Gussie P, all of whom have been instrumental in helping him reach a wider audience. 'Wickedest Thing In Life', 'You Must Be Fool' and 'Too Much Gun Talk' revealed a shift from mildly 'slack' themes to something altogether more cultural, much as 'Ten' had done when released by Penthouse in 1991.

Throughout 1991-92 he also recorded for Soljie, Top Rank, Bee Cat and Taxi before Sinbad coaxed him into writing a combative 'burial' tune called 'Brush Dem', which became his biggest hit to date. During 1993 a stay in the UK found him guesting on the Aswad/Yazz collaboration 'Hold On', and enjoying further exposure with both Fashion and Sinbad, occasionally in combination, as with John McLean on *Romantic Ragga*.

● ALBUMS: Various *Romantic Ragga* (Sinbad 1993)★★★★.

GRANT, EDDY

b. Edmond Montague Grant, 5 March 1948, Plaisance, Guyana, West Indies. Grant was 24 years old, with several hits to his credit, when he left the Equals to form his own production company. After producing other acts, he made his own debut in 1977 with *Message Man*. It was certainly a solo effort: not only did he sing and play every note, but it was recorded in his own studio, the Coach House, and released on his own label, Ice Records. Grant had developed his own sound - part reggae, part funk, with strong musical motifs and strong melodies - producing pop with credibility. More than 10 years after the Equals' first hit, 'Living On The Front Line' (1979) was a UK number 11 hit, and the now dreadlocked Grant had found himself a whole new audience. 'Do You Feel My Love' and 'Can't Get Enough Of You' kept him in the UK Top 20. In 1982 he moved his home and studio to Barbados, signed Ice Records to RCA, and achieved a memorable UK number 1 hit with 'I Don't Wanna Dance'. The following year 'Electric Avenue' reached number 2 on both sides of the Atlantic, and the parent album *Killer On The Rampage* proved his biggest seller. The huge hits eluded him for four years until he stormed back in January 1988 with 'Gimme Hope Jo'anna', as if he had never been away. The dressing of the anti-Apartheid message in the apparent simplicity of a pop song was typically inspired.

● ALBUMS: *Message Man* (Ice 1977)★★★, *Walking On Sunshine* (Ice 1979)★★★, *Love In Exile* (Ice 1980)★★★, *Can't Get Enough* (Ice 1981)★★★, *Live At Notting Hill* (Ice 1981)★★, *Paintings Of The Soul* (Ice 1982)★★★, *Killer On The Rampage* (Ice/RCA 1982)★★★, *Can't Get Enough* (Ice/RCA 1983)★★★, *Going For Broke* (Ice/RCA 1984)★★, *Born Tuff* (Ice 1987)★★,

File Under Rock (Parlophone 1988)★★.
● COMPILATIONS: *All the Hits: The Killer At His Best* (K-Tel 1984)★★, *Hits* (Starr 1988)★★, *Walking On Sunshine (The Best Of Eddy Grant)* (Parlophone 1989)★★★.
● VIDEOS: *Live In London* (PMI 1986), *Walking On Sunshine* (PMI 1989).

GRAY, OWEN

b. 5 July 1939, Jamaica, West Indies. Gray's singing won him a local talent contest at the age of nine, and three years later he began to appear in public, playing drums, guitar and keyboards. In 1960 he became one of the first artists produced by Chris Blackwell, later the owner of Island Records. His first single, 'Please Let Me Go', with its easy shuffle rhythm and hard Ernest Ranglin guitar solo adding to the singer's appeal, was a number 1 hit in Jamaica. Gray's voice, light but with a cutting edge, won him favour throughout the decade; he turned his hand to R&B ('Let Me Go Free', based on Professor Longhair's 'Tipitina'), ska ('Millie Girl') and ballads ('Far Love') before emigrating to Britain. He maintained a prodigious output, following the trends of ska, rocksteady and reggae, scoring a big seller with 'Cupid' (1968) and recording one of the steamiest soul dances ever issued in England in 'Help Me' (1966). By the late 70s he was no longer in the forefront of British black music, and a 1982 attempt at 'Sexual Healing' was less than successful. He now lives in Miami where he still finds an audience for his extensive oldies repertoire.
● ALBUMS: *Cupid* (1969)★★★, *Fire And Bullets* (Trojan 1977)★★★★, *Dreams Of Owen Gray* (Trojan 1978)★★★★, *Forward On The Scene* (Third World 1978)★★★, with Pluggy Satchmo *Battle Of The Giants Round 1* (Vista Sounds 1983)★★★, with Delroy Wilson *Oldies But Goldies* (Vista Sounds 1983)★★★, with Max Romeo *Owen Gray Meets Max Romeo* (Culture Press 1984)★★★, *Little Girl* (Vista Sounds 1984)★★★, *Owen Gray Sings Bob Marley* (Sarge 1984)★★, *Room At The Top* (World Enterprise 1986)★★, *Watch This Sound* (Sky Note 1986)★★, *Stand By Me* (Hitbound 1986)★★, *Instant Rapport* (Bushranger 1989)★★★, *Ready Willing And Able* (Park Heights 1989)★★★.
● COMPILATIONS: *Hit After Hit Vols. 1, 2 & 3* (Carib Gems 1980, Vista Sounds 1983)★★★★.

GREENE, TONY

b. Anthony Greene, March 1957, Kingston, Jamaica, West Indies. Greene's earliest involvement in music came at the renowned Alpha Boys School in Jamaica, whose alumni included the Skatalites' horn section (featuring Don Drummond, Tommy McCook and Roland Alphonso). Greene initially played the clarinet, although on joining the Jamaican Military Band he switched to playing the saxophone. His playing skills led to a scholarship in the UK at the Royal Academy Of Music from 1975-77. During the late 70s Greene returned to Jamaica, where he played on sessions for the Roots Radics and joined Sonny Bradshaw's Band, followed by a spell with Lloyd Parks' We The People Band. In this respect, his career duplicated that of the distinguished saxophonist Dean Fraser, who had also performed with both bands. However, by the mid-80s their careers diverged as Fraser continued to perform over the emerging digital reggae beat, while Greene accompanied visiting R&B acts. He performed alongside Gladys Knight, Lou Rawls and Aretha Franklin on the island, which led to Greene being employed as a saxophonist on the international circuit. In the 90s Greene returned to his roots with the release of *Sax Man*. Although instrumental albums rarely enjoy the commercial success of their vocal counterparts, Greene's work led to further solo recording sessions. His releases proved especially popular in North America, although reggae purists considered his work too jazzy. Greene's follow-up featured vocal contributions from Tanya Stephens, and samples from Beenie Man, Bounty Killer and Capleton. In addition to releasing his own work Greene established the Sax Man label with the aim of promoting local talent.
● ALBUMS: *Mean Greene* (Gone Clear 1997)★★★, *Square From Cuba* (Sax Man 1998)★★★.

GREENSLEEVES RECORDS

Despite its humble origins as a record shop in West Ealing, London, in 1975, Greensleeves continues to thrive in the keenly contested environs of the reggae marketplace. The label's first releases were Reggae Regular's 'Where Is Jah' and Doctor Alimantado's 'Born For A Purpose'. The latter artist also offered them their first long-player, the *Best Dressed Chicken In Town* compilation. Tony McDermott's distinctive artwork soon established Greensleeves' visual image and identity. The label further consolidated its name with the emergence of dancehall, licensing much of Henry 'Junjo' Lawes' catalogue for domestic release. Others included Scientist, Channel One's technical guru, and Prince (later King) Jammy's productions, notably his early works with Black Uhuru. The UK side were equally productive with their UK Bubblers label, peaking commercially with Tippa Irie's UK Top 30 hit, 'Hello Darling', in 1986. Other notable successes on the domestic front included Clint Eastwood And General Saint. The mid-80s saw impressive repackagings of Jamaican standards (Hugh Mundell, Burning Spear, Yabby You) as well as major new works from Eek A Mouse, Josey Wales, Junior Reid and Yellowman. Their profile was enhanced further via the UK release of two groundbreaking singles: Wayne Smith's 'Under Me Sleng Ten', which kickstarted the digital revolution, and Gregory Isaacs' 'Rumours', the bestselling reggae record of 1988, and an important staging post in the development of ragga. A new wave of artists had their records released in the UK by Greensleeves: Shabba Ranks, Cocoa Tea and Papa San among them. The English lovers rock scene was represented by Deborahe Glasgow, while the company scored their biggest seller to date when they picked up Shaggy's 'Oh Carolina'. They also market several other independent labels, notably Jah Shaka's idiosyncratic roster.

● COMPILATIONS: *Greensleeves Sampler Volumes 1 - 8* (Greensleeves 1983-93)★★★★.

GREYHOUND

Greyhound evolved from the Rudies, subsequently known as Freddie Notes And The Rudies. The band was formed by Danny Smith and Freddie Notes in the second half of the 60s. Working with Dandy Livingstone, then known as Dandy, they had a hit in 1969 with 'Night Train'. They enjoyed hits in the reggae charts including 'Down On The Farm' and a version of Clarence Carter's 'Patches'. Their version of Bobby Bloom's 'Montego Bay' was almost a crossover hit. While collectively known as the Rudies, they released *Unity* and *Montego Bay*,

both of which were titled after their hit singles. In the early 70s Notes left the band and was replaced by Glenroy Oakley, and it was at this stage that the transformation took place. Trojan Records had several unsuccessful attempts at recording a live album, but the release of *Trojan Reggae Party Volume One* resolved this with musical backing provided by Greyhound. The group accompanied a host of top reggae artists at the show, as well as performing 'You Made Me So Very Happy' and 'Move On Up'. In June 1971 the new line-up had a Top 10 hit with 'Black And White', a song that has since been covered by Gregory Isaacs, the Maytones and King Sounds (who also covered 'Patches'). In January 1972, following successful touring, the group covered Andy Williams' number 1 hit 'Moon River', and entered the UK Top 20. Their sound had by now been diluted and the addition of strings did nothing to enhance the recordings. The final hit, 'I Am What I Am', a plea for recognition in a white-dominated society, peaked at number 20 in March of that same year. A combination of the Pioneers and Greyhound, known as the Uniques, released a cover version of Paul Simon's 'Mother And Child Reunion', followed by 'Lonely For Your Love'. The singles did not reap the rewards they deserved and resulted in confusion within the group, which also featured Slim Smith, Lloyd Charmers and Jimmy Riley. The release of 'Floating' did not match the success of the earlier recordings in either the reggae or national chart, although the later output had more of a reggae feel. Disillusioned with the lack of promotion, a change of labels ensued and despite national airplay the follow-up releases, 'Wily', 'Only Love Can Win' and 'Dream Lover', failed to attain chart status. Shortly after the release of *Mango Rock* the group disbanded, and Sonny Binns joined the Cimarons while the others emerged as Dansak, who toured the UK in 1974 with Jimmy Cliff and Dave Barker.

● ALBUMS: as Freddie Notes And The Rudies *Unity* (Trojan 1969)★★, as Freddie Notes And The Rudies *Montego Bay* (Trojan 1970)★★★, *Black And White* (Trojan 1971)★★★, *Mango Rock* (Trans Atlantic 1975)★★.

● COMPILATIONS: *Black And White* (Tring 1990)★★.

GRIFFITHS, MARCIA

b. 1954, Kingston, Jamaica, West Indies. Griffiths is arguably the most consistently successful female vocalist in the history of reggae music, having recorded in every one of the myriad of styles in Jamaican music, from ska through to an 80s rap crossover record. Her precocious talent was recognized very early by producers Coxsone Dodd and Byron Lee, who were competing for her father's signature on a recording contract even before Marcia's tenth birthday. Dodd was the winner because she 'liked his vibes' and Dodd's Studio One set-up was like a 'musical college'. It was there that Griffiths achieved her first Jamaican number 1 in 1968 with the rocksteady hit 'Feel Like Jumping', a record that can still fill dance floors. She had worked very closely with Bob Andy during this period and he had written many of her biggest hits for her. In 1969, they recorded, as Bob And Marcia, an interpretation of Nina Simone's 'Young, Gifted And Black' for producer Harry J., and their bright, lilting reading of the song touched a nerve with UK buyers, particularly among the reggae-obsessed skinhead audience. The popularity of the record ensured crossover success and it rode high in the UK charts in 1970 and became a hit all over Europe. Their follow-up, 'Pied Piper', in 1971 was equally pop-oriented and another big hit in the UK. The duo toured extensively but both felt that there was very little financial reward during this period and they returned to Jamaica to reassess their respective careers. Griffiths made some beautiful records for Sonia Pottinger's High Note label and in 1975, she became one of Bob Marley's I-Threes backing vocalists, along with Rita Marley and Judy Mowatt - recruited to fill the musical gap left by the departure of Bunny Wailer and Peter Tosh from the Wailers. For the remainder of the decade and on into the 80s she recorded and toured with Marley, still continuing with her solo career, but after Marley's death in 1981, she returned to extensive recording as a solo artist. Her 'Electric Boogie' with Bunny Wailer was a hit in the USA in 1989 - seven years after it was recorded - and even inspired its own dance - 'The Electric Slide'. She continues to record and, furthermore, to make records that matter.

● ALBUMS: *The Original - At Studio One* (Studio One 1973)★★★★, *Sweet Bitter Love* (Trojan 1974)★★★★, *Naturally* (Sky Note 1978)★★★, *Steppin'* (Sky Note/Shanachie 1979)★★★, *Rock My Soul* (Pioneer International 1984)★★★, *I Love Music* (Mountain Sounds 1986)★★, *Marcia* (Germain 1988)★★★, *Carousel* (Mango/Island 1990)★★★, *Indomitable* (Penthouse 1993)★★★.

● COMPILATIONS: *Put A Little Love In Your Heart: The Best Of ... 1969-1974* (Trojan 1993)★★★★.

GROOVY, WINSTON

b. Winston Tucker, 1946, Kingston, Jamaica, West Indies. Before leaving Jamaica, Winston Groovy enjoyed minor hits with 'Yellow Bird' and 'Standing On The Corner'. Recording with Lee Perry, he enjoyed his first big hit, 'Want To Be Loved', which was also released in the UK. Inspired by a popular dance, the 'Funky Chicken', Groovy recorded a reggae version, and any similarity to the Rufus Thomas hit was in the title alone. A huge success for the Jackpot label, it was produced by Laurel Aitken. The hit led to a various artists compilation, *Funky Chicken*, using the song as its theme, which included contributions from Dave Barker, Freddie Notes And The Rudies and Rita Alston. Groovy's arrival in the UK coincided with the release of a cover version of Dr. Hook's 'Sylvia's Mother', with this version given a-side status and aimed firmly at the pop market, while the b-side was more traditional reggae. Other hits followed, including 'Oh My My', 'I've Got A Nose For Trouble' and 'Please Don't Make Me Cry'. He continued to record throughout the 80s, the most notable releases being 'Don't Blame Me', 'Paradise In Your Eyes' and 'So In Love With You'. The UK pop reggae band UB40 recorded a compilation of cover versions of old reggae that included 'Please Don't Make Me Cry', giving them a UK Top 10 hit in 1983. Inspired by the success of the cover version, Groovy re-recorded the song. Trojan Records also responded by releasing the original version, along with Jimmy Cliff's 'Many Rivers To Cross', Tony Tribe's 'Red Red Wine' and Eric Donaldson's 'Cherry Oh Baby', under the collective title *Reggae Classics*.

● ALBUMS: *Presenting Winston Groovy* (Trojan 1972)★★★★, *The Groovy Collection* (Trojan 1978)★★★★.

HALF PINT

b. Lyndon Roberts, *c.*1962, Western Kingston, Jamaica, West Indies. One of the first and finest dancehall reggae singers, Half Pint has never entirely maintained his career at the highest level, but nonetheless has had an impressive, if sporadic, string of huge Jamaican hits. An enthusiastic and exciting singer, Half Pint, one of seven children, left school in 1976 and spent the next six years trying to break into the music business before recording a debut single, 'Sally'. 'Money Man Skank' was a major hit and kicked off a five-track debut album for Jammy's. Early hits 'One In A Million' and 'Pouchie Lou' for producer Prince (later King) Jammy established his style, and Half Pint's diminutive figure traversed the world on Sly And Robbie's 1985 Taxi Tour, paying the duo back with the singles 'World Inflation', 'Hold On', and 'Night Life Lady'. A visit to producer George Phang brought about his biggest hit, 'Greetings' (1985), an unavoidable refrain in the world's reggae cities, and then the Rolling Stones covered his 'Winsome', to the complete astonishment of the singer. *Victory* followed the blueprint of *Greetings* to the letter and sold well in America. Since then, Half Pint has been less successful, but he has a considerable following, eagerly waiting for another *Greetings*, and in 1992 the big reggae hit 'Substitute Lover' was a sign of his reviving fortunes.

● ALBUMS: *Money Man Skank* (Jammys 1984)★★★, *Can't You Wait Till I Get You Home* (Power House 1984)★★★, *One In A Million* (Greensleeves 1984)★★★, *In Fine Style* (Sunset/Sonic Sounds 1984)★★★, with Michael Prophet *Joint Favourites* (Greensleeves 1985)★★★, *Greetings* (Power House 1986)★★★★, *Victory* (RAS 1988)★★★★, *One Big Family* (Powerhouse 1989)★★★, *Pick Your Choice* (1993)★★★.

● COMPILATIONS: *20 Super Hits* (Sonic Sounds 1993)★★★★.

HALL, AUDREY

b. *c.*1948, Jamaica, West Indies. Hall's first recording session was with Dandy Livingstone. The latter had previously recorded as Sugar And Dandy with Tito Simon, and the success of the duets by Jackie Edwards And Millie Small, Keith And Enid and Derrick And Patsy prompted the pairing of Dandy And Audrey. In 1969 the duo recorded 'Morning Side Of The Mountain', which led to an album of the same name on Trojan Records. Inspired by the duo's success, a year later, Trojan compiled a further release, *I Need You*, which contained a number of tracks from the initial album including 'Storybook Children', 'Once Upon A Time' and 'I Need You'. Livingstone also produced Hall's solo recordings, including versions of R&B classics originally recorded by the Toys, 'A Lovers Concerto', and Barbara Lynn, 'You'll Lose A Good Thing', for his Down Town productions. In Jamaica it appeared that Hall's solo career was over and she found employment as a backing singer alongside her sister Pam Hall. In 1985 she made a comeback when she recorded an answer to Beres Hammond's hit, 'What One Dance Can Do'. 'One Dance Just Won't Do', produced by Donovan Germain, took her into the pop chart after 15 years in the music business. She followed the hit with 'The Best Thing For Me', though it was the ensuing 'Smile' that repeated her success in the pop market. In 1986 she returned to recording duets with Don Evans (ex-Paragon) and they released 'Heart Made Of Stone' and *Dynamic Duo* on Trojan Records.

● ALBUMS: *Eight Little Notes* (Germain 1985)★★★, *Just You Just Me* (Germain 1987)★★★.

HALL, PAM

Hall has provided backing vocals, often alongside her brother Raymond, on numerous recording sessions in Jamaica. The family involvement in the music business also includes her sister Audrey Hall, who has been recording since the late 60s, peaking with her crossover chart success in the 80s with Donovan Germain. In 1976 Pam recorded in her own right for her performance on a duet with Tinga Stewart, 'You Should Never Do That'. In 1986 her quest for recognition as a soloist came to fruition with the release of 'Dear Boopsie', which topped the reggae chart and crossed over into the mainstream, spending four weeks at the lower end of the UK Top 50. She followed the hit with 'How Glad I Am', produced by Danny Brownie at Music Mountain, but in spite of suitable promotion she was unable to emulate her earlier success. The singles were both coupled with productions by Errol Wilson who has remained with the singer throughout her career as her manager and producer. Her debut album, *Perfidia*, took its title from the Phylis Dillon classic. While pursuing her aspirations towards a career as a soloist she continued to provide back-up vocals for many of Jamaica's top performers, including Peter Tosh, Bunny Wailer, Dennis Brown, Jimmy Cliff and Gussie Clarke. Following a period of anonymity she re-emerged in 1994 with the release of 'Missing You Baby'. She followed the hit with her interpretation of 'I Will Always Love You', inspired by the phenomenal success of Whitney Houston's version of the Dolly Parton composition. Hall's version, recorded for Joe Frasier, topped the reggae chart and was followed by the equally successful 'Young Hearts Run Free'. Although a competent DJ in her own right in 1995, she also performed in combination with General Degree for 'Lonely Days', which provided the basis and title for the Nardo Ranks hit several months later. Her interpretation of Michael Jackson's 'You Are Not Alone' provided Hall with a massive solo hit, topping the reggae charts in the early summer of 1996. She continues to perform on stage, having supported the I-Threes in Judy Mowatt's absence, as well as with Toots Hibbert and Ziggy Marley. It was through the latter's involvement in the Fugees' version of 'No Woman No Cry' that she was asked to provide backing vocals on the Ziggy Marley remix. In 1996 she joined the growing number of popular reggae artists in Japan, where she released *Magic*, which included her Jamaican hits alongside a version of Toni Braxton's 'Unbreak My Heart'. The album was heavily promoted in early 1997 when the premier US reggae distributor released her second compilation with the label.

● ALBUMS: *Perfidia* (Blue Mountain 1987)★★★★, *Missing You Baby* (VP 1995)★★★, *Magic* (VP 1997)★★★.

HAMMOND, BERES

b. Beresford Hammond, 1955, St. Mary, Jamaica, West Indies. Winning a string of awards for Best Male Vocalist throughout the early 90s meant that success had come late to Beres Hammond. He was still in his teens when he joined Zap Pow in 1975, after singing on local amateur shows. He had met guitarist and producer Willie Lindo prior to that, and by the time Hammond left the group in 1980, Lindo had produced his debut album, *Soul Reggae*, and was already working on *Just A Man*, which followed in 1981. It was to prove a harmonious partnership; although *Let's Make A Song* was self-produced, Lindo was back in the chair for *Coming At You* in 1983. With his smoky, soulful vocals, Hammond was gaining a reputation as a master stylist, and his choice of material reflected this, often bearing a distinctly R&B flavour. All that changed with his fifth album, *Beres Hammond*. 'Groovy Little Thing', 'One Dance Will Do' (which sparked off a saga of answer versions) and 'She Loves Me Now' all became bestselling singles and established his name on the dancehall scene.

It was not until he was coerced into recording for Donovan Germain's Penthouse label in 1990 that he experienced similar success. A major label contract with Cooltempo had failed in presenting his talents to a wider audience, and despite a high-profile duet with Maxi Priest for 'How Can We Ease The Pain' in 1988, he had seemingly lost direction. Germain voiced him over popular dancehall rhythms and 'Tempted To Touch' proved to be a runaway hit, resulting in the release of *A Love Affair* in 1992. By that time Hammond was in demand, and a wealth of material ensued from producers such as Lindo, Richard Bell from Star Trail, Steely And Clevie and Philip 'Fatis' Burrell, who was based at Music Works, adjoining the Penthouse studio. The hits flowed thick and fast, often in the shape of collaborations with artists such as Marcia Griffiths, Buju Banton, Cobra, Cutty Ranks, Reggie Stepper and Tony Rebel. In 1992 Sly Dunbar remixed earlier tracks Hammond had voiced for Tapper Zukie and 'Putting Up Resistance' won a JAMI award for the year's Best Song. The following year, Burrell built on the existence of a growing number of great tracks for his Exterminator label and issued the *Full*

Attention album, which showcased Hammond in unstoppable form over a selection of weighty rhythms. The result highlighted his abilities not only as a magnificent singer of ballads, reality and dancehall material, but also revealed him to be a writer of genuine merit. After recording further hits for New York producers Sting and Robert Livingston, he signed for Elektra in the autumn of 1993, releasing one album before moving to Harmony House for *Love From A Distance* in 1996. On this release, Shaggy and the Dream Warriors add some excellent harmony.
● ALBUMS: *Soul Reggae* (Water Lily 1977)★★★, *Just A Man* (Joe Gibbs 1981)★★★, *Let's Make A Song* (1982)★★★, *Coming At You* (WKS 1983)★★★★, *Beres Hammond* (Charm 1986)★★★, *Have A Nice Weekend* (WKS 1987)★★★, *Live & Learn Present* (Live & Learn 1988)★★★, *Putting Up Resistance* (Tuff Gong 1989)★★★, *Just A Vibes* (Star Trail 1990)★★★, *A Love Affair* (Penthouse 1992)★★★, *Full Attention* (Exterminator 1993)★★★★, *Sweetness* (VP 1993)★★★, *In Control* (Elektra 1994)★★★, *Love From A Distance* (Harmony House 1996)★★★★, *Lifetime Guarantee* (Greensleeves 1997)★★★.

HARDER THEY COME, THE

One of the pivotal music films, *The Harder They Come* played a vital role in introducing Jamaican reggae to an international audience. Filmed in 1971 and released in 1973, it has since become a cult movie, and its attendant soundtrack album proved as crucial to reggae's popularization as Bob Marley And The Wailers' *Catch A Fire*. The film starred Jimmy Cliff as Ivan O. Martin, inspired by the Jamaican legend of Vincent 'Rhygin' Martin, a real-life outlaw who hit the Jamaican headlines in 1948. Cliff is superb in his role, and, indeed, the entire film bristles with atmosphere, humour and action. However, the strengths of *The Harder They Come* are equally drawn from its sub-plot: a portrait of the island's music industry. Rivalries between different entrepreneurs, who run labels and recording studios, are pointedly encapsulated. Producer Perry Henzell, who had previously forged a career in Jamaica producing commercials, judiciously chose a soundtrack spanning five years of Jamaican music, including Toots And The Maytals, Scotty, the Slickers - whose 'Johnny Too Bad' pre-empts the film's plot - and Cliff himself.

The film's plot revolves around Martin, an aspiring singer, who, unable to shake off the 'rude boy' subculture, becomes a folk-hero through his often violent brushes with authority. Having travelled to the Kingston ghetto to inform his mother that his grandmother has died, he quickly learns the harsh reality of life in the city. After being robbed, he begins work for the local minister, and upon visiting a recording studio, successfully persuades the record company boss Mr. Hilton to give him an audition. He records 'The Harder They Come', but subsequently rejects Hilton's paltry offer of $20. His efforts at self-promotion are thwarted when the DJs advise him that Hilton controls the record industry, and although Martin finally signs over the rights to the song, Hilton refuses to promote it. Disillusioned with the recording industry, Martin drifts into dealing in ganja, but soon learns that this industry is also controlled by dominant forces. Martin encourages solidarity among the other dealers, who at first support his stance until they begin to feel pressure. Martin becomes a fugitive and, when exposed, he finds the informant and shoots him. Hilton realizes that Martin's notoriety could prove lucrative and promotes his song, which sails to the top of the charts. Forced underground, Martin attempts to escape to Cuba, but having missed the boat, he is hunted down by the police and is ultimately gunned down. The film also starred Carl Bradshaw and featured comedy act Ed 'Bim' Lewis and Aston 'Bam' Winter with Ken Boothe's elder sister Hyacinth Lewis (née Clover); it also included cameo appearances from Prince Buster and the Maytals. *The Harder They Come* inspired a lengthy piece in *Rolling Stone* magazine, and did much to introduce the history of reggae to the USA.
● ALBUMS: *The Harder They Come* film soundtrack (Island 1972)★★★★★.

HARRIOTT, DERRICK

b. *c.*1942, Kingston, Jamaica, West Indies. While a pupil at Excelsior High School, Harriott formed a duo with Claude Sang Junior, and in 1958 formed the Jiving Juniors with Eugene Dwyer, Herman Sang, and Maurice Winter. In

1960-61 they had hits with 'Over The River' for Coxsone Dodd and 'Lollipop Girl' for Duke Reid. In 1962, Harriott left the group and formed his own label, Crystal. His first solo recording, 'I Care', was a hit, as were 'What Can I Do' (1964), 'The Jerk' (1965) and 'I'm Only Human' (1965). All of these were included on his debut, *The Best Of Derrick Harriott*. In 1967 he had hits with his own 'The Loser' and 'Solomon', the Ethiopians' 'No Baptism' and Keith And Tex's 'Tonight' and 'Stop That Train'. Harriott's sophisticated, soul-styled sound caught the imagination of the Jamaican public - his recordings in the rock-steady style were superlative and still sound fresh and vibrant today. In 1970 he issued the Crystalites' *The Undertaker*, an excellent instrumental album in a similar vein to the early music of the Upsetters, which had been highly popular with the skinhead audience in the UK. Other albums included DJ Scotty's *Schooldays*, Dennis Brown's *Super Reggae And Soul Hits* and his own *14 Chartbuster Hits*. Under the Crystalites banner he issued one of the earliest dub albums, *Scrub A Dub*, becoming one of the first producers to use the talents of King Tubby at his Waterhouse Studio. He followed it with the sublime *More Scrubbing The Dub*, a collection of dub and instrumental versions of his best rhythms.

In the late 70s he utilized the Revolutionaries for Winston McAnuff's *Pick Hits To Click* (1978), DJ Ray I's *Rasta Revival* (1978) and his own *Enter The Chariot* and *Disco 6*, a fine compilation featuring Dennis Brown, Cornell Campbell and Horace Andy. In the 80s he continued to have hits with soul cover versions such as 'Skin To Skin' and 'Checking Out', and in 1988 scored with 'Starting All Over Again', a duet with Yellowman, concerning the affects of Hurricane Gilbert.

● ALBUMS: *The Best Of Derrick Harriott* (Island 1965)★★★★, *The Best Of Derrick Harriott Volume Two* (Trojan 1968)★★★★, *14 Chartbuster Hits* (Crystal 1973)★★★★, *Greatest Reggae Hits* (Trojan 1975)★★★, *Songs For Midnight Lovers* (Trojan 1976)★★★, *Disco 6* (1977)★★★★, *Reggae Disco Rockers* (Charmers 1977)★★★, *Chartbusters 70s Style* (1978)★★★, *Enter The Chariot* (1978)★★★, *Songs For Midnight Lovers* (Trojan 1985)★★★, as Derrick Harriott And Friends *Step Softly* (Trojan 1988)★★★★, *Skin To Skin* (Sarge 1989)★★★, *Musical Chariot* (Charly 1990), as Derrick Harriott And The Jiving Juniors *The Donkey Years 1961-65* (Jamaican Gold 1994)★★★. Productions including Various: *Rock Steady Party* (1967)★★★, *Disco 6* (1977)★★★, *Those Reggae Oldies* covers 1967-72 (1978)★★★, *Riding The Musical Chariot* (1990)★★★★; Dennis Brown *Super Reggae And Soul Hits* (Trojan 1972)★★★★; Crystalites: *The Undertaker* (1970)★★★, *Scrub A Dub* (Crystal 1974)★★★★, *More Scrubbing The Dub* (Crystal 1975)★★★, *Sensimilla Dub* (1980); Winston McAnuff *Pick Hits To Click* (1978)★★★; Ray I *Rasta Revival* (1978)★★★; Scotty *Schooldays* (1972)★★★★; Sly And The Revolutionaries *Go Deh Wid Ridim* (Crystal 1977)★★★; Keith And Tex *Stop That Train* (Crystal 1992)★★★.

HARRIS, DENNIS

b. Jamaica, West Indies. Harris is credited with introducing the term lovers rock to reggae. His initial involvement was marketing recordings from Jamaica under the collective banner of Eve Records, securing a contract to release work from such luminaries as Winston Edwards, Lee Perry and Yabby You. Notable Upsetters releases included Jimmy Riley's cover version of Pluto Shervington's hit, 'Ram Goat Liver', which included a version on the b-side performed by the young Perrys, Omar And Marsha, who also appeared on a different cut of the Mighty Diamonds' 'Talk About It'. Other releases included 'Cutting Razor' by the Versatiles and 'Hurt So Good' by Susan Cadogan, which entered the UK pop chart, peaking at number 4 in 1975 when Harris licensed the release to Magnet. The song also influenced a pop remake by Jimmy Somerville in 1995, revitalizing interest in the original version. Magnet were also licensed to release the classic Junior Byles tune, 'Curly Locks', but disappointingly failed to secure an entry in the UK pop chart. With Yabby You, the label released *Ram A Dam*, considered by many to be a classic, along with Big Youth's 'Lightning Flash (Weakheart Drop)'.

Inspired by his success, Harris began recording in the UK, producing hits with Two In Love ('You Are Mine') and with white singer T.T. Ross (a version of 'Imagine' and a remake of 'Last Date'). 'Last Date' was licensed to Polydor

Records as both parties were hoping to emulate the success of Cadogon's hit. His initial releases surfaced on the Dip, Lucky and Eve labels, but it was the introduction of the Lovers Rock label that coined the phrase that lives on to this day. Harris recorded Brown Sugar for their hits 'I'm In Love With A Dreadlocks', 'Hello Stranger' and 'Black Pride'. Other Lovers Rock productions were Vivian Clark's 'Come And Take Me' and Carolyn And Roland's 'You're Having My Baby', both of which had crossover potential but were sadly overlooked by the media. By 1976 Harris was offering a dub plate service, where anybody could make a trip to Upper Brockley Road and purchase a unique disc similar to those heard in the sound systems, as well as take advantage of his generous rates to hire Eve's eight-track recording studio facilities. He enjoyed enormous success with his dub albums *Leggo Ah Fe We Dis* and *Ah Who Seh Go Deh*, credited to the 4th Street Orchestra whose albums were originally thought to have been recorded in Jamaica. The musicians who had successfully recreated the Jamaican sound were reported to be members of Matumbi, who had recorded the tunes in Harris's south London studio. He also introduced Sunday afternoon auditions in the same way that Coxsone Dodd had done in Jamaica in the early 60s.

In 1977 Laurel Aitken ventured to Harris's studio where he cut a version of the Demis Roussos tune 'Forever And Ever', which worked surprisingly well given a reggae beat. Sadly, by the early 80s Eve Records had vanished, but not before making an important contribution to the history of reggae.

● COMPILATIONS: *Kung Fu Meets The Dragon* (DIP 1975)★★★, *DIP All Stars* (DIP 1976)★★★, *Beautiful People From Jamaica* (Eve 1976)★★★, *Golden Hits* (Lucky 1976)★★★, *Concrete Jungle Dub* (DIP 1976)★★, *Leggo Ah Fe We Dis* (Rama 1976)★★★, *Ah Who Seh Go Deh* (Rama 1977)★★.

HARTLEY, TREVOR

b. c.1958, Morant Bay, St. Thomas, Jamaica, West Indies. Dreaming of becoming a singer in his youth, Hartley managed to voice two sides on rhythms recycled from the Morwells at Joe Gibbs' studio, which eventually saw release on the Pele label. He moved to London in the late 70s, recording with Dennis Bovell on the 1978 double a-side, 'Selassie I'/'Skip Away', followed by sessions with Phill Pratt for his debut album. Unfortunately, shortly after its release the record label went under, neutering its impact. Following a liaison with Sugar Minott's Black Roots label on 'Africa', Hartley worked with Arawak on two 45s before a placement with Top Ranking. Neither yielded the breakthrough Hartley's obvious talents deserved. A revision of the Frankie Beverley/Maze nugget, 'Call On Me,' at least pushed him back into the reggae charts, and his profile was boosted by his participation in the British Reggae Artists Famine Appeal (BRAPA) as a featured vocalist, alongside Aswad and many others. He topped the UK reggae charts again in 1988 with 'Hooked On You', which brought him a contract with London Records. However, like so many before him, the liaison between raw reggae talent and a major label proved a mismatch. Their relationship was not a happy one, although it did yield one minor hit, 'Nine Til Five'. The 90s saw him recording with a variety of production teams, notably Mad Professor and Mafia And Fluxy, work that bodes well for his future.

● ALBUMS: *Innocent Lover* (Burning Sounds 1979)★★★, *Hartical* (Jove 1993)★★.

HEARTLAND REGGAE

Released in 1980, this Canadian film documents a memorable concert, held in Kingston, Jamaica, to commemorate the twelfth anniversary of a visit by the Ethiopian emperor, Haile Selassie. Although technically poor and marred by distorted sound, *Heartland Reggae* includes performances by many of the island's most popular musicians, notably Bob Marley And The Wailers, Peter Tosh, vocalist Dennis Brown, DJ U-Roy, Inner Circle and pop duo Althea And Donna. The event was held during a rancorous general election campaign, marred by gang violence and murder. In one memorable scene, Marley, himself the subject of an assassination attempt, brings together Jamaican Prime Minister Michael Manley and opposition leader Edward Seaga in a symbolic gesture of greater unity. Coincidentally, involvement in the music industry was among businessman Seaga's many interests. Although not essential viewing, *Heartland Reggae* captures a crucial time in

Jamaican politics and documents a concert held in celebration of a figurehead crucial to the island's Rastafarian subculture.

HENRY, MARCIA

(see Sister Love)

HEPTONES

Leroy Sibbles (b. 1949, Jamaica, West Indies), Barry Llewellyn (b. 1947, Jamaica) and Earl Morgan (b. 1945, Jamaica) were without doubt the foremost rocksteady and reggae vocal trio, and their work together, especially for Studio One, set the standards by which all other Jamaican harmony groups are measured. They started with Ken Lack's Caltone label, but failed to record any hits, although they produced a memorable and bizarre version of the 'William Tell Overture' entitled 'Gun Men Coming To Town'. Their next move, to Coxsone Dodd's Studio One set-up in 1966, coincided with the rise of rocksteady, and the Heptones proved to be masters of the genre. Not only did Sibbles possess a pure and delicate lead voice and a masterly songwriting talent, he was also responsible for many of the music's most popular (and versioned) bass lines, which were sufficiently versatile and melodic to be able to record any number of different instrumental and vocal takes. The Heptones quickly became the most imitated and influential vocal group in Jamaica. After their first big hit in Jamaica and the UK, the lewd and suggestive 'Fattie Fattie', which was a big seller despite being banned from the radio, nothing could hold them back. Sibbles wrote love songs and social/protest/reality songs almost to order, but he excelled with the sly misogyny of 'Tripe Girl': 'You tried to hurt me but you can't', and 'I Hold The Handle': 'I hold the handle, you've got the blade ... When I wake up in the morning fix me some orange juice ... When I wake up in the morning just put yourself to use'. His voice swooped and soared, and all the time Morgan and Llewellyn filled in beautifully behind him, taking occasional lead and even contributing songs, such as Llewellyn's 'Pretty Looks', which proved just as popular and enduring as Sibbles' own compositions.

The Heptones left Studio One in 1971, a bitter parting for Sibbles in particular, who had been employed at Brentford Road as a bassist, musical arranger and talent scout, and, while Dodd is reluctant to discuss the past, Sibbles has voiced many accusations. It was a sad end to an association that gave the world so much great music. This was by no means the end for the Heptones, however, and they went on to work for Joe Gibbs, Harry J., Augustus Pablo, Harry Mudie, Geoffrey Chung, Phill Pratt, Rupie Edwards and many more - a veritable who's who of the Jamaican music world of the early 70s - and they produced hit after hit. In 1973 they relocated briefly to Canada, but returned to Jamaica and recorded what was their most commercially successful album, *Party Time*, for the Upsetter - Lee Perry - consisting mainly of recuts of their Studio One hits. It appeared, for a time, that the Heptones would follow Bob Marley And The Wailers into the realms of international stardom, but for some reason - and it was certainly nothing to do with the power and strength of their music - it did not happen. Sibbles left for a solo career, returning again to Canada where he has based himself intermittently ever since, and he continues to tour and sporadically release interesting records. Llewellyn and Morgan recruited Naggo Morris and continued as the Heptones; although they were solid and workmanlike, they unfortunately failed to match the power and beauty of their earlier recordings.

● ALBUMS: *The Heptones* (Studio One 1967)★★★★, *On Top* (Studio One 1968)★★★★, *Black Is Black* (Studio One 60s)★★★, *Ting A Ling* (Studio One 60s)★★★, *Freedom Line* (Studio One 1971)★★★, *Heptones & Friends Meet the Now Generation* (Trojan 1972)★★★, *Party Time* (Island 1976)★★★, *Night Food* (Island 1976)★★★, *Better Days* (Third World 1979)★★★, *Good Life* (Greensleeves 1979)★★★, *Back On Top* (Vista Sounds 1983)★★★, *In A Dance Hall Style* (Vista Sound 1983)★★★, *Swing Low* (Burning Sounds 1985)★★★, *Changing Time* (Thunderbolt 1987)★★, *On The Run* (Shanachie 1987)★★, *Sing Good Vibes* (Clarendon 1988)★★.

● COMPILATIONS: *Legends From Studio One* (Trenchtown 1985)★★★★, *22 Golden Hits* (TTP 1986)★★★★, *Big And Free* (Trenchtown 1989)★★★, *Original Heptones* (Trenchtown 1989)★★★★, *Nightfood In A Party Time* (Trenchtown 1989)★★★, *On The Road Again*

(Trenchtown 1990)★★★, *20 Golden Hits* (Sonic Sounds 1992)★★★★.

HIGGS, JOE

b. 3 June 1940, Kingston, Jamaica, West Indies. In the late 50s Higgs joined Roy Wilson to form the duo Higgs And Wilson. In 1959 they recorded their first single, 'Mammy Oh', for politico Edward Seaga, and it became a massive hit. In the early 60s they worked for Coxsone Dodd, and had several further hits including 'How Can I Be Sure' and 'There's A Reward'. Higgs was also coaching a young group called the Wailers, and he subsequently introduced them to Dodd, who launched their career. In the mid-60s Higgs decided to pursue a solo career, and made further recordings for Dodd including 'Change Of Plans' and 'Neighbour Neighbour'. In the early 70s Higgs recorded for a variety of producers, and outstanding songs from this period include 'The Wave Of War' and 'The World Is Spinning Round' (1972) for Harry J., 'Burning Fire' (1974) for Rupie Edwards, 'More Slavery' (1975) for Jack Ruby, and 'Creation' (1975), a self-production. In 1975, Higgs finally had an album released, the excellent *Life Of Contradiction*. The imaginatively arranged songs were given faultless jazz-tinged performances by a group that included jazz guitarist Eric Gale. Further albums followed, with 1979's *Unity Is Power* and 1985's *Triumph* particularly strong collections. Higgs' thoughtful lyrics and expressive voice have made him one of the most singular artists to come from Jamaica.
● ALBUMS: *Life Of Contradiction* (Grounation 1975)★★★★, *Unity Is Power* (One Stop/Island 1979)★★★, *Triumph* (Alligator 1985)★★★, *Family* (Blue Mountain 1988)★★, *Blackman Know Thyself* (Shanachie 1990)★★.

HIGH NOTE RECORDS

(see Pottinger, Sonia)

HINDS, JUSTIN

b. 7 May 1942, Steertown, St. Anns, Jamaica, West Indies. Justin Hinds, together with backing vocalists the Dominoes (Dennis Sinclair and Junior Dixon), first recorded in late 1963 for producer Duke Reid. That first session produced an instant hit, 'Carry Go Bring Come', recorded in one take, and set a pattern from which Hinds

rarely deviated - Hinds' expressive country/gospel tenor lead vocals, with empathetic support from the two Dominoes, backed by the Treasure Isle studio band led by Tommy McCook and Herman Marquis. Hinds was Reid's most successful artist in the period from 1964 to 1966, reputedly recording 70 singles. He stayed with Reid until 1972; the relationship produced some of the finest Jamaican music, through ska, rocksteady and reggae. In the former style, 'King Samuel', 'Botheration', 'Jump Out Of The Frying Pan' (all 1964), 'The Ark', 'Peace And Love' and the bawdy 'Rub Up Push Up' (all 1965) are exemplary. The transition to the rocksteady format during 1966-67 resulted in hits such as 'The Higher The Monkey Climbs', 'No Good Rudy', a new rocksteady version of 'Carry Go Bring Come', 'On A Saturday Night', 'Once A Man', an anguished cover version of the Rip Chords' 'Here I Stand' and the sublime 'Save A Bread', both in 1968. Lyrically, Hinds utilized the rich Jamaican tradition of proverb and parable to reflect the wide range of issues thrown up by a society in transition from country to city. After Reid's death in 1975, Hinds made two albums with sound system owner and producer Jack Ruby. In 1978 he also recorded a handful of discs for producer Sonia Pottinger. Titles such as 'What A Weeping', 'Rig-Ma'Roe Game' and 'Wipe Your Weeping Eyes' showcased Hind's beautiful and expressive voice, and highlighted his lyrical concerns. Since 1985, when he recorded the excellent album *Travel With Love* for Nighthawk Records of St. Louis, he has apparently preferred the rural lifestyle to the 'rat race' of Kingston. He is also part of the Wingless Angels, a group of Nyahbingi Rastafarian drummers.
● ALBUMS: *Best Of Justin Hinds & The Dominoes* (1968)★★★, *Jezebel* (Island 1976)★★★, *From Jamaica With Reggae* (High Note 1984)★★★, *Travel With Love* (Night Hawk 1985)★★★★, *Justin Hinds* (Jwyanza 1990)★★, *Early Recordings* (Esoldun/Treasure Isle 1992)★★★.

HOLNESS, WINSTON 'NINEY'

b. 1951, Montego Bay, Jamaica, West Indies. Winston 'Niney' Holness, aka The Observer, is one of the great characters of reggae music. Nicknamed 'Niney' when he lost a thumb in a workshop accident, he has been a singer, producer, engineer, DJ, fixer, arranger, manager and virtually everything else in reggae. Although Holness had organized bands to play at school dances in the 50s, it was not until he came under the tutelage of producer Bunny Lee in the late 60s that he achieved his entry into the professional music business. In 1967/8 he worked with Lee Perry for Joe Gibbs, taking over when Perry left in mid-1968 to start his own label. By 1970 he had set up his own operation, with his first production entitled 'Mr Brown'/'Everybody Bawling' by DJs Dennis Alcapone and Lizzy. It sold modestly, but his next record, 'Blood & Fire', released in December 1970, was an immediate smash, eventually selling 30,000 copies in Jamaica alone. The tune propelled Holness into the front rank of the new 'rebel' vanguard, establishing him as a producer fully capable of building original rhythms. The record bore a slight resemblance to Bob Marley's 'Duppy Conqueror' but far outsold it, and the pair clashed when Marley heard the record. Holness productions of the early 70s are characterized by their sparse simplicity and heaviness, often cultural/political in sentiment, and frequently espousing Rasta themes.

During 1973 he began an association with Dennis Brown, with the results released initially by Joe Gibbs, but later that year records began appearing on Holness's 'Observer' label. Again Holness had changed the beat, and Brown became the hottest singer of 1974. The local hits of the period included 'Westbound Train' (1973), 'Cassandra', 'I Am The Conqueror', and 'No More Will I Roam' (all 1974). Brown's sessions with Holness constitute a high point in the development of reggae during the 70s. Holness also issued records by Gregory Isaacs, Michael Rose, Junior Delgado, Sang Hugh, Horace Andy, Delroy Wilson, Leroy Smart, Junior Byles and Cornell Campbell. He issued a dub album - *Dubbing With The Observer* - mixed by King Tubby's, and DJ music by the likes of U-Roy, Big Youth, I. Roy, Dillinger and Trinity. At the end of the 70s Holness vanished from view, only to materialize in Paris in 1982. During the mid-80s he worked at Kingston's Channel One studio in an unspecified capacity, and issued a few singles and an album. He was next spotted in New York, apparently retired, although he went on to release his first new work in years, with record-ings by Frankie Paul and Andrew Tosh.

● ALBUMS: *Dubbing With The Observer* (Attack 1975)★★★★, *Live At The Turntable Club* (1975)★★★, *Sledgehammer Dub* (1976)★★★, *Niney The Observer* (Charly 1990)★★★, *Turbo Charge* (Rounder 1991)★★★.

● COMPILATIONS: *Blood & Fire 1971-1972* (Trojan 1988)★★★★, *Bring The Couchie 1974-1976* (Trojan 1989)★★★.

HOLT, ERROL

b. *c.*1959, Kingston, Jamaica, West Indies. Holt began recording in the mid-70s with Prince Far I and Ja Man. Early hits included 'Who Have Eyes To See', 'Gimme Gimme' and 'Shark Out Deh'. In 1976 he recorded 'A You Lick Me First', a sound system hit that provided the foundation to the Jah Woosh hit 'Lick Him With The Dustbin'. In the same year he was enrolled as part of Maurice Wellington's group the Morwells. He stayed with the group until its demise in the early 80s. While with the band he performed on the hits 'Kingston 12 Tuffy' and 'Africa We Want To Go'. With fellow band member Bingi Bunny he formed the Roots Radics, who became the most in-demand session band on the island. Holt also shared production credits with Gregory Isaacs for *Out Deh*. The band's performance with Isaacs on his UK tour led to their being in demand to support the island's top performers. In 1985 Roots Radics released 'Earsay', with Holt singing on the b-side a cover version of Delroy Wilson's 'I'm Not A King'.

● ALBUMS: *Vision Of Africa* (Dread & Dread 1982)★★★★.

HOLT, JOHN

b. 1947, Kingston, Jamaica, West Indies. At the age of 12 Holt's voice was a regular feature of the talent contests run by Vere Johns at various Jamaican theatres, and by 1963 Holt had cut his first single, 'I Cried A Tear'/'Forever I'll Stay', for Leslie Kong's Beverley's label. Holt also recorded duets with Alton Ellis for Randy's, including 'Rum Bumper' (1964). Between 1965 and 1970 he was lead singer with the Paragons, one of the smoothest, most accomplished vocal trios in reggae, and heavily dependent on Holt's precise, creamy tenor. The group's work with producer Duke Reid was impeccable, and they enjoyed a string of hits, 'Ali Baba', 'Tonight' and

'I See Your Face', among them. Holt, sometimes with the Paragons, also worked with Studio One on sides such as 'Fancy Make-Up', 'A Love I Can Feel', 'Let's Build Our Dreams' and 'OK Fred' (later a chart smash for Errol Dunkley), as well as Prince Buster ('Oh Girl', 'My Heart Is Gone'). By the early 70s Holt was one of reggae's biggest stars and ready to cross over into the pop market. His 'Stick By Me', one of dozens of songs he cut with producer Bunny Lee, was the biggest-selling Jamaican record of 1972. Just over a year later, his *Time Is The Master* set for producer Harry Mudie proved a masterpiece, and pointed the way ahead: fine songs (among them cover versions of Ivory Joe Hunter's 'It May Sound Silly' and Brook Benton's 'Looking Back'), heavy rhythms, and a sweet addition of lush, orchestral arrangements recorded in London. Trojan Records issued a bestselling series of Bunny Lee-produced John Holt albums, including the *1,000/2,000/3,000 Volts* series, and brought him to London to work with Tony Ashfield, who again used string arrangements. In December 1974 he achieved a huge pop hit across Europe with 'Help Me Make It Through The Night', but Holt was more than a balladeer, and by 1976 he was enjoying further Jamaican success with 'Up Park Camp', a massive roots hit for producer Joseph 'Joe Joe' Hookim. A brief experiment with disco (*Holt Goes Disco*) was virtually the only blot on his copybook during the 70s, and he has continued to work in a contemporary style to the present day, occasionally enjoying enormous roots reggae hits ('Police In Helicopter' in 1987) while still being willing to work in other styles, as demonstrated by the *Reggae, Hip House, R&B Flavor* album title he employed in 1993. He remains a unique talent, perhaps underrated among more élitist fans because of his flirtation with the pop world.

● ALBUMS: *A Love I Can Feel* (Studio One 1971)★★★, *Greatest Hits* (Studio One 1972)★★★★, *Presenting The Fabulous John Holt* (Trojan 1973)★★★★, *Holt* (Trojan 1973)★★★, *Still In Chains* (Trojan 1973)★★★, *1,000 Volts Of Holt* (Trojan 1973)★★★, *Time Is The Master* (Creole 1974)★★★★, *Dusty Roads* (Trojan 1974)★★★, *Sings For I* (Trojan 1974)★★, *Pledging My Love* (Trojan 1975)★★★, *Before The Next Teardrop Falls* (Klik 1976)★★★, *Up Park Camp* (Channel One 1977)★★★, *Holt Goes Disco* (Trojan 1977)★★, *2,000 Volts Of Holt* (Trojan 1979)★★★, *Just The Two Of Us* (CSA 1982)★★★, *Sweetie Come Brush Me* (Volcano 1982)★★★, *Police In Helicopter* (Greensleeves 1983)★★★, *Further You Look* (Trojan 1983)★★, *Let It Go On* (Trojan 1983)★★★, *For Lovers And Dancers* (Trojan 1984)★★★, *Live In London* (Very Good 1984)★★★, with Dennis Brown *Wild Fire* (Natty Congo 1986)★★★, *3,000 Volts Of Holt* (Trojan 1986)★★★, *Reggae Christmas Album* (Trojan 1986)★★, with Horace Andy *From One Extreme To Another* (Beta 1986)★★★, *OK Fred* (Spartan 1987)★★, *Time Is The Master* (Creole 1988)★★★, *Rock With Me Baby* (Trojan 1988)★★★, *If I Were A Carpenter* (1989)★★, *Why I Care* (Greensleeves 1989)★★★, *Reggae, Hip House, R&B Flavor* (1993)★★★, *Peacemaker* (1993).

● COMPILATIONS: *Roots Of Holt* (Trojan 1983)★★★, *Greatest Hits* (Prince Buster 1984)★★★, *Pure Gold* (Vista Sounds 1985)★★★, *16 Songs For Soulful Lovers* (Platinum 1986)★★★, *Living Legend* (Classic 1986)★★★, *20 Golden Love Songs* (Trojan 1986)★★★★, *Let Your Love Flow* (CSA 1988)★★★, *Best Of* (Action Replay 1990)★★★★, *Love Songs Volume 2* (Parish 1992)★★★.

HOME T

b. Michael Bennet, c.1962, Kingston, Jamaica, West Indies. Bennet began his career as a vocalist in the quartet Home T4, and in 1980 had a hit with 'Irons In The Fire'. The group later became known for covering popular standards, including versions of Bunny Wailer's 'Cool Runnings' and Marvin Gaye's 'What's Going On'. They established their popularity with live performances at the Reggae Sunsplash Show in 1984 and were the only vocal group to appear on the Dancehall '84 stage show in Kingston alongside Half Pint, Michael Palmer, Edi Fitzroy, Charlie Chaplin and Ini Kamoze. The group's recorded output never reached the top of the charts despite working with Sly Dunbar and Robbie Shakespeare. They were, however, able to find some success on their collaborations with Josie Wales ('Changing'), Yellowman ('Mr Counsellor') and Phillip Papa Levi ('Dear Pastor') in the mid-80s, which brought them to the attention of a wider audience. Following the reduction of the group to a trio, Bennet continued recording as Home T, with Tony Anderson and Winston 'Diego' Tucker at Gussie Clarke's Music Works Studio. They had hits with 'Rockers Don't Move You', 'Are You Going My Way', 'How Hot' and 'Same Friend'. In 1988 they recorded a version of 'Telephone Love' as 'Single Life', while also providing backing vocals and helping to arrange the original version for J.C. Lodge. In 1990 Gussie Clarke recorded the combined talents of Shabba Ranks, Cocoa Tea and Home T for 'Pirates Anthem'. When the London-based pirate radio station Kiss FM was granted a license the track was selected as the first tune to be played on the now legal transmission. Home T continued working with Clarke until the early 90s when he set up his Philadelphia-based Two Friends label with Patrick Lindsay. They continued to utilize the Music Works Recording Studio, producing hits for Dennis Brown, Cocoa Tea, Shabba Ranks and Cutty Ranks. With Brown, the duo produced 'No More Walls', which became a massive hit. The combined talents of Home T, Cocoa Tea and Shabba were also produced by the Two Friends crew in 1991 and they had a hit on the reggae charts with a version of the Philadelphia Sounds track 'Your Body's Here With Me'. Other hits for the duo included Gregory Isaacs' 'Loverman', Brian and Tony Gold's, 'Ram Dance' and Daddy Lizard's 'Show Them The Way'. When Shabba was unavailable to record a follow-up to the successful combination single, Cutty Ranks took the DJ role. This coalition topped the reggae chart with 'The Going Is Rough' and the equally successful 'Another One For The Road'. By 1992 Mikey Melody had moved on to producing with Clifton 'Specialist' Dillon as Twin City productions, and enjoyed international success with a remake of 'Mr Loverman' by Shabba Ranks and Chevelle Franklin (originally a Deborahe Glasgow hit) and 'Housecall' with Maxi Priest and Shabba. Twin City enjoyed a number of hits but competition from Steely And Clevie overshadowed the duo's success.

● ALBUMS: *Sly & Robbie Present Home T4* (Taxi 1983)★★★★, with Cocoa Tea, Shabba Ranks *Holding On* (Greensleeves 1989)★★★, with Cocoa Tea, Cutty Ranks *Another One For The Road* (Greensleeves 1991)★★★, *Red Hot* (Two Friends 1992)★★★.

HONEY BOY

b. Keith Williams, *c*.1955, St. Elizabeth, Jamaica, West Indies. Williams moved to Britain in the late 60s and settled in Oxford before moving to London. He began his career working with Laurel Aitken on the session that resulted in 'Guilty' by Tiger (one of Aitken's pseudonyms) for the Palmer brothers. Honey Boy's first session as a vocalist came when working for Junior Lincoln, who had set up an independent label after leaving B&C Music. Lincoln's label Banana had been an outlet for Coxsone Dodd's Studio One recordings in the UK, but also released Honey Boy's debut, 'Homeward Bound'. His alias was appropriate because his vocal cords were considered to be sweeter than honey. Although the single did not make a big impact, many releases followed, including 'I'm Not Going Down', 'Sweet Cherie' and 'Happiness Comes'.

He also recorded under different guises, as Happy Junior on 'Sugar Dandy', and as Boy Wonder on 'All On The House'. His vocals also graced *Trojan Reggae Party Volume One* when he performed alongside the Pioneers, Greyhound, Bruce Ruffin, Nicky Thomas, Delroy Wilson and Count Prince Miller. By 1976 he had teamed up with Winston Curtis, a Studio One veteran who had taken up residence in the UK, and a number of releases followed, notably 'Rock Me' and 'Who Baby'. He was also a featured vocalist on *Winston's Greats*. In 1977 Honey Boy recorded for Count Shelley cover versions of Derrick Harriott's 'Penny For Your Song' and Jackie Edwards' 'Keep On Running'. In 1980, Honey Boy returned to Curtis, and with the nucleus of Aswad, Angus 'Drummie Zeb' Gaye, Tony 'Gad' Robinson and George Oban, he released *Arise*. Although a major hit has eluded him, he has been involved in the UK reggae scene for many years and is considered to be one of the pioneers of lovers rock.

● ALBUMS: *Sweet Cherries Impossible Love* (Cactus 1974)★★★, *Taste Of Honey* (Cactus 1975)★★★, *This Is Honey Boy* (Third World 1975)★★★, *Strange Thoughts* (Trojan 1977)★★★, *Arise* (Diamond 1980)★★.

HONOURABLE APACHE

b. Richard Bailey, Kingston, Jamaica, West Indies. Bailey's academic achievements led to his initial aspiration to become a teacher. He may well have fulfilled his ambition had he not been drawn to the delights of the dancehall and remarkably emulated his DJ heroes.

In the mid-80s he emigrated to Baltimore, USA. He soon found solace with a local sound system, where he nurtured his career. Although he proved a competent performer, his location in Baltimore offered little opportunity to sustain a career as a DJ. In 1988 he moved to Miami where his reputation quickly spread, and he attracted the attention of Willie Lindo who took him into the studio. The sessions resulted in 'Stamina Man', 'Hurricane' and 'Gangsta Roll' for Lindo's Heavy Beat label. The historic end to Nelson Mandela's incarceration was described in Apache's 1990 hit, 'Them Free Mandela'. In the same year, he recorded in combination with Screwdriver the local hit 'Long Time'. His success led to live appearances at the Jamaican Reggae Sunsplash Festival in 1992 and 1993, as well as the Miami Reggae Festival, previously known as the Jamaica Awareness Reggae Festival, for four consecutive years.

In 1994 Honourable Apache produced his biggest hit, 'Yardie Anthem'. His prominence led to a signing with Clifton 'Specialist' Dillon, who, through his Shang production stable, successfully exposed works by Shabba Ranks, Mad Cobra and Patra to a global audience. By the mid-90s he became the Hono Rebel Apache, a name emphasizing his unwillingness to compromise his music for commercial purposes.

HOOKIM, JOSEPH 'JOE JOE'

b. Jamaica, West Indies. One of four brothers involved with music from an early age (the other brothers were Kenneth, Ernest and Paulie), Joe Joe and his brother Ernest started on the bottom rung of the entertainment industry ladder, controlling juke-boxes and one-armed bandits, but in 1970 the Jamaican government outlawed gaming machines. The brothers subsequently decided to branch out and build their own recording studio - Channel One - in the heart of the Kingston ghetto on Maxfield Avenue. At first, Joe Joe hired veteran Sid Bucknor as engineer, since none of his family were particularly adept at the technical side of the business, but before long, Ernest took over at the mixing desk. By this time, the

Hookims also had their own pressing plant and label-printing workshop. Channel One slowly established a name for itself with releases on a variety of different labels from established singers such as Leroy Smart, Junior Byles and Horace Andy, but it was when the Mighty Diamonds started work for them that everything came together, particularly after the release of 'Right Time' in 1976. The Diamonds offered an exciting and different rockers rhythm, dominated by 'militant' double drumming courtesy of Sly Dunbar of the in-house Revolutionaries band. The sound influenced the entire Jamaican music business for the next two years, with every producer on the island formulating their own variation on the beat.

The bestsellers continued for the Diamonds, along with DJs Dillinger and Trinity, plus countless instrumental records from the Revolutionaries that appeared in the charts; Joe Joe professed embarrassment at seeing nine out of the Top 10 records on his own Well Charge label! Many of the rhythms were versions of Studio One classics, which caused some friction, and Joe Joe was the object of a great deal of criticism. He was, however, always open about the fact that he copied some of Coxsone Dodd's rhythms. Throughout the 70s and on into the mid-80s, the Maxfield Avenue Studio was in constant demand by artists and producers, all hoping to capture a little of the magic, and in 1979 the set-up was upgraded to sixteen tracks to accommodate the demand. The Hookim brothers were the first to introduce 12-inch 45 rpm records to Jamaica with 'Truly' by the Jayes (a version of an old Marcia Griffiths Studio One hit), which was released with a DJ version by Ranking Trevor. The dynamic range of these 12-inch releases was a vast improvement on the 7-inch, and the 12-inch 'Disco-Mix' went on to become an integral part of reggae music, with vocal, DJ and instrumental cuts of the same rhythm all together on one release. Less successful were the 'Channel One Economic Packages' - 7-inch releases that played at 33 and a third rpm, but, sadly, the sound quality left much to be desired and these were soon discontinued. Joe Joe founded a New York branch of Channel One and in the early 80s their future looked assured as he released a highly successful and much imitated series of 'Clash' albums from the USA - featuring a different artist on each side. Even with hindsight it is difficult to see exactly what went wrong at Channel One, but the Kingston and New York operations were summarily shut down in the late 80s and the innovative Hookim brothers are no longer active in the music business.

● COMPILATIONS: Various Artists: *Jonkanoo Dub* (Cha Cha 1978)★★★, *General For All General - Dance Hall Style* (Hitbound 1984)★★★★, *Hit Bound! Revolutionary Sound Of Channel One* 1976-79 recordings (Heartbeat 1990)★★★★

H.R.

b. Paul Hudson, USA. Former Bad Brains vocalist H.R., aka Joseph I, left his former employees in the mid-80s to follow his religious beliefs more closely. His subsequent work, although much more closely allied to dub and reggae, still betrayed the abrasive punk energy of Bad Brains on some tracks. Releases progressively minimized that influence, however, and his second set featured not only his brother and Bad Brains drummer Earl Hudson, but also Oscar Brown Jnr. The textured reggae funk that resulted was surprisingly pop-orientated. *Singin' In The Heart* offered a more straight-up, quasi-religious feel. The lyrics reflect the eagerness of H.R.'s Rasta vision, though there was also space for more soulful ballads.

It is difficult to perceive a more authentic roots reggae artefact than *Charge*. Composed entirely of old-school reggae songs, the album was so unswerving in its dedications to Jah that all other attributes faded into the background. He also worked with roots lynchpin Ras Michael on a set of songs that H.R. co-wrote and produced. H.R. returned to Bad Brains in 1994, but was dismissed a year later after he assaulted band members before a show. He was then arrested at the Canadian border and charged with a drugs offence.

● ALBUMS: *Its About Luv* (Olive Tree 1985)★★★, *Human Rights* (SST 1987)★★★, *HR Tapes '84 - '86* (SST 1988)★★★, with Ras Michael *Zion Train* (SST 1988)★★★, *Singin' In The Heart* (SST 1989)★★, *Charge* (SST 1990)★★★.

HUDSON, KEITH

b. 1946, Kingston, Jamaica, West Indies, d. 14 November 1984, New York, USA. As a youth, Hudson attended Boys Town School where his fellow pupils included Bob Marley, Delroy Wilson, Ken Boothe and the Heptones, with whom he organized school concerts. From an early age, he was a sound system fanatic, and became an ardent follower of Coxsone Dodd's Downbeat. He also came to know members of the Skatalites, and gained entry to Studio One recording sessions by carrying Don Drummond's trombone. He was only 14 years old when he produced his first recording, an instrumental featuring members of the Skatalites that eventually saw release with a blank label in 1968, and two years later was reused for Dennis Alcapone's 'Shades Of Hudson'. After leaving school, he served an apprenticeship in dentistry, and subsidized his early recordings with money earned from these skills. In late 1967, he launched his Inbidimts label with Ken Boothe's 'Old Fashioned Way', which subsequently became a number 1 in Jamaica. Over the next two years he released hits by Delroy Wilson ('Run Run') and John Holt ('Never Will I Hurt My Baby'). In 1970 he began to feature himself as a vocalist with 'Working Like A Slave' and 'Don't Get Confused', which caused a sensation at the time. Over the next two years, he had hits with U-Roy's 'Dynamic Fashion Way', Alton Ellis' 'Big Bad Boy', Dennis Alcapone's 'The Sky's The Limits', Big Youth's 'S.90 Skank' and Soul Syndicate's 'Riot', and released a host of other singles on his Imbidimts, Mafia, Rebind and other labels. His willingness to experiment was evident on U-Roy's 'Dynamic Fashion Way', on which he re-employed the 'Old Fashioned Way' rhythm, added a string bass to lay a new bassline, and overdubbed saxophone to transform the track completely. For 'S.90 Skank' he arranged for a motorcycle to be surreptitiously brought into Byron Lee's recording studio so that he could record it being revved up. It created such an impact on motorcycle-mad Jamaica that Coxsone Dodd, Lee Perry and other producers were soon wheeling motorcycles into their recording sessions.

In 1972 Hudson released his first LP, *Furnace*, on his Imbidimts label, which featured four songs by himself, together with DJ, instrumental and dub tracks. He followed this with *Class And Subject*, and though he continued to record other artists, from this point in time he concentrated on his own career. In 1973 he emigrated to London, issuing *Entering The Dragon*, which showed him continuing to experiment and develop, even if the results at this stage were inconsistent. In particular, his practice of utilizing one rhythm track for two or more different songs on one album was an innovation that only fully entered the reggae mainstream some ten years later. In 1974 he released *Flesh Of My Skin, Blood Of My Blood*, which still stands as a masterpiece. Sandwiched between two atmospheric instrumentals was a series of uplifting laments set to bare, understated rhythms, which sounded like nothing that had preceded them and nothing that has followed them, forcefully conveying not only a feeling of pain and oppression, but also an iron resolve to endure and defeat those obstacles. There were two further stunning releases in 1975: *Torch of Freedom* and *Pick A Dub*. The latter is simply one of the greatest dub albums ever issued, featuring versions of his classic singles plus cover versions of the Abyssinians' 'Satta Massa Gana' and 'Declaration Of Rights'. It also included both the vocal and dub cuts of his cover version of the Dramatics' Stax hit, 'In The Rain', on which he makes the song wholly his own. *Torch Of Freedom* was another one-off stroke of genius, featuring an understated, introverted sound with a distinct soul influence, for a series of songs on the theme of love, before eventually changing its focus for the final song, the visionary title track.

In 1976 he moved to New York and signed a four-year contract with Virgin Records, who had followed Island Records' lead in signing reggae acts in response to increased interest in the music, primarily from a new, predominantly white audience. If Hudson had released a strong mainstream reggae album at this juncture, then he would probably have become at least as big a star as Burning Spear or Dennis Brown. However, Hudson's insatiable desire to keep moving artistically and try new things compelled him to follow his own course, and he duly delivered to Virgin a fully blown soul album, *Too Expensive*. Virgin marketed it along with their

reggae releases, but it sounded so out of step with prevailing tastes and expectations that it received a savaging at the hands of the press, and generated poor sales. In truth, it is a strong album, let down only by two poor tracks and an irritating, thin saxophone sound. The reaction to the album severely strained Hudson's relationship with Virgin, and he released his next single, '(Jonah) Come Out Now', under the pseudonym of Lloyd Linberg on his wryly titled Tell A Tale label. Hudson had moved on again, returning to reggae and reusing the rhythm he had previously employed for 'The Betrayer' to build a classic track. Virgin were evidently underwhelmed by their artist's intention to make each album entirely different, and they terminated Hudson's contract. In October, he released another excellent single in Jamaica, 'Rasta Country', before starting Joint, his new label in New York.

In 1977 a dub album, *Brand* (aka *The Joint*) was issued, followed the next year by its companion vocal set, *Rasta Communication*, which included 'Rasta Country' and a remade 'Jonah'. The brilliant, militant songs, outstanding rhythms and inspired playing made both of these albums masterpieces. An unusual feature enhancing several tracks was the excellent slide guitar work of Willy Barratt, who added a ghostly shimmer to the sound. In 1979, he again preceded his new vocal album with its dub counterpart, but *Nuh Skin Up Dub* and *From One Extreme To Another* were less inspired than their predecessors and were marred by overuse of in-vogue synth-drums. Nevertheless, they still contained some fine music. That year, Hudson also issued a strong DJ album to back *Brand*, Militant Barry's *Green Valley*. *Playing It Cool* was an excellent set, featuring new songs built over six of his earlier rhythms. The following year *Steaming Jungle* was issued, but proved to be his most disappointing release.

In early 1984 rumours circulated that Hudson was recording with the Wailers in New York, but nothing was ever released. In August he was diagnosed as having lung cancer. He received radiation therapy, and appeared to be responding well to the treatment, but on the morning of 14 November he complained of stomach pains, collapsed and died. Very little of his music has remained on catalogue. Hopefully this situation will change, and allow his music to be appreciated by the wider audience it deserves.

● ALBUMS: *Furnace* (Imbidimts 1972)★★★, *Class And Subject* (1972)★★★, *Entering The Dragon* (1973)★★★, *Flesh Of My Skin, Blood Of My Blood* (Mamba 1974)★★★★, *Torch Of Freedom* (Altra 1975)★★★★, *Pick A Dub* (1975)★★★★, *Too Expensive* (Virgin 1976)★★★, *Brand/The Joint* (Joint 1977)★★★★, *Rasta Communication* (Joint 1978)★★★★, *Nuh Skin Up Dub* (1979)★★, *From One Extreme To Another* (1979)★★, *Playing It Cool* (1981)★★★★, *Steaming Jungle* (Vista Sounds 1982)★★.

● COMPILATIONS: various artists *The Big J Of Reggae* covers 1970-75 (1978)★★★, various artists *Studio Kinda Cloudy* covers 1967-72 (Trojan 1988)★★★★.

HUNNINGALE, PETER

b. *c*.1962, London, England. Hunningale, aka Mr Honey Vibes, established his reputation in the lovers rock idiom. He began his musical career playing bass as part of the Vibes Corner Collective, which also featured Barrington Levine, Jimmy Simpson, Ray Simpson and Fitzroy Blake. In 1982 he released his debut as a singer, 'Slipping Away'/'Swing And Dine', which sold respectably on LGR Records. 'Got To Know You'/'Money Money' was then issued on his own Street Vibes label, which he co-founded with long-term collaborator Blake (it is now run in association with Tippa Irie and Crucial Robbie). In 1987 he topped the UK reggae chart with 'Be My Lady', regarded by many as his debut. The success of this single and his debut album led to a prolific period that included the singles 'Falling', 'Its My Turn', 'If You Want It' and 'Mr Vibes'. The popularity of combination hits from Jamaica inspired Hunningale and Tippa Irie to team up for 'Ragamuffin Girl' in 1989, which went straight to number 1 in the UK reggae charts, and was voted Best British Reggae Record by *Echoes* newspaper at the close of the year; the single led to a long and fruitful partnership with Irie. With this success behind them they embarked on two album collaborations - *The New Decade* for Island Records and *Done Cook And Currie* for Rebel MC's Tribal Base label. The former collection was produced by

Hunningale himself and featured two songs popular on the UK sound system circuit, 'Shocking Out' and 'Dibi Dibi'. He also produced and played all the instruments on *Done Cook And Currie*, which produced another major domestic reggae hit with 'Inner City'. His second solo album, *Mr Vibes*, followed in the same year. Hunningale's next collaboration with Irie came in 1993, this time a single, 'Shouting For The Gunners', to celebrate their mutual fondness for the London football club Arsenal. The following year's *Mr Government* was a more roots-flavoured offering, released on the Mad Professor's Ariwa Sounds label, after which Hunningale worked with Crucial Robbie once more on a version of Desmond Dekker's '007'.

Throughout Hunningale's career awards have been bestowed upon him, including Best Newcomer in 1987, Best Reggae Vocalist Of The Year in 1989 and 1991 and in the mid-90s he made a rare television appearance after winning additional accolades in the Black Music Association Awards. Hunningale also demonstrated his versatility when he performed in the reggae musical *Johnny Dollar* and secured his independence with the inauguration of the Street Vibes label. As well as recording many hits in the UK, Hunningale also worked with legendary Jamaican producer Gussie Clarke, which resulted in 'Love Like This'.

Hunningale's outstanding achievements continued in 1995 when Lloyd 'Musclehead' Francis's production of his hit 'Baby Please' knocked his Gussie P production of 'Perfect Lady' from the number 1 position in the reggae chart. In 1995 Hunningale recorded a version of 'Declaration Of Rights' in a reunion with Tippa Irie, which featured on his *Nah Give Up* compilation, alongside such reggae chart hits as 'Trust Me' and 'Sorry'. Hunningale displayed his honeyed voice on songs including 'Out In The Country', 'Candy', 'Crazy Love', 'How Could I Leave' and 'Love Is Here To Stay'. A series of popular duets with Dennis Brown, Lloyd Brown and Janet Lee Davis, performing 'Cupid', 'Lonely Girl' and 'We Can Work It Out', respectively, all met with approval. His distinguished career has also seen him work with artists such as the Original Pioneers, Maxi Priest (writing the title track to his *Best Of Me* hit album), Chosen Few, Trevor Hartley, Double Trouble,

Tinga Stewart and B.B. Seaton, as well as many others, either as musician, producer or writer. Late in 1996 Hunningale performed as part of the combination Passion, which also included Glamma Kid and Nerious Joseph, among others. 'Share Your Love', their version of Teddy Riley's R&B hit, 'No Diggity', spent over eight weeks at number 1 on the reggae chart.

● ALBUMS: *In This Time* (Level Vibes 1987)★★★, with Tippa Irie *The New Decade* (Mango/Island 1991)★★★★, *Mr Vibes* (Street Vibes 1992)★★★, with Tippa Irie *Done Cook And Currie* (Tribal Base 1992)★★★, *Mr Government* (Ariwa Sounds 1994)★★★.
● COMPILATIONS: *Nah Give Up* (Kalymazoo 1995)★★★★, *Reggae Max* (Jet Star 1996)★★★.

HUNT, CLIVE

b. *c*.1955, Linstead, St. Catherine, Jamaica, West Indies. Hunt originally trained as a tailor and learnt to play the trumpet while at school. At the age of 17 he joined the Jamaican Military Band, where he honed his trumpeting skills. He was initially recruited by Byron Lee as part of the Dragonaires and joined them on their tour of North America. On his return, Hunt became involved in playing on a number of sessions in Jamaica, including Culture's *Combolo*, which was produced by Sonia Pottinger at the reactivated Treasure Isle Studios in Bond Street. In the latter half of the 70s Hunt emigrated to New York, USA, where he teamed up with Chalice and co-wrote the hit for Joe Gibbs, 'Good To Be There', although there was subsequently some dispute regarding the origins of the song. Hunt's association with Gibbs also resulted in the composition 'Milk And Honey' for Dennis Brown; Hunt played trumpet on the sessions for Brown's *Spellbound* and co-produced his 1981 A&M Records debut, *Foul Play*. Hunt then began working with Wackies, where he played on sessions and performed as a soloist, recording 'Rockfort Rock' as Clive 'Azul' Hunt. He remained a US citizen until 1987 but then returned to Jamaica, where his career as a producer and arranger flourished. He produced a number of singles with Beres Hammond, including the perennial 'Putting Up Resistance'. Hunt's reputation grew and he worked on the internationally successful 'I Can See Clearly Now' for Jimmy Cliff, the Steely And Clevie

remake of 'You Don't Love (No No No)' for Dawn Penn, and was employed by veteran rockers the Rolling Stones. In 1994 Hunt co-produced Judy Mowatt's *Life* on her own Judy M label, later released by Pow Wow as *Rock Me*. Much of Hunt's production work was based at Bob Marley's Tuff Gong studio where he worked with the Abyssinians remaking their classic hits, and also with Tyrone Taylor, the I-Threes, Yvad, Richie Spice and Garnett Silk.

HYLTON, SHEILA

b. 1956, London, England. Hylton's family moved to Jamaica in 1959, and she later attended the Jamaica Commercial Institute. Her first association with the music business came when she worked as a secretary at Total Sounds. Uninspired by secretarial work, she later divided her time between working as an air hostess for Air Jamaica and singing under the guidance of Harry J. In 1979 her debut, 'Don't Ask My Neighbour', became a local chart hit and heralded the beginning of a fruitful partnership. In the early 70s Harry J. had produced a version of Jeanette Washington's 'Breakfast In Bed', which became an international hit for Lorna Bennett, and following Hylton's successful debut, Harry J. persuaded her to re-record the song; it entered the UK pop chart, and even surpassed his previous production. In 1980 she enjoyed a second foray into the pop charts with her interpretation of 'Bed's Too Big Without You', arranged by Sly And Robbie with Harry J. taking the production credits. Third I productions in the UK recorded an identical version of the Sly And Robbie cut with vocals supplied by Julie Roberts. The television documentary *Deep Roots Music* featured Hylton recording in the studio, with her proud mentor Harry J. producing. In 1983 she recorded 'Let's Dance', which was a minor hit in the reggae charts. Hylton left for the USA in 1984, where she found occasional employment and a husband. In 1995 she returned to Jamaica, where she signed a contract with Tommy Cowan's Talent Corporation and recorded a version of Diana Ross And The Supremes' 'My World Is Empty Without You'.
● ALBUMS: *Sheila Hylton* (Harry J 1979)★★★.

I. Roy

b. Roy Reid, *c.*1949, Spanish Town, Jamaica, West Indies. I. Roy, aka Roy Reid, aka Roy Senior, is one of the great originals of Jamaican music. Always the most intellectual of his peers, he arrived at the start of the 70s as an accomplished DJ with a neat line in storytelling and the ability to ride a rhythm as if it was first recorded for him and not simply 'borrowed'. He drew his name from U-Roy, the first truly popular reggae star, and his first records were slightly derivative of the older man's style, and also owed a little to another DJ pioneer, Dennis Alcapone. However, I. Roy soon hit his stride and recorded a mighty series of singles for producer Gussie Clarke, including 'Black Man Time', 'Tripe Girl' and 'Magnificent Seven'. 'Brother Toby Is A Movie From London' emerged for Glen Brown; 'Dr Who' for Lee Perry and innumerable sides for Bunny Lee. His debut album *Presenting* was magnificent, collating most of his hits for Gussie Clarke. It remains a classic of its genre today. Further albums *Hell And Sorrow* and *Many Moods Of* were nearly as strong.

In 1975 he became involved in an on-record slanging match with fellow DJ Prince Jazzbo, a bizarre name-calling affair that nonetheless presented the public with a new twist to such rivalries and helped to maintain sales. In 1976 a liaison with producer Prince Tony Robinson brought I. Roy a contract with Virgin Records and Roy's albums graced the label five times: *General*, *Musical Shark Attack*, *World On Fire*, *Crisis Time* and the excellent 1977 set *Heart Of A Lion*. By the early 80s I. Roy had burnt out his lyrical store and was overtaken by younger DJs. However, he is still to be found on the periphery of reggae today, sometimes, ironically, on Ujama, the label owned by his old rival, Prince Jazzbo.

● ALBUMS: *Presenting* (Gussie/Trojan 1973)★★★★★, *Hell And Sorrow* (Trojan 1974)★★★★, *Many Moods Of* (Trojan 1974)★★★★, *Truths & Rights* (Grounation 1975)★★★, with Prince Jazzbo *Step Forward Youth* (Live & Love 1975)★★★★, *Can't Conquer Rasta* (Justice 1976)★★★, *Crisis Time* (Caroline/Virgin 1976)★★★, *Dread Baldhead* (Klik 1976)★★★, *Ten Commandments* (Micron 1977)★★★, *Heart Of A Lion* (Front Line 1977)★★★★, *Musical Shark Attack* (Front Line 1977)★★★, *The Best Of* (GG's 1977)★★★, *The Godfather* (Third World 1977)★★★, *The General* (Front Line 1977)★★★, *World On Fire* (Front Line 1978)★★★, *African Herbsman* (Joe Gibbs 1979)★★★, *Hotter Yatta* (Harry J 1980)★★★, *I. Roy's Doctor Fish* (Imperial 1981)★★★, *Outer Limits* (Intense/Hawkeye 1983)★★★, with Jah Woosh *We Chat You Rock* (Trojan 1987)★★★, *The Lyrics Man* (Witty 1990)★★★, with Prince Jazzbo *Head To Head Clash* (Ujama 1990)★★★, *Straight To The Heart* reissue of *Truths & Rights* with four non-I. Roy dub tracks (Esoldun 1991)★★★.

● COMPILATIONS: *Crucial Cuts* (Virgin 1983)★★★, *Classic I. Roy* (Mr. Tipsy 1986)★★★, *Crisis Time - Extra Version* (Front Line 1991)★★★, *Don't Check Me With No Lightweight Stuff (1972-75)* (Blood & Fire 1997)★★★.

I-Threes

The I-Threes were formed, at the instigation of Bob Marley, on the departure of Peter Tosh and Bunny Wailer. Having lost his two main backing vocalists, he recruited Marcia Griffiths, Judy Mowatt and Rita Marley to fill out the Wailers' sound. The trio's harmonies added substantially to many of Marley's most successful records, and they also added visual depth to live concerts, with dance steps choreographed by Mowatt. All three had recorded solo previously, and returned to those careers following the death of their band leader. They have not recorded as a trio outside of the Wailers' legacy, aside from the 'Music For The World' 12-inch, credited to Marley, Mowatt and Griffiths, in 1983, although there have been several reunion concerts.

ICHO CANDY

b. Winston Evans, Jamaica, West Indies. Probably the first the world heard of roots enigma Icho Candy was his anonymous appearance on Channel 4's *Deep Roots* programme in 1982, where he was seen twisting his tortured, Horace Andy-styled tonsils around 'Where Do The Children Play' in company with DJ Bobby Culture, singing live on the late Jack Ruby's sound system. His earliest vinyl outing, 'Little Children No Cry', was for Ruby, followed by 'Bandulu' for Joe Gibbs, finally achieving some prominence with titles such as 'Captain Selassie I', on the Jwyanza label, and 'Mr User' and 'Bloodsuckers' for Prince Jazzbo's Ujama label, thereby establishing a small cult following for himself in the UK. Never the most prolific of singers, he embarked on, what was for him, a burst of recording activity during the latter part of the decade, with singles such as 'In Texas Town' (1987), a bizarre cowboy variation on the Cajun standard 'Jambalaya', the apocalyptic roots anthem 'Babylon' (1987) for Augustus Pablo's Rockers label, 'Cool Down Sufferer' (1989) for Tesfa McDonald, and 'Jah Calling All Over The World' (1990) for Cashima Steel's Creation label, for whom he also recorded a (so far) unreleased album. He also provided an album's worth of material for Finnish producer Tero Kaski, of which only one track, 'Resign Babylon' (1994), has so far emerged. Another period of obscurity was broken in 1993 by the release of *Glory To The King*, issued on Jah Shaka's King Of The Zulu Tribe label.
● ALBUMS: *Glory To The King* (King Of The Zulu Tribe 1993)★★★.

IN CROWD

The In Crowd was a popular showband in the late 70s led by Phil Callender (lead guitar, vocals, percussion), supported by Errol Walker (lead vocals), Clevie Browne (drums, vocals), Tony Lewis (bass guitar, vocals), Freddie Butler (keyboards) and Wigmore Francis (guitar), with a horn section featuring Egbert Evans (tenor saxophone, alto saxophone, flute) and Barry Bailey (trombone). Browne had performed with his brothers as part of the Browne Bunch in the latter half of the 70s prior to joining the In Crowd. The band initially came to prominence with the chart-topping 'We Play Reggae', a laid-back tune that encapsulated the feeling of the summer of 1978. The success of the single prompted eager anticipation for the follow-up. The expectations were fulfilled with the sublime 'Back A Yard', which surpassed its predecessor and was regarded as an all-time classic of the genre, with its cheery celebration of Jamaican life. Encouraged by the achievements of the two singles, the band recorded their debut album, *His Majesty Is Coming*, which mingled various styles in contrast to the melodious single releases. The group performed in their ethereal style covering topics that demanded a heavier sound. 'Slave Ship', 'You Facety Whitey' and 'Beg You A Ten Cent' did not lend themselves to the sugar-coated harmonies of the group. The band enjoyed a further hit with the title track from their debut and signed to Island Records, who released *Man From New Guinea*, with less success. The album featured the three earlier single releases alongside six new tracks, notably 'Marcus Garvey's Back In Town' and the prophetic 'Time Is Running Out'. Despite the short history of the group, they provided reggae lovers with two classic hits, guaranteed to provoke much lighter-waving on the revival circuit. Following the group's demise, Callender pursued a solo career, notably with the celebratory 'Island Music', while Browne went on to become one half of the eminent duo Steely And Clevie.
● ALBUMS: *His Majesty Is Coming* (Cactus 1978)★★★, *Man From New Guinea* (Island 1979)★★★.

INNER CIRCLE

Inner Circle first emerged in the early 70s, comprising brothers Ian and Roger Lewis (guitars) and three future members of Third World, Stephen 'Cat' Coore, Richard Daley and Michael 'Ibo' Cooper. As Third World reassembled, the Lewis brothers recruited drummer Calvin McKenzie, keyboard players Charles Farquharson and Bernard 'Touter' Harvey. Together they won the prestigious Best Band Contest on the *Johnny Golding Show*. Although they later enjoyed moderately successful album sales and a hit single, 'I See You', it was not until the brothers brought in singer Jacob 'Killer' Miller (b. *c*.1955, Jamaica, West Indies, d. 23 March, 1980) that they became a viable commercial proposition. Miller had been a child prodigy, and had created a series of classic roots records ('Tenement Yard', 'Forward Jah Jah Children') before joining Inner Circle. Miller and the Lewis brothers were all of fairly heavy build, and together, the trio made a formidable, imposing combination. Early albums showed the band fusing dancefloor rhythms and reggae with reasonable success. In 1976, however, they signed to Capitol Records, releasing two albums for the label, *Reggae Thing* and *Ready For The World*, rising rapidly up the reggae hierarchy in the process. At one point Miller was more popular in Jamaica than Bob Marley: at the now-legendary Peace Concert in 1978, the band appeared above him on the bill.

Everything Is Great, their first album for Island Records gave the band an overdue international hit with its title song, and its disco rhythms made it a huge seller in Europe. 'Stop Breaking My Heart' was also a hit single, and *New Age Music* consolidated their position. However, disaster struck in 1980 when Jacob Miller was killed in a car crash. The remainder of Inner Circle quit, with the Lewis brothers and Harvey eventually opening a studio in Miami. However, in 1987 the band recorded an album for RAS, *One Way*, with new singer Carlton Coffey. US dates were critically acclaimed, and the band, with the addition of Lance Hall (drums) and Lester Adderley (guitar), signed to WEA/Metronome. *Identified*, their first LP for the label, brought the band to wider recognition with 'Bad Boys', which was employed as the theme to the US television series *Cops*. In 1993 pop success eventually returned with 'Sweat (A La La La La La Long)', a catchy, upbeat single from the *Bad To the Bone* album. Bright, unsentimental, and thoroughly professional, Inner Circle deserve their long-overdue success.

● ALBUMS: *Dread Reggae Hits* (Top Ranking 1973)★★★, *Heavy Reggae* (Top Ranking 1974)★★★, *Blame It On The Sun* (Trojan 1975)★★★, *Rock The Boat* (Trojan 1975)★★★, *Reggae Thing* (Capitol 1976)★★★, *Ready For The World* (Capitol 1977)★★★, *Everything Is Great* (Island 1978)★★★★, *New Age Music* (Island 1979)★★★, *One Way* (RAS 1987)★★★, *Identified* (Warners 1989)★★★★, *Bad To The Bone* (RAS 1993)★★★.

● COMPILATIONS: *Reggae Greats* (Island 1985)★★★.

INSTIGATORS

The Instigators were a north London-based reggae band formed in 1976, featuring the illustrious duo Mafia And Fluxy. Attributed to the original line-up were Toyin (b. Toyin Adekale, 21 December 1963, London, England; lead vocals), Leroy 'Mafia' Heywood (b. 1962, London, England; bass guitar), David 'Fluxy' Heywood (b. 1963, London, England; drums), Dingle Heywood (rhythm guitar), Conway Keeler (lead guitar), Tony Cooper (keyboards) and Oliver Robinson (percussion). The band recorded their debut, 'Let's Make Love', which was an instant hit but also marked the departure of Toyin, who embarked on a solo career. The group were employed to provide backing on the live circuit for a number of tours including the UK's Pablo Gad, as well as Studio One's finest, Johnny Osbourne, Delroy Wilson and Sugar Minott. The band were also employed as session musicians, notably on the 1980 reggae chart-topper, 'Late Night Blues', for Roy Ranking and Raymond Naptali.

In addition to their supportive role they continued to record their own material, having enrolled Courtney Bartlett to provide lead vocals. The group released 'Boom' for the Mighty Fatman, alongside 'Pretty Girl', 'Your Love', 'Five O' and 'Blessing From Above'. Leroy and David also performed as soloists, releasing 'Can't Get Enough Love' and 'Stranger In Love', respectively. While pursuing individual careers, the duo of Mafia And Fluxy concurrently performed with the Instigators, who were voted the best reggae band in 1989 and in the same year reached number 4 in the UK reggae chart with 'Aint Been Getting Along'. Owing to Leroy and David's extensive commitments, the band dissolved, and the duo released further solo outings alongside production obligations, notably with the A Class Crew. By 1996 they recorded alongside Peter Hunningale, Nerious Joseph and Glamma Kid, performing in the revered supergroup Passion for the hit 'Share Your Love'. There are no Instigators albums, although Mafia And Fluxy have released a popular series of *Revival Hits*.

INTERNS

(see Viceroys)

INVESTIGATORS

The Investigators were based in Battersea, south London, England, as a lovers rock band formed in 1975. The line-up included Lorenzo Hall (lead vocals), Michael Gordon (lead vocals), Ian Austin (bass guitar), Reg Graham (keyboards) and Martin Christie (percussion); the remaining instrumentalists were session players. The group were no strangers to the UK reggae scene, having performed as the Private I's, working alongside Chris Lane of Fashion Records. As the Private I's they recorded Otis Gayle's Studio One classic, 'I'll Be Around', although it was the b-side, 'Love Won't Let Me Wait', that secured a placing in the reggae chart, along with a version of Black Uhuru's 'Folk Song'. The band recorded numerous melodies including 'Living In A World Of Magic', 'What Love Has Done' and 'Loving Feeling' on their Private Eye label, 'Love Is What You Make It, and the seductive 'Turn Out The Lights'.

For Inner City they recorded their number 1 reggae hit, 'Baby I'm Yours', followed by 'Summertime Blues' and 'Close To You'. The line-up was also responsible for providing the foundation to Dee Sharp's debut, 'Let's Dub It Up', which topped the reggae chart in 1980, closely followed by 'Its Too Late Baby'. The releases did much to acquaint reggae followers with the newly formed Fashion label. In 1981 the group toured the UK and USA supporting Black Uhuru, but to little acclaim. In 1984 the band gained recognition with 'Woman I Need Your Loving'. They continued to maintain a high profile releasing lovers hits, and in 1985 they performed as the opening act at the second Reggae Sunsplash festival in the UK. The showcase was a prelude to the European leg of the Sunsplash world tour, which has since flourished, although not in the UK. Following the demise of the Investigators, both Lorenzo Hall and Michael Gordon have pursued successful solo careers, Gordon having a notable chart hit with 'Don't Want No More', while Hall recorded the popular 'Don't Let Go'.

● ALBUMS: *First Case* (Investigator 1982)★★.
● COMPILATIONS: *Greatest Hits* (Jet Star 1990)★★★.

ISAAC, OWEN

Isaac began his career demonstrating his dextrous dance steps in bars in Kingston, Jamaica. He saved up the money earned through his dancing in order to pursue a career in music. His first experience in the business was as part of the Seven Seals band, whose line-up also included Errol Dunkley. Isaac concurrently began producing other artists and was responsible for the foundation of the Seven I's youth clubs in St. Mary and St. Elizabeth. The clubs exposed young Jamaicans to many opportunities that might otherwise have bypassed them, and the success of the organization led to expansion in London and Kingston. As a producer he had amassed a considerable collection of master tapes from his recording sessions, although the masters were never stamped. The tapes were apparently *en route* to the pressing plant when they mysteriously disappeared, a fate also experienced by the singer Chris Wayne. Both artists have suggested that they were the victims of subversive tactics. In Isaac's case, it resulted in the loss of his life savings, although his disillusionment with the music business was tempered by the collective support of friends such as Dennis Brown and Gregory Isaacs. In 1980 he formed an allegiance with Frankie Davis, founding the Natami Music label and releasing their DJ debut, 'Three Little Birds'. The single proved a hit both in Jamaica and abroad and was swiftly followed by the equally popular 'Girls'. Sounding relatively simple upon first hearing, the song in fact proved to be rather complex, and eventually provided the duo with a commercial success. In 1983 Isaac released the solo 'Heavy Load', which sadly faltered, and he returned to relative anonymity.

ISAACS, BARRY

b. 23 August 1955, Portland, Jamaica, West Indies. In 1966 Isaacs joined his parents in the UK where he continued his education. He initially formed a band in the mid-70s known as Ras Isaacs And The Rasses, prior to the emergence of the Royal Rasses. The band enjoyed a strong local following in north London and the Midlands where they performed in the roots and culture style. The group disbanded in 1980 and Isaacs concentrated on a solo career, releasing 'Special King Of Love', which featured backing vocals from Trevor Walters. Isaacs' initial success led to the 1980 release of 'Come Turn Me On', followed by a combination with Eli Emmanuel, the inane 'Tickle Me Medley'. In 1985 with other artists he released 'One More Rub A Dub' for Three Kings. In the late 80s Isaacs formed the Reggae On Top label, working with the cream of UK roots performers. He continued to record his own songs, including the 90s hits 'Revelation Time' and 'Happiness', but concentrated his efforts on promoting his increasing roster of artists, including UK roots stalwart Pablo Gad, I Jah Man's former right-hand man Steven Wright, and Hughie Izachaar. In 1997 Isaacs released his own 'Birthday Song' and embarked on a promotional tour.

● ALBUMS: *Revolutionary Man* (Reggae On Top 1995)★★, *Jah Mek I* (Reggae On Top 1997)★★★.

ISAACS, GREGORY

b. 1951, Kingston, Jamaica, West Indies. Reggae superstar Gregory Isaacs has seldom looked back during a three-decade career that has gone from strength to strength, and while many rock stars like to toy with an 'outlaw' image, Isaacs is the real thing - the ultimate rude boy reggae star - who shows no signs of slowing down in the 90s. Like so many other others before him, he began by doing the rounds of Kingston's producers and entering various talent competitions, before recording with Rupie Edwards' Success Records in the early 70s. He set up his own African Museum shop and label in 1973 with Errol Dunkley, in order to gain artistic and financial control of his own work. He continued to record for many other producers during the rest of the decade to finance his own label, notably Winston 'Niney' Holness, Gussie Clarke, Lloyd F. Campbell, Glen Brown, Alvin 'GG' Ranglin and Phil Pratt. His early recordings were romantic ballads crooned in the inimitable Isaacs style, cool, leisurely, and always sounding vulnerable or pained by his adventures in love. However, these translated effortlessly into social protest or 'reality' songs as the decade progressed and the preoccupations of reggae music shifted towards songs with a more cultural emphasis. By 1980 Gregory was the number one star in the reggae world, touring the UK and the USA extensively, and his live appearances resulted in frenzied crowd scenes, with audiences eating out of the palm of his hand. He had by this time signed with Virgin Records' Front Line label and was gaining a considerable name for himself outside of the confines of the traditional reggae music audience and, even though he had recorded many classic sides for outside producers, he still managed to release his best 45s on African Museum (and subsequently Front Line). His pre-eminence during this period was confirmed by the mantle of 'Cool Ruler', chosen for him by critics and fans after the title of the album.

A new contract with Charisma Records' Pre label led to the UK release of two further classic albums, though he was never less than prodigious even by Jamaican standards. He was, however, beset by personal and legal problems in the mid-80s and was even jailed in Kingston's notorious General Penitentiary. His release was celebrated with *Out Deh!*. His spell inside left him short of money and he proceeded to record for anyone and everyone who was prepared to pay him. Because of his name, he was inundated with offers of work and the market was soon flooded with Gregory Isaacs releases on any number of different labels. Incredibly, his standards did not drop, and he generally recorded original material that was still head and shoulders above the competition. In the latter half of the decade, virtually every week saw the release of yet more Isaacs material, voiced with current hot producers such as Jammys, Red Man, Bobby Digital and Steely And Clevie, among others; in so doing, he took on the youth of Jamaica at their own game and won. Rumours abound about Isaacs' rude boy lifestyle - but he would claim he has to be tough to maintain his position within Kingston's notorious musical industry. Certainly the reasons for his lofty seat in the reggae hierarchy are purely musical - a combination of his boundless talent and his uncompromising attitude. Of all reggae's star performers, Isaacs alone has actually improved over the years. The anticipation of more high-quality releases is not merely wishful thinking, but a justifiable expectation, inspired by his high standards. It is very difficult to see how anyone could take away his crown - his legendary status and reputation in the reggae business are truly second to none.

● ALBUMS: *Gregory Isaacs Meets Ronnie Davis*

(Plant 1970)★★★, *In Person* (Trojan 1975)★★★, *All I Have Is Love* (Trojan 1976)★★★, *Extra Classic* (Conflict 1977, Shanachie 1981)★★★, *Mr Isaacs* (Earthquake 1977)★★★, *Slum Dub* (Burning Sounds 1978)★★★★, *Best Of Volumes 1 & 2* not compilations (GG's 1976, 1981)★★★, *Cool Ruler* (Front Line 1978)★★★★, *Soon Forward* (Front Line 1979)★★★★, *Showcase* (Taxi 1980)★★★, *The Lonely Lover* (Pre 1980)★★★, *For Everyone* (Success 1980)★★★, *More Gregory* (Pre 1981)★★★, *Night Nurse* (Mango/Island 1982)★★★, *The Sensational Gregory Isaacs* (Vista 1982)★★★, *Out Deh!* (Mango/Island 1983)★★★★, *Reggae Greats (Live)* (Mango/Island 1984)★★★, *Live At The Academy Brixton* (Rough Trade 1984)★★★, with Dennis Brown *Two Bad Superstars Meet* (Burning Sounds 1984)★★★, *Judge Not* (Greensleeves 1984)★★★, with Jah Mel *Double Explosive* (Andys 1984)★★★, *Private Beach Party* (RAS 1985)★★★, *Easy* (Tad's 1985)★★★, *All I Have Is Love, Love Love* (Tad's 1986)★★★, with Sugar Minott *Double Dose* (Blue Mountain 1987)★★★, *Victim* (C&E 1987)★★★, *Watchman Of The City* (Rohit 1988)★★★, *Sly And Robbie Presents Gregory Isaacs* (RAS 1988)★★★, *Talk Don't Bother Me* (Skengdon 1988)★★★, *Come Along* (Live & Love 1988)★★★, *Encore* (Kingdom 1988)★★★, *Red Rose For Gregory* (Greensleeves 1988)★★★, *I.O.U.* (RAS 1989)★★★, *No Contest* (Music Works 1989)★★★, *Call Me Collect* (RAS 1990)★★★, *Dancing Floor* (Heartbeat 1990)★★★, *Come Again Dub* (ROIR 1991)★★★, *Can't Stay Away* (1992)★★★, *Pardon Me* (1992)★★★, *No Luck* (1993)★★★, *Absent* (Greensleeves 1993)★★★, *Over The Bridge* (Musidisc/I&I Sound 1994)★★★, *Reggae Greats - Live* 1982 recording (1994)★★★, *Midnight Confidential* (Greensleeves 1994)★★★, *Mr Love* (Virgin Front Line 1995)★★★, *Memories* (Musidisc 1995)★★★, *Dem Talk Too Much* (Trojan 1995)★★★.
● COMPILATIONS: *The Early Years* (Trojan 1981)★★★, *Lover's Rock* double album comprising *The Lonely Lover* and *More Gregory* (Pre 1982)★★★, *Crucial Cuts* (Virgin 1983)★★★, *My Number One* (Heartbeat 1990)★★★, *Love Is Overdue* (Network 1991)★★★, *The Cool Ruler Rides Again - 22 Classics From 1978-81* (Music Club 1993)★★★.

ISRAEL VIBRATION
Comprising Cecil 'Skeleton' Spence, Albert 'Apple' Craig and Lascelles 'Wiss' Bulgrin, this vocal group was formed while the members, all crippled in infancy during the polio epidemic that swept the Jamaica in the 50s, were inmates at Kingston's Mona Rehabilitation Centre. Resident since childhood, they were expelled after they began to grow dreadlocks in accordance with their Rastafarian beliefs. For six years they lived rough, literally singing for their supper. Their attempts to survive on handouts from the institution they had lived in for most of their lives were met with indifference, hostility, and sometimes brutality. Their first release, 'Why Worry' (1976), financed by the Twelve Tribes organization to whom they had become affiliated, and recorded at Treasure Isle Studio, was a big success, as were their live shows supporting Dennis Brown and Bob Marley, among others. In 1978 they teamed up with Inner Circle's Lewis Brothers, Ian and Roger aka the Fatman Riddim Section, to record their debut, *The Same Song*, for Tommy Cowan's Top Ranking label. It swiftly became hailed as an instant roots classic, as did its dub companion, *Israel Tafari*. *Same Song* and its follow-up, *Unconquered People* (1980), appeared through a licensing agreement with Harvest Records in the UK, as did the 12-inch 'Crisis', which featured a melodica version by Augustus Pablo. The group's unique brand of gentle, rural-sounding harmonies and sincere Rasta lyrics has sustained them across a number of albums - mostly released through RAS Records in the USA - over the years, especially in the international market, where they continue to flourish.
● ALBUMS: *The Same Song* (Top Ranking 1978)★★★★, *Same Song Dub* (Top Ranking 1978)★★★, *Israel Tafari* (Top Ranking 1978)★★★★, *Unconquered People* (Israel Vibes/Greensleeves 1980)★★★, *Strength Of My Life* (RAS 1988)★★★, *Praises* (RAS 1990)★★★, *Forever* (RAS 1991)★★★, *Israel Dub* remixed version of *Same Song Dub* (Greensleeves 1992)★★★, *Why You So Craven* (RAS 1992)★★★★, *Free To Move* (Ras 1996)★★★.
● COMPILATIONS: *Best Of* (Sonic Sounds 1988)★★★★.

ITALS

The Itals were a vocal group that formed in 1976 and comprised Keith Porter, Ronnie Davis and Lloyd Ricketts. Porter began his career in 1967 at Studio One as part of the Westmorelites, who recorded 'Miss Hitie Titie'. Before joining the Itals, Porter also sang lead vocals for the Future Generation and the Soul Hermit. Davis and Ricketts had performed as part of the rocksteady group the Tennors and recorded with Duke Reid at Treasure Isle and Coxsone Dodd at Studio One. The trio enjoyed a number of hits, including 'Hopeful Village', 'Weather Report', 'Ride Your Donkey' and the powerful 'Pressure And Slide'. Davis pursued a successful solo career, enjoying hits such as 'Stop Yu Loafing', and a showcase album with Gregory Isaacs. Comparable to the Mighty Diamonds and Tamlins, the Itals were inspired by the late 60s/early 70s American R&B groups, although their themes were Rastafarian-orientated. Their debut was the popular 'In Dis A Time'. By 1977 the group established a distinguished reputation with the release of 'You Don't Care' and 'Brutal'; the US Nighthawk label signed the trio and the group enjoyed unprecedented success in America. 'Herbs Pirate' featured on a specially commissioned compilation, *Calling Rastafari*, and sessions and studio time were secured with Harry J. Through the Itals the record company recruited the Mighty Diamonds, the Gladiators, Culture and the Wailing Souls for a historic recording session, which is still widely available. Throughout the 80s and 90s the Itals maintained a high profile with a number of hits, including the Rastafarian-influenced 'Truth Must Reveal', 'Jah Glory' and 'Run Baldhead Run'.

● ALBUMS: *Brutal Out Deh* (Nighthawk 1978)★★★★, *Give Me Power* (Nighthawk 1980)★★★, *Easy To Catch* (Rhythm Safari 1985)★★★, *Cool And Dread* (Nighthawk 1989)★★, *Rasta Philosophy* (Nighthawk 1992)★★.

● COMPILATIONS: *The Early Recordings* (Nighthawk 1995)★★★★.

IVANAY

b. Rosalin Thompson, February 1972, St. Thomas, Jamaica, West Indies. Thompson was the youngest of 13 siblings, all reared in a Christian environment, and her initial vocal training was in the local church and school choirs. In 1994 she began singing professionally through Howlers International Music, performing as Rosie T. Although her initial recordings were all cover versions, they proved moderately successful, and she was invited to appear at the 1995 Reggae Sumfest in Montego Bay, where she gave a triumphant performance on the International Night alongside the likes of Buju Banton, Everton Blender and Freddie McGregor. This gained her a following, and prompted invitations to perform with other renowned artists. She recorded 'Empower Me' as Ivanay, a song co-written with Tony Rochester, combining a steadfast rhythm with masterful lyricism. Her name change emphasized her individuality, and she recorded self-compositions alongside the earlier cover versions for the long-awaited debut album, which demonstrated both her vocal and writing skills. The set featured guest vocals from Angie Angel on a ragga remix of 'Empower Me', Louie Culture on the dancehall mover 'Make Love To You', and a version of a Peter Tosh hit, retitled 'God Is My Keeper'.

● ALBUMS: *Empower Me* (Howlers 1997)★★★.

J

J., HARRY

b. Harry Johnson, *c.*1945, Kingston, Jamaica, West Indies. After completing his education, Johnson joined a band called the Virtues, playing bass guitar. The group recorded a few tunes, notably a version of 'Amen'. Intrigued by the business side of music, he became the band's manager until his partners decided to disperse. Following the group's demise he concentrated on a career in insurance but was drawn back into the music business as a producer in 1968. His first sessions resulted in 'No More Heartaches' by the Beltones, which became a big local hit. The song was covered in the 80s by Keble Drummond of the Cables with Harry producing. His skilful negotiating with Coxsone Dodd won him the use of Studio One's facilities, when he recorded Lloyd Robinson performing 'Cuss Cuss'. He employed some of the island's top session men, notably Hux Brown, Winston Wright and Boris Gardiner, collectively known as the Harry J. Allstars. The studio band enjoyed a UK number 9 crossover hit with 'The Liquidator' in October 1969, which re-entered the chart in March 1980. The success of the single led to a compilation of instrumentals taking its title from the hit, and featuring 'Jay Moon Walk', 'The Big Three' and a version of 'Je T'Aime (Moi Non Plus)'. In March 1970 his production of Bob And Marcia's 'Young Gifted And Black', one of the first reggae records to use strings, reached the Top 5 in the UK. In July 1971 the duo enjoyed a second hit with 'Pied Piper' (number 11 UK pop chart) with Bob Andy in the producer's chair.

In 1972 Harry sold his record shop and invested the money, and the profits from his UK hits, into his 16-track studio at 10 Roosevelt Avenue. He later installed former Studio One engineer Sylvan Morris at the controls in place of Sid Bucknor, who moved to England. Harry J's became one of the most popular recording studios on the island, utilized by the likes of Burning Spear, Augustus Pablo, and, prior to the advent of Tuff Gong, Bob Marley. Harry J. also produced work by the Cables, the Heptones, Busty Brown, Lloyd Robinson and Lorna Bennett. His production of Bennett's 'Breakfast In Bed', originally a Nashville country tune, was a financial success but failed to make an impression on the UK chart. Some of the pressings of her hit were released with a Scotty toast, 'Skank In Bed', on the b-side. The song was also covered by another of Harry's protégés, Sheila Hylton, who entered the UK chart in 1979, peaking at number 57. In the late 70s Harry moved down a gear and produced mainly DJ records for the local market. His studio remained popular, however, and in 1981 he was tempted back into the production seat to achieve another international hit with Hylton's 'The Bed's Too Big Without You', which reached number 35 in the UK chart in February of that year. Another substantial hit was the Heptones' 'Book Of Rules', which lost its appeal when Island Records inadvisably added strings. The version without strings can be found on *Night Food*.

Over the years, Harry J.'s studio facilities have been used by some of reggae's finest musicians, and Bob Marley And The Wailers' *Catch A Fire*, *Burning*, *Natty Dread* and *Rastaman Vibration*, and their collaborations with Johnny Nash (including 'Guava Jelly', 'Stir It Up' and 'Nice Time'), were all recorded there. By the 80s Harry had set up his own distribution network in Jamaica with Sunset, 10 Roosevelt Avenue, Junjo and, of course, the Harry J label. In 1996 the 'Cuss Cuss' rhythm resurfaced, providing hits for a number of DJs where a loop of the original recording was clearly audible.

● ALBUMS: *Liquidator* (Trojan 1970)★★★★.

JACKSON, CARLTON

b. *c.*1955, Greenwich Town, Jamaica, West Indies. Jackson began his musical career on the Ethiopian Hi Fi Sound System in the early 70s. To be a serious contender on the sound system circuit, the operators would secure unique dub plates, and this led Jackson to Lee Perry's Black Ark studio in Washington Gardens. At the studio, Perry persuaded Jackson to record his debut, the timeless 'History'. The song related the history of Afro-Caribbeans from slavery to

the awakening of Rastafari: 'I was bound in chains and taken to the Caribbean - The new faces that I met - Sayin' they are my master - to teach I to be like fools - Jah Jah'. The song surfaced in the UK on a limited-edition Upsetter disco mix, where it was snapped up by Perry enthusiasts, and it was later remixed and re-released in Jamaica on Jackson's own Ital International label. Jackson followed the song with 'Only Jah Can Do It', but elected to concentrate on working with other artists, including the Soul Syndicate, Prince Allah, Sammy Dread and Bunny Wailer. There was a brief return to performing in 1982 when he recorded 'Disarmament', ably supported by Roots Radics. By the mid-80s he returned to production and promotional work in the USA on behalf of reggae. While based in New York, Jackson worked with a variety of contemporary dancehall singers, including Cocoa Tea, Pinchers and Sanchez. In the late 80s Jackson toured Europe with Pinchers and settled in London, when the release of *Open The Gate*, featuring 'History', ensured the performer cult status.
● ALBUMS: with Lee Perry *Open The Gate* (Trojan 1988)★★★.

JAH FREE

Jah Free began his musical career with the band Tallowah, who later evolved into Bushfire. The band built a solid reputation on the European live circuit until their premature demise. This was followed by the inauguration of Jah Free Music, set up to record, design and release Jah Free records. He released the favoured roots hit 'Wicked Can't Run', followed by the equally popular discomix, 'Lighting Clap'. Both hits proved to be especially popular on the sound system circuit, notably with Jah Shaka. Shaka's sound is notorious for its reverberating bass levels, and his releases and mixing works attracted the attention of Zion Train, who enrolled Jah Free into the Universal Egg collective. With the organization he released his debut, *Breaking Out*, which featured his earlier releases and the disparaging 'Jacques Chirac'. Echoing the Motown Revues of the 60s, he was enrolled as a compere on the Egg Experience '97 tour, a showcase that featured various artists from the label. In addition to his collaboration with Zion Train, he also produced the classic 'Rich Man' for Martin

Campbell of the Jah Works posse. At the close of 1997 he had completed an exhaustive schedule, having worked with the Mad Professor, Iration Steppas, Conscious Sounds, Armagideon (sic) and the Belgium dub heroes Bong Messages. He embarked on a series of sessions in 1998 with Vibronics that led to a series of Live 'Dub Conferences' across Europe, promoting the duo's album. Jah Free also released his solo plea that we should 'Love One And Other'.
● ALBUMS: *Breaking Out* (Universal Egg 1995)★★★, with Vibronics *Outernational Dub Conference Volume One* (Universal Egg 1998)★★★★.

JAH LION

b. Pat Francis, c.1950, Kingston, Jamaica, West Indies. Pat Francis has recorded under a variety of aliases including Jah Lion, Jah Lloyd and the Black Lion Of Judah. In the mid-60s he sang alongside Fitzroy 'Bunny' Simpson as the Mediators and also as a soloist, notably with 'Soldier Round The Corner' and 'Know Yourself Blackman' for producer Rupie Edwards. In the early 70s he turned to production when he recorded his sparring partner Simpson alongside Donald 'Tabby' Shaw and Lloyd 'Judge' Ferguson, known collectively as the Diamonds. In 1976 he introduced the renamed Mighty Diamonds to Joseph 'Joe Joe' Hookim at Channel One, where they recorded the legendary *Right Time*, which proved to be the beginning of the vocal trio's lengthy career. As Jah Lloyd he turned to the art of the DJ, recording the hits 'Black Snowfall', 'World Class', and a comment on a report about a batch of poisoned flour discovered in Kingston, 'Beware Of The Flour'. With Lee Perry Francis recorded, as Jah Lion, *Columbia Collie*. The project was critically acclaimed and enjoyed a prolonged stay on the reggae album chart. 'Wisdom' was lifted from the album and featured in the film *Countryman*, and his version of Junior Murvin's 'Police And Thieves', 'Soldier And Police War', topped the reggae charts. In 1978 he reverted to the pseudonym of Jah Lloyd and secured a two-album contract with Virgin Records' Front Line label. With Maurice 'Blacka' Wellington and Bingi Bunny producing, he recorded *The Humble One*, which included 'Jah Lion' and 'Cocaine'. The latter surfaced as a single through Front

Line, although it failed to make a significant impact on the charts. In 1979 he returned to production, initially his own recordings at Channel One, assisted by Sly And Robbie; together, they recorded 'Green Bay Incident' and 'Dispenser', a return to lyrics relating to hard drugs. His final appearance as Jah Lloyd came in 1982 when he recorded the unusual 'Shake And Flicker'. By the mid-80s he was promoting his latest protégé, Julie Charles, with her debut 'As Long As You Love Me', and reverted to the pseudonym of Jah Lion.

● ALBUMS: *Columbia Collie* (Island 1977)★★★★, *The Humble One* (Front Line 1978)★★★, *Black Moses* (Front Line 1979)★★, *In Action With The Revolutionaries* (Vista 1983)★★★.

JAH SCREW

b. Paul Love, *c.*1955, Kingston, Jamaica, West Indies. Love began his musical career as the operator for Echo Bell and later U-Roy's Stur Gav sound system with DJ Little Joe, aka Ranking Joe. Love's period as Stur Gav's operator ended when the sound was destroyed during the 1980 elections in Jamaica. The duo then joined Ray Symbolics Hi Fi. The sound system toured the UK to rave reviews, but was marred by tragedy when Ray returned to Jamaica. Stories relating to Ray's death were plentiful, and varied from drink-driving to a shoot-out with the police. Ranking Joe and Love embarked on a production partnership with their own Sharp Axe label and had hits in 1982 with 'Ice Cream Style' and *Armageddon*. In 1984 Love produced Barrington Levy's 'Under Mi Sensi', which led to a long and successful partnership. His production of 'Here I Come' was accompanied by national radio and television exposure when licensed to London Records. The label also released 'Money Moves', which flopped. Love also set up his own Time One production stable. In 1988 Love released his production of Levy's 'She's Mine', and 'Step Up In Life' with Sassafras. In the late 80s, as a performer he recorded 'Original Soundboy Killer' for Wildfire, although he found greater success in the role of producer. In 1991 'Dancehall Rock', a variation on Bob Marley's 'Trenchtown Rock', topped the reggae charts when Love, now known as Jah Screw, teamed Levy with DJ Cutty Ranks. A year later Jah Screw produced a

number of notable hits with artists including Dennis Brown, Reggie Stepper and Chaka Demus. In 1994 he produced DJ Beenie Man for the ragga remix of 'Under Mi Sensi 94 Spliff', resulting in another reggae chart-topper. Following Jah Screw's success in pairing up Levy with the DJs, he then recruited Bounty Killer for 1995's 'Living Dangerously'.

● ALBUMS: *Original Experience* (Time One 1991)★★★, *Jah Screw Presents Dancehall Glamity* (Time One 1994)★★★.

JAH SHAKA

An enigmatic and highly individual performer on the UK sound system scene, Jah Shaka (his real name remains a mystery) came with his parents to the UK from Jamaica at the age of eight, settling in south-east London. Succumbing to his passion for music, he began his career a few years later in the late 60s, playing in a band and travelling around in an obscure local sound system named Freddie Cloudburst. Inspired spiritually by his interest in Rastafari, and consciously by the American Civil Rights movement (particularly such exponents of black awareness as Angela Davis and George Jackson), he began to assemble equipment for his own sound, named after the great eighteenth century Zulu, King Shaka, the 'Black Napoleon'. From quite modest beginnings in the early 70s, by the end of the decade Shaka's sound had become one of the top three in the country, alongside such luminaries as Lloyd Coxsone and the Mighty Fatman, specializing in heavyweight, dubwise steppers material, and exclusive cuts on dub plates. However, whereas these and other sounds usually supported a team of selectors and DJs, Shaka performed all these functions alone, assistance in setting up the sound coming from a team of devoted youths for whom Shaka's music was almost a way of life.

His dances became famous for their spiritually charged atmosphere and the acrobatic, stylized dancing of the participants. Shaka would operate his sound like a single instrument, the music played at ear-splitting distortion levels, the air torn by his trademark sirens and syndrums, the man himself caught up in the spirit, alternatively chanting, singing and dancing as furiously as many of those in the crowd. In 1980

Shaka inaugurated his Jah Shaka King Of The Zulu Tribe label with the release of 'Jah Children Cry' by African Princess, which sold well in the reggae market. This was followed by the first instalment in his long-running *Commandments Of Dub* series. Over the years the label has carried well over 50 releases by UK-based artists such as Junior Brown, Sgt Pepper, Vivian Jones, Sis Nya and the Twinkle Brothers, as well as dozens of releases by Shaka himself, and Jamaican artists such as Horace Andy, Icho Candy and Max Romeo. With the decline of interest in Rastafarianism in the 80s, Shaka's dances became more and more isolated affairs, the crowd thinning to a hardcore of older followers. However, Shaka's adherence to Rasta, and the particular type of heavy, spiritual reggae with which his name has become synonymous, remained unswerving. By the latter part of the decade a new, young, multiracial crowd of disaffected roots fans had begun to appear. Out of this crowd emerged a number of artists and sound systems who largely shunned contemporary reggae in favour of the revived sounds of the 70s and early 80s in which Shaka still specialised. Though seen by some observers as anachronistic and irrelevant, this 'new dub school', predominantly inspired by Shaka, has nevertheless gained much support over the last few years, nurturing and sustaining its own network of musicians, record labels, studios, sound systems, clubs and radio shows.

● ALBUMS: *Commandments Of Dub Chapters 1-10* (Jah Shaka 1980-1991)★★★★, *Revelation Songs* (Jah Shaka 1983)★★★, *Kings Music* (Jah Shaka 1984)★★★, *Message From Africa* (Jah Shaka 1985)★★, *The Music Message* (Jah Shaka 1988)★★★, *My Prayer* (Jah Shaka 1990)★★, and Mad Professor *A New Decade Of Dub* (RAS 1996)★★★.

JAH STITCH

b. Melbourne James, 1949, Kingston, Jamaica, West Indies. Jah Stitch was one of the pioneering DJs. Although famed as a DJ, he began his career singing in a music yard alongside Roy Shirley, Stranger Cole, the Wailers and the Heptones. Jah Stitch soon became the leading DJ with the Lord Tippertone and Black Harmony sound systems. Errol Holt produced his debut, 'Danger Zone', and his vocals bore a

resemblance to Big Youth, who was an influence on the young DJ. Many of Jah Stitch's early hits were DJ versions of Johnny Clarke's extensive back catalogue, such as 'Legalise It' as 'Collie Bud', 'My Conversation' as 'How Long Jah Jah', and 'Roots Natty Roots Natty Congo' as 'True Born African'. Other hits included 'Crazy Joe', 'King In The Arena' and, with Yabby You, 'African Queen'. Prior to the One Love Peace Concert in Jamaica, organized in an attempt to thwart the escalating street violence and bring an end to the State Of Emergency, Jah Stitch was shot. Although scarred by the event, he returned to the recording studio, responding with 'No Dread Can't Dead'. By 1977 his hits included 'Militant Man' and 'Jah Jah Forgive You' and he successfully toured the UK. In 1985 he re-emerged as Major Stitch, selecting the tunes for Sugar Minott's Youth Promotion sound system. A number of up-and-coming vocalists began their careers with the sound, including Tenor Saw, Jah Mikey, Dickie Ranking and Yammie Bolo. A prolonged period of anonymity came to end when, in 1995, he recorded with Trevor Douglas and Jah Woosh and his career was documented on a compilation released through Simply Red's Blood & Fire label.

● ALBUMS: *No Dread Can't Dead* (1976)★★★, *Watch Your Step Youthman* (Third World 1977)★★★, with Prince Jazzbo *Straight To Babylon Chest* (1979)★★★, *Moving Away* (Live And Love 1979)★★★, with Jah Woosh *Jah Woosh Meets Jah Stitch At Leggo Sounds* (Leggo 1995)★★.

● COMPILATIONS: *Jah Stitch, Original Ragga Muffin 1975 -77* (Blood & Fire 1996)★★★★.

JAH STONE

b. Gladstone Fisher, *c.*1953, Jamaica, West Indies. After working as a DJ on a variety of sound systems, Fisher recorded as Jah Stone with Bim Sherman. In 1977 Sherman inaugurated his own Scorpio label and due to financial restraints, was forced to employ Jah Stone to deliver two separate chants over the same rhythm track. The association with Sherman led to the dancehall favourites 'Fat Ting' and 'Burning'. His notoriety led to work with producer Alvin 'GG' Ranglin, who featured the DJ in combination with Freddie McKay on his remake of 'Picture On The Wall' and the solo hit

'Ten Ton Woman'. He was also employed on the Sonia Pottinger production of 'Baby Love' by the reactivated vocal group the Sensations. In 1978 Jah Stone recorded for Doctor Alimantado, the sessions producing the assertive 'Militant Dread'. In 1979 Jah Stone recorded in session with Winston Jarrett of the Righteous Flames, resulting in the release of 'War' and 'Kaya', both of which were later featured on *The Messiah*. Notable album tracks included the admonishing 'Sergeant Black', the bizarre 'Kung Fu Ballet' and the chauvinistic 'Irie Lickle Filly'. Sadly, the album signalled his swan-song, and in spite of this and his work with a number of Jamaican producers, Jah Stone is usually only recalled as the DJ who recorded with Bim Sherman. The 1997 release of a Freddie McKay compilation featuring Jah Stone demonstrated the latter's versatility and rekindled interest in the DJ's work.

● ALBUMS: *The Messiah* (Gorgon 1979)★★★.
● COMPILATIONS: with Freddie McKay *The Right Time* 1977-78 recordings (GG's 1997)★★★★.

JAH WARRIORS

Jah Warriors were a UK-based reggae band from Ipswich, Suffolk. The line-up included Lloyd 'Captain' Morgan (lead vocals), Ira Jones (vocals, lead guitar), Gordon Mulraine (bass guitar), Joseph White (drums), Aubrey Mulraine (keyboards), Lloyd Clarke (saxophone) and Trevor Jones (trombone). In 1982 the band released their debut, 'If Only You Knew'/'Can't Take It No More', which was met with critical acclaim but failed commercially. Undeterred, the group built a solid reputation touring, and in 1984 they were asked to support the legendary Curtis Mayfield. Although an R&B performer, Mayfield and the Impressions had influenced many of Jamaica's top performers, notably Bob Marley, Black Uhuru, Pat Kelly, the Mighty Diamonds and Brown Sugar. Conscious and respectful of the singer's eminence, the young group gave their all in support of the influential performer. The group performed 'Tribute To Bob Marley' alongside tracks from their forthcoming album, including 'Drug Squad', 'Can't Cook' and their earlier singles releases. Mayfield was impressed by the band's performance and predicted a bright future for the group. The experi-

ence proved beneficial and the band released *Poor Mans Story*, which covered a diversity of subjects including abortion ('Innocent Ones') and an interpretation of an advertising jingle, 'Liquor'. The album was recorded locally by the band at a studio owned by the 60s pop singer Chris Andrews, who had a Top 10 hit with 'Yesterday Man', later covered in a reggae version by Nicky Thomas. The group continued to work with Andrews for their second album, which included the Bob Marley tribute. The track featured the playing skills of one-time Wailer Al Anderson, and has since become a standard for the group. The group also released the lovers rock hit 'What's This Feeling', followed by 'Love Has A Way'. While performing lovers rock tracks, they also continued in a roots vein for the haunting 'Apartheid' and still enjoy cult status. Their status as UK rockers was endorsed when they were invited to perform alongside the reggae élite as part of the British Reggae Artists Famine Appeal. In the 90s the group enjoyed a revival as dubmasters, releasing *Great Kings Of Israel In Dub* and *African Tribes Dub*.

● ALBUMS: *Poor Mans Story* (Vista 1984)★★★, *No Illusions* (A Records 1985)★★

JAH WOOSH

b. Neville Beckford, 1952, Kingston, Jamaica, West Indies. Before entering a recording studio, Beckford served an apprenticeship as a mechanic. He and his friend Reggae George attended auditions with the island's top producers under the name of Neville And George, but their partnership was short-lived and both went on to pursue solo careers. Beckford's career took off when he became resident DJ on Prince Lloyd's sound system, and producer George Bell liked what he heard. The result was 'Angela Davis', a tribute to the black freedom fighter credited under his new pseudonym, Jah Woosh. Despite the strong lyrics, it was not a hit, but he was able to impress producer Rupie Edwards. The sessions with Edwards led to the release of *Jah Woosh*, through Cactus in the UK. He subsequently enjoyed a brief spell of fame, recording for a number of producers, and enjoying hits with 'Psalm 121', 'Ital Feast' and 'Zion Sound'. Following his success, he recorded a self-production with the Mighty Clouds band, resulting in the release of *Dreadlocks Affair*, which featured the popular 'Natty Bal' Head', 'Shimi Skank' and the title track. Other records followed, but it was the release of *Religious Dread* that produced a successful run in the Jamaican reggae charts, including 'Marcus Say', 'Chant Freedom' and a tribute to the Four Aces club, a popular dance venue in the UK. With Sydney Crooks of the Pioneers in the production seat and a host of top sessioners assembled, *Loaded With TNT* was the follow-up. Despite excellent musicianship from Lloyd Parks and keyboard wizard Ansell Collins, the set was destined not to repeat the success of his earlier recordings.

● ALBUMS: *Jah Woosh* (Cactus 1974)★★, *Dreadlocks Affair* (Trojan 1974)★★★, *Rebellion* (1975)★★★, *Religious Dread* (Trojan 1976)★★★★, *Loaded With TNT* (Trenchtown 1976)★★★, with I-Roy *We Chat You Rock* (Trojan 1987)★★★, with Mixman *Fire In A Blackamix* (Blackamix 1993)★★, with Jah Stitch *Jah Woosh Meets Jah Stitch At Leggo Sounds* (Leggo 1995)★★.

JAHMALI

b. Ryan Thomas, 5 April 1972, Vere, Clarendon, Jamaica, West Indies. Thomas was the ninth of 10 children and was raised among the sugar plantations in the Jamaican countryside. His love for the dancehall sounds of Shabba Ranks, Pinchers, Red Dragon and Wayne Wonder inspired a move to Kingston, where he embarked on his own musical career. He received encouragement from King Jammy, Philip 'Fatis' Burrell and Tony Rebel, although they remained hesitant about producing his work. Rebel subsequently introduced Thomas to the Rastafarian faith, which prompted a radical change in the young singer's approach. Performing as Jahmali, he began voicing hits for Donovan Germain, Bobby Digital and Roof International's Barry O'Hare.

A string of hits followed, including the inspired 'Victory', 'Let Me Live', 'Wake Up' and 'El Shaddai'. Jahmali's association with O'Hare led to a collaboration with Mikey Spice, who had set up his own Ingredients label. Spice produced for Jahmali's 'Let Jah Be Praised' and 'Only Love', both of which demonstrated his new, conscientious stance. Jahmali's critically acclaimed debut album featured many top Jamaican per-

formers, including Earl 'Chinna' Smith, Sly Dunbar, Robbie Shakespeare, Stephen 'Cat' Coore and Aston 'Familyman' Barrett. Jahmali's reputation was further enhanced when he recorded 'Mother's Cry' with Buju Banton, featured on the latter's accomplished *Inna Heights*. Following his combination success, Jahmali released his own 'Cry People' and the haunting 'Politics'.

● ALBUMS: *Jahmali* (High Times 1997)★★★.

JAHSON, DAVID

b. Everald Pickersgill, 4 November 1954, Kingston, Jamaica, West Indies. Jahson embarked on his recording career with his debut, 'For I', which peaked at number 7 on the JBC chart in Jamaica. His overnight success led to the release of a number of hits, including 'Ruff Neck Soldier', 'Give Thanks And Praise' and the melancholy 'People Bawling'. By 1977 he joined the line-up of the Well Pleased And Satisfied band who enjoyed a string of hits during their brief career, including 'Black On Black', 'West Man Rock', 'News Carrier Dem A Warrior', 'Barberman Bawling' and 'Open The Gates'. Following the band's demise, Jahson reactivated his solo career, working with brothers Ian and Roger Lewis of Inner Circle. The alliance led to Jahson's pivotal hit, 'Natty Chase The Barber', which reiterated his acrimonious attitude towards hairdressers. The song inspired a series of barber-related tunes in the late 70s, including Doctor Alimantado riding the same rhythm for 'I Killed The Barber'. Jahson simultaneously accompanied the Inner Circle band on their promotional tour for *Everything Is Great*, where he is credited as percussionist. He remained with the band under the guise of 'Black Spy' until Jacob Miller's untimely demise in March 1980, which led to the band's temporary dissolution.

He settled in the UK throughout the 80s, initially recording with fellow expatriate Errol Dunkley. Jahson's sporadic releases include 'True Believer', 'She Loves The Rub A Dub', 'Lips Of Wine', 'Stop Your Gun Shooting' and 'Zion Home'. In the mid-90s the release of two retrospective anthologies rekindled interest in the performer.

● ALBUMS: *Natty Chase The Barber* (Top Ranking 1978)★★★, *Past And Present* (Spy

1982)★★, *Come Again Showcase* (Top Ranking 1985)★★.
● COMPILATIONS: *Natty Chase* (Lagoon 1996)★★★, *Root Of David* (Pick A Skill 1997)★★★★.

JAMES, JIMMY

b. Michael James, 13 September 1940, USA. James was raised in Jamaica where he began his career in the late 50s. His debut, 'Bewildered And Blue', appeared through Tip Top productions and topped the Jamaican charts. He followed this hit with the equally successful 'Come To Me Softly', which he re-recorded in the UK during the mid-60s. The latter version appeared on the *Billboard* Hot 100, an unprecedented achievement for a Jamaican performer. By 1960 he accepted the role of lead vocalist with the Vagabonds. The band performed around Jamaica, regarded as second only to Byron Lee And The Dragonaires as the island's top showband. The group performed prosaic refrains to the tourists, including 'Love Letters In The Sand', 'Anchors Aweigh' and 'Happy Wanderer', which featured on their debut album. In an attempt to promote their career, the group financed a trip to the UK, where, after supporting the Who at the Marquee club in London, they were enlisted to perform weekly at the venue. The shows were highly acclaimed and enhanced the band's reputation, notably through the stage antics of Count Prince Miller. His charismatic charm and unique style earned him a huge following, which led to his reggae hit 'Mule Train', in 1971. James and the Vagabonds released a number of singles that failed to cross over, but in 1968 the band recorded their most popular hit, Neil Diamond's 'Red Red Wine', also their debut on the UK pop chart. It was James's interpretation that inspired Tony Tribe's reggae hit, later covered by UB40. By 1970, the original Vagabonds decided to relinquish the band although James retained the rights to the name. In 1970 he recorded the commercially successful 'A Man Like Me' with producer Biddu. He released a few singles for Trojan Records before his breakthrough into the pop world with the classic 'Help Yourself'. Consolidating his association with Biddu, he released 'Dancing To The Music Of Love' and 'Whatever Happened To The Love We Knew'. The newly formed

Vagabonds featured an all-white line-up who supported him through the 70s, touring and playing on the 1976 pop hits 'Now Is The Time' and 'I'll Go Where The Music Takes Me'. He remained in relative obscurity throughout the 80s, although in 1984 he released the effervescent but overlooked 'Love Fire', before returning to obscurity. In 1987 another bid for a pop hit arose when he reworked 'I'll Go Where The Music Takes Me' and 'Now Is The Time', but a return to the chart eluded the performer. He restored his credibility when he returned to his Jamaican roots in the 90s, performing alongside Winston Curtis on the Count Prince Miller-produced hit 'Muriel'.
● ALBUMS: as the Vagabonds: *Presenting The Fabulous Vagabonds* (Island 1964)★★, *The New Religion* (Picadilly 1967)★★, *Live At The Marquee* (Pye 1967)★★★, *Open Up Your Soul* (Pye 1968)★★.

JARRETT, WINSTON

b. 1941, St. Ann, Jamaica, West Indies. Jarrett began his career with Alton Ellis's group the Flames and is widely acknowledged as the writer of Ellis's classic 'Sunday Coming' and 'True Born African', although he is not always credited as such. The Flames shared in Ellis's fame during Jamaica's fleeting flirtation with rocksteady. By 1967 the newly emerging reggae beat had gained favour and the original Flames disbanded. Jarrett enrolled Junior Green and Egga Gardner, and they collectively embarked on a recording career, performing as the Righteous Flames. With Coxsone Dodd they released their debut, 'Born To Be Loved', followed by a string of credible hits including 'Ease Up', 'You Don't Know' and 'I Was Born To Be Loved'. In 1969 the group recorded sessions with Lee Perry, resulting in the excellent 'Zion I Love You'. Returning to Studio One, the group became known as Winston Jarrett And The Flames and released the bizarrely titled 'Peck Up A Pagan'. The group returned in 1978 with 'War'. By the early 80s, Jarrett concentrated on his solo career, enjoying a modicum of success throughout the decade. In the early 90s he reformed the Flames to pay homage and acknowledge their debt to Bob Marley when he performed alongside Peter Tosh and Bunny Wailer. Some cynics suggested the motivation for the sessions was purely fiscal and the songs were greeted with indifference, sadly eclipsing Jarrett's virtuoso performance. The 10-track album featured five vocal cuts with their respective dub versions; notable tracks include 'Selassie Is The Chapel', 'African Herb Man' and 'Pound Get A Blow'.

● ALBUMS: *Wise Man* (Wambesi 1980)★★★, *Kingston Vibrations* (Ras 1994)★★★, *Solid Foundation* (Heartbeat 1995)★★★, *Too Many Boundaries* (Ras 1996)★★★★, with the Righteous Flames *Sings Tribute To Bob Marley* (Original 1994)★★★.

JAZZ JAMAICA

Jazz Jamaica was the brainchild of Gary Crosby, who in 1991, inspired by the rhythms of traditional Jamaican music and the largely improvisational nature of jazz, turned his concept into a reality. He enrolled a number of talented young jazz musicians from the jazz and reggae circuits, including himself on double bass, Clifton 'Bigga' Morrison (keyboards), Alan Weekes (guitar), Kenrick Rowe (drums), Tony Uter (percussion) and a horn section featuring the legendary Rico Rodriguez (trombone), Eddie 'Tan Tan' Thornton (trumpet), and Michael 'Bammi' Rose (alto saxophone, flute). The group toured extensively, playing worldwide festivals from 1993 to the present day. In 1993 the Roots and Reminiscence Tour included performances from Crosby's uncle, Ernest Ranglin, and Majorie Whylie, who played the piano, provided vocals and followed in the tradition of an African griot as the storyteller. Also featured on the tour was Lord Tanamo who performed in his own distinctive style. Following the tour the band set up workshops specifically for elderly Caribbean expatriates, although these were, in fact, attended by a cosmopolitan audience encompassing all ages and races. In 1994 the band played the St. Lucia Jazz Festival, where they proved so successful that the great George Benson had to wait in the wings until the band played an encore. The band also released *Skaravan*, initially through the Japanese Quattro label. Tracks included ska versions of 'Peanut Vendor', Charlie Parker's 'Barbados', Don Drummond's 'Don Cosmic' and 'Confucius', the Skatalites' 'Green Island' and Rodriguez's 'Africa'. By the autumn of 1994 the group secured a Japanese-based major label contract. The release of *The Jamaican Beat - Blue Note Blue Beat Volume One* found the musicians playing alongside Courtney Pine, Brian Edwards, Cleveland Watkiss and Julie Dexter. The album leant heavily towards jazz while remaining faithful to the initial concept of a ska fusion. In 1995, sponsored by the British Council, the group toured Senegal and Nigeria, featuring a performance at the British Embassy in Senegal, and a live jamming session with the Nigerian ensemble Fran And Tunde Kuboye And The Extended Family Band, who supported Jazz Jamaica on their UK tour in October. As well as the constant touring, the band's recording sessions included Dennis Rollins, Denys Baptiste, Tony Kofi, Byron Wallen, Kevin Robinson, and the sublime vocals of lovers rock singer Carroll Thompson. Despite their increasing touring schedule, the band has, ironically, never actually played together in Jamaica. In addition to his Jazz Jamaica commitments, Crosby also leads a jazz ensemble known as Gary Crosby's Nu Troop. In 1997 the group contributed a competent skazz version of 'Wrapped Around Your Finger' to the Police tribute album.

● ALBUMS: *Skaravan* (Skazz/Rykodisc 1994)★★★, *The Jamaican Beat - Blue Note Blue Beat Volume One* (Toshiba EMI 1994)★★★★, *The Jamaican Beat - Blue Note Blue Beat Volume Two* (Toshiba EMI 1995)★★★.

JEMINI THE GIFTED ONE

b. *c*.1959, Brooklyn, New York, USA. Brooklyn-based Mercury Records recording artist Jemini made his mainstream debut with the *Scars And Pain* EP in 1995. Its title was taken from the artist's own struggle to gain recognition and a recording contract: 'I spent all of my formative years trying to get to where I am now. There were a whole lot of hard times, trials and tribulations. I made many sacrifices'. The EP, which was initially shipped on vinyl before emerging on CD, featured a variety of producers on its seven tracks, including Minesota, Prince Poetry (Organized Konfusion), Rah Boogie, Buckwild and Fatman. Prior to this release, there had been a single, 'Funk Soul Sensation', which married a booming reggae bassline with more traditional west coast sounds. It was backed by his hometown pride anthem, 'Brooklyn Kids'.

JET STAR
(see Pama Records)

JEWELS

The Jewels were a Kingston, Jamaica-based vocal group formed in the early 70s. The line-up revolved around Glasford Manning, who had until 1975 recorded alongside Junior Delgado, Orville Smith and Hugh Marshall in Time Unlimited. Manning descended from the revered Jamaican lineage that spawned Carlton And His Shoes and, later, the Abyssinians. In common with his predecessors, Manning recorded conscientious songs, initially produced by Winston 'Niney' Holness. In 1977 the group released 'Jah I', coupled with Leroy Smart and I. Roy's performance of 'Jah Is My Light'. The single was one of the first 12-inch vinyl discomixes, at the time referred to as a 'mastermix'. The success of the track resulted in further releases through Holness, including 'One Lick', 'Highest City', 'Prophecy Call' and *Mastermix 5*. The group also recorded 'Mr Big Man' under the guise of Porti. During the late 70s occasional releases surfaced, including the classic 'Love And Livity' through the combined support of Gregory Isaac, Bunny Wailer, Big Youth and Trevor 'Leggo Beast' Douglas, who formed the Cash & Carry collective. The paean hailed the second coming, appealing for 'Love and livity - A so Jah seh - 'Til I Jah will be forward'. The song provided the foundation to Big Youth's classic 'Political Confusion' which, along with the Jewels' original, has become a prized collector's item. In 1981 the group followed their hit with 'Fountain Of Tears', which, although produced by Bunny Wailer, regrettably faltered.

JOHNSON, LINTON KWESI

b. 1952, Chapelton, Jamaica, West Indies. Johnson's family emigrated to London in 1963, and he quickly developed a keen awareness of both literature and politics, culminating in a degree in sociology at Goldsmith's College, London, in 1973. An interest in poetry manifested itself in two books, *Voices Of The Living And The Dead* (1974) and *Dread Beat And Blood* (1975), both written in a style that put on paper the patois spoken in black Britain, often with a rhythm reminiscent of Jamaican DJs. Johnson also wrote about reggae for *New Musical Express*, *Melody Maker* and *Black Music*, as well as being writer-in-residence for the London Borough of Lambeth and heavily involved in the *Race Today* co-operative newspaper. Experiments with reggae bands at his poetry readings culminated in 1977's *Dread Beat An' Blood*, recorded as Poet And The Roots, an album that virtually defined the 'dub poetry' genre. An intoxicating mixture of Johnson's lucid, plain-spoken commonsense and rhetoric, and Dennis Bovell's intriguing dub rhythms, it sold well. In 1978 Johnson changed labels from Virgin to Island and issued the strong *Forces Of Victory*, this time under his own name. Johnson became a media face, introducing radio histories of reggae and cropping up on television arts shows, but to his credit he did not exploit his position, preferring instead to remain politically active at grass-roots level in Brixton, London. *Bass Culture* was a more ambitious project that met with a mixed reception, with tracks including the love-chat 'Lorraine' and the title song offering a far broader sweep of subjects than his previous work. *LKJ In Dub* featured Dennis Bovell dub mixes of tracks from his two Island albums. In the same year *Inglan Is A Bitch*, his third book, was published and he also started a record label, LKJ, which introduced Jamaican poet Michael Smith to a UK audience. In the early 80s Johnson seemed to tire of the 'dub poet' tag and became far less active in the music business. In 1986 he issued *In Concert With The Dub Band*, a double live set that consisted chiefly of old material. He finally returned to the studio in 1990 to record *Tings An' Times* for his own label, a more reflective, slightly less brash set. While Johnson has undoubtedly added a notch to reggae's canon in providing a solid focus for the dub poetry movement, offering an alternative stance to that of straightforward reggae DJs, he appears to view his musical involvement as secondary to his political and social activities, and is not therefore the 'name' in the media he might have been. However, no other artist would have tackled subjects such as 'Black Petty Booshwah' (petit-bourgeois) or 'Inglan' (England) Is A Bitch', and for that, his place in reggae history is assured.

● ALBUMS: as Poet And The Roots *Dread Beat An' Blood* (Front Line 1977)★★★, *Forces Of Victory* (Island 1979)★★★★, *Bass Culture*

(Island 1980)★★★★, *LKJ In Dub* (Island 1980)★★★, *Making History* (Island 1984)★★★★, *Linton Kwesi Johnson Live* (Rough Trade 1985)★★★, *In Concert With The Dub Band* (LKJ 1986)★★★, *Tings An' Times* (LKJ 1990)★★★★, *LKJ In Dub Volume 2* (1992)★★★, *A Cappalla Live* (LKJ 1997)★★★.
● COMPILATIONS: *Reggae Greats* (Island 1985)★★★★.

JOHNSON, TEX

b. 30 October 1960, St. Vincent, West Indies. Johnson emigrated with his family to the UK in the 60s, completing his education in Stratford, east London. His initial recording was a self-production with David Tyrone of Venture, 'I Wanna Hold You All Night Long'. Encouraged by the sales of his debut he decided to take control of his career with the inauguration of the Discotex label. The project proved encouraging with the release of Johnson's successful follow-up, 'Pillow Talk', which proved a massive hit in 1981. In 1982 he recorded 'Cork Inna Dance' with the UK-based producer Lloyd Cave, which helped to finance further releases under the Discotex banner, including 'Reggae Rhumba' and 'Love To Love You'. His Christmas release was a double a-sided chart buster in the lovers rock style, 'Honey', and an exhibition of his DJ style on 'Girls Girls Girls'. By 1983 he released 'Body Snatch' and 'Crowd Of People', both in combination with DJ Ranking Ivan, alongside 'Womaniser' and 'Can't Get By Without You'. The hits continued with 'The Girl Next Door', 'Song Book Of Love', 'Ask For A Dance' and an outstanding combination hit with Annette Brisset, 'Eye To Eye'. Throughout his career he has released a number of successful albums but has been unable to emulate the runaway success of 'Pillow Talk' in the singles market. As a producer he carved a considerable niche in the revival market when he enrolled Errol V, Blacksteel and Hector Cross, brother of Sandra Cross, to perform as Klearview Harmonix for the phenomenally successful *Happy Memories* compilations. The albums featured faultless cover versions of reggae classics produced by Johnson. *Volume 5* of the series featured Paulette Tajah performing classic lovers rock hits. In the 90s he concentrated on his production skills, although in 1992 he recorded 'That's Life'. He continues to produce and release lovers and roots compilations, asserting his aspirations towards 'Keeping reggae music sweet, clean, loving and conscious'.
● ALBUMS: *Heart Beat* (Discotex 1988)★★★, *Pure Bliss* (Discotex 1989)★★, *The Collection* (Discotex 1989)★★★★, *For Lovers Only* (Discotex 1990)★★★★, *That's Life* (Discotex 1992)★★★, with Klearview Harmonix *Those Were The Days* (Discotex 1993)★★★, with Klearview Harmonix *Happy Memories Volumes 1 - 5* (Discotex 90s)★★★★.

JONES, FRANKIE

b. Greenwich Farm, Kingston, Jamaica, West Indies. Influenced by local celebrities including Brent Dowe, Tony Brevett, Tapper Zukie and Earl 'Chinna' Smith, Jones set his sights on a career as a vocalist. In 1978 he began recording at Channel One and enjoyed his first hit with 'Sweeten My Coffee'. During the late 70s and early 80s he performed on the live circuit on the fashionable north coast of Jamaica. By the mid-80s Jones was back in the studio recording with Errol 'Myrie' Lewis and John Marshall. In 1984 he enjoyed hits with 'Settle For Me', 'Best Love', 'Modelling Girl' and with DJ Schreecha Nice, 'Get Out Of My Life'. A collaboration with Triston Palmer, who had enjoyed success as a dancehall vocalist, resulted in recording sessions at Music Mountain and Harry J. The sessions were supervised by Keith Wignall with Robbie Lynn and Sylvan Morris. The productions were released in the UK as *The Best Of Frankie Jones Volume One* and included 'Sweet Leoni', 'Mr Bad Boy' and 'Vegetarian'. The compilation confusingly featured a photograph of the legendary drummer and film star Leroy 'Horsemouth' Wallace on the cover, with Jones in the background. Trojan Records proclaimed that a *Volume Two* would be released in 1988 but it did not appear.
● ALBUMS: with Michael Palmer *Showdown Volume Four* (Empire 1984)★★, with Patrick Andy *Two New Superstars* (Burning Sounds 1985)★★★.
● COMPILATIONS: *The Best Of...* (Trojan 1986)★★★★.

JONES, VIVIAN

Jones has established a long and fruitful career as a reggae vocalist, having initially been regarded as a lovers rock performer. He emerged in the late 70s as the lead singer with the Doctor Birds, but by 1980 Jones was pursuing a solo career. 'Good Morning' topped the reggae chart and signalled the beginning of a run of hits for the singer. His popularity spread from the UK to Jamaica where his reputation continued to prosper. In 1988 he was acclaimed as the best reggae performer and won the award for four consecutive years. He released a series of reggae hits, including the chart-topping 'Strong Love', 'Extra Classic', 'I Care', 'A Woman Should Be' and 'Sugar Love'. He also performed on duets with the élite of female UK reggae vocalists, including Sylvia Tella on 'Nu Chat To Me', Debbie Gordon for 'Mr Right' and Deborahe Glasgow on the acclaimed 'The First'. By the mid-90s Jones had established his own Imperial House label, and he escaped his lovers rock image when in 1994 he released the rootsy *Iyaman*, an approach that continued with *The King*. In 1994, 'Happiness' reaffirmed his status as one of the UK's top lovers rock performers. In 1995 he recorded his debut for Fashion Records, 'Dedicated To His Majesty', which featured an outstanding performance from the contemporary DJ Nico Junior. On his own label he released 'Love Is For Lovers' and an album of the same name, and maintained a high profile throughout 1996/7 with a series of hits including 'Let's Go Again' and 'Very Thought Of You'. His international notoriety was enhanced when the US-based Wooligan label released 'Jah See Dem A Come', providing the singer with a Top 10 hit in reggae charts worldwide.
● ALBUMS: *Jah Works* (Shaka 1990)★★★★, *Strong Love* (Jet Star 1993)★★★, *Iyaman* (Imperial House 1994)★★, *Love Is For Lovers* (Imperial House 1995)★★★, *Reggae Max* (Jet Star 1997)★★★★.

JOSEPH, NERIOUS

b. Nereus Mwalimu, St. Lucia, West Indies. Mwalimu began his career with UK-based Fashion Records, who suggested a name change on the basis that 'Nerious' rhymed with 'serious', and would therefore be easier to pronounce. In 1985 his debut 'Sensi Crisis' was an instant hit, and led to the equally popular 'Let's Play' and the 1990 classic, 'Guidance'. His run of hits resulted in a long association with the A Class Crew. The UK-based DJ Top Cat enrolled Joseph to provide the vocals on his combination hit with Tenor Fly, 'Hurry Up', while Gussie P and Chris Lane produced the duo for 'My Girl'. In spite of Joseph's ardent following, his adaptability, whether as a lovers rock, dancehall or roots singer, was not fully recognized, although the critics often suggested that he would be the 'next big thing'. Frustrated by this apparent indifference, Joseph decided to pursue his career with other producers, which led to an amicable break with Fashion and a long sabbatical through to the mid-90s. The critics' predictions came to fruition when in 1996 his return was heralded by the results of sessions with Saxon's Musclehead, who produced 'Giving All My Time', 'Wonderful Feeling', and the sublime 'Shouldn't Touch It'. He became part of reggae's first supergroup, Passion, recording in combination with Peter Hunningale, Mafia And Fluxy and Glamma Kid, and the group enjoyed the smash hit 'Share Your Love'. The single was a dextrous modification of BLACKstreet's 'No Diggity', which crossed over into the UK pop chart and occupied the number 1 position in the reggae charts for two months. Following on from his success with Passion, Joseph released a double a-side, 'Rejoice' and 'I'll Keep Loving You', produced by Gussie P. who had previously engineered most of his Fashion output. The success of the single led to the release of *Rejoice*, featuring contributions from Frankie Paul, Tad Hunter, Claudia Fontaine and Ruff Cut, celebrating his long-overdue recognition.
● ALBUMS: *Loves Gotta Take Its Time* (Fashion 1988)★★★, *Yours To Keep* (Fashion 1992)★★, *Guidance* (Fashion 1990)★★★, *Rejoice* (Charm 1997)★★★★.

JUDGE DREAD

b. Alex Hughes, 1942, Kent, England, d. 13 March 1998, Canterbury, Kent, England. Hughes was a bouncer in London clubs at the end of the 60s and became familiar with reggae through his work, where he had become acquainted with the likes of Derrick Morgan and Prince Buster. In 1969 Buster had a huge underground hit with the obscene 'Big 5', a version of

Brook Benton's 'Rainy Night In Georgia'. It was clear there was a yawning gap waiting to be filled when Buster failed to follow up on his hit, so Hughes, aka Judge Dread (a name borrowed from a Prince Buster character), plunged in. His first single, 'Big Six', went to number 11 in 1972, and spent more than six months in the charts. No-one heard it on air: it was a filthy nursery rhyme. 'Big Seven' did better than 'Big Six', and from this point onwards Dread scored hits with 'Big Eight', a ridiculous version of 'Je T'Aime', and a string of other novelty reggae records, often co-penned by his friend and manager, Fred Lemon. Incidentally, 'Big Six' was also a hit in Jamaica. Five years and 11 hits later (including such musical delicacies as 'Y Viva Suspenders' and 'Up With The Cock'), the good-natured Hughes, one of just two acts success-fully to combine music-hall with reggae (the other was Count Prince Miller, whose 'Mule Train' rivalled Dread for sheer chutzpah), had finally ground to a halt in chart terms. In later years he was found occasionally working the clubs, and he had also sought employment as a local newspaper columnist in Snodland, Kent. In March 1998 he suffered a fatal heart attack while performing in concert at the Penny Whistle Theatre in Canterbury.

● ALBUMS: *Dreadmania: It's All In The Mind* (Trojan 1972)★★★, *Working Class 'Ero* (Trojan 1974)★★★, *Bedtime Stories* (Creole 1975)★★★, *Last Of The Skinheads* (Cactus 1976)★★★, *40 Big Ones* (Creole 1977)★★★, *Reggae And Ska* (TTR 1980)★★★, *Rub-A-Dub* (Creole 1981)★★★, *Not Guilty* (Creole 1984)★★, *Live And Lewd* (Skank 1988)★★, *Never Mind Up With The Cock, Here's Judge Dread* (Tring 1994)★★, *Ska'd For Life* (Magnum 1996)★★, *Dread White And Blue* (Skank 1996)★★★.

● COMPILATIONS: *The Best Of Judge Dread* (Klik 1976)★★★, *The Best Worst Of Judge Dread* (Creole 1978)★★★, *The Legendary Judge Dread Volume 1* (Link 1989)★★★, *The Legendary Judge Dread Volume 2* (Link 1989)★★★, *The Very Worst Of Judge Dread* (Creole 1991)★★★, *The Big 24* (Trojan 1994)★★★, *Big 14* (Hallmark 1995)★★★, *Greatest Hits* (K-Tel 1997)★★★, *Big Hits* (Summit 1997)★★★.

K

KAMOZE, INI

b. 9 October 1957, Port Maria, St. Mary, Jamaica, West Indies. In 1981 Kamoze recorded his debut release, 'World Affairs'; other singles followed and he soon became known as the Voice Of Jamaica. His reputation brought him to the attention of the Taxi Gang, led by Sly Dunbar and Robbie Shakespeare. In 1983 the duo pro-duced a mini-album, *Ini Kamoze*, released through Island Records, which earned him inter-national acclaim, but at the same time his local success faltered, as message music was becoming less popular in the dancehall. At the 1984 Jamaican Sunsplash, however, Kamoze appeared in the line-up on dancehall night, giving an impressive performance to an audi-ence in the grip of DJ mania. The release of *Statement* followed in the same year, including the track 'Call The Police', which was included on the soundtrack of *Good To Go*. His debut per-formance in the UK was at the 1985 Reggae Sunsplash, as part of Sly And Robbie's showcase, which also featured Gregory Isaacs and Sugar Minott. His performance was greeted with enthusiasm and the tour was equally successful in Europe. In 1986 *Pirate* did not enjoy similar success to its predecessors, despite the inclusion of some notable tracks, including 'Betty Brown's Mother', 'Gunshot', a warning about the dangers of firearms, and 'Queen Of My House'. In the same year he toured with Yellowman, Half Pint and the Taxi Gang, including a show at the Town & Country Club that was recorded and released as *The Taxi Connection Live In London*. A con-densed showcase of the tour was featured on the UK television music show *The Tube*. In 1987 Kamoze left the Taxi Gang and began working with the One Two Crew, where he shared pro-duction duties on *Shocking Out*. He won new fans with his single 'Stress', featured on the one rhythm album *Selekta Showcase*. His work remained popular in reggae charts, resulting in a compilation of his earlier Taxi recordings, *Pirate*, and tracks from another two albums on *16 Vibes Of Ini Kamoze*. The ever popular 'Stalag' rhythm found the singer winning dancehall approval when he enjoyed a hit with 'Another Sound'.

By the winter of 1994 he had a number 1 in the US charts with 'Here Comes The Hotstepper' from the movie soundtrack of *Prêt A Porter*, which was also a UK Top 5 hit in January 1995. The song was originally recorded for the *Strictly Dancehall* compilation on the Epic label, which also sponsored a tour featuring the artists involved. The success of the single led to a contract with Elektra Records.

● ALBUMS: *Ini Kamoze* mini-album (Island 1983)★★★, *Statement* (Island 1984)★★★, *Pirate* (Island 1986)★★★, *Shocking Out* (Greensleeves 1987)★★★, *Here Comes The Hotstepper* (Sony 1995)★★★★, *Lyrical Gangsta* (East West 1995)★★★.

● COMPILATIONS: *16 Vibes Of Ini Kamoze* (Sonic Sounds 1992)★★★.

KAY, JANET

b. Janet Kay Bogle, 17 January 1958, London, England. Kay attended Brondesbury High School, Wembley, and later took up secretarial studies, skills to which she has returned at various junctures in her recording career. Her first recordings came under the aegis of Alton Ellis in 1977. This had been brought about by a chance meeting with members of Aswad that summer, who recommended her to the reggae stalwart. The first result of the collaboration, 'Loving You', topped the reggae charts. In many ways she was the prototype lovers rock singer, with her spirited vocals floating over some of the genre's most inspired basslines. 'That's What Friends Are For' and 'I Do Love You' followed. However, her breakthrough came with 'Silly Games', produced by Dennis Bovell for the Arawak label. It became a huge crossover hit, reaching number 2 in 1979. Kay has returned intermittently to recording, predominantly in the lovers rock style, and has also acted extensively as part of the Black Theatre Co-operative, appearing in several straight acting roles on television. Her work has never lost its popularity with the reggae audience, despite her low profile for much of the 80s and 90s, and she has the

talent and personality to be successful on her own terms.

● ALBUMS: *Capricorn Woman* (Solid Groove 1979)★★★, *Silly Games* (Arawak 1980)★★, with Dennis Brown *So Amazing* (Body Work 1987)★★★, *Loving You* (Burning Sounds 1988)★★★, *Sweet Surrender* (Body Music 1989)★★★, with Dennis Bovell *Dub Dem Silly* (Arawak 1994)★★★★.

KEITH AND ENID

In Jamaica Keith Stewart and Enid Cumberland recorded as a duo throughout the early 60s. In 1961 they notched up a number of hits, 'Only A Pity', 'Never Leave Me Throne' and 'What Have I Done'. In 1964 the duo recorded 'Lost My Love', an early example of the new ska beat, produced by D Darling. Many of the singles were released in the UK, albeit marketed within the Jamaican community. By the mid-60s Cumberland found a new partner, Roy Richards, who joined her on 'He'll Have To Go'. The single curiously featured an all-time ska classic, 'Love Me Forever' by Carlton And His Shoes, on the b-side when released in the UK on the Coxsone label. Working with Richards and producer Coxsone Dodd at Studio One she also recorded the up-tempo 'Rocking Time'. Both Stewart and Cumberland have faded into obscurity, while Richards was last seen entertaining tourists by playing his harmonica at a hotel in Kingston.

● ALBUMS: *Keith And Enid Sing* (Island 1963)★★★.

KEITH AND TEX

Texas Dixon and Keith Rowe first auditioned for Derrick Harriott in the late 60s, and the producer was so enamoured with their voices that he immediately took them under his wing and into his studio. Backed by musicians of the calibre of Lynn Tait and Hux Brown, they recorded two of reggae's most enduring and versioned staples, 'Tonight' and 'Stop That Train'. However, they faded into obscurity soon after these releases, although 'Hypnotizing Eyes' and a cover version of the Temptations' 'Don't Look Back' prolonged their career. Rowe went on to release 'Groovy Situation' for Lee Perry, but afterwards emigrated to the USA and joined the army, while Dixon relocated to Canada. The duo might well have languished in obscurity had it not been for rapper Vanilla Ice's version of 'Stop That Train'. In its wake, Crystal Records put together an admirable retrospective package of early recordings, which, rather than bursting the bubble, served to reaffirm their legendary status.

● COMPILATIONS: *Stop That Train* (Crystal 1992)★★★.

KELLY, DAVE 'RUDE BOY'

Kelly worked with Donovan Germain in the late 80s, and was employed as the resident engineer at the Penthouse studio in Slipe Road, Kingston, Jamaica. In 1990 he was introduced to Buju Banton, and together they wrote many of the songs that helped to earn the DJ an award as the Most Exciting Newcomer Of 1991. Kelly continued to work at Penthouse while he set up his own Mad House label, which was eventually launched with Buju Banton's 'Big It Up', featured on the DJ's Penthouse debut *Mr Mention*. Kelly is widely regarded as an innovator, contriving distinctive rhythms including the 'Pepperseed', 'Joyride', 'Arab', 'Stink' and 'Medicine'. He has worked with many top performers in the 90s, including Beenie Man ('Old Dawg' and 'Slam'), Frisco Kid ('Rubbers'), Lady Saw ('Sycamore Tree') and Nadine Sutherland with Terror Fabulous ('Action'). In 1997 Kelly embarked on an adventurous musical project known as Alias, electing to avoid any media hype; he refused to be photographed and formed a co-operative with Wayne Wonder, Frisco Kid, Spragga Benz, Alley Cat, Baby Cham, Textra and Mr. Easy. Working on a totally non-hierarchical basis, the enterprise featured Kelly as producer, writer, musician and even performing as a DJ (hiding behind an alias). He courted controversy when he produced Beenie Man's 'Nuff Slam' jingle to promote a new condom known as 'the Slam'. The sheath's packaging featured Carlene the dancehall queen in an alluring pose and the proclamation 'Slam Country' over the Jamaican flag, which led to protests in Gordon House.

● ALBUMS: *Pepperseed* (Mad House 1996)★★★, *Joyride* (Mad House 1997)★★★.

KELLY, PAT

b. 1949, Kingston, Jamaica, West Indies. Kelly spent a year in Springfield, Massachusetts, USA, during 1966, studying electronics, before returning to Jamaica. In 1967 he replaced Slim Smith as lead singer of the Techniques, who along with Alton Ellis, the Paragons and the Melodians were spearheading Duke Reid's campaign to dominate Jamaican music via his epochal rocksteady productions. With Kelly's wholly distinctive and utterly beautiful falsetto soaring over the impeccable harmonies of Winston Riley and Bruce Ruffin, the trio easily maintained the flow of hits they had begun when Smith had been lead singer. Their first record, an adaptation of a Curtis Mayfield tune, 'You'll Want Me Back', retitled 'You Don't Care' in Jamaica, held the number 1 position in the local chart for six weeks. Their next, another Mayfield cover version, this time adapted from the Impressions' 'Minstrel And Queen' and retitled 'Queen Majesty', enjoyed similar hit status, as did the subsequent 'My Girl' and 'Love Is Not A Gamble'. All are *bona fide* classics of Jamaican vocal harmony, rocksteady style. In 1968 Kelly went solo, joining the roster of artists under the wing of the leading producer Bunny Lee. His first effort for Lee was another Mayfield cover version, 'Little Boy Blue'. Subsequently, he provided Lee with the biggest-selling Jamaican hit of 1969, 'How Long Will It Take', a landmark recording in that it was the first Jamaican record to feature a string arrangement, overdubbed when the song was released in the UK by the Palmer Brothers on their Unity label. Other hits and an album for Lee soon followed, and Kelly's superb, Sam Cooke-derived falsetto even came to the attention of the Beatles' Apple label, who reputedly offered Kelly a £25,000 contract. Unable to act on this offer because of prior contractual commitments, he returned to Jamaica disillusioned, where he recorded sporadically, enjoying a huge local hit for producer Phill Pratt in 1972, 'Talk About Love', as well as recording songs at Treasure Isle studios in the same period with former Gaylad, B.B. Seaton. He then returned to engineering, principally for the Channel One studios owned by the Hookim brothers. Throughout the late 70s and early 80s he continued recording, for Winston Riley, Phill Pratt, Bunny Lee and the London-based sound system owner Fatman. He still records occasionally, and his contribution as one of the great Jamaican soul voices cannot be underestimated.

● ALBUMS: *Pat Kelly Sings* (Pama 1969)★★★,

Talk About Love (Terminal 1975)★★★★, *Lonely Man* (Burning Sounds 1978)★★, *One Man Stand* (Third World 1979)★★, *From Both Sides* (Ital 1980)★★★, *I Wish It Would Rain* (Joe Gibbs 1980)★★★, *Pat Kelly And Friends* (Chanan-Jah 1984)★★★, *One In A Million* (Sky Note 1984)★★, *Ordinary Man* (Body Music 1987)★★★, *Cry For You No More* (Blue Moon 1988)★★★.
● COMPILATIONS: *The Best Of Pat Kelly* (Vista Sounds 1983)★★★★.

KENTE

The term Kente is associated with a hand-woven cloth made up of radiant and dynamic shades of striped material, the strips being assembled to symbolize unity in diversity. This theme inspired the name of the popular Ghanaian group Kente, who have played their brand of roots reggae promoting black awareness since their formation in the early 90s. They are among several Ghanaian performers, including Felix Bell and Swapo, to have embraced and been inspired by Jamaican music. In 1992 the group hosted and successfully supported Ziggy Marley And The Melody Makers on a tour of Ghana. They also played at both the 1992 and 1994 Panafest festivals, where they performed with Stevie Wonder, Jermaine Jackson, Public Enemy, and the Sounds Of Blackness, alongside African reggae stars Lucky Dube and Alpha Blondy. In 1995 the group came to the attention of the German-based African Dance Records organization, who produced and released their debut, *Keep On Moving*. The album led to a successful winter tour of Germany. In their early years the band had provided support to Jah Shaka during a tour of West Africa, and in 1997 they were reunited with him on an acclaimed UK tour celebrating Ghana's 40 years of independence. The tour included a stunning performance by the group at the Essential Festival.
● ALBUMS: *Keep On Moving* (African Dance 1995)★★★.

KING JAMMY

b. Lloyd James, Kingston, Jamaica, West Indies. Jammy, the undisputed king of computerized, digital reggae music for the 80s, was interested in little else but the sound system business from a very early age. He began by building ampli-fiers and repairing electrical equipment from his mother's house in the Waterhouse area of downtown Kingston, and was soon playing live with his own sound system. His prowess earned him a deserved local reputation and as Prince Jammy, he built equipment for many Waterhouse sounds - he was even acknowledged by the legendary King Tubby, another Waterhouse resident, with whom Jammy often worked. In the early 70s Jammy left Jamaica to work in Canada, where his reputation had preceded him, and he was soon working in live stage shows, and employed in various studio activities and sound system work. He stayed for a few years but returned to Kingston and set up his first studio (with extremely limited facilities) at his in-laws' home in Waterhouse. At the same time Tubby's top engineer, Phillip Smart, left for New York and Jammy joined Tubby's team. It was during his time with Tubby that Jammy met the most influential people in reggae; he acknowledges, in particular, the inspiration provided by Bunny Lee and Yabby You. Jammy was continually expanding his own studio and sound system and in the late 70s he began to release his own productions, including the debut Black Uhuru album, coming into contact with many rising dancehall artists such as Half Pint, Junior Reid and Echo Minott.

His constant involvement with the grass-roots side of the business gave Jammy a keen sense of what was currently happening in the music, and also allowed him to anticipate new trends. In 1985 he recorded a youth singer called Wayne Smith with a tune called 'Under Me Sleng Teng', which was to alter irrevocably the nature, and revolutionize the sound, of reggae music. The basis for 'Sleng Teng' was a Casio 'Music Box' and one of the 'rock' rhythms from the box was adapted and slowed down to become a 'reggae' rhythm. The shockwaves were scarcely believable and before long there were over two hundred different versions of the rhythm available, as every producer and artist jumped on the bandwagon. More than anything else, it opened the music to young independent producers and artists, since expensive studio time and 'real' musicians were no longer a prerequisite for recording. Digital reggae ruled, and Jammy, the originator, rode the crest of the wave. His records and sound system dominated and controlled reggae music for the remainder of the decade and on into the 90s. Bobby Digital, now an established producer in his own right, was brought into Jammy's camp and he soon became right-hand man in the set-up, with Steely And Clevie providing the rhythms. Both were established musicians with a real feeling for the new sound, and a bewildering array of 7-inch and 12-inch singles and albums were released every month. Most were massive Jamaican hits and with the help of long-time associate Count Shelly, the records were released simultaneously in New York and London while Jammy administered the business in Jamaica. Countless artists made their debut on the Jammys label, but veteran singers and vocal groups were all keen to play their part in the new sound. There was no one to rival him and in 1987, Jammy won the coveted Rockers Award for best producer. Jammy's 90s output is not as prolific (by his standards), but he still continues to lead while others follow. In 1995, he revived his most innovative tune on *Sleng Teng Extravaganza '95*, featuring the modish stars updating the rhythm with their own interpretations.

It is impossible to overstate his contribution to Jamaican music, because, as the top producer throughout the digital era, he has altered the sound of reggae music without ever losing touch with its foundation - the sound system.

● COMPILATIONS: Various Artists: *Superstar Hit Parade Volumes 1 - 7* (Greensleeves 1984-1992)★★★★, *Ten To One* (Jammys 1985)★★★★, *Sleng Teng Extravaganza Volumes 1 & 2* (Jammys 1986)★★★, *A Man And His Music Volumes 1, 2 & 3* (RAS 1991)★★★★, *Sleng Teng Extravaganza '95* (Greensleeves 1995)★★★.

● FURTHER READING: *King Jammy's*, Beth Lesser.

KING KONG

b. Dennis Anthony Thomas, Kingston, Jamaica, West Indies. First named Junior Kong after his father, he started out as a DJ at Tuff Gong, releasing his debut, 'Pink Eye', in 1982. After stints with GT and his own Love Bunch sound system, he went on to record for King Tubby's Firehouse label, using a powerful, gospel-tinged wail not dissimilar to that of Tenor Saw. The

gravity and realism of early songs such as 'Aids' and 'Babylon', when matched to Tubby's prototype digital 'riddims' in 1985, quickly established his reputation alongside Anthony Red Rose, with whom Tubby teamed him for their debut album, *Two Big Bull Inna One Pen*, on the Firehouse label.

By the following year he was voicing for King Jammy, with 'Trouble Again', 'Mix Up' and 'Legal We Legal' becoming notable hits and leading to his first solo album release in the UK via Greensleeves Records. Jammy was one of many producers in both the UK and Jamaica to record him throughout 1986/7. Others included Black Scorpio, Harry J. ('Musical Terrorist'), Errol T., Ossie Hibbert, Prince Jazzbo, Java ('Toots Boops') and Jah Life. Albums for Bunny Lee, Black Solidarity and King Jammy ensued before he took up residency first in New York, then Canada, as the 80s drew to a close, recording only intermittently on his own short-lived Conscious Music label. 'He Was A Friend' was prompted by the death of Tenor Saw in 1988. The following year he relocated to England and attempted a comeback with strong work for Mafia And Fluxy and Gussie P. in 1991/2, since which time he has been inactive.

● ALBUMS: *Legal We Legal* UK title *Trouble Again* (King Jammys 1986/Greensleeves 1986)★★★★, with Anthony Red Rose *Two Big Bull Inna One Pen* (Firehouse 1986)★★★, *Dancehall Session* (Striker Lee 1986)★★★★, with Nitty Gritty *Musical Confrontation* (Jammys 1986)★★★, *Big Heavy Load* (Striker Lee 1987)★★★, *Identify Me* (Black Solidarity 1987)★★★.

KING SOUNDS

b. *c.*1948, St. Elizabeth, Jamaica, West Indies. King Sounds emigrated to the UK in 1974 , but his first foray into the music business was back in Jamaica, where he danced to ska music in talent shows. His friend Alton Ellis asked him to compere a show, which led to further bookings showcasing his ability to work crowds into a frenzy before an artist's stage appearance ; a cameo as an MC in *Babylon* captured an early performance in this role.

In 1975 he recorded 'Rock & Roll Lullaby', which was a minor hit, before jointly founding the Grove Music collective based in Ladbroke

Grove, London. Together with Mikey Campbell, he introduced Aswad, Delroy Washington and the Sons Of Jah as well as distributing Yabby You's productions from Jamaica. His debut recording was re-released by the label, but his 'Spend One Night In A Babylon', featuring DJ Trinity, captivated the market. Sharing the production with Yabby You, the duo gained a number of hits as the Prophets, including a remake of Slim Smith's 'Blessed Are The Meek'. He was frequently involved in performances at the annual Notting Hill Carnival where, with the Israelites, he proved a popular live act. King Sounds often performed as a support to Aswad, and the energetic Israelites, including Clifton 'Bigga' Morrison, Eddie 'Tan Tan' Thornton and Michael 'Bammi' Rose, provided the horns and keyboards for both acts. *Forward To Africa*, a 1981 release featuring the title track, a version of Clarence Carter's 'Patches' and 'Batman', was successful in Europe. Sounds also made successful appearances at the British Invasion to Reggae Sunsplash, performing alongside Winston Reedy and Steel Pulse. His success was followed by a hit in Jamaica when he covered the Heptones' 'Book Of Rules', released through his own King & I label. The track was lifted from *There Is A Reward* which featured some of the top session musicians in Jamaica, including Sly Dunbar, Pam Hall, J.C. Lodge and Dean Fraser. King Sounds 'bubbled under' the UK charts when he worked with Lloyd Charmers and B.B. Seaton for the singles 'Black & White', 'I Really Don't Want To Hurt You' and 'Would You Like To Be Happy'.

King Sounds' membership of the Twelve Tribes Of Israel, alongside Freddie McGregor, Dennis Brown and Bob Marley, has influenced much of his work. His desire to educate the youth has not always been popular, but he is regarded with 'nuff respect'. Now seen as an elder statesman of British Reggae he was one of the representatives in the House Of Parliament for the launch of COBRA, aiming to look after the interests of performers who had previously suffered exploitation in the music industry. In 1996 he performed and toured with Freddie McGregor.

● ALBUMS: *Come Zion Side* (Grove 1979)★★★, *Forward To Africa* (Island 1981)★★★★, *Moving Forward* (King & I 1983)★★★, *There Is A Reward* (King & I 1985)★★★, *Strength To Strength* (King & I 1988)★★★, *I Shall Sing* (King & I 1992)★★★.

KING SPORTY

b. Noel Williams, *c*.1945, Kingston, Jamaica, West Indies. King Sporty was one of the first DJs to record with Coxsone Dodd at Studio One, where he chanted over Delroy Wilson's 'Feel Good All Over' and 'I'm Not A King', the latter of which enjoyed an enormous revival through Cocoa Tea's 1997 remake of the song. King Sporty also provided the DJ version of the Heptones' classic 'Choice Of Music', which has since become a much sought-after collector's item. By the early 70s King Sporty had relocated to Miami where he continued to be involved in the music. He linked up with the TK organization, working with KC And The Sunshine Band, who in 1975 played on sessions for King Sporty's production of *The Chosen Few In Miami*. His songwriting skills were to prove advantageous when Bob Marley recorded 'Buffalo Soldier', a posthumous hit; King Sporty was involved in the original production. As well as producing, King Sporty continued to perform in Florida where in 1983, backed by the Ex-tras he enjoyed the disco hits 'Do You Wanna Dance' and 'Meet Me At The Disco', the latter of which led to an album of the same name. With the Ex-tras he also released '(The) Boomerang', 'Haven't Been Funked Enough' and 'I Can't Keep Still'. By the early 90s the disco-orientated albums were marketed by Receiver who also controlled Trojan Records' vast back catalogue. In 1995 he had set up Sporty's Studio in Miami, patronized by a number of top reggae performers including the Wailers Band. He is married to the US singer Betty Wright, noted for her R&B hits 'Clean Up Woman' and 'Shoorah Shoorah', as well as for her tour with the Bob Marley And The Wailers in the 70s.

● ALBUMS: *Meet Me At The Disco* (Dancefloor 1983)★★, with the Ex-tras *Extra Funky* (Dancefloor 1983)★, with the Ex-tras *Can't Keep Still* (Dancefloor 1984)★★★.

KING STITT

The 'Ugly One', apparently born Winston Spark, never let his seriously disfigured facial features inhibit his progress in the highly competitive Kingston music world. By 1969 he was the regular DJ for Coxsone Dodd's Number One Set. His success paved the way for U-Roy, I. Roy and Big Youth, but unfortunately, their new style and approach soon superseded Stitt. His style was firmly rooted in the older tradition of Jamaican DJing, influenced by American radio DJs - shouted introductions and interjections as opposed to 'riding the rhythm' and filling out the entire length of the record. Stitt's contributions were fragmentary and explosive as hit followed hit for Clancy Eccles in the early 70s - 'Herbman', 'Fire Corner', 'The Ugly One' and, possibly the most interesting of all, 'Dance Beat', where Eccles and Stitt reminisce about the old ska days, the dances and the dancehalls. Sadly, there is no album of strictly King Stitt material, although *Fire Corner*, credited to the Dynamites (Clancy's Studio band), features a fairly representative cross-section of his work. His few recordings at Studio One failed to match the quality of his Clancy's output, but he has continued to work there in a non-recording capacity. In 1997 the DJ recorded 'Small Axe' alongside Buju Banton.

● ALBUMS: with The Dynamites *Fire Corner* (Trojan/Clandisc 1969)★★★★, various artists *Dance Hall '63* (Studio One 1994)★★★.

● COMPILATIONS: *Reggae Fire Beat* (Jamaican Gold 1997)★★★★.

KING TUBBY

b. Osbourne Ruddock, 28 January 1941, Kingston, Jamaica, West Indies, d. 6 February 1989. King Tubby grew up around High Holborn Street in Central Kingston before moving to Waterhouse in 1955. He started repairing radios and by the late 50s had begun to experiment with sound system amplifiers. By 1968 he was operating his own Tubby's Home Town Hi-Fi, where he later incorporated a custom reverb and echo facility into his system. At the same time he was working as disc-cutter for Duke Reid and it was here that he discovered that he could make special versions of well-known rocksteady tunes. By cutting out most of the vocal track, fading it in at suitable points, reducing the mix down to the bass only, and dropping other instrumental tracks in or out, Tubby invented dub. Initially the technique was used for 'specials' or dub plates - custom acetates made exclusively for sound system use. The spaces left in the mix allowed sound system DJs to stretch out lyrically, predating the emergence of US rappers by some years. Record producers soon began to see the potential of these versions. Joe Gibbs' engineer, Errol Thompson, working at Randy's Studio 17, had started employing rhythm versions as b-sides by 1971. To keep ahead of the competition, Tubby acquired an old four-track mixing console from Dynamic Studios. He then introduced further refinements - delay echo, slide faders, and phasing. By late 1971 he was working with producers such as Bunny Lee, Lee Perry, Glen Brown, Augustus Pablo and 'Prince' Tony Robinson. The latter issued records that credited Tubby as mixer, including 'Tubby's In Full Swing', the b-side to a DJ track by Winston Scotland.

Throughout the 70s Tubby mixed dubs for all the aforementioned producers, in addition to Roy Cousins, Yabby You, Winston Riley, Carlton Patterson and Bertram Brown's Freedom Sounds. His most important work, in terms of sheer quantity, was with Bunny Lee. Lee used Tubby for dub and voicing on rhythms he had built elsewhere with the Aggrovators session band. All the singers who worked with Lee at this time - Johnny Clarke, Cornell Campbell, Linval Thompson, Jackie Edwards, Derrick Morgan, Delroy Wilson, Horace Andy, John Holt and Owen Grey - made records with Aggrovators rhythms, voiced and mixed at King Tubby's. Lee began to issue dub albums featuring Tubby's mixes, and other producers soon followed that lead. Tubby's name as mixer soon appeared on well over 100 albums. A generation of engineers trained under Tubby's supervision, including King Jammy and 'Prince' Phillip Smart, both subsequently finding success on their own terms. Throughout this period Tubby planned to build his own studio, and by 1988 he had begun to issue computer-generated digital music, featuring many of the new-wave ragga singers and DJs, including Pad Anthony, Courtney Melody, Anthony Red Rose, Pliers and Ninjaman, as well as established talents such as Cornell Campbell. Just when it seemed Tubby was poised to challenge top producers such as Jammy and Gussie Clarke, tragedy struck. On 6 February 1989, a lone gunman murdered King Tubby outside his home, the motive apparently robbery. The loss shocked Jamaican music fans and artists. Many innovations, not only in Jamaican music but in other 'dance' forms as well - the 'dub mix', the practice of DJing extended lyrics over rhythm tracks, the prominence of bass and drums in the mix - were developed by King Tubby, both on his sound system and in the studio during the period 1969-74. His place as a seminal figure in the music's development through three decades is assured.

● ALBUMS: *Black Board Jungle* (Upsetter 1974)★★★★, *Dub From The Roots* (Total Sounds 1974)★★★, *The Roots Of Dub* (Grounation 1975)★★★★, *Shalom Dub* (Klik 1975)★★★, *King Tubby Meets the Aggrovators At Dub Station* (Live & Love 1975)★★★★, *King Tubby Meets The Upsetter At The Grass Roots Of Dub* (Fay Music 1975)★★★, *Harry Mudie Meets King Tubby In Dub Conference Volumes 1, 2 & 3* (Mudies 1975/76/77)★★★★, *Dubbing With The Observer* (Trojan 1975)★★★, *King Tubby Meets Rockers Uptown* (Clocktower 1976)★★★★, *King Tubby's Prophecy Of Dub* (Prophet 1976)★★★★, *Ital Dub* (Trojan 1976)★★★, *Beware Dub* (Grove Music 1978)★★★, *Rockers Meets King Tubby In A Firehouse* (Yard Music 1980)★★★, *Dangerous Dub: King Tubby Meets Roots Radics* (Copasetic 1981)★★★★, *King Tubby's Presents Soundclash Dubplate Style* (Taurus 1989)★★★, *King Tubby's Special 1973-1976* (Trojan 1989)★★★, *Dub Gone Crazy: The Evolution Of Dub At King Tubby's 1975-79* (Blood & Fire 1994)★★★★, *Creation Dub* (Roir 1995)★★★, *King Tubby & Friends* (Trojan 1996)★★★★, *Dub Gone 2* (Blood & Fire 1996)★★★.

KING, DIANA

b. *c*.1972, Spanish Town, Jamaica, West Indies. As a child King lived in the Hope Road neighbourhood, Kingston, famous for number 56, the Jamaican home of Bob Marley and his family. She often played with his children Cedella and Sharon, who in the early 80s continued their father's work as the Melody Makers. King began her singing career performing on the tourism circuit in the north of Jamaica at hotels between Negril and Ocho Rios. She soon found work in the studios; in 1990 she recorded with Junior Tucker, the child prodigy-turned-ragga star, for 'Stop To Start', included on his album *Don't Test*. The track was featured on two single releases,

'Sixteen' and the 'Junior Tucker EP'. In 1993 an album of Bob Marley cover versions, *Stir It Up*, by a variety of Jamaican performers included a version of the title track by King which bought her to the attention of major label Sony. Her initial release, 'Shy Guy', crossed over into the pop charts in 1995 which led to the release of *Tougher Than Love*, which showcased her skills both as a singer and DJ. The album included a version of Alton Ellis's 'I'm Still In Love' produced by Sugar Minott and Coxsone Dodd. The follow-up single, 'Ain't Nobody', failed to match its predecessor's performance. *Think Like A Girl* featured King's version of 'I Say A Little Prayer', and was included on the soundtrack for the film *My Best Friend's Wedding*.

● ALBUMS: *Tougher Than Love* (Sony 1995)★★★, *Think Like A Girl* (Work 1997)★★.

KING, JIGSY

b. Errol King, *c*.1970, Kingston, Jamaica, West Indies. In 1993, King developed his DJ skills chanting on various sound systems. He voiced a number of hits at various studios with a number of producers in Jamaica and gained a reputation as the youths' DJ. His vocal style and delivery was similar to Buju Banton, whose gritty delivery over popular rhythms guaranteed a hit. An early example of his style can be found on 'Cock Up And Ride'; the tune was produced by King Jammy's son John John and was a dancehall smash. The lyrics ('Push out your foot and do the bogle dance') and the 'bogle' rhythm inspired a provocative dancing style and led to an adult rating for dancehall videos! In 1994 a combination with Barrington Levy, 'Work', was an international hit that 'bubbled' under the pop chart. The single crossed many barriers and proved especially popular among the East Indian population. Ragga had influenced many Asian performers, notably Apache Indian, and the tune was a guaranteed floor filler at bhangra dances. King's other 1994 hits, 'Have What It Takes' and 'Kick Up', were unable to generate similar enthusiasm. In 1995, he recorded 'God Never Fail Me' and 'Give Me The Weed' with Courtney Cole at Roof International. Other recordings have maintained his profile in the reggae charts, including 'Judge The Book', 'Mr Bate' and 'Ragga Ragga'. In 1996 he topped the Jamaican chart in combination with an English

singer known as Jamie Irie, for an ode to mari-
juana, 'Sweet Sensimella'.
● ALBUMS: *Load It Back* (VP 1994)★★★, *Have
To Get You* (Jet Star 1995)★★, *Ashes To Ashes*
(VP 1995)★★★.

KING, PETER

In 1976 a sound system known as Imperial
Rockers, based in Lewisham, London, surfaced
through Lloyd 'Musclehead' Francis and Dennis
Rowe. By the early 80s the sound had evolved
into the phenomenally successful Saxon sound.
Many of the UK's top performers served their
apprenticeships there, including Maxi Priest,
Tippa Irie and Phillip Papa Levi. In 1981 King
regularly performed with the posse alongside
Papa Levi and is acknowledged as the DJ who
conceived the 'fast style mic chat'. At the Dick
Shepherd Youth Club in 1982, King unleashed
his spectacular speed rap, which instantly
caught on and a number of other DJs immediately emulated his style. His unique, rapid-fire
lyricism earned him a reputation as the originator, although the foundation of the style was
soon forgotten when a myriad of fast-style tunes
surfaced; Papa Levi's 'Mi God Mi King' builds up
to a speed rap in the closing verses and Tippa
Irie's 'All The Time The Lyric A Rhyme' is also
modelled around the style. While his cohorts
have reaped the rewards, King's recorded output
is not as abundant, but he is still respected in
the reggae world. On the Fashion label, notable
releases include 'Me Neat Me Sweet' and 'Step
On The Gas'. Fellow Saxon crew members
Smiley Culture and Asher Senator recorded both
in combination and as soloists and acknowledged King's influence. When Smiley Culture
crossed over into the mainstream King and
Senator joined forces and gave a memorable performance on the television show *Club X*. The
programme, hosted by Smiley, featured some of
Jamaica's best musicians, including Ernest
Wilson, Bloodfire Posse, Delroy Wilson and
Freddie McGregor. King and Senator performed
'You Too Lie Fib Fib'. King has remained a popular MC on the dancehall circuit and should not
be confused with the UK-based mellow saxophonist who records sentimental lovers rock.
● ALBUMS: various artists *Live At DSYC
Volume One* (Raiders 1984)★★★.

KNOWLEDGE

Knowledge were based in the Rema area of
Kingston, Jamaica, West Indies, where they
established a solid reputation. The group began
their career in the late 70s under the guidance of
DJ Tapper Zukie. The line-up included Anthony
Doyley, Delroy Folding, Earl MacFarlane,
Michael Smith, Michael Samuels, and later, Paul
Freeman. The group's debut, 'Make Faith', featured Zukie introducing the band as his protégés, and proved a winning combination. They
released a number of hits through Zukie's Stars
label, which culminated in a major label signing
in 1978. The contract was short-lived and in the
early 80s the group went through a period of
anonymity. During this unproductive time,
Freeman, under the pseudonym of Jah Showie,
linked up with Trevor 'Leggo Beast' Douglas to
set up his own Sunshine label. In 1981 Samuels,
under the guise of Michael Knowledge,
attempted a solo career with the release of
'Dreadlock Time'. In the early 90s the band
began recording for Roy Cousins, resulting in
the hits 'Na Buy Apartheid', 'Chant Rasta Man'
and 'Fire Burn', for his Tamoki-Wambesi label.
The group avoided the digital sound, preferring
to use real musicians, and enlisted some of
Jamaica's top players including Pablove Black,
Winston Wright, Leroy 'Horsemouth' Wallace
and Sowell Radics. After a lengthy delay, the sessions eventually appeared on a CD compilation
in 1995.
● ALBUMS: *Hail Dread* (A&M 1978)★★★.
● COMPILATIONS: *Stumbling Block* (Tamoki-
Wambesi 1995)★★★★.

KOFI

b. Carol Simms. Formerly with female lovers
rock trio Brown Sugar, Simms pursued an
equally prolific career as Kofi following the
former's demise in the mid-80s. She worked
with the Mad Professor, revisiting Brown Sugar's
past glories on 'I Am So Proud' and 'I'm In Love
With A Dreadlocks', alongside versions of 'Place
In The Sun' and 'Didn't I'. She also recorded a
duet with John McLean on 'I'm Still In Love
With You'. Kofi released three albums on Ariwa
Sounds and one on Atlantic Records. In 1990 her
remake of the Brown Sugar songs, 'Proud Of
Mandella' and 'Dread A Who She Love', were
also used as the basis for combination hits with

DJ Macka B. In the 90s she released the popular 'Coming Down To See Me' and continued to maintain a high profile as a lovers rock performer.

● ALBUMS *Black With Sugar* (Ariwa 1989)★★★, *Wishing Well* (Ariwa 1992)★★, *Fridays Child* (Ariwa 1994)★★, *A Very Reggae Christmas* (Atlantic 1994)★.

KOJAK AND LIZA

Kojak (b. Floyd Anthony Perch, 30 September 1959, Kingston, Jamaica, West Indies) began his career chanting on various sound systems under the guise of Pretty Boy Floyd. He adopted the gangster image that had proved successful for Dennis Alcapone and Dillinger, but was unable to emulate the fortunes of his role models and changed his stage name to Nigger Kojak in response to a title given to him by his followers. Inspired by the 70s television series *Kojak*, he emulated the show's star with a shaved head and often appeared with the obligatory lollipop. His debut, 'Massacre', proved a local hit and led on to many others. In 1978 Dennis Brown had an international hit with the remake of 'Money In My Pocket', which was followed by 'Ain't That Loving You', featuring Kojak And Liza performing 'Hole In De Bucket'. The hit proved a success in the dancehall, which resulted in the inauguration of a popular winning combination. The partnership led to conflicting reports as to the identity of Kojak's fellow artist, as there were in fact two Mama Lizas, Beverly Brown and Jacqueline Boland. His female partner was always labelled simply as Liza, which hindered the women's careers, making it impossible to judge them on their individual merits. The duo performed 'Fist To Fist Rub A Dub', a tribute to the soft drink Sky Juice, the modest 'One Thousand Gal' and the festive 'Christmas Stylee'. By 1981 Kojak And Liza had become well established and the unprecedented success of 'Nice Up Jamaica' was endorsed by the Jamaican tourist board. The song, although on some pressings credited to the duo, was actually a solo from Floyd Perch that verged on the surreal. By 1982 he became known as Papa Kojak and was a featured DJ at the acclaimed Skateland show, recorded live as *A Dee Jay Explosion*. By 1996, his resurgence as a singer, performing 'What Time Is It', was met with enthusiasm. The song was included on his distinguished comeback album of soul cover versions, which featured backing vocals from Nadine Sutherland, J.C. Lodge, Marcia Griffiths and Judy Mowatt. The paucity of female DJ performers has often been criticized, along with the fact that early performances were only in a supporting role. The pioneering efforts of the two Lizas have since been acknowledged on record as influencing the likes of Sister Nancy and Lady Saw.

● ALBUMS: *Kojak And Liza Showcase* (Gorgon 1981)★★★, *Floyd Perch A/K/A Papa Kojak* (Mouthpiece 1996)★★.

KONG, LESLIE

b. 1933, Kingston, Jamaica, West Indies, d. 1971. In partnership with his three brothers, Chinese Jamaican Kong ran a combination ice-cream parlour and record shop called Beverley's, on Orange Street in Kingston. He became a record producer in 1961 after hearing Jimmy Cliff sing 'Dearest Beverley' outside his establishment, which he subsequently recorded and released on the Beverley's label. The following year he recorded Bob Marley's first records, 'Judge Not' and 'One Cup Of Coffee', and had huge hits with Cliff's 'Miss Jamaica' and Derrick and Patsy's 'Housewives Choice'. For the rest of the decade he worked with nearly all of the top names in Jamaican music, including John Holt, Joe Higgs, Derrick Morgan, Stranger Cole, Desmond Dekker, the Maytals, the Melodians and the Pioneers, and many of these recordings were licensed for release in the UK on Chris Blackwell's Island Records.

In 1967 Kong achieved a big international hit with Desmond Dekker's '007', and a massive worldwide smash with the same artist in 1969 with 'Israelites'. In late 1969 Kong again recorded Bob Marley, this time with the Wailers, and he released these sessions as *The Best Of The Wailers*. He crossed over again into the UK national charts with the Pioneers' 'Long Shot Kick The Bucket', the Melodians' 'Rivers Of Babylon' (the blueprint for Boney M's hit version a decade later) and 'Sweet Sensation', and the Maytals' 'Monkey Man' - only one of a long series of hits that he enjoyed with the group. Kong's work has for too long been viewed as 'unfashionable' by reggae's self-appointed experts. Much of this is owing to professional jealousy - few producers ever came near to matching Beverley's in terms of hit records, and many of Beverley's releases were also huge international successes - Kong was one of the first producers to popularize Jamaican music outside of its immediate target audience. His productions were always clean and sharp and he used the best available musicians. His reputation has sadly never matched these achievements - a highly unusual situation in the reggae field - but time will, hopefully, redress the balance, and allow his work to be appreciated on its true merits.

● COMPILATIONS: various artists *Reggae Party* (MFP 1970)★★★, *The Best Of Beverley's* (Trojan 1981)★★★★, *The King Kong Compilation* (Island 1981)★★★★.

KOTCH

Kotch have been in existence since 1981, although only drummer Steven Lee and his guitarist uncle Pablo Stewart have remained constant. First called Psalms, the band offered straightforward roots reggae at a time when dancehall was starting to become popular. Their first single, 'In The Hills', produced by themselves and Third World's Willie Stewart, flopped, but it was followed by the better-received 'Skaba', produced by Ibo Cooper, also from Third World. By that time, in 1982, their lead singer, Parry Hinds, had been replaced by the distinctive, soulful baritone of Rueben 'Norman' Espuet and the line-up settled to Espuet, Lee, Pablo Stewart, Ian Heard (saxophone), Al Wilson (trombone), Earl Thorpe (bass) and Herbie Harris (keyboards). Four singles arrived in 1983, the last two, 'Head Over Heels' and 'Jean', charting in Jamaica. Their first album, *Sticks And Stones*, was also issued that year. Steven Lee's other job, at his father's Sonic Sounds record distribution company in Kingston, gave Kotch an important connection. Upstairs at Sonic Sounds was a tiny computerized studio, Megabyte, that Sly Dunbar rented. Kotch's keyboard player, Herbie Harris, became resident programmer and, with reggae changing in 1986 to a fully digital sound, Sly was looking for his Taxi label to follow suit. In 1988 it arrived: a rocking, woodblock snare, a subsonic, growling bass, and a simple keyboard and guitar arrangement that owed something to rocksteady. When

Dunbar needed a voice, he simply called on the band downstairs, but Kotch's first new hit, 'Cruising', caused confusion. Many believed that it was the work of a girl group, as Espuet's baritone had been sidelined for a falsetto worthy of the Stylistics. An appearance at the Reggae Sunsplash festival in 1988 confirmed that it was Espuet with the high-rise larynx. 'Cruising' hit number 1 in Jamaica, and it was quickly followed by 'Tears' (a Top 10 hit) and a cover version of Smokey Robinson's 'Ooh Baby Baby', which Mango issued in England to considerable reggae chart success. 'Heartbreak', a cover version of Eric Clapton's 'Wonderful Tonight', and 'Tracks Of My Tears' have all since sold well. The album *Kotch* was released internationally and to support it they toured Africa, South America and Europe and played extensively, backing singers and DJs in Jamaica - a facet of their work that success forced them to abandon. 'Don't Take Away' with U-Roy, and 'Clock' maintained their profile into the 90s.

● ALBUMS: *Sticks And Stones* (Sonic Sounds 1983)★★★, *Kotch* (Mango/Island 1989)★★★★.

KPIAYE, JOHN

b. John Ogetti Kpiaye, 1948, London, England. Kpiaye was born to an English mother and Nigerian father, spending his formative years in the English countryside. He left school in London at the age of 15 and, emulating luminaries such as Bob Marley and Desmond Dekker, he embarked on an apprenticeship in welding. In 1966 his mother bought him his first guitar, and he joined a band called the Hustling Kind, who later changed their name to the Cats. In 1968 Kpiaye encouraged the band to record a reggae rendition of Tchaikovsky's 'Swan Lake', working out the piano melody line on his sister's piano at home, and the Cats secured their first British reggae UK Top 50 chart hit. The success of the single resulted in a European tour, but by 1971 the group disbanded. Kpiaye soon found work playing for the In Brackets, who provided backing for a number of top performers including Dandy, Ginger Williams, Owen Gray, Winston Groovy and Joy White. In 1973 the band was dissolved and Kpiaye became immersed in production work, initially for Dennis Harris, and provided direction for notable lovers rock performers Brown Sugar and

15-16-17. In the latter half of the 70s he became an in-demand guitarist, playing for Ijahman Levi, Aswad, Dennis Brown, Janet Kay and Linton Kwesi Johnson, Eddy Grant and Georgie Fame. In 1982 Kpiaye became the resident guitarist in Dennis Bovell's Dub Band, touring the globe and providing backing to Linton Kwesi Johnson's acclaimed appearances. In 1997 Kpiaye released *Red, Gold And Blues*, a reggae instrumental album drawing from his many influences.

● ALBUMS: *Red, Gold And Blues* (LKJ 1997)★★★★.

KRYZTAL

b. Henry Buckley, 1972, Jamaica, West Indies. Chicago-based Pancho Kryztal was working as a desktop publishing consultant before an inspirational return trip to Jamaica convinced him to pursue a career in music. Returning to Chicago, he was introduced to Jeremy Freeman, who was setting up the Scratchie label with James Iha and D'arcy Wretzky of Smashing Pumpkins, and Adam Schlesinger of Fountains Of Wayne. Kryztal signed to Scratchie, but retained Caribbean rights for his own label, Skinny Bway. An initial 12-inch DJ promo, 'Girl A Chat'/'I Need You Badly', gained extensive airplay in Jamaica and the USA. Subsequent singles, 'Lethal Weapon' and 'Sweet Gal', generated further interest in Krystal's 'dancehall R&B', which blended the contrasting styles of R&B balladeer and macho toaster. His self-titled debut was released in October 1997 on Scratchie/Mercury, drawing favourable comparisons with both the current crop of urban R&B singers and established ragga artists such as Shaggy and Chaka Demus And Pliers. The album's diverse production credits included dancehall stalwart Tony Kelly and rapper DJ Spinner.

● ALBUMS: *Kryztal* (Scratchie/Mercury 1997)★★★★.

KY-MANI

b. *c*.1975, Jamaica, West Indies. In addition to Bob Marley's musical legacy, his lifestyle was evidently irresistible to the media, who considered his consumption of ganja and his siring of many offspring newsworthy. Following Bob's demise many of his relatives have entered the music business, notably Ziggy Marley And The Melody Makers, Julian Marley, Damien 'Jr Gong' Marley and Ky-mani Marley. Critics tended to approach releases by members of the Marley family with accusations of nepotism, and to avoid this Ky-mani refused to capitalize on his father's name, in spite of the title of his debut, *Like Father Like Son*. The album featured cover versions of his father's hits complete with their respective dub versions, which gave the singer the opportunity to establish his recording career. He relocated to the USA with his mother when he was eight years old. He initially followed in Bunny Wailer's footsteps as a percussionist, although he was attracted by the dancehall style, and by the early 90s emerged as a DJ. In common with his siblings, Ky-mani's vocal styling is very reminiscent of his father, particularly on 'Thank You Lord', the 1997 combination hit with DJ Shaggy. The single, lifted from *Midnite Lover*, was originally recorded with Brian And Tony Gold until Clifton 'Specialist' Dillon suggested adding Ky-mani's vocals. The project resulted in commercial success, topping a number of specialist charts worldwide. Further hits included 'Judge Not' with Patra, the stimulating 'Sensimella' and the stirring 'Dear Dad'. In late 1997 Ky-mani joined forces with Tito Puente Jnr., fulfilling the Bronx-born singer's desire to record in combination with a reggae artist. Puente, a notable salsa performer, dabbled with the Jamaican sound, having recorded a version of Musical Youth's 'Pass The Dutchie'. The duo appeared at the annual MIDEM seminar in Miami, where both artists achieved critical acclaim for their performance.

● ALBUMS: *Like Father Like Son* (Rhino 1997)★★.

LADY ANNE

b. Anne Smith, *c*.1960, Jamaica, West Indies. In the late 70s a new wave of DJs including Charlie Chaplin, Josie Wales and Brigadier Jerry were plying their trade in the dancehalls. The number of female performers in the same area was small, and when they rendered a chant it was mainly in a supporting role, as in Liza's assistance to Papa Kojak. The situation was rectified when Sister Nancy began performing, and ushered in a new dimension to dancehall entertainment. Lady Anne was one of the first, alongside Nancy, who won the support of the crowds and her popularity led to studio sessions. Lady Anne's debut was with Roots Tradition, where she recorded an answer to 'Shine Eye Girl' as 'Shine Eye Boy'. Other hits included 'Take A Set', 'Heroes Connection', 'Talk Talk Talk' and 'Lady Anne You're Sweet', as well as combinations with Peter Metro ('Bossanova') and reggae's Santana ('Love Life'). She continued to record and appear on various sound systems and in 1982 her hit 'Informer', for Joe Gibbs, enjoyed a lengthy spell in the Jamaican Top 10. She was known for her cheerful disposition and sense of humour, but the song revealed another side of her character in her condemnation of ghetto informants. Plans for an international tour were thwarted owing to problems with the immigration authorities, and this undermined her chance of wider recognition. The trailblazing spirit of Nancy and Anne has since inspired many performers, including Sister Carol, Lady Shabba, Lady Saw, Lady G and Patra.
● ALBUMS: *Informer* limited pressing (Joe Gibbs 1983)★★★★, with Peter Metro And Friends *Dedicated To You* (CSA 1984)★★★, *Vanity* (Pre 1984)★★★.

LADY G

b. Janice Fyffe, *c*.1974, Kingston, Jamaica, West Indies. Fyffe began DJing with the Black Scorpio sound system and her reputation soon spread. Her initial recording came in 1988 with producer Gussie Clarke who utilized J.C. Lodge's hit 'Telephone Love' for Lady G's 'Nuff Respect'. The song was a warning to all chauvinists and has since become an anthem among ragga girls. Championed as the sisters' DJ, she recorded in combination with Papa San the hit 'Round Table Talk', which topped the Jamaican charts. The duo performed a comical altercation, in which Lady G won the squabble. Other hits prior to a temporary sabbatical included 'Rock Back' and 'Is It Me Or The Gun'. The lapse in her career allowed Lady G as a single mother to spend more time with her two children. In 1994 she returned to the stage, performing a stunning presentation at the annual Fresh concert. In the spring of 1995 she performed in combination with Chevelle Franklin 'The Real Slam', in response to the many male DJ records on that theme initiated by Beenie Man. Lady G and Franklin also recorded with Exterminator the conscientious 'Thank You', riding the 'No Woman No Cry' rhythm, and also 'Love And Hate' at Donovan Germain's Penthouse studio, reaffirming the success of the duo.
● ALBUMS: *God Daughter* (Pre 1995)★★★★.

LADY SAW

b. Marion Hall, 1969, St. Mary, Jamaica, West Indies. Lady Saw began chatting on the microphone at the age of 15. Being located some distance from the recording studios, she served an apprenticeship on local sound systems before appearing on vinyl. Inspired by the popularity of the slackness style, she performed lewd songs, which earned her a reputation as an X-rated DJ. Her earliest tunes, 'Stab Up De Meat' and 'Just Anuddah Day', reinforced her bad girl image which she eloquently defended on the controversial television documentary *Yardies*. In 1994 her shows were banned in certain Jamaican parishes, to which she responded with 'Freedom Of Speech'. She complained that many male performers had performed slack lyrics without having to endure the censorship to which she was exposed. Her grievance faltered when she performed 'Peanut Punch Mek Man Shit Up Gal Bed' on her video *The Legend Returns* with Lady G, Shamara, Michelle and Lo Lo. In spite of the controversies, she maintained

a high musical profile with the hits 'Me Naw Lock Mi Mouth', 'Lonely Without You' and the popular 'Good Wuk'. Other releases followed, including the celebratory 'Glory Be To God' and 'Ask God For A Miracle'. She enjoyed her biggest hit in 1995 with 'Hardcore', while with King Jammy's son John John, her rendition of 'Welding Torch' left little doubt as to the subject matter. The controversy surrounding the AIDS virus resulted in Buju Banton's recording of 'Don't Be Silly (Put A Rubber On Your Willy)'. The tune and a television report inspired Lady Saw to advise girls of the dangers of unprotected sex with her recording of 'Condom'. By the autumn of 1995, the continued drive towards conscientious lyrics found Lady Saw being drawn into the roots and culture style, though her audiences demanded to see the more notorious raunchy performances. In 1996 she enjoyed hits with 'Give Me A Reason' and 'You Yuh Husband Of Mine'. The same year, *Give Me The Reason* was released and included 'Condom' and 'Saturday Night At The Movies' in combination with Brian and Tony Gold.
● ALBUMS: *Bare As You Dare* (VP 1994)★★★, *Lover Girl* (Pre 1995)★★★★, *Give Me The Reason* (VP 1996)★★★, *Passion* (VP 1997)★★★.
● COMPILATIONS: *The Collection* (Diamond Rush 1997)★★★.

LARA, JENNIFER

b. *c*.1959, Kingston, Jamaica, West Indies. In 1974 she recorded her debut album with Coxsone Dodd at Studio One in Brentford Road. The results of the sessions appeared on *Studio One Presents Jennifer Lara*, which was an instant success. She also enjoyed a massive hit with the single 'Where Have All The Good Men Gone', which has since become an anthem. Other Downbeat-produced hits followed, including 'Consider Me' and 'Do That To Me One More Time'. While working in Brentford Road she was also employed as a backing singer and is recognized for her notable contribution on Freddie McGregor's *I Am Ready*. She has toured in Europe and her appearances in the UK were greeted with enthusiasm by both media and audiences. In the autumn of 1980 she recorded three tracks on the six-track compilation *Sir Coxsone's Family Christmas Album*. Her contributions included 'Lonely Christmas', 'Hands Of

The Lord' and a duet with Johnny Osbourne and the family group, 'Christmas Medley'. The success of her Studio One output has overshadowed her later work, although she enjoyed minor hits with 'All My Love For You' and 'Mark My Words'. By the mid-80s she had recorded with Prince Far I, Henry 'Junjo' Lawes and Tristan Palmer. Her work with Palmer included a duet, 'Midnight Confession'. Into the 90s she worked with King Jammy, lending her vocal skills to 'I Wanna Sex You Up' with Thriller U, 'You Turn Me On', with a host of Jamaica's top DJs including Bounty Killer, and 'Stop' with Major Mackerel.
● ALBUMS: *Studio One Presents* (Studio One 1974)★★★★, *Across The Line* (Sonic Sounds 1980)★★★, *Dancehall Roots And Lovers* (Rads 1994)★★★.

LAUREL AND HARDY

Laurel (b. Paul Dawkins, October 1962, London, England) and Hardy (b. Anthony Robinson, April 1962, London, England). Before entering the reggae scene in 1978 the duo tried their luck at performing soul but found the DJ style more absorbing. The pair followed the sound systems of the day, such as Neville King, Moa Ambassa and Sufferer. They began performing with a young girl known as the Virgin Mary, while they were known as Reverend T and Pope Paul. Following in the combination style of Clint Eastwood And General Saint, Yellowman And Fathead, and Michigan And Smiley they became known as the Holy Two. Located in Battersea, London, it was not long before their debut single appeared on the locally based Fashion label, and they became known as Laurel And Hardy. Emulating Stan and Ollie, they would appear in bowler hats, bow ties, white gloves and suits, to the delight of the audience. The release of 'You're Nicked' surfaced on a 10-inch disc, a popular fad at the time, and the success of the single brought them to the attention of CBS Records. The signing led to a tour of universities supporting the funk fusion group Pigbag. Following the rave reviews on campus another tour of universities was arranged, using a band as opposed to backing tapes, and supported by the dub poet Benjamin Zephaniah. The pair were also featured in the national press and appeared on Saturday morning television shows promoting the release of 'Clunk Click' in 1983. However, major label contracts frequently prompted the demise of reggae performers' careers, and the duo were no exception. Following the second release, 'Lots Of Loving And She's Gone', Laurel And Hardy returned to an independent label and recorded with Papa Face. Sadly, the duo's credibility was already low and they were unable to recapture the popularity that they had previously enjoyed. Other outings followed, notably 'Dangerous Shoes', but they were unable to maintain a high profile in the reggae chart. During a quiet spell they set up their own recording studio and worked in the background, although an appearance on the television series *Black On Black* was met with enthusiasm.

● ALBUMS: *What A Bargain* (Upright 1983)★★★.

LAWES, HENRY 'JUNJO'

b. Henry Lawes, Kingston, Jamaica, West Indies. One of the most prolific and influential producers of the 80s, Lawes was born and raised in Olympic Way, West Kingston. In 1978 he made his musical debut singing in the trio Grooving Locks. The following year, he took Barrington Levy to Channel One. Subsequently, 'Collie Weed', 'Looking My Love' and 'Shine Eye Gal' all reached number 1 on the Jamaican charts, and the resulting *Bounty Hunter* album is generally considered to be the first of the new dancehall era. With the Roots Radics and Scientist working on the majority of his releases, Lawes began voicing a dazzling array of talent. Michael Prophet ('Gun Man'), Papa Tullo, General Echo, Ranking Toyan ('How The West Was Won'), Billy Boyo, Little Harry, Little John ('Dancehall Style'), Barry Brown ('Give Another Israel A Try'), Anthony Johnson and Eek A Mouse ('Wa Do Dem') were among those who recorded for his Arrival and Volcano labels throughout 1980-82.

Apart from pioneering the concept of two artist 'clash' albums and presenting dubmixer Scientist as an artist in his own right, his next step was to instigate albums of live dancehall sessions, often featuring Yellowman, whose rapid rise owed much to the many hit singles and albums recorded for Lawes. Early B, Josey Wales ('Outlaw Josey Wales'), Nicodemus, Buru Banton, Michigan And Smiley ('Diseases'), Peter Metro, Charlie Chaplin, Audie Murphy and Lord Sassafras all recorded over his rhythm tracks, which began to dominate the dancehall market. Quick to spot new talent, he also revived the careers of several established acts who had slipped into decline. Under his direction, John Holt enjoyed a revival, voicing hits such as 'Sweetie Come Brush Me' and then 'Police In Helicopter'; Alton Ellis, Ken Boothe, Johnny Osbourne ('Fally Lover'/'Ice Cream Love'), Al Campbell, the Wailing Souls and Earl Sixteen similarly benefited from his winning touch. In 1983 he formed his own Volcano sound system. With access to unlimited dub plates and using state-of-the-art equipment, Volcano soon became the top sound in Jamaica. By 1984, Yellowman ('Zungguzungguguzungguzeng'), Barrington Levy ('Prison Oval Rock') and Eek A Mouse ('Anaxerol') were vying for the top slot, and he had already added new talents such as Cocoa Tea ('Rocking Dolly'/'Lost My Sonia') and Frankie Paul ('Pass The Tushenpeng') to his roster, co-writing an ever-increasing number of hit songs himself. In 1985 he took Volcano to New York, where he remained for six years. He had missed out on the digital revolution that had swept through Jamaican music during those years, but worked with several of his former artists on his return, including John Holt, Linval Thompson, Cocoa Tea ('Kingston Hot') and Yellowman, to varying degrees of success. By 1994 he had recorded albums with Ninjaman, General TK and Shaka Shamba, voiced an increasing number of younger artists and had plans for his own studio in Kingston. With his uncanny eye for new talent, his lyrical ability and shrewd marketing sense, few would bet against him making further significant contributions to reggae music in the future.

Productions include: Barrington Levy *Bounty Hunter* (1979), *Englishman* (1980), *Robin Hood* (1980); Scientist *Heavyweight Dub Champion* (1980), *Scientist Wins The World Cup* (1983); Ranking Toyan *How The West Was Won* (1982); Eek A Mouse *Wa Do Dem* (1981), *The Mouse And The Man* (1983), *Mouseketeer* (1984); Yellowman *Mr Yellowman* (1982), *Zungguzungguguzungguzeng* (1983); Yellowman with Josey Wales *Two Giants Clash* (1984); Josey Wales *The Outlaw Josey Wales* (1983); John Holt *Police In Helicopter* (1983); Johnny Osbourne *Fally Lover* (1980); Don Carlos *Day*

To Day Living (1983); Wailing Souls *Inch Pinchers* (1983); Frankie Paul *Pass The Tu-Sheng Peng* (1984); Cocoa Tea *Wha Dem A Go Do, Can't Stop Cocoa Tea* (1985), *Kingston Hot* (1992); Ninjaman *Booyakka! Booyakka!* (1994).
● COMPILATIONS: various artists *Live At Aces International* (1983)★★★, *Total Recall* (VP 1991)★★★, *Total Recall Volume 2* (VP 1992)★★★.
● FURTHER READING: *Reggae Inna Dancehall Style*, Tero Kaski and Pekka Vuorinen.

LAZARUS, KEN

Lazarus began his career from the inception of ska in the early 60s. He performed lead vocals for Byron Lee And The Dragonaires, playing on tours of the West Indies and North America. In 1965, credited as performing with the Byron Lee Orchestra, he relished his first taste of international fame when 'Funny' was released through Island Records in the UK. He also performed as part of an idiosyncratic, neglected Jamaican rock band, Tomorrow's Children. His sporadic output resulted in a few releases of note, although in 1971 he maintained a high profile with 'Girl' and the bewildering 'Tomorrow's Children'. Although Lazarus's releases were erratic he worked in the studios as an arranger, producer and songwriter. In 1972, as a performer, he secured a one-single contract with a major label for the release of 'Hail The Man', but failed to satisfy the company's expectations. By the 90s, having relocated to California, he joined Pluto and Ernie Smith on a small island tour. The jaunt was to promote his solo release, *Reflections*, which featured Lazarus's unique renditions of reggae classics including the Maytals' 'Peeping Tom', Ken Boothe's 'Freedom Street' and Jimmy Cliff's 'Wonderful World Beautiful People'.
● ALBUMS: *Reflections* (Laz Rec 1997)★★.

LEE DAVIS, JANET

b. 1966, London, England. Lee Davis moved to Jamaica at the age of three and was raised in the Old Harbour Bay area of St. Catherine. Following the customary path of many Jamaican singers, her vocals were nurtured singing in the local church choir. Although a competent chorister, she was influenced by the country, R&B, pop and reggae hits that she per-

formed in neighbourhood shows. In 1981 she progressed into the sound system circuit, forming an allegiance with the St. Catherine-based Ghetto Sound, performing both as a vocalist and in the DJ style. Her versatility gained her notoriety and she proved that she was equally proficient at performing in stage shows. Lee Davis relocated to the UK and her initial recording session came when she met up with DJ Jah Walton through soundman Vego Wales. She was asked to chat on the massive number 1 hit for Fashion Records, 'No Touch The Style', with the DJ performing as Joseph Cotton. Although Lee Davis was not credited for her performance on the hit, she quickly gained recognition with her solo hit for Flash, 'Never Gonna Let You Go'. In 1987 she returned to Fashion for 'Two Timing Lover', while the b-side, 'Call Me An Angel', featured her DJ skills, recorded under the name of Shako Lee. The song was written by Philip Leo who also worked with her for the vocal/DJ release 'I'm Gonna Make You Happy Again' and 'I'm In Love'. She also worked with High Power, resulting in the concurrent release of 'Prisoner Of Love'. In 1990 she topped the reggae charts in combination with CJ Lewis, performing a version of the 60s hit from Keith And Enid, 'Worried Over You'. Lee Davis's success led to a four-album contract with Island Records, and although no album surfaced, the label released 'Spoilt By Your Love' and 'Pleasure Seekers'. The Island sessions were supervised by Barry Boom, who released 'Just The Lonely Talking Again', 'Love Is Alive', 'Never Say Never' and the classic 'Hello Stranger'. Following from his success with the late Deborahe Glasgow, Gussie Clarke recruited Lee Davis to perform backing vocals on Cocoa Tea's *Authorised* and released her solo hit, 'Oops There Goes My Heart'. Following from her disappointing brush with the majors she returned to Fashion, secure in the knowledge that she could compete on the wider market while maintaining her credibility within the reggae community. By 1992 she dominated the UK lovers rock scene with a continuous profile on the reggae chart, including the hits 'Ooh Baby Baby', 'Big Mistake', 'Ready To Learn' and another chart-topper, in combination with Tippa Irie, 'Baby I've Been Missing You'. Another DJ combination came with General Levy for a version of the Joya Landis Treasure Isle hit, 'Moonlight Lover'. In 1994 her series of Fashion hits surfaced on *Missing You*, alongside an array of self-composed new tracks and has proved to be an all-time classic in the lovers rock genre. In 1995 she was awarded a number of accolades including Best Female Singer and Best UK Album by the British Reggae Industry and the Bob Marley Award for Best Female Singer by the Black Arts, Sports And Enterprise Awards. By 1997 her quest for international recognition was almost complete, having been described as the 'queen' of contemporary lovers rock. Her collaboration with Mr. G Spot, Wayne Marshall and Barry Boom highlighted her songwriting, singing and DJ skills, as well as consolidating her reputation for sheer hard work and professionalism.

● ALBUMS: *Missing You* (Fashion 1994)★★★.

LEE, BUNNY

b. Edward O'Sullivan Lee, 23 August 1941, Jamaica, West Indies. Bunny Lee, aka Bunny and Striker, was introduced to the music business by vocalist Derrick Morgan in 1962. Morgan, at that time one of Jamaica's most prolific and successful performers, took Lee to producer/sound system operator Duke Reid, who gave him a job as record plugger for his Treasure Isle label. Following his stay with Reid, Lee began working with Ken Lack, erstwhile road manager for the Skatalites band. By 1966, Lack had started releasing records by Ken Boothe, the Clarendonians, Max Romeo, the Tartans, the Heptones and others. Lee's first production, 'Listen To The Beat' by Lloyd Jackson And The Groovers, was released on Lack's Caltone label in 1967. His first hit was 'Music Field' by Roy Shirley (1967), on the WIRL label. He then began releasing his productions on his own label, Lee's. He enjoyed local hits during 1967-68 with Derrick Morgan's 'Hold You Jack', Slim Smith And The Uniques' 'My Conversation', Lester Sterling and Stranger Cole's 'Bangarang', Pat Kelly's 'Little Boy Blue' and the Sensation's 'Long Time Me No See You Girl'. Lee's talent for producing music that was commercially and artistically satisfying ensured his position as the leading hitmaker in Jamaica by 1969. During the following four years Lee enjoyed hits with Slim Smith's 'Everybody Needs Love' (1969), Pat

Kelly's 'How Long?' (1970), Delroy Wilson's 'Better Must Come' (1971) and the Jamaica Song Festival winner, Eric Donaldson's 'Cherry Oh Baby' (1971), later a UK hit for UB40, and John Holt's 'Stick By Me' (1972). By 1974 he was producing Johnny Clarke on a string of local hits, beginning with 'None Shall Escape The Judgement' and 'Move Out Of Babylon'. Owen Grey had showcased 'Bongo Natty' that same year, while 1975 saw Cornell Campbell release a series of strong-selling tunes, beginning with 'The Gorgon'.

Lee, along with producer Lee Perry and engineer King Tubby, had changed the face of Jamaican music, breaking the dominance of the big producers such as Coxsone Dodd and Duke Reid. Bunny Lee's contribution had been to grasp the commercial opportunities created by technological innovations such as the multi-track studio. A rhythm track could be made that could then be used as the backing for many songs or 'versions', often remixed or 'dubbed'. In addition to King Tubby, engineers such as King Jammy and Philip Smart developed their talents on Bunny Lee productions. During the period 1969-77, Lee produced literally thousands of tracks - vocals, DJ records and dubs - with a wide range of artists. As well as those already mentioned, he produced music for singers, including Jackie Edwards, Leroy Smart, Linval Thompson, David Isaacs, Alton Ellis, Dave Barker, Ken Boothe and Frankie Jones, and for DJs such as Dennis Alcapone, U-Roy, I. Roy, Prince Jazzbo, U Brown, Big Joe, Trinity, Dr. Alimantado, Jah Stitch and Tapper Zukie, most with additional corresponding dub versions. The early 80s saw a reduction in output; Lee was hampered because he did not control his own studio, although he continued to release music through his connection with Count Shelley in London and New York. He bought Joe Gibbs' old studio in North Parade, Kingston, and released material in the late 80s using computer-generated rhythms, but seems content to hire his studio to newer producers.

● ALBUMS: *Leaping With Mr. Lee* (1968)★★★.
● COMPILATIONS: *Jumping With Mr Lee 1967-68* (Trojan 1989)★★★★.

LEE, BYRON, AND THE DRAGONAIRES

b. 27 June 1935, Jamaica, West Indies. Lee and his manager, Ronnie Nasralla, first put together the Dragonaires in 1956 and worked as a support act for touring singers including Harry Belafonte, and their debut single 'Dumplins' in 1960 was the first release on the UK's Blue Beat label (although it originally came out on his own Dragons Breath label in Jamaica). The 14-piece Dragonaires featured an ever fluctuating line-up and are often cited as one of Jamaica's first ska bands, although they were firmly an 'establishment' band and their success was largely due to Lee's business and political connections. They toured extensively in the West Indies, North America and Canada and did much to popularize the ska sound. In 1969 Lee bought out the old WIRL set-up and established Dynamic Sounds as the best equipped and most popular studio in the Caribbean. As well as supporting home-grown talent, visiting stars such as the Rolling Stones, Eric Clapton and Paul Simon all recorded at Dynamic hoping for a piece of the reggae action. Lee still records occasionally but concentrates on the soca style these days.

● ALBUMS: *Rocksteady Explosion* (Trojan 1968; reissued as *Reggay Eyes*, Jamaican Gold 1993)★★★★, *Reggae With Byron Lee* (Trojan 1969)★★★★, *Sparrow Meets The Dragon* (1970)★★★, *Reggae Roun' The World* (Dragon 1973)★★★, *Reggae Fever* (Polydor 1974)★★★★, *The Midas Touch* (Dragon 1975)★★★, *Mighty Sparrow* (Dynamic 1976)★★★, *Reggae International* (Dynamic 1976)★★★, *Six Million Dollar Man* (Dynamic 1976)★★★, *This Is Carnival* (Dynamic 1976)★★★, *Art Of Mas* (Dynamic 1977)★★★, *Jamaica's Golden Hits* (Stylus 1977)★★★, *More Carnival* (Dynamic 1978)★★★, *Carnival Experience* (Dynamic 1979)★★★, *Jamaican Ska* (Rhino 1980)★★★★, *Soft Lee Volume 3* (Vista 1983)★★★, *Soul-Ska* (Vista 1983)★★★★, *Best Of Carnival* (Dynamic 1984)★★★, *Jamaica's Golden Hits Volume 2* (Dynamic 1984)★★★, *Wine Miss Tiny* (Creole 1985)★★★, *Soca Girl* (Dynamic 1986)★★★, *Soca Thunder* (Dynamic 1987)★★★, *De Music Hot Mama* (Dynamic 1988)★★★, *Reggae Blast Off* (Trojan 1988)★★★, *Soca Bachannal* (Dynamic 1989)★★★, *Play Dynamite Ska* (Dr Buster Dynamite 1992)★★★, *Wine Down* (Dynamic 1992)★★★, *Play Dynamite Ska With The Jamaican Allstars* (Jamaican Gold 1994)★★★.

LEO, PHILIP

b. Philip Pottinger, Greenwich, London, England. Leo is widely known for his work with C.J. Lewis, who enjoyed crossover success in the early 90s. Leo and Lewis shared a love of music from childhood and both pursued careers within the music industry. Leo's first musical experience was at the Roger Manwood school, playing in the institute's steel band, which led to his mastering of both kit drums and keyboards. He began his professional involvement in the music business as a songwriter, following the presentation of his initial 90-minute demo to Fashion Records. The latter were suitably impressed and stated that when they asked whether Leo could provide any more, 'two further tapes arrived within the week!'. Some of the songs on the introductory demos provided hits for a number of the UK's top singers, including Janet Lee Davis ('Two Timing Lover'), Peter Spence ('Crazy Feeling') and Nerious Joseph ('Show The World' and 'She Gone And Left Me'). Leo's long-time cohort Lewis was enrolled to provide the DJ skills on the 1989 reggae chart-topper 'Why Do Fools Fall In Love', and in 1990, 'Good Thing Going'. In 1993 Leo recorded the entrancing 'Hypnotic Love', which featured his sparring partner on the ragga mix. Shortly after the hit, Lewis secured a major label contract that included Leo as the DJ's co-producer, and the duo subsequently released a succession of crossover hits. Following his success with Lewis, Leo diversified into an R&B style for the 1994 release of 'Second Chance', which sadly faltered. He had always demonstrated a willingness to expand his repertoire regardless of genre, but his enthusiasm was not greeted sympathetically; he continues to work within the industry and is a much-loved character.

● ALBUMS: *Today* (1991)★★★, *Down To Earth* (1997)★★, *Space Dub* (1997)★★★.

LEVI, IJAHMAN

b. Trevor Sutherland, 1946, Manchester, Jamaica, West Indies. Levi received his earliest musical tutoring as a youth living in Trenchtown from Joe Higgs, eventually becoming proficient enough to appear on Vere John's 'Opportunity Hour', the launching pad for many a reggae career. He made his first recording, 'Red Eyed People', under the name Youth for producer Duke Reid in 1961. Levi emigrated to England in 1963, settling in Harlesden, London, and formed a short-lived group called the Vibrations. Once the Vibrations folded, he and another singer, Carl Simmons, formed a stage act called Youth And Rudie And The Shell Shock Show, performing a Tamla-Motown and Stax-style soul revue at the famous London niterie the Q Club, as well as touring Europe. He recorded a number of obscure singles at this time for various labels including Polydor, Pama and Deram, for whom he cut a reggae version of P.P. Arnold's 'Angel Of The Morning', as well as a reggae version of 'White Christmas' for Trojan Records, under the unlikely name of Nyah And The Snowflakes. None of these recordings made any impact, and Levi put his career on hold while he settled down to pursue a normal family life.

His career was resuscitated in 1972 when he was reborn as Ijahman Levi, after turning to the Bible. In 1976 he recorded three excellent singles for Dennis 'Dip' Harris: 'Chariot Of Love', 'I'm A Levi' and 'Jah Heavy Load'. At this time he also contributed some vocal harmonies to Rico Rodriguez's 'Man From Warieka'. This brought him to the attention of Island Records boss Chris Blackwell, who set about producing his 1978 debut, *Haile I Hymn*. Hampered by Blackwell's stated intention of creating a reggae *Astral Weeks*, the album contained only four extended tracks, including new versions of 'Jah Heavy Load' and 'I'm A Levi', and garnered mixed reviews. Nevertheless, despite accusations of self-indulgence and pretension, *Haile I Hymn* remains Levi's most important and popular album. After the follow-up, *Are We A Warrior*, Levi parted company with Island. He set up his own labels, Tree Roots and Jahmani, releasing several Jamaican pressed singles in the early 80s including 'Thank You', another version of 'Jah Heavy Load' and 'Tradesman', as well as a new, more conventional album, *Tell It To The Children*. During the 80s Levi's style of roots Rasta reggae fared less well, in common with many of his contemporaries. Nevertheless, in 1985 he enjoyed perhaps his biggest reggae hit with the sentimental 'I Do', a duet with his wife Madge, a radical departure from his usual militant spiritual style.

● ALBUMS: *Haile I Hymn (Chapter 1)* (Island 1978)★★★★, *Are We A Warrior* (Mango/Island 1979)★★★, *Tell It To The Children* (Jahmani/Tree Roots 1982)★★, *Africa* (Jahmani/Tree Roots 1984)★★★, *Lily Of My Valley* (Jahmani 1985)★★, with Maj *I Do* (Jahmani 1986)★★, *Culture Country* (Tree Roots 1987)★★★, *Forward Rastaman* (Fat Shadow 1987)★★, *Ijahman & Friends* (Tree Roots 1988)★★★, *Inside Out* (Tree Roots 1989)★★★, *Live Over Europe* (Jamaica Sound 1989)★★, *Love Smiles* (Jahmani 1991)★★★, *On Track* (Jahmani 1991)★★.

LEVY, BARRINGTON

b. 1964, Kingston, Jamaica, West Indies. Barrington Levy was one of the first singers to challenge the dominance of DJs in 80s dancehall reggae, although his earliest recording, under the name of the Mighty Multitude ('My Black Girl' in 1977), predated that era. Another early single, 'A Long Long Time Since We Don't Have No Love' in 1978, followed the first into obscurity, but Barrington, undaunted, went into the dancehalls. By 1981 Levy's effortlessly buoyant voice had spread his fame to the point where Henry 'Junjo' Lawes, at the time the most in-demand producer in Jamaica, pursued him. His first Junjo single was 'Ah Yah We Deh', which sold moderately well, as did two further releases. His fourth single, 'Collie Weed', was a great success. Levy did not sound like anyone else: he perhaps revealed some of Jacob Miller's style, and a little of Bob Andy's influence, but his phrasing evoked the raw energy of the dancehalls. While other singers were struggling, Levy was slugging it out at the top. His first album, *Bounty Hunter*, sold well and a string of singles consolidated his position: 'Robber Man', 'Black Rose', 'Like A Soldier', the massive 'Money Move', the huge hit 'Shine Eye Gal', and the stunning 'Prison Oval Rock', and a series of albums were released between 1982-85 to capitalize on his success. He later denounced many of these as 'joke business', being packaged with old singles, out-takes and one-off private sound system recordings. He performed his first UK gigs in 1984, including an appearance as a winner at the UK Reggae Awards. He then linked with young producer Jah Screw and enjoyed a big hit with the anthemic 'Under Me Sensi'. He followed it with 'Here I Come', which was a hit in the soul clubs and scraped the UK charts when licensed by London Records, who also issued an album of the same title. However, Screw and Levy made the mistake of courting crossover success and he sounded lost on subsequent rocky singles. Levy travelled between Jamaica, London and New York, and although he lost momentum at the end of the 80s, he still had all the talent of his peak period, as *Love The Life You Live* made clear. Two Bob Andy cover versions, 'Too Experienced' and 'My Time', brought him back to the forefront of reggae, and he signed to Island Records in 1991 for the fine *Divine* set. While it remains to be seen whether he can ever achieve the broader success that seemed to be his in the mid-80s, he remains one of reggae's most powerful and original voices.

● ALBUMS: *Bounty Hunter* (Jah Life 1979)★★★, *Shine Eye Gal* (Burning Sounds 1979)★★★, *Englishman* (Greensleeves 1980)★★★, *Robin Hood* (Greensleeves 1980)★★★, *21 Girls Salute* (Jah Life 1983)★★★, *Poor Man Style* (Trojan 1983)★★★, *Run Come Yah* (1983)★★★, *Lifestyle* (GG's 1983)★★★, *Teach Me Culture* (Live & Learn 1983)★★★, with Frankie Paul *Barrington Levy Meets Frankie Paul* (Ariwa 1984)★★★, *Barrington Levy* (Clock Tower 1984)★★★★, *Here I Come* (Time/London 1985)★★★★, *Hunter Man* (Burning Sounds 1988)★★★, *Love The Life You Live* (Time/London 1988)★★★★, *Open Book* (Tuff Gong 1988)★★, *Prison Oval Rock* (Volcano 1989)★★, *Divine* (Mango/Island 1991)★★★, *Turning Point* (Greensleeves 1992)★★★, *D.J. Counteraction* ragga mixes (Greensleeves 1995)★★★.

● COMPILATIONS: *The Collection* (Time/London 1991)★★★★, *20 Vintage Hits* (Sonic Sounds 1992)★★★★.

LEWIS, C.J.

b. Stephen Lewis, London, England. Lewis shadowed the sound systems around London with his childhood friend Philip 'Leo' Pottinger, and soon established himself as a respected DJ. Philip Leo himself began a recording career as a singer-songwriter with two successful releases for Fashion Records. For his third release, 'Why Do Fools Fall In Love', a reworking of Frankie Lymon And The Teenagers' 1956 chart-topper, he introduced Lewis to a wider audience. The single had considerable exposure through ffrr Records, and narrowly missed reaching the UK pop chart. In 1990 Lewis appeared on a number of releases, notably in combination with Janet Lee Davis for a version of Keith And Enid's 'Worried Over You', while with Pottinger he recorded a version of the Michael Jackson/Sugar Minott hit, 'Good Thing Going'. In 1993 the duo recorded the reggae chart-topper 'Hypnotic Love', which was number 1 for seven weeks. This success resulted in Lewis signing with Black Market/MCA, with Pottinger as co-producer. The arrangement led to crossover success when 'Sweets For My Sweet' peaked at number 3 in the UK Top 10. He followed the hit with a version of Stevie Wonder's 'Everything Is Alright (Uptight)', Earth, Wind And Fire's 'Best Of My Love' and an original composition, 'Dollars', utilizing Prince Buster's 'Ten Commandments' rhythm. In 1994 he toured Europe, Asia and the Far East and began working on his second album for the label. He continued to play the live circuit on a 28-day tour of the UK, resulting in an award for Best P.A. Of The Year In Britain. His popularity in Japan resulted in his second album selling 150,000 copies in one day, increasing to 250,000 in the first two weeks of its release. In September 1995 he played seven sell-out dates in the Far East, and had a UK Top 40 summer hit with 'R To The A'. By the beginning of 1996, he had returned to the UK to promote the release of 'Can't Take It (Street Life)'. The release of 'Phat Ting' went some way towards soothing the disaffected hardcore reggae fans, who had become somewhat disillusioned by Lewis's crossover success.

● ALBUMS: *Dollars* (MCA 1993)★, *Rough And Smooth* (MCA 1995)★★.

LEWIS, HOPETON

Lewis began recording in the mid-60s, and found fame with 'Take It Easy'. The song was an instant hit and heralded the arrival of the less frenzied rocksteady beat. The song has frequently been reworked, notably on versions by Johnny Clarke ('Rockers Time Now') and Joyce Bond ('Do The Teasy'). He continued to record a number of hits through to the early 70s, including 'Sound And Pressure' and 'Music Got Soul'. In 1970 he entered and won the Jamaican Song Festival with 'Boom Shaka Lacka' and began working as a vocalist with Byron Lee And The Dragonaires. In 1971 he released 'Grooving Out On Life', supported by the Dragonaires, which led to an album of the same name. The songs proved to be too lightweight for the reggae audience and he similarly failed to cross over into the mainstream. In 1973 he released 'Good Together' and 'City Of New Orleans', neither of which made an impression on the charts.

● ALBUMS: *Take It Easy* (Island 1968)★★, *Grooving Out On Life* (Trojan 1973)★★, *Dynamic Hopeton Lewis* (Dragon 1974)★★.

LIEUTENANT STITCHIE

b. Cleveland Laing, Spanish Town, Jamaica, West Indies. In 1979 the young Stitchie was a singer, eventually joining the Django sound system as the DJ Ranking Noseworthy in 1983, while still working as a biology teacher in a Spanish Town school. Within two years he had graduated from City Lights Disco and Lightning Super Mix to Stereo One, adapting the name Citchie from his love of citrus fruit. His first tune was 'If I Don't Care' for Nonsul as Ranking Citrus. By his second ('Two Is Better Than Too Many'), he was Stitchie thanks to a label misspelling. Hits for Stereo One ('Nice Girl', 'Story Time' and 'Natty Dread') followed before he visited King Jammy in 1986. Immediately, his perfectly observed and humorous lyrics caught the popular imagination, with 'Wear Yuh Size' and 'Broad Hips' attaining instant success. In 1987 he was voted DJ Of The Year in Jamaica and celebrated with a debut album, *Great Ambition*. Atlantic signed him in 1988, releasing *The Governor* album but failing to retain his dancehall audience with the next (*Wild Jamaican Romances*). In 1993 he returned to the Kingston studios eager to recapture lost ground, recording a spate of local hits for Danny Browne, Penthouse, Digital B, King Jammy's ('Hot Like The Sun'), Shocking Vibes ('Bun It Down'), Carib ('Bandy Leg'), John John and his own Drum And Bass label, on which he produced emergent talents such as the late Pan Head. His third Atlantic album, *Rude Boy*, was released that year and he made successful tours of both

Europe and America. Always entertaining on stage or record, he is currently enjoying his most popular spell since his 1987 heyday.

● ALBUMS: *Great Ambition* (King Jammys 1987)★★★★, *The Governor* (Atlantic 1989)★★, *Wild Jamaican Romances* (Atlantic 1991)★★, *Rude Boy* (Atlantic 1993)★★★, with Beenie Man, Mad Cobra *Mad Cobra Meets Lt Stitchie And Beenie Man* (VP 1995)★★★★.

LINDO, KASHIEF

b. c.1978, Kingston, Jamaica, West Indies. The Lindo dynasty has featured heavily in the reggae industry: Earl 'Wire' Lindo played keyboards for Bob Marley, the singer Hopeton Lindo has enjoyed many hits, the producer Jack Ruby was born Laurence Lindo and Willie Lindo played guitar for the Hi Times Band. Kashief spent his childhood years surrounded by music - his father is Willie Lindo, who formed his own production stable. Although Willie produced dancehall hits, including 'Girlie Girlie' for Sophia George, he is celebrated for his tender ballads, including UK chart-topping hits for Boris Gardiner in the mid-80s. In 1992 Willie produced his son's recording debut, which surfaced on the one rhythm *Rougher Yet* compilation. Kashief's earliest success came in late 1993 with 'Hard Times', performed over the evergreen 'Satta A Massa Gana' rhythm. In 1996, inspired by the Fugees' success with their cover version of Roberta Flack's 'Killing Me Softly With His Song', Kashief recorded his own version, which was enthusiastically received within the contemporary market. As a youthful performer, he remains unperturbed by the fact that he has yet to produce a commercially successful dancehall hit.

● ALBUMS: *Trouble Free* (Heavy Beat 1994)★★★, *Sings Christmas* (Heavy Beat 1995)★, *Soul And Inspiration* (Heavy Beat 1996)★★.

LINDSAY, JIMMY

b. 1950, Kingston, Jamaica, West Indies. At the age of nine Lindsay and his family relocated to the UK. His first venture into music began in 1965 with a soul group named the Healers, followed by a short term with the Nighthawks. Other ventures included a spell with the rock band Pure Medicine, back to soul with the

Garments, and notably as a member of the more successful group Cymande. In the early 70s his first recordings surfaced, 'Tribute To Jimi Hendrix', and on the Cymande album, *Promised Heights*. By 1976 he began concentrating on reggae and recorded lead vocals on the sound system hit, 'What You Gonna Do'. This encouraged Lloyd Coxsone to produce him as a soloist. The first release, 'Motion', surfaced through Cactus, followed by 'Easy', a cover version of the Commodores hit, on Lloyd's own Tribesman label. The latter was picked up for release by Island Records, appearing on the revived Black Swan logo. The single's success led Lindsay to put his energies into his own Music Hive label and, sharing lead vocals with Larry Walker under the collective name of Dambala, they enjoyed a big hit with 'Zimbabwe'. The song, featuring the lyrics, 'Crucify Smith and take back Zimbabwe, crucify Smith and take back Namibia, crucify Vorster and take back Anzania', was released shortly before Bob Marley's plea for the country then known as Rhodesia. The group consisted of a multiracial line-up including members from Nigeria, Guyana, St. Lucia, Barbados and the UK. The group were commissioned by the BBC to record a theme to a six-part current affairs programme, *Babylon*. Lindsay began to concentrate on his solo career when he signed a contract with the Gem label, and in the autumn of 1979 he released *Where Is Your Love*, produced by Lloyd Coxsone. To promote the album he toured with his new band Rasuji, including members from Dambala in the line-up. In 1980 he released *Children Of Rastafari*, which conveyed a more spiritual message, notably on the track 'It's Hard (For A Dread To Live In Babylon)'. It was lifted for single release and promoted on a tour of the UK when supporting Steel Pulse.

● ALBUMS: *Where Is Your Love* (Gem 1979)★★★, *Children Of Rastafari* (Gem 1980)★★.

LIONESS

Founded by lead singer and songwriter Teri Owens, and largely inspired by her staunch Rastafarian beliefs and morals, Lioness's sound is rendered unique by the employment of instrumentation drawn from outside of reggae's normal canon, notably Janet Irvine's flute. Their 'cultural' lyrics are equally refreshing, a return to the roots flavour that has been overshadowed by modern dancehall tastes.

● ALBUMS: *Jah Works* (1989)★★★, *Jah Victory* (Dawter 1991)★★★.

LITTLE JOHN

b. John McMorris, *c*.1970, Kingston, Jamaica, West Indies. McMorris first recorded with Captain Sinbad for the Youth In Progress label at the tender age of nine, where his piping interjections contrasted neatly with Sinbad's gruff style, and throughout the 80s he was seldom out of the reggae charts. Claimed by many to be the first dancehall singer, his ability to fit lyrics over any rhythm or backing track became something of a legend in a business that has scant regard for second takes and 'dropping in'. Little John did it every time - and he rode on the crest of the 80s' dancehall music explosion, becoming a superstar by the age of 17. He began his career on Romantic Hi Fi, moving up through Killimanjaro, Gemini and Volcano Hi Power, where he honed and perfected his craft with a lengthy string of live appearances. Simultaneously, he was recording for virtually every producer in Jamaica, notably Henry 'Junjo' Lawes, Joseph 'Joe Joe' Hookim, George Phang, Jah Thomas and Jammys, and he has released countless records on a bewildering string of labels. He no longer records as extensively as he once did, and limits his live appearances to a minimum. Hits for Exterminator proved that he was not relying on his past glories, and his talent, warm personality and skill as a raconteur remained.

● ALBUMS: *True Confession* (Power House 1984)★★★★, *Unite* (Vista Sounds 1984)★★★★, with Frankie Paul *Showdown Volume 6* (Empire 1984)★★, *Clark's Booty* (Live & Love/Jammys 1985)★★★, *River To The Bank* (Power House 1985)★★★, *Warriors & Trouble* (World Enterprise 1986)★★★, *Youth Of Today* (Skengdon 1987)★★★, *Reggae Dance* (Midnight Rock 1989)★★★.

● COMPILATIONS: *Best Of Little John* (R&M 1985)★★★★, *Junjo Presents A Live Session With Aces International* includes Little John (Volcano/Greensleeves)★★★.

LITTLE ROY

b. Earl Lowe, c.1950, Jamaica, West Indies. Little Roy began his career at Studio One, with Jackie Mittoo as the producer, initially recording 'Cool It'. He retired for a time but returned and pursued his career performing as a member of an unsigned vocal group alongside Bunny Maloney and George Thompson. Following his departure from Studio One and the group, Little Roy recorded as a soloist with Prince Buster the singles 'It's You I Love' and 'Reggae Soul'. In the late 60s Little Roy achieved immense popularity with Lloyd Daley with the classic 'Bongo Nyah', and alongside Joy Lindsay as Roy And Joy, notably with 'Keep On Trying' and 'Righteous Man'. From the outset he wrote about Rasta themes - slavery, the wearing of dreadlocks and exile. By 1972 he had formed the Tafari label with the help of Lloyd Barnes and Munchie Jackson, and his records soon received simultaneous release in New York through Barnes' Aries label. Often part of a trio alongside two mysterious characters, Ian and Rock, he recorded some alluring and atmospheric tracks: 'Tribal War', 'Blackbird' and 'Prophecy'. Barnes put them together to form an album, *Tribal War*, which had a decidedly limited pressing. In 1978 he recorded *Columbus Ship*, a far less artistically successful set, and then dropped below reggae's horizon altogether, though there were occasional sightings of him in New York. His business associate Munchie Jackson was shot by his own son in a bizarre Brooklyn domestic killing in 1977. However, in one of those twists unique to reggae, ragga rulers Steely And Clevie decided to remake the 'Prophecy' rhythm in 1990, and it was an instant hit for Freddie McGregor. Not slow to spot an opportunity, Little Roy emerged from nowhere with a 10-track compilation of his now in-demand old material, *Prophecy*, and then recorded the excellent *Live On* the following year. In 1994 he began residing in the UK and he was invited to record with On-U-Sound, releasing the results of the sessions in 1996.

● ALBUMS: *Tribal War* (Tafari 1975)★★★, *Free For All Dub* (1975)★★★, *Columbus Ship* (Copasetic 1978)★★, *Live On* (1991)★★★★, *Long Time* (On-U-Sound 1996)★★★.

● COMPILATIONS: *Prophecy* (1990)★★★, *Tafari Earth Uprising* (Pressure Sounds 1996)★★★★.

LIVINGSTONE, DANDY

b. Robert Livingstone Thompson, 1944, Kingston, Jamaica, West Indies. Livingstone was at one time a member of the 60s duo Sugar And Dandy with Sugar Simone, and he became a very popular performer in the UK as a solo artist after he relocated there at the age of 15. His records appeared on a variety of different labels under different names and he was responsible for many of the UK's rocksteady and reggae hits throughout the 60s, 'Reggae In Your Jeggae' proving particularly popular in 1969. His first UK chart entry was 'Suzanne Beware of the Devil' in 1972, when reggae was briefly enjoying great popularity in the charts due to the skinhead connection. The follow-up, 'Big City', was a smaller hit the following year. His name was revered by many ska/2-Tone fans who recalled his 60s heyday, and the Specials recorded a cover version of his 'A Message To You Rudy'.

● ALBUMS: *Your Musical Doctor* (Downtown 1965)★★★, *Dandy Livingstone* (Trojan 1972)★★★★, *South African Experience* (Night Owl 1978)★★★.

LIZZY

The DJ phenomenon began in the early 60s, but it was the unprecedented success of U-Roy that signalled the turning point in the development of Jamaican music. By 1970 there was a considerable number of new DJs, including Dennis Alcapone, I. Roy, Big Youth and Lizzy. The young DJs were inspired by the scat toasting of Count Matchuki, Sir Lord Comic and King Stitt, but the newcomers took the art to a different level. Lizzy recorded in the innovative 'sing talk' style for Duke Reid, initially enjoying hits with 'Love Is A Treasure', which employed Freddie McKay's original rocksteady hit, and 'I See Your Face (Version)', which utilized the John Holt hit. Inspired by this success, Duke Reid encouraged Lizzy to join forces with his sparring partner, Dennis Alcapone, for a string of classic combination hits, notably 'Baba Riba Skank' (based on Ken Parker's 'I Can't Hide'), 'The Right Song' (the Paragons' 'Same Song') and the excellent 'Cry Tough', which further embellished the Alton Ellis classic. By 1973 Lizzy's association with Alcapone ended when the El Paso DJ relocated to the UK. Lizzy remained in Jamaica where he embarked on sessions with Joe Gibbs, who produced the hit 'Aquarius' and a remake of the Paragons' 'Wear You To The Ball' aka 'Harmony Hall'. Lizzy continued to release sporadic hits, including 'Double Attack' with Delroy Wilson. Although he was often considered as a sidekick of Dennis Alcapone, his individual efforts were recognized in the mid-90s. He savoured a revival and interest in his early work resulted in the release of two similar compilations.

● ALBUMS: with Dennis Alcapone *Soul To Soul DJ's Choice* reissued 1996 (Trojan 1973)★★★, *Baba Riba Skank* (Esoldun 1996)★★★★.

LOCKS, FRED

b. Stafford Elliot, *c.*1955, Kingston, Jamaica, West Indies. Locks began his sporadic recording career as a member of the Lyrics, who recorded tracks such as 'A Get It', 'Girls Like Dirt', and 'Hear What The Old Man Say' for Coxsone Dodd in the late 60s, 'Give Praises' for Randy's, and the self-financed 'Sing A Long', both in 1971. The Lyrics disbanded shortly afterwards, and Locks, discouraged by the lack of financial reward endemic to the Jamaican music business, immersed himself in the Rasta faith, which was at the time gaining significant ground amongst Jamaica's ghetto youth, and he retired to live a spartan existence on the beach at Harbour View. During this time, Locks allowed his dreads to grow to a formidable length - hence his nickname - and continued to write songs, one of which, a prophetic Garveyite vision of repatriation entitled 'Black Star Liners', he was persuaded to record by producer Hugh Boothe.

Released in 1975 on the Jahmikmusic label in Jamaica, and on Grounation in the UK, 'Black Star Liners' struck a resounding chord with the new generation of Rastafarian youth on both islands, propelling Locks to cult status in the process. Two years later Grounation offshoot Vulcan officially released the long-awaited *Black Star Liners/True Rastaman*, a classic example of 70s roots Rasta reggae, packed with fine songs including former singles 'Last Days' (retitled 'Time To Change') and 'Wolf Wolf', and raw, guileless vocals. Throughout this time Locks had also been a member of the vocal trio Creation Steppers with Eric Griffiths and Willy Stepper, who had been releasing singles on their Star Of The East label in Jamaica, achieving consider-

able local success with 'Stormy Night' - later covered at Channel One by the Rolands. A various artists album entitled *Love & Harmony* featured the title track (also a 12-inch in Jamaica) credited to Fred Locks, and 'Kill Nebuchadnezzar' by the Creation Steppers also emerged, in 1979. In 1980 Locks and the Creation Steppers went to the UK for several shows and linked up with the legendary sound system operator and record producer Lloyd Coxsone, who released a number of discs by both the group and Locks, including the classic 'steppers' 'Homeward Bound', 'Love And Only Love' and 'Voice Of The Poor'. These and other tracks were eventually released on *Love And Only Love*. Locks moved to the USA in 1982, effectively halting his and the Steppers' career. Settling in Philadelphia, he immersed himself in the local Twelve Tribes organization, after which he recorded only sporadically.

● ALBUMS: *Black Star Liners/True Rastaman* (Vulcan 1977)★★★★, *Love And Only Love* (Tribesman 1981)★★★.

LODGE, J.C.

b. June Carol Lodge. Lodge's entrance into the reggae world came courtesy of an audition for Joe Gibbs. Their first recording together was a version of Charley Pride's 'Someone Loves You, Honey', which went to the top of the Jamaican charts. Ironically, the result for Gibbs was bankruptcy, after he failed to pay royalties to the songwriter. In 1988 she recorded 'Telephone Love' for Gussie Clarke, which subsequently became a big hit in Jamaica and America, where, after being housed on the Pow Wow label, it achieved crossover status. Its success brought her to the attention of the predominantly hip-hop-focused, Warners-owned Tommy Boy subsidiary. In the process she became the first female reggae star to secure a major label contract. Her debut for Tommy Boy played safe by revisiting 'Telephone Love', and branching out musically to encompass soul and rock. Also a talented painter, Lodge has exhibited in Kingston art galleries, and acted in several theatrical productions.

● ALBUMS: *I Believe In You* (Greensleeves 1987)★★★, *Revealed* (RAS 1988)★★★, *Tropic Of Love* (Tommy Boy 1992)★★.

LONDON, JIMMY

b. c.1953, Kingston, Jamaica, West Indies. In the late 60s London recorded, with the Inspirations, the Joe Gibbs-directed hits 'Take Back Your Duck', 'La La' and 'The Train Is Coming'. He achieved international renown in the early 70s with the Impact All Stars at Randy's studios. His version of Simon And Garfunkel's 'Bridge Over Troubled Waters' topped the Jamaican chart and was equally successful in the UK reggae charts. This was swiftly followed by 'A Little Love', and both songs were featured on *Bridge Over Troubled Waters*. Versions of the Temptations' 'Just My Imagination' and 'It's Now Or Never' were also lifted from the album for release as singles. In 1974 'Rock And Roll Lullaby' made a significant impression on the reggae chart with its infectious 'Na Na Na It'll Be Alright' chorus. He then topped the reggae chart for two consecutive months with 'No Letter Today', which was released on the Dragon label. With a variety of producers, the hits 'Together', 'Jim Say Hello' and 'Don't Keep The Kids', sustained his high profile in the specialist charts. In 1975 London toured the UK, making his debut at the Lyceum in London supporting soul artist George McCrae. London joined forces with Pat Rhoden, releasing the first single on the newly formed Jama label, 'What Good Am I', which was soon followed by 'I'm Your Puppet' and 'Am I That Easy To Forget'. By 1976 he had recorded 'Thank The Lord', featured on *Welcome To My World*, which included a remake of his earlier hit 'A Little Love', a version of the Drifters' 'Kissing At The Back Row Of The Movies' and the particularly popular 'Hold On'. Jimmy London continued to record throughout the 70s and 80s.

● ALBUMS: *Bridge Over Troubled Waters* (Trojan 1972)★★★★, *Welcome To My World* (Burning Sounds 1977)★★★, *Crying In The Ghetto* (Imp 1977)★★, *Hold On* (Lagoon 1996)★★★.

LONE RANGER

b. Anthony Waldron, the Lone Ranger was one of the late 70s' most lyrically inventive DJs, with a considerable influence on the British school of MCing. Waldron spent a large proportion of his formative years in the UK, which perhaps accounted for his radically different stance, and, like so many others, he began his own recording career at Studio One. Welton Irie partnered him

at first, but he soon graduated to working solo, tackling several classic Studio One rhythms, after which he became virtually unstoppable. His version of Slim Smith's seminal 'Rougher Yet', retitled 'Love Bump', was a major success. So too was his reading of Smith's 'Never Let Go', a version known as 'The Answer', which has become more famous than the original. As top DJ for Kingston's Virgo Sound, he kept up appearances in the dancehalls and Virgo Hi Fi were voted the top sound of 1980. His recordings for Alvin 'GG' Ranglin assured his legendary status. 'Barnabas Collins' (about a vampire show on television) included the classic line, 'chew ya neck like a Wrigley's', and was a UK reggae chart number 1 in 1980. His additional work for Winston Riley and Channel One, which included the memorable 'M16', proved almost as popular. His tour of the UK that year reiterated that he could perform on stage as well as on record and for the sound systems. His repertoire of strange voices, 'oinks' and 'ribbits', was widely imitated. Lone Ranger recorded sparingly, sometimes branching out into self-production, like many other DJs, and his catalogue has always been assembled with style, class and a dash of great humour.

● ALBUMS: *Barnabas Collins* (GG's 1980)★★★, *On The Other Side Of Dub* (Studio One 1981)★★★, *M16* (Channel One 1982)★★★, *Hi-Yo Silver Away!* (Greensleeves 1982)★★★★, *Badda Dan Dem* (Studio One 1982)★★★, *Dee Jay Daddy* (Techniques 1984)★★★, *Learn To Drive* (Bebo's Music 1985)★★★.

● COMPILATIONS: *Collection* (Grapevine)★★★★.

LORD CREATOR

b. Kentrick Patrick, c.1940, San Fernando, Trinidad, West Indies. As his imperious name suggests, Lord Creator began his career as a calypso singer. Some time in the mid- to late 50s he arrived in Jamaica, just as the music scene was starting to take off. Lord Creator's smooth, honeyed tones were not ideal for the raucous jump to R&B soon to emerge from ska, but as a big band crooner in Jamaica, he had no equal. 'Evening News' (1959) was his first huge hit, and it was a song to which he returned at several points during his career. The narrative of a barefoot child feeding his siblings by selling newspapers he could not even read, had greater resonance at a time when Jamaica was struggling for its independence. In 1962 his 'Independent Jamaica' was the first single on the Island label in the UK, although legend has it that Owen Gray's 'Twist Baby', scheduled as Island 002, reached the shops first. 'Don't Stay Out Late' (1963) was a major Jamaican hit, and made Lord Creator the island's biggest star at the time. 'Little Princess' (1964) helped to maintain his status. He also released a calypso album for the Studio One label. However, he was overtaken by other smooth voices such as Ken Boothe and Bob Andy, both of whom offered more contemporary songs.

In 1969, he teamed up with producer Clancy Eccles and recorded the single 'Kingston Town', perhaps the finest sentimental reggae record ever released. By this time, Creator was in financial trouble and a week after recording the record, he borrowed $30 from Eccles. A couple of months later, Eccles spotted Creator in a Kingston street and the singer ran off. Eventually, Eccles caught him, and Creator immediately began to make excuses for not paying back the money he owed; Eccles explained that he owed Creator $1,000 in royalties for 'Kingston Town'. The record sold thousands of copies in Britain without ever making the charts. During the 70s, Lord Creator's croon became obsolete in a reggae music obsessed with roots, Rasta and heavy dub. He did record one powerful single in 1977, 'Life', a new version of a 1967 single, 'Such Is Life'. During the 80s rumour had it that Lord Creator had succumbed to a life as a homeless rum-drinker on the streets of Kingston, and eventually Eccles helped to organize enough money for Creator to be returned to his family in Trinidad. In 1989 UB40 covered 'Kingston Town', and Clancy Eccles and Creator were recruited to give their seal of approval in the accompanying video. While it seems sadly ironic that he never had the hit he deserved with his own version, at least UB40's success meant that a royalty cheque would go to the song's creator.

● ALBUMS: *Songs My Mother Never Taught Me* (Port O Jam 1964)★★★★, *Big Bamboo* (Dynamic 1974)★★★★.

LOUCHIE LOU AND MICHIE ONE

Female duo Louchie Lou and Michie One met at a Rebel MC gig in 1991, and quickly found the backing of independent label Fashion Records for their debut single 'Rich Girl'. Switching to London Records in 1993, they released an exuberant version of Lulu's 'Shout' which stayed in the UK Top 10 for eight weeks. After protracted legal wranglings they eventually signed to China Records in 1994, working on their delayed debut album in Jamaica with Sly & Robbie, and then in Los Angeles, California with Quincy Jones' son QDIII (Ice Cube, Tupac Shakur). A diverse blend of reggae rhythms with elements of dancehall, pop, R&B and hip-hop, *I'll Be Free*'s material did not always do justice to the production talent on show, although the club hit 'Champagne And Wine' and the funky 'Free' were notable highlights. The video for the Top 40 'Good Sweet Lovin'' included a cameo appearance from Suggs, resulting in the duo guesting on the ex-Madness singer's hit single 'Cecilia'. They also went on to headline the Japansplash Festival alongside Shaggy, Snow and Barrington Levy, performing to audiences of over 100,000, while further tours of Japan and the Far East served to strengthen their popularity in the Asian market. *Danger-Us* was released in September 1997, with a more mature and full sound replacing the shallow grooves of their debut. Ranging from the reggae/dancehall workouts 'Before The Night Is Over' and 'Kingman', through an excursion into salsa ('The Crickets Sing For Ana Maria'), to the modern urban soul of 'You'll Never Know' and 'I Knew I Blew It', the album again featured QDIII and Sly & Robbie, with additional production work by the in-demand Jazzwad (Buju Banton, Shabba Ranks) and Buzz Productions (Maxi Priest, Barrington Levy). Confident and upfront, Louchie Lou and Michie One look set for further success.

● ALBUMS: *I'll Be Free* (China 1995)★★★, *Danger-Us* (IndoChina 1997)★★★.

LOVERS ROCK

Although love songs have always been staple fare in reggae, and other musics, lovers rock as a genre did not emerge until the mid-70s, chiefly in London. Mixing Philly soul with sweet skanking rhythms, it was the antithesis of the roots reggae movement and provided non-Rasta

reggae fans with something with which to identify in an era otherwise dominated by dub. Early exponents such as 15-16-17, Brown Sugar (who featured Caron Wheeler, later of Soul II Soul) and Carroll Thompson, all sold incredibly well. The critics reviled them for their sickly, barely trained harmonies and schoolgirl voices, but this truly working-class music was to be found in teenagers' bedrooms in every British city centre. There were few lovers chart hits, one exception being Janet Kay's 'Silly Games' (number 2 in 1979), but the music thrived away from the mainstream music business, and some records, such as Louisa Mark's 'Caught You In A Lie' and 'Six Sixth Street', were real artistic successes, albeit largely unheralded ones. Throughout the 80s and early 90s lovers rock has remained a largely underground music, while artists such as Winsome, the Investigators, the Instigators, Deborahe Glasgow and Sandra Cross have built huge followings. One international success has been Maxi Priest, who combined lovers with ragga, roots and soul to produce that long-awaited breakthrough fusion.
● COMPILATIONS: various artists *Fashion Revives Classic Lovers* (Fashion 1989)★★★, *Pure Lovers Volume 2* (Charm 1992)★★★, *Lovers For Lovers Volume 6* (Business 1992)★★★.

LUCIANO

b. Jepther McClymont, 1974, Davey Town, Jamaica, West Indies. Luciano was one of the most promising new singer-songwriters to emerge in 1993. He began singing in his local parish church before assuming the name of Stepper John and migrating to Kingston in April 1992. There he voiced his debut tune for Herman Chin-Loy at Aquarius, then half an album with Pressley for Mau Mau producer Sky High. Homer Harris of Blue Mountain had by that time changed McClymont's name to Luciano. His first Jamaican hit, 'Give My Love A Try', was for Castro Brown and a clutch of ballads and self-penned reality songs soon followed, initially for Brown's New Name label. Philip 'Fatis' Burrell produced his first two UK hits, 'Chant Out' and 'Poor And Simple', in the summer of 1993 on Exterminator, and was later to release his debut solo album *Moving Up*. Singles for Exterminator, Blacka Dread ('Time Is The Master') and Sly And Robbie's Taxi label

helped to establish Luciano's fast-growing reputation before he joined Freddie McGregor's Big Ship organization. 'Shake It Up Tonight' became his first UK reggae number 1 and led to a well-received album of the same name. He earned a contract with Island Records, and his association with Burrell continued with the critically acclaimed *Where There Is Life*, which featured the Jamaican chart-topper 'It's Me Again Jah'.
● ALBUMS: with Pressley *Luciano Meets Pressley* (Sky High 1992)★★★, *Moving Up* (RAS/Exterminator 1993)★★★★, *Shake It Up Tonight* (Big Ship 1993)★★★, *Back To Africa* (Xterminator 1994)★★★, *One Way Ticket* (Xterminator 1995)★★★, *Where There Is Life* (Island 1995)★★★, *The Messenger* (Xterminator 1996)★★★.

LUKIE D

b. Michael Kennedy, 1972, Cockburn Pen, Kingston, Jamaica, West Indies. Kennedy began his career performing on various local sound systems, building a solid reputation as a dance-hall singer. His influences included local heroes Frankie Paul, Tenor Saw and ragga DJ Supercat. His popularity led to recording sessions that produced his biggest hit, 'Centre Of Attraction', alongside combination hits with Lieutenant Stitchie ('Don't Deny Me') and Beenie Man and Black Pearl ('Bag It Up'). Lukie D joined the Firehouse Crew, noted for fostering the careers of Luciano and Sizzla. While with the Firehouse crew he released his debut, *Centre Of Attraction*, featuring combinations with Mikey Spice and DJ Determine. He also released a series of hits, including 'I Won't Let You Go', 'Lonely Nights', 'Let Me Love You Now', 'Heavy Load' and 'You've Got It Going'. His success allowed him to commute between Jamaica and the USA, where he became acquainted with more diverse musical influences, resulting in the broadening of his repertoire. In 1997 he released a 20-track compilation featuring, unconventionally, versions of AC/DC's 'You Shook Me' and Queen's 'We Will Rock You'. His alternative approach garnered attention in the USA, but alienated the partisan dancehall crew.
● ALBUMS: *Centre Of Attraction* (VP 1995)★★★, *The Place To Be* (Down Sound 1997)★★.

MACKA B

b. Christopher MacFarlane, Wolverhampton, England. Macka B is one of the most productive, distinctive and talented of MCs to emerge in Britain in the 80s. He first rose to local fame chatting for the Birmingham-based Wassifa hi-fi, with a melodic but gruff voice that perhaps most closely resembled that of Prince Far I, although Macka B was of the new breed and capable of a pace of delivery that made his predecessors look lazy by comparison. His large physique, stunning, topical lyrics and dreadlocked features made him an imposing presence on the mic, and after one local release his fame quickly spread to London, occasioning the release of a well-received single, 'Bible Reader', for Fashion Records in 1985. Perhaps recognizing that Macka B's future did not lie in the dancehall MC trade, Fashion suggested that Macka B try his luck at Ariwa Sounds, their south London rivals. With the help of fellow Wolverhamptonite Macka Dub, Ariwa producer Mad Professor unleashed a monster with Macka B's debut LP, *Sign Of The Times*, which remains a classic to this day. Mixing comic material with roots anthems such as 'Invasion', drenched in tight horns and heavy dub mixing, the album was a huge hit within the reggae community. Macka B appeared on ITV's *Club Mix* and was something of a celebrity, but he shunned the limelight, preferring instead to work in the roots market, issuing a series of strong albums over the next five years, among them *We've Had Enough*, *Natural Suntan* and *Peace Cup*. He retains his credibility and goodwill, and has even made the occasional trip to Jamaica to record with producer Black Scorpio on a few tracks, as well as cutting 'DJ Unity' at Penthouse Studio, Kingston, with Jamaican counterpart Tony Rebel.

● ALBUMS: *Sign Of the Times* (Ariwa 1986)★★★★, *We've Had Enough* (Ariwa 1987)★★★★, *Looks Are Deceiving* (Ariwa 1988)★★★, *Buppie Culture* (Ariwa 1989)★★★, *Natural Suntan* (Ariwa 1990)★★★★, *Peace Cup* (Ariwa 1991)★★★★, *Jamaica No Problem* (Ariwa 1992)★★★, *Here Comes Trouble* (Ariwa 1993)★★★.

MAD COBRA

b. Everton Brown, *c*.1969, Kingston, Jamaica, West Indies. Brown began his career earnestly following his musical roots - his uncle was an engineer at Bob Marley's Tuff Gong studios. While still at school, Brown chanted on sound systems including the Mighty Ruler and Stereo One. After gaining his qualifications, he pursued a career in the music business. He recorded with a number of producers including Bobby Digital, King Jammy and Donovan Germain. In 1991 Brown recorded 'Tek Him', riding a version of Eric Donaldson's 20-year old Jamaican Music Festival winner, 'Cherry Oh Baby'. The song has since become an anthem and a myriad of versions to the rhythm surfaced, including a remake by Donaldson himself. The hits continued, including 'OPP' (Other Peoples Property), with Conroy Smith, 'Body Basics', 'Be Patient', 'Yush' and 'Gundelero'. His success led to a number of compilations, including *Cobra Gold*, which featured a variety of tracks from a number of producers, and *Ex-Clusive* produced by Clive Kennedy. By 1993, following the success of Shabba Ranks, the major labels took an interest in Jamaican performers and Sony signed Brown; he subsequently became known as Mad Cobra. With production credits to Clifton 'Specialist' Dillon and Sly Dunbar, the release of 'Flex' earned him international fame. The success of the tune was eclipsed when the rhythm was used for Buju Banton's infamous 'Boom Bye Bye', but Mad Cobra's earlier homophobic song, 'Crucifixion', was ignored by the media. In Jamaica he recorded 'Fat And Buff' for Jammys and, inspired by the revival of conscious lyrics, 'Selassie I Rules' in 1994, sounding much like the ever popular Bounty Killer. Throughout 1995 his prolific output continued with notable hits such as 'Poor Mans Shoes', 'Live Good', 'Hell Swell', 'Send Them Come' and 'Dun Wife'. He was also the featured DJ on Bunny Rugs' remake of his Third World hit, 'Now That We've Found Love'. At the 1995 Sting concert, pro-

moted by Isaiah Lang, Mad Cobra faced Ninjaman in a clash of the DJs. Unfortunately, on this Boxing Day event Mad Cobra had to accept defeat, but a rematch was scheduled in Montego Bay on New Year's Eve. The clash never took place and the two protagonists embraced, with Ninjaman announcing, 'Cobra ah mi bwoy, we come outa de same camp'.
● ALBUMS: *Ex-Clusive* (Charm 1991)★★★, *Bad Boy Talk* (Penthouse 1991)★★★, *Merciless Bad Boy* (Sinbad 1992)★★★, *Your Wish* (Esoldun 1992)★★★, *Spotlight* (Top Rank 1992)★★★, *Hard To Wet Easy To Dry* (Columbia 1993)★★★, *Venom* (Greensleeves 1994)★★★★, *Step Aside* (VP 1994)★★★, with Beenie Man, Lieutenant Stitchie *Meets Lt Stitchie And Beenie Man* (VP 1995)★★★★, *Sexperience* (Breadfruit 1996)★★★, *Exclusive Decision* (VP 1996)★★★★, *Milkman* (EMI America 1996)★★★.
● COMPILATIONS: *Cobra Gold* (Charm 1991)★★★, *Goldmine* (VP 1993)★★★, *Shoot To Kill* (VP 1993)★★★, *Mad Cobra* (Sonic 1994)★★★, *Sexperience* (Critique 1996)★★★.

MAD LION
b. Oswald Preist, London, England. The reggae/hip-hop connection has been strengthened with top performers from the two diverse styles recording together: Yellowman with Bill Laswell's Material, Shabba Ranks performing with KRS-1, Shaggy with Grand Puba and Buju Banton alongside Heavy D. In Brooklyn, New York, the Mad Lion (acronym for Musical Assassin Delivering Lyrical Intelligence Over Nations) began performing a combination of ragga and hip-hop in verbal battles fought in parking lots, or any location where opposing rappers could set up their decks, amps and speakers, the equivalent of Jamaica's sound system battles. Mad Lion's reputation spread and he began recording in his own unique style. Kris Parker aka KRS-1 had worked with Shelly Thunder and Ziggy Marley, although it is his association with the Mad Lion that proved to be the most enduring. While the projects with Thunder, Shabba and Ziggy Marley were brief encounters, the partnership with the Lion continued throughout the mid-90s. The Lion's debut, 'Shoot To Kill', was a phenomenal success in New York. The hit was swiftly followed by 'Take It Easy', which became an international

hit and led to an album release of the same name. He topped *Billboard*'s reggae chart and introduced female DJ Lady Apache to Nervous Records, with whom he had enjoyed his notable accomplishments. By the end of 1994, with producer Gyasi Addae, he recorded 'Real Lover', which also led to an album of the same name. Notable inclusions were 'Idiot Drumpan Sound', 'Murderah Man', 'Bad Boy Life' and 'Fluffy'. In the summer of 1995 in the Paramount Theatre, a show, *Hot 97*, was organized by the New York-based radio station featuring legendary hip-hop performers. The aim was to demonstrate that the negative image created by the gangster and drug culture was detrimental to the music's progression. Supporting the show were Doug E. Fresh, Lovebug Starski, the Furious Four, KRS-1, MC Shan and Mad Lion. Also in 1995, the Lloyd Campbell-produced 'Love Woman So' almost crossed over into the international reggae charts. Two years later, 'Carpenter' topped the US reggae chart. Mad Lion has enjoyed tremendous success on the rap scene but has as yet failed to make a significant impression with dancehall devotees.
● ALBUMS: *Take It Easy* (Nervous 1994)★★, *Real Ting* (Nervous 1994)★★, *Real Lover* (VP 1995)★★★, *Ghetto Gold And Platinum Respect* (Nervous 1997)★★★.

MAD PROFESSOR
(See Ariwa Sounds)

MAFIA AND FLUXY
Initially inspired by Sly And Robbie, brothers Mafia (b. Leroy Heywood, 1962, London, England; bass) and Fluxy (b. David Heywood, 1963, London, England; drums) are the UK's foremost rhythm section, and are becoming increasingly well known for their own productions. Early encouragement came via Uncle Wizard's sound system and then Fatman, who released their debut, 'Let's Make Love', after they had formed the Instigators in 1977. By 1985 they had enjoyed several hits and gained valuable experience backing touring Jamaican acts, quickly coming to terms with the new digital technology.
In 1987 they visited Jamaica, building rhythm tracks for Bunny Lee, Blacker Dread, King Jammy and Exterminator. That year they

started their own self-titled label, producing Cinderella, Billy Melody, Sugar Minott and, later, Private Collection ('Dreamer'). Their debut album, *Dancehall Connection Volume 1*, featured such diverse talents as General Trees, King Kong and General Levy when released in 1990. That year, Mafia And Fluxy returned to Jamaica, providing many notable hits for Penthouse, Black Scorpio, Jammys, Gussie Clarke, Mikey Bennett, Mr Doo and Roy Francis. In the UK they backed Maxi Priest and Lloyd Brown, and were voted Producers Of The Year, the Instigators winning the Best Reggae Band Award. On their own label, tracks by Tiger ('Winery'), Gregory Isaacs, Johnny Osbourne, Sugar Black, Cornell Campbell, Sanchez ('Whip Appeal') and Sugar Minott were released at regular intervals.

In 1992 Mafia issued his debut album, *Finders Keepers*, while hits by Cobra ('Off Guard'), Dirtsman, Poison Chang ('Do Me A Favour'), Sweetie Irie, Red Dragon, Cutty Ranks ('Armed And Dangerous'), Tenor Fly and Chaka Demus And Pliers ('Wining Machine') witnessed no shortage of success throughout 1992/3. Back in Jamaica, Mafia And Fluxy laid further tracks for Bobby Digital, Penthouse and Stone Love, with whom they won a Jamaican award for 'Best Juggling (mixing) Record'.

By 1994 they were remixing the likes of Boy George, Barrington Levy and the Rhythm Kings, Mega Banton's 'First Position' was a number 1 hit and they had become one of the most in-demand rhythm sections in reggae music, even occasionally pairing with Sly (Mafia) and Steely (Fluxy).

● ALBUMS: various artists *Dancehall Collection Volume 1* (Mafia & Fluxy 1990)★★★, *Mafia And Fluxy Revival Hits Volume 1* (Mafia & Fluxy 1992)★★★.
Solo: Mafia *Finders Keepers* (Mafia & Fluxy 1992)★★★★.

MALCOLM, CARL

b. July 1952, Black River, St. Elizabeth, Jamaica, West Indies. Malcolm learnt to play the keyboard by ear at the local Methodist church and his musical talents were recognized by those around him from an early age. After leaving the St. Elizabeth Technical High School he spent two years working for a shoe company in Kingston and was a reserve for the Jamaica Defence Force. Music remained his passion and in 1965 he became involved in a band called the Volcanoes alongside Al Brown. The two artists shared vocal duties and stayed with the group until they disbanded four years later. Malcolm retired from music and returned to studying. It was in his second year of study that he was involved in a car accident in which he sustained a broken leg and cracked ribs. Returning to music, he joined a band called Big Relations, led by Jo Jo Bennett. Malcolm recorded with Coxsone Dodd on his first tune, 'Father Free Us', before leaving the island for the USA, where he performed at various clubs and house parties. He then returned to Jamaica where he found employment with Rupie Edwards as the branch manager of Success Records, located at Half Way Tree. While working for Edwards he was allowed studio time to record 'Make It When You Try', but, like his earlier effort, it was overlooked by Jamaican music lovers. Accompanied by Skin Flesh And Bones in 1973, he recorded 'No Jestering', and two years later when released in the UK, it held the number 1 position in the reggae charts. Malcolm's career took off with the follow-up, 'Miss Wire Waist', which demonstrated his smooth vocals. In an effort to appease his fans, he also acknowledged his love of larger ladies in the song 'Fattie Bum Bum', which became a UK Top 10 hit in September 1975. The lyrics, 'Hey fatty bum bum, you sweet sugar dumpling, hey fatty bum bum let me tell you something, no not because your so big and fat, don't believe I'm afraid of that, never let the big size fool you', appealed to many, but in the eyes of the British record-buying public he was a one-hit-wonder. The song was covered by a UK-based group, the Diversions, who diverted enough sales from Malcom to enjoy a chart hit alongside the original version. He returned to the reggae charts in the late 70s with the release of 'Repatriation' with Ranking Trevor. In 1992 Scotty reactivated Malcolm's career when he covered 'Miss Wire Waist'. Even though Malcom had a UK Top 10 hit, no album was released to capitalize on his success. *DJ Specials* (VP 1981) featured both 'No Jestering' and 'Miss Wire Waist', providing the foundation to the DJ tracks.

MALVO, ANTHONY

b. 4 January 1962, Kingston, Jamaica, West Indies. Malvo has voiced many hits for a number of Jamaica's top producers in the style of a dancehall singer. His initial hits include 'Come Back To Me' and 'Rain From The Sky', both with Tiger, and 'Take You To The Dance' with Lizard. The combination hits were followed by a solo venture recorded with Bobby Digital, 'Can't Control The Feeling' and 'History Sound'. Malvo is best known for his work with dancehall singer Anthony 'Red Rose' Cameron when his career peaked in 1994. The duo enjoyed individual hits on their How Yu Fi Sey Dat label: Cameron sang about the 'Ganja Man' while Malvo performed 'Sensi' on an identical rhythm in combination with Josey Wales. In the history of reggae, the dancehall has always played an important role in inspiring recording trends. In the early days the selector would play one rhythm and the DJs would take turns to chant over the same tune. By the early 90s the selector would mix various recorded tracks of the same rhythm, creating the impression that a number of performers were taking a turn at the microphone. Although many sound systems would play the rhythm without an apparent interruption, the practice induced the duo to create 'Informer'. As well as producing the song, they performed alongside Frankie Paul, Red Dragon, Snagga Puss, Lizard and Flourgon. The idea proved a success and a number of multi-combination tunes followed. In 1994 the duo performed 'Never Get', which was rendered in a call-and-response style. They also produced a number of Jamaica's top performers, including Red Dragon ('Sweetheart'), Beenie Man ('Name Brand'), Chuckleberry ('Woman You're Hard') and combinations with Merciless ('You A Mi Heart'), President Brown ('Red Alert') and Spragga Benz ('Reminiscing'). In 1996, after maintaining a low profile, Malvo released the popular 'Main Ingredient', as well as producing successful hits for How Yu Fi Sey Dat.
● ALBUMS: various artists *Quarter To Twelve* (HYFSD 1995)★★★.

MANDATORS

In Africa many performers have been influenced by the music of Jamaica, including Lucky Dube and O'Yaba from South Africa, Alpha Blondy and ex-boxer Waby Spider from the Ivory Coast, along with Majeck Fasheck and the Mandators from Nigeria. The group are fronted by Victor Essiet and though not renowned outside of the dark continent play to large audiences in their homeland. Rounder Records, pioneers of world music, signed the group for *Power Of The People*, released through their Heartbeat outlet. In spite of the reawakening of African consciousness, these performers mainly appeal to followers of world music and although popular, rarely make an impression on the reggae chart.
● ALBUMS: *Power Of The People* (Heartbeat 1994)★★

MARIE, DONNA

Donna Marie was born in the UK, although her formative years were spent in Jamaica. It was while living in Jamaica that she demonstrated her talent singing lead in her local Pentecostal Church choir. After leaving the choir she joined a band performing lead and backing vocals. By 1989 Marie began recording as a soloist with the Pioneers, heralding her emergence in the UK as a lovers rock singer. She released her first single, 'On The Outside', which was a cover version of the theme to the Australian soap opera *Prisoner Cell Block H*. She then released four neglected albums with the group before concentrating on sessions with Delroy Wilson, which resulted in the enticing 'Dance With Me'. Marie maintained a credible profile within the industry for a number of years, including notable sessions with vocalist Don Campbell. By July 1994 her performance at the Intermezzo nightspot in London inspired Jeff Peart of the Boiler Room production team to sign the singer. With Peart and the crew she recorded *Now*, which featured the chart-topping song 'Think Twice', a version of the Celine Dion hit. Marie's interpretation of the song sold particularly well in South America, topped the Italian charts and held the number 1 position in the reggae charts. In 1995 she continued to maintain a high profile, appearing alongside Bunny Wailer at his prestigious concert in Finsbury Park, London, as well as performing with Beres Hammond in the UK and Shabba Ranks in Jamaica. In 1997 Marie toured Brazil and other parts of South America, where her arrival was greeted with rapturous enthusiasm. She featured on television shows, the streets were adorned with banners detailing her tour and her face appeared on the front of the daily nationals. The unprecedented welcome showed Donna Marie as the Queen of Reggae in South American eyes.

● ALBUMS: *Now* (Londisc 1994)★★★, *Thinking Of You* (Londisc 1996)★★★, *Feel Good* (Londisc 1997)★★★★.

● COMPILATIONS: *Love Music Volumes 1-4* (Golden Age/Pioneer 1989-92)★★.

MARK, LOUISA

b. 1960, Shepherds Bush, London, England. Mark first ventured into showbusiness through the regular talent competitions held at the Four Aces Club in London, where she won for 10 consecutive weeks. Competitors would sing over acetates provided by Lloyd Coxsone, who, impressed with her popularity, took her into Gooseberry Studios for a recording session. The result was a cover version of the soul hit by Robert Parker, 'Caught You In A Lie'. With backing provided by Matumbi it was an instant hit, almost breaking through into the pop charts. The second release with Coxsone was 'All My Loving' but it lacked the original winning formula. As Mark was only 15 years old and attending Hammersmith County School at the time, she became a celebrity among the pupils. After leaving school, further releases surfaced, including the Clement Bushay-produced 'Keep It Like It Is', which was later used by Trinity for his hit 'Step It Brother Clem'. Her preference for lyrics relating to infidelity continued unabashed when she released the beautifully crafted 'Six Sixth Street'. In 1980 Bushay released *Markswoman*, although Mark felt that the album was rush-released and improperly mixed; she did not record during the following year as a result. By 1982, she had resolved these disagreements and recorded a version of the Jones Girls' 'Mum And Dad', arranged by Sly And Robbie. As one of the forerunners of lovers rock, before the phrase was inaugurated by Dennis Harris, Mark is still held in high esteem, as demonstrated by the popularity of her debut single, which is still played in dancehalls 20 years after its initial release.

● ALBUMS: *Markswoman* (Bushranger 1980)★★, *Breakout* (Bushays 1982)★★★.

MARLEY, BOB

This legendary singer's vocal group, the Wailers, originally comprised six members: Robert Nesta Marley (b. 6 February 1945, St. Anns, Jamaica, West Indies, d. 11 May 1981, Miami, Florida, USA), Bunny Wailer (b. Neville O'Riley Livingston, 10 April 1947, Kingston, Jamaica, West Indies), Peter Tosh (b. Winston Hubert McIntosh, 19 October 1944, Westmoreland, Jamaica, d. 11 September 1987, Kingston, Jamaica), Junior Braithwaite, Beverley Kelso and Cherry Smith. Bob Marley And The Wailers are the sole Jamaican group to have achieved global superstar status, together with genuine penetration of world markets. The original group was formed during 1963. After extensive tuition with the great vocalist Joe Higgs, they began their recording career later that year for Coxsone Dodd, although Marley had made two singles for producer Leslie Kong in 1962 - 'Judge Not' and 'One Cup Of Coffee'. Their first record, 'Simmer Down', released just before Christmas 1963 under the group name Bob Marley And The Wailers, went to number 1 on the JBC Radio chart in January 1964, holding that position for the ensuing two months and reputedly selling over 80,000 copies. This big local hit was followed by 'It Hurts To Be Alone', featuring Junior Braithwaite on lead vocal, and 'Lonesome Feeling', with lead vocal by Bunny Wailer. During the period 1963-66, the Wailers made over 70 tracks for Dodd, over 20 of which were local hits, covering a wide stylistic base - from cover versions of US soul and doo-wop with ska backing, to the newer, less frantic 'rude-boy' sounds that presaged the development of rock-steady, and including many songs that Marley re-recorded in the 70s. In late 1965, Braithwaite left to go to America, and Kelso and Smith also departed that year.

On 10 February 1966, Marley married Rita Anderson, at the time a member of the Soulettes, later to become one of the I-Threes and a solo vocalist in her own right. The next day he left to join his mother in Wilmington, Delaware, returning to Jamaica in October 1966; the Wailers were now a vocal trio. They recorded the local hit 'Bend Down Low' at Studio One late in 1967 (though it was actually self-produced and released on their own label, Wail 'N' Soul 'M'). This and other self-produced output of the time is among the rarest, least reissued Wailers music, and catches the group on the brink of a new maturity; for the first time there were overtly Rasta songs. By the end of that year, following Bunny Wailer's release from prison, they were making demos for Danny Sims, the manager of soft-soul singer Johnny Nash, who hit the UK charts in April 1972 with the 1968 Marley composition, 'Stir It Up'. This association proved incapable of supporting them, and they began recording for producer Leslie Kong, who had already enjoyed international success with Desmond Dekker, the Pioneers and Jimmy Cliff. Kong released several singles and an album called *The Best Of The Wailers* in 1970. By the end of 1969, wider commercial success still eluded them. Marley, who had spent the summer of 1969 working at the Chrysler car factory in Wilmington, Delaware, returned to Jamaica, and the trio began a collaboration with Lee Perry that proved crucially important to their future development. Not only did Perry help to focus more effectively the trio's rebel stance, but they worked with the bass and drum team of the Barrett brothers, Aston 'Family Man' (b. 22 November 1946, Kingston, Jamaica) and Carlton (b. 17 December 1950, Kingston, Jamaica, d. 1987, Kingston, Jamaica), who became an integral part of the Wailers' sound.

The music Bob Marley And The Wailers made with Perry during 1969-71 represents possibly the height of their collective powers. Combining brilliant new songs such as 'Duppy Conqueror', 'Small Axe' and 'Sun Is Shining' with definitive reworkings of old material, backed by the innovative rhythms of the Upsetters and the equally innovative influence of Perry, this body of work stands as a zenith in Jamaican music. It was also the blueprint for Bob Marley's international success. The group continued to record for their own Tuff Gong label after the Perry sessions and came to the attention of Chris Blackwell, then owner of Island Records. Island had released much of the Wailers' early music from the Studio One period, although the label had concentrated on the rock market since the late 60s. Their first album for the company, 1973's *Catch A Fire*, was packaged like a rock album, and targeted at the album market in which Island had been very successful. The band arrived in the UK in April 1973 to tour and appear on television. In July 1973 they supported Bruce Springsteen at Max's Kansas City club in New York. Backed by an astute promotional campaign, *Catch A Fire* sold well enough to warrant the issue of *Burnin'*, adding Earl 'Wire' Lindo to the group, which signalled a return to a militant, rootsy approach, unencumbered by any rock production values.

The rock/blues guitarist Eric Clapton covered 'I Shot The Sheriff' from this album, taking the tune to the number 9 position in the UK chart during the autumn of 1974, and reinforcing the impact of the Wailers in the process. Just as the band was poised on the brink of wider success, internal differences caused Tosh and Livingston to depart, both embarking on substantial solo careers, and Lindo left to join Taj Mahal. The new Wailers band, formed in mid-1974, included Marley, the Barrett brothers and Bernard 'Touter' Harvey on keyboards, with vocal harmonies by the I-Threes, comprising Marcia Griffiths, Rita Marley and Judy Mowatt. This line-up, with later additions, would come to define the so-called 'international' reggae sound that Bob Marley And The Wailers played until Marley's death in 1981.

In establishing that form, not only on the series of albums recorded for Island but also by extensive touring, the band moved from the mainstream of Jamaican music into the global market. As the influence of Bob Marley spread, not only as a musician but also as a symbol of success from the so-called 'Third World', the music made locally pursued its own distinct course. 1975 was the year in which the group consolidated their position, with the release of the massively successful *Natty Dread* and rapturously received concerts at the London Lyceum. These concerts attracted both black and white patrons - the crossover had begun. At the end of the year Marley achieved his first UK chart hit, the autobiographical 'No Woman No Cry'. His first live album, comprising material from the Lyceum concerts, was also released in that year. He continued to release an album a year until his death, at which time a spokesman for Island Records estimated worldwide sales of $190 million. Marley survived an assassination attempt on 3 December 1976, leaving Jamaica for 18 months in early 1977. In July he had an operation in Miami to remove cancer cells from his right toe.

His albums *Exodus* and *Kaya* enjoyed massive international sales. In April 1978, he played the One Love Peace Concert in Kingston, bringing the two leaders of the violently warring Jamaican political parties together in a largely symbolic peacemaking gesture. The band then undertook a huge worldwide tour that took in the USA, Canada, Japan, Australia and New Zealand. His own label, Tuff Gong, was expanding its interests, developing new talent. The album *Survival* was released to the usual acclaim, being particularly successful in Africa. The song 'Zimbabwe' was subsequently covered many times by African artists. In 1980, Marley and the Wailers played a momentous concert in the newly liberated Zimbabwe to an audience of 40,000. In the summer of 1980, his cancer began to spread; he collapsed at Madison Square Garden during a concert. Late in 1980 he began treatment with the controversial cancer specialist Dr. Josef Issels. By 3 May, the doctor had given up. Marley flew to Miami, Florida, where he died on 11 May. Marley was rightly celebrated in 1992 with the release of an outstanding CD box set chronicling his entire career, although his discography remains cluttered due to the legal ramifications of his estate. His global success had been an inspiration to all Jamaican artists; his name became synonymous with Jamaican music, of which he had been the first authentic superstar. His contribution is thus immense: his career did much to focus attention on Jamaican music and to establish credibility for it. In addition, he was a charismatic performer, a great singer and superb songwriter - a hard act to follow for other Jamaican artists.

● ALBUMS: Bob Marley And The Wailers *Wailing Wailers* (Studio One 1965)★★★, *The Best Of The Wailers* (Beverley's 1970)★★★, *Soul Rebels* (Trojan/Upsetter 1970)★★★, *Catch A Fire* (Island 1973)★★★★★, *Burnin'* (Island 1973)★★★★, *African Herbsman* (Trojan 1974)★★★, *Rasta Revolution* (Trojan 1974)★★★, *Natty Dread* (Island 1975)★★★★★, *Live!* later retitled *Live At The Lyceum* (Island 1975)★★★★, *Rastaman Vibration* (Island 1976)★★★★, *Exodus* (Island 1977)★★★★, *Kaya* (Island 1978)★★★★, *Babylon By Bus* (Island 1978)★★★, *Survival* (Tuff Gong/Island 1979)★★★★, *Uprising* (Tuff Gong/Island 1980)★★★★, *Marley, Tosh Livingston & Associates* (Studio One 1980)★★★.

● COMPILATIONS: Bob Marley And The Wailers *In The Beginning* (Psycho/Trojan 1979)★★★, *Chances Are* (Warners 1981)★★★, *Bob Marley - The Boxed Set* 9-LP box set (Island 1982)★★★, *Confrontation* (Tuff Gong/Island 1983)★★★, *Legend* (Island 1984)★★★★★, *Mellow Mood* (Topline 1984)★★, *Reggae Greats* (Island 1985)★★★, *Soul Revolution I & II* the first UK release of the 70s Jamaican double album (Trojan 1988)★★★, *Interviews* (Tuff Gong 1988)★★, *One Love: Bob Marley And The Wailers At Studio One* (Heartbeat 1991)★★★, *Talkin' Blues* (Tuff Gong 1991)★★★, *All The Hits* (Rohit 1991)★★★, *Upsetter Record Shop Parts 1&2* (Esoldun 1992)★★★, *Songs Of Freedom* 4-CD box set (Island 1992)★★★★, *Never Ending Wailers* (RAS 1993)★★★, *Natural Mystic: The Legend Continues* (Island 1995)★★★★, *Power* (More Music 1995)★★★, *Soul Almighty - The Formative Years Volume 1* (JAD 1996)★★★, *Dreams Of Freedom: Ambient Translations Of Bob Marley In Dub* (Axiom/Island 1997)★★★, *Roots Of A Legend* (Trojan 1997)★★★.

● VIDEOS: *One Love Peace Concert* (Hendring Video 1988), *Live At The Rainbow* (Channel 5 1988), *Caribbean Nights* (Island Video 1988), *Legend* (Island Video 1991), *Time Will Tell* (1992), *The Bob Marley Story* (Island Video 1994).

● FURTHER READING: *Bob Marley: Music, Myth & The Rastas*, Henderson Dalrymple. *Bob Marley: The Roots Of Reggae*, Cathy McKnight and John Tobler. *Bob Marley: Soul Rebel - Natural Mystic*, Adrian Boot and Vivien Goldman. *Bob Marley: The Biography*, Stephen Davis. *Catch A Fire, The Life Of Bob Marley*, Timothy White. *Bob Marley: Reggae King Of The World*, Malika Lee Whitney. *Bob Marley: In His Own Words*, Ian McCann. *Bob Marley: Conquering Lion Of Reggae*, Stephen Davis. *So Much Things To Say: My Life As Bob Marley's Manager*, Don Taylor. *The Illustrated Legend 1945-1981*, Barry Lazell. *Spirit Dancer*, Bruce W. Talamon, *The Complete Guide To The Music Of...*, Ian McCann. *Bob Marley: An Intimate Portrait By His Mother*, Cedella Booker with Anthony Winkler.

MARLEY, CEDELLA BOOKER

b. Cedella Malcom, Nine Miles, Jamaica, West Indies. Cedella Marley, the sixth of nine children, gave birth to reggae's foremost emissary. In the early 40s, still in her teens, she began a clandestine relationship with Norval Sinclair Marley. He was a white patriarchal figure whom she married in June 1944. Her husband left for Kingston following the wedding and visited Cedella twice while she was carrying their child. Bob was born on 6 February 1945, and was brought up by Cedella and her father, Omeriah, with only occasional visits from Norval. Years later, Cedella moved with Bob to Kingston to join her boyfriend, Toddy Livingston, and the latter's son, Bunny, who joined them in 1955. Cedella's estranged husband had married bigamously and following a legal battle, he died of a heart attack. In 1962 Cedella accompanied Bob to Montego Bay where he performed his debut, 'Judge Not'. In 1964 Cedella was carrying her second child and decided that the USA offered better opportunities. In Wilmington, Delaware, she gave birth to her daughter Pearl, followed by sons Richard and Anthony. In 1966 Cedella encouraged Bob to join her in the USA, unaware that he married Rita Anderson on the day before he left Jamaica. Bob stayed with Cedella for six months before the draft board necessitated a hasty return to Jamaica. Bob's career came to fruition, and throughout, he maintained a loyal relationship with his mother, providing the family with a new home in Miami. In 1981 Cedella supported her son during his infirmity and continued his works following his untimely demise. Cedella's other sons, Richard and Anthony, formed the band Copasetic, who in 1988 released *Five And Dime*. The boys also supported their mother in her musical endeavours through to 1990, when Anthony played his last concert at a Bob Marley birthday celebration in Kingston, before being shot dead in a Miami shopping mall. Cedella has since recorded a series of Rastafarian-influenced melodies, remaining majestically impassive in the face of the inevitable criticism. She has also organized and performed at a number of Bob Marley Festivals, earning the nickname of 'Mother B'. She was still active within the industry in 1997, working on the eagerly awaited *My Altar*.
● ALBUMS: *Awake Zion* (Tuff Gong 1990)★★.

● FURTHER READING: *Bob Marley: An Intimate Portrait By His Mother*, Cedella Booker with Anthony Winkler.

MARLEY, RITA

b. Rita Anderson, Jamaica, West Indies. Wife of Bob Marley, Rita has enjoyed a successful solo career in her own right, both before and after her husband's death. She had originally worked with the Soulettes, a Studio One trio, where she first met Bob. She subsequently enjoyed several solo hits in Jamaica, among them 'Pied Piper'. Prophetically, she would back the Wailers on several early recordings before linking up with Marcia Griffiths and Judy Mowatt to form the I-Threes. Perhaps her most poignant statement is the album *Who Feels It Knows It*, recorded while Bob was dying of cancer. Rita's biggest hit came with 'One Draw', a pro-marijuana lyric recorded in 1981, shortly after Bob's death. However, she continued to enjoy single successes with 'Many Are Called' and 'Play Play'. By the mid-80s she was largely retired, concentrating on untangling Bob's legal estate, and fostering the career of her children, Ziggy Marley And The Melody Makers.
● ALBUMS: *Who Feels It Knows It* (Shanachie 1980)★★★, *Harambe* (Teldec 1984)★★.

MARLEY, ZIGGY, AND THE MELODY MAKERS

b. David Marley, 1968, Kingston, Jamaica, West Indies. 'Ziggy' Marley, one of Bob Marley's four children with his wife Rita Marley, started his career as one of the Melody Makers with siblings Sharon, Cedella and Stephen, whose appearance at their father's funeral in 1981 marked their introduction to the rest of the world. The following year, 'What A Plot', released on Rita's label, was a big hit, and Ziggy's lead vocals sounded uncannily similar to his late father's. The Melody Makers were allowed the time and space to mature and practise before committing themselves needlessly to vinyl - unlike so many of their Jamaican counterparts, where recording activities were an economic necessity - and by the late 80s they were a headline act, especially in the USA. Their *Play The Game Right* debut, the only album to be credited simply to the Melody Makers, included one notable excerpt from their father's songbook, 'Children Playing In The Street', which he had originally written for them. Despite their tender years, the record stands up to repeated listening and suggests that Marley's maturity and wisdom were hereditary. The album to confirm this was *Conscious Party*. Produced by Chris Frantz and Tina Weymouth from Talking Heads, and featuring an inspired selection of backing musicians, the set boasted high-calibre material such as 'Tomorrow People' and 'We Propose', which would not have disgraced any Wailers album. *One Bright Day* is a similarly delightful collection, comprising slick dance reggae with articulate rebuttals of the South African apartheid system. The Melody Makers have resisted the obvious temptation to re-record too many of their father's songs, and instead have forged a career in their own right. In his excellent book *Bob Marley - Conquering Lion Of Reggae*, Stephen Davis illustrates the group's popularity in America by detailing a short exchange between two youngsters after seeing Bob Marley on video; one's question, 'Who's that?', is met with the cursory response, 'Ziggy Marley's father'. In his own lifetime, Bob and the Wailers did not break the American market with the same level of success as the Melody Makers. They are also very popular in Jamaica - and not just because of Ziggy's lineage, though his ability to sing over his father's songs as 'specials' for some of Kingston's top sound systems, adapting the lyrics for each particular system, has made him widely popular. Ziggy And The Melody Makers have transcended the 'famous parent' tag to become stars in their own right, following on from their father's tradition without ever leaning on it too heavily. As Bob once remarked: 'All a my family are music'.

● ALBUMS: *Play The Game Right* (EMI 1985)★★★, *Hey World* (EMI 1986)★★, *Conscious Party* (Virgin 1988)★★★★, *One Bright Day* (Virgin 1989)★★★★, *Jahmekya* (Virgin 1991)★★★, *Joy & Blues - Ghetto Youths United* (Virgin 1993)★★★, *Free Like We Want 2 B* (Elektra 1995)★★★, *Fallen Is Babylon* (Elektra 1997)★★★.

● COMPILATIONS: *Time Has Come: The Best Of Ziggy Marley And The Melody Makers* (EMI/Manhattan 1988)★★★★, *The Best Of Ziggy Marley 1988-1993* (Virgin 1997)★★★.

MARSHALL, CARLA

b. Kingston, Jamaica, although she grew up in Toronto, Canada, when her mother emigrated. Inspired by Sister Nancy's rendition of 'No Borrow, No Lend' in the mid-80s, Marshall began her quest as a contender for the crown of the queen of the DJs. A notable recording, 'Champion', was also her biggest hit when released on Sly And Robbie's Fourth And Broadway outlet. By 1995 she had worked with Diana King who had an international hit with 'Shy Guy', although her own career came first. In the winter of 1995 she released 'Puny Puny' for Columbia, with little impact. Undeterred, the record company followed it with her version of Marvin Gaye's 'Sexual Healing' (co-written with author David Ritz). Marshall has as yet been unable to equal the success of other female dancehall DJs, although by 1996, her reputation had grown internationally and her debut album was issued.

● ALBUMS: *Fire On The Mountain* (Columbia 1996)★★★.

MARSHALL, LARRY

b. *c*.1945, St. Anns, Jamaica, West Indies. In 1963, Marshall had minor hits with 'Too Young To Love' for E Henry, and 'Please Stay' for Coxsone Dodd's Studio One label. He subsequently enjoyed a big hit with 'Snake In The Grass', a Top Deck production, and, in 1967, recorded 'I've Got Another Girl' and 'Suspicion' for Prince Buster. However, he had his greatest successes at Studio One where, in addition to singing in a duo with Alvin Leslie, he also worked as an engineer. Larry And Alvin had a massive hit with 'Nanny Goat' (1968), and followed with 'Hush Up' (1968), 'Your Love' (1969) and 'Mean Girl' (1969). Another of their songs, 'Throw Me Corn', became hugely popular at dances through 1969-70 when played on acetate, and was eventually released in 1971. Marshall then recorded solo, and had a further hit with 'Thelma'. A compilation of his Studio One recordings, *Presenting Larry Marshall*, was issued around 1973. By this time, he was also doing production work at Studio One. He left around 1974, and had success with his self-produced 'I Admire You' (1975), with a strong album of the same name following. Since then, he has issued a steady stream of singles, and had moderate hits with remakes of 'Throw Me Corn' (1984) and 'I Admire You' (1985), both Gussie Clarke productions.

● ALBUMS: *Presenting Larry Marshall* 1968-71 recordings (Studio One 1973)★★★★, *I Admire You* (Java 1975)★★★, *Dance With Me Across The Floor* (1988)★★★, *Come Let Us Reason* (1992)★★★.

MARTIN, HORACE

Martin was an underrated singer who released a large number of recordings but received little recognition. He began his recording career in 1980 with Robert Palmer's Negus Roots, releasing 'Zuggy Zuggy' and 'Sweet Something', while with the fiercely unconstrained Big Ben label he released 'Africa Is Calling', 'We Are All One', 'Beautiful Dream' and 'Jah Jah Children'. Throughout the 80s he maintained a high profile as a singles artist, although he was unable to achieve crossover success. In 1985 his fortunes changed when he recorded 'War', produced by veteran DJ Jah Thomas over the legendary Stalag rhythm. The song led to sessions with Prince Huntley, whose print shop Modernize Printery led to the formation of his Modernize Music and Greedy Puppy labels. Huntley had recorded 'Pressure In A Babylon' but found greater success as a producer. Martin recorded a succession of hits for Huntley, including 'Na Fry No Fat', 'Sonia' and 'Mi Rule'. The popularity of Patrick Andy's 'Sting Me A Sting' led Martin to respond with 'Shock Me A Shock'. In 1987 he recorded for Harold McLarty the hit 'Type Of Loving', which featured the fledgling DJ skills of Tiger, supported by the Riddim Kings Band. The release gave Martin the wider exposure he deserved, although this was overshadowed by the unprecedented demand for the newly acclaimed DJ. Martin followed his hit with the less successful 'Can't Get Used To Losing You', which heralded a return to anonymity.

● ALBUMS: *Watermelon Man* (Mr Tipsy 1984)★★★.

MASSIVE DREAD

b. Dennis James, *c.*1960, Trenchtown, Jamaica, West Indies. James began his career in 1982 touring with Byron Lee And The Dragonaires, which led to an appearance at the Jamaican Reggae Sunsplash show. His live appearances culminated in the Crazy Jim show, where he introduced the new DJ style that became known as 'bubbling' to an ecstatic audience. A adherent of the concept of leaving the audience 'wanting more', he withdrew from appearing on the live circuit. His reputation grew and he was soon recording for a number of Jamaican producers, including Tommy Cowan's first wife, Valerie, at Music Mountain. He enjoyed his greatest achievements as a recording artist with Winston 'Pipe' Matthews and Lloyd 'Bread' McDonald of the Wailing Souls. The vocal group, like so many other reggae performers, focused their aims towards both artistic and financial independence by establishing their own record label. The Upfront Organisation released his version of the Wailing Souls' 'Things And Time' as 'Nice Dem Up' as well as 'One Way', 'Just Cool Melba' and the Jamaican chart-topping 'This Is Massive'. The Wailing Souls were asked to perform 'Things And Time', for Tyne Tees Television, which was included in a documentary of Jamaican music for the *Tube*. The programme also featured a rare performance from Massive Dread in his riding hat, worn in recognition of the then current craze of the jockey-ride dance. He performed at the Valentines dance alongside Yellowman, Eek A Mouse, Buro Banton and Billy Boyo at Aces. The DJs appeared as a showcase of the Volcano sound system's top performers under the guiding light of Henry 'Junjo' Lawes. In 1984 the hits continued with 'Young Gal No Sell Your Body' and 'Justice Love And Harmony' lifted from his second album. Following his association with Volcano, Massive Dread joined the Metro Media sound where he performed alongside Peter Metro and Zu Zu.

● ALBUMS: *Strictly Bubbling* (Upfront 1982)★★★, *Its Massive* (Upfront 1984)★★.

MATCHUKI, COUNT

b. Winston Cooper, *c.*1939, Kingston, Jamaica, West Indies, d. 1995. Matchuki, whose nickname came from his habit of chewing matchsticks, is widely acknowledged as the first Jamaican DJ. In the 50s R&B was the prevailing popular sound, and he would simply add local phraseology to enhance the tunes, whereas U-Roy, who is often referred to as the innovator, rode the reggae rhythms with his chantings. R&B is acknowledged to have influenced Jamaican musicians and in the 50s Coxsone Dodd made frequent visits to secure new releases for his Downbeat Sound System. While on his visits, he heard the US DJs' jive talk and felt that the style would augment his status as the top sound man on the island. Following the departure of Dodd's resident DJ Duke Vin, Matchuki was offered and accepted the role, where he emulated the US radio hosts. By the late 50s Jamaican musicians began recording their own sound, initially with an American influence, but it soon developed its own identity. The Skatalites performed a number of ska instrumentals for Dodd and the Count was invited to add his vocals on a number of recordings, although he was often uncredited. Having not been acknowledged, it is difficult to identify recordings involving his voice-overs, although he certainly appeared on the Sound Dimension's 'More Scorcher', 'Doctor Sappa Too' and 'Pepper Pot'. By the late 60s, disillusioned with the lack of either financial reward or recognition, he decided to abandon his career, remaining unobtrusive within the industry. He resurfaced 10 years later in the television series *Deep Roots Music*. The production team secured a rare interview with the pre-eminent DJs Sir Lord Comic and Count Matchuki, although the duo spent most of the interview in a heated debate relating to the Jiving Juniors' 'Lollipop Girl'. Matchuki's appearance enabled him to set the record straight as to the embryonic role he played in the DJ phenomenon.

MATUMBI

Nowadays largely remembered for being home to Dennis Bovell's first musical adventures, Matumbi should nevertheless be considered in their own right as a leading voice in the UK's 70s reggae scene. Formed in south London in 1972 by Tex Dixon (vocals), the latter assembled a nucleus that comprised Euton Jones (drums), Errol Pottinger (guitar), Eaton 'Jah' Blake (bass), Bevin Fagan and Nicholas Bailey (vocals), alongside the aforementioned Bovell (guitar). They took their name from the African word for 'rebirth', and in the customary manner of early UK reggae bands, first found employment backing visiting Jamaican musicians. After signing to Trojan Records, early singles included 'Brother Louie' and 'Wipe Them Out', but it was

the subsequent singles, 'After Tonight' and 'Man In Me', that brought them major commercial recognition. The latter was the biggest-selling UK reggae single of 1976. However, success almost immediately brought internal friction, exacerbated by Trojan's attitude. They were concerned over individual members' involvement in outside projects, rather than concentrating solely on establishing the band as a top name. An injunction was finally served, with the result that Bailey and Dixon quit, the former, who went on to solo 'pop' successes with Nick Straker, being replaced by Webster Johnson (keyboards). Pottinger had already been replaced by Glaister Fagan, while Jah 'Bunny' Donaldson joined in 1976 in place of Euton Jones. The remaining members moved on to a contract with EMI subsidiary Harvest, bolstering their profile by joining Ian Dury And The Blockheads on tour. *Seven Seals* was an effective long-playing debut, but it was the follow-up, *Point Of View*, that garnered most plaudits. The title track, a mix of reggae, soul and Glen Miller, reached the Top 40, and for a time it seemed Matumbi might occupy the commercial high ground to which many UK reggae bands had aspired. It was not to be, however; a further album followed but popular taste had bypassed Matumbi, and the members resumed their solo projects. Donaldson joined the Cimarons, and Fagan and Blake came to be known as the Squad, experiencing some chart success as such. Bovell pursued his own idiosyncratic vision, working both inside and outside of the reggae medium.

● ALBUMS: *Seven Seals* (Harvest 1978)★★★, *Point Of View* (EMI 1979)★★★★, *Dub Planet* (Extinguish 1980)★★.
● COMPILATIONS: *Best Of* (Trojan 1978)★★★.

MAYTALS

Arguably, the Maytals were only ever kept from becoming 'international' artists by the runaway success of Bob Marley And The Wailers in the 70s. Rumour has it that Island Records' Chris Blackwell originally only signed the Wailers because he was unable to obtain the Maytals' signatures at the time. Frederick 'Toots' Hibbert, Nathaniel 'Jerry' Matthias/McCarthy and Henry 'Raleigh' Gordon came together in 1962 at the start of Jamaica's ska craze and began recording for Coxsone Dodd's Studio One organization. With a hoarse vocal from Hibbert, backed by an impenetrable wall of sound, it was not long before the Maytals were the number one vocal group in Jamaica - a position they maintained throughout the 60s and on into the 70s.

They left Dodd after some massive hits and moved on to his ex-employee and arch-rival Prince Buster, celebrating with the vengeful 'Broadway Jungle'/'Dog War'. However, their stay with Buster was also short-lived and the Maytals moved on again to Byron Lee's BMN stable. In 1965 they made Jamaican musical history when both sides of 'Daddy'/'It's You' topped the Jamaican charts, and in 1966 they won the prestigious Jamaican Festival Song Competition with 'Bam Bam'. Many of their releases in these early days were credited to 'The Vikings' or 'The Flames', because, as Hibbert explained: 'Promoters in Jamaica called us all kinds of different names because they didn't want us to get our royalties'. The future was looking bright for the group, but Hibbert was imprisoned in late 1966 for possession of marijuana and was not released until 1968. The Maytals began work for Leslie Kong's Beverley's label, and their first release was a huge hit in Jamaica and the UK - '54-46 That's My Number' featured one of reggae's most enduring basslines as Hibbert detailed his prison experiences in song. This was the beginning of a hugely successful period for the group, both artistically and financially, and they recorded many classic records for Beverley's, including 'Do The Reggay', one of the first songs ever to use 'reggae' in the title, 'Monkey Man', which actually reached the UK charts, and 'Sweet and Dandy', which won the Festival Song Competition again for them in 1969. They also appeared in a cameo role in the hugely popular film The Harder They Come, singing one of their most popular tracks, 'Pressure Drop'.

Kong's untimely death in 1971 from a heart attack robbed them of their mentor. Many believed that their best work was recorded while at Beverley's; evidence of its popularity was found in the 2-Tone craze of the late 70s, when new bands took a large part of their repertoire from Hibbert's Beverley's songbook. The Maytals subsequently returned to Byron Lee, now the successful owner of Dynamic Sounds, a state-of-the-art recording, mastering and record pressing complex. In 1972 they won the Festival Song Competition yet again with 'Pomps and Pride'. Through their work with Dynamic they attracted the attention of Chris Blackwell and became Toots And The Maytals. For the first time in 14 years they became widely known outside of reggae circles. Their UK and US tours were sell-outs, and Island Records released what became their biggest-selling album, Reggae Got Soul, which took them into the UK album charts. They made history again in 1980 when, on 29 September, they recorded a live show at London's Hammersmith Palais, which was mastered, processed, pressed and in the shops 24 hours later. Few live excursions have been able to capture the feel and spontaneity of this album, which showcases the Maytals at their best - live without any embellishments. By this time, they had left their Jamaican audiences far behind, but their nebulous 'pop' audience soon moved on to the next big sensation. Hibbert dispensed with the services of Matthias/McCarthy and Gordon for his 1982 tour and has even experimented with non-reggae line-ups. While the Maytals continued to tour and make records in the 90s, real lasting international success always seemed to elude them.

● ALBUMS: Presenting The Maytals (Ska Beat 1964)★★★★, The Sensational (Wirl 1965)★★★★, Never Grow Old (Studio One 1966)★★★, Original Golden Oldies (Volume Three) (Fab Prince Buster 1967)★★★, Sweet & Dandy (Beverley's 1969)★★★, From The Roots (Trojan 1970)★★★, Monkey Man (Trojan 1970)★★★, Funky Kingston (Dragon 1973)★★★★, In The Dark (Dragon/Dynamic 1974)★★★, Slatyam Stoot (Dynamic)★★★, Reggae Got Soul (Mango/Island 1976)★★★★, Pass The Pipe (Mango/Island 1979)★★★, Just Like That (Mango/Island 1980)★★★, Toots Live (Mango/Island 1980)★★★, Toots In Memphis (Mango 1988)★★★, Life Could Be A Dream (Studio One 1992)★★★.
● COMPILATIONS: Reggae Greats (Mango/Island 1988)★★★★, Do The Reggae 1966-70 (Trojan 1988)★★★, Sensational Ska Explosion (Jamaica Gold 1993)★★★, Time Tough (Mango/Island 1996)★★★.

MAYTONES

The Maytones comprised Vernon Buckley and Gladstone Grant and began recording in the late 60s with Alvin 'GG' Ranglin. In 1970 they released 'Black And White', which was considered to be the alternative reggae cut to Greyhound's successful pop hit. They also enjoyed hits in the early 70s with 'Preaching Love', 'If Loving You Was Wrong', 'Brown Girl' and 'Funny Man'. These successes were generally love songs, but with subsequent releases they recorded in a more serious vein, concentrating on a Rastafarian theme. 'Judas', 'Babylon A Fall' and 'Run Babylon' signalled the direction in which reggae was heading. Conscientious lyrics and a clarion call for black pride resulted in the duo achieving cult status. They continued releasing hits through to the mid-70s, then returned to Ranglin at the Channel One Recording Studio, securing a success with *Madness*, which surfaced in the UK through Burning Sounds. The group were inauspiciously overlooked by Virgin Records when the latter were signing all the major acts in Jamaica. Fellow vocal group and Virgin signing the Mighty Diamonds had previously recorded as the Diamonds. This inspired Ranglin and Clement Bushay to promote the duo as the Mighty Maytones. The release of *Boat To Zion*, including the title track, was a hit within the West Indian community but failed to match the success of other Rastafarian-influenced vocal groups. The duo recorded in heavy patois and this may have been the reason why they were overlooked. Their image did not portray the media idea of the typical Rastafarian, without locks or red, gold and green outfits, and they were therefore generally ignored. In 1980 Ranglin compiled a collection of the duo's work, including recordings from 1976 sessions. Bushay also compiled a *Best Of*, which featured tracks lifted from the two earlier releases.

● ALBUMS: *Madness* (Burning Sounds 1976)★★★★, *Boat To Zion* (Burning Sounds 1978)★★★, *Madness 2* (Pioneer 1995)★★.
● COMPILATIONS: *One Way* (GG's 1980)★★★, *Best Of The Mighty Maytones* (Burning Sounds 1983)★★★, *Funny Man* (GG's 1990)★★★, *Brown Girl In The Ring* (Trojan 1995)★★★.

McCLEAN, BITTY

b. *c.*1972, Birmingham, England. Bitty was so named by his grandmother because he was underweight as a baby. As a teenager he went on to study Sound Recording and Media at Sandwell College in Birmingham. He impressed in his studies, and lecturer Alan Cave, previously engineer to UB40 on *Labour Of Love*, recommended him to his former employers as a tape operator. He went to the band's Abattoir Studio and remained there for three years. Although nominally recording local bands, McClean would more often find himself sneaking back into the studio late at night to record demos. By chance, the band's Ali Campbell heard some of his material and was impressed enough to invite McClean to provide backing vocals and harmonies on UB40's UK number 1, 'Can't Help Falling In Love'. He also co-produced and engineered their subsequent album, *Promises And Lies*. Having given notice of his talents, he was signed by the newly established Brilliant Record Company in June 1993. His debut single, 'It Keeps Rainin', surged to number 2 in the UK charts in September of that year, and was a good example of the fare on offer for his debut long-playing set - as Bitty himself described it: 'Fresh, infectious, accessible reggae'. The immediate follow-ups were versions of Bunny Wailer's 'Pass It On' and Justin Hinds' 'Here I Stand', both of which followed a similar pattern.

● ALBUMS: *Just To Let You Know* (Brilliant 1994)★★★.

McCOOK, TOMMY

b. *c.*1932, Jamaica, West Indies. From the age of 10, McCook attended the Alpha Catholic School For Boys, where he learnt tenor saxophone, flute and music theory. He left Alpha at 14, and played with the dance bands of Eric Deans and Ray Coburn, subsequently developing into a fine jazz player. During the late 40s and early 50s he was a frequent visitor to Count Ossie's camp, where he jammed with Ossie's Rastafarian hand-drummers, developing a deep love for their music in the process. In 1954 McCook joined a dance band in the Bahamas, and further developed his jazz technique. On his return to Jamaica in 1962, he became involved in the development of ska, emerging as a founder-member of the Skatalites in 1963. His understanding of jazz, R&B and Jamaican musical forms enabled him to make a huge contribution to the group, which changed the course of Jamaican music. The group backed all of the major ska vocalists, and recorded a huge body of instrumental music. Some of the best examples of his work with the Skatalites are compiled on *Ska Authentic*. After the Skatalites split up in 1965, McCook formed the Supersonics, who became Duke Reid's house band at Treasure Isle studios. Their sublime, cool style made Treasure Isle the most popular studio of the rocksteady era with hits from the Techniques, Alton Ellis And The Flames, Justin Hinds And The Dominoes and many more. A compilation of Supersonics instrumentals from this period, simply entitled *Tommy McCook*, was later released in the UK. Since this time, he has played on many recordings for Coxsone Dodd, Bunny Lee, Channel One, Joe Gibbs, Randys and other producers. Solo albums released by Bunny Lee include *Cookin'*, *Brass Rockers* and *Hot Lava*. Glen Brown also issued an excellent blank-labelled album, usually called *Horny Dub*, and with trumpeter Bobby Ellis he made an album (*Blazing Horns*)for Yabby You. He is also a featured soloist on most Aggrovators, Revolutionaries and Professionals instrumentals from this period. He continues to tour and work as a session player.

● ALBUMS: *Tommy McCook* 1965-66 recordings (Attack 1974)★★★, *Cookin'* (1974)★★★, with the Aggrovators *Brass Rockers* (Total Sounds 1975)★★★, *Horny Dub* white label (Grounation 1976)★★★★, *Hot Lava* (Third World 1977)★★★, *Instrumental* (Justice 1978)★★★★, with Bobby Ellis *Blazing Horns* (Grove Music 1978)★★★.

● COMPILATIONS: *Down On Bond Street* (Trojan 1993)★★★.

MCGREGOR, FREDDIE

b. *c*.1955, Clarendon, Jamaica, West Indies. McGregor entered the Jamaican music business at the precocious age of seven, singing backing vocals with ska duo the Clarendonians at Coxsone Dodd's Studio One. He stayed with Dodd throughout the rest of the decade and into the early 70s, acting as a session drummer and backing singer as well as cutting sides such as

'Why Did You Do It', and 'Do Good' (*c*.1965) with Clarendonian Ernest 'Fitzroy' Wilson as Freddie And Fitzy, versions of Johnny Ace's 'Pledging My Love' and Junior Byles' 'Beat Down Babylon' (*c*.1972), and his own compositions, 'Go Away Pretty Woman', 'What Difference Does It Make' and 'Why Is Tomorrow Like Today'. In 1975, after adopting the Rastafarian faith through the Twelve Tribes organization, he recorded two of his finest singles, 'I Man A Rasta' and 'Rastaman Camp', both heavyweight slices of roots Rasta reggae. In the early 70s he worked stage shows as lead singer with the Generation Gap and Soul Syndicate bands and maintained strong links with both sets of musicians throughout his career. The late 70s saw his star rise with excellent singles such as 'Jogging' for Tuff Gong, the herbsman anthem 'Natural Collie', based around the melody and arrangement of Norman Collins' soul opus, 'You Are My Starship', and 'Mark Of The Beast', 'Leave Yah', and a cover version of George Benson's 'Love Ballad', all for Earl 'Chinna' Smith. Winston 'Niney' Holness produced his debut set, *Mr McGregor*, and there were further recordings for Studio One including 'Homeward Bound', 'Come Now Sister', 'Africa Here I Come', and the classic *Bobby Babylon*. In 1979 McGregor was also involved in the production of Judy Mowatt's excellent *Black Woman*.

McGregor's reputation as one of the most vocally gifted singers in reggae, able to turn his hand to lovers or roots material with equal potency, had been increasing steadily when he recorded *Big Ship* for Linval Thompson. Released in the UK on Greensleeves, the album was a great success. He followed this up with *Love At First Sight* (1982) for Joe Gibbs. Coxsone capitalized on McGregor's popularity, which by that time was rivalling that of Dennis Brown and Gregory Isaacs, with the same year's *I Am Ready*, which, like its predecessor, was comprised mainly of singles and previously unreleased tracks from the singer's sojourn at Studio One in the early 70s. In 1984 McGregor inaugurated his own Big Ship label with *Across The Border*, and secured a licensing agreement with RAS Records in the USA for the release of *Come On Over*. In 1985 he recorded the duet 'Raggamuffin' with Dennis Brown for Gussie Clarke, and the dancehall hit 'Don't Hurt My

Feelings' for George Phang's Powerhouse label. Throughout the 80s, McGregor enjoyed a position as one of reggae's most popular performers, touring the world with the Studio One Band, and enjoying a huge hit in Colombia with a version of the Sandpipers' 'Guantanamera', sung in Spanish, for RAS. He signed a contact with Polydor Records which resulted in the UK chart-nudging 'Push Come To Shove' (1987) and 'That Girl', finally achieving a UK hit with a cover version of Main Ingredient's 'Just Don't Wanna Be Lonely', which reached number 9 in August 1987. Now established as a senior reggae statesman, McGregor completed a pair of albums, *Sings Jamaican Classics* and *Jamaican Classic Volume 2*, on which he sang reggae standards such as Little Roy's 'Prophecy' and Derrick Harriott's 'The Loser', retitled 'The Winner'. McGregor again narrowly missed the UK charts with his interpretation of Justin Hinds And The Dominoes' 'Carry Go Bring Come' (1993), but has since had huge success in the reggae charts with his production of Luciano's 'Shake It Up Tonight', sung over the rhythm used for his own 'Seek And You Will Find', which also provided the vehicle for Big Youth's excellent 'Jah Judgement'. Already a veteran in reggae McGregor's future as a superstar looks assured.

● ALBUMS: *Mr McGregor* (Observer 1979)★★★, *Bobby Babylon* (Studio One 1980)★★★★, *Lovers Rock Showcase JA Style* (Third World 1981)★★★, *Big Ship* (Greensleeves 1982)★★★, *Love At First Sight* (Intense/Vista Sounds 1982)★★★, *I Am Ready* (Studio One 1982)★★★, *Come On Over* (RAS 1983)★★★, *Freddie* (Vista Sounds 1983)★★★, *Across The Border* (Big Ship 1984)★★★, *All In The Same Boat* (RAS 1986)★★★, *Freddie McGregor* (Dynamic/Polydor 1987)★★★, *Rhythm So Nice* (Dynamic 1988)★★★, *Don't Want To Be Lonely* (Studio One 1988)★★★, *Now* (Steely & Clevie/VP 1991)★★★, *Sings Jamaican Classics* (Jetstar/VP 1991)★★★, *Hard To Get* (Greensleeves 1992)★★★, *Jamaican Classics Volume 2* (Jetstar/VP 1992)★★★, *Push On* (Big Ship 1994)★★★, *Rumours* (Greensleeves 1997)★★★.

● COMPILATIONS: *Reggae Rockers* (Rohit 1989)★★★.

● VIDEOS: *So I Wait* (Polygram Music Video 1989).

McKAY, FREDDIE

b. 1947, St. Catherine, Jamaica, West Indies. McKay recorded for producer Prince Buster in 1967 and gained his first hit, 'Love Is A Treasure', for Duke Reid in that same year. Later he moved from Treasure Isle to Coxsone Dodd's Studio One to record a number of popular titles in the early reggae idiom, including 'High School Dance', 'Sweet You Sour You', 'Drunken Sailor' and 'Picture On The Wall'. The latter was also the title of his debut album, which remains McKay's most consistent set. Never in the major league of Jamaican singers, McKay nevertheless commanded a faithful following and continued to make excellent records right up to his untimely death in the mid-80s.

● ALBUMS: *Picture On The Wall* (Studio One 1971)★★★, *Lonely Man* (Dragon 1974)★★★, *The Best Of Freddie McKay* (GG's 1977)★★★, *Creation* (Plant 1979)★★★, *Tribal In A Yard* (Move/Charly 1983)★★.

● COMPILATIONS: with Jah Stone *The Right Time* 1977-78 recordings (GG's 1997)★★★★.

McLEAN, NANA

b. c.1960, Jamaica, West Indies. McLean began singing in her childhood, and won various local carnival contests. A notable success came at the Donkey Carnival in Linstead Market, where her performance led to her singing for the Soul Defenders, and she made her debut recording sessions at Studio One in 1977. Coxsone Dodd released her interpretation of 'Til I Kissed You', which announced McLean's arrival and showcased her characteristic style. She continued to maintain a high profile within the industry through to 1979, when she was commissioned to record *Dream Of Life*, released through A&M Records. As with many major label signings, the relationship was brief and she returned to an independent recording career. In 1987 she was recording with King Jammy ('Single Girl') and for the Youth & Youth co-operative ('Take Me Higher'). By the early 90s she had gained prominence for her work with Donovan Germain and Dave 'Rude Boy' Kelly. 'Take Me I'm Yours' was followed by the retrospective 'Nana's Medley', which featured 50s doo-wop over the popular 'Love I Can Feel' rhythm. A popular medley including versions of 'Daddy's Home', 'Eddie My Love' and 'Sincerely' led to a series of hits, such

as 'Let Me Cover You' and 'I Will Follow You', which cemented her association with the duo. Although McLean relocated to Canada, she remained loyal to the producer's Penthouse organization, and in 1997 she earned a Juno award for her release *Collectors Series*.
● ALBUMS: *Dream Of Life* (A&M 1979)★★, *Modern Day Romance* (Paradise 1996)★★★, *Collectors Series* (Penthouse 1997)★★★★.

McLEOD, ENOS

b. 1946, Trenchtown, Kingston, Jamaica, West Indies. Prior to his involvement in music McLeod served an apprenticeship as a cabinet-maker and trained as a boxer. His early work surfaced in the mid-60s with the debut 'Mackie', produced by Sid Bucknor, the resident engineer at Studio One. Bucknor coached McLeod in record production and this led to his initial success as a producer, with the release of 'Young Love' by Lloyd Clarke. The single surfaced on a UK release in the mid-60s through Blue Beat Records. McLeod followed this achievement by working with many of Jamaica's top performers, including Gregory Isaacs, Ken Boothe and the Gaylads, as well as the debut release from Prince Far I, who had until this session recorded under the name of King Cry Cry.

In addition to production work, McLeod continued to voice his own hits, including 'Tel Aviv', 'Hello Carol', 'Bad Times', 'Hi-Jacking', 'Come Running Back' and 'If You Love Jah', while in combination he released 'Jestering' (with Shorty The President) and 'Jericho' (alongside the Mighty Diamonds). In the mid-70s McLeod was approached by Joe Gibbs, mindful of his boxing skills, to act as the bouncer at the producer's Retirement Crescent studio. While keeping out gatecrashers he also worked on recording sessions with the resident engineer, Errol Thompson, resulting in the scarcely available 'Money Worries' and, by contrast, his biggest hit, 'By The Look', released in the UK through Hawkeye. McLeod's intermittent output is eagerly consumed by his faithful followers and he continued recording through to the 90s, latterly in Europe, where he maintained flourishing business ventures.
● ALBUMS: *By The Look In Your Eyes* (Soul Beat 1978)★★★, *Goodies Best* (White Label 1995)★★★, *Ram Jam Party* (President

1996)★★★, *Enos In Dub* (Grapevine 1996)★★★.
● COMPILATIONS: *The Genius Of Enos* (Pressure Sounds 1996)★★★★.

ME AND YOU

Me and You were a vocal duo featuring the talents of a brother and sister team, Norman McLean (b. 1959, Jamaica) and Sonia McLean (b. 1963, Jamaica, d. 1995). They came from a musical family and were aware of the pitfalls in the industry through their sister Shirley's earlier experiences in the Jamaican music scene. The duo began their recording career in 1979 with DEB music, one of the more successful independent labels, which evolved from the Morpheus group initiated by Castro Brown. (It was wrongly assumed that there was a family connection when Castro formed a partnership with Dennis Emanuel Brown, whose initials inspired the label's name.) The duo's debut, 'This Love', was a Top 10 hit in the reggae charts, maintaining a healthy position throughout the spring season. They were then taken to the studio by Dennis and Castro Brown, who produced a version of the Philly hit 'You Never Know What You Got', featuring Jamaican session players the Professionals, later known as the We The People Band, and including Lloyd Parks and Sly Dunbar. The single topped the reggae chart and crossed over into the mainstream, staying in the chart for nine weeks and peaking at number 31 in the UK Top 40. The song was licensed to the Lazer group who had promoted 'Money In My Pocket' for Dennis Brown, repeating the accomplishment with the duo's major label debut. During the summer months the group toured as part of a DEB music showcase featuring Black Harmony, 15-16-17, Destiny and George Burrell, pipped from the top slot by Black Harmony. In spite of this phenomenal rise to stardom Norman and Sonia maintained a cautious approach to their success. Their decision to be wary was proved correct when 'In The Future', released on DEB, was unable to match the fortunes of its predecessor. In 1980 the previous year's efforts were rewarded when they were voted among the best newcomers in the *Black Echoes* Awards. They continued to record a number of hits, including 'Railway Station', alongside their 1982 self-production of 'Casual Affair', with a sublime version of Jackie Edwards' 'Who Told You So'. The duo had carved a respectable position in the history of UK reggae and the industry suffered a great loss when Sonia died in 1995.

MEDITATIONS

Jamaican vocal group comprising Ansel Cridland, Danny Clarke and Winston Watson. Clarke had previously been a member of The Righteous Flames, the group fronted by Winston Jarrett (which had, in turn, been formed from the ashes of Alton Ellis's Flames). Clarke left in 1975, forming the Meditations alongside Cridland and Watson. The trio, a roots group similar in style to the Mighty Diamonds, recorded a series of strong singles for producers Dobby Dobson and Lee Perry: 'Running From Jamaica', 'No Peace', 'House Of Parliament' and 'Much Smarter', songs that cast them as righteous Rastafarians who would have nothing to do with the system. Further hits for a variety of producers revealed their pedigree: 'Wake Up', 'Fly Your Natty Dread' and the massive 'Woman Is Like A Shadow' (1978). Their first LP, *Message From The Meditations*, was a minor classic. Resourceful beyond the limits of most bands, the Meditations rode out the dancehall era, cutting a series of strong, if hardly spectacularly successful, albums for a variety of labels. Their 1983 set, *No More Friend*, was favourably received, and they remain revered ambassadors of rasta reggae, and retain much goodwill in America to this day.
● ALBUMS: *Message From the Meditations* (Wild Flower 1977)★★★★, *Wake Up* (Third World 1978)★★★, *No More Friend* (Greensleeves 1983)★★★★, *For The Good Of Man* (Greensleeves 1988)★★★, *Return Of* (1993)★★★.
● COMPILATIONS: *Greatest Hits* (Greensleeves 1984)★★★★, *Deeper Roots: The Best Of* (Heartbeat)★★★.

MEEKS, CARL

b. 1962, Kingston, Jamaica, West Indies. As a schoolboy, Meeks emulated the singing styles of top Jamaican musicians, and, determined to pursue a career in the recording industry, he realized that he would have to develop his own original style. In the mid-80s he auditioned with George Lemon who released his debut, 'No More Secrets', which led to a series of singles. He also worked with other producers, including the prolific Hugh 'Redman' James. James was proving to be one of Jamaica's top producers, releasing smash hits from Clement Irie, Thriller U and Meeks's 1987 hits, 'Weh Dem Fah', 'Haul And Pull Up Selector' and 'Rude Girl Sandra'. By 1988 Meeks performed alongside DJ Daddy Lilly for 'Lean On Me', and a classic tale of wasted emotions, 'Heard About My Love'. As a soloist, Meeks continued to enjoy hits with the conscientious 'Danger' and 'Tuff Scout'.
● ALBUMS: *Weh Dem Fah* (Redman International 1987)★★★★, *Jackmandora* (Greensleeves 1988)★★★, *Righteousness* (Ellis 1997)★★★.

MELODIANS

Vocal trio comprising Brent Dowe, Tony Brevett and Trevor McNaughton. Robert Cogle was also a member of the group throughout their career. He made a major contribution as songwriter on many of the trio's biggest hits, but apparently not as a vocalist. They started singing in Kingston's amateur talent contests from 1960, but did not record until April 1966, when they made four titles for Coxsone Dodd, only two of which were released. During 1967-68 the Melodians recorded a series of big local hits for the Treasure Isle label, owned by producer Duke Reid, that endure to this day as classics of the rocksteady school. The trio's cool, precise harmonies are showcased to near-perfection on 'You Don't Need Me', 'I Will Get Along', 'I Caught You', all released in 1967, and 'Come On Little Girl' in 1968. Later in 1968, the group made two more massive local hits for Sonia Pottinger - 'Little Nut Tree', freely adapted from the nursery rhyme, and the celebratory 'Swing And Dine'. The following year, while still continuing to record occasional titles for Pottinger's Tip-Top label ('No Nola'), they began an association with the producer Leslie Kong that was to bring them international success, firstly with 'Sweet Sensation' and then with the Rasta-influenced, anthemic 'Rivers Of Babylon', the latter reputedly selling 75,000 copies in the UK alone.
They continued recording for Kong until his death in 1971, not only as a trio but as solo vocalists. Following this they recorded for Lee Perry,

Harry J., Dynamics and Sonia Pottinger and Duke Reid again in 1972. Two years later the group split up. Brent Dowe recorded for Lee Perry in 1975 ('Down Here In Babylon'), and produced himself at Channel One the same year on the sublime 'Deh Pon The Wicked'. Tony Brevett enjoyed success again with 'Don't Get Weary', a self-production. In 1976, they reformed, recording many of their old hits for producer Harry J., with backing by the Soul Syndicate band, but failed to maintain momentum. In the mid-80s the trio attempted a reunion, with little success; nevertheless, much of the music they made in the 60s remains emblematic of the best in rocksteady and reggae, and their recent stage shows at revival concerts have proved to be hugely popular.
● ALBUMS: *Rivers Of Babylon* (1970)★★★, *Sweet Sensation* (1976)★★★, *Sweet Sensation: The Original Reggae Hit Sound* (Island 1980)★★★, *Premeditation* (Skynote 1986)★★★.
● COMPILATIONS: *Swing And Dine* (Heartbeat 1993)★★★.

MERCILESS

b. Leonard Bartley, 1971, Kingston, Jamaica, West Indies. Merciless learnt his craft on the sound systems and in 1994, his debut with singer and producer Rula Brown, 'Lend Out Mi Mercy', was an international success. Sounding not dissimilar to Bounty Killer he warned, 'The reason why they call mi Merciless - I len out no mercy - mi no get it back yet - you dis Merciless - well a dead'. The chant led to numerous hits, assuring his status as one of the island's top DJs. Collaborations with Anthony Red Rose and Malvo ('You Are Mi Heart') and Little Hero with Action Fire ('Thief In The Night' and 'God Alone') were dancehall favourites. The Big Yard label released Merciless's 'Mavis', which made references to domestic violence, and became the top reggae single of 1995 (the rhythm was also used for Shaggy's chart-topping 'Mr Boombastic'). His follow-up at the end of 1995, 'Gun From Paris', signalled a return to the Annex label, where the majority of his hits originated. The in-house producers at Annex, Harvel Hart and Delroy Schobourgh, recorded him in combination with Queen Yemisi for 'Sexy Lover'. Through the Taxi production team of Sly Dunbar and Robbie Shakespeare, he entered the Jamaican Top 10, praising 'Girls From Near And Far', and a version of the Melodians' 'Rivers Of Baylon', retitled 'Rivers Of Girls', ensured that his high profile was maintained. The conscientious revival found Merciless praising his mother over a Rastafarian burra-drumming version of Bob Marley's 'Redemption Song', entitled 'Mama Cooking'.
● ALBUMS: *Len' Out Mi Mercy* (Annex 1995)★★★.

MERGER

Merger formed in the mid-70s, and the line-up comprised Barry Ford (lead vocals, guitar), Winston Bennett (vocals, guitar), Ivor Steadman (bass), Mike Osei (drums) and Tony Osei (keyboards). Their 1977 debut, *Exiles In A Babylon*, featured the keyboard skills of Mike Dorane, who had been involved in the UK reggae scene for a number of years. Initially, the set was released in West Africa, only surfacing in the UK following a remix. Bennett had previously recorded in 1968 as part of Errol Daniels And The Garments, and prior to Merger, recorded *Seeds Of The Earth* with Ivor Steadman for EMI Records. The name Merger described the fusion of reggae and other sounds, along with the fact that the band members were of Ghanaian and Jamaican parentage. The group played their first gig at Brixton's Cloud club, a concert that resulted in an ardent following. Their reputation spread and they attracted an abundance of media attention. The release of 'Ghetto Child' and a tribute to Steve Biko were popular releases. In 1978 Barry Ford elected to pursue a solo career and was replaced by Far I and Ras Damjuma. The group maintained a low profile until Bob Dylan chose them to play at his outdoor concert in Blackbushe Aerodrome. Following his departure from the group, Ford returned to Jamaica where he teamed up with Pablo Black, Bagga Walker and Freddie McGregor to record *Cool Breeze Blowing*, featuring the title track, 'JA People' and 'Curfew'. Ford was also reacquainted with Pam Nestor, and they recorded 'Hiding And Seeking No More', which was remixed in the UK by Dennis Bovell in 1979.

In 1980 Merger's new line-up recorded *Armageddon Time* at the Rock City Studios in London. In 1996 Winston Bennett released

Prisoner Of Love which contained two tracks recorded in 1980 with Merger.

● ALBUMS: *Exiles In A Babylon* (Sun Star 1977)★★★, *Armageddon Time* (1980)★★★.

METRO, PETER

b. Donovan Harris, *c*.1960, Western Kingston, Jamaica, West Indies. After leaving school he worked as a welder, following in the footsteps of many legendary reggae performers. In his leisure time he went to the local dances, and when given the opportunity to chat on the sound, the enthusiastic audience response inspired him to pursue a career as a DJ. He initially decided to call himself Peter Ranking, but discovered that another DJ used that name and had enjoyed a minor hit with 'Sukiyaki'. Harris was a resident DJ on the sound Metromedia and adopted the pseudonym Peter Metro. He recorded his debut outing, 'Jamaica Salute', and was soon found voicing a number of recordings for a variety of producers. An unusual characteristic of his recordings was his use of Spanish, which won him many fans in South America, and this is particularly notable on 'Water Jelly' and the introduction to 'Fisherman Connection'. Working with Yellowman and Fathead, his popularity increased following the release of 'Water Pumpee'. He also recorded a version of Michael Jackson's 'The Girl Is Mine' in combination with Yellowman, which became a big hit. Metro's success inspired his brother Squiddly Ranking to become resident DJ on the Gemini Sound System, where he frequently clashed with Yellowman. Always an innovative performer, Metro recorded 'Yardie And Cockney' in combination with a white English DJ, Dominic, and is acknowledged as the first multilingual toaster. The duo gave a respectable performance at the 10th Reggae Sunsplash festival, but the novelty was short-lived.

● ALBUMS: with Yellowman, Fathead *Yellowman, Fathead And The One Peter Metro* (Abissa 1982)★★★★, with Little John, Captain Sinbad *Sinbad And The Metric System* (CSA 1983)★★★, with various artists *Dedicated To You* (CSA 1984)★★★, *Live With Yellowman And Sassafrass* (White Label 1984)★★★★, *No Problem* (VP 1989)★★★.

● VIDEOS: *Reggae Sunsplash Dancehall X '87* (1987).

MEXICANO

b. Rudolph Grant, Plaisance, Guyana. Grant and his family settled in the UK in 1967. Grant made his debut in 1969 as Little Brother Grant for the release of 'Let's Do It Tonight'. His brother Eddy Grant began performing in the Equals, who had a number of hits in the late 60s. Rudy, recording as the Mexicano, began his career as a DJ with 'Gorilla In Manilla' and 'Cut Throat', a tale of the Mexicano's quest to find I. Roy and Prince Jazzbo so that he could spit in their eyes. While Mexicano pursued his career in recording, Eddy Grant used the royalties from his time with the Equals to set up his own Coach House Recording Studio, working with various groups including the Pioneers.

Mexicano's career surged when in 1977 at the Coach House he recorded a tribute to the popular television series *Starsky And Hutch*, entitled 'Move Up Starsky', a DJ version of Bob Marley's 'I'm Still Waiting'. The single topped the UK reggae chart and inspired a response from the modestly titled Superstar, 'Move Up Hutch', which failed to match the success of the original. Mexicano's hit was followed by 'Lover's Conversation', which did not enjoy the success of its predecessor. He voiced further Pioneers tracks (most significantly 'Harry The Fool', 'Rock It' and Lonely Street') with a number of notable reggae celebrities including Sidney Crooks, Danny Ray, Clement Bushay and Jackie Edwards. In 1980 Mexicano was the featured DJ on Jackie Robinson's interpretation of 'Jamaican Child' with the Lloyd Charmers-produced 'Better Love Next Time'.

By 1981 Mexicano's career changed direction when he decided to sing as Rudy Grant. He recorded a version of John Lennon's 'Woman' and Stevie Wonder's 'Lately' for Ensign Records, the latter of which entered the UK pop chart. The success of the single led to a contract with Stiff Records, who released 'Trial By Television', which failed to generate interest within the reggae community. In 1983, still courting the major labels, he recorded 'Everyday People' for RAK Records.

● ALBUMS: *Move Up Starsky* (Golden Age/Pioneer 1977)★★★, as Rudy Grant *Sings The Hits* (Pinnacle 1982)★★★.

MICHIGAN AND SMILEY

Papa Michigan Fairclough and General Smiley Bennett began their career in the early 80s at Studio One under the direction of Coxsone Dodd. The duo recorded their number 1 hit 'Rub A Dub Style' over the original master tape for Alton Ellis's 'I'm Just A Guy', followed by the equally popular 'Nice Up The Dance'. Although Dodd released hits in the dancehall style, the sessions proved to be his swan-song before relocating to New York. The duo were able to overcome this setback by recording at Tuff Gong Studio the classic 'One Love Jamdown', produced by Jahmet Enwright, which was released as a double a-side with Freddie McGregor's 'Jogging'. Michigan And Smiley gave a dynamic performance at the annual Reggae Sunsplash Festival in 1981, which led to a debut appearance in the UK where they topped the bill at the *Black Echoes* Reggae Awards Show. In 1982 Henry 'Junjo' Lawes productions dominated the dancehall, introducing current DJs to a wider audience without attenuating the sound. Michigan And Smiley recorded a grim warning to prospective philanderers, 'Diseases', and the song inspired Yellowman to record an identical version alongside his sparring partner, Fathead. Throughout the 80s Michigan And Smiley sustained attention in the album charts with the releases *Step By Step*, *Sugar Daddy*, *Back In The Biz* and *Reality Must Rule Again*. The duo enjoyed a revival in the 90s when some of their earlier hits resurfaced through VP in the USA.
● ALBUMS: *Rub A Dub Style* (Studio One 1980)★★★★, *Downpression* (Greensleeves 1982)★★★, with Eek A Mouse *Live At Reggae Sunsplash* (Sunsplash 1982)★, *Up Town/Downtown* (VP 1995)★★.

MIGHTY DIAMONDS

One of the most famous Jamaican vocal groups of the 70s and 80s, the Diamonds consisted of Donald 'Tabby' Shaw (lead vocals), with Fitzroy 'Bunny' Simpson and Lloyd 'Judge' Ferguson providing the harmonies and occasional lead. They recorded unsuccessfully for Stranger Cole and Rupie Edwards, among others, before their breakthrough in 1975 with Joseph 'Joe Joe' Hookim's Channel One studio. 'Hey Girl' and 'Country Living' were big reggae hits, but their next release, 'Right Time', on Hookim's Well Charge label, consolidated that success. The Diamonds' initial popularity was boosted by a number of factors: the influence of Burning Spear's championing of Jamaican national hero, Marcus Garvey; the definitive three-part rock-steady harmonies of the Heptones, together with Sly Dunbar's militant rockers style of drumming on 'do-overs' of timeless Studio One rhythms; and, of course, their own superb songwriting, vocal abilities and the odd knack of somehow managing to sound urgent and relaxed at the same time. Jamaica erupted into Diamonds-mania, while the Channel One 'rockers' sound they had brought to prominence was to dominate reggae music for the next few years, with every drummer in the business developing his very own Sly Dunbar impersonation. Virgin Records was busy acquiring reggae artists in 1976, and the Diamonds and Hookim signed with them for the release of their debut, *Right Time*. It was a classic collection, showcasing perfectly the Diamonds' uncanny ability to write catchy, meaningful songs - whether about 'love' or 'reality' - and set them to updated versions of some of the greatest Studio One rhythms. They sold throughout the reggae world and picked up many crossover sales. Virgin sent the Diamonds to New Orleans to work with veteran producer Allen Toussaint, which resulted in *Ice On Fire*. It was not well received, and sold poorly - mainly because its misguided approach baffled reggae fans, while the Diamonds name still meant very little to a wider audience.

They continued to work at Channel One, and many more hit singles emerged during the 70s. In 1981, the dub plates of tunes they had recorded for Gussie Clarke were the most played on the Kingston and London sound system circuits. The most popular of these tunes was released on a 10-inch, dub plate-style record in New York, a 7-inch in Jamaica and a 12-inch in England; 'Pass The Kouchie', an updating of a 60s Studio One instrumental 'Full Up', was a massive hit. This eventually became 'Pass The Dutchie' for the English group Musical Youth, which was a worldwide pop hit. (A 'kouchie' is a pipe for smoking ganja, while a 'dutchie' is a type of cooking pot.) The rest of their work with Clarke was released on *Changes*, which consisted of the same combination of new songs and old rhythms, with some classic reggae ongs, including 'Party Time' and 'Hurting nside', performed in the inimitable Diamonds tyle. For the rest of the decade and on into the 0s, the Diamonds have continued to build on heir reputation as one of the best vocal harmony trios in the business with regular releases or a variety of different producers and some ovely self-produced records. Their harmonies re always tight, and their songs usually manage o avoid obvious and naïve statements. In the onstantly changing world of reggae, they are lways a reliable and dependable source of top-uality music, and if their performances have ot quite reached the exalted standards of *Right 'ime* and *Changes*, it is perhaps too much to xpect any radical change in direction at this tage in their career.

ALBUMS: *Right Time* (Well Charge/Virgin 976)★★★★, *Ice On Fire* (Front Line 977)★★★, *Stand Up To Your Judgement* Channel One 1978)★★★, *Planet Earth* (Virgin 978)★★★, *Tell Me What's Wrong* (JJ 979)★★★, *Deeper Roots - Back To The Channel* Front Line 1979)★★★, *Changes* (Music Works 981)★★★★, *Vital Selection* (Virgin 1981)★★★, *eader Of Black Countrys* (Mobiliser 1983)★★★, *ouchie Vibes* (Burning Sounds 1984)★★★, *truggling* (Live & Love 1985)★★★, *If You're ooking For Trouble* (Live & Love 1986)★★★, *he Roots Is There* (Shanachie 1987)★★, *Real nemy* (Greensleeves 1987)★★, *Reggae Street* Shanachie 1987)★★, *Dubwise* (Music Works 988)★★★, *Get Ready* (Greensleeves 988)★★★, *Never Get Weary* (Live & Love 988)★★★, *Live In Europe* (Greensleeves 989)★★, *Go Seek Your Rights* (Frontline 990)★★★, *The Moment Of Truth* Mango/Island 1992)★★★, *Bust Out* Greensleeves 1993)★★★, with The Tamlins *rom The Foundation* (Music Works 996)★★★★.

MIKEY GENERAL

. Michael Taylor, 9 October 1963, London, ngland. Taylor spent his formative years com-nuting between London and Jamaica. Inspired y the established singers on the island, ncluding Dennis Brown and Barrington Levy, e embarked on his own singing career; his ocal style was initially in the high tenor dance-all style of Pinchers, Sanchez and Pliers. He

began his recording career during the mid-80s in the UK, recording with Studio One producer Jackie Mittoo. The recordings surfaced on Mikey's own MGR label through Omega, and other notable recordings followed, including 'Kuff N Dem', 'A Sound Gonna Die Tonight', and the allegorical 'Cowboy Life'. In combination he found success with Richie Davis ('Back To Life' and 'Suzy Wong'), while he joined Skipper Ranking for the anti-cocaine anthem, 'Don't Nose It Up'. He accepted a starring role in the television play *We The Raggamuffin*, for which he also provided the theme tune. In 1992 Mikey returned to Jamaica, where he met Luciano during a recording session - the association led to his becoming part of the Firehouse Crew alongside DJ Sizzla and saxophonist Dean Fraser. In 1997 the Firehouse Crew shared top billing with Buju Banton and Bunny Wailer at the Essential Roots Day festival, and by this time, Mikey's recording career was enjoying a renaissance; Philip 'Fatis' Burrell produced his Firehouse debut, *Stronger Rastaman*, while his combination with Sizzla, 'Babylon A Listen/Unseen Blessings', became a dancehall anthem.

● ALBUMS: with Andrew Paul *Sound Bwoy Burial* (1989)★★★, *Sinners* (Charm 1995)★★, *Stronger Rastaman* (VP 1996)★★★.

MILLER, COUNT PRINCE

b. *c.*1948, Jamaica, West Indies. Count Prince Miller is a veteran performer having been involved in black entertainment for over 30 years. In the early 60s he was initially a baritone singer, singing with the Downbeats. He learnt his craft performing on the hotel circuit on the north coast of Jamaica. His reputation led to his being enrolled to perform with Jimmy James And The Vagabonds, joining the group in the UK. The band released a number of singles, including 'Red Red Wine' prior to Tony Tribe's reggae version of the Neil Diamond classic. The song gave the group their only UK Top 40 hit in 1968 and it was not until 1976 that they returned to the chart. After Miller departed from the group he became more involved in the UK reggae scene. He appeared at the Wembley Reggae Festival in 1971, the recording of which was planned as a live album by Trojan Records, but the project faltered. Undeterred, the label persevered, and a live album was successfully recorded at Alexandra Palace featuring the Pioneers, Greyhound, Nicky Thomas, Delroy Wilson, Bruce Ruffin, and compered by Miller. In 1971 he had recorded a novelty hit for the label, 'Mule Train Parts One And Two', which he performed at the show. Further releases included 'Bewildered' and a comment on man's follies, 'The Monkey'. He also performed along-side his compatriot Danny Ray and was instru-mental in securing the singer a contract with MCA Records. In 1974 as a soloist, he released 'Call Me' on the Trojan subsidiary Ashanti. His reputation as an MC led to his introducing a number of top Jamaican artists, including the Rainbow Theatre performance of the Jamaica Showcase in 1974, featuring Al Brown, Dennis Brown, Cynthia Richards and Sharon Forrester. He was also invited to introduce Bob Marley And The Wailers at the same theatre in June 1977. The event was filmed and has the distinc-tion of being the first official reggae video. In the early 80s, he re-recorded 'Mule Train' with Sly And Robbie, reviving his popularity as a per-former. He continued to whip up enthusiasm at live events, and pursued his aspirations towards an acting career. By the 90s, his determination resulted in a role in the popular television situa-tion comedy *Desmond's*. In 1996 he returned to the studios to produce Jimmy James and Winston Curtis's 'Muriel'.

● ALBUMS: *Trojan Reggae Party Volume One* (Trojan 1972)★★★★.

MILLER, JACOB

b. c.1955, Jamaica, West Indies, d. 23 March 1980. Miller recorded his first record for Coxsone Dodd, entitled 'Love Is A Message' (aka 'Let Me Love You') in 1968, aged just 13. The song was not a hit, however, and Miller had to wait a few years before he returned to the studio. In 1974 he recorded a number of singles for Augustus Pablo, including 'Each One Teach One', 'Keep On Knocking', 'False Rasta', 'Who Say Jah No Dread' and 'Baby I Love You So', most of which were popular on the pre-release circuit in the UK. Unfortunately, when Island released 'Baby I Love You So', they failed to credit Miller, and even relegated his vocal to the b-side in favour of its thrashing King Tubby's/Pablo dub, 'King Tubby's Meets Rockers

Uptown'. Miller's biggest hits came as a member of Inner Circle. In 1976 they enjoyed a couple of roots hits with 'Tenement Yard' and 'Tired Fe Lick Weed In A Bush' (both credited to Miller). These hits, combined with Miller's explosive stage act made them the top act in Jamaica in the latter part of the 70s. Miller, an exuberant, amply proportioned man, possessed of a fine tenor that often featured a trademark stutter, went on to make a number of excellent records with Inner Circle, including 'All Night Till Daylight' and 'Forward Jah Jah Children'. He took part in the famous 1978 One Love Peace Concert in Kingston, where Bob Marley joined hands with Edward Seaga and Michael Manley, and had an amusing cameo role in the 1979 film *Rockers*. He died in a road crash on 23 March 1980.

● ALBUMS: *Killer Miller* (Top Ranking 1978/RAS 1988)★★★★, *Natty Christmas* (Top Ranking 1978, RAS 1988)★★, *Unfinished Symphony* (Circle 1984)★★★, *Who Say Jah No Dread* (Greensleeves 1992)★★★.

● COMPILATIONS: *Reggae Greats* (Island 1985)★★★★, *Greatest Hits* (RAS 1988)★★★★.

MILLIE

b. Millicent Small, 6 October 1942, Clarendon, Jamaica, West Indies. After leaving home at the age of 13 to further her singing career in Kingston, Millie recorded several tracks with producer Coxsone Dodd, who teamed her with Roy Panton. As Roy And Millie, they achieved local success with 'We'll Meet' and 'Oh, Shirley' and caught the attention of entrepreneur Chris Blackwell. On 22 June 1964, Millie accompanied Blackwell to the UK and recorded Harry Edwards' 'Don't You Know', before being pre-sented with the catchy 'My Boy Lollipop', for-merly a US R&B hit for Barbie Gaye, which became a transatlantic Top 5 hit, the first crossover ska record. However, chart fame proved ephemeral. A carbon-copy follow-up, 'Sweet William', was only a minor hit, and 'Bloodshot Eyes' failed to reach the Top 40. Thereafter, she languished in relative obscurity. Even a brief collaboration with Jackie Edwards in Jackie And Millie, and a nude photo-spread in a men's magazine failed to revitalize her career. Ultimately handicapped by her novelty hit, Millie's more serious work, such as the self-chosen *Millie Sings Fats Domino*, was sadly ignored.

● ALBUMS: with Jackie Edwards *Pledging My Love* (1967)★★★.

● COMPILATIONS: with Jackie Edwards *The Best Of Jackie & Millie* (1968)★★★, *The Best Of* (Trojan 1970)★★★.

MINOTT, ECHO

b. Noel Philips, *c*.1962, Kingston, Jamaica, West Indies. Philips began his career in 1981 with King Jammy when he recorded 'Youthman' and an obscure album under his own name. He decided to start afresh with Michael 'Myrie' Taylor and Marshall who had set up the Sunset label. Owing to confusion over the Harry J. label of the same name, the duo discontinued Sunset and resurfaced with the Reggae Sting logo. The result of Philips' association with the team was 'Ten Miles', recording as Echo Minott. He performed in the 'sing-jay' style that was immensely popular in the early 80s. In 1982 he recorded 'Emilio Bimbo' with Prince Hammer, who took control of Minott's career on his own Berris label. Minott's popularity grew when he performed 'What The Hell The Police Can Do', a reference to the security forces' reluctance to become involved in domestic disputes. With producer Jack Scorpio he recorded 'Lazy Body', an early product of the digital age, as the rhythm was accompanied with a drum machine, considered sacrilegious by the purists. The result of the song's popularity was the release of two one-rhythm albums, *Lively Body* and *Lively Move*. At the 10th Reggae Sunsplash in Jamaica, Minott virtually stole the show at the dancehall night when he performed alongside Peter Metro, Red Dragon, Leroy Smart, Lovindeer and General Trees. Minott continued to record irregular hits through to the 90s, including 'Wherever You Go', 'Cool And Deadly', 'Jealousy Fe Done', 'When My Little Girl Is Smiling' and 'New Dimension'. In 1993 he enjoyed a dancehall success with 'Murder Weapon', which used similar vocal phrasing to Burning Spear and led to various dance remixes. In 1995 Minott had a minor hit with 'Girl Of My Complexion', which reaffirmed his enduring talent.

● ALBUMS: *What The Hell* (Sonic 1985)★★★, with Frankie Paul *Meets Frankie Paul* (Empire 1986)★★★★, *Familiar Face* (VP 1989)★★★.

MINOTT, SUGAR

b. Lincoln Minott, 25 May 1956, Kingston, Jamaica, West Indies. Minott was probably reggae music's brightest hope throughout the early 80s, but his refusal to compromise and turn his back on either his roots or his ghetto companions has marginalized his influence, and he is now a peripheral figure, as opposed to the major force that he arguably deserves to be. Minott first recorded in the mid-70s as one of the African Brothers with Tony Tuff and Derrick Howard for a variety of Kingston producers; a couple of all-time classics evolved from this period, including 'Torturing' and 'Party Night'. The African Brothers eventually arrived at Studio One, where Minott's precocious talent was immediately recognized, and he was taken on as a studio apprentice, singing whatever was required, and often providing percussion and guitar where necessary. His sweet vocals were only one facet of his talent, and his ability to write new songs to fit over existing rhythms was remarkable, the results, in many cases, eclipsing the originals. He had a few steady sellers for Studio One, but it was his debut long-player, *Live Loving*, that made his name and extended his popularity. He became a bigger star in the UK than in his homeland, and his first release in Britain, the self-produced 'Hard Time Pressure', was a major underground hit in 1979. He travelled to England later that year, and stayed for a lengthy period, contributing immeasurably to the indigenous reggae scene. He became a focus for UK reggae, while releasing many records in the accepted local lovers rock style, which demonstrated his ability to work successfully in any style of reggae music. A national chart hit, for Hawkeye Records, followed in 1980, and crossover success seemed to be the obvious next step for Minott.

He had previously parted company with Studio One because of his desire for independence, and set up his own Youth Promotion/Black Roots collective organization to foster and develop the abundant talent in the Kingston ghettos. Consequently, when he was offered contracts for recording and concert work with established companies, Minott refused to sign unless the rest of the Youth Promotion team were a part of the arrangement. This proved too altruistic for the large labels, and Minott continued to work in his own way, recording solo outings for many independent producers to finance his ideals. Sadly, his single-minded determination to help the youths in the ghetto did not work in his favour, and many young singers and DJs who came to prominence on Minott's Youth Promotion sound system went on to greater success elsewhere, while his personal strength, too, seemed to be sapped by his constant concern for the less fortunate. His releases during the latter part of the decade were often lacklustre, relying too heavily on the stringing together of dancehall catchphrases and clichés. However, in the 90s he began to make some excellent records both for himself and other producers, including King Jammy, that at last recalled former glories.

● ALBUMS: *Live Loving* (Studio One 1978)★★★★, *Showcase* (Studio One 1979)★★★, *Black Roots* (Island 1979)★★★★, *Bittersweet* (Ballistic 1979)★★★, *Ghetto-ology* (Trojan 1979)★★★★, *Roots Lovers* (Black Roots 1980)★★★★, *Give The People* (Ballistic 1980)★★★, *African Girl* (Black Roots 1981)★★★, *Good Thing Going* (RCA 1981)★★★, *Dancehall Showcase* (Black Roots 1983)★★★★, *With Lots Of Extra* (Hitbound 1983)★★★, *Herbman Hustling* (Black Roots 1984)★★★, *Slice Of The Cake* (Heartbeat 1984)★★★, *Wicked A Go Feel It* (Wackies 1984)★★★, *Leader Of The Pack* (Striker Lee 1985)★★★, *Rydim* (Greensleeves 1985)★★★, *Time Longer Than Rope* (Greensleeves 1985)★★★, with Leroy Smart *Rockers Award Winners* (Greensleeves 1985)★★★, *Inna Reggae Dancehall* (Heartbeat 1986)★★, *Sugar And Spice* (Taxi 1986)★★, with Gregory Isaacs *Double Dose* (Blue Mountain 1987)★★★, *Them Ah Wolf* (C&F 1987)★★, *Jamming In The Streets* (Wackies 1987)★★, with the African Brothers *Collectors Item* (Uptempo 1987)★★★, *African Soldier* (Heartbeat 1988)★★, *Buy Off The Bar* (Sonic Sounds 1988)★★, *Sugar Minott And Youth Promotion* (NEC 1988)★★, *Lovers Rock Inna Dancehall* (Youth Promotion 1988)★★★, *Ghetto Youth Dem Rising* (Heartbeat 1988)★★, *Sufferer's Choice* (Heartbeat 1988)★★★, *The Boss Is Back* (RAS 1989)★★, *Smile* (L&M 1990)★★★, *A Touch Of Class* (Jammys 1991)★★★★, *Run Things* (Exterminator 1993)★★★★.

● COMPILATIONS: *Best Of Volume 1* (Black Roots 1988)★★★★, *The Artist* (L&M 1989)★★★, *20 Super Hits* (Sonic Sounds 1990)★★★, *Reggae Max* (Jetstar 1997)★★★★.

● VIDEOS: *Official Sugar Minott Dance Hall Video* (Jetstar 1988).

MISTY IN ROOTS

Misty In Roots are one of Britain's foremost roots reggae groups, fronted by brothers Walford (lead vocals) and Delvin Tyson (rhythm guitar, vocals), with other regular members including Delbert McKay (guitar, vocals), Chesley Samson (lead guitar), Tony Henry (bass) and Dennis Augustine (rhythm guitar), who took over Delvin's role on the instrument when he elected to concentrate on vocal duties. Samson was replaced by Lorrance Crossfield in 1983, though this represented the most serious of numerous line-up revisions. Through eight John Peel Radio 1 sessions (he numbered them among his favourite groups for several years in the early 80s) they exhibited radically different line-ups for each, happily adding and subtracting musicians and vocalists as the occasion demanded.

The band originated in Southall, Middlesex, where they formed in 1974, backing Jamaican singer Nicky Thomas on his British tour a year later. From early on, their commercial brand of reggae attracted supporters, but they relinquished the opportunity of signing to a major in order to set up their own People Unite label. On successive releases they honed a crafted, pleasing sound that would later see them become the first band in the reggae idiom invited to play in Russia. They were also heavily involved in the Rock Against Racism movement, playing alongside punk bands such as 999 and the Ruts. The fact that their staunch Rastafarian views were aired regularly on Radio 1 via Peel served to strengthen links between the two musical camps. Their Rasta beliefs were reinforced in the 80s by playing shows in their spiritual homeland of Africa.

In 1987 the band toured West Africa, but the euphoria was marred when Delvyn Tyson drowned in a swinning accident. Alongside Steel Pulse and Aswad, Misty In Roots rank as the most important UK reggae band of their generation.

● ALBUMS: *Live At The Counter-Eurovision* (People Unite 1979)★★, *Wise And Foolish* (People Unite 1981)★★★★, *Earth* (People

Unite 1983)★★★★, *Musi O Tunya* (People Unite 1985)★★★, *Forward* (Kaz 1989)★★★.

MITTOO, JACKIE

b. 1948, Kingston, Jamaica, West Indies, d. 1990. The self-effacing Mittoo was probably reggae's premier keyboard player, and had as much influence on the direction of reggae in the 60s and 70s as any single musician. He was taught to play the piano by his grandmother, first performing in public before he was 10 years old. After playing with local Kingston bands the Rivals and the Sheiks, Mittoo came to the attention of Coxsone Dodd at Studio One. At 15 Mittoo was playing piano and organ in the Skatalites, thereafter performing scouting and arranging duties for Dodd's labels. His own 'Got My Bugaloo' (1966), a rare vocal outing, was one of the best records of the ska era and presaged the arrival of rocksteady, and his work with the Soul Brothers, and later, Soul Vendors bands, helped to keep Studio One ahead of rival production houses. His playing behind the Heptones, Cables, Wailers and innumerable solo acts helped to create the sound of reggae for years; later artists and studios, such as Augustus Pablo, Channel One, and virtually the entire dancehall movement of the early 80s, based their rhythm arrangements on material that Mittoo had pioneered in the 60s. Dodd also issued solo albums by Mittoo from 1967 onwards, and they (*Now* and *Macka Fat*, particularly) rank among the most artistically pleasing organ instrumental albums outside of Booker T and jazz maestros such as Jimmy Smith.

In the mid-70s Mittoo left Dodd to work in Canada, where he set up the moderately successful Stine-Jac label, which produced music in a similar vein to Studio One's output, and he cut several albums for producer Bunny Lee in both Jamaica and London. He also worked extensively on some fine sessions for Sugar Minott's Youth Promotion outlet, still displaying the same taste and rhythmic acumen that had always been his trademark. He was deeply respected as an elder statesman among Minott's young reggae hopefuls.

Mittoo died in 1990, an event that brought about a long-overdue reassessment of his work among the reggae cognoscenti. Undoubtedly, had he been an American musician, his name would be mentioned in the same breath as the greats of black music.

● ALBUMS: with the Soul Vendors *On Tour* (Studio One 1966)★★★, *Evening Time* (1967)★★★, *In London* (Coxsone 1967)★★★, *Keep On Dancing* (1969)★★★, *Now* (Studio One 1969)★★★★, *Macka Fat* (Studio One 1970)★★★★, *Hot Blood* (1977)★★★, *Cold Blood* (1978)★★★, *Keyboard King* (1978)★★★, *Showcase* (Studio One 1983)★★★.
● COMPILATIONS: *The Original Jackie Mittoo* (Third World 1979)★★★★, *Tribute To Jackie Mittoo* (Heartbeat 1995)★★★★.

MODIBO, ASKIA

b. *c.*1968, Ke-Macina, Mali. In his formative years, Modibo sang ancestral Bambara songs accompanied on the flute while he travelled with his nomadic family. Following his schooling and a stint in the army, he pursued a career in music. He became known as Modibo Kone, recording in the traditional Wassoulou sound as part of Le Super Tentemba. They cut *Wass Manding L'An 2000*, which elicited a positive response from critics and punters alike. When exposed to music from the West, including that of Bob Marley, Peter Tosh and Bunny Livingstone, he found reggae to be inspirational. Many African performers have turned to reggae, notably Lucky Dube and Alpha Blondy, and Modibo was no exception. He moved to the Ivory Coast where he found work with Alpha Blondy and in 1988 formed his own group.

In 1988 Modibo released his own tape, *Allah Akbar*. Its success led to a tour of West Africa and further tapes in his African reggae style followed. Following a meeting with Ibrahma Sylla, Modibo took his band Tjiladeh to record in Paris. The result of these sessions was *Les Aigles*, a cassette devoted to the Malian football team who almost won the African Nations Cup in 1994. By 1996 the UK-based World Music specialist Stern's Records released a compilation of his earlier cassettes, including 'Les Aigles Du Mali' and, in the style of Buju Banton's 'Untold Stories', the haunting 'Devaluation'.
● COMPILATIONS: *Wass Reggae* (Stern's 1996)★★★.

MONYAKA

This six-piece, Jamaican-born reggae act, based in Brooklyn, New York, USA, was led by guitarist/vocalist Errol Moore. At the time of their hit in 1983 other group members included Beres Barnet (guitar, vocals), Paul Henton (bass, vocals), Richard Bertram (drums, percussion), William Brown and John Allen (keyboards). Formed in 1974 as the Soul Supersonics, they backed visiting reggae stars and released their first single, 'Rocking Time', in 1977. They followed this with *Classical Roots*, both records being released in the USA on their Hevyaka label. Under the new name Monyaka (Swahili for 'good luck'), they recorded 'Stand Up Strong' in 1982. A year later, with just three original members left, they had a UK Top 20 hit with 'Go Deh Yaka' (patois for 'go to the top'), which cleverly fused reggae and contemporary R&B. The follow-up, 'Reggae-matic Funk', failed to sustain the interest and this unique band joined the ranks of reggae one-hit-wonders.

● ALBUMS: *Classical Roots* (Monyaka 1977)★★★.

MORGAN HERITAGE

Morgan Heritage initially consisted of Denroy Morgan's (b. c.1954, Spanish Town, Jamaica, West Indies) eight children. The line-up featured Jamaican-born drummer Denroy Junior (b. 1970) and lead guitarist Jeffrey (b. 1971). The remaining six siblings were born in New York, USA: vocalist and keyboard player Una (b. 1973), bass guitarist David (b. 1974), vocalists and keyboardists Roy (b. 1976) and Peter (b. 1977), rhythm guitarist Nakamyah (b. 1977) and percussionist Memmalatel (b. 1981). Morgan's interest in the music business began after witnessing the annual Junkanoo celebrations in 1965. His enthusiasm led to him following local artists, although the recording industry was still in its infancy. At 19 years of age, Denroy emigrated to the USA, where he formed the Mad Creators, performing US chart hits on the live circuit. By the early 70s Denroy had written his debut recording, 'Cheating', which inspired him to pursue a new direction with a new band, the Black Eagles. The group followed the session with 'I Come From Jamaica', which led to a recording contract with CBS Records. In 1977 a change of line-up ensued, and the group reappeared winning a talent show at the New York Reggae Festival. The group continued performing through to the 80s, releasing local hits including 'I'll Do Anything For You', 'Reggae' and 'Last Change'. The Morgan family were based in Brooklyn, New York, although the children were educated in Springfield, Massachusetts, returning home at weekends to practise in their father's studio. In 1992 Denroy introduced his family band Morgan Heritage on the international night at the Jamaican Reggae Sunsplash Festival, where they caused a sensation. The family group had spent time supporting Sister Carol and Judy Mowatt, appearing at prestigious venues including the Apollo Theatre, the Lincoln Centre and Brooklyn Academy Of Music, but the media hype surrounding this performance resulted in the band securing a major label contract. Recording sessions were greeted with indifference, however, in spite of the collection featuring guest performances from Nona Hendryx, and Donald Kinsey alongside Sly And Robbie performing 'Love Police', 'Mother Africa' and the title track. The band attracted increased interest with a series of popular singles including 'Rasta Know Seh', 'Chant We A Chant' and 'Return Of Jah Son'. The group has since performed at Reggae Sunsplash in 1995/6, Reggae Sumfest and Tony Rebel's acclaimed Solution event. By early 1997 the group's line-up had reduced to five, but success continued when they released further hit singles, including the King Jammy-produced collaboration with Lady Saw, 'Ladies', and 'Gimme A License', while Bobby Digital released 'Let's Make Up', 'Mama And Papa', 'Set Yourself Free' and 'People Are Fighting'. In 1997 the group embarked on a tour of Africa and Europe, securing a hit in the UK reggae chart with 'Pray For Love'.

● ALBUMS: *Miracle* (MCA 1994)★★, *Protect Us Jah* (VP 1997)★★★, *One Calling* (Greensleeves 1997)★★★★.

MORGAN, DERRICK

b. March 1940, Stewarton, Jamaica, West Indies. Morgan's recording career stretches back to the birth of the Jamaican record industry, c.1959-60. An imposing figure, invariably topped with an almost brimless pork-pie hat, his cool, hip and rhythmic voice, enlivened by the occasional excited yelp, was successfully applied to a variety of styles in those formative years, such as the Latin beat of 'Fat Man' (1960), the gospel fervour of 'I Pray For You' (1961) and the shuffling R&B of his Jamaican Independence anthem, 'Forward March' (1962). He duetted with female singer Patsy on a series of Shirley And Lee-styled numbers, that duo being popular at the time in Jamaica, before settling into a ska style with 'Shake A Leg' (1962) and other recordings for Prince Buster. His split from Buster to join the Chinese-owned Beverley's Records led to an entertaining and successful exchange of insults on singles such as Morgan's 'Blazing Fire' and Buster's unequivocal 'Blackhead China Man' (Buster resented the idea of the Jamaican music industry being controlled by non-blacks). Morgan recorded prolifically throughout the 60s and into the 70s, recording rocksteady cuts such as 'Greedy Gal' (1967). He quickly became a very popular figure with reggae's UK skinhead followers. Around this time, his sight, always impaired, deteriorated to the extent where he could see only 'light and clouds', and he is now musically less active, though as recently as 1990 he travelled to London for a ska revival concert.

● ALBUMS: *Forward March* (Island 1963)★★★, *Seven Letters* (1969)★★★, *Moon Hop* (1970)★★★, *In The Mood* (Magnet 1974), *Development* (1975)★★★, *People Decision* (Third World 1977)★★★.

● COMPILATIONS: *Blazing Fire Volumes 1 & 2* (1988)★★★★, *I Am The Ruler* (Trojan 1993)★★★, *Ska Man Classics* (Heartbeat 1995)★★★.

MORRISON, NEVILLE

b. *c.*1965, Manchester, England. Although born in the UK, Morrison spent his formative years in Jamaica. His route to stardom included several successful appearances on local talent shows in Kingston and singing over dub plates on sound systems. By 1986 he was encouraged by dancehall singer Half Pint to go for an audition with George Phang, who had produced the singer's classic 'Greetings'. Having convinced the producer of his abilities, Morrison recorded his debut, 'Lovers Feeling'. By 1988 Morrison had returned to the UK where his cousin Dennis Rowe asked him to sing on the legendary Saxon sound system, and produced his UK debut, 'Got

To Make A Change'. By the early 90s he had a string of hits for a number of producers, including 'Best Of Me', 'Wanna Make Love', 'Phone Me', 'You're Gonna Leave' and his number 1 hit 'Crying Over You'. In 1995 Morrison accepted the role of Mango in Devon Morgan's musical play, *Johnny Dollar*. The show featured a number of top UK performers including Sylvia Tella, Peter Hunningale and Tippa Irie. He returned to the recording scene with the Christmas 1995 release of his biggest-selling single to date, 'True Friends', which reached the top of the reggae chart in the spring of 1996. A year later he repeated his chart success with 'This Game Called Love', enhanced by an infectious loop including the horn riff from Delroy Wilson's 'Dancing Mood'.

● ALBUMS: *True Friends* (Fashion 1996)★★★.

MORWELLS

Formed in 1973, in Kingston, Jamaica, this group featured Maurice 'Blacka' Wellington (vocals, percussion) and Eric 'Bingi Bunny' Lamont (b. *c.*1956, Kingston, Jamaica, West Indies, d. January 1994; vocals, guitar). Prior to forming the group (the group's name is a contraction of Maurice Wellington), Wellington had been a record salesman, and Lamont had recorded with Bongo Herman for Derrick Harriott. In 1974 they released 'Mafia Boss' and 'You Got To Be Holy' on their own Morwell Esquire label, and followed these with their debut, *Presenting The Morwells*. A dub version of the album, *Dub Me*, was also released, and proved even more popular than the vocal album. In 1976 Wellington became an engineer and producer for Joe Gibbs, and Lamont became the rhythm guitarist with the Revolutionaries, Channel One's house band. This gave them considerable access to the island's top musicians and studios, and in this period they reached peak form. Singles on Morwell Esquire included 'Proverb' (1976) and 'Crab In A Bag' (1977), and eight tracks from their first album plus four singles were released in the UK as *Crab Race*. Bassist Errol 'Flabba' Holt joined the group on a permanent basis, and further singles in 1977 included ''77 Festival' for Joe Gibbs, 'Mix-up' for Winston 'Niney' Holness and 'Africa We Want To Go' for Tony Robinson. Excellent albums followed with *Cool Runnings, Kingston 12 Toughie* and *The Best Of The Morwells*. The group then broke up, with Wellington continuing with the Morwell label, and Eric Lamont and Errol Holt forming the Roots Radics.

● ALBUMS: *Presenting The Morwells* (Morwells 1975)★★★, *Dub Me* (1975)★★★★, *Crab Race* (Burning Sounds 1978)★★★, *Cool Runnings* (Bushays 1979)★★★★, *Kingston 12 Toughies* (Carib Gems 1980)★★★.

● COMPILATIONS: *The Best Of The Morwells* (Night Hawk 1981)★★★★.

MOSES, PABLO

b. Pablo Henry, c.1953, Jamaica, West Indies. In 1975 Moses made his debut recording, 'I Man A Grasshopper'. It was immediately evident that an extraordinary talent was at work, an impression that was sustained by the release of 'We Should Be In Angola' (1976), produced by Clive Hunt. His first album, *Revolutionary Dream*, was released in 1977, and it still stands as a genuine mid-70s reggae classic. Moses's detached delivery of his parable-like songs coalesced with Geoffrey Chung's brilliant production and arrangements to form a truly remarkable whole. Two further excellent albums under Chung's supervision followed, *A Song* and *Pave The Way*. Moses then decided to produce himself, but was unable to sustain the quality of his previous releases. Since the early 80s, he has toured extensively, and gained a strong reputation internationally as a live performer.

● ALBUMS: *Revolutionary Dream* (Tropical Sound Track 1977)★★★★, *A Song* (Island 1980)★★★, *Pave The Way* (Mango/Island 1981)★★★, *In The Future* (Alligator/Mercury 1983)★★, *Tension* (Alligator/Mercury 1985)★★, *Live To Love* (Rohit 1985)★★, *We Refuse* (Profile 1990)★★, *Charlie* (Profile 1990)★★, *The Confessions Of A Rastaman* (Musidisc 1993)★★.

MOWATT, JUDY

b. c.1952, Kingston, Jamaica, West Indies. In her teens Mowatt joined a dance troupe that toured the Caribbean. There she met up with Beryl Lawson and Merle Clemonson, with whom she formed the Gaylettes (aka the Gaytones). Together they backed many artists on releases for the Federal label in the mid-60s, until Mowatt's two companions left for America in 1970. Deciding to persevere with a solo career,

she recorded widely in both soul and reggae styles, under a variety of names due to contractual complications. The most notable of these releases was 'I Shall Sing', the first of a string of reggae chart successes. Subsequently, Mowatt joined the Twelve Tribes Of Israel organization, aligning herself with fellow Jamaican musicians such as Dennis Brown and Freddie McGregor. She formed her own label, Ashandan, and in the early 70s joined Marcia Griffiths on stage, alongside Rita Marley. Eventually, the trio was cemented as the I-Threes, Bob Marley having been suitably impressed by their performance. While working with Marley, she continued her solo career, and also managed to find time to raise a family. She also had the honour of being the first to record at Bob Marley's Tuff Gong studio in Kingston, sessions that produced *Black Woman*. It was the first time that a female artist had produced her own album in Jamaica. Not only was it an outstanding work in its own right, but it offered an articulate voice for Jamaican women, who had previously been either under- or mis-represented in the reggae idiom. Largely self-penned (with notable contributions from Bob Marley and Freddie McGregor), it proved a landmark work, showcasing her sweet and plaintive voice.

She has continued to forge a solo career and rivals her old sparring partner Griffiths for the title of Jamaica's first woman of reggae. However, attempts to cross over have been less successful, notably *Love Is Overdue*, which included takes on 'Try A Little Tenderness' and UB40's 'Sing Our Own Song'. The album did bring her a Grammy nomination, however, the first occasion on which a female reggae artist had been honoured in this way.

● ALBUMS: *Mellow Mood* (Ashandan 1975)★★★, *Black Woman* (Tuff Gong/Shanachie 1979)★★★★, *Only A Woman* (Shanachie 1982)★★★, *Mr D.J.* (Ashandan 1982)★★★, *Working Wonders* (Shanachie 1985)★★★, *Love Is Overdue* (Greensleeves 1986)★★.

MUDIE, HARRY

b. c.1940, Spanish Town, Jamaica, West Indies. One of the unsung pioneers of Jamaican recording, Mudie first developed his interest in music while a pupil at St. Jago High School during the mid-50s. His debut with the legendary Rasta drummer Count Ossie and saxophonist Wilton Gaynair, entitled 'Babylon Gone', aka 'Going Home', backed with 'So Long' by Winston And Roy, was released in the UK on the Blue Beat label in 1962. In the same year, he opened the Scaramouch Garden Amusement Center in Spanish Town. Little seems to have emerged, however, between 1962 and 1970, when Trojan Records began releasing his productions on the specially formed Moodisc label. A year later, Rita and Benny King's R&B Discs Ltd created their own Moodisc label. Using a studio band led by pianist Gladstone Anderson, Mudie deftly combined sweet, tuneful melodies with heavy rhythms. The records issued on these and his Jamaican labels, including organist Winston Wright's 'Musically Red', Winston Shand's 'Time Is The Master', the Eternal's 'Push Me In The Corner', the Ebony Sisters' 'Let Me Tell You Boy', John Holt's 'It May Sound Silly', Dennis Walks' 'The Drifter' and 'Heart Don't Leap', Count Ossie's 'Whispering Drums', Lloyd Jones' 'Rome' and trumpeter Jo Jo Bennett's instrumental version, 'Leaving Rome', established Mudie's name among the very best of the reggae producers of the day. He launched DJ I. Roy on record with 'Musical Pleasure' and a version of 'The Drifter'. He was probably the first to use strings in the music, notably on John Holt's classic love song album, 1973's *Time Is The Master*, and it is arguably this fact that seems to have prejudiced his standing among some of the more reactionary elements of the reggae audience.

In 1973 he enjoyed a big reggae hit with Dennis Walks' calypso-flavoured 'Margaret', released on the Cactus label in the UK, following it with vibist Lennie Hibbert's version, 'Margaret's Dream'. He also produced the Heptones on the classic 'Love Without Feeling', DJ tunes by Count Sticky, Big Joe ('Set Your Face At Ease' on the 'Rome' rhythm), and Jah Lloyd, and a number of 'Drifter' cuts by Bongo Herman and others. During the mid-70s Mudie issued three classic dub albums mixed by King Tubby, instrumental sets by Gladstone Anderson and Ossie Scott, vocal albums by Dennis Walks and Bunny Maloney, for whom he produced 'Baby I've Been Missing You', and two excellent various artists collections. During the 80s and 90s he concentrated on his back catalogue with re-presses and some excellent new compilations such as *Reggae History Volume One* and *Reggae Bible*, the latter being a whole album based on the 'Drifter' rhythm. This prolific period produced over 100 singles and several 12-inch 'discomix' singles as the decade closed. Mudie recorded a variety of other artists, including Gregory Isaacs, Freddie McKay, Joe White, Cornell Campbell, Jah Walton (now known as Joseph Cotton), and Prince Heron. During the 80s he kept a low profile, moving to Miami, Florida, issuing his back catalogue and an album by Bunny Maloney.

● ALBUMS: with King Tubby *Harry Mudie Meets King Tubby In Dub Conference Volumes 1, 2 & 3* (Moodisc 1975/76/77)★★★, Harry Mudie And Friends *Let Me Tell You Boy 1970-71* (Trojan 1988)★★★, various *Quad Star Revolution Volume 1* (1974)★★★, *Quad Star Revolution Volume 2* (1976)★★★, *Reggae History Volume 1* (Moods 1985)★★★.

MUNDELL, HUGH

b. 14 June 1962, Kingston, Jamaica, West Indies, d. 1983. Hugh Mundell made his first recording for producer Joe Gibbs, the unreleased 'Where Is Natty Dread', while barely in his teens. After this false start, his career really began when his precocious talent impressed session player/producer Augustus Pablo. Pablo enlisted his services as a DJ alongside Jah Bull on his Rockers sound system, and produced his first single release, 'Africa Must Be Free', in 1975. Several more singles were released over the next two years, including 'My Mind', 'Don't Stay Away Too Long', 'Let's All Unite' and 'Book Of Life', before the classic *Africa Must Be Free By 1983*, which was released in 1978, swiftly establishing Mundell's name as a bright new roots star in the ascendant. Pablo further recorded Mundell on such sides as 'That Little Short Man', 'Feeling Alright', 'Jah Says The Time Has Come', 'One Jah One Aim And Destiny' and 'Great Tribulation'. Sundry other recordings were undertaken in his DJ mode as Jah Levi, surfacing mainly on 12-inch releases. In 1979 Mundell tried his hand at self-production on 'Stop Them Jah' and 'Blackman's Foundation', as well as producing the teenage 'Little' Junior Reid on his debut, 'Speak The Truth', which emerged on Pablo's Rockers label in Jamaica.

Another excellent song, 'Rastafari's Call' appeared on Mundell's own Muni Music label, while 'Can't Pop No Style' surfaced in 1981 on Greensleeves, coupled with Junior Reid's 'Know Myself'. The same year, Mundell issued a co-produced album with Pablo entitled *Time And Place*, containing many of tracks previously released as singles, after which he broke with Pablo altogether, going on to record 'Jah Fire Will Be Burning' for Prince Jammy and *Mundell* for Henry 'Junjo' Lawes. Ironically, it was in 1983, the year he prophesied for Africa's emancipation on his first record, that Mundell was shot and killed after an argument over a fridge.
● ALBUMS: *Africa Must Be Free By 1983* (Message 1978)★★★★, *Time & Place* (Ja Mun Rock 1981)★★★, *Mundell* (Greensleeves 1982)★★★, *Black Man Foundation* (Shanachie 1985)★★★, *Arise* (Atra 1987)★★★.

MURVIN, JUNIOR

b. *c*.1949, Port Antonio, Jamaica, West Indies. Murvin first recorded for producers Sonia Pottinger and Derrick Harriott in the early 70s as Junior Soul (not to be confused with the New York-based reggae singer of the same name). 'Solomon', a traditional Jamaican air, sold fairly well in 1972, but shortly afterwards, Murvin vanished from the public eye. In 1976 he appeared, guitar in hand, at Lee Perry's Black Ark studio in Kingston, with a song on which he had been working for some time. No-one was aware that this singer, now calling himself Junior Murvin, had ever recorded before, but Perry liked what he heard, and within weeks, 'Police And Thieves' was the biggest-selling Jamaican record of the year. Its popularity crossed the Atlantic to the UK and, released on Island Records, it became the anthem for that year's violence-troubled Notting Hill Carnival. Perry recorded another couple of versions of the rhythm before issuing a strong album of the same title in 1977. The single was finally a UK chart hit in 1978. Murvin's Curtis Mayfield-styled falsetto (he covered Mayfield's 'People Get Ready' and 'Closer Together') worked well with Perry's silky, complex arrangements, but the pair never put together another album; Perry was on the verge of a nervous breakdown and subsequently demolished his studio. Murvin moved on to work with Joe Gibbs,

Mikey Dread, Henry 'Junjo' Lawes and Prince Jammy, but he has never managed to recapture the spirit of 'Police And Thieves'. Murvin's influence spilled over into rock, however, with the song's right-on, rude-boy image suiting the Clash's first album.
● ALBUMS: *Police And Thieves* (Island 1977)★★★★, *Bad Man Posse* (Dread At The Controls 1982)★★★, *Muggers In The Street* (Greensleeves 1984)★★★★, *Apartheid* (1986)★★★, *Signs And Wonders* (Live & Love 1989)★★★.

MUSICAL YOUTH

Formed at Duddeston Manor School, Birmingham, England, this pop/reggae-influenced group featured two sets of brothers, Kelvin and Michael Grant and Junior and Patrick Waite (b. *c*.1969, d. 18 February 1993). The latter pair's father, Frederick Waite, was a former member of Jamaican group the Techniques, and sang lead with Junior at the start of the group's career in the late 70s. Although schoolboys, the group managed to secure gigs at certain Birmingham pubs and released a single, 'Political'/'Generals', on local label 021 Records. An appearance on BBC disc jockey John Peel's evening show brought further attention to the group and they were signed to MCA Records. By that time, founding father Frederick Waite had backed down to be replaced by Dennis Seaton as lead singer. During the winter of 1982, the group issued one of the fastest-selling singles of the year in 'Pass The Dutchie'. Based on the Mighty Diamonds' 'Pass The Kouchie' (a song about marijuana), the title had been subtly altered to feature the patois 'dutchie' (literally a 'cooking pot'). The infectious enthusiasm of the group's performance captured the public's imagination and propelled the record to number 1 in the UK charts. A US Top 10 hit also followed. The catchy follow-up, 'Youth Of Today', also reached the UK Top 20 and early in 1983 'Never Gonna Give You Up' climbed to number 6. Minor successes with 'Heartbreaker' and 'Tell Me Why' were succeeded by a surprise collaboration with Donna Summer on the UK Top 20 hit 'Unconditional Love'. A revival of Desmond Dekker's '007' saw them back in the Top 30, but after one final hit with 'Sixteen', they fell from commercial grace and subsequently split up in 1985 when Seaton left the band. Plans to re-form were scotched when Patrick Waite, who had gone on to a career of juvenile crime, died of natural causes while awaiting a court appearance on drug charges. The Grant brothers remain involved in music, while Seaton released a solo set and formed his own band, XMY.

● ALBUMS: *The Youth Of Today* (MCA 1982)★★★, *Different Style* (MCA 1983)★★. Solo: Dennis Seaton *Imagine That* (Bellaphon 1989)★★.

● FURTHER READING: *Musical Youth: Their Own Story*, no editor listed.

MUTABARUKA

b. Allan Hope, Jamaica, West Indies. Hope is a dub poet who combines social commentary with scathing personal analysis and endearing humour. Having published several volumes of poetry and having written for *Swing* magazine, Mutabaruka (his stage name is a Rwandan term for 'one who is always victorious') reserves his performances for his most effective tirades against hypocrisy, injustice, or more particularly, stupidity. His favoured means of denouncing his enemies rests strongly with the latter, vilifying them and the contradictions of their positions by means of a languid, inviting slur. His debut album for Earl 'Chinna' Smith's High Times label was a genre classic. Muta tore through a set that railed against oppression on all fronts, aided and abetted by Smith's imaginative rhythms and arrangements. 'Everytime A Ear De Soun', from the album, was also a hit as a single. In the interim he has ensured his position as Jamaica's most popular radical poet, with a series of inspiring albums. Despite such militancy, he retains his day job - running a health food store in Jamaica and broadcasting on Jamaica's Irie FM radio station The Cutting Edge. He also appeared in the film *Sankofa*.

● ALBUMS: *Check It* (High Times 1982)★★★★, *The Mystery Unfolds* (Shanachie 1986)★★★, *Out Cry* (Shanachie 1987)★★★, *Any Which Way* (Greensleeves 1989)★★★, *Blakk Wi Black ... Kkk* (Shanachie 1991)★★★.

● COMPILATIONS: *The Ultimate Collection* (Shanachie 1996)★★★★.

● VIDEOS: *Live At Reggae Sumfest* (Shanachie 1996).

MYSTIC REVEALERS

The Mystic Revealers performed for most of their career on the fringe of the Jamaican music industry, in and around the Bull Bay area. Led by the enigmatic Billy Mystic (b. Anthony Wilmott), and featuring Nicky Henry (drums), Chris Burth (percussion), Leroy Edwards (bass), Paul Smith (keyboards) and Dexton Davis (guitar), the band initially released *Young Revolutionaries*, which was met with critical acclaim but failed to attract Jamaican reggae fans. The group's righteous stance established a significant US following, which led to an association with the Washington-based entrepreneur Dr. Dread. In 1995 the band appeared alongside Robert Ffrench who was promoting his compilation *With Heavy D And Friends*, following an exhaustive European tour. Live performances brought the band further praise, and their promotional videos featured cameos from leading Jamaican entertainers, including Carl Bradshaw and Judy Mowatt. The ensemble released a number of singles, notably 'Religion', 'Space And Time', 'Remember Romeo' and the celebratory, 60s-styled 'I Believe In Love'. Many of the singles featured on the band's third and final album with Dr. Dread, which also included the classic 'Righteous Man'. The Mystic Revealers maintained their profile through to the mid-90s, continuing with their brand of conscientious lyricism. The band subsequently changed label and released a successful single, 'I'm Gonna Tell You', with Anthony B. In addition to his recording commitments, Wilmott concurrently pursued an acting career playing CC, the lead singer of a band, in the Jamaican soap opera *Royal Palms Estate*. The Mystic Revealers also featured in the series when they performed 'There's Got To Be A Better Way', appearing as CC's backing band.

● ALBUMS: *Young Revolutionaries* (Ras 1994)★★★, *Jah Works* (Ras 1995)★★★, *Space And Time* (Ras 1996)★★★, *Space And Dub* (Ras 1996)★★★.

● COMPILATIONS: *Portrait* (Ras 1997)★★, with Anthony B. *This One's For Jah* (Mesa 1997)★★★★.

NAPTALI, RAYMOND

b. Raymond McCook, 1961, Jamaica, West Indies. Naptali spent his formative years in Jamaica, where he witnessed the phenomenal rise of Dennis Al Capone, Big Youth, I. Roy and U-Roy. By the early 70s, he and his family had settled in the UK, where, inspired by the sound systems, he gradually built up his reputation as a DJ with Fatman Hi Fi. In 1980 the duo of Raymond And Roy recorded the classic 'Late Night Blues' with the Instigators, and Naptali embarked on a prolific recording career, including Anthony 'Sir George' Brightly's production of 'Dirty Rat' and 'ABC', and with Clive Stanhope, the popular 'Mr Talkative' and 'Automatic Boom'. Fatman produced the reggae Top 10 hit 'Love Trap/No Chat To Credel', which also featured backing by the Instigators, with vocals from Cornell Campbell. Although his recorded output tapered off, he made a dramatic reappearance in 1996 when he performed at the Bunny Wailer Unity Showcase, alongside Chaka Demus And Pliers, Spanner Banner and Prince Lincoln. In 1997 Naptali continued to appear with the renowned Fatman, performing at London's illustrious Dub Club as Fatman And Sons At The Controls With Raymond Naptali.
● ALBUMS: *Trouble Posse* (CSA 1982)★★, with Roy Ranking *Late Night Session* (KG 1982)★★★.

NASH, JOHNNY

b. 9 August 1940, Houston, Texas, USA. The story of Nash's association with Bob Marley has been well documented. His background is similar to that of many Jamaican performers in that he first started singing in a church choir. By his early teens he performed cover versions of popular R&B hits of the 50s on a television show called *Matinee*. He enjoyed his first US chart entry in 1957 with a cover version of Doris Day's 'A Very Special Love'. ABC Records decided to market the young singer as another Johnny

Mathis, which did little to enhance his career. Disillusioned with the label, he concentrated on a career in films. In 1958 he starred in *Take A Giant Step*, and in 1960 he appeared alongside Dennis Hopper in *Key Witness*, which was critically acclaimed in Europe. Returning to the recording studio he persevered with middle-of-the-road material but was unable to generate a hit. A number of label and style changes did not improve his chart potential. By 1965 he finally achieved a Top 5 hit in the R&B chart with the ballad 'Lets Move And Groove Together'. He was unable to maintain the winning formula, but in 1967 his R&B hit was enjoying chart success in Jamaica. The good fortunes in Jamaica led Nash to the island to promote his hit. It was here that he was exposed to ska and arranged a return visit to the island to record at Federal Studios. Accompanied by Byron Lee And The Dragonaires, the sessions resulted in 'Cupid', 'Hold Me Tight' and 'You Got Soul'. When he released 'Hold Me Tight', the song became an international hit, achieving Top 5 success in the UK as well as a return to the Jamaican chart. He formed a partnership with Danny Simms, and a label, JAD (Johnny and Danny), releasing recordings by Bob Marley, Byron Lee, Lloyd Price and Kim Weston as well as his own material until the label folded in the early 70s. He returned to recording in Jamaica at Harry J.'s studio where he met Marley, who wrote 'Stir It Up', which revived Nash's career by peaking at number 13 on the UK chart in June 1972. He continued to enjoy popularity with 'I Can See Clearly Now', a UK Top 5 hit that was successfully covered by Jimmy Cliff in 1994 for the film *Cool Runnings*. Other hits followed, including 'Ooh What A Feeling' and 'There Are More Questions Than Answers', but the further he drifted from reggae, the less successful the single. He covered other Bob Marley compositions, including 'Nice Time' and 'Guava Jelly', but they were not picked up for single release, although the latter was on the b-side to 'There Are More Questions Than Answers'. His career subsequently took another downward turn but was revived yet again when he returned to Jamaica to record an Ernie Smith composition, 'Tears On My Pillow', which reached number 1 in the UK Top 10 in June 1975. He also reached the UK chart with 'Let's Be Friends' and '(What)

A Wonderful World' before choosing to devote more energy to films and his West Indian recording complex.

● ALBUMS: *A Teenager Sings The Blues* (ABC 1957)★★★, *I Got Rhythm* (ABC 1959)★★★, *Hold Me Tight* (JAD 1968)★★★, *Let's Go Dancing* (Columbia 1969)★★★, *I Can See Clearly Now* (Columbia 1972)★★★, *My Merry Go Round* (Columbia 1973)★★, *Celebrate Life* (Columbia 1974)★★★, *Tears On My Pillow* (Columbia 1975)★★★, *What A Wonderful World* (Columbia 1977)★★, *Johnny Nash Album* (Columbia 1980)★★★, *Stir It Up* (Hallmark 1981)★★, *Here Again* (London 1986)★★.

● COMPILATIONS: *Greatest Hits* (Columbia 1975)★★★, *The Johnny Nash Collection* (Epic 1977)★★★, *The Best Of* (Columbia 1996)★★★.

NICODEMUS

b. Cecil Willington, 1957, Jamaica, West Indies, d. 1996. Nicodemus came to notoriety as a DJ in the late 70s/early 80s performing on the Socialist Roots sound system alongside selector Danny Dread. In 1978 King Jammy (then Prince Jammy) gave his name to the Tapetown sound, which flourished when Nicodemus joined the crew. He delivered his chantings in a style similar to Prince Far I and Prince Jazzbo. He recorded a number of hits, including memorable work with the Roots Radics and notable sessions at Channel One Studio. In 1980 Nicodemus released a combination tune with Ranking Trevor, 'Jamaican Rockers Hop', announcing his arrival. He enjoyed a string of hits in 1981, including the adjoining hits 'Gunman Connection' and 'Bone Connection'. The *DJ Clash*, with Ranking Toyan, which was issued with a voting card, featured the exceptional 'Hail Nico Dread', 'Bubble Nicodemus Bubble' and 'Tubby's Daddy'. Nicodemus was the featured DJ on Bingi Bunny's 'Him A Natty Dread', which introduced his idiosyncratic style to a wider audience. His reputation was further enhanced by the equally popular combination hits with Linval Thompson ('Holding On To My Girlfriend') and Leroy Sibbles ('Rock Steady Party'), while his solo 'Natty Sell A Million' was credited to the Top Ranking Deejay Nicadeamus (sic). Nicodemus's popularity inspired the up-and-coming John Taylor, who called himself Nicodemus Junior as a mark of respect to the DJ

responsible for motivating his career. Taylor's fortune changed when he changed his stage name to Chaka Demus and joined with Pliers. Sporadic hits continued through to the late 80s when Nicodemus linked up with Early B's protégé Supercat. His career prospered and he enjoyed a revival, recording for Don Dada's Wild Apache label. His combination venture in 1988 with Supercat, 'Cabin Stabbin', resulted in an all-important US hit, generating new interest in his past repertoire. The veteran DJs recorded two successful albums with their protégés Junior Demus and Junior Cat, joining forces as the Wild Apache crew. The four DJs also featured in a promotional video for the release of 'Scalp Dem' which was considered unorthodox in opting for a Western theme. Nicodemus succumbed to complications from diabetes and died in 1996.

● ALBUMS: *Gunman Connection* (Cha Cha 1981)★★★, *Dancehall Style* (Black Joy 1982)★★★, with Ranking Toyan *DJ Clash* (Greensleeves 1983)★★★★, with Wild Apache Crew *The Good The Bad The Ugly And The Crazy* (Wild Apache 1994)★★★, with Wild Apache Crew *Cabin Stabbin'* (Wild Apache 1994)★★★, with Flabba Holt *King Tubby On The Mix Volume One* (Ernie B 1996)★★★.

NINJAMAN

b. Desmond Ballantine, Kingston, Jamaica, West Indies. Notorious from his long history of fearless controversy on record, stage show and sound system, Ninjaman's popularity in the Jamaican dancehalls has been unrivalled. He began DJing when he was 12, progressing to the Black Culture sound system and then Killimanjaro, where from 1984 onwards he was apprentice to Supercat and Early B, known as Double Ugly. When another DJ appeared with the same name, he became Uglyman, recording his debut for the Soul Carib label. That name, too, was short-lived; a second Uglyman arrived and, determined to forge an identity of his own, 'Ugly' quickly became Ninja. His first hit, 'Protection', was self-produced, and voiced alongside Courtney Melody in 1987. The following year Lloyd Dennis teamed him with Tinga Stewart for a notable string of hits including 'Cover Me' and then 'Zig It Up', duetted with Flourgon. His early producers included King Jammy, Witty, Redman and Ini Kamoze, but it was with the advent of the Gulf War in 1990 that he became transformed into the archetypal outlaw, brandishing the title of 'Original Front Tooth, Gold Tooth, Gun Pon Tooth Don Gorgon', and recording a bounty of apocalyptic 'burial' tunes interspersed with the most uncompromising 'reality' lyrics heard from any DJ of the ragga era. His sense of melodrama and stuttering verbal walkabouts were unique; he spread his fiery invective over many fine sides for Bobby Digital ('Permit To Bury', 'Fulfilment'), King Jammy ('Border Clash'/'Reality Yuh Want'), Mr. Doo ('Murder Weapon'), Gussie Clarke ('Above The Law'), Steely And Clevie ('Murder Dem') and Exterminator throughout 1991-92. Among his many targets has been Shabba Ranks, who has had to endure an incessant stream of taunts over the years. By the end of 1992, after surviving a bout of Christianity, an arrest on gun charges and a flood of imitators, his talents had become overexposed, though he remained one of the few genuinely original DJs to remain without a major record contract. Instead, he made unremarkable albums for Henry 'Junjo' Lawes and then Junior Reid, still waiting for a much-deserved wider audience.

● ALBUMS: *Super Star* (Witty 1989)★★★, with Courtney Melody *Protection* (1989)★★★, *Kill Them & Done* (Tassa 1990)★★★, *Out Pon Bail* (Exterminator 1990)★★★★, *Move From Here* (1990)★★★, *Run Come Test* (RAS 1990)★★★, with Capleton And Tony Rebel *Real Rough* (1990)★★★, with Johnny P And Japanese *Rough, Mean & Deadly - Ninja Man With Johnny P* (Pickout 1990)★★, *Reggae Sunsplash* (Pickout 1991)★★, *Warning You Now* (Jammys 1991)★★★, *Nobody's Business But My Own* (Shanachie 1991)★★, *My Weapon* (Mr Doo 1991)★★★, *Bounty Hunter* (Blue Mountain 1991)★★★★, *Target Practice* (Jammys 1992)★★★, *Original Front Tooth, Gold Tooth, Gun Pon Tooth Don Gorgon* (Greensleeves 1992)★★★★, *Sing-A-Ling-A-Ling School Pickney Sing Ting* (Greensleeves 1992)★★★, *Hardcore Killing* (Greensleeves 1993)★★★, *Booyakka! Booyakka!* (Greensleeves 1994)★★.

● VIDEOS: with Shabba Ranks *Reggae Sting Volume 1* (1992).

NITTY GRITTY

b. Glen Augustus Holness, 1957, August Town, Kingston, Jamaica, West Indies, d. 24 June 1991, Brooklyn, New York, USA. Nitty Gritty rose to prominence as computerized rhythms took hold in Jamaica, alongside Tenor Saw, King Kong and Anthony Red Rose, all of whom shared a similar vocal style. Gritty's was a deep-throated, gospel-tinged wail distinguished by improvised catch-phrases. He was born the second eldest of 11 children in a church-going family, and he trained as an electrician before founding a local group called the Soulites. In 1973 he sang 'Let The Power Fall On I' with Dennis Brown, George Nooks and the Mighty Diamonds for Joe Gibbs, but his first solo release, 'Every Man Is A Seller', did not arrive for another decade, being voiced for Sugar Minott's Youth Promotion label. After a spell on the Zodiac sound system with Danny Dread he cut several sides at Channel One, and two for Eric 'Bubbles' Howard of the African Brothers, before moving on to George Phang in 1984. By the following April he had joined forces with King Jammy and their first release together, 'Hog In A Minty', was an instant success, with its haunting vocal refrain and shuffling 'tempo' rhythm track. It was promptly followed by 'Good Morning Teacher', 'Sweet Reggae Music', 'Run Down The World' and 'Gimme Some Of Your Something', all of them sizeable hits. His debut album, *Turbo Charged*, was released in 1986 as did *Musical Confrontation*, on which credits were shared with King Kong. Soon afterwards, he moved to London and then to New York, his output becoming more varied but lacking the impact of his work with Jammys. Singles appeared on the Uptempo, Black Solidarity and Skengdon labels. He returned to form with *General Penitentiary*, recorded with the Studio One Band in 1987, which was far more like the Nitty Gritty of old. By 1989 an album for Blacker Dread had arrived with material dating back to his first visit to England in 1986, after which he became relatively inactive. At the age of 34 he was shot dead outside Super Power record shop in Brooklyn, New York.

● ALBUMS: *Turbo Charged* (Greensleeves 1986)★★★, with King Kong *Musical Confrontation* (Jammys 1986)★★★, *General Penitentiary* (Black Victory 1987)★★★★, *Nitty*

Gritty (Witty 1988)★★★, *Jah In The Family* (Blacker Dread/SCOM 1989)★★, with Tenor Saw *Powerhouse Presents* (Powerhouse 1989)★★★.

NOOKS, GEORGE
(see Prince Mohammed)

NOTES, FREDDIE, AND THE RUDIES
(see Greyhound)

NOW GENERATION
One of the great unsung bands (or session teams) in the history of Jamaican music. Led by Geoffrey Chung on keyboards, the band included Mikey Chung on lead guitar, Val Douglas on bass, Mikey 'Boo' Richards on drums, Robert Lynn on keyboards and Earl 'Wire' Lindo on organ. They worked on sessions for all the top producers in the early 70s, including Derrick Harriott, Herman Chin-Loy, Ken Khouri, Sonia Pottinger, Joe Gibbs and some of the late Duke Reid's reggae recordings. Their music was 'uptown' and soul-influenced (they covered many soul classics), but they proved that they could provide raw roots records too - Glen Brown's better work, or Herman's 'Aquarius Dub' being notable examples. Their tightness and all-round panache distinguished them from other session bands at the time, but they have never, sadly, been quite as celebrated as other less skilful outfits - perhaps due to a lack of show and stage work. They certainly deserve much wider recognition.
● ALBUMS: *For The Good Times* (Trojan 1974)★★★★.

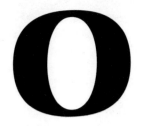

OGHOLI, EVI-EDNA
Evi-Edna Ogholi is widely recognized as the 'queen of Nigerian reggae'. Specializing in a cool, romantic style, sung in her native Isoko tongue, the sound is a little akin to UK's lovers rock idiom. Ogholi began her career in the late 80s. A contract with Polydor Nigeria produced *Happy Birthday*, but it was not successful enough for her contract to be renewed. She recovered her equilibrium, however, and within a few months had re-established her reputation throughout West Africa. A national tour of Nigeria followed, sponsored by the Pepsi soft drink company.
● ALBUMS: *Happy Birthday* (Polydor Nigeria 1989)★★.

OLIVER, FRANKIE
b. 1970, Bow, London, England. Oliver's initial introduction to reggae was through his cousin, who first played him Bob Marley's *Kaya*. Impressed by the power of the playing and song-writing, Oliver decided to pursue a career in the reggae industry, despite lacking the usual credentials, being a white East-ender of Greek/Cypriot descent; however, undeterred, he fought against these obstacles. He began performing in clubs and pubs in the East End of London and neighbouring Essex, where he was spotted by Christine Atkins of Island Records. She asked him to provide a demo, which led to requests for further examples of his work. Unfamiliar with the recording industry, Oliver had no other demo versions, although he was able to overcome this drawback through a chance meeting with Delroy Pinnock. Pinnock had been involved in the UK reggae scene for a number of years in various guises, best remembered for his 1981 S&G hit, 'I Want To Be', and became responsible for launching Oliver's recording career. The second demo arrived at Island when Sly Dunbar and Robbie Shakespeare were in the office, and having

heard the results, they invited the singer to record in Jamaica. The sessions led to his debut single, 'She Lied To Me', which faltered, although the b-side, 'What Is Life', proved acceptable within the reggae industry. His record company was determined to promote him as Britain's answer to Snow, following the hapless debut with the heavily promoted 'Give Her What She Wants'. The release demonstrated a vocal style similar to Ali Campbell of UB40, with DJ vocals provided by Bigga Ranks, but despite all the promotional efforts, his follow-up suffered the same fate. In an effort to increase his profile the label secured a billing at the Essential Festival Roots Day, the Respect Festival and as the support act for Ziggy Marley's showcase at the Forum in London.
● ALBUMS: *Looking For The Twist* (Island Jamaica 1997)★★★.

ONUORA, OKU

b. Orlando Wong, March 1952, Kingston, Jamaica, West Indies. In 1971, at the start of a 15-year prison sentence for his part in an armed robbery, Onuora began writing poetry. In true Robin Hood style, the funds from the misdemeanour were to finance projects to help the underprivileged. Not considering himself a criminal, the poems reflected his assertion that he was a political prisoner. In the mid-70s much of his work had been smuggled out against the wishes of the authorities. It was probably owing to the praise bestowed upon his writing by the Jamaican Literary Festival Commission that the Jamaican Government was compelled to grant an early release in 1977. Soon after securing freedom, his first collection of poems, *Echo*, was published in Jamaica by Sangsters and later in Europe by the Cultural Media Collective. Onuora's debut in the recording studio was at Tuff Gong where backed by the Wailers drum and bass duo, Aston 'Familyman' Barrett and Carlton Barrett, he read 'Reflection In Red' over a heavy dub sound. The poem was a sceptical chronicle of the peace truce between rival gangs led by Bucky Marshall and Claudie Massop. The single won critical acclaim but was not to make an impression in the reggae charts. He began performing his poetry around the world and incongruously appeared at the One Love Peace Concert, a commemoration of the reprieve,

alongside Jacob Miller, Culture, Leroy Smart, Big Youth, Peter Tosh and Bob Marley. His numerous awards and notoriety inevitably led to a working relationship with the first successful dub poet Linton Kwesi Johnson. In 1982 following a tour of Europe with Rico Rodriguez, he released 'I A Tell' on his own Kuya label with 'Reflection in Red' on the b-side. By the mid-80s he released his debut, *Pressure Drop*, with backing supplied by AK7 (Armageddon Knights Column 7), demonstrating his uncompromising lyrics and inventive reggae style. In the early 90s Oku began experimenting with dub, working alongside Courtney Panton who played and programmed all the instruments. Although Onuora's recorded work is sporadic he enjoys a cult following and occasional releases are snapped up by his dedicated followers.
● ALBUMS: *Pressure Drop* (Heartbeat 1986)★★★★, *New Jerusalem Dub* (ROIR 1991)★★★, *I A Tell Dubwise And Otherwise* (ROIR 1994)★★★.

OSBOURNE, JOHNNY

b. *c*.1948, Jamaica, West Indies. During 1967 Osbourne became lead vocalist of the Wildcats, and recorded for producer Winston Riley, although nothing was issued. The Wildcats' manager then financed a session at Coxsone Dodd's Studio One, from which his debut single, 'All I Have Is Love', was released. In 1969 he recorded an album, *Come Back Darling*, for Riley. It was a strong collection on which Osbourne was supported by the Sensations on harmony vocals. On the day that he completed the album, he emigrated to Toronto, Canada, to join his family. After singing with various soul and reggae groups, he became lead vocalist for Ishan People, and recorded two albums with them. The group broke up in 1979, and Osbourne decided to return to Jamaica. Shortly after returning, he recorded 'Forgive Them' and 'Jealousy, Heartache And Pain' for the Studio One label. Through late 1979 and early 1980 he recorded extensively for Dodd, with these sessions culminating in a stunning album, *Truths And Rights*. This beautifully understated set of classic songs is Osbourne's major work. In 1979 he also had a hit for King Jammy (then Prince Jammy) with 'Folly Ranking', and an excellent album of the same name followed in 1980. The success of these recordings made him one of the most in-demand vocalists on the island, and a glut of material was released, including *Fally Lover, Warrior, Innah Disco Style* and *Never Stop Fighting*, between 1980 and 1982. In 1983, he began the year with two big hits, 'Yo Yo' and 'Lend Me A Chopper', and later in the year enjoyed massive success with 'Water Pumping', an adaptation of Hopeton Lewis's 'Take It Easy', which had also served as the basis for Johnny Clarke's 1976 hit 'Rockers Time Now'. The hits continued with 'Get Cracking', 'Check For You', 'Rewind' (1984), 'Buddy Bye', 'No Sound Like We' and 'In The Area' (1985). In the late 80s he was particularly successful when recording for Bobby Digital, and had hits with 'Good Time Rock' (1988) and 'Rude Boy Skank' (1988), both of which are included on the 1989 album *Rougher Than Them*. Throughout the 80s he continued to record for Coxsone Dodd, and excellent singles included 'Keep That Light', 'Unity' and 'A We Run Things', but a long-promised second album from Dodd has not materialized. Osbourne's versatility and talent have enabled him to remain at the forefront of reggae, and no matter how thin the lyrics he has sung have been, often no more than encouragements to dance or endorsements of a particular sound system, he always manages to inject artistry and vitality into the proceedings. He is doubtless capable of another *Truths And Rights*, but it has been a long time coming.

● ALBUMS: *Come Back Darling* (Trojan 1969)★★★, *Truths And Rights* (Studio One 1980)★★★★, *Folly Ranking* (Jammys 1980)★★★, *Fally Lover* (Greensleeves 1980)★★★, *Never Stop Fighting* (Greensleeves 1982)★★★, *Water Pumping* (Greensleeves 1984)★★★, *Reggae On Broadway* (Vista Sounds 1984)★★, *Dancing Time* (Londisc 1984)★★★, *Johnny Osbourne* (Lix 1984)★★★, *In The Area* (Greensleeves 1984)★★★, *Michael Palmer Meets Johnny Osbourne* (Vibes & Vibes 1984)★★, *Rub A Dub Soldier* (Jammys 1985)★★★, *Bring The Sensi Come* (Midnight Rock 1985)★★, *Reality* (Selection 1985)★★★, *Rock Me Rock Me* (Top Rank 1986)★★★, *Cool Down* (1989)★★★, *Johnny Osbourne* (Jetstar 1989)★★★, *Rougher Than Them* (1989)★★★★, *Smiling Faces* (Blue Mountain 1989)★★★, *Nuh Dis (Come Ya Fe Drink Milk)* (Star 1990)★★★.

PABLO GAD

In 1977 Pablo Gad was introduced to Joe Sinclair by his benefactor Winston Fergus. Sinclair had set up the Klik label following his departure from Trojan Records with a view to releasing authentic Jamaican sounds. Both Fergus and Gad were British-based but were able to maintain an appeal within the roots market. Fergus was the lead singer of the Equators who provided the backing to Gad's debut recordings. Surfacing on the Caribbean subsidiary, 'International Dread' and 'Kunte Kinte' enhanced his position as a top vocalist. In 1978 Gad emerged with the classic 'Blood Suckers', which surfaced through Clement Bushay's Burning Sounds empire. Further singles surfaced through Bushay, including 'Natty Loving', 'Trafalgar Square', 'Throw Your Dreams' and 'Riddle I Dis'. The success of 'Blood Suckers' overshadowed his later output which probably inspired the revival of the rhythm for 'Hard Time'. The outcome was another smash hit that has become an anthem for revival DJs. 1980 was a prolific year when a successful run of hits encompassed 'Guns Fever', 'Nursery Rhyme', 'Oh Jah' and 'Fly Away Home'. Pablo Gad continues to record in the 90s, including the self-penned 'Johnny Reggae' and the haunting 'Lash On My Back', the latter being featured on the Brixton-based *Lion Roots* compilation.

● ALBUMS: *Trafalgar Square* (Burning Rockers 1980)★★★, *Hard Time* (Form 1980)★★★★, *Life Without Death* (Reggae On Top 1993)★★.

● COMPILATIONS: *The Best Of* (Reggae On Top 1993)★★★★.

PABLO, AUGUSTUS

b. Horace Swaby, *c*.1954, St. Andrew, Jamaica, West Indies. Pablo was responsible for putting the humble melodica on the musical map when one day in 1969, he walked into Herman Chin-Loy's Aquarius Records shop clutching the instrument, and was taken to Randy's studio the following day to cut his first record, 'Iggy Iggy'. His next release for the same producer was the prototype 'Far East' sound of 'East Of The River Nile'. Moving from Chin-Loy to Clive Chin as his new producer at Randy's, the next single, 'Java', proved to be Pablo's biggest, and one of his most influential. Chin later worked on the classic instrumental set *This Is Augustus Pablo*, on which Pablo played a number of lead keyboard instruments. He worked with other producers at this time, cutting 'Lovers Mood' for Leonard Chin, 'Hot And Cold' with Lee Perry, and others for Gussie Clarke, Keith Hudson and Bunny Lee. Dissatisfied with the financial and artistic arrangements with the producers, Pablo set up his own label named Rockers, after the sound system he and his brother Garth operated. His first releases were a mixture of new versions of old Studio One rhythms - 'Skanking Easy' (from 'Swing Easy') and 'Frozen Dub' (from 'Frozen Soul'), plus original compositions 'Cassava Piece', '555 Crown Street' and 'Pablo's Theme Song'. *King Tubby Meets Rockers Uptown* is regarded by many as one of the finest dub albums of all time. It contains dubwise versions of most of Pablo's productions, mixed by the legendary independent studio engineer King Tubby. Other artists have benefitted from Pablo's skills as a producer, notably Jacob Miller, Hugh Mundell and Tetrack. Pablo was also in demand as a session musician and played on countless recordings throughout the 70s. *East Of The River Nile* in 1978 remains his most compelling instrumental set after *This Is Augustus Pablo*. On this release, Pablo and his Rockers All Stars band, featuring guitarist Earl 'Chinna' Smith, created vast landscapes of rhythmic sound awash with Pablo's string synthesizer and melodica. The sound bore the unmistakable production stamp of Lee Perry's Black Ark studios. The early 80s saw Pablo floundering somewhat in the early throes of the dancehall revolution, though he later rallied with his production of Junior Delgado's 'Raggamuffin Year' single and album in 1986. Since then he has released a number of recordings with varying degrees of artistic success, both of his own music and that of artists such as Yammie Bolo, Icho Candy, Delroy Williams, Norris Reid and Blacka T. Ironically, he has managed to adapt to the new computerized technology, which many of his fans blame for what they see as the decline in musicianship in reggae music in the 80s and 90s. A withdrawn slip of a man, often in ill health, Pablo's music has, at its best, always reflected a humility and inner peace. Although most critics agree his influential and commercially successful period was over by the end of the 70s, his 1990 instrumental set *Blowing With The Wind* was his best since *East Of The River Nile*, and belied criticisms of artistic demise.

● ALBUMS: *This Is Augustus Pablo* (Tropical 1974)★★★★, *Thriller* (Tropical/Nationwide 1975)★★★, *Ital Dub* (Trojan 1975)★★★, *King Tubby Meets Rockers Uptown* (Clocktower 1976)★★★★, *East Of The River Nile* (Message 1978)★★★★, *Africa Must Be Free By 1983 Dub* (Greensleeves 1979)★★★, *Dubbing In A Africa* same tracks as *Thriller* (Abraham 1979)★★★, *Earths Rightful Ruler* (Message 1982)★★★, *Rockers Meet King Tubby In A Fire House* (Shanachie 1982)★★★, *King David's Melody* (Alligator 1983)★★★, *Rising Sun* (Greensleeves 1986)★★★, *East Man Dub* (Greensleeves 1988)★★★, *Rockers Comes East* (Greensleeves 1988)★★★, *Blowing With The Wind* (Greensleeves 1990)★★★, with Junior Delgado *Raggamuffin Dub* (Rockers International 1990)★★★, with Delgado *One Step Dub* (Greensleeves 1990)★★★, *Heartical Chant* (Rockers International 1992)★★★, *Pablo And Friends* (1992)★★★.

● COMPILATIONS: *Original Rockers* (Greensleeves 1979)★★★★, *Original Rockers 2* (Greensleeves 1989)★★★, *Authentic Golden Melodies* (Rockers International 1992)★★★, *Augustus Pablo Presents DJs From 70s To 80s* (Big Cat 1997)★★★★.

PALMA, TRISTON

b. 1962, Waltham Park, Kingston, Jamaica, West Indies. Palma is widely acknowledged as being introduced to the recording scene by DJ and producer Jah Thomas. He was hailed as a master of the sing-jay style that enjoyed enormous popularity in the early 80s. In 1980, prior to his alliance with Jah Thomas, the She Get Up And Skank label released 'Bad Boys', which accelerated his career. He recorded 'A Class Girl', credited to Triston And Tony, which inspired Thomas to work with Palma. His initial hits, 'Entertainment' and 'Spliff Tail', made a significant impression with the reggae audience. He also recorded in combination with Ranking Toyan 'Run Around Woman', and with Badoo 'Yes I'm Ready'. Palma's initial success led to a large number of recordings, including 'Raving' and 'Joker Smoker', which were both in combination with Thomas. In 1982 Palma was still topping the reggae charts with 'Darling When', 'If You Knew Baby' and 'Rub A Dub Session'. By the end of the year Thomas began concentrating on Michael Palmer's career as he felt that his association with Palma had reached its pinnacle. In 1983 Palma had a succession of hits including 'Mr False Preacher' with Nicker Smart, 'Settle Down Girl', 'I'm Leaving' with Ranking Joe, 'Woman Woman', 'Undying Love', 'Buy Out The Bar', 'No Shot No Fire', 'Folly Ranking' and 'It's Not What You Say'. By 1985 Palma became involved in the Music Is Life project, alongside a host of top performers, including Freddie McGregor, Mutabaruka, Gregory Isaacs, Third World, Edi Fitzroy and Steel Pulse, for the famine relief single 'Land Of Africa'. His popularity continued throughout the 80s including a number of hits with Pants produced by Castro Brown and then into the 90s when he recorded with Dennis Brown and Beenie Man for the hit compilation *Three Against War*.

● ALBUMS: *Showcase In A Roots Radics Drum And Bass* (Midnite Rock 1982)★★★★, *Entertainment* (Sonic 1982)★★★, *Joker Smoker* (Greensleeves 1982)★★★, *Touch Me Take Me* (Echo 1982)★★, *Settle Down Girl* (Trojan 1983)★★, with Ranking Toyan *Nice Time* (Pre 1983)★★, with Philip Frazier *I & I In Inity* (Black Solidarity 1985)★★★, with Pants *Triston Palma And Pants* (New Name Music 1993)★★★, with Dennis Brown, Beenie Man *Three Against War* (VP 1995)★★★★.

PALMER, MICHAEL

b. 1964, Maxfield Park, Kingston, Jamaica, West Indies. Inspired by his neighbour, Leroy Smart, Palmer began his career singing on the Echo Tone Hi Fi Sound. The sound system featured Big John, Flux and owner General Echo, who were all killed in 1980 following a shooting incident in Kingston. Working with producer Oswald Thomas, Palmer's debut release, 'Mr Landlord', faltered and with the demise of the

sound system he maintained a low profile. By 1983 he was back in the studio with Jah Thomas, who had enjoyed success with Triston Palma, resulting in the release of 'Ghetto Dance' with Jim Brown and 'Different Love'. A number of recordings followed with a variety of producers, including King Jammy, Sugar Minott and Joseph 'Joe Joe' Hookim. Palmer's career began to prosper and while Aswad were recording in Jamaica they utilized Palmer's voice for the release of 'Me Nah Run'. By the mid-80s his career was firmly established. He enjoyed a number 1 in Jamaica with 'Lickshot' and his appearance at the Reggae Sunsplash festival was one of the high points of the event. Numerous albums followed and those producers that did not have enough material to release a complete set compiled duo artist sets. As is often the case when a glut of material becomes available, interest began to dwindle and a lean period followed. He decided to test his production skills and enjoyed a smash hit with 'Haul And Pull Up' by Neville Brown. Palmer returned in fine style by the early 90s with a condemnation of licentiousness with the single 'Juggling', and alternatively, 'Everyone Makes Love'.

● ALBUMS: *Star Performer* (Tonus 1983)★★★, *Lickshot* (Powerhouse 1984)★★★, *Pull It Up Now* (Greensleeves 1984)★★★, *Angelia* (Vista 1984)★★, with Frankie Jones *Showdown Volume 4* (Empire 1984)★★, with Frankie Paul *Double Trouble* (Greensleeves 1985)★★★, with Kelly Ranks *Chucky No Lucky* (Vista 1985)★★.

PAMA RECORDS

Once the chief rival to Trojan Records, Pama has since evolved into Jet Star, the main reggae distributors in the UK. Originally the brainchild of occasional Jamaican record producers the Palmer Brothers, Pama was founded in London in 1967, releasing an almost endless supply of Jamaican productions on a series of labels that were less high-profile than Trojan's in the white market, but were just as musically strong as its rival's. Among Pama's subsidiary labels were Pama Supreme, Supreme, Crab, Bullet, Gas, New/Nu Beat, Success, Camel, Escort, Unity and Punch, the latter perhaps epitomizing reggae's attitude, depicting a fist punching through a Top 10 pop chart. Through these labels, the brothers worked with nearly all of the top reggae producers, including Laurel Aitken (chiefly Nu Beat), Lee Perry (chiefly Punch), Rupie Edwards (Success), Bunny Lee (Unity, which enjoyed a massive hit with Max Romeo's 'Wet Dream' in 1969) and virtually everyone who was anyone in reggae at the time. They also issued a series of *Straighten Up* albums in competition with Trojan's *Tighten Up* series, which remain highly collectable today, plus a smattering of non-reggae LPs, including *Butlins Red Coat Revue* and an album commemorating the investiture of the Prince Of Wales! By the mid-70s the business was chiefly in the hands of the youngest Palmer brother, Carl, who began to concentrate on establishing a distribution network in the UK, which has gradually expanded to the point of ubiquity: if Jet Star do not distribute it, then it probably is not reggae.

● COMPILATIONS: various artists *Crab's Biggest Hits* (Crab 1969)★★★, various artists *Straighten Up Volume 1* (Pama 1970)★★★★.

PAN HEAD

b. Anthony Johnson, 1966, St. Mary, d. October 1993, Spanish Town. Pan Head was a dancehall DJ who made his initial impact in 1990. Complying with the dancehall fascination for guns, rude-boy lyrics and homophobia, he associated himself with all the current trends. His initial releases, 'Respect Gunman', 'Punny Printer' and 'Gunman Tune', proved especially popular. His notoriety grew, leading to performances alongside Buju Banton, Capleton, Beenie Man and the Mad Cobra. By 1993 his recorded output revealed a more conscientious stance with the release of 'African Princess', which utilized the 'full up' rhythm, 'Under Bondage', a lucid condemnation of servitude, and, in combination with Yoruba, 'Teaser'. It was evident that he was fighting hard to establish his own style, and there were media predictions that his career would flourish. However, his potential success was ended by a gunman in October 1993, when he was leaving a dance; Pan Head left a widow, two children and a stunned community. The dancehall DJs were united in their condemnation of the event, as demonstrated on their vinyl outpourings: Capleton released 'Cold Blooded Murderer', Beenie Man's denunciation of the homicide resulted in 'No Mama No Cry' with Luciano, while Buju Banton

responded with 'Murderer'. Pan Head's untimely demise signalled a depressing era in the history of dancehall, as numerous DJs met with a similar fate, including Early B and Dirtsman.

● ALBUMS: *Punny Printer* (Imp 1994)★★★, *Tribute To Pan Head* (Imp 1995)★★★.

PAPA LEVI, PHILLIP

b. Phillip Williams. Papa Levi originally rose to fame on south London's Saxon sound system in the early 80s. His committed and uncompromising stance has, perhaps, denied him the kind of mainstream success that his talent deserves. As the premier UK MC of the period he was notable for a number of firsts: he was the first from the Saxon posse to make a record - 'Mi God Mi King' (for Barry Boom), the first UK MC to have a number 1 record in Jamaica when the same record was released on the Taxi label - and the first to sign a major recording contract - with Island Records. However, while others reaped the subsidiary benefits of these achievements, Papa Levi never moved from the Saxon sound system. In his live performances, he dominated the proceedings and little was lost in the transfer to vinyl, as demonstrated on 'Mi God Mi King', when he dropped into the 'fast style' at the end of the record, to shattering effect. The rest of the decade saw him notching up some notable performances in both Kingston and New York with Saxon on tour. Sadly he has never actually recorded that often, although when he does the results are always of interest. The 90s have neither seen nor heard much from Papa Levi, but judging by his past performances the fireworks will start again when he returns to the studio.

● ALBUMS: *Trouble In Africa* (1987)★★★★, *Code Of Practice* (Ariwa 1990)★★★, various artists *Coughing Up Fire - Saxon Studio Live* (Greensleeves 1985)★★, *Great British MCs* (Fashion 1985)★★★.

PAPA SAN

b. Tyrone Thompson, 1966, Spanish Town, Jamaica, West Indies. Probably the fastest DJ in the world and certainly one of the most inventive, Papa San began his career on the People's Choice, Small Axe and Creation sound systems, based around Spanish Town, where he spent most of his early years. In 1983 he joined Lee's

Unlimited and by the following year could be heard on Metromedia. He first recorded in 1985, 'Animal Party' on Black Solidarity being one of his earliest releases, so too 'Talking Parrot' for Rosie's Uprising, and both were distinguished by an ingenious lyrical slant and a quick-fire delivery, inspired in part by the fast-talking style instigated by UK MCs on the Saxon sound system.

Over the next two years he recorded for Isiah Laing's Supreme label, Bunny Lee, Prince Jazzbo, Harmodio, King Jammy and the late King Tubby, among others, voicing mainly cultural material and intricate tales of ghetto living complete with vivid descriptions of local characters. In 1988, after a successful spell in New York with the African Love and Papa Mike sets, he recorded 'DJ Business' for Fashion Records in London, an eight-minute *tour de force* that listed in detail the entire history of reggae DJs. By all accounts it was voiced in one take and remains an essential illustration of his unique abilities. Fashion later teamed him with Tippa Irie for their *JA To UK MC Clash (Volume 2)* album. The next two years were spent recording in Jamaica with varying degrees of success. Gussie Clarke reunited him with his former Creation partner Lady G for 'Round Table Talk', but it was not until 1990 that he found another winning streak, sharpening his skills with Black Scorpio on both sound and record, voicing for Mikey Bennett, Captain Sinbad, Penthouse, Digital B and King Jammy's son, John John, before really hitting his stride around 1991-92. He produced his own 'Strange' and the bizarre 'Maddy Maddy Cry'. 'Hippity Hippity Hop' arrived on Robbie Shakespeare's Powermatic label, and fine tunes for Exterminator, Tan Yah, Shocking Vibes, Wild Apache and Lloyd Honeyghan followed. He then began a rewarding stint with Sly And Robbie's Taxi label in 1993, though in December of that year his elder brother Dirtsman, also a DJ, was shot and killed in Jamaica.

● ALBUMS: *Animal Party* (Sonic Sounds 1986)★★★, *Lyric Shop* (Black Solidarity 1988)★★★★, with Tippa Irie *JA To UK MC Clash* (Fashion 1988)★★★★, *Style And Fashion* (Black Scorpio 1989)★★★★, *Fire Inna Dancehall* (Pipper 1991)★★★.

PARAGONS

One of the classic reggae vocal groups, the Paragons recorded extensively throughout the 60s, and, by the time of their disbandment in 1970, had left behind a string of classic sides with which few of their rivals could compete. Originally a quartet comprising Garth 'Tyrone' Evans, Bob Andy, Leroy Stamp and Junior Menz, the Paragons evolved from a group called the Binders. In 1964 Stamp left, and was replaced by John Holt, whose controlled lead vocals, supported by sumptuous, never-wavering harmonies, became the group's trademark. Junior Menz also left that year, to join the Techniques, his place taken by Howard Barrett. During 1964-65 the group cut a few singles for Coxsone Dodd at Studio One, including 'Good Luck And Goodbye'. In 1965 Bob Andy left to go solo, and in 1966 the trio began recording for Duke Reid, achieving a series of Jamaican number 1 hits in the new rocksteady style. Reid's productions were almost serene compared to those of his rivals, somehow utterly harmonious, and the Paragons came to epitomize the classy, warm sound of Reid's Treasure Isle Studio with a heap of wonderful releases: 'Happy Go Lucky Girl', 'On The Beach', 'Riding High On A Windy Day', 'Wear You To The Ball', 'The Tide Is High' and 'Only A Smile', among them. The trio also recorded a couple of singles that showed them to be just as adept at the more furious early reggae beat as they were at rocksteady - 'Left With A Broken Heart' and 'A Quiet Place'. In 1970 the trio split, with Holt rising to even dizzier heights as a solo act and Evans and Barrett relocating to New York, where Evans occasionally recorded for Lloyd Barnes' Bullwackies label. The pop world belatedly discovered the Paragons' genius in the following decade, when the Slits murdered 'A Quiet Place' as 'The Man Next Door', and Blondie enjoyed a worldwide number 1 with an inferior remake of 'The Tide Is High'. The original trio re-formed in 1983 to record a few sides for Island under Sly And Robbie's production aegis.

● ALBUMS: *On The Beach* (Treasure Isle 1968)★★★, *The Paragons With Roslyn Sweat* (1971)★★★, *The Paragons Return* (Island 1981)★★★, *Sly & Robbie Meet The Paragons* (Island 1981)★★★★, *Now* (Starlite 1982)★★★.

● COMPILATIONS: *The Original Paragons*

(Treasure Isle 1990)★★★, *My Best Girl Wears My Crown* (Trojan 1992)★★★, *Golden Hits* (1993)★★★.

PARKER, KEN

b. *c*.1948, Jamaica, West Indies. Parker began singing in church where his father was a preacher. Inspired by the gospel tunes, he formed a group called the Blues Blenders and in 1967 they recorded 'Honeymoon By The Sea'. The group decided to audition with Coxsone Dodd at Studio One, but owing to a misunderstanding only Parker arrived. He decided to audition as a soloist and thus began his recording career. His output included 'Choking Kind', 'Run Come' and My Whole World Is Falling Down'. Following his departure from Studio One he recorded with Duke Reid at Treasure Isle, where he cut some of his classic hits, including 'Jimmy Brown', 'Help Me Make It Through The Night' and 'Kiss An Angel Good Morning'. Lesser-known Duke Reid productions include 'Sugar Pantie', 'I Can't Hide' and 'True True True', the latter being covered by U-Roy. Parker's popularity escalated, resulting in further hits produced with Bunny Lee ('Guilty'), Rupie Edwards ('Talk About Love' and 'Wanna Be Loved'), Byron Lee ('Will The Circle Be Unbroken'), Lloyd Charmers ('Queen Majesty'), and Joe Gibbs ('Only Yesterday' and 'It's Alright'). By 1972 Parker became disillusioned with the industry and took a break from the recording scene. In the early 80s he returned to music, recording in the UK, where he set up his own record label and production company. In 1982 the release of 'God Bless Our Love' on the reactivated Pama label maintained his profile prior to the inauguration of his own production company, which released his gospel-inspired recordings.
● ALBUMS: *Peace In The Valley* (Studio One 1968)★★, *A Touch Of Inspiration* (Pisces 1984)★★★, *I Shall Not Be Moved* (Pisces 1984)★★★, *Jesus On The Main Line* (Pisces 1985)★★★.

PARKS, LLOYD

b. 26 May 1948, Walton Gardens, Jamaica, West Indies. A renowned singer and bass player, after completing his studies in music, Parks toured the north coast of Jamaica, performing on stage with his uncle. In the late 60s, Parks performed with the Invincibles band, whose personnel at that time also included Ansell Collins on organ, Sly Dunbar on drums and Ranchie Mclean on guitar. He then teamed up with Wentworth Vernon as half of the vocal duo the Termites, who recorded one album for Studio One and enjoyed a number of hits produced by Coxsone Dodd, including 'Do It Right Now', 'Have Mercy Mr Percy', 'My Last Love' and the legendary 'Rub Up Push Up'. After three years, the duo split and Parks was drafted into the Techniques to replace Pat Kelly, joining Dave Barker and producer Winston Riley. Although he was only in the line-up for a brief period, he was reputed to have sung on the classic 'You Don't Care', which he later recorded as a soloist in a medley of his hits. His solo recording 'Stars' was a minor hit but it was his version of 'Slaving' that won him international acclaim. The song was used by I. Roy for his classic 'Black Man Time' and by Big Youth for 'Honesty'. He recorded 'Say You Love Me' for Riley in 1969, and played bass on Dave Barker and Ansell Collins' international hits 'Double Barrel' (1970) and 'Monkey Spanner' (1970). By 1970 he was recording for producers Sonia Pottinger ('We Will Make Love') and Harry J. ('A Little Better'). In addition to his singing, Parks is also regarded as one of Jamaica's top bassists and his work in the line-up of Skin Flesh And Bones, alongside Sly Dunbar, Errol Nelson and Bertram 'Ranchie' Mclean, is legendary. The group's cover version of Neil Diamond's 'Solitary Man' was a hit in the reggae chart. He also joined the Thoroughbreds house band, playing Kingston's 'Tit-for-Tat' club. Parks continued making records in an expressive falsetto/tenor voice for a variety of producers including Glen Brown ('Slaving') and Prince Tony Robinson, and when Parks launched his own label in 1973 it was initially distributed from Robinson's shop. Among his Jamaican hits were the huge smashes 'Officially' (1974), 'Mafia' (1974), 'Girl In The Morning' and 'Baby Hang Up The Phone' (1975). Parks continued session work on bass with Skin Flesh and Bones, and by 1976 was playing bass in both the Revolutionaries and Professionals studio bands. When Skin Flesh And Bones evolved into Joe Gibbs' house band, the Professionals, the group performed on classic mid-70s hits backing

Culture, Dennis Brown, Prince Far I, Trinity and the UK number one hit for Althea And Donna, 'Up Town Top Ranking'. The sessions also resulted in a series of dub albums that still enjoy healthy sales over 20 years later. In 1978 he formed We The People Band, recording and touring, principally with Dennis Brown. He continued to combine session work and touring with the same band into the early 90s, touring with fellow Studio One veterans Freddie McGregor and Marcia Griffiths.

● ALBUMS: with the Termites *Presenting The Termites* (Studio One 1968)★★★, *Officially* (Trojan 1974)★★★★, *Girl In The Morning* (Trojan 1975)★★★, *Loving You* (Trojan 1976)★★★, with the Professionals *African Dub Chapters 1, 2, 3 & 4* (Joe Gibbs mid-70s)★★★★, with the Professionals *Earthquake Dub* (Joe Gibbs 1978)★★★.

PATRA

b. Dorothy Smith, 22 November 1972, Kingston, Jamaica, West Indies. A DJ, singer and hopeful actor widely touted/hyped as the female equivalent of Shabba Ranks, Patra (formerly Lady Patra) signed to the same management, under the aegis of Clifton 'Specialist' Dillon, in 1989. She also shares the same record company, Epic. Accordingly, with the new, commercial expectations placed on her shoulders, her material has moved from strict dancehall to include smooth love songs. Patra was brought up singing in churches in Westmoreland, where she moved from Kingston at an early age. Her ambition as a child was always evident, and she soon entered neighbourhood singing/DJing competitions in high school. Early supporters, who included Major Mackerel, encouraged her to return to Kingston and try her luck in the studios. Gussie Clarke was the first to 'voice' her after she had been declined by several others. Such rejections were only a short-term problem, however. Following the sessions with Clarke, she found herself in demand by Shocking Vibes, Exterminator and several others. Sides such as 'Holler Fe The Wok', 'Visa Hole', 'Man Me Love' and 'Worky Worky' showcased her considerable talents. On the back of this moderate success she played her first major show at the Sting '88 celebrations. By the time the contract with Epic was secured, Patra's singing voice had taken

precedence over her DJ skills, as highlighted by the single 'Sweet Memories', the first product of new sessions (though it was actually released by Tachyon's Sonny Ochai). Curiously, it rose to number 1 in the Japanese reggae charts, but Epic will surely demand more concrete domestic success in return for their investment.

● ALBUMS: *Queen Of The Pack* (Epic 1993)★★★★, *Scent Of Attraction* (Epic 1995)★★.

PAUL, FRANKIE

b. Paul Blake, Jamaica, West Indies. Blind from birth, Paul had his sight partially restored as a child on a hospital ship. When Stevie Wonder visited Paul's special school, he was encouraged by his schoolfriends and teachers to sing for him. Legend has it that Stevie was so impressed by the youth's precocious talent that from that point, Paul Blake decided to make singing his career. He first came to the record-buying public's attention in the early 80s, as Frankie Paul, when he shared the honours with Sugar Minott (one side each) on a Channel One 'clash' album. Minott was already established, while Paul was billed as the 'up and coming superstar', but it was not long before he became one of the most prolific singers in the history of reggae music. Every producer in dancehall reggae from Jamaica, the USA and the UK queued up for Frankie Paul and his consistency was amazing. Although, at first, the Dennis Brown and Stevie Wonder influences were apparent, Paul quickly developed his own style. His voice had a power and dignity too often lacking in 80s reggae and his interpretations of other artists' material were masterful. Like many other reggae artists, Paul recorded for a number of labels and producers, but, through his talent, managed to avoid the 'overkill' syndrome suffered by so many others. He released a staggering number of records, the majority of a consistently good quality. A major label contract appears to be on the horizon for Paul, though a mooted arrangement with Motown Records fell through.

● ALBUMS: *Strange Feeling* (Techniques 1983)★★★, *Be My Lady* (Joe Gibbs 1984)★★★★, *Strictly Reggae Music* (Londisc 1984)★★★, *Pass The Tu-Sheng-Peng* (Greensleeves 1984)★★★, with Little John *Showdown Volume 6* (Empire 1984)★★, *Tidal*

Wave (Greensleeves 1985)★★★★, with Michael Palmer *Double Trouble* (Greensleeves 1985)★★★, *Rich And Poor* (Classic 1986)★★★, *Alesha* (Powerhouse 1987)★★★, *Sara* (Jammys 1987)★★★, *Warning* (RAS 1987)★★★, *Give Me That Feeling* (Moodies 1987)★★★, *Rub A Dub Market* (Mango/Island 1987)★★★★, *Casanova* (Live & Love 1988)★★★, *The Classic* (Tappa Zukie 1988)★★★★, *Easy Mover* (Vena 1988)★★★, *True* (Black Scorpio 1988)★★★, *Ripe Mango* (Scom 1988)★★★, *Reaching Out* (Blue Mountain 1988)★★★★, *Shut Up B'way* (Ujama 1988)★★★, *Sizzling* (Skengdon 1988)★★★, *Slow Down* (Redman 1988)★★★, with Leroy Sibbles *The Champions Clash* (Kingdom 1988)★★★, with Pinchers *Dancehall Duo* (RAS 1988)★★★, with Pinchers *Turbo Charge* (Super Supreme 1988)★★★, *Love Affair* (Techniques 1989)★★★, *Love Line* (Glory Gold 1989)★★★, *Frankie Paul* (Blacka Dread 1989)★★★, *Can't Get You Out Of My Mind* (Rohit 1990)★★★, *Heartical Don* (Superpower 1990)★★★, *Close To You* (Jammys 1991)★★★, *Star Of A Romance* (Black Scorpio 1991)★★, *At His Best* (Techniques 1991)★★★★, *At Studio One* (Studio One 1992)★★★, *Fire Deh A Mus Mus Tail* (1992)★★★, *Should I?* (Heartbeat 1992)★★★, with Pinchers *If You Love Me Girl* (Trojan 1995)★★★.
● COMPILATIONS: *The Best Of* (Abraham 1988)★★★★, *20 Massive Hits* (Sonic Sounds 1990)★★★★, *FP The Greatest* (Fashion 1992)★★★★.
● VIDEOS: *Musical Explosion* (Jettisoundz 1991).

PEART, JEFF

b. Jamaica, West Indies. In the late 60s Peart relocated to the UK, and after completing his studies, began working for a telephone company. He later became self-employed and formed a partnership in a driving school. Although this proved a successful venture, Peart remained unfulfilled. He had been influenced by Jamaican music from childhood, and as an adult, his extensive spending on records led to his eventual purchase of a record shop. In 1974 Peart set up Londisc Records, releasing Jamaican recordings. His debut signing was a little-known Jamaican fireman performing as Jah Ted, but his failure prompted Peart to resort to a career in retail. He pursued a successful career as a retailer until he was persuaded by Trevor Walters and the Santic band to record their first album. The record inspired him to set up the Boiler Room production team, who released high-quality recordings for a number of top performers including Winston Reedy, Bunny Maloney, Rockie Campbell, Jimmy Mack and Donna Marie. His unprecedented success with Donna Marie, who recorded the popular 'Think Twice', led to Peart and the crew performing on a memorable and enthusiastically received tour of South America in the summer of 1997. Peart continues to provide solid foundations for his artists' careers, maintaining realistic aspirations of Londisc becoming the reggae equivalent of Motown Records.

PENN, DAWN

b. c.1952, Kingston, Jamaica, West Indies. Penn studied classical piano and violin from the age of five. Her tuition led to her entering and winning a musical scholarship at the Jamaica Independent Festival for the classical section and also a second prize in the pop category. While still at school she began recording with Coxsone Dodd at Studio One in Brentford Road. Her initial hit, 'You Don't Love Me', backed with 'Portabello Road' by the Soul Vendors, proved a popular hit, although not particularly lucrative. Other recording work included 'Don't Sleep In The Subway' and 'To Sir With Love', along with 'Long Day Short Night' and 'Blue Yes Blue' with Prince Buster. When Johnny Nash recorded 'I Can See Clearly Now' and 'Guava Jelly' in Jamaica, Penn provided the backing vocals. By 1970 she had left Jamaica for Tortola in the Virgin Islands, where she raised her children and pursued an administrative career within a bank and airline company. She moved back to Jamaica in 1987 and four years later returned to the recording studio, although she was initially unwilling to sing over dancehall rhythms. She re-recorded her debut single for Steely And Clevie as well as for King Jammy. The Jammy-produced version, 'No, No, No (World A Respect)' featured her solo vocal cut as well as the more popular dancehall version employing the vocal skills of Dennis Brown, Ken Boothe and Beenie Man. While King Jammy's recording proved a dancehall smash, the Steely And Clevie version crossed over into mainstream pop charts. The single entered the UK Top 10 in June 1994 and stayed there for 12 weeks, peaking at number 3. The UK chart version was initially recorded for *Steely & Clevie Play Vintage Studio One* and Penn's discerning manager secured the rights for a single release. She followed the hit with an interpretation of Jacob Miller's 'Baby I Love You So', as 'Night And Day', which featured special mixes by Augustus Pablo. However, her follow-up failed to generate a similar level of enthusiasm and left her as a one-hit-wonder. In spite of this, she continued to tour and record, and enjoyed several local hits, notably her rendition of 'What Do You Do' in 1995. In 1996 Penn teamed up with UK-based producer and performer Delroy Williams, who produced her second album and joined her in a European tour alongside George Dekker, formerly a member of the Pioneers.

● ALBUMS: *No No No* (Big Beat 1994)★★★, *Come Again* (Trojan 1996)★★★.

PENTHOUSE RECORDS
(see Germain, Donovan)

PERRY, LEE
b. Rainford Hugh Perry, 28 March 1936, Hanover, Jamaica, West Indies, aka Scratch and the Upsetter. Small in stature, but larger than life, 'Little' Lee Perry began his musical career working for seminal producer Coxsone Dodd during the late 50s and early 60s, acting as a record scout, organizing recording sessions, and later supervising auditions at Dodd's record shop in Orange Street, Kingston. By 1963, as well as handling production and songwriting for Delroy Wilson ('Joe Liges', 'Spit In The Sky') and the Maytals, Perry had released the first of his own vocal records through Dodd. Featuring a bluesy, declamatory vocal style over superb backing from the legendary Skatalites, these tracks set a pattern from which Perry, throughout his career, rarely deviated. Social and personal justice, bawdy, sometimes lewd, sexual commentary, and, like the material he wrote for Delroy Wilson, stinging attacks on musical rivals - mainly former Coxsone employee Prince Buster - are all prefigured on these early tracks such as 'Prince In The Pack', 'Trial And Crosses', 'Help The Weak', 'Give Me

Justice', 'Chicken Scratch' (from which he acquired his nickname), 'Doctor Dick' with Rita Marley and the Soulettes on backing vocals, and 'Madhead', recorded between 1963 and 1966. Incidentally, there was evidently no acrimony between Buster and Perry, as the latter often appeared on Buster's records, including 'Ghost Dance' and 'Judge Dread'. Also during his sojourn with Dodd, he began an association with the Wailers that had repercussions later in the decade.

In 1966 Perry fell out with Dodd and began working with other producers including J.J. Johnson, Clancy Eccles and, in 1968, Joe Gibbs, for whom he wrote songs and produced artists such as Errol Dunkley and the Pioneers. With Gibbs, he also voiced a bitter snipe directed at Dodd entitled 'The Upsetter', from which he gained his next epithet. On parting with Gibbs, Perry recorded several fine titles, including the big local hit, 'People Funny Boy' (1968), a vicious record, featuring a chugging rhythm in the new reggae style given to him by Clancy Eccles, wherein Perry castigated his former employer for allegedly ignoring his role in Gibbs' success, the slight made all the more pointed by his use of the melody from the Pioneers' hit 'Longshot'. In 1968 Perry set up his own Upsetter label in Jamaica, again with help from Clancy Eccles. Immediately, he began having hits with David Isaacs ('Place In The Sun') and the Untouchables ('Tighten Up', which lent its title to the classic series of early 70s reggae compilations on Trojan Records), and, in common with other early reggae producers, secured a contract with Trojan whereby his records were released under his label in the UK.

Perry experienced his first taste of UK chart success with tenor saxophonist Val Bennett's spaghetti western-inspired title, 'Return Of Django', which spent three weeks at number 5 in the UK charts during October 1969. At the same time, he began producing the Wailers on a series of records including 'Small Axe', 'Duppy Conqueror', and 'Soul Rebel', mostly available on a number of recent compilations, and which are now considered to be among that group's finest work. Just over 100 singles were released on Upsetter between 1969 and 1974 by artists such as Dave Barker (Dave And Ansell Collins)

('Shocks Of Mighty', 'Upsetting Station'), Dennis Alcapone ('Alpha & Omega'), the Stingers ('Give Me Power'), the Bleechers ('Come Into My Parlour', 'Check Him Out'), Neville Hinds ('Blackmans Time'), Leo Graham ('Newsflash'), Big Youth ('Mooving (sic) Version'), and the legendary Junior Byles ('Beat Down Babylon', 'Place Called Africa'). He also unleashed a welter of intense, energetic, and just plain barmy instrumentals: 'Night Doctor', 'Live Injection', 'Cold Sweat', 'Django Shoots First', 'The Vampire' and 'Drugs & Poison'. Other productions such as 'Selassie' by the Reggae Boys, the instrumentals 'Dry Acid', 'Return Of The Ugly', 'Clint Eastwood', and many more, appeared on other B&C and Pama labels.

From 1972-74 Perry slowed down the rhythm and consolidated his position as one of the leading innovators in Jamaican music. He released instrumentals including 'French Connection' and 'Black Ipa', and DJ tracks by artists such as U-Roy (who had recorded two of his earliest records, 'Earths Rightful Ruler' and the demented 'OK Corral', for Perry in the late 60s), Dillinger, Dr. Alimantado, I. Roy and Charlie Ace (on the unique and bizarre cut-and-mix extravaganza, 'Cow Thief Skak'). Perry was also one of the first producers to utilize the talents of King Tubby, then just starting his own operations, and released important early dub albums such as *Rhythm Shower* (1973) and the glorious *Blackboard Jungle* (1973). Perry's productions from this period - the Gatherers' monolithic 'Words Of My Mouth', Milton Henry's 'This World', whose rhythm also served Junior Byles' reading of Little Willie John's 'Fever' and Augustus Pablo's melodic workout 'Hot & Cold', Perry's own 'Jungle Lion', the Classics' 'Civilisation', and many others - are among the heaviest and most exciting reggae records of their day. In 1974 Perry opened his own studio, dubbed the Black Ark, situated in his backyard at Washington Gardens, Kingston. Almost immediately, he achieved a big Jamaican hit with Junior Byles' hugely influential 'Curly Locks'. In 1975 his production of Susan Cadogan's seminal lovers rock tune, 'Hurt So Good', reached number 4 in the UK charts. He also released the overlooked but innovative dub album *Revolution Dub* (1975), featuring some of his heaviest contemporary productions such as Bunny And

Rickey's 'Bushweed Corntrash', Junior Byles' 'The Long Way', and Jimmy Riley's 'Womans Gotta Have It', all garnished with Perry's crazy singalong rhymes and bursts of dialogue 'sampled' from the television. From 1975 he began to employ studio technology, notably phase shifters and rudimentary drum machines, to produce a dense, multi-layered mixing style that is instantly recognizable, and eminently inimitable. It is all the more remarkable for the fact that all this was achieved in a four-track studio. By 1976 Island Records had begun to release the fruits of this latest phase, including music by the Heptones (*Party Time*), Max Romeo (*War Inna Babylon*), Bob Marley And The Wailers ('Jah Live', 'Punky Reggae Party'), George Faith (*To Be A Lover*), Junior Murvin (*Police & Thieves*, the single of the same title being very popular in Jamaica at the time, and becoming a belated chart hit in the UK in May 1980), Prince Jazzbo (*Natty Passing Through*, released on Black Wax), and the Upsetters (the classic *Super Ape*). However, Island rejected his own vocal album, *Roast Fish, Collie Weed & Corn Bread* (1978), and missed out on the Congos classic, *Heart Of The Congos*, which finally gained a UK release some years later on the Beat's Go Feet label.

With commercial success now coming infrequently, Perry's frustrations and personal problems began to increase. He was still making wonderful records - 'Mr Money Man' by Danny Hensworth, 'Open The Gate' by Watty Burnett, 'Garden Of Life' by Leroy Sibbles, and many others - but his style was now so far removed from the reggae mainstream that they met with little success either in Jamaica or abroad. Perry's behaviour became increasingly strange and bewildering, and in 1980 he destroyed his studio and left for Britain, where he conducted a number of puzzling interviews that seemed to add credence to reports of his mental decline. Since then, he has made a long series of eccentric, often self-indulgent solo albums with a variety of different collaborators, including Adrian Sherwood, Lloyd Barnes, and Mad Professor, completely outside the mainstream of Jamaican music. Simultaneously, his earlier work began to receive significant critical and cult attention as well as commanding high prices in the collector's market. After living in the Netherlands in the mid-80s, he moved back to London, occasionally performing live. In 1990 he went to Switzerland, worked with a new management team, and married a Swiss millionairess. He also returned to Jamaica with the intention of rebuilding the trashed and burnt-out Black Ark. Whatever the future holds, Lee 'Scratch' Perry, the Upsetter, the man Bob Marley once described as a 'genius', has already made one of the most individual contributions to the development of Jamaican music, as a producer, arranger and writer, and also simply as a singularly powerful guiding force during several crucial phases. The lovingly prepared three-CD box set *Arkology* is indispensable for anyone interested in reggae. It presents some of the most vital music ever to have come from Jamaica - all the more remarkable on seeing the Black Ark and realizing that this great music emanated from a mere wooden shack.

● ALBUMS: as Lee Perry/Lee Perry And The Upsetters: *The Upsetter* (Trojan 1969)★★★★, *Many Moods Of The Upsetter* (1970)★★★, *Scratch The Upsetter Again* (1970)★★★★, with Dave Barker *Prisoner Of Love: Dave Barker Meets The Upsetters* (Trojan 1970)★★★★, *Africa's Blood* (1972)★★★, *Battle Axe* (1972)★★★, *Cloak & Dagger* (Rhino 1972)★★★, *Double Seven* (Trojan 1973)★★★, *Rhythm Shower* (Upsetter 1973)★★★★, *Blackboard Jungle* (Upsetter 1973)★★★★, *Return Of Wax* (Upsetter 1974)★★★, *Musical Bones* (Upsetter 1974)★★★, *Kung Fu Meets The Dragon* (D.I.P. 1974)★★★, *D.I.P. Presents The Upsetter* (D.I.P. 1974)★★★, *Revolution Dub* (Cactus 1975)★★★★, *Super Ape* (Mango/Island 1976)★★★★, with Prince Jazzbo *Natty Passing Through* aka *Ital Corner* (Black Wax 1976)★★★★, with Jah Lion, as producer *Colombia Collie* (Island 1977)★★★★, *Return Of The Super Ape* (Lion Of Judah/Mango 1977)★★★, *Roast Fish, Collie Weed & Corn Bread* (Lion Of Judah 1978)★★★, *Scratch On The Wire* (Island 1979)★★★, *Scratch And Company: Chapter 1* (Clocktower 1980)★★★, *Return Of Pipecock Jackson* (Black Star 1981)★★★, *Mystic Miracle Star* (Heartbeat 1982)★★★, *History Mystery & Prophecy* (Mango/Island 1984)★★★, *Black Ark Volumes 1 & 2* (Black Ark 1984)★★★, *Black Ark In Dub* (Black Ark 1985)★★★, *Battle Of Armagideon: Millionaire Liquidator* (Trojan 1986)★★★, with

Dub Syndicate *Time Boom X De Devil Dead* (On-U-Sound 1987)★★★, *Satan Kicked The Bucket* (Wackies 1988)★★★, *Scratch Attack* (RAS 1988)★★★, *Chicken Scratch* (Heartbeat 1989)★★★, *Turn And Fire* (Anachron 1989)★★★, with Bullwackie *Lee 'Scratch' Perry Meets Bullwackie - Satan's Dub* (ROIR 1990)★★★, *From The Secret Laboratory* (Mango/Island 1990)★★★, *Message From Yard* (Rohit 1990)★★★, *Blood Vapour* (La/Unicorn 1990)★★★, *Magnetic Mirror Master Mix* (Anachron 1990)★★★, with Mad Professor *Lee Scratch Perry Meets The Mad Professor, Volumes 1 & 2* (Ariwa 1990)★★★, with Mad Professor *Lee 'Scratch' Perry Meets The Mad Professor In Dub, Volumes 1 & 2* (Angella 1991)★★★, *Spiritual Healing* (Black Cat 1991)★★★, *God Muzick* (Network/Kook Kat 1991)★★★, *The Upsetter And The Beat* (Heartbeat 1992)★★★, *Soundz From The Hot Line* (Heartbeat 1993)★★★, *Technomajikal* (ROIR 1997)★★★.

● COMPILATIONS: *Reggae Greats* (Island 1984)★★★, *Best Of* (Pama 1984)★★★★, *The Upsetter Box Set* (Trojan 1985)★★★★, *Some Of The Best* (Heartbeat 1986)★★★, *The Upsetter Compact Set* (1988)★★★★, *All The Hits* (Rohit 1989)★★★★, *Larks From The Ark* (Nectar Masters 1995)★★★, *Voodooism* (Pressure Sounds 1996)★★★. As Lee Perry And Friends: *Give Me Power* (Trojan 1988)★★★, *Open The Gate* (Trojan 1989)★★★, *Shocks Of Mighty 1969-1974* (Attack 1989)★★★, *Build The Ark* (Trojan 1990)★★★, *Public Jestering* (Attack 1990). As the Upsetters *The Upsetter Collection* (Trojan 1981)★★★★, *Version Like Rain* (Trojan 1990)★★★, *Upsetters A Go Go* (Heartbeat 1996)★★★. Various Artists: *Heart Of The Ark, Volume 1* (Seven Leaves 1982)★★★, *Heart Of The Ark, Volume 2* (Seven Leaves 1983)★★★, *Megaton Dub* (Seven Leaves 1983)★★★, *Megaton Dub 2* (Seven Leaves 1983)★★★, *Turn & Fire: Upsetter Disco Dub* (1989)★★★, *Arkology* 3-CD box set (Island/Chronicles 1997)★★★★★.

● VIDEOS: *The Ultimate Destruction* (1992).

PINCHERS

When Pinchers first came to England from Jamaica in 1985, he had already recorded an album for Blue Trac, alongside Peter Chemist. It was the release of 'Abracadabra' that first won him significant attention. He followed up with minor hits for a variety of producers, including Philip 'Fatis' Burrell and Redman. The single to make the breakthrough, however, was 'Agony', recorded for King Jammy. It quickly made him a minor celebrity in Jamaica, to the point where he was offered (and accepted) advertising endorsements from a local vineyard. His other notable hits include 'Bandolero', the wild west imagery of which neatly seduced the dancehall audience, whose preoccupation with guns and violence it echoed. However, Pinchers' main source of fame continues to centre on sound system 'specials', live appearances at which he excels, and on which he has built a considerable reputation as one of reggae's emerging stars.

● ALBUMS: *Agony* (Live & Love 1987)★★★, *Mass Out* (Exterminator/RAS 1987)★★★★, *Lift It Up Again* (Exterminator/Vena 1987)★★★, *Got To Be Me* (Live & Love 1987)★★, with Frankie Paul *Dancehall Duo* (RAS 1988)★★★, with Paul *Turbo Charge* (Super Supreme 1988)★★★, with Pliers *Pinchers With Pliers* (Black Scorpio 1988)★★★, *Return Of The Don* (Supreme 1989)★★, with Sanchez *Pinchers Meets Sanchez* (Exterminator 1989)★★★★, with Tweetie Bird *Two Originals* (King Dragon 1990)★★, *Hotter* (Blue Mountain 1992)★★★, *Dirt Low* (Exterminator 1993)★★★, with Paul *If You Love Me Girl* (Trojan 1995)★★★.

PINKNEY, DWIGHT

b. 1945, Manchester, Jamaica, West Indies. Pinkney began his musical career after graduating from the Jamaican School of Music. In the mid-60s he performed as lead guitarist alongside drummer Lloyd Robinson, bassist Alfred Crossley and keyboardist Danny MacFarlane, collectively known as the Sharks. The group recorded at Studio One, where they were approached by the Wailers to provide backing on their 1965 Jamaican chart-topper 'Put It On'. Following his departure from the Sharks, Pinkney joined Zap Pow. The band formed around the nucleus of Mike Williams, Beres Hammond and Max Edwards alongside David Madden and Glen DaCosta. They recorded two albums and are principally remembered for the classic 'This Is Reggae Music', of which Pinkney was co-author. In the mid-70s Pinkney's career followed an alternative course when he returned to the Jamaican School of Music in a teaching role. In 1979, after collecting the Guinness Jamaica award for best arrangement on the Astronauts' song festival winner, 'Born Jamaican', he relinquished his capacities as coach to revert to performing. He later replaced Sowell Radics in the Roots Radics band, where he performed alongside a variable line-up that featured Bingi Bunny, Errol Holt and Lincoln 'Style' Scott, among others. In addition to his Radics commitments, Pinkney's guitar playing embellished a number of Donovan Germain and Dave 'Rude Boy' Kelly productions.

● ALBUMS: with Zap Pow *Zap Pow Now* (Vulcan 1976)★★★, with Roots Radics *Scientist Meets The Space Invaders* (Greensleeves 1981)★★★.

PIONEERS

The original Pioneers, formed in 1962, consisted of the brothers Sidney and Derrick Crooks, and Glen Adams. The latter later enjoyed a career as a vocalist and studio musician, playing organ as a member of Lee Perry's Upsetters. The Pioneers' debut, 'Sometime', was recorded for Leslie Kong's Beverley's label during 1965. By late 1967 they were recording for the Caltone label, owned by Ken Lack, former road manager of the Skatalites. In 1968, Sidney teamed up with Jackie Robinson to record a series of local hits for producer Joe Gibbs, hitting number 1 in the Jamaican chart with their first attempt, 'Gimme Little Loving'. They followed up with another number 1, 'Long Shot', a song celebrating the victories of a famous Jamaican racehorse. Further successes for Gibbs included 'Dem A Laugh', 'No Dope Me Pony', 'Me Nah Go A Bellevue', 'Catch The Beat', and 'Mama Look Deh', which the Maytals used as the basis for their huge local hit of 1968, 'Monkey Man'. Sidney and Robinson then teamed up with Desmond Dekker's brother George, and returned to record for Leslie Kong, initially releasing another local hit, 'Nana', under the group name the Slickers. Subsequent records for Kong were recorded under the name of the Pioneers, including their famous continuation of the racehorse saga, 'Long Shot Kick De Bucket', which tells how Long Shot and a horse named Combat died in a race at Caymanas Park track in Kingston. Other local hits for Kong included the Jamaican chart-topper 'Easy Come Easy Go' (a return volley against rival group the Royals), the frenetic 'Samfie Man', about a confidence trickster, and 'Mother Rittie'. After their sojourn at Beverley's, they took up residence in England, where 'Long Shot Kick De Bucket' had reached the UK chart, peaking at number 21 in early 1970. They toured Egypt and the Lebanon later that year, returning in 1971 to record in a much more lightweight 'pop' reggae style. Their greatest success came with the Jimmy Cliff-penned 'Let Your Yeah Be Yeah', which reached number 5 in the autumn of 1971. Lesser success came with the cover versions '100 lbs Of Clay' and 'A Little Bit Of Soap'. Since 1973, Dekker has pursued a singing and composing career, Robinson has been a solo vocalist, while Sidney Crooks has concentrated on production, since the late 80s operating his own studio in Luton, Bedfordshire, England. Their best records remain those they recorded for Joe Gibbs and Leslie Kong during 1968-70.

● ALBUMS: *Greetings From The Pioneers* Amalgam 1968)★★★, *Long Shot* (Trojan 1969)★★★★, *Battle Of The Giants* (Trojan 1970)★★★, *Let Your Yeah Be Yeah* (Trojan 1972)★★★, *I Believe In Love* (1973)★★, *Freedom Feeling* (1973)★★, *Roll On Muddy River* (1974)★★, *I'm Gonna Knock On Your Door* (1974)★★, *Pusher Man* (1974)★★.

COMPILATIONS: *Greatest Hits* (1975)★★★, *Longshot Kick De Bucket* (Trojan 1997)★★★.

PLIERS
(see Chaka Demus And Pliers)

POTTINGER, PHILIP 'LEO'
(see Leo, Philip)

POTTINGER, SONIA
b. c.1943, Jamaica, West Indies. In the mid-60s Pottinger opened her Tip Top Record Shop on Orange Street, Kingston, and in 1966, launched her career as a record producer with 'Every Night' by Joe White And Chuck with the Baba Brooks Band, recorded at Federal Recording Studios. This sentimental C&W ballad with an R&B beat became a massive hit and stayed high in the Jamaican charts for months. As the music changed to rocksteady, she recorded a string of sweet-sounding hits such as 'The Whip' by the Ethiopians (1967), 'That's Life' by Delano

Stewart (1968), and 'Swing And Dine' by the Melodians (1968), all released on her Gayfeet and High Note labels. In 1974, after Duke Reid's death, she took over his business and reissued and repackaged the Treasure Isle catalogue. In the late 70s, she issued several bestselling albums by Bob Andy, Marcia Griffiths and Culture. She retired from the recording business in 1985, deservedly remembered as the most successful woman producer in Jamaican music.
● COMPILATIONS: Various Artists: *Put On Your Best Dress* 1967-68 recordings (Trojan 1990)★★★, *Musical Feast* 1967-70 recordings (Heartbeat 1990)★★★★.

POWER STEPPERS
Power Steppers' true identity remains a mystery as he shuns publicity. Interviews with the elusive performer can only be conducted through facsimile or e-mail. The main force behind Power Steppers had no previous experience in the field of music, but had been active in the areas of eco-agriculture, conservation and primate research. His credentials led to preservation work in Africa and South America. His musical influence began in north London's dancehall scene, primarily through the eminent Jah Shaka. Although predominately inspired by Shaka, his other influences include Ash Ra Temple, Faust and Brain Ticket, resulting in a definitive dub sound. Power Steppers utilized the bass guitar and delay as the fundamental instruments of protest, producing minimal dubs that captivate and stimulate. He recorded with gabba gabba dubbers Zion Train through the band's own Universal Egg outlet, and his sound was promoted through the band's Bass Odyssey system. Power Steppers' dub outings particularly appealed to the rapidly expanding audience of the prevalent ambient dub sound. Zion Train have stated: 'Power Steppers is one of the strangest people it has ever been our pleasure to meet'.
● ALBUMS: *Bass Enforcer* (Universal Egg 1995)★★★, *Bass Re-Enforcement* (Universal Egg 1996)★★★.

PRATT, PHIL
b. George Philip Pratt, c.1950, Kingston, Jamaica, West Indies. In 1972 a young Big Youth chanted the introduction, 'Hail dread! - Irie! -

Now this 'appen to the Phil Pratt Thing', uti-
lizing the hit song 'Riding For A Fall'. 'Phil Pratt
Thing' and another Phil Pratt production, 'Tell It
Black', were two of Big Youth's earliest record-
ings and appeared on Pratt's own Sunshot and
Terminal labels. He produced a number of
Jamaica's top singers, including Dennis Brown
('Black Magic Woman' and 'Let Love In'), Ken
Boothe ('Artibella'), John Holt ('My Heart Is
Gone'), Keith Poppin ('Envious') and Pat Kelly
('Talk About Love' and 'How Long'). Many of his
productions are now regarded as classics and
have become collector's items. One particular
rarity is the Trojan Records affiliate label
Explosion's pressing of 'Black Magic Woman',
credited as being performed by the producer.
Inspired by the popularity of DJs, Pratt recorded
many of the island's top performers in the early
70s, including I. Roy ('My Food Is Ration'), U-
Roy ('Real Cool'), Dillinger ('Platt Skank') and
Dennis Alcapone ('This A Butter'). By 1975 Pratt
was producing the up-and-coming Jah Woosh,
resulting in the hits 'Psalm 121' and 'Zion
Sound'. Big Youth was also reunited with Pratt,
performing over the 'Artibella' rhythm for 'Keep
Your Dread', and the amazing 'Love Jah Jah
Children' on the newly formed Channan Jah
label. Pratt was one of the first producers to
release a 12-inch single, often referred to as a
discomix, that was a remake of 'Talk About
Love/First The Girl' by Pat Kelly and Dillinger.
He established his own Terminal outlet in east
London, ensuring his product would reach an
international market. The 10-track release of
Talk About Love first surfaced on his own
Terminal label, but later reappeared with eight
tracks as So Proud on Burning Rockers.
Throughout the 70s Pratt maintained a
respectable profile in his production role,
employing the best musicians, who in 1976
became known the Revolutionaries, recording
the bulk of his output at Channel One Studios.
In the 90s, 'revival' has become extremely popular and many Sunshot/Terminal releases have
resurfaced and are snapped up by eager collectors.
● ALBUMS: DJ Round Up (Trojan 1976)★★★★,
Hits Of The Past Volume One (Sunshot
1994)★★★★.

PRIEST, MAXI
b. Max Elliot, 10 June 1962, Lewisham, London,
England. Former carpenter Maxi Priest is now a
hugely successful solo reggae artist. Named by
his mother after her fondness for Max Bygraves,
Elliot took his new name upon his conversion to
Rastafarianism (from Priest Levi, one of the fig-
ureheads of the 12 tribes of Israel). He made his
initial music industry breakthrough by
employing his artisan's skills in building sound
systems. He went on to tour with Saxon
International, the UK's premier reggae
assembly, where he rubbed shoulders with Peter
King, Phillip Levi, Smiley Culture and Asher
Senator. He made his name and reputation as a
'singing' DJ, vocalizing improvised observation
over prime 70s roots music, but he soon progressed to a more soulful style that was captured
by producer Paul Robinson (aka Barry Boom) on
his debut, You're Safe. After recording this
album, he began a run of hits in 1986 with
'Strollin' On', 'In The Springtime' and 'Crazy
Love'. In 1987 he gained a minor hit single with
a cover version of Robert Palmer's 'Some Guys
Have All The Luck'. However, most successful
was his 1988 cover version of Cat Stevens' 'Wild
World', though it owed more of a debt to the
Jimmy Cliff reggae version. Further chart
appearances followed with 'Close To You', 'Peace
Throughout The World' and 'Human Work Of
Art'. Bona Fide included contributions from
among others, Soul II Soul, a group undoubtedly
influenced by Priest's mellow but evocative
brand of lovers rock. In 1996 Priest enjoyed a
Top 20 hit in the UK with 'That Girl', in combination with Shaggy.
● ALBUMS: You're Safe (Virgin 1985)★★,
Intentions (Virgin 1986)★★, Maxi (Ten
1987)★★, Bona Fide (Ten 1990)★★★, Fe Real
(Ten 1992)★★, Man With The Fun (Virgin
1996)★★.
● COMPILATIONS: The Best Of Me (Ten
1991)★★★.

PRINCE ALLAH
b. Keith Blake, 10 May 1950, Denham Town,
Kingston, Jamaica, West Indies. Blake began his
recording career with producer Joe Gibbs as part
of the Leaders vocal group during 1967/8. Gibbs
licensed three releases from the group through
B&C Music in the UK before the Leaders dis-

banded. Blake remained with Gibbs, who produced his first solo recording, 'Woo Oh Oh', which, like the early Leaders recordings, was relegated to a b-side. In 1969 he became strongly involved in the Rastafarian movement, living in the island's camp community until the mid-70s, when he re-emerged through Bertram Brown's Freedom Sounds with a series of records that have since proved landmarks in the history of roots music. As Prince Allah, he recorded 'Sun Is Shining', 'Mama Don't Fight' and 'Come Away', all featured on the *Ethiopian Kings* compilation, which described him as: 'The singer that has ability to capture the musicians, and have them play whatever he wants. A truly talented young man. With great promise for the future'. The prediction proved to be true, with classic recordings over the following years, such as 'Bucket Bottom', 'Lot's Wife', 'Stone', and 'Nah Go A Funeral', the latter marking a reunion with Gibbs. He continued sporadically to release material throughout the late 70s and early 80s, and in 1996/7 a retrospective compilation of his Freedom Sounds work appeared through the archive label established by members of Simply Red. The release of the roots anthem 'Born A Fighter' demonstrated that his career was not yet over.
● ALBUMS: *Heaven Is My Roof* (Imp 1979)★★★, *King Of The Road Showcase* (Vista 1984)★★, *Jah Children Gather Round* (Shaka 1994)★★★.
● COMPILATIONS: *The Best Of Prince Allah* (Redemption Sounds 1980)★★★★, with various artists *Ethiopian Kings* (RRR 1981)★★★, *Only Love Can Conquer (1976-79)* (Blood & Fire 1997)★★★★.

PRINCE BUSTER

b. Cecil Bustamante Campbell, 28 May 1938, Kingston, Jamaica, West Indies. Buster was named after Alexandra Bustamante, the leader of the Jamaican Labour Party, and began his career as a boxer, but soon found his pugilistic talents being put to use as a bouncer/strong-arm man and minder for Coxsone Dodd's Down Beat sound system. Competition was fierce in the early days, with fights frequently breaking out between the supporters of rival sounds, and with wires (and people) being cut regularly; Buster still carries the scars (literally). He claims, like so many others, personally to have invented the ska sound, and he was certainly involved from the very early stages - at first, with his work for Dodd, and after they had parted company, with his own Voice Of The People sound system, record label and shop. His very first recording session produced one of the all-time classics of Jamaican music, 'Oh Carolina', with vocals by the Folks Brothers and musical accompaniment from Count Ossie. Inventive and innovative at the time, the record still sounds every bit as exciting. Buster released countless records both by himself and other top acts on his Wild Bells, Voice Of The People and Buster's Record Shack labels, which were subsequently released in the UK on the Blue Beat imprint. They proved as popular there as they had been in Jamaica, firstly with the Jamaican community and secondly with the mods, who took Buster to their hearts with songs such as 'Al Capone' and 'Madness'. He toured the UK in the mid-60s to ecstatic crowds and appeared on the hugely popular *Ready, Steady, Go* television show.
He recorded in many different styles but his talking records were the most popular, including the hilarious 'Judge Dread', in which he admonishes rude boys, the wildly misogynistic 'Ten Commandments', the evocative 'Ghost Dance' - a look back at his early Kingston dancehall days, the confused and confusing 'Johnny Cool', and the less well-known but equally wonderful 'Shepherd Beng Beng'. He also claims to have taught Georgie Fame to play ska and he influenced other white pop acts - Madness named themselves after his song (debuting with a tribute, 'The Prince') - and he inspired doorman/bouncer Alex Hughes to adopt the name Judge Dread and have UK chart hits with variations on Prince Buster's lewd original, 'Big Five'. Towards the end of the 60s, Buster tended towards 'slack' or rude records that were only mildly risqué compared with what was to follow; nevertheless, they caused a sensation at the time. He wisely invested his money in record shops and juke-box operations throughout the Caribbean, and in the early 70s, he took to recording many top names, including Big Youth, Dennis Alcapone, John Holt, Dennis Brown and Alton Ellis, with varying degrees of success. He soon realized that his older recordings consis-

tently outsold his newer efforts and he turned to re-pressing his extensive back catalogue on single and releasing his old albums both in Jamaica and the UK. He also put together some excellent compilations where the superb sleeve-notes, written by the Prince himself, attack in no uncertain terms the music of the day: 'They have used guns to spoil the fun and force taste-less and meaningless music upon the land.'

Throughout the rest of the 70s and on into the 80s he lived on his shops, his juke-boxes and his past glories, but he returned to live work in the latter half of the 80s. He has become a crowd-puller again, for, as he says: 'The people know my songs and loved them.' In 1992, he even started, for the first time in years, to record new music again. 'Whine & Grine' was used as a soundtrack to a Levi's commercial, resulting in a return to the UK charts in April 1998.

Regardless of the quality of his more recent work, Prince Buster's music has already inspired generations of performers. He is respected abroad - probably more than in his native Jamaica - but he will always retain his place as one of the few Jamaican artists to reach directly to the international audience. Many more have played their part indirectly, but his name was known both through his own recordings ('Al Capone' reached the lower regions of the UK national charts) and his work with other people. It is unlikely that any other Jamaican artist (apart from Bob Marley) still has his records so regularly played in clubs and dances throughout the world.

● ALBUMS: with various artists *I Feel The Spirit* (Blue Beat 1963)★★★★, with various artists *Pain In My Belly* (Islam/Blue Beat 1966)★★★★, *On Tour* (1966)★★★, *Judge Dread Rock Steady* (Blue Beat 1967)★★★, *Wreck A Pum Pum* (Blue Beat 1968)★★★★, *She Was A Rough Rider* (Melodisc 1969)★★★★, *Big Five* (Melodisc 1972)★★★, *Tutti Fruitti* (Melodisc)★★★.

● COMPILATIONS: *Prince Buster's Fabulous Greatest Hits* (Fab 1967)★★★★, *Original Golden Oldies Volumes 1 & 2* (Prince Buster 1989)★★★★.

PRINCE FAR I

b. Michael Williams, *c*.1944, Spanish Town, Jamaica, d. 15 September 1983. Prince Far I, the voice of thunder, was originally a bouncer at the premises of Studio One, Jamaica's premier record label of the 60s and early 70s. A huge, muscular figure with impressive facial scars, he was known as a gentle giant with hidden depths. One day in 1970 King Stitt, the regular DJ at Studio One, had failed to arrive to voice a track, and Williams, the bouncer, persuaded producer Coxsone Dodd to allow him to try. Impressed, Dodd named the new artist King Cry-Cry and a legend was born. After a couple of records as Cry-Cry, he renamed himself Prince Far I. A gruff, deep, slow-burning rhymer, his talents at first appeared limited, although Far I was built to last: while other DJs' careers fizzled like fire-crackers, Far I retained his status throughout his life. When he really let rip, as on his 1977 album *Under Heavy Manners*, he was awesome. His *Psalms For I* (1976) remains a roots classic today, and his Trojan Records albums, *Free From Sin*, *Jamaican Heroes* and *Voice Of Thunder*, were all of a high standard. A brief liaison with Virgin Records brought him a wider, rockier audience, as did his *Cry Tuff Dub Encounter* (1976-79) series of dub albums, originally cut for his own Jamaican label Cry Tuff. Eventually, Far I spent a fair portion of his time in England, where he recorded as part of Singers And Players for Adrian Sherwood's On-U-Sound label. The pair worked together well, particularly on the 'Virgin' single, an undisguised swipe at Far I's previous label. UK gigs were frequent, with Far I, dressed in biblical robes, 'chanting down babylon' with the help of hundreds of white youths, whom he genially met and offered signed autographs after the show. However, just as he was starting to build this new following, he was shot dead in Jamaica, yet another victim of Kingston's regular street violence, one year short of his 40th birthday.

● ALBUMS: *Psalms For I* (Carib Gems 1976)★★★★, *Under Heavy Manners* (Joe Gibbs 1977)★★★★, *Message From The King* (Front Line 1978)★★, *Long Life* (Front Line 1978)★★, *Cry Tuff Dub Encounter* (Cry Tuff/Hit Run 1978)★★, *Free From Sin* (Trojan 1979)★★★★, *Cry Tuff Dub Encounter Chapter 3* (Cry Tuff/Daddy Kool 1979)★★, *Livity* (Pre 1979)★★, *Cry Tuff Dub Encounter, Part 2* (Cry Tuff/Front Line 1979)★★, *Jamaican Heroes* (Trojan 1980)★★★★, *Showcase In A Suitcase* (Pre 1980)★★★, *Cry Tuff Dub Encounter*

Chapter 4 (Cry Tuff/Trojan 1981)★★★, *Voice Of Thunder* (Trojan 1981)★★★★, *Musical History* (Trojan 1983)★★★, *Spear Of The Nation* (Kingdom 1984)★★★, with the Suns Of Arqa *The Musical Revue* 1983 recording - cassette only (1989)★★, with the Arabs *Dub To Africa* (Pressure Sounds 1995)★★, *Health And Strength* recorded late-70s (Pressure Sounds 1998)★★★.

● COMPILATIONS: *Black Man Land* (Front Line 1990)★★★, *Dubwise* (Front Line 1991)★★★★.

PRINCE HAMMER

b. Beresford Simpson, *c.*1962, Kingston, Jamaica, West Indies. Simpson began his recording career with Glen Brown, who produced 'Daughter A Whole Lotta Sugar Down Deh', which surfaced in the UK as the b-side to 'Two Wedden Skank'. Other singles appeared, notably 'Tel Aviv Skank'. His early recordings were in his own name but he chose the pseudonym Prince Hammer for his own production, 'King Of Kings'. The film *Rockers* included cameo appearances from nearly all of Jamaica's top performers including Prince Hammer, although he did not contribute to the soundtrack. He gained international notoriety when produced by Blacka Morwell, who licensed his work to Virgin Records in the UK. The result, *Bible*, was a popular compilation with liner notes from dub poet Linton Kwesi Johnson, who stated, 'There is no doubt in my mind that *Bible* will win a large following for the Prince and we will be hearing a lot more from him'. His success led to a visit to the UK and a move to the forerunner of On-U-Sound, Hit Run. In 1979 he was featured in a reggae showcase called Roots Encounter, although some of the gigs were cancelled at the last minute. Those lucky enough to witness the events were able to enjoy performances from Prince Hammer along with Bim Sherman and Prince Far I. While in the UK, he released his production of Rod Taylor's 'If Jah Should Come Now' and enjoyed a big hit, although the album of the same name did not achieve similar success. He also released '10,000 Lions', which featured his singing and DJ style on the same disc/mix. He continued producing other artists, enjoying moderate success with Echo Minott, Jennifer Lara, Toyan and George Nooks, and he was one of the first producers to record DJ Trinity singing. Many of Prince Hammer's early productions surfaced on the compilation *Africa Iron Gate Showcase*.

● ALBUMS: *Bible* (Front Line 1978)★★★★, *Roots And Roots* (Hit Run 1979)★★★, *Roots Me Roots* (Little Luke 1980)★★★, *World War Dub Part 1* (Baby Mother 1980)★★★, *Dancehall Style* (Hit Run 1981)★★★, *World War Dub Part 2* (Baby Mother 1981)★★★.

PRINCE JAZZBO

b. Linval Carter, *c.*1950, Jamaica, West Indies. Prince Jazzbo is one of the survivors of reggae music. While he has never been as important as other 70s DJs such as U-Roy or Big Youth, it is Jazzbo who retains a charismatic personal style and a reasonably healthy following through his label, Ujama, for which he produces and occasionally records. Like many others, Jazzbo first recorded for the Studio One label in the early 70s. Legend has it that Jazzbo had come to Kingston from the countryside and was initially passed over by Coxsone Dodd, the studio and label owner, who expected little from the skinny youth. However, Jazzbo eventually pestered his way into the studio and took the microphone. Dodd ran a backing track at random - Horace Andy's 'Skylarking' - and Jazzbo delivered on the first take what was to become a monster hit, 'Crabwalking'. For the next 18 months, Jazzbo remained with Dodd, cutting a string of flawless roots records: 'Crime Don't Pay', 'Pepper Rock', 'School' and 'Imperial I'. However, the promised album with Dodd failed to materialize, so Jazzbo, disillusioned, began to record for other producers, including Glen Brown and Bunny Lee. A liaison with Lee Perry on 'Penny Reel', originally intended as a one-off single, eventually produced the superb 1976 album *Natty Passing Thru*, aka *Ital Corner*, for which he was paid a mere 1,000 Jamaican dollars (about £100 at the time). Other albums from this time include *Kick Boy Face* and *Step Forward Youth*, the latter shared with I. Roy. By 1977 Jazzbo had launched Ujama, recording as a singer for the label, under the name Johnny Cool. Neither his alter ego nor his label was commercially successful. Jazzbo reached the start of the 80s, and the impending dancehall boom, in much the same state as his fellow DJ pioneers I. Roy, U-Roy and Big Youth: he had talent but reggae's styles were changing fast. Jazzbo decided that Ujama had to become a viable operation, and from around 1983 onwards, it has been just that - even if his idiosyncratic production style and somewhat off-the-wall ideas have held it back in the larger marketplace. Besides offering a shelter for older DJs such as U-Roy and I. Roy, Ujama specializes in finding the sorts of reggae acts other producers overlook, including Zebra, Manchez and Horace Ferguson. None of them have reached the status of Jazzbo's most famous ally, Frankie Paul, but this is wholly in keeping with Ujama's symbol of a donkey, because, as Jazzbo frequently tells people, 'a donkey may not arrive quickly, but it was good enough to carry Jesus and will not suffer a mechanical breakdown on the way'. The cheaply produced sleeves of his albums nearly always feature a cartoon donkey carrying Jazzbo or taking part in a horse race. While Jazzbo is unlikely ever to achieve great international success, his career received an unexpected boost in 1991 when Studio One finally released his album *Choice Of Version*, some 18 years late, to ecstatic reviews and considerable excitement. If it had been issued in 1973, Jazzbo might have been in a far stronger position today.

● ALBUMS: *Kick Boy Face* (Third World 1975)★★★★, with I. Roy *Step Forward Youth* (Live & Love 1975)★★★★, *Natty Passing Thru* aka *Ital Corner* (Black Wax 1976)★★★★, with Jah Stitch *Straight To Babylon Chest* (1979)★★★, with I. Roy *Head To Head Clash* (Ujama 1990)★★★, *Choice Of Version* (Studio One 1991)★★★★.

PRINCE LINCOLN (THE ROYAL RASSES)

b. Lincoln Thompson. Lincoln Thompson's solo career began at Studio One, where he made three singles in the early 70s that failed to make any impact, but established his name with the committed following for 'roots' music. He had been involved in the music business in the 60s as a member of the Tartans, and their 'Dance All Night' on Merritone Records was a big rock-steady hit, but they disbanded soon after this early taste of success. 'Live Up To Your Name', 'True Experience' and 'Daughters Of Zion' are still sought-after records, and immediately sell out every time Coxsone Dodd re-presses them.

Prince Lincoln left Studio One to establish his own label, God Sent, and released three more singles - this time as the Royal Rasses (Royal Princes) - that were effectively solo efforts with harmonies provided by an assortment of back-up singers, including Cedric Myton (of Congos fame), Keith Peterkin and Studio One stalwart Jennifer Lara. 'Love The Way It Should Be', 'Kingston 11' - a musical tour of the ghetto - and 'Old Time Friend' were all good sellers both in Jamaica and the UK, and attracted the attention of Ballistic Records who signed them and heavily promoted their debut, *Humanity*. The album featured the three hit singles and songs of similar calibre, including 'San Salvador', a hugely in-demand dub plate popularized on Lloyd Coxsone's London-based sound system. The set was issued in a full colour (and very expensive) sleeve with lyric sheet and backed up with a lengthy European tour in 1979. The group were poised on the brink of international stardom and Prince Lincoln's carefully crafted, thoughtful songs and soaring vocals were exactly right for the time. Sadly, it all went wrong. Although the Royal Rasses were making music that Lincoln defined as 'inter-reg' or crossover music, their follow-up album, *Experience*, failed to scale the heights that *Humanity* had reached and was not particularly popular with either the reggae audience or the pop audience at which it was aimed. The third album release, a very brave step and one that brought Lincoln much critical acclaim, but failed to sell in any quantity, was a collaboration with English singer Joe Jackson. The cost of these admirable ventures was borne by Ballistic Records, who went out of business in the process, and Thompson returned to Jamaica in 1981. There was nothing from Prince Lincoln for the rest of the decade but the early 90s have seen a handful of interesting UK releases on God Sent, which might signal a return to the business for one of reggae's most gifted singers, songwriters and arrangers. He is one of the few with the vision the music requires.

● ALBUMS: *Humanity* (Ballistic 1979)★★★★, *Experience* (Ballistic 1980)★★, *Ride With The Rasses* (God Sent 1981)★★★, with Joe Jackson *Roots Man Blues* (Ballistic 1981)★★, *21st Century* (1-5 South 1996)★★★.

PRINCE MOHAMMED

b. George Nooks, *c*.1958, Jamaica, West Indies. Initially a DJ appearing on discomix hits for *Joe Gibbs Record Globe*, in 1978 Nooks featured as Prince Mohammed on the remake of Dennis Brown's 'Money In My Pocket'. The b-side, 'Cool Runnings', was co-written with George and Errol Thompson and showed Nooks giving an exceptional performance. He also featured alongside Brown on 'How Could I Leave', identified as George Knooks (sic), the name under which he also recorded for Prince Tony Robinson on his hit 'Light Up Your Spliff'. Nooks' distinctive style was soon gracing releases for other producers, including Alvin 'GG' Ranglin's 'Hallelujah I Love Her So'. Nooks' success led to sessions with Bunny Riley, resulting in 'People Are You Ready', which was remarkably similar to Tapper Zukie's chant-and-response hit 'Oh Lord', and Nooks subsequently released his debut album, which included 'Fat John Tom', 'Great Sounds Ska' and 'Natty Going Back To Africa'. The increasing violence in Kingston influenced Nooks, now recording under his real name, to record as a singer with his interpretation of Little Roy's 'Tribal War', and the follow-up single, Errol Dunkley's 'Darling Ooh'. Nooks continued to concentrate on his singing career and with Donovan Germain released 'We're In This Love Together', which crossed over into the mainstream, almost reaching the UK pop chart. Other releases include 'Time For Love', 'My Heart Is Gone', 'Be Your Lover', 'Rocking Time' and 'Freedom Blues'. In the 90s Nooks continued to release the occasional song, notably 'No One Else Will Do', which when played as a dub plate was mistaken for a Dennis Brown tune. Examples of Nooks' work surfaced on the Acid Jazz Records roots offshoot.

● ALBUMS: *People Are You Ready* (Ballistic 1978)★★, *African Roots* (Burning Rockers 1979)★★★, *George Nooks* (Correct 1997)★★.

PRINCESS SHARIFA

b. Michelle Gibb, 1969, Scotland. Sharifa loved to sing and recite poetry from an early age and demonstrated her burgeoning vocal skills when she joined her primary school choir. In her adolescence she formed a vocal group with two schoolfriends, accompanied by the drum 'n' bass of Lawrence and Chris 'Scratchy Fingers' Lecky, initially performing in school concerts. By the early 80s Sharifa began to follow the sound systems and moved with Dennis Rowe's Saxon Sounds. Although Sharifa had not performed on the sound herself, she has acknowledged being influenced by Maxi Priest, Phillip Papa Levi, Smiley Culture and Tippa Irie. During her formative years she loved to write poetry, and, inspired by the excitement generated in the dancehall, she began to develop her songwriting skills. In 1985 Sharifa had her first opportunity to set her songs to music when the drummer from her school band invited her to perform with Jah Foundation. By the mid-80s Sharifa's catalogue consisted of songs relating to the experiences of the African communities in the UK, as demonstrated in her debut, 'Fight This Fight Together'. She also embraced Ras Tafari, as Head Creator, in her search for truth and cultural identity. This indoctrination led to a significant change of lifestyle and appearance. With Jah Foundation she gained notoriety when she performed in a gala concert for Africa staged in Paris, France. The concert led to her being in constant demand as a backing vocalist from 1986-91, with performances throughout Europe, the USA and Jamaica. In 1992 she was invited to sing on the Haile Selassie Centenary compilation, on which she performed 'Get Ready'. In addition to her solo contribution, she provided backing vocals for Earl Sixteen, Horace Andy, Junior Delgado and Aqua Levi. The project also led to her initial encounter with Norman Grant, lead singer of the Twinkle Brothers and proprietor of the ethical Twinkle label. In 1990 she began recording with the Mad Professor at Ariwa Sounds where, as far back as 1984, she had provided backing vocals on 'Kookoo Macka'. In 1994 Ariwa released *Roots Daughters Part 3* featuring the Princess, and her solo debut *Heritage*, which included tracks recorded in Jamaica with Sly Dunbar and Lloyd 'Gitsy' Willis. In 1995 Sharifa was reunited with Norman Grant with whom she recorded 'The Truth Will Prevail' and 'A Fi Reach Back A Africa', culminating in her first album with the Twinkle production team.

● ALBUMS: *Heritage* (Ariwa 1994)★★★, *Time Will Tell* (Twinkle 1997)★★★★.

PROPHET, MICHAEL

b. Michael George Haynes, 1957, Kingston, Jamaica, West Indies. Prophet's singular crying vocal style was first heard in 1977 when he was discovered by Yabby You, who took him to Channel One for his debut, 'Praise You Jah Jah', written some five years earlier. 'Fight It To The Top' was his first hit. With Yabby he made several highly regarded roots albums, inevitably featuring the Gladiators in support and mixed by either Scientist or King Tubby; Island released *Serious Reasoning* in 1980. By that time Prophet had left for Henry 'Junjo' Lawes, who successfully steered him towards dancehall popularity. 'Gunman', voiced in response to the violent Jamaican elections of that year, became his biggest hit. After two albums with Lawes, he freelanced with varying results, recording *Blood Stain* for Satta Blue and tunes for Don Mais, Al Campbell, Sugar Minott, Winston 'Niney' Holness, Soul Syndicate, Winston Riley and others. All helped to maintain his presence throughout the early 80s. By 1986 he was recording for Delroy Wright's Live & Learn label, then left Jamaica for Miami, where he briefly voiced for Skengdon. In 1988 he moved to England and within two years had teamed up with former Stur-Mars and Coxsone Outernational DJ, Ricky Tuffy. Their debut single, 'Your Love', was a number 1 reggae hit in 1990 and preceded the bestselling *Get Ready* album for Brixton label Passion a year later. The self-produced *Bull Talk* was released in 1993. Since then, Prophet has recorded solo singles with a variety of UK producers, including General Saint, Ruff Cutt and Lloydie Crucial. He remains one of the most enduring singers to emerge from the roots era.

● ALBUMS: *Serious Reasoning* (Island 1980)★★★★, *Righteous Are The Conqueror* (Greensleeves 1980)★★★, *Michael Prophet* (Greensleeves 1981)★★, with Yabby You, Wayne Wade *Prophecy* (WLN 1983)★★★, *Love Is An Earthly Thing* (CSA 1983)★★★, *Blood Stain* (Satta Blue 1984)★★★, *Cease Fire* (Move 1985)★★, with Half Pint *Joint Favourites* (Greensleeves 1985)★★★, *Settle Yu Fe Settle* (Live & Love 1986)★★★, *Certify* (Burning Sounds 1988)★★★, *Get Ready* (Passion 1991)★★★★, *Bull Talk* (Greensleeves 1993)★★★, with Dread Flimstone *Flimmy And The Prophet* (Acid Jazz 1995)★★★.

● COMPILATIONS: *Gunman* comprises *Righteous Are The Conqueror* and *Michael Prophet* (Greensleeves 1991)★★★★.

PYRAMIDS

The Pyramids were a seven-piece, UK-based ska/rocksteady band, although they began their career as a straight 'pop' group, consisting of Josh Roberts, Ray Knight, Roy Barrington, Monty Naismith, Ray Ellis, Mick Thomas and Frank Pitter. A popular live attraction in Britain in the late 60s, they hit with 'Train Tour To Rainbow City', an appropriately chugging piece written and produced by Eddy Grant, which ran through many of the period's most popular records and bore a close resemblance to Prince Buster's 'Train To Girls Town'. As rocksteady gave way to reggae, elements of the band, including Ellis, Naismith and Thomas, resurfaced in 1969 as Symarip with 'Skinhead Moon Stomp', based on Derrick Morgan's 'Moon Hop' hit, which was one of the anthems of the skinhead era but had to wait until its 1980 reissue to gain a chart placing.

● ALBUMS: *Pyramids* (President 1968)★★★.

QUAYE, FINLEY

b. 25 March 1974, Edinburgh, Scotland. Quaye comes from a musical background with Ghanaian lineage - his father is the jazz composer Cab Quaye, while his brother Caleb Quaye played guitar for Hookfoot and Elton John in the 70s, followed by a stint with Hall And Oates in the 80s. Quaye was raised in Manchester and on leaving school he returned to Edinburgh, where he embarked on a career as a paint sprayer, and spent his free time driving to Newcastle to attend gigs by the likes of 808 State and Soft Cell. Disenchanted with the motor industry, he moved back to Manchester where he embarked on a BTEC course in music and sound engineering, but did not complete his tuition. He relocated to London where he joined the Donga Tribe and practised drumming. His aspirations towards a singing career began when he returned to Manchester, where he voiced a track for A Guy Called Gerald in one take. Shortly after the session, he returned to Edinburgh, where he unexpectedly heard the track on the radio, and subsequently began listening to dub music. His initial inspiration came from an unorthodox source, the New York-based avant-gardist John Zorn's 'Black Hole Dub', although he was later inspired by more conventional performers. Quaye recorded his first solo outing on a four-track tape, singing and playing drums, bass and guitar. In March 1997, he released the *Ultra Stimulation* EP which demonstrated his diverse influences, including Charles Mingus, Jimi Hendrix and Bob Marley. He also embarked on the live circuit, debuting at Bristol's Malcolm X centre, where he supported Luciano. In June he released 'Sunday Shining', which gave a nod to Bob Marley's 'Sun Is Shining', as well as other reggae hits including Dennis Brown's 'Money In My Pocket'. The song, delivered in a style similar to that of a young Burning Spear, became his first UK chart hit and Quaye's unique style was much lauded by the critics. The promotional wheels were set in motion with appearances at the major summer festivals, including the Essential Roots Day alongside Everton Blender, Cocoa Tea and Anthony B. in Finsbury Park, London, and the release of his debut album. Further chart success followed with the singles 'Even After All', 'It's Great When We're Together' and 'Your Love Gets Sweeter', and he was voted Best Male Singer at the 1998 BRIT awards.

● ALBUMS: *Maverick A Strike* (Epic 1997)★★★★.

QUEEN YEMISI

b. Deborahe Owen, *c*.1972, South Carolina, USA. Owen began her career in Chicago, Illinois, where she performed as a jazz singer, although it was evident that her vocal style was influenced by Jamaican music. As she was an enthusiastic supporter of reggae, she travelled to Jamaica and linked up with DJ Merciless. The duo wrote and recorded 'Sexy Lover' with Harvel Hart and Delroy Schoborough at Annex Productions, which soon topped the reggae charts. The sensuous hit, with its seductive comments and sexy interplay between the two, led to a further Jamaican recording session that resulted in 'I'll Always Come Back To You', for Fat Eyes. In 1997 she returned to prominence with Merciless, performing 'Rocking Chair' over a sample of the Four Tops' 'Used To Be My Girl'.

● ALBUMS: *Lovefire* (Tres Belle 1997)★★★.

R

RADICS, JACK

b. Jordan Bailey, Kingston, Jamaica, West Indies. As a teenager, Radics had become involved with the New World sound system in 1975, and made one recording, a cover version of Kool And The Gang's 'Get Down On It', before moving to London in the early 80s. There he met up with producer Blacker Dread who released 'Easy' (a duet with Debbie Ryvers) and 'Walk On By' in 1985, the year he was signed to Island Records under his real name. Despite recording an album for them, only a handful of tracks ever emerged. When the contract expired in 1988 he returned to Jamaica and promptly achieved two local hits with 'Dream Merchant' and 'Conversation'. It was at the Sting '90 festival that he made his reputation for singing in a dramatic and exaggerated baritone, which, once harnessed to dancehall rhythms, provided a barrage of releases for a variety of Jamaican producers. 'Set My Heart On Fire' for Shocking Vibes, 'All Of Me' on Freddie McGregor's Big Ship label, 'Good Loving' for boxer Lloyd Honeyghan and 'I'll Be Sweeter' and 'My Love Is On Fire' for Penthouse were all substantial hits in 1991, the year Castro Brown released Radics' debut album, *Jack*. The following year he repeated the process all over again, increasing his volume of cover versions and also his producers, who by now had grown to include numerous labels in Jamaica, England and America. The list increased throughout 1993 when there was a growing shift towards more self-penned, cultural material, resulting in several fine sides for Star Trail, Shocking Vibes, Bobby Digital and Taxi. That summer, the Montego Bay label Top Rank released *Something*, which was followed by his belated Penthouse set, *I'll Be Sweeter*, in October. In December 1993 Sly And Robbie teamed Radics with Chaka Demus And Pliers on a version of 'Twist And Shout', which became an international hit,

reaching number 1 on the UK chart in January 1994.
● ALBUMS: *Jack* (New Name 1991)★★★, *Something* (Top Rank 1993)★★★, *I'll Be Sweeter* (Penthouse 1993)★★.

RADICS, SOWELL

b. Noel Bailey, 1953, Kingston, Jamaica, West Indies. Bailey began his career as a singer performing under his own name. His debut, 'What Am I To Do Now', was recorded at Harry J.'s and was a Top 10 hit in Jamaica. Disenchanted with the lack of financial rewards for his hit he found work playing guitar alongside the drum and bass section of the Hippy Boys, Aston 'Familyman' Barret and Carlton 'Carly' Barrett, playing the hotel circuit as Youth Professionals. In the early 70s Sowell was invited to play in sessions alongside Errol Holt, Bingi Bunny and Lincoln 'Style' Scott, who became known as the Roots Radics. The group became the most in-demand session band in Jamaica, playing on recordings for the island's top vocalists, notably Gregory Isaacs and Bunny Wailer. The unit was also frequently employed by producers Linval Thompson and Henry 'Junjo' Lawes to provide rhythms for successful vocal, DJ and (when remixed by Scientist) dub albums. They were also employed to tour with Gregory Isaacs, but it came to an end in 1982 when Sowell left the group. He decided to revive his career as a vocalist and his association with Mikey Dread resulted in the release of 'All Nite Jamming'. The single was followed by 'Wheel O' Matilda', which, along with the Mikey Dread release, enjoyed a respectable placing in the reggae charts.
● ALBUMS: *Freelance* (Kingdom 1985)★★★.

RAGGAMUFFIN/RAGGA

It is rare that an entire genre of music can be traced to one particular record, but ragga undoubtedly began with one single, Wayne Smith's 'Under Me Sleng Teng' (1985). Legend states that one of the musicians working in King Jammy's studio in Waterhouse, Kingston, was experimenting with a Casio electronic keyboard and found a pre-set demo rhythm. With the addition of a keyboard bassline, he provided the basis for Wayne Smith's 'voicing', and the digital era of reggae began. More than 200 other versions of the backing track were recorded, such was its popularity. Ragga is, therefore, barely distinguishable from the earlier dancehall, the main differences being its slightly more aggressive attitude, an alignment with the concerns of its youthful audience - one-upmanship, guns, sex - and an all-important, rocking electronic beat. The early years of the genre (1986-89) were dominated by King Jammy's production house, Donovan Germain's Penthouse Studio and a variety of other producers, such as Mixing Lab, Exterminator, Black Scorpio and King Tubby's. Veteran producer Gussie Clarke added a roots edge at his Music Works studio, and released the next biggest watershed record, Gregory Isaacs' 'Rumours'. Leading ragga musicians include Steely And Clevie, Mafia And Fluxy and the Firehouse Crew. Just like dancehall before it, ragga has also created its own set of stars, including Cutty Ranks, General Levy, Tiger, and, the biggest of them all, Shabba Ranks.

● COMPILATIONS: Various artists: *Ragga Clash Volume 1* (Fashion 1990)★★★★, *Ragga Clash Volume 2* (Fashion 1990)★★★, *Just Ragga Volume 5* (Charm 1994)★★★, *Ragga Ragga Ragga* (Greensleeves 1994)★★★★.

RAMACON, PHIL

b. Philip Ramacon, London, England. Ramacon started playing piano while at school in Hackney, east London. Following constant practising and performances at local youth clubs, his playing skills won him a scholarship and the chance to perform on BBC Television's *Full House*. His appearance on the programme led to him being asked to chronicle life as a black youth for the documentary series *Man Alive*, which in turn led to a plea from the *That's Life* television programme to support his tuition at a music school in Devon. Following his training, he was enrolled to play in Rico's band, promoting *Man From Warieka*, which included appearances alongside Bob Marley And The Wailers on the group's 1977 European tour. He then played piano for a punk duo, followed by work with Lene Lovich and the Automatics. By the early 80s he was enrolled to play for Jimmy Cliff, both on tour and in session for *I Am The Living*. Although in demand as a session musician, Ramacon's aspirations as a recording artist led to the unsuccessful release of his debut,

'Take A Trip'. He continued in session work, playing with Talk Talk, and appeared as the resident pianist on the television show *Club Mix*. His minor celebrity status and renowned session work have earned him prestige and a reputation as an innovator.

RANGLIN, ERNEST

b. 1932, Manchester, Jamaica, West Indies. Ranglin had two uncles who played guitar and ukulele, and as a child he would pick up their instruments and try to imitate their playing. He was also influenced by the recordings of Charlie Christian, and by Cecil Hawkins, an unrecorded local guitarist. At the age of 15, Ranglin joined his first group, the Val Bennett band, and subsequently played with Eric Deans and Count Boysie. By the early 50s, he had developed into a proficient jazz guitarist, and started to tour overseas. Around 1959, he joined bassist Cluett Johnson in a studio group called Clue J And His Blues Blasters, who recorded several instrumentals for Coxsone Dodd at JBC studio. The first of these recordings, 'Shuffling Jug', is widely regarded as one of the first ska recordings. Ranglin's beautiful, versatile guitar playing ensured that he was in demand as a session musician throughout the ska era, and he provided the musical accompaniment for Millie's worldwide smash, 'My Boy Lollipop'. In the mid-60s he recorded two jazz albums for the Merritone label, *Wranglin* (1964) and *Reflections* (1965). Around this time, Duke Reid employed him as musical director at his Treasure Isle recording studio, where he worked for several years. From the late 60s and all through the 70s he worked as a studio musician and arranger for many of the island's top producers, such as Coxsone Dodd, Lee Perry and Clancy Eccles. His other albums have included *Ranglin Roots* and *From Kingston JA To Miami USA*. He continues to record, but spends most of his time playing live, both locally and abroad. In 1996 Ranglin and his musical colleague Monty Alexander were the first to have albums issued on the Jamaica Jazz label, under the Island imprint.

● ALBUMS: *Wranglin* (Island 1964)★★★, *Reflections* (Island 1965)★★★★, *Ranglin Roots* (Water Lily 1977)★★, *From Kingston JA To Miami USA* (1982)★★★, *Below The Bassline* (Island Jamaica Jazz 1996)★★★.

RANKING ANN

Ranking Ann came to prominence on her brother's Black Rock sound system playing in and around London. She began her recording career with an uncompromising debut, 'Liberated Woman'. This resulted in her being categorized as the music's feminist DJ. When labelled as such, she announced, 'No Rasta me's a individualist'. In 1982 she released 'Love On A Mountain Top' but returned to her revolutionary style for 'Dangerous MC'. Her popularity led to the release of *A Slice Of English Toast*, produced by Mad Professor. She appeared on the UK's black magazine television programme, *Black On Black*, which was noted for featuring live appearances of visiting Jamaican performers. As an exception to the rule, the show's producer focused on the Saxon sound system with performances from Tippa Irie, Daddy Colonel and Lorna 'G' Gale alongside Ann. Demonstrating her charisma in an extraordinary performance of 'Militant Style', she paraphrased the expression 'All Dem Want Is Coal Not Dole'. In 1984 her career advanced further with the release of 'Something Fishy Going On' and an excursion to the USA as part of the Ariwa Posse Tour. In 1985 she made known her opposition to the parliamentary act allowing the police wider powers to stop and search suspects, of which the majority were black - 'Kill The Police Bill' was a pertinent piece that tackled the issue. It received strong support from the Red Wedge group, and as a result, Ranking Ann toured alongside some of the UK's leading pop stars promoting socialist ideals.

● ALBUMS: *A Slice Of English Toast* (Ariwa 1983)★★★★, *Something Fishy Going On* (Ariwa 1984)★★★, *Feminine Gender* (Ariwa 1985)★★★★.

RANKING DREAD

b. Winston Brown, Kingston, Jamaica, West Indies. Ranking Dread established his reputation as a live DJ for Lloyd Coxsone's London-based sound system as yet another in the long line of eccentric, idiosyncratic microphone men associated with reggae music. His particular style of delivery was based around a slurring, almost whining, vocal, constantly interrupted by comments and interjections, and offered definite proof that it was not what you said, but how you said it that mattered. His early recordings were inauspicious and failed to make any impact, but *Lots Of Loving* was among the most played records in UK reggae in 1979/1980, where the combination of Dread's delivery and some of Sly And Robbie's and Sugar Minott's best rhythms assured his popularity. A number of big-selling 12-inch singles followed, a couple of which hovered in the lower reaches of the national charts. He is now believed to be residing in Canada but no longer records or works live.

● ALBUMS: *Lots Of Loving* (Stand Firm/Freedom Sounds 1980)★★★.

RANKING JOE

b. Joe Jackson, c.1960, Kingston, Jamaica, West Indies. Ranking Joe cut his musical teeth toasting on a sound system known as Smith The Weapon. Working his way up through the ranks he became resident DJ on the El Paso sound, performing as Little Joe. His name was inspired by DJ Big Joe, who had enjoyed a hit with 'Selassie Skank', and not, as many believed, by the character from Western television series *Bonanza*. As with so many of his Jamaican counterparts he began recording with Coxsone Dodd at Studio One. His first session resulted in 'Gun Court', which saw him toasting over the Heptones' 'Love Me Girl', but this did not make an impression on the charts. He subsequently studied electronics before pursuing his recording career. Encouraged by his father, he enjoyed a major breakthrough when he returned to the studio to record the highly infectious '750'. The hit resulted in many recordings for a number of producers, notably 'Don't Give Up', 'Psalm 54', 'Natty Don't Make War', 'Tradition', and a tribute to the bionic man, 'Steve Austin'. He also returned to the sound system circuit as resident DJ for U-Roy's King Sturgav, alongside Jah Screw, before it was destroyed in the violent election campaign of 1980. Later in the same year, the Jamaican sound system Ray Symbolic Hi Fi toured the UK, giving British audiences their first taste of a real 'yard' sound. As he had become the resident DJ with the system, Ranking Joe featured on the tour and a new wave of enthusiasm for his recordings followed. By 1982 he had become an international figure with the release of *Weakheart Fadeaway* and *Saturday Night*

Jamdown Style. Tracks included the popular 'Natty The Collie Smoker', 'Nine Month Belly' and 'Step It Down A Shepherds Bush'. The popularity of the lewd slackness style of 'Lift Up Your Frock', 'Rub Sister Rub It' and 'Sex Maniac' ensured an enthusiastic response to his output. *Dub It In A Dance* included 'Clarks Booty Style', 'Slackness Style' and the title track, but was not as successful. In 1982/3 he enjoyed renewed success with *Disco Skate* and the reissued *Armageddon*. Shortly after Ray Symbolic's system returned to Jamaica the promoter's life was bought to a sudden end in the streets of Kingston. The tragedy cut short Ranking Joe's career, but many of his albums are still available and remain cherished by discerning reggae fans.

● ALBUMS: *Best Of Ranking Joe* (TR International 1977)★★, *Round The World* (Ital 1978)★★★, *Weakheart Fadeaway* (Greensleeves 1982)★★★★, *Showcase* (Tads 1982)★★★, *Armageddon* (Kingdom 1982)★★★, *Saturday Night Jamdown Style* (Cha Cha 1982)★★★★, *Disco Skate* (Copasetic 1982)★★, *Dub It In A Dance* (Trojan 1983)★★, *Check It Out* (Vista 1983)★★, *Natty Superstar* (Joe Gibbs 1983)★★★.

RANKING TOYAN

Jamaican DJ Ranking Toyan enjoyed a succession of hits during the 80s although he began his career in 1974, progressing through the top sound systems, playing in and around Kingston. By the late 70s he recorded his debut, 'Disco Pants', with producer Don Mais. A myriad of sessions resulted in productions at Channel One with Joseph 'Joe Joe' Hookim and later with DJ-turned-producer Jah Thomas. A string of hits ensued, including 'Girls Nowadays', 'Kill No Man', 'John Tom', 'Talk Of The Town', 'Just Love' and 'Sodom In Jamaica', while his combination hits included 'Pretty Woman' with the Mighty Diamonds, 'Rocking The 5000' with Badoo, and 'Roots Man Skanking' with Freddie McGregor. Further combination hits resulted in his being acclaimed as a top DJ; he joined Anthony Johnson on the hits 'Gunshot' and 'Don't Let Me Down', and an alliance with John McLean proclaimed the release of 'Starliner'. The success of these releases inspired an eclectic assortment of Jamaican producers to dust off the master tapes for a number of tracks

demonstrating his unique delivery. By 1982 he joined Henry 'Junjo' Lawes' Volcano sound system working alongside Billy Boyo, Little Harry, Welton Irie, Buro Banton and Little John, with whom he shared the stage on an aborted Canadian tour. Working with Lawes, he recorded 'How The West Was Won', which led to an album of the same name that is regarded as the definitive example of his style. He appeared on several live dancehall albums, including *A Dee Jay Explosion*, where he performed 'No More War', and in combination with Lee Van Cliff, 'Dreadlocks Party'. A resolute determination towards independence resulted in the self-produced hit, 'Joycie Gwan'. He found greater success producing others, including the favoured 'Bushmaster Connection' and 'Hoity Toity' with Billy Boyo performing alongside Little John and Bunny Lie-Lie, respectively. His illustrious reputation resulted in a UK tour with the Jah Prophecy Band, which included a prominent showcase with Michael Prophet followed by a unique appearance in Jamaica alongside Dennis Brown and We The People.

● ALBUMS: *Toyan* (J&L 1981)★★★, *How The West Was Won* (Arrival 1982)★★★★, with Yellowman *Yellowman Has Arrived With Toyan* (Joe Gibbs 1982)★, *DJ Daddy* (Upfront 1983)★★★, with Nicodemus *DJ Clash* (Greensleeves 1983)★★★★, with Triston Palma *Nice Time* (Pre 1983)★★, *Hot Bubble Gum* (Powerhouse 1984)★★.

RANKS, CUTTY

b. Philip Thomas, 12 February 1965, Kingston, Jamaica, West Indies. Thomas began his working life as a butcher, and it is tempting to suggest that he continued his DJing career as if he was still working with his cleaver - cutting through rhythms and rivals like slices of meat. Cutty is a friendly and personable character, but his style is strictly no-holds-barred, and his career during the 90s has progressed from strength to strength as a result of his uncompromising musical stance. He first took up the microphone for local sound system Feathertone, and moved on to Stereo Mars, Arrows and Metro Media. He began his recording career for Winston Riley of Techniques Records and then moved to Miami with Skeng Don, learning his craft from Super Cat and Nicodemus. He then moved on to Patrick Roberts at Shocking Vibes where he recorded his first - and highly influential - hit, 'The Bomber'. His next move, to Donovan Germain's Penthouse, further consolidated his popularity, and he hit again with 'Pon Me Nozzle'. His 'rock-stone' ranting attracted the attention of London-based Fashion Records, and his 1990 recording, 'The Stopper', became a huge international reggae hit both in the original and hip-hop remix versions. The album of the same name became a bestseller, while its catchphrases and hooklines have been endlessly sampled and reworked. Cutty has since established himself as one of the foremost exponents of the 90s DJing style. He was even able to deal with a decline in his popularity on record in 1992 with 'A Who Seh Me Dun', where he dismissed rivals with his customary blend of venom and humour and emerged victorious. He has only ever worked with the best producers in the business, such as Sly And Robbie, Roof International and the aforementioned Germain, Fashion and Shocking Vibes, and has always resisted the temptation to 'voice out' too many tunes for too many producers. 'Limb By Limb', a massive hit in the USA in 1993, suggested he would cross over in the same way as fellow travellers Buju Banton and Shabba Ranks.

● ALBUMS: *The Stopper* (Fashion 1991)★★★, *Lethal Weapon* (Penthouse 1991)★★★★, with Cocoa Tea, Home T *Another One For The Road* (Greensleeves 1991)★★★, with Tony Rebel *Die Hard (Volumes 1 & 2)* (Penthouse 1991)★★★★, with Rebel *20 Man Dead* (Charm 1991)★★★, *From Mi Heart* (Shanachie 1992)★★.

● VIDEOS: *Champions Of The Dance* (1992).

RANKS, SHABBA

b. Rexton Gordon, 1965, St. Ann's, Jamaica, West Indies. Although born in a country parish, his family moved to Kingston when he was eight; by the age of 12 he was studying DJs such as General Echo, Brigadier Jerry, Yellowman and especially Josey Wales, who took him to King Jammy's after Shabba had served his apprenticeship on the Roots Melody sound system alongside Admiral Bailey, recording his debut, 'Heat Under Sufferers Feet', in 1985. 'Original Fresh', a year later, was his first for Jammys. Unable firmly to establish himself despite an album shared with Chakademus (*Rough And Rugged*), his initial reputation for 'slackness' came with hits for Wittys ('Needle Eye Punany'), voiced while visiting New York in 1988. Shortly afterwards, he left King Jammy's for Bobby Digital's new label and Heatwave sound system, finding immediate success with 'Mama Man', 'Peanie Peanie' and then 'Wicked In Bed', which proved highly successful in 1989. Digital, previously the engineer with Jammys, had known Shabba since he was 15 and the special relationship between the two is still very much in evidence today.

Mike 'Home T' Bennett had also worked for Jammys and first teamed Shabba with Cocoa Tea and his vocal group, Home T4, for 'Who She Love' then 'Stop Spreading Rumours'. They took the formula to Gussie Clarke, who produced a subsequent album, *Holding On*, and big hits including 'Pirate's Anthem', 'Twice My Age' (with Krystal) and 'Mr Loverman' (with Deborahe Glasgow). The song was later re-voiced with Chevelle Franklin and become an international success in 1993. Throughout 1989, however, Shabba's presence dominated reggae music, although he recorded for few producers outside of Bobby Digital and Gussie Clarke. His personal appearances in London resulted in riots and, in one tragic case, a shooting. He also attracted the attention of the hip-hop fraternity, which had previously forged strong links with reggae before breaking into the mainstream. He was signed to Epic Records in late 1990, the year his duet with Maxi Priest on 'Housecall' became a major crossover hit. The first Epic album, *Raw As Ever*, wisely continued to use the top Jamaican producers and won him a US Grammy in 1991. By now his gruff, commanding voice had become known worldwide and the follow-up album, *X-Tra Naked*, repeated the feat, with Shabba becoming the first DJ to win two consecutive Grammy awards. After releasing a number of commercially successful singles, in 1993 he returned to the dancehall arena with a flourish - 'Shine And Criss' and 'Respect' pleased his still fanatical reggae following immensely, and he had further hits with 'Mr Loverman' and 'Family Affair'. In 1995 he released 'Let's Get It On' as a trailer for his 1995 album *A Mi Shabba*.

● ALBUMS: with Chaka Demus *Rough & Rugged* (Jammys 1988)★★★, with Chaka Demus *Best Baby Father* (John John/Blue

Mountain 1989)★★★, with Home T, Cocoa Tea *Holding On* (Greensleeves 1989)★★★, *Just Reality* (Blue Mountain 1990)★★★, *Star Of The 90s* (Jammys 1990)★★★, *Rappin' With The Ladies* (Greensleeves 1990)★★★, *As Raw As Ever* (Epic 1991)★★★, *Rough & Ready Volume 1* (Epic 1992)★★★★, *Mr Maximum* (Greensleeves 1992)★★★, *X-Tra Naked* (Epic 1992)★★★, *Rough & Ready Volume 2* (Epic 1993)★★★, *A Mi Shabba* (Epic 1995)★★★.
● VIDEOS: *Fresh And Wild X Rated* (1992), with Ninjaman *Reggae Sting Volume 1* (1992).

RAS MICHAEL AND THE SONS OF NEGUS

b. Michael George Henry, *c*.1943, Kingston, Jamaica, West Indies. Michael grew up in a Rastafarian community at St. Mary where he learned hand-drumming, eventually becoming a master-drummer. In the early 60s, he formed the Sons Of Negus, a Rastafarian group of drummers and singers. In the mid-60s he founded his own Zion Disc label, and started to release a series of singles including 'Lion Of Judah', 'Ethiopian National Anthem' and 'Salvation'. These recordings, on which the group is usually augmented by guitar and bass, show a remarkable degree of invention and subtlety. Around 1966, he recorded at Studio One as a percussionist, playing with Jackie Mittoo And The Soul Vendors in exchange for studio time. In the early 70s he recorded *Dadawah Peace And Love*, on which his group was augmented by studio musicians, a blend of Rastafarian chant, reggae, Southern soul and psychedelia, greatly enhanced by its imaginative arrangements. *Nyahbinghi* was a collection of chants and hymns in the style of his Zion disc singles. In 1975, he recorded *Rastafari*, on which his group was augmented by several well-known reggae musicians. The album's tight arrangements and excellent songs brought him into the reggae mainstream, but the momentum was lost with 1976's *Tribute To The Emperor* with Jazzboe Abubaka and *Freedom Sounds*. He augmented his group again for 1978's *Kabir Am Lak* (Glory To God) and *Movements*, both of which are strong albums. In 1979, *Rastafari In Dub* was issued, an excellent collection of material culled from *Rastafari* and *Kibir Am Lak*. Further releases included *Promised Land Sounds Live*,

Disarmament and *Revelation*. His last outstanding album was *Love Thy Neighbour*, whose imaginative production was the work of Lee Perry. During the late 80s Michael spent a great deal of time teaching drumming. He returned to recording with *Zion Train*, a mediocre album made without the Sons Of Negus, followed by *Know How*, a disappointing set that tried to incorporate world music elements.
● ALBUMS: *Dadawah Peace And Love* (Trojan 1975)★★★, *Nyahbinghi* (1975)★★, *Rastafari* (Grounation 1975)★★★, *Freedom Sounds* (Dynamic 1976)★★★, with Jazzboe Abubaka *Tribute To The Emperor* (Trojan 1976)★★, *Irations Of Ras Michael* (Top Ranking 1977)★★★, *Kibir Am Lak* (Rastafari 1978)★★★★, *Movements* (Dynamic 1978)★★★★, *Rastafari In Dub* (Grounation 1979)★★★★, *Promised Land Sounds Live* (Lions Gate 1980)★★★, *Revelation* (Trojan 1982)★★★, *Disarmament* (Trojan 1983)★★★, *Love Thy Neighbour* (Live & Love 1984)★★★★, *Rally Round* (Shanachie 1985)★★★, with HR *Zion Train* (SST 1988)★★★, *Know How* (Shanachie 1990)★★.

RASTA MUSIC

Rasta music refers to the 'burru' or 'nyabhingi' drumming, as practised by outfits such as Count Ossie And The Mystic Revelation Of Rastafari, and Ras Michael And The Sons Of Negus. There are three types of drum used in such music: first, the large bass drum of between two and three feet in diameter, played by striking with a stick, the end of which is padded. This is used to mark time and keep the pace with a deeply resonant, almost sub-frequency thump. The smaller funde and repeater hand drums lay down the rhythm, with the repeater improvising across the top. These are often complemented by a selection of percussion instruments and home-made bottle horns or saxes. Rasta music derives from the Afro-Jamaican burru and kumina traditions, themselves said to have descended from traditional West African dances. Prior to the late 50s, such music was confined to Rastafarian strongholds at Wareika Hill, Dungle, and other locations. Count Ossie was instrumental in bringing such music to wider public attention, especially when he agreed to provide the backing for Prince Buster's production of the

Folks Brothers' 'Oh Carolina'. Count Ossie and his drummers were subsequently used on a number of recordings throughout the next ten years, including 'Babylon Gone' aka 'Going Home' (c.1961), featuring saxophonist Wilton Gatnair, producer Harry Mudie's first record; 'Lumumba' (1961) by Bonny And Skitter; and 'Another Moses' (1961) by the Mellowcats for Coxsone Dodd. 'Cassavubu' (1961) aka 'Chubby' provided another hit for Buster. Other notable releases included 'Ducksoup' (1962) by Drumbago's Orchestra, 'Down The Train Line' (1967) by Stranger Cole And Patsy, and 'Pata Pata Rock Steady' (1967) by Patsy, both for Sonia Pottinger. They also recorded 'So Long Rastafari Calling' (1971) for Studio One, 'Rasta Reggae' for Arnold Wedderburn's Right On label, 'Whispering Drums' (1969) for Harry Mudie, and 'Blacker Black' (1968), wrongly credited to the Ethiopians, and released on Pama's Crab label in the UK in 1968.

In 1973 Count Ossie linked up with Rasta saxophonist Cedric Brooks to record the classic triple set, *Grounation*, released in the UK on the Ashanti label. This remains the essential Rasta music artefact, a compelling *tour de force* of heartbeat drumming, dread philosophy and free jazz-styled horn playing. Count Ossie died in 1976, crushed when a storm panicked the crowd during a cricket match at Kingston's National Stadium. Cedric Brooks carried out further experimentation with the basic Rasta music structure, with some satisfying results on *United Africa* (1977), and went on to form the Light Of Saba, from whom 'Lambs Bread Collie' (1978) is a fine example. Ras Michael follows much in the tradition of Count Ossie, though his music often fits more easily into the orthodox reggae format. His early albums, *Peace & Love* (1975) and *Freedom Sounds* (1976), remain fairly conventional examples of Rasta music. Later albums such as *Rastafari* (1976) and *Irations Of Ras Michael* (1977) combined burru drumming and standard reggae rhythms to good effect. While Rasta music has never been at the forefront of reggae music itself, it is a uniquely Jamaican aspect that was incorporated into the earliest R&B-derived, pre-ska forms. Its influence has been felt in subtle ways ever since.

RASTAFARIANISM

Rastafari emerged out of the ghettos of Kingston, Jamaica, West Indies, during the 30s. Its rise in popularity among Jamaica's youth in the late 60s and 70s promoted its worldwide recognition as the driving philosophical force behind the music of prominent reggae artists such as Burning Spear, Culture, Big Youth, Black Uhuru and, of course, the three main Wailers - Bunny Wailer, Peter Tosh and Bob Marley. So strongly has Rasta become associated with reggae music that for many people, the one is unthinkable without the other. However, reggae reflects all the aspects and concerns of Jamaican life, whether spiritual, temporal, or purely hedonistic. Rastafarianism was felt most keenly during the 70s, but though it is less crucial to the music's identity nowadays, its reverberations are still felt.

Religion has always played a large part in the lives of Jamaicans, partly a hangover from the days of the slavemasters' indoctrination of slaves. The African religions and traditions practised prior to enslavement were severely discouraged, but they were, however, retained in coded forms, through music, dance and folk tales, which still survive in modern Jamaica. The majority of the island's population, however, adhere to Christian forms such as Anglican, Methodist and Roman Catholic churches, and The Church of God, as well as a strong following for the Ethiopian Orthodox Church. More than 80 per cent of Jamaica's population is Christian. The roots of Rasta may be found in the rise of black awareness in Jamaica during the early part of the twentieth century. Some African-Jamaicans began to feel increasingly dissatisfied with the Caucasian bias of the Christian churches, and the image of God as a white man. A new interest in African affairs also burgeoned. This new-found consciousness was manifested in many ways by many different individuals and organizations, but in particular, in the activities and speeches of Marcus Mosiah Garvey (b. 17 August 1887, St. Ann's Bay, Jamaica, West Indies, d. 1940). Garvey had established the Universal Negro Improvement Association (UNIA) in Jamaica in 1914 with the aim of providing an impetus for disenfranchised blacks to learn about their history, their African roots, and to make provision for a hopeful future despite their humble present. The limitations of working within the confines of Jamaica soon prompted Garvey's relocation to America, where UNIA blossomed among the black ghettos and tenements of Harlem and, naturally, attracted the attention of the authorities. Garvey attempted to launch a steamship company, the Black Star Line, that would establish a firm business base for the organization and with which he hoped to provide free passage back to Africa for those African-Americans who wished to return. This eventually proved to be his undoing when he was jailed in Atlanta and deported to Jamaica on trumped-up charges of fraud. Garvey died in obscurity in London in 1940, but when his body was returned to Jamaica for burial he was received as a hero.

Garvey was an important figure in what eventually became the Civil Rights Movement in the USA, but it was his pronouncements that influenced the rise of Rasta, particularly his assertion: 'Look to Africa, when a black king shall be crowned, for the day of deliverance is near.' In Jamaica, among his followers (known as Garveyites) this was received literally as prophecy, and when in November 1930, Haile Selassie, the latest in the Ethiopian line of royalty, was crowned Ras Tafari, King of Kings, Lord of Lords, Conquering Lion of the Tribe of Judah, Emperor of Ethiopia, many Garveyites and sympathizers felt that Garvey's prophecy had been fulfilled. Another key figure was preacher Leonard P. Howell, who was arrested in 1933 for sedition and blasphemy. Howell had been selling postcards of Emperor Haile Selassie, claiming him to be 'the spirit of our Lord . . . returned', and suggesting that blacks in the west were really Jews, the Biblical lost tribe of Israel. The Rastafarian movement began to flourish in the Jamaican ghettos, its followers marked out, in accordance with certain Old Testament passages, by the adoption of dreadlocks, in which the hair is not combed but is allowed to grow in wild coils, frequently tucked into knitted tams adorned with the colours of the Ethiopian flag: red, green and gold. Frowned upon by the authorities, life was made difficult for the Rastas during these early years. Howell's stronghold in Pinnacle, where hundreds of Rastas lived in isolation from the rest of Jamaican society, was raided twice, and finally closed down by police, after which the faithful settled in the ghetto districts of Kingston. This allowed the movement to gain currency among Jamaica's poor. By the mid-60s it was established that there were at least 70,000 Rastafarians living in Jamaica.

Rastafarians are deeply spiritual individuals who hold their faith uppermost in their lives. There are many misconceptions about their faith in terms of behaviour and speech - the headline-grabbing use of marijuana (aka ganga, the holy herb), the dreadlocks (though neither ganga smoking or dreadlocks are necessary requirements), the deliberate lack of an organized church and hierarchy (until the inauguration of the Twelve Tribes in the early 70s), the grounations (gatherings where brethren would partake of the herb by way of the chalice, play drums, chant, and sing adapted hymns - see Rasta Music), the desire for repatriation in Africa, and the apocalyptic view of the world's present state of affairs. Throughout the 60s, interest in Rasta grew among Jamaica's youth and this was reflected in the popular music of the day, on records such as 'Oh Carolina' by the Folks Brothers, which utilized the burru drumming of master Rasta musician Count Ossie and his group, and 'Beardman Ska' (1965) by the Skatalites. This influence found its fullest expression in the 70s with Rasta sentiments clearly conveyed in popular records such as 'Beat Down Babylon' and 'A Place Called Africa' (both 1971) by Junior Byles, and 'Satta Massa Gana' (recorded in 1969 but only becoming a hit in 1971) by the Abyssinians. The movement achieved worldwide recognition in the mid-70s with the success of Bob Marley And The Wailers. Marley, like many of his contemporaries, had been interested in the faith since the mid-60s, finally capitulating fully at the turn of the 70s. The release of the epochal *Natty Dread* (1976), and the extensive touring that Marley undertook subsequently, brought Rasta to the attention of the world's media, and also alerted many in Europe and America to the faith. Rastafarianism's influence waned to some extent during the 80s - many of those attracted to the faith found it hard to adhere to the strict moral, dietary, and philosophical guidelines of fundamental Rastafarianism, and in some cases its practitioners adapted and compromised the faith to a more easily assimilable lifestyle. Rastafari still struggles to be recognized as a 'proper' religion, and this is probably because many Rastas practise their faith in a personal way rather than adhering to any organization. Its popularity in the 70s among Jamaica's youth was for many a transitional phase, later dropped when it became unfashionable. It has also suffered from the bad publicity it has received at the hands of criminals affecting the outward appearance of Rastafarians. It has survived the 'death' of its godhead Haile Selassie (who never officially recognized, nor denounced, the faith) in 1976 after Ethiopia had endured a communist-backed military coup. Nevertheless, Rasta has been and still remains a strong and positive influence for many people, of all races, all over the world.

RAY, DANNY

b. c.1951, Kingston, Jamaica, West Indies. Ray began singing in his teens and followed in the footsteps of many reggae veterans, performing in local talent shows. In 1967 he left the island for the UK, where he signed up with the Royal Air Force and found himself posted in Germany. During his time in the service he formed a band known as Danny Ray And The Vibrations, performing at a number of American airbases, which led to further exposure on European television and radio. After buying himself out of the forces Ray returned to Jamaica in 1970 for a brief period. His success in the UK inspired his return, where he formed Danny Ray And The Falcons and signed with MCA who released his debut, 'The Scorpion'. He was one of the first reggae performers to experience the pitfalls of major label signings and a year later signed with Trojan Records. A series of successful singles surfaced, including 'Don't Stop', 'Playboy', 'Sister Big Stuff', 'I'm Gonna Get Married', 'Just Because', 'Your Eyes Are Dreaming' and 'Miss White And Wonderful, Miss Black And Beautiful'. Ray stayed with the label until the mid-70s when it was declared bankrupt, and then re-emerged through Saga. In 1974 Ray starred alongside Sharon Forrester in a film financed by the British Film Institute, *Moon Over The Alley*, a tale of the Jamaican experience with the immigration authorities. He linked up with the Pioneers, who had established their own label, releasing hits from Gregory Isaacs, 'Mr. Cop', and Mexicano, for the classic 'Move Up Starsky'. Ray recorded a number of hits, notably 'Dip And Fall Back' and 'Revolution Rock', and a version of Bob Marley's 'I'm Still Waiting', which provided the backing to the Mexicano's chart-topper. Ray set up his own Black Jack label, re-releasing Christine Joy White's 'You'll Lose A Good Thing' and *Pure Love*, as well as his own works. Other notable performers to benefit from his production skills included Dave Barker and Studio One veteran Winston Francis. In 1982 Danny performed a duet, 'Why Don't You Spend The Night', with the then unknown singer Shirley James, which bubbled under the UK pop chart. The success of the single led to another major label signing, this time with Arista Records who re-released the single. The duet was followed by 'Right Time Of The Night' which, although less successful, led to recording sessions in Jamaica for the duo's album and a reggae version of Paul Anka's 'Hey Paula'. Ray joined forces with the British Reggae Artists Famine Appeal, performing the verse alongside the Chosen Few, Junior English and B.B. Seaton for the release of 'Let's Make Africa Green Again'. By the mid-80s Ray returned to Jamaica where he recorded a Dandy Livingstone composition, 'No Love Today'. Into the 90s Ray continues to record in the popular sentimental lovers rock style, including another remake of 'Playboy', which has since become his anthem, being regularly played on the revival circuit.

● ALBUMS: *The Same One* (Trojan 1973)★★★, *Playboy* (Black Jack 1989)★★★.

RAYVON

b Bruce Brewster. Rayvon is widely considered to be Shaggy's sparring partner, first gaining prominence on the DJ's 'Big Up', which topped the New York reggae chart in 1992. Rayvon has in fact been involved in the New York reggae scene for a number of years and is considered a veteran. His recordings with Shaggy included the adroit jazzy hit 'Nice And Lovely', in 1993, and three years later, Rayvon found international success providing vocals on the duo's interpretation of Mungo Jerry's 'In The Summertime'. The unprecedented success with Shaggy, the latter being the only reggae artist to have topped the European pop charts twice, resulted in Rayvon joining him on a world tour encompassing the Far East, Eastern Europe and Africa. His acclaimed appearances on the tour prompted recognition of Rayvon as a performer in his own right. In 1994 he teamed up with Funkmaster Flex and Frank Cutlass for 'No Guns No Murder'. His continued involvement with Shaggy and the Sting International crew led to an affiliation with the DJ's label, and the release of an inspired debut that showcased Rayvon's unique talent. In 1997 the corporation released *Hear My Cry*, utilizing the production skills of Robert Livingstone and Gemma Corfield. Notable inclusions were 'Party Vibe', which sampled KC And The Sunshine Band, the much-hyped 'Stallion Ride', and the conscientious title track. He also performed 'Some People' on the soundtrack to *Speed 2*. Rayvon continues to record with Shaggy, most recently with the combination hit 'Get Up Stand Up', which also featured Maxi Priest on vocals.

● ALBUMS: *Hear My Cry* (Virgin 1997)★★★.

REBEL, TONY

b. Patrick Barrett, Manchester, Jamaica, West Indies. Rebel is one of the few dreadlocked 'cultural' DJs of the ragga era, but actually started out as a singer, winning local talent competitions as Papa Tony or Tony Ranking on sound systems such as Destiny Outernational, Thunderstorm, Wha Dat and Sugar Minott's Youth Promotion. In 1988 he recorded 'Casino' for the MGB label, his first ever release. Sides for Delroy 'Callo' Collins and Shocking Vibes followed, but it was at Penthouse where his true potential began to be realized. 'Fresh Dee-Jay', 'Music Fraternity' and 'Mandella Story' announced his arrival, before he was matched with Cutty Ranks for *Die Hard*. It included two of his first hit singles, 'The Armour' and 'Instant Death'. Although notable for their combative zeal, both revealed an uncompromisingly spiritual approach, and were voiced in a melodic sing-jay fashion that was unique. 'Fresh Vegetable' was the unlikeliest love song of 1990, but proved a sizeable hit; so too, 'D.J. Unity' (with Macka B), 'The Herb', 'War And Crime' and 'Hush', the latter voiced for Bobby Digital. Throughout 1991-92 he recorded for a number of different producers, including Exterminator,

Redman, Star Trail and the Two Friends label, who teamed him first with Anthony Red Rose ('Gun Talk') and then Judy Mowatt ('Guilty'). Penthouse released his debut album, *Rebel With A Cause*, in 1992 and this was followed by *Rebellious*, a more rootsy set produced by Sky High that included duets with Half Pint and Garnett Silk. 'Chatty Chatty Mouth' continued his winning run with Penthouse before he recorded the anthemic 'Reggae On Top' for Steely And Clevie. By the end of the year he had signed to Columbia Records for *Vibes Of The Times*, released in 1993. 'Sweet Jamaica', a song voiced for Bobby Digital, was chosen for the soundtrack of the film *Cool Runnings* that November.

● ALBUMS: with Capleton And Ninjaman *Real Rough* (1990)★★★, with Cutty Ranks *Die Hard (Volumes 1 & 2)* (Penthouse 1991)★★★★, with Ranks *20 Man Dead* (Charm 1991)★★★, *Rebel With A Cause* (Penthouse 1992)★★★, *Rebellious* (RAS 1992)★★★, *Vibes Of The Times* (Columbia 1993)★★★.

RED DRAGON

b. Leroy May, Kingston, Jamaica, West Indies. One of the most enduring and dependable DJs to emerge from Jamaica, Dragon - or Redman, as he was then known - learnt his trade on Barrington Hi-Fi in 1981, progressing to Stone Love, Small Axe, Rambo Mango (which he owned) and People's Choice sound systems, before changing his name in 1984 after the popularity of his 'Laughing Dragon' lyric on a dub plate. Fellow DJ Charlie Chaplin had also passed through the ranks of People's Choice and produced his debut tune, 'Computer', in 1985. The following year, Dragon went to Harry J., who released 'Nah Get Nutten' and 'Commander' to a welcoming dancehall audience. In 1987 'Hol A Fresh' was a massive hit for Winston Riley, but failed to cross over as predicted owing to poor promotion. Nevertheless, its local success ensured a wealth of releases for the late King Tubby ('Canter Mi Horse'), Redman, Vena and King Jammy's, where 'Duck Dance' and 'Della Skank' confirmed his ability to define the latest dancehall moves. In 1989 Riley's Techniques label issued an album pairing him with his DJ brother, Flourgon. That same year witnessed the birth of his own Dragon label, on which he

released tunes by young artists such as John Mouse as well as himself, 'Old', 'Love Unuh' and 'My Anthem' achieving the most recognition. Throughout 1990-91 he recorded very little, concentrating instead on encouraging the fresh talent emerging through Rambo Mango and Flourgon's Sweet Love set. Buju Banton and Terry Ganzie both started their careers with Dragon. In 1992 he made a return to the dancehall market with the uncharacteristic *Pum Pum Shorts*, and then several sides for Shang, Steely And Clevie, Mafia And Fluxy and Parrish. The momentum increased during 1993 and there was a proliferation of hits for the likes of Bobby Digital, Danny Browne, Winston Riley, Fashion and Sly And Robbie's Taxi label, all capturing his deep, rolling vocals and adept rhythm-riding to perfection. In 1994, Red Dragon enjoyed a huge crossover hit in combination with Brian And Tony Gold with 'Compliments On Your Kiss', which peaked at number 2 in the UK chart.
● ALBUMS: *Red Dragon Vs Flourgon* (Techniques 1989)★★★, *Pum Pum Shorts* (Dragon 1992)★★★★.

RED RAT

b. Wallace Wilson, 17 January 1978, St. Ann's Bay, Jamaica, West Indies. Wilson came from a musical family - his father played guitar as part of Byron Lee And The Dragonaires, while his eldest brother played bass for Diana King, and another brother played keyboards and drums in the band KRU. By his fourth birthday, Wilson was performing in front of audiences in Jamaica, although he cited his first notable performance as being at a school barbecue in 1990. He was DJing under the guise of Mice (a name given to him by his football coach) when the MC halted the proceedings, stating that if the crowd wanted more they should throw money onto the stage. The crowd obliged and inspired the young DJ to persevere on his chosen path. The event encouraged Danny Brownie to sign Wilson, who subsequently gained considerable experience with the Main Street Crew, also featuring General Degree, Buccaneer, Goofy and Hawkeye. Wilson recorded his debut, 'Can't Live Without You', in 1995 as a guest DJ with his brother's band KRU; this was followed by 'Itsy Bitsy' under his new name, Red Rat (there were already two other DJs using the Mice name - his

new name was inspired by General Degree's comment, 'yah red and yah look like a rat'). On completing his education, Red Rat was greeted with two encores when he played at the annual Sting Festival. His recording career went into overdrive with the exuberant 'Shelly Ann', 'Dwayne' and 'Good Boy'. His distinctive cry, audacious lyrics, babyface looks, red medusa hairstyle and infectious catchphrase, 'oooh nooo', resulted in international notoriety. 'Shelly Ann' topped the reggae charts worldwide and was acknowledged as the ragga anthem of 1997. His popularity resulted in international tours with the Main Street Crew, including highly acclaimed performances at London's Notting Hill carnival. He released a succession of Jamaican hits including combinations with Buju Banton ('Charlene') and Goofy ('Big Man Little Yute'), alongside the solo hits 'Wrigley's' and 'Can't Manage'.
● ALBUMS: *Oh No ... It's Red Rat* (Greensleeves 1997)★★★★.

RED ROSE, ANTHONY

b. Anthony Cameron, *c.*1962, Kingston, Jamaica, West Indies. At the start of his career, Michael Rose recorded as Tony Rose, which led to Anthony performing as Red Rose to avoid confusion. Anthony Red Rose has the distinction of recording the first hit from King Tubby's new studio in 1985. The song 'Tempo' was recorded in the Waterhouse style initially popularized by Tenor Saw, and the latter's popular song 'Fever' was almost identical to the Red Rose hit. He continued recording sporadic hits, including 'Reminisce', with haunting backing vocals from Brian And Tony Gold, 'Vanity Rush', 'Babylon Be Still' and 'Not Ready For My Loving'. By 1994 he enjoyed a number of combination hits with 'Gun Talk', alongside Tony Rebel's 'You A Mi Heart', featuring the up-and-coming DJ Merciless, and 'Ragga Reggae' with Don Youth, while 'Never Get' featured Anthony Malvo, who also performed with Red Rose alongside Cobra for 'Rumours' and President Brown for 'Red Alert'. The US release of *Family Man* was met with critical acclaim. With the increasing popularity of jungle music, Red Rose's 'Tempo' enjoyed a revival hit when remixed in the fast style. While he continued to record dancehall hits he also pursued a career as a producer and

formed a partnership with Anthony Malvo for the How Yu Fi Seh Dat? and RR&M productions. The duo produced their own vocal excursions alongside hits for Beenie Man ('Name Brand') and Red Dragon ('Sweet Heart'). In 1995 they produced Simpleton's smash hit, 'Quarter To Twelve'. The rhythm led to numerous versions and the release of the one-rhythm *Quarter To Twelve*, featuring contributions from Beenie Man, Cobra and Snagga Puss. The album initially surfaced in typical dancehall fashion as strictly vinyl and without a sleeve. In 1996 the team followed their success with the equally popular hit 'Explode Gal' for Red Dragon, restoring the DJ's credibility after his crossover hit with Brian And Tony Gold. Red Rose and Malvo demonstrated their versatility when they produced Brown Sugar for the classic 'Sensimilia Babe', an ode to marijuana in a lovers rock style.
● ALBUMS: *Family Man* (VP 1994)★★.

RED, DANNY

b. Daniel Clarke, *c*.1962, London, England. Clarke's formative years in London were followed by an adolescence in Jamaica where he became acquainted with reggae, blues, R&B, gospel, country and jazz. In 1980 he returned to the UK where he was introduced to the Jah Marcus sound system by his cousins. Initially performing as a DJ, he joined the City Dread sound system, leading to further notoriety when he joined the Fine Style Crew. His reputation as a cultural DJ flourished when he toured Europe alongside General Kelly as Danny Dread. It was under this appellation that in 1986, he recorded his debut 'Duppy Conqueror', a moderate hit, followed by 'Skateboard'. A return to Jamaica resulted in a session at Music Mountain alongside the Bloodfire Posse, who supplied the rhythms to 'Blackness Awareness' and 'Who Say Jah Jah'. Danny changed his surname to Red to avoid confusion with two other Jamaican DJs using the Dread banner. The name change coincided with his first singing track, 'Jah Jah Me'. By 1991 he was firmly established as a roots performer, enjoying hits with 'Armageddon', 'Original Formula', 'Don Gorgon' and 'Dance Get Overload'. In 1993 Red's blend of roots and dancehall proved a considerable success, with releases such as 'Sons Of Jah' for Surzima Selassie and 'Jah Is Here' for Abba Jahnoi and Dredbeat. He recorded a number of tracks for Dredbeat including a tribute to Big Youth, 'Warn Them', and a showcase compilation, *Rebirth*, with Ras Tyah, Ras Natural, and of Lidj Incorporated, Lidj Ishu and Lidj Xylon. In 1994 he recorded 'Riddimwize', combining his vocal and DJ skills, followed by a combination with Gospel Fish, 'Teaser'. His success led to a contract with Columbia Records, who released 'Wise Up', which featured Top Cat as well as remixes from Mafia And Fluxy and the Mad Professor. The single proved a moderate success and in 1995 he returned with 'Rolling Stone', produced by Sly And Robbie featuring Starkey Banton. The single, promotional video and an appearance on the *Radio One Roadshow* resulted in a crossover hit, although it marked the end of Red's association with Columbia. He returned to the roots market with a strong compilation, and worked with a number of top producers, including Donovan Germain, Mikey Bennett and Steely And Cleevie, performing 'Keep On Moving', 'Jah Is Here' and 'I Don't Care'.
● ALBUMS: *Riddimwize* (Columbia 1995)★★★, *I Don't Care* (Roots 1996)★★.

REGGAE

Although used as the generic title for all Jamaican music, reggae first arrived in 1968, with Larry And Alvin's 'Nanny Goat' and the Beltones' 'No More Heartaches' competing for the status of first reggae record. The beat was distinctive from rocksteady in that it dropped any of the pretensions to the smooth, soulful sound that characterized slick American R&B, and instead was closer in kinship to US southern funk, being heavily dependent on the rhythm section to drive it along. Reggae's great advantage was its almost limitless flexibility: from the early, jerky sound of Lee Perry's 'People Funny Boy', to the uptown sounds of Third World's 'Now That We've Found Love', it was an enormous leap through the years and styles, yet both are instantly recognizable as reggae. Like ska before it, reggae found favour in the UK with the mods' successors, skinheads. They supported the music to a degree that enabled a roll-call of reggae acts to hit the charts between 1968 and 1972, among them, Desmond Dekker, Dave And Ansell Collins, Jimmy Cliff and Bob And Marcia. Many similar acts also received a bite of the commercial cherry. By 1972 skinheads had tired of the Jamaican sound, which had diversified away from the quirky love songs (Clancy Eccles, Pat Kelly) and stomping organ instrumentals (Upsetters, Lloyd Charmers) of its early days to embrace Rasta philosophy (Junior Byles, Bob Marley, Abyssinians, etc.), DJ music (U-Roy, I. Roy, Dennis Alcapone) and black rights (Burning Spear, Heptones). Other subgenres, such as skank, dub, rockers and steppers, unfolded through the 70s, before all were more or less supplanted by dancehall and ragga for the 80s. Each style, however, remained under the collective banner of reggae, a flag of convenience that never seems to outstay its welcome.

● COMPILATIONS: *Tougher Than Tough - The Story Of Jamaican Music* 4-CD box set (Mango/Island 1993)★★★★★.

● FURTHER READING: *Jamaica: Babylon On A Thin Wire*, Adrian Boot and Michael Thomas. *Reggae: A People's Music*, Rolston Kallyndyr. *Reggae Bloodlines: In Search Of The Music And Culture Of Jamaica*, Stephen Davis. *Jah Music*, Sebastian Clarke. *Steelbands & Reggae*, Paul Farmer. *Reggae: Deep Roots Music*, Howard Johnson. *Reggae International*, Stephen Davis and Peter Simon. *Rastafari & Raggae: A Dictionary & Sourcebook*, Rebekah Michele Mulvaney. *Reggae Island: Jamaican Music In The Digital Age*, Tom Weber. *Words Like Fire: Dancehall Reggae And Ragga Muffin*, Stascha Bader. *Two-tone Story*, George Marshall. *Boss Sounds: Classic Skinhead Reggae*, Mark Griffiths. *Noises In The Blood*, Carolyn Cooper. *Reggae On CD: The Essential Guide*, Lloyd Bradley. *Reggae In View*, Maverick Lensman.

REGGAE GEORGE

b. George Daley, *c.*1950, Kingston, Jamaica, West Indies. With Neville Beckford, Daley would attend auditions as one half of the duo Neville and George. His partner went on to record in the DJ style as Jah Woosh, while George recorded 'Babylon Kingdom Fall' as Prince George - an alias he used only once. His second release, 'Fig Root', credited to Reggae George, was produced by Sonia Pottinger for her High Note label. The success of 'Fig Root' led to recording sessions with producer Hartnell Henry, featuring Bingi Bunny and Sowell Radics, who later formed part of the Roots Radics session band. The most

notable release was 'Read The Bible', which was followed by 'Vision', 'Stop Push The Fire' and a version of the classic Dennis Walks hit, 'Drifter'. The big break came with producer Winston 'Niney' Holness and the release of 'Trodding', which achieved international acclaim and an appearance in the reggae chart. 'Three Wicked Men' followed for 56 Hope Road, an offshoot label of Bob Marley's Tuff Gong empire. It was in the studio that gave the label its name that Rita Marley engineered the recording, ably assisted by Sylvan Morris who had worked on much of Marley's output, notably *Rastaman Vibration.* With such an impressive track record Trojan were keen to release *Mix Up*, which included the hit 'Stop Push The Fire', alongside 'No Fuss Nor Fight', 'Sister Dawn', 'Gimme Gimme Your Love' and a version of John Holt's 'My Eyes'. The set was produced by the late Prince Far I and musicians on the set included Jah Lloyd, Sowell Radics, Errol 'Flabba Holt' and Professor Larry. Despite critical acclaim and the obvious pedigree, *Mix Up* made little impression on the album charts. In 1983 his Tuff Gong recordings surfaced on Dennis Brown's Yvonne's Special label in the UK, while Greensleeves Records released 'Walla Walla' and the more popular 'You'll Never Know'/'We Still Survive'. A follow-up to *Mix Up* was scheduled, but due to the untimely death of Prince Far I, the project was abandoned. By the mid 80s, reunited with his old friend Neville Beckford and employing a host of the island's top session men, he released *Fight On My Own*.

● ALBUMS: *Mix Up* (Trojan 1981)★★★★, *Fight On My Own* (Sky Juice 1985)★★.

REGGAE PHILHARMONIC ORCHESTRA

Formed by original Steel Pulse member Mykaell S. Riley, the Reggae Philharmonic was a noble and bizarre experiment that crossed reggae rhythms with orchestral themes, despite the fact that Riley can neither read nor write music. The idea was to employ the most talented black classical musicians, with Riley adding vocals on top of these arrangements to surprisingly good effect.

● ALBUMS: *Reggae Philharmonic Orchestra* (Mango/Island 1988)★★★, *Time* (Mango/Island 1990)★★★.

REGGAE REGULAR

Reggae Regular formed in 1976, supporting live acts from Jamaica in the UK. The line-up featured George 'Flee' Clark (keyboards), Allan 'Kingping' King (lead vocals and harmony), Anthony 'Benjamin' Rookwood (lead vocals and harmony), Trevor 'Seal' Salmon (bass), Errol 'Sly Jnr.' Francis (drums) and Patrick 'Chiki' Donegan (rhythm guitar and harmony), who were later joined by Norman Junior Ebanks (lead guitar). Initially, the group supported Maurice Wellington's group the Morwells on their first visit to the UK. As the group were managed at the time by Castro Brown, their skills were also utilized for the musical backing for the popular lovers rock trio 15-16-17. A change of management in 1977 led to a recording session in the UK with Lloyd 'TCB' Patten producing. The session resulted in one of the UK's biggest reggae hits of the year, 'Where Is Jah', a haunting tribute to Rastafari. The single introduced Greensleeves Records, which has since become an exceptionally successful independent. The hit was followed by 'The Black Star Liner', a reference to Marcus Garvey's projected shipping company, which was equally popular. The success of the two singles attracted the attention of CBS Records, who signed Reggae Regular, though the group suffered as a consequence. The company insisted that they become known as the Regulars, as the A&R department believed that the inclusion of the word 'reggae' in the group's title would curtail their career prospects. Sadly, in spite of the promotion associated with majors, including a picture disc and gatefold album with a free 12-inch single, their popularity plummeted. The album, although produced by Lloyd 'TCB' Patten, was considered mediocre and they were asked to re-record their principal hit, which lost its appeal when diluted. The label decreed a change of direction influenced by the 2-Tone fad. In 1980 the release of the group's interpretation of the Wailers' ska hit, 'Rude Boy Gone A Jail', and Kenrick Patrick's 'Don't Stay Out Late' curiously surfaced on the label's Epic subsidiary, although it had been allocated a CBS matrix number. The group disbanded, with various members concentrating on individual projects. In 1984 Trevor Salmon and Patrick Donegan returned to Greensleeves as the Reggae Regular, accompanied by Weston Salmon and Brian Campbell. The sessions were engineered by Mad Professor. In spite of the indisputable effort devoted to the project, notably 'Violence In The Streets', 'Tribute To The DJ' and 'Aristocrat', they were unable to match their previous achievements. Allan 'Kingping' King recorded two albums, *Letter From Jail* and *God Of Love*, both of which garnered a respectable response. In the spring of 1996, Patrick Donegan released an album as the Dub Teacher, *Dub Teachings Lesson One*.

● ALBUMS: *Victim* (Columbia 1979)★★★, *Ghetto Rock* (Greensleeves 1980)★★★★.

REID, DUKE

b. *c*.1915, Jamaica, West Indies, d. 1974. Perhaps the single biggest influence on reggae music after his close rival, Coxsone Dodd, Duke Reid's marvellous productions were, at their best, reggae at its absolute peak. Reid spent 10 years as a Kingston policeman, a sometimes dangerous profession that enabled him to develop the no-nonsense style he displayed while conducting business negotiations in later life. He and his wife Lucille bought the Treasure Isle Liquor Store in the 50s, and in a sponsorship agreement, Reid hosted his own radio show, *Treasure Isle Time*, airing US R&B: his theme song was Tab Smith's 'My Mother's Eyes'. Reid also ran his own sound system, Duke Reid The Trojan, and visited America to find obscure R&B tunes with which to baffle rivals such as Coxsone Dodd's Downbeat sound system. After flirting with the record business for three years, recording tunes such as 'Duke's Cookies', 'What Makes Honey' and 'Joker', he took up record production seriously in 1962, enjoying ska hits galore with Stranger Cole, the Techniques, Justin Hinds And The Dominoes and Alton Ellis And The Flames, issuing them on three labels: Treasure Isle, Duke Reid and Dutchess. Reid was a formidable presence in the music business: he was notorious for carrying a loaded gun and ensuring that his ammunition belt was clearly visible. However, he was more than mere muscle and had an astute musical sensibility, as the fast-approaching rocksteady era proved beyond doubt.

By 1966 ska was evolving into a slower, more stately beat, and with help from guitarist Ernest Ranglin and the band of sax player Tommy

McCook And the Supersonics, Reid's productions at his own Treasure Isle Studio epitomized the absolute peak of the style. Hits such as the Paragons' 'Ali Baba' and 'Wear You To the Ball', Alton Ellis's 'Cry Tough', 'Breaking Up', 'Rock Steady' and 'Ain't That Loving You', the Melodians' 'You Don't Need Me', 'I Will Get Along', 'I Caught You' and 'Last Train To Expo '67', the Jamaicans' 'Things You Say You Love' and the Techniques' 'Queen Majesty' were only the tip of an impressive iceberg. All were tasteful, irresistibly danceable, soul-soaked rocksteady classics, released on Reid's own labels in Jamaica and on Trojan Records (the label was named after his sound) or its imprints in the UK. By 1969 rocksteady had died, and Reid was apparently struggling, stuck in a musical revolution he himself had created. However, in 1970 he did it again, taking a sparsely recorded toaster named U-Roy, and single-handedly founded the modern DJ era. At one point U-Roy held four out of the top five Jamaican chart positions and both he and Reid watched the records swap places over a period of months - 'Wake The Town', 'Wear You To the Ball', 'Everybody Bawlin'' and 'Version Galore'. Reid simply dropped the chatter over his old rocksteady hits to start a whole new genre of reggae music. He also had hits with other DJs, such as Dennis Alcapone and Lizzy. Reid's legend in the reggae pantheon was assured. By 1973 Reid's fortunes had again begun to wane, perhaps because he was notorious for not wanting to record rasta lyrics in an era dominated by roots themes, and was considered to be an establishment figure as the senior reggae producer in Jamaica. He died in 1974, his extensive back catalogue going on to sell thousands of singles and albums through a variety of licensees, his name on a record almost a guarantee of sheer joy for the duration of its playing time.

● COMPILATIONS: Various Artists: *Golden Hits 1966-69* recordings (Trojan 1969)★★★★, *The Birth Of Ska 1962-65* recordings (Trojan 1972)★★★★, *Hottest Hits 1966-69* recordings (Front Line)★★★★, *Hottest Hits Volume Two 1966-69* recordings (Front Line 1979)★★★, *Ba Ba Boom Time 1967-68* recordings (Trojan 1988)★★★.

REID, JUNIOR

b. Delroy Reid, 1965, Kingston, Jamaica, West Indies. Born in the Tower Hill area of Kingston, Reid grew up in the infamous Waterhouse ghetto. He made his first recording in 1979 at the age of 13 for the equally youthful singer Hugh Mundell, entitled 'Speak The Truth', and released through Augustus Pablo's Rockers label. Another Mundell production, 'Know Myself', a version of Dennis Walks' classic, 'Drifter', appeared on Greensleeves in 1981. After Mundell's untimely death - Reid was in the car when he was murdered - he achieved some success as part of the Voice Of Progress group, with a single and album entitled *Mini-Bus Driver* for producer Robert Palmer's Negus Roots label. Recording throughout the rest of the early 80s as a solo artist, Reid found success with tracks such as 'Jailhouse', 'Sister Dawn', 'Pallaving Street' and 'Give Thanks & Praise' for King Jammy. Other singles included 'The Original Foreign Mind', a self-production on Sugar Minott's Youth Promotion label, on which he adopted a fast delivery similar to that of the new wave of UK DJs such as Phillip 'Papa' Levi and Smiley Culture. Further notable recordings included 'Babylon Release The Chain' for Errol Thompson, 'Chanting' for Delroy Wright and the monster 'Boom Shack A Lack' for Jammys, released in the UK on Greensleeves.

In 1985 Reid's solo career was interrupted when he was enlisted into the ranks of Grammy award-winners Black Uhuru, after lead singer Michael Rose's departure. The first release with Uhuru, 'Fit You A Fe Fit', met with approval from the reggae audience. However, subsequent material, particularly the experimental, rock-influenced Arthur Baker production, 'Great Train Robbery', and Grammy-nominated *Brutal* album, made more of an impact on the international market, serving only to alienate the grassroots following he had worked so hard to establish. Aware of this credibility gap, Reid inaugurated his own label, JR Productions, and began to issue roots tunes such as 'Pain On The Poor Man's Brain' and 'Nah Get Rich And Switch', credited to Black Uhuru, but far more in the vein of his previous solo material. After recording Uhuru's *Positive* in 1988, Reid left the group to concentrate once more on his own career. Teaming up with English dance outfit

Coldcut for 'Stop This Crazy Thing', he reached number 21 in the UK pop chart in September 1988. In 1990, he made another appearance in the singles chart when he joined forces with indie-dance band the Soup Dragons, for a version of the Rolling Stones' 'I'm Free', reaching number 5 in August of that year. Back in the reggae world, Reid's return to grass-roots favour came in 1989 with the anthemic 'One Blood', followed by a well-received album of the same title. Its raw digital rhythms and roughneck ragga production firmly re-established his name at the forefront of the reggae scene. Since then he has issued a flood of tunes on his own label, including 'Married Life', 'Good Man Scarce', 'Can't Tek the Gun Gun', a new version of 'Mini-Bus Driver', 'Friend Enemy', 'Banana Boat Man', 'Strong Survive', and the popular 'All Fruits Ripe', as well as producing other artists such as Junior Demus, Ninjaman, Dennis Brown, and Gregory Isaacs.

He has also opened his own studio, one more step towards complete artistic independence. Junior Reid, like that other Waterhouse singer, Yammie Bolo, is an artist who has continued to display his commitment to roots reggae music, and looks set to carry on the winning formula into the millennium.

● ALBUMS: with Voice Of Progress *Mini-Bus Driver* (Negus Roots 1982)★★★★, *Boom Shack A Lack* (Greensleeves 1983)★★★★, *Back To Back* (Volcano 1985)★★★, *Original Foreign Mind* (Black Roots 1985)★★★, *One Blood* (JR Music 1989)★★★, *Visa* (Greensleeves 1993)★★★, *Junior Reid And The Bloods* (Ras 1995)★★★.

REVOLUTIONARIES

The Revolutionaries were formed in 1976 and consisted of the in-house session band at Channel One Recording Studio, Maxfield Avenue, Kingston. The line-up featured Sly Dunbar, Robbie Shakespeare, Earl 'Wire' Lindo, Rad Bryan and Ansell Collins. If any of the musicians were unavailable, others would step in, including Lloyd Parks, Uziah 'Sticky' Thompson, Barnabus, Bo Peep, Errol 'Tarzan' Nelson and Skully. They were accompanied by the horn section which consisted of ex-Skatalite Tommy McCook, 'Deadly' Headley Bennett and Vin Gordon. The line-up evolved from Skin, Flesh And Bones who were the resident band at the Tit For Tat club. Their notoriety spread and they were considered to be the island's top session band. They accompanied Al Brown on his track 'Here I Am Baby (Come And Take Me)' which led to them supporting him and others on the Jamaica Showcase tour in 1974. Dunbar's drumming, with its innovative beat, helped the group provide hits for the Mighty Diamonds ('Right Time'), Junior Byles ('Fade Away'), Johnny Osbourne ('Kiss Somebody') and Dillinger ('CB 200'). The Mighty Diamonds cut led to an album of the same name which was released through Virgin Records in the UK. The musicians on *Simple Sly Man* and *Sly Wicked And Slick* were the nucleus of the Revolutionaries, accompanied by Mikey Chung, The Tamlins, Black Uhuru and Beres Hammond. The Revolutionaries' recording style became known as Rockers and the other studios in Jamaica emulated the band's winning formula. The ensemble were criticized for utilizing Coxsone Dodd's old Studio One rhythms; nevertheless, the record-buying public approved. The group also recorded a number of dub and instrumental albums *Vital Dub*, *Goldmine Dub*, *Black Ash Dub* and *Negrea Love Dub*, all of which were greeted with enthusiasm and sold in large quantities. The group's demise occurred when Sly And Robbie's services were enrolled by Peter Tosh for his backing band, Word Sound And Power, while the other members joined forces with Bunny Lee's Aggrovators. Ironically, a dub compilation, *The Revolutionaries Meet The Aggrovators At Channel One*, surfaced and has proved to be the most enduring set.

● ALBUMS: *Vital Dub* (Virgin 1976)★★★★, *Goldmine Dub* (Greensleeves 1978)★★★, *Guerilla Dub* (Burning Sounds 1978)★★★★, *Negrea Love Dub* (Trojan 1978)★★★, *Black Ash Dub* (Trojan 1978)★★★★, *Macca Roots Man Dub* (GG's 1978)★★★, *Outlaw Dub* (Trojan 1978)★★★, *Junkanoo Dub* (Cha Cha 1978)★★, *Dutch Man* (Burning Vibrations 1979)★★★.

● COMPILATIONS: *Revolutionaries Part One* (United Artists 1981)★★★, *Revolutionaries Part Two* (United Artists 1981)★★★, *Hit Bound! The Revolutionary Sound Of Channel One* 1976-79 recordings (Heartbeat 1990)★★★★.

RHODEN, DONNA

b. September 1964, London, England. Rhoden gained notoriety as a lovers rock performer in the early 80s. She began her career performing on the Silver Slate sound system based in Stockwell, south London. Her vocal skills led to an association with members of the Well Pack band, who had provided backing for Brown Sugar - the latter's delicate harmonies alongside 15-16-17 inspired Rhoden to embark on a recording career. Unfortunately, her work with the group made little impact but led to a collaboration with Leonard Chin, the lead guitarist from UK rockers Santic, who had successfully produced hits for Carroll Thompson and Jean Adebambo. Her initial hit, 'It's True', proved a success and was followed by the equally popular 'Be Kind To My Man'. The winning formula resulted in her third release, 'Shy Girl', which did not make a significant impression on the charts. The failure of the single led to an effective change of direction, which resulted in the release of 'I've Fallen In Love'. In 1982 the similarly titled 'I'm Falling In Love', the poignant 'Don't You' and the celebratory 'We Are In Love' were released, all demonstrating the professionalism of the close-knit Ital group. Rhoden has since been recognized as one of the key performers in the development of lovers rock.

RHODEN, PAT

b. Winston Patrick Rhoden, c.1950, Jamaica, West Indies. In 1963 Rhoden left Jamaica to take up residence in the UK. Four years later he recorded his first record, 'Jezebel', for Rita King's R&B label. While with R&B Records he recorded soul ballads and duets with a rising starlet, under the name of Pat And Maureen. Rhoden began working with Dandy Livingstone, who had also recorded for Rita King, and signed with Trojan Records. In 1969 Rhoden successfully signed with Philips Records, who released 'Let The Red Wine Flow' and 'I Need Help', credited to Pat And Brother Lloyd's All Stars. The major label contract was short-lived and Rhoden resurfaced in 1970 with his biggest-selling hit, 'Maybe The Next Time', and 'Do What You Wanna Do' for the Pama label. Three years later he was back with Trojan, where his hit 'I've Got A Nose For Trouble' recalled his experiences within the music industry. Other releases with

the label included versions of Stevie Wonder's 'Boogie On Reggae Woman' and 'Living For The City'. By 1975 Rhoden had become involved in the Jama group, an independent partnership alongside Tito Simon and B.B. Seaton. Two releases by Rhoden, 'Sweet Sunshine' and 'Happiness', maintained his chart profile. He ventured into production work with the Meditations, who recorded 'Sympathy' and 'Johnny', while also promoting other productions for the label. Notable releases for Jama include Junior Byles' 'Fade Away' and I. Roy's 'Welding', which were licensed to a major label but failed to cross over into the mainstream. The label survived into the 80s with the re-releases of Rhoden's 'Stop' and 'Sweet Sunshine', which were minor hits. 'Stop' had previously topped the reggae chart in 1976, although it was originally the b-side to 'Let's Move A Mountain'.

RHYTHM ALBUMS

Rhythm albums are reggae LPs that are all based on one backing track. The first such artefact was Rupie Edwards' 'Yamaha Skank', which featured a dozen different mixes and vocals over the 'My Conversation' rhythm in 1975. Rhythm albums gradually increased in popularity until, by 1990, they constituted around a third of all Jamaican LP releases. Their advantages were obvious: if the listener likes the rhythm, it was reasonable to assume that they would like even more of it, and for producers, it represented the minimum outlay in terms of musicians and studio time. It is also cheaper to buy one LP containing 10 versions of a track than 10 singles.
● COMPILATIONS: Various Artists: *Yamaha Skank* (1975)★★★, *Stalag 17, 18, 19* (1985)★★★★, *Music Works Showcase '88* (1988)★★★, *Funky Punany* (Fashion 1991)★★★.

RICHARDS, CYNTHIA

b. 1944, Duhaney Park, Jamaica, West Indies. Richards' voice won the adoration of fellow pupils at the Denham Town Primary school, where she impressed them at end-of-term concerts. On the suggestion of one of her teachers, she appeared on Vere John's Talent Show, and utilized the financial rewards to further her career. She worked outside music as a magistrate's clerk, as well as with veteran guitarist

Bobby Aitken's Carib Beats Band. Following her departure from the group, her vocal skills were employed by the Falcons, Byron Lee's Dragonaires and the Mighty Vikings. In 1969 she recorded her first single, 'How Could I', for Coxsone Dodd at Studio One. The song did not make any waves but, encouraged by what he had heard, Clancy Eccles recorded her and 'Foolish Fool' was a smash hit in Jamaica. The single was also released in the UK where it bubbled under the pop chart. Continuing with her live performances, in 1970 she also linked up with Skin Flesh And Bones, performing at the Tit For Tat club while maintaining her solo career. Frustrated with the lack of financial reward for her recordings, she did not return to the studio until summoned by Duke Reid. She recorded a version of 'Clean Up Woman', 'Sentimental Reason' and the more rootsy 'Aily I', the latter proving a UK reggae smash when released on the Attack label in 1972. With other producers, including Alvin 'GG' Ranglin and Larry Lawrence, she released the minor hits 'Place In My Heart' and 'Change Partners'. With the business side of the industry thwarting her efforts, Richards decided to go it alone. By 1972 she had recorded 'Mr Postman', which, assisted by Al Brown, was written, produced and arranged by Richards. In 1973 she enjoyed a hit with the Staple Singers' 'If You're Ready (Come Go With Me)'. The success of the single led her to be voted Top Female Artist Of 1973 and she toured as part of the Jamaica showcase alongside Dennis Brown, Toots And The Maytals, Sharon Forrester and Al Brown, all backed by Skin Flesh And Bones.
● ALBUMS: with various artists *Foolish Fool* (Trojan 1972)★★★.

RILEY, JIMMY

b. Martin James Riley, *c.*1954, Kingston, Jamaica, West Indies. Riley began his recording career with Duke Reid at Treasure Isle. He provided harmonies in the Sensations, who enjoyed a number of successes including 'Everyday Is Just A Holiday' and 'Those Guys', both of which have been frequently covered by other artists. Following his departure from the group, Riley joined the Uniques with Slim Smith and Lloyd Charmers; the group enjoyed hits with 'Watch This Sound' and 'Gypsy Woman'. While with the group, Riley also recorded *Absolutely The Uniques*, released in the late 60s and including the classic 'My Conversation' and 'Run Come'. They remained together for almost a year before concentrating on solo careers. Riley initially recorded for Bunny Lee before electing to record independently. In the early 70s he wrote and produced his own work as well as working with other artists, including Slim Smith and Delroy Wilson. Riley enjoyed hits with 'Tell The Youths The Truth', 'Nyah Bingi', 'Clean Up The Streets' and 'Poor Immigrants' which championed the exploited. His success continued through to the early 80s, working with Sly And Robbie's Taxi productions, whose global reputation ensured Riley's solo recordings attracted international interest. The Taxi sessions resulted in the hits 'My Woman's Love', written by Curtis Mayfield, and Riley's own 'Love And Devotion'. Both songs were featured on his album alongside interpretations of the Motown Records hits 'I Wish It Would Rain', 'I'm Gonna Make You Love Me' and 'You'll Lose A Precious Love'. In 1983 Riley topped the reggae chart with his version of Marvin Gaye's 'Sexual Healing', also produced by Sly And Robbie.
● ALBUMS: *Tell The Youths The Truth* (Sonic 1975)★★★, *The Jimmy Riley Explosive Showcase* (Burning Sounds 1978)★★, *Rydim Driven* (Taxi 1982)★★★, *Magic* (Imp 1984)★★★★, *Love Fa Real* (1995)★★★, *Attention* (Love & Promotion 1996)★★★.

RILEY, WINSTON

Riley started out as a singer, forming the legendary rocksteady outfit the Techniques as a schoolboy in 1962. In 1968 the group broke away from their producer Duke Reid, and Riley, with his brother Buster, borrowed enough money from his mother to form his own label. Their first production, Johnny Osbourne's 'Come Back Darling', was an immediate success followed by an album of the same name. Other early productions included Osbourne's 'See And Blind' and 'Purify Your Heart', Alton Ellis's 'I'll Be Waiting', Lloyd Young's 'High Explosion', Dennis Alcapone's 'Look Into Yourself', Jimmy Riley's 'Prophecy', the Ethiopians' 'Promises', and various Techniques sides. These appeared on a variety of labels in Jamaica - Techniques, Wind, Serpent, Romax and Riley Inc. - and a licensing agreement with the B&C group resulted in the appearance of many of them on the Techniques label in the UK. He enjoyed a number 1 UK hit in May 1971 with 'Double Barrel' by Dave And Ansell Collins, which spawned an album of the same title in 1971. The follow-up, 'Monkey Spanner', reached number 7 in July of the following year. In 1973 he achieved a huge Jamaican hit with his production of Ansell Collins' 'Stalag 17', with DJ versions by Big Youth; 'Jim Screechy' and 'All Nations' were also popular. During the mid-70s other fine productions appeared in the then popular roots style, including the Interns' (aka the Viceroys) 'Missions Impossible' and two melodica cuts of the rhythm, both entitled 'Black Out', by Augustus Pablo and Ansell Collins, 'Cheer Up Blackman' by former Technique Morvin Brooks, 'Don't Mock Jah' by Donovan Addams and a pair of fine dub albums, *Meditation Dub* and *Concrete Jungle Dub* (both 1976).

As the decade drew to a close, Riley was responsible for producing one of the first and most influential of the new breed of dancehall DJs, General Echo, enjoying a big reggae hit with 'Arleen' which rode the original 'Stalag' rhythm, and releasing the popular *Ranking Slackness* (1980), which inaugurated the trend for lewd lyrics that has prospered ever since. When quizzed on this in an interview in Canada's *Reggae Quarterly* in 1986, he remarked, with admirable candour: 'Let's face it, that record was a big seller! People would pass by the shop [Techniques Records, at 2 Chancery Lane, Kingston] and say "You don't have to make a record like that!" But somebody have to do it.' This period also saw numerous sides by Johnny Osbourne, including 'Politician', 'Inflation' and a recut of 'Purify Your Heart'. In 1982 Riley revived the Techniques with Morvin Brooks and ex-Paragon Tyrone (aka Don) Evans to record an album, *Never Fall In Love*. In 1985 Riley resurrected the durable 'Stalag' rhythm once more for Tenor Saw's massive dancehall hit, 'Ring The Alarm', which prompted the classic one-rhythm album, *Stalag 17, 18 And 19* (1985). The following year, another of his productions, 'Boops' (Jamaican slang for a sugar daddy) by DJ Supercat, became a massive hit, breaking the artist internationally, and starting another trend for records dealing with the same subject. Riley has been one of the most successful Jamaican producers of the past 25 years, and many artists have benefited from his expertise, including Frankie Paul (*Strange Feeling*, 1984), Michael Prophet, Don Evans (*Don Evans*, 1983), Admiral Tibet (*Leave People's Business*, 1988), Sister Nancy, Red Dragon ('Hol' A Fresh', 1987), Courtney Melody (*Bad Boy*, 1988), Ernest Wilson, Gregory Isaacs, Papa San And Lady G ('Legal Rights', 1989), Cutty Ranks, Yammie Bolo, who recorded his debut 'When A Man's In Love' (1985) for Riley, and many others.

RINGO, JOHNNY

b. 1961, Jones Town, Kingston, Jamaica, West Indies. Johnny Ringo first began his career working in a record shop where he met Welton Irie, which proved to be the start of a long association. Both were influenced by, and shared their enthusiasm for, the popular DJ Ranking Trevor. Ringo joined the Soul Express and Ripper Tone sound systems as an operator. In the late 70s he was given an opportunity to chat on the microphone, which led to a number of recording sessions. His observations on life in Jamaica became a success, although it was the fashionable slackness (lewd) lyrics that proved most popular. His recordings of the hits 'Two Lesbians' and 'Push Lady Push' represent the archetype of this fad. The latter's lyrics were often used by other DJs, such as Jah Bull's 'Push Daughter Push'. In 1982 Ringo had an international hit with 'Dub And Lef', backed with Edi Fitzroy's 'First Class Citizen', produced by the Musical Ambassador. With the Roots Radics he chronicled the advent of the video recorder in Jamaica with the succinctly titled 'Video', which led to numerous DJ hits on the subject. Other bestsellers included 'Pain A Back (Me Can't Rhumba)', 'The Boss', 'Nah Fight Over Woman', 'Model With Me' and 'Married For The Opportunity'. He joined Lees Unlimited and the Gemini sound system, which was widely acknowledged as the sound that introduced Yellowman to the world. The sound followed Ray Symbolic's Hi Fi on an international tour, visiting the UK in 1983. The show was a major success and featured Peter Metro's brother Squiddly Ranking and Welton Irie with Ringo. It was while touring the UK with Gemini that Ringo voiced 'New Yorker' and 'Nice And Easy' at Fashion's A Class studios. He also worked with Sugar Minott, who had recorded dub plates for the sound and also produced Ringo's 1983 hit, 'One O'Clock Rock'. Often credited as simply Ringo, he continued to record throughout the 80s, including the first in a series of clash albums for the Fashion label featuring the two singles and other voicings from the A Class sessions.

● ALBUMS: *Two Cocksman* (Duracell 1981)★★★, *Woman A Ginal* (Sonic 1982)★★★★, with Asher Senator *JA To UK MC Clash* (Fashion 1983)★★★, *Cool Profile* (Negus Roots 1984)★★★, *Eyewitness* (Imp 1990)★★★.

ROCHESTER, ANTHONY

b. 27 June 1970, Kingston, Jamaica, West Indies. Rochester's initial involvement in the Jamaican music scene was with Neville Lee's sound system. Under the guise of Fire, he performed with Lee's until an argument ended the association; shortly afterwards, Rochester embraced Rastafari. A meeting in Jamaica's Pembroke Hall with the conscientious DJ Tony Rebel led to an encounter with the then unknown Garnett Silk. Fire demonstrated his songs to the young performer and together they co-wrote the singer's solo debut, 'You're Gonna Need Love'. Discarding the Fire appellation, Rochester accompanied the late singer when he embarked on sessions at Roof International, which led to sessions for Silk's debut, *It's Growing*, produced by Bobby Digital. The album is widely considered to be his masterpiece and demonstrated the superior writing skills of the partnership of Rochester and Silk. The duo subsequently embarked on a world tour and after their return to Jamaica, the partnership was ended by Silk's death. Rochester continued writing songs, providing Everton Blender with the classic 'Family Man', while he co-wrote 'I'm In Love' with songstress Nadine Sutherland. With Rose 'Ivanay' Thompson, he wrote 'Empower Me', which lent its title to her debut album and featured DJ Angie Angel on the ragga remix. He continued writing and working with a number of Jamaican stars, including Junior Tucker, Uton Green, Thriller U, Sugar Black and Marcia Griffiths.

ROCKERS

Rockers is the name given to the 'militant' double drumming style of reggae that dominated the music from 1975-78. Pioneered by Sly Dunbar, the drummer for Channel One Studio's house band the Revolutionaries, it became immediately popular and Dunbar not only worked for Channel One but also recorded rhythms for most of Jamaica's other top producers. With his unique drumming style, Dunbar made his presence felt on every tune he recorded, but it was not long before every other drummer in reggae had developed his own variation on the Sly Dunbar style. Bunny Lee, Joe Gibbs, Yabby You and, ironically, Coxsone Dodd (on whose original rhythms many of the hit records were based) all enjoyed success with their versions of the sound. This would ordinarily have been of purely parochial interest to reggae fans only, but the rise of Rockers coincided with the first considerable outside investments in Jamaican music - notably from Island Records and Virgin Records. Both were anxious to capitalize on the then current international success of Bob Marley And The Wailers, and the subsequent interest and greater availability of 'roots' reggae meant that the 'Rockers' sound became both well known and influential worldwide. Much of the musical output of the period sounds more dated now than the originals that were being 'updated' but, as always, the best still sounds as fresh and innovative as when it was first released.

ROCKERS (FILM)

Rockers is the story of drummer Leroy 'Horsemouth' Wallace and his fictional attempt to become involved in the Jamaican music business. The film featured a host of reggae stars, including Big Youth, Jacob Miller, Gregory Isaacs, Richard 'Dirty Harry' Hall, Robbie Shakespeare and Kiddus I. The film also included cameos from Burning Spear, the Mighty Diamonds, Doctor Alimantado, Leroy Smart, Big Joe, Jack Ruby and Joe Gibbs, to name but a few. The story begins with Horsemouth buying a motorbike which he decorates with the Lion Of Judah. Once his bike is suitably embellished, he successfully attempts to secure records from Joe Gibbs and Jack Ruby. His music business aspirations are encouraged

by a host of Jamaican stars, including Tommy McCook, who is seen rehearsing in his backyard with Herman Marquis and Bobby Ellis. In addition to selling records, Horsemouth is asked to support Inner Circle for a regular booking. While at the venue, he trifles with the affections of the owner's daughter, Sunshine, which leads to a violent confrontation. In addition, Horsemouth's bike is stolen by an organized crime group led by Sunshine's father. Horsemouth discovers that his bike is in a warehouse along with an extraordinary haul. Supported by the all-star line-up, he recovers his bike along with the spoils, and in a clandestine operation distributes the 'ill-gotten' gains around Trenchtown. The film's soundtrack featured classic songs from Bunny Wailer, Peter Tosh, Junior Byles, the Mighty Maytones, the Heptones, Junior Murvin, Third World, the Upsetters, Kiddus I, Burning Spear, Gregory Isaacs and Jacob Miller. Though not earning the cult status of *The Harder They Come*, the movie was greeted with enthusiasm in Jamaica, particularly on account of the numerous cameo appearances. In promoting the film Horsemouth made a triumphant appearance at the One Love Peace Concert, where he was hailed as Jamaica's biggest movie star.
● ALBUMS: Various Artists *Rockers* (Island 1979)★★★★.

ROCKSTEADY

Rocksteady, among the most elegant and rhythmically pleasing of all pop music forms, grew out of ska, spanning the period *c.*1966-68. Ska's furious high-tempo beat had driven dancers into frenzies in Jamaica for five years, at that point, and a new, more confident breed of singers had emerged in Jamaica, with the likes of the Ethiopians, the Maytals, Ken Boothe, Alton Ellis and the Wailers. Ska, however, offered limited possibilities for the singer, who either had to fight with it or flow through it, but the chances of stamping one's personality on a song, in the same way that American soul stars could, were minimal. As Jamaica's singers began to offer more than just the icing on ska's cake, with the idea of being real songwriters with something to say, so the beat slowed to allow them the time to say it. The bass parts took a distinctive character for the first time, leaving a space in the rhythm

that came to characterize all of Jamaican music from this point onwards. Bearing in mind the frantic currents of Jamaican music, it is almost impossible to pinpoint exactly when ska became rocksteady, though certain records such as Peter Tosh's 'I'm The Toughest', the Wailers' 'Rasta Put It On' and Alton Ellis And The Flames' 'Cry Tough' were rocksteady in all but name, before the genre was defined as such. By 1967 the rocksteady era was in full flow, perhaps best epitomized by the sounds emanating from Duke Reid's Treasure Isle Studio in Bond Street, Kingston. Reid's productions were heavily dependent on the arrangements of saxophonist Tommy McCook, and together the pair of them created a pantheon of hits from the likes of Alton Ellis, the Paragons, the Melodians and Joya Landis that remain unsurpassed today in terms of their sheer melodic strength. Other producers who worked on distinctive rocksteady sides include Coxsone Dodd, Sonia Pottinger and Prince Buster. The shift of emphasis away from costly horn sections meant that more people could afford to become involved in record production, and many new producers began to make their mark. The rocksteady bubble burst around 1968, when the new, faster and more manic style of reggae began to emerge. However, the lines between new and old styles of Jamaican music were blurred, and remain so today - reggae's DJ boom was started by U-Roy's use of old rocksteady backing tracks at Treasure Isle, and both dancehall and ragga styles owe plenty to the format.
● COMPILATIONS: Various Artists *Put It On - Its Rocksteady* (Island 1968)★★★★, *Rocksteady Coxsone Style* (Studio One 1968)★★★★, *Get Ready Rock Steady* (Studio One 1968)★★★★, *Hottest Hits (Vols. 1, 2 & 3)* (Treasure Isle 1979)★★★, *Rocksteady Years* (Island 1980)★★★★, *Mojo Rock Steady* (Heartbeat/Studio One 1994)★★★.

RODRIGUEZ, RICO

b. Emmanuel Rodriguez, 17 October 1934, Kingston, Jamaica, West Indies. With the exception of Don Drummond, Rico aka Reco aka El Reco, was undoubtedly the most gifted trombonist working in the early years of Jamaican music. In the 40s he attended the famous Catholic Alpha Boys School, where, by the age of

10, he had learned to play the trombone under the strict tutelage of the nuns, though he had originally wanted to play the saxophone. In the early 50s he began appearing at and winning local talent contests. He became a Rasta and formed a close musical association with master Rasta drummer Count Ossie at his encampment at Wareika Hill, to the east of Kingston. Rodriguez's first recording session was for Coxsone Dodd, playing on the Jiving Juniors' 'Over The River' and Theophilius Beckford's seminal 'Easy Snappin'', and his own 'Stew Peas And Cornflakes'. He went on to work on literally hundreds of sessions for Dodd and most of the top producers of the day, including Duke Reid ('Let George Do It'), Leslie Kong, Vincent Chin (Randy's, for whom he cut 'Rico Special') and Prince Buster, who released a few sides credited to Rico himself, such as 'Luke Lane Shuffle', 'August 1962', 'This Day', 'Blues From The Hills', and the amazing 'Soul Of Africa'. In an interview with Carl Gayle for *Black Music* magazine in 1977, Rodriguez claimed that some records, issued after he moved to Britain but recorded years earlier ('Let George Do It', 'Salt Lane Shuffle') and credited to his successor, Don Drummond, were really by him. In 1966 while resident in the UK, Rodriguez joined Buster when the latter toured the country, and was enlisted to play on 'Barrister Pardon', the follow-up to the infamous 'Judge Dread', during recording sessions in London.

Rodriguez left Jamaica in 1961 and settled in the UK, where he continued recording as a session musician for artists such as Laurel Aitken, Georgie Fame, Joe 'Brixton Cat' Mansano and others, and also in his own right with many singles, including the popular 'The Bullet', and a number of albums released on various UK reggae labels throughout the 60s. In March 1964 he experienced a taste of pop chart success with a reworking of Jimmy Cliff's 'King Of Kings' as Ezz Reco And The Launchers, with Boysie Grant on vocals. The record entered the chart one week before Millie's 'My Boy Lollipop' and spent four weeks in the lower reaches of the UK Top 50, but follow-ups 'Little Girl' and 'Please Come Back' failed to sell in any quantity and the band folded. He spent the early 70s in the doldrums, rarely recording, but passing the time by playing live with the Undivided, a band made up of expatriate Jamaican musicians. In 1976 he returned to Jamaica to record the well-received *Man From Wareika*, utilizing many of the key Jamaican session musicians of the day, including Sly And Robbie. With the arrival of 2-Tone in the early 80s Rodriguez enjoyed great success playing on stage and on record with the Specials, on whose label his next album, *That Man Is Forward*, was released. This was followed by *Jama Rico* a year later. Since a protracted stay in Jamaica, where he spent eight years living once more in Wareika, Rodriguez has returned to London and regularly appears on stage with double bassist Gary Crosby's Jazz Jamaica.

● ALBUMS: *Reco In Reggae Land* (1969)★★★, *Blow Your Horn* (1969)★★★, *Brixton Cat* (1969)★★★★, *Man From Wareika* (1976)★★★★, *That Man Is Forward* (2-Tone 1981)★★★, *Jama Rico* (2-Tone 1982)★★★.

ROMEO, MAX

b. Max Smith, *c*.1947, Jamaica, West Indies. It was Romeo who first introduced to Britain the concept of rude reggae with 'Wet Dream', which, despite a total radio ban, reached number 10 in the UK charts. He toured the UK several times in the space of a year and issued two albums, *A Dream* being the better selling. However, despite other similarly styled singles such as 'Mini Skirt Vision', he did not enjoy chart success again. Romeo was, essentially, something of a gospel singer, with an ability to convey a revivalist fervour on his records, which included 'Let The Power Fall' (a Jamaican political anthem in 1972) and 'Pray For Me'. Furthermore, he had an ability to convey the trials, tribulations and amusements of Jamaican life in a song, as evinced by 'Eating Competition', 'Sixpence' and 'Aily And Ailaloo'. In 1972 Romeo began a liaison with producers Lee Perry and Winston 'Niney' Holness, and from this point onwards, his records had a musical fire to match his apocalyptical vision and contrasting humour. 'Babylose Burning', 'Three Blind Mice' and 'The Coming Of Jah' all maintained his star status in Jamaica between 1972 and 1975. *Revelation Time* was one of the best albums of 1975, and 1976's *War Ina Babylon* was hailed by the rock press as an all-time classic reggae album. However, Perry had much to do with the artistic success of those records, and following a much-publicized split between the pair - with Perry recording 'White Belly Rat' about Romeo, and scrawling 'Judas' over the singer's picture in Perry's studio - Romeo was cast adrift without musical roots. *I Love My Music*, recorded with the help of Keith Richards, was a flop, and the stronger *Reconstruction* fared no better. A move to New York's Wackies' label in the early 80s did little to reverse his fortunes, and by the late 80s Max Romeo's name was forgotten in the mainstream reggae market. However, in the spring of 1992, London producer Jah Shaka recorded *Far I Captain Of My Ship* on Jah Shaka Records, an unabashed, Jamaican-recorded roots album, generally reckoned to be Romeo's best work for over 15 years.

● ALBUMS: *A Dream* (1970)★★★, *Let The Power Fall* (1972)★★★, *Revelation Time* (Tropical Sound Tracs 1975)★★★★, *War Ina Babylon* (Island 1976)★★★★, *Reconstruction* (1978)★★★, *I Love My Music* (1979)★★, *Rondos* (1980)★★, *Holding Out My Love For You* (Shanachie 1987)★★, *Far I Captain Of My Ship* (Jah Shaka 1992)★★★★, *On The Beach* (1993)★★★.

RONDO, GENE

b. Winston Lara, May 1943, d. June 1994, Kingston, Jamaica, West Indies. Rondo was involved in the music business from the late 50s. He entered the Vere Johns Opportunity Hour where he found success with his partner Satch. By 1960 he recorded 'Love My Little Queenie' and 'Squeeze Me', and in 1962 he left Jamaica for the UK, where he continued with his musical career. Rondo initially trained as a classical vocalist, studying at a school in Hammersmith, London, and performing the classics in Covent Garden. He worked on numerous recording sessions in a R&B style, including the local hits 'Because You're Mine', 'Its Got To Be Mellow' and 'Grey Life'. In 1970 he formed a band called the Undivided, who performed around the UK and released a pop reggae album for Decca Records, although the lack of promotion resulted in an ambiguous collection. Rondo continued to record as a soloist with Trojan Records, including 'Sentimental Reasons' and 'A Lovers Question'. With Magnet Records he recorded with Mike Dorane for 'Valley Of Tears' and 'Impossible Dream'. Rondo

worked for a number of UK-based producers, including Clement Bushay ('You Said You Love Me'), Dennis Harris ('Ms Grace'), and Count Shelley ('I'm In A Different World'). Proving to be a prolific artist both in the studios and performing live, Rondo was invited to accompany Susan Cadogan when she sang 'Hurts So Good' on *Top Of The Pops*. In the mid-70s Rondo embraced Rastafari and with Bunny Lee recorded 'A Land Far Away', as well as the more conventional 'Why You Do That' and 'Everything Going Up Love'. Often regarded as an erratic recording artist, in 1983 he had a success with 'Prisoner In Love', although his solo work is overshadowed by his extraordinary efforts in the BRAFA project. The British Reggae Artists Famine Appeal formed an allegiance in 1985, resulting in the recording of 'Let's Make Africa Green Again'. The various artists that gathered for the song included Rondo alongside Dennis Brown, Ken Parker, B.B. Seaton, Trevor Walters, Danny Ray, Winston Reedy, Janet Kay, Aswad, and the Chosen Few. The music was provided by Undivided Roots, who, it is claimed, evolved from Rondo's original incarnation in the early 70s. Following his death in 1994, a memorial concert featuring Alton Ellis, Prince Lincoln, Justin Hinds, Dennis Alcapone, Owen Gray and Carroll Thompson was held in honour of Rondo.

● ALBUMS: *On My Way* (Trojan 1972)★★★, with Mike Dorane *Reggae Desire* (Magnet 1974)★★, with Undivided *Listen To The World* (Decca 1974)★★★.

ROOTS RADICS

Jamaican session band centred around a nucleus of Errol 'Flabba' Holt (bass), Lincoln Valentine 'Style' Scott (drums) and Eric 'Bingi Bunny' Lamont (guitar). Other members at various times included Roy Hamilton (lead guitar), Noel 'Sowell' Bailey (lead guitar), Dwight Pinkney (formerly of the Sharks and Zap Pow, on lead guitar), Carlton 'Santz' Davis (drums), Fish Clarke (drums) and Steely Johnson (later of Steely And Clevie fame, on keyboards). Holt and Bingi Bunny were previously active as part of Morris 'Blacker' Wellington's Morwells set-up, recording such popular tunes as 'Swing & Dine' (1974), 'They Hold Us Down' (1978) and 'Kingston Twelve Tuffy' (1979). Prior to this,

Bunny had been teamed with bongo player Bongo Herman, the pair enjoying a big hit, 'Know Far I', in 1971 for producer/singer Derrick Harriott. He had also produced Peter Broggs' *Progressive Youth* LP, and played in the crack Channel One session band the Revolutionaries, whose demise at the end of the 70s was prompted by Sly And Robbie's production work for their Taxi label, and live work with Peter Tosh, which had left a vacuum the Radics were only too pleased to fill. Errol Holt was already noted for his many fine singles during the mid-70s, including 'A You Lick Me First', 'Gimme Gimme' and 'Who Have Eyes To See'. Their initial impact was in partially slowing down the beat from the militant rockers sound of the Revolutionaries. This is perhaps best showcased on an album on which they worked for producer Henry 'Junjo' Lawes; *Bounty Hunter* (1979) was Barrington Levy's debut, as it was for the Radics, and it revolutionized reggae music in the same way that the Mighty Diamonds' *Right Time* had done five years earlier. Both productions included old Studio One rhythms, which were central to the success of both groups. The Radics worked on innumerable sessions for as many different producers, including Linval Thompson - it was with their rhythms that Scientist destroyed space invaders and won the World Cup, as the titles of his LPs suggest - and worked for a while as Gregory Isaacs' backing band on tour and record; they were responsible for the rhythms on his classic *Night Nurse* (1982), the title track of which enjoyed a revival in 1997 as a pop hit for Simply Red and provided the basis for a number of dancehall hits. The Roots Radics also did sessions for Bunny Wailer and Israel Vibration, among many others. While in the UK on tour with Prince Far I (for whom they recorded under the name the Arabs), the group forged a social and musical friendship with maverick reggae/rock producer Adrian Sherwood, for whom they worked on many sessions as part of the loose conglomerates Creation Rebel and Singers & Players. The Roots Radics came in at the birth of, and were partly responsible for, the dancehall style that dominated in the first half of the 80s. However, as their commitment to live work increased, particularly in the USA, they were eventually usurped by other outfits. The digital/ragga revolution sparked off by King Jammy's production of Wayne Smith's massive hit, 'Under Me Sleng Teng', virtually eradicated the need for live musicians overnight, and the Radics lost their position as Jamaica's number one session band, although they remained in demand for stage shows. Eric Lamont died of prostate cancer in January 1994.

● ALBUMS: *Roots Radics Dub Session* (Solid Groove 1982)★★★★, *Freelance* (Kingdom 1985)★★★, *Forwards Never Backwards* (Heartbeat 1990)★★★, *World Peace Three* (Heartbeat 1992)★★★, *Radically Radics* (Ras 1996)★★★★.

ROSE, MICHAEL

b. Jamaica, West Indies. Rose is the former vocalist with Black Uhuru, but he left that group shortly after they had received a Grammy award for 1984's *Anthem*. He took an extended rest from the music business and became a coffee plantation owner. His solo career began with 'Demonstration' for his own Grammy Rose label. 'Bogus Badge', the follow-up, gained strong reviews, but it was not until he signed with RCA Records that he began to gain serious commercial exposure. However, by this time Rose's music had begun to gravitate to the pop/soul mainstream. A cover version of Paul Simon's early 70s song, 'Mother And Child Reunion', was indicative of this, being closer to contemporary hip-hop than the roots sound with which Black Uhuru had been so closely associated. Whatever its style, it was an undeniably effective single that impressed the critics. His singles for Sly And Robbie's Taxi label heralded a return to roots reggae, and 'Monkey Business', 'Visit Them' and 'One A We: To A We' are already regarded as minor classics of contemporary roots music. However, his relationship with RCA soured and it was not until 1995 and his self-titled debut for Heartbeat Records that he recovered the lost ground. This set included excellent singles such as 'Short Temper', and paired him with Winston 'Niney' Holness. For *Be Yourself* Rose elected to plot his own destiny, producing the rhythms in association with a select group of collaborators. This included remakes of Black Uhuru classics such as 'I Love King Selassie' and 'Guess Who's Coming To Dinner', as well as powerful original compositions including 'From Babylon To Timbuktu' and 'Agony'.

● ALBUMS: *Free Yourself* aka *Proud* (RCA 1990)★★★, *Michael Rose* (Heartbeat 1995)★★★, *Be Yourself* (Heartbeat 1996)★★★★, *Nuh Carbon* (Greensleeves 1996)★★★, *Dance Wicked* (Heartbeat 1997)★★★.

ROSE, SAMANTHA

b. 1954, Kingston, Jamaica, West Indies. Rose left Jamaica for the UK when she was 15, although she began singing prior to her departure. She made her recording debut when she was 21 with the UK-based producer Les Cliff, 'Your Tender Lips'. The single was released through Dennis Harris, whose independent Eve organization spawned the lovers rock label and genre. Rose continued recording with Cliff, who had established his own Saturn label, releasing the classic 'Undying Love' alongside 'My Only Chance', 'Could This Be True' and 'How I Need You'. By 1978 she began recording with Winston Curtis, who released her debut, *In Person*, which included remakes of her earlier hits alongside the chart-topping 'Kiss You All Over' and 'Hello I Love You'. Also on the album was a cover version of 'Angel Of The Morning' which, although originally an R&B hit, has become a reggae standard. In 1980 she released 'Angel In Your Arms' and 'Stay With Me Baby', as well as notable duets with Ray Mondo, which included a version of the Heptones' 'Book Of Rules' and 'Easy Loving'. By 1981 Rose was reunited with Les Cliff, who not only produced, but also performed on, the duet 'Together In Love'. Other examples of her work in this period surfaced on the popular *Reggae For Lovers* compilation. In 1982 her distinctive vocals were recorded by Count Shelly who released 'Go Away Little Girl', 'You'll Never Get Your Hooks In My Man' and her second album of lovers tunes. By the early 90s she was reputed to have relocated to Miami where she joined the growing number of South Florida Reggae Artists celebrated at a concert that included appearances from Wayne Wade and Jimmy Riley.

● ALBUMS: *In Person* (Empire 1978)★★, *Tell Me Why* (Third World 1981)★★★.

ROYAL RASSES

(see Prince Lincoln)

ROYALS

Formed by Roy Cousins (b. *c*.1945, Cockburn Pen, Kingston, Jamaica, West Indies) in 1964, the group also featured Bertram Johnson, Keith Smith and Errol Wilson, although the line-up remained largely fluid, with Cousins remaining a constant. The Royals recorded for Duke Reid and Federal in the mid-60s, and for Coxsone Dodd in 1967, though no releases were forthcoming until 1968 when they cut 'Never See Come See' for producer Joe Gibbs, a dig at the Pioneers. The following year, the group recorded 'Never Gonna Give You Up' for Byron Smith, 'Pick Out Me Eye', and, in 1969, '100 Pounds Of Clay' for Lloyd Daley. Although they achieved a measure of popular, if not fiscal, success with these records, Cousins disbanded the group and took a two-year sabbatical. He eventually saved enough money from his job in the Jamaican Post Office to finance a self-produced single, 'Down Comes The Rain', issued in Jamaica on his own Tamoki label. In 1973 the Royals again recorded the classic 'Pick Up The Pieces', the success of which prompted Coxsone Dodd to release his original version of the song, which had been languishing ignored since the group's stint with him in the late 60s. This too became very popular, particularly the rhythm, which has been versioned countless times since. More self-produced releases followed throughout the decade including 'Promised Land', 'When You Are Wrong', 'Ghetto Man', 'Blacker Black', 'Only For A Time' and 'Sufferer Of The Ghetto', all collected on the essential *Pick Up The Pieces*, which ranks alongside the finest works of contemporaries such as the Abyssinians, the Wailing Souls and the Mighty Diamonds. Cousins also produced records by other artists, including 'Jah Jah Children' by the Kingstonians, 'Genuine Way' by Lloyd Ruddock (King Tubby's brother), 'Heart In Pain' by Vinni O'Brien, 'Monkey Fashion' by I. Roy and 'Way Of Life' by Gregory Isaacs, many included on the various artists set *Herb Dust Volume 1* (1983). In 1975, the Royals split yet again, the rest of the group going on to record for Channel One as the Jayes. Cousins enlisted two new members with whom he recorded the single 'Make Believe', followed by two more albums, *Ten Years After* and *Israel Be Wise*, featuring Heptones Barry Llewelyn and Naggo Morris on harmonies. Cousins has been resident in the UK since the early 80s, concentrating mainly on producing other artists for his Wambesi and Dove labels, including the Gaylads, Derrick Pitter, Cornell Campbell, Earl Sixteen (*Julia* and *Crazy Woman*), Prince Far I, Charlie Chaplin (*Diet Rock*) and Don Carlos (*Plantation*).

● ALBUMS: *Ten Years After* (Ballistic 1978)★★★, *Israel Be Wise* (Ballistic 1978)★★, *Moving On* (Kingdom 1983)★★★.
● COMPILATIONS: *Pick Up The Pieces* (Magnum 1978)★★★★, *Royals Collection* (Trojan 1983)★★★★.

RUFFIN, BRUCE

b. Bernardo Constantine Balderamus, 17 February 1952, St. Catherine, Jamaica. Ruffin served his vocal apprenticeship in 1968 along-side Pat Kelly, Winston Riley and Junior Menns as the Techniques. He also sang with Morvin Brooks on 'Travelling Man', credited to the same group. Other members of the Techniques included Dave Barker, who replaced Pat Kelly. Each went on to pursue successful solo careers and Ruffin was no exception. Working with Leslie Kong at Beverly's studio, successful singles such as 'Dry Up Your Tears', 'I'm The One' and 'Bitterness Of Life' followed. With Kong licensing his recordings to Trojan Records, the hits soon became international, appearing on the Summit offshoot. Following Kong's death in 1971, Ruffin went on to record with Herman Chin-Loy for 'One Big Happy Family' and a cover version of Jose Felancio's 'Rain', which took him into the UK Top 20 in May 1971. The flip-side featured 'Geronimo', wrongly credited to Bruce Antony (Bruce White and Tony Cousins of Creole Records) and originally released in 1970 on the Duke label. The success led to a compilation set, *Rain*, which featured the overtly commercial 'Candida', 'C.C. Child', 'Heaven Child' and 'Bitterness Of Life', as well as the title track. In an effort to capitalize on the first hit, the release of 'Songs Of Peace', 'You Are The Best' and 'We Can Make It', as a maxi-single, failed to achieve chart entries. In 1972 Ruffin switched to the Rhino label, a subsidiary of Creole, and enjoyed a Top 10 hit with the bla-

tantly commercial 'I'm Mad About You'. The track featured squawking backing vocals and when he appeared on the television show *Top Of The Pops* with a parrot in the background, the purists were aghast. The hit was followed with the release of 'Coming On Strong', but this flopped. In an effort to regain chart status he returned to the style of 'Mad About You' with 'Tickle Me' and 'In The Thick Of It'. Further releases, including 'I Like Everything About You' and 'Little Boys And Little Girls', followed, but neither improved his profile in the reggae or pop charts. In 1976 Bruce was reunited with Dave Barker as part of the British soul group Chain Reaction. They released *Never Lose Never Win*, and the notable contributions from Ruffin included a cover version of Lamont Dozier's 'Why Can't We Be Lovers', and a self-composition, 'I'm Indebted To You'. Ruffin now runs his own Genius management and publishing companies in north London.

● ALBUMS: *Rain* (Trojan 1971)★★★, *Bruce Ruffin* (Rhino 1972)★★★★. With Chain Reaction: *Never Lose Never Win* (Gull 1976)★★, *Change Of Action* (Vista 1983)★★★, *Chase A Miracle* (Vista 1983)★★★.
● COMPILATIONS: With the Techniques: *Classics* (Techniques 1991)★★★★, *Run Come Celebrate - Their Greatest Reggae Hits* (Heartbeat 1993)★★★★.

RUSSELL, DEVON

Russell began his career in Jamaica, West Indies, where he performed alongside Watty Burnett, Cedric Myton and Lloyd Robinson as part of the rocksteady group the Tartans, remembered for the classic 'Dance All Night'. Following the group's demise, the individual members pursued solo careers, although Myton and Burnett performed together as the Congos, originally for Lee Perry. In the mid-70s Russell recorded at Perry's Black Ark Studio under the alias Devon Irons for 'Vampire', which featured a DJ performance on the now rare *Upsetter* discomix from Doctor Alimantado. By the early 80s, Russell was recording with Coxsone Dodd at Studio One; the results of the sessions included the celebrated 'Make Me Believe In You', 'Sexual Healing' and 'Let Sleeping Dogs Lie'. His recording of 'Make Me Believe In You' was an interpretation of the Impressions' R&B hit, 'You

Must Believe Me'. That group featured Curtis Mayfield, who also inspired Russell's later hits, 'Move On Up' and 'Darker Than Blue', produced by Earl 'Chinna' Smith. His deference for the R&B superstar resulted in *Darker Than Blue*, a compilation of Mayfield compositions featuring 'Keep On Moving', 'I'm Still Waiting' and remakes of his earlier renditions. Smith was also responsible for producing the underrated 'Gully Bank' which demonstrated Russell's flawless vocal abilities. He also released the critically acclaimed 'Come A Me Girl', which inexplicably languished in obscurity. Undeterred by these impediments, Russell has remained an influential force within the industry, releasing a series of commercially successful albums. Russell was asked to join the line-up of the Congos for a promotional European tour in 1983 following the group's major label contract. He accompanied the group and the jaunt resulted in the singer eventually relocating in the UK where he was constantly in demand for recording sessions. In the early 90s, Zion Train enrolled Russell to record on sessions which included his revitalization of the roots chart-topper, 'Jah Holds The Key'. His cult status in the industry was maintained with consistently acclaimed quality roots compilations, including the now rare *Jah Homebound Train*, *Something Special*, *This Cloak And Dagger* and *Prison Life*.

● ALBUMS: *Roots Music* (Studio One 1980)★★★★, *Darker Than Blue* reissued through Roots/Southern Records (High Times 1981)★★★★, *Money Sex And Violence* (Jet Star 1992)★★, with Zion Train *Devon Russell Sings Roots Classics* (Universal Egg Records 1993)★★, *Bible And The Gun* (Fire House 1996)★★★.

SAGITTARIUS BAND

The Sagittarius Band was the collective name of session musicians formed around the bass playing skills of Derrick Barnett. He first appeared playing bass in the 1982 Reggae Sunsplash Festival, which was filmed for a television broadcast. Accompanied by an all-star horn section featuring Tommy McCook, Michael Hanson and Everod Gale, Barnett played bass behind Marcia Griffiths, Sister Nancy, Eek A Mouse (who also appeared in the same year with Lloyd Parks' We The People Band) and Yellowman. As well as televising the event, Synergy, the company behind the annual Sunsplash Festival, recorded it for a series of live albums. Highlights of the series included recordings of Yellowman, Toots And The Maytals, Big Youth, Chalice, the Twinkle Brothers and Eek A Mouse with Michigan And Smiley. The Yellowman album highlighted the playing skills of the group, although the album credits the Sagittarius Band as Derrick Barnett And Company. The success backing Yellowman resulted in the group accompanying the star on his European tour, where the combined playing skills and dance routines of the band became legendary. They were acknowledged as the successors to the Roots Radics, although competition from the High Times and Black Roots Band led to intense rivalry.

By 1983 Barnett was recording with Mikey 'Boo' Richards, Franklin 'Bubbler' Waul and Willie Lindo, and backing Ruddy Thomas and Desi Roots. Barnett also backed Susan Cadogan for her duets with Ruddy Thomas. The sessions were recorded for Roy 'Hawkeye' Forbes Allen who encouraged Barnett to embark on a solo career as a vocalist. In 1984 he covered 'You Make It Happen' under the pseudonym of Rikki Barnett. The single proved a hit in the reggae chart and was swiftly followed by the equally successful 'Figures Can't Calculate'. He maintained his position as leader of the band, and their reputation for professionalism resulted in further appearances at the Sunsplash Festivals. This involved them playing non-stop rhythms for DJs such as Charlie Chaplin, Brigadier Jerry, Josie Wales and Yellowman.

By the autumn of 1984 the group stole the show at the Heat In De Place concert, headlined by the Mighty Sparrow. The group were the most in-demand support band in Jamaica but the advent of the digital era resulted in less call for session work.

SANCHEZ

b. 28 November 1967, Kingston, Jamaica, West Indies. In the autumn of 1987, the first record releases by a singer called Sanchez D arrived in the reggae shops. His voice was distinctive but untutored, and its roughness matched the equally gritty dancehall rhythms of the time. His first hit was 'Lady In Red' for Red Man, and by November 1987 he was drawing attention with 'Zim Bam Zim', riding a scorching, bizarre Sly And Robbie rhythm. The more traditional 'Tears' followed and almost immediately gave him his debut UK chart appearance, becoming the lead track on Sanchez a few months later. By the spring of 1988, Sanchez was the number one singer of love songs in reggae. He became highly popular, with a strong female following, and 60s-style screaming was de rigueur at his concerts. His skinny frame, boyish demeanour and exciting stage act appealed to the predominantly female audiences. Hit followed hit, including 'Old Friend', 'Green Green Grass Of Home', 'Let It Be Me', 'Impossible', 'Joy', 'Hello Josephine', 'Let Me Love You Now', 'Lonely Won't Leave', 'My Girl' and 'Tell Him I'm Not Home' - in typical reggae style, every producer and label in Jamaica was demanding a share of the singer. His first UK gigs in the summer of 1988 revealed a massive following there too: Sanchez-mania brought screaming to every show. A second album, Loneliness, orchestrated by veteran producer Winston Riley, dominated the reggae charts for months and the title cut, 'Loneliness Leave Me Alone', was a massive seller. Sweetest Girl, named after yet another hit, was his second 1988 album. Critically dismissed as a cover-singing fad whose own lyrics were slight, Sanchez was capable of writing his own, serious

songs, such as 'South Africa', which became yet another hit. Further doubts about his vocal abilities were shattered when he recorded a superb version of 'End Of The World' in the spring of 1989, followed by Wild Sanchez.

Hit singles continued to arrive: 'Me Love Me Girl Bad' with ragga DJ Flourgon, a cover version of Bobby Brown's (with whom Sanchez has often been compared) 'My Prerogative', 'Come To Rule' and Tracy Chapman's 'Baby Can I Hold You Tonight' for his original producer Philip 'Fatis' Burrell. Number One was released in the UK on Island Records, and in 1990 he released a 'clash' album with Pinchers (Meets Pinchers), followed by two sets with Wayne Wonder. He reunited with Burrell for 1993's Boom Boom Bye Bye.

● ALBUMS: Sanchez (Vena 1987)★★★★, Loneliness (Techniques 1988)★★★, Sweetest Girl (Dennis Star 1988)★★★, Wild Sanchez! (Greensleeves 1988)★★★, Number One (Mango/Island 1989)★★★, with Pinchers Pinchers Meets Sanchez (Exterminator 1989)★★★★, In Fine Style (Charm 1990)★★, with Wayne Wonder Penthouse Presents (Volume One & Two) (Penthouse 1990/91)★★★, I Can't Wait (Blue Mountain 1991)★★, Bring Back The Love (World Enterprise 1992)★★★, The One For Me (1993)★★★, Boom Boom Bye Bye (Greensleeves 1993)★★★, Missing You (VP 1994)★★.

SANTANA, STEVE

b. Steve Campbell, c.1970, Falmouth, Trelawny, Jamaica, West Indies. Campbell's big break came in 1987 when he was invited to open a show at his school's annual fair. The line-up also featured an early appearance by Patra, while Foxy Brown, Lady G and Papa San topped the bill. At the time of the concert, Papa San was managed by Sassafras (The People's Promoter), who was sufficiently impressed with Campbell to offer his services to the young singer. The promoter gave Campbell his first taste of stardom, but this was short-lived, owing to Sassafras apparently being ostracized through legal issues raised by the Jamaican Federation of Musicians. Campbell, however, found a niche singing on the sound system circuit, which led to him being invited to perform on the north coast of Jamaica as part of a cabaret show. He performed to the tourists for five years, playing six nights a week, which developed his skills and provided a stable income. By 1993 his association with Norman Grant's son led to an introduction to the lead singer of the Twinkle Brothers, who produced his debut, 'Beware'. The singer initially performed as Santana, but to avoid confusion with the US band, Grant suggested that the singer should precede his name with Steve. Santana's career began to develop and by 1997 the singles 'Until There Is Justice', produced by Roy Cousins, 'Time Will Tell', produced by Mafia And Fluxy, and Norman Grant's production of the roots anthem 'Heavily Protected', signalled his arrival. A number of sessions also resulted in white label releases appearing in the UK, where Santana had by this time chosen to base himself. His recordings are a regular feature of roots and culture shows and have been endorsed by the Mighty Jah Shaka. Santana claimed that to augment his position 'you have to lay the foundation'. He is a widely admired performer who makes music for the mind and asserted: 'Too many people believe in God - Yet only a handful know him'.

● ALBUMS: *Such Is Life* (Twinkle 1993)★★★, *Heavily Protected* (Twinkle 1997)★★★★.

SASSAFRAS (THE PEOPLES PROMOTER)

b. Denzil Naar, Kingston Jamaica, West Indies. In 1975 Naar began designing posters for the sound systems in Jamaica. His unique compositions soon gained popularity and he became known as Sassafras The Peoples Promoter. His successful advertising campaigns led to his association with the Gemini sound, noted for elevating Yellowman's career. In the early 80s he moved on to Lees Unlimited who were successful in promoting DJs Johnny Ringo, Welton Irie and sing-jay Echo Minott. Naar's artwork was featured on many vinyl dancehall recordings including *A Dee Jay Explosion* and *Special Request And A Popular Demand*. He continued working in publicity, known as the 'original' Sassafras, to avoid confusion with the DJ often referred to as the Horseman. Naar was also responsible for promoting the prolific career of Lady G.

SCIENTIST

b. Overton Brown, Jamaica, West Indies. Scientist burst onto the reggae scene in the early 80s with a reckless mixing style that seemed to outdo even King Tubby's wildest extravaganzas. He began his career as an engineer at Studio One in 1978, mixing the dub to Sugar Minott's 'Oh Mr DC', among others. Shortly afterwards he became a protégé of King Tubby, and swiftly gained a reputation with his fresh mixing style. In 1980 Greensleeves Records began to release the productions of top Jamaican producer Henry 'Junjo' Lawes. Lawes, finding success with new singing sensation Barrington Levy, used Tubby's studio for his voicing and final mix-downs and offered Greensleeves a couple of dub albums mixed by Tubby's sensational young engineer. *Scientist v Prince Jammy*, mostly consisting of dub mixes of Barrington Levy tracks, was presented as a 'Big Showdown' between the two dubmasters, with the first track mixed by Scientist, the second by King Jammy (as he was later known), and so on. The combination of heavyweight Roots Radics rhythms pitted against one another (the cover depicted the two protagonists in a cartoon style, sitting at their mixing desks in a boxing ring surrounded by a crowd of dreads) made for exciting listening. Greensleeves followed this with an album proclaiming Scientist to be the *Heavyweight Dub Champion*, a similar brew of Roots Radics/Barrington Levy rhythms. Dub albums mixed by Scientist soon began to appear with bewildering regularity from various sources. Greensleeves, in particular, continued to issue album after album which, despite their increasingly unlikely titles and garish covers, remain essential listening. Scientist moved from Tubby's four-track studio to Joseph 'Joe Joe' Hookim's 16-track Channel One studio in 1982, where he also learned to record live.His popularity resurrected dub's fading fortunes for a few years, but the form had lost ground in the Jamaican dancehalls to the new breed of dancehall DJs and vocalists, and by the mid-80s few Jamaican producers felt it prudent to produce dub albums. He continued as resident engineer at Channel One until the mid-80s, when he moved to New York to continue his career.

● ALBUMS: *Introducing* (JB Music/Greensleeves 1979)★★★, *Scientist v*

Prince Jammy (Greensleeves 1980)★★★★, *Heavyweight Dub Champion* (Greensleeves 1980)★★★, *Scientist Meets The Space Invaders* (Greensleeves 1981)★★★, *Dub Landing Vol 1 & 2* (Starlight 1981)★★★, *Scientist Rids The World Of The Evil Curse Of The Vampires* (Greensleeves 1981)★★★, *Scientist Encounters Pacman* (Greensleeves 1982)★★, *Scientist Wins The World Cup* (Greensleeves 1983)★★★, *The People's Choice* (Kingdom 1983)★★★, *Dub Duel At King Tubbys* (Kingdom 1983)★★★, *High Priest Of Dub* (Kingdom 1983)★★★, *In The Kingdom Of Dub* (Kingdom 1983)★★★, *King Of Dub* (Kingdom 1987)★★, *1999 Dub* (Heartbeat 1988)★★★.
● COMPILATIONS: *Crucial Cuts* (Kingdom 1984)★★★★.

SCORCHER, ERROL

b. Errol Archer, 1956, St. Catherine, Jamaica, West Indies, d. 1982. Scorcher began his career as a DJ in the early 70s performing for a number of sound systems, where he cultivated his unique style. Although his debut, 'Leggo Mi Hand Babylon', was a crowd-pleaser in the dancehall, it failed to achieve chart success. This initial disappointment did not deter the DJ, and his perseverance came to fruition when he released a series of hits through the mid-70s, including the popular 'Jolly Bus-Ting' and 'Engineers Affair'. His notoriety was enhanced further when in 1978 he recorded the celebratory 'Peace Truce', utilizing Culture's 'Stop This Fussing And Fighting'. The song extolled the signing of an armistice between rival factions in Western Kingston on 11 January 1978; the treaty led to the acclaimed One Love Peace Concert in Jamaica, which featured the legendary return of Bob Marley to the Jamaican stage. In the same year, Scorcher joined the Tapetone sound system, widely acknowledged as King Jammy's first dancehall venture. The combination of Scorcher alongside Nicodemus, Mama Liza and Kojak promoted the system to a position as the island's number one sound. In 1979 Scorcher released the popular 'Roach In The Corner', which led to the similar 'Frog In The Water'. By 1980 Scorcher embarked on a series of recording sessions with Ansell Collins, resulting in the renowned 'Mosquitoes', which described the DJ's love-hate relationship with Jamaican insect-life. The hit led to Scorcher forming his own label for the releases of 'Rope In' and 'DJ Spirit', as well as Tony Tuff's 'Hustling'. By 1982 Scorcher was regarded as a veteran, although he had hits with 'Rude Boy Step' and 'Letting Go', and also featured on the *Dee Jay Explosion* compilation, performing 'Wife And Sweetheart' (originally recorded over the 'Johnny Dollar' rhythm by Winston Riley). The same year, in an attempt to arrest a suspected criminal, an over zealous group of law enforcers shot eight men, fatally wounding the DJ. He is widely acknowledged by his Jamaican counterparts as being an influential performer, contradicting unfounded accusations that he was 'an infamous plagiarist'.
● ALBUMS: *Rasta Fire* (Pre 1978)★★★, with Horace Andy *Unity Showcase* (Pre 1981)★★★.

SCOTTY

b. David Scott, c.1950, Jamaica, West Indies. A singer and DJ, Scotty started out in late 1967 as a member of the Federals vocal group, gaining a massive local hit with 'Penny For Your Song' for producer Derrick Harriott the same year. They also recorded 'By The River' and 'Shocking Love' for Harriott, the original group breaking up after the Jamaican Song Festival in 1969. Scotty then joined the original line-up of the Chosen Few with Noel Brown and Franklin Spence, again at the instigation of Harriott. In July 1970, Scotty recorded his first DJ title, 'Musical Chariot'; this was followed by 'Sesame Street' (1970, Jamaican chart number 3), 'Riddle I This'/'Musical Chariot' (1970, Jamaican chart number 1), 'Jam Rock Style' (1971), later featured in the film *The Harder They Come*, and 'Draw Your Brakes'. Scotty and Harriott had followed the trend set by DJs such as U-Roy and Dennis Alcapone for Duke Reid, combining witty lyrics with classic rocksteady rhythms. He continued recording with Harriott until 1972. He later worked under the supervision of Harry J. (the original DJ version of 'Breakfast In Bed'), Lloyd Charmers and Sonia Pottinger. Scotty moved to the USA during the mid-70s. During the late 80s, having returned to live in Jamaica, he began recording in a ragga style, with considerable local success.
● ALBUMS: *Schooldays* (1972)★★★★, *Unbelievable Sounds* (Trojan 1988)★★★★.

SCREWDRIVER

b. Dalton Lindo, c.1960, St. James, Jamaica, West Indies. Inspired by the dancehall singers Pinchers, Pliers, Spanner Banner and Tenor Saw, Lindo utilized the pseudonym of Screwdriver. In the mid-80s he went to Kingston where he met Beres Hammond, who encouraged his musical aspirations. Screwdriver began his career in 1986, recording the hits 'We Rule', 'Soundboy Killa', 'Family Counsellor' and 'Here I Come'. In 1989 he topped the Jamaican chart with 'No Mama', which became a major hit throughout the Caribbean and inspired many DJs to mimic the chorus. Following his success, Screwdriver toured America and Canada before settling in Florida, USA. Further hits followed, including 'Reggae On Broadway', 'Learning The Ways Of Love', 'Roots And Culture', 'Teach Dem' and 'HIV'. By 1995, influenced by the music of his domicile, he blended R&B and hip-hop with Jamaican dancehall rhythms, a sound that he demonstrated on *Calling Calling* for the Miami-based Ikus label. The album featured 'She Too Young', 'African Woman', 'Got To Be Love' and 'Selassie Live'. His earlier hit, 'Teach Dem', was given a 90s hip-hop/reggae-style remix.

● ALBUMS: *Teach Dem* (Imp 1992)★★★, *Calling Calling* (Ikus 1995)★★★★, *Let Me Remind You* (1996)★★★.

SEATON, B.B.

b. Harris Seaton, 3 September 1944, Kingston, Jamaica, West Indies. Seaton, sometimes known as 'Bibby', was initially encouraged to enter the music business by Boris Gardiner, who asked him to sing in a group known as the Rhythm Aces. When his vocal skills attracted the attention of Coxsone Dodd, the producer took him to the studio and recorded 'Only You'. While at Studio One he recorded alongside Delano Stewart and Maurice Roberts as the Gaylads, originally performing in the mento style. The group initially recorded their debut in 1958 but soon afterwards split up. By 1960 they had re-formed as Bibby And The Astronauts, enjoying hits with 'Rub It Down' and, as the Gaylads, 'Lady In The Red Dress'. In 1972 Seaton recommenced his solo career and developed his songwriting skills. He enjoyed a number of hits, including 'The Thin Line Between Love And Hate', 'Miss My Schooldays' and a version of Bill Withers' 'Lean On Me'. His composing abilities resulted in hit songs for Ken Boothe ('Freedom Street'), the Melodians ('Swing And Dine') and Delroy Wilson ('Gave You My Love'). He returned to harmonizing when he joined forces with Boothe alongside Lloyd Charmers and Busty Brown in the Messengers, who enjoyed hits with 'Cherry Baby' and 'Crowded City'. Following on from the group's demise, he was the first reggae performer to be signed by Virgin Records, which led to the inauguration of the notorious Front Line label. His production was not well received, as the final mix was overwhelmed by the use of synthesizers and electric piano. By the mid-70s Seaton was based in the UK, where he secured a producer's contract with the Jama label and released his own cover version of 'Born Free', which, in spite of the song's middle of the road reputation, was a big hit. He has remained active within the industry, including a memorable performance at the British Reggae Awards and a worthy contribution on the BRAFA single, and although he has not achieved chart-busting hits, he has maintained a loyal following among the major figures in the industry. His son Richard has followed in his father's footsteps, working with Mary J. Blige, Boyz II Men and Shabba Ranks. In 1996 B.B. Seaton was involved in sessions alongside Little Roy, whose debut, 'Cool It', was erroneously credited to the Gaylads.

● ALBUMS: *Thin Line Between Love And Hate* (Trojan 1973)★★★, *Dancing Shoes* (Virgin 1974)★, *Colour Is Not The Answer* (Jama 1976)★★★, *In Control* (Soul Beat 1995)★★.

● COMPILATIONS: *Greatest Hits* (Rhino 1996)★★★

SHAGGY

b. Orville Richard Burrell, 22 October 1968, Kingston, Jamaica, West Indies. Shaggy is, effectively, the man who put New York reggae on the map, thanks to his worldwide hit, 'Oh Carolina'. The same record also helped to start the ragga boom of 1993, an explosion that also carried the likes of Shabba Ranks, Chaka Demus And Pliers and Snow into the international pop charts. An amusing vocal stylist who can be rude without ever descending into a leer, Shaggy learned his trade on Brooklyn's Gibraltar Musik sound system. He had moved there with his parents at the age of 18, and at 19 he had joined the Marines, based at Lejeune, North Carolina. Following active service in the Gulf War, Shaggy began to record singles for a variety of labels, among them 'Man A Me Yard'/'Bullet Proof Baddie' for Don One, and 'Big Hood'/'Duppy Or Uglyman' for Spiderman. A chance meeting with Sting, a radio DJ at KISS-FM/WNNK, led to Shaggy's first New York reggae chart number 1, 'Mampie', a version of the 'Drum Song' rhythm, produced by Sting for New York reggae ruler Phillip Smart's Tan-Yah label. His next single, 'Big Up', released on Sting International and recorded in tandem with singer Rayvon, also hit number 1, as did 'Oh Carolina'. A mighty cover version of the Folks Brothers classic, replete with samples of the original, the record became a huge hit on import charts wherever reggae was sold. At the time, Shaggy was still in the Marines, and was forced to make an 18-hour round trip to Brooklyn for dates and studio sessions. At the end of 1992, Greensleeves Records picked up 'Oh Carolina' for UK release, and by spring 1993 Shaggy had achieved a pop chart hit all over Europe with the song, reaching number 1 in the UK and several other countries. His next single, the slow, raucous 'Soon Be Done' failed, however, to capitalize on his success. Apparently unruffled by this, a liaison with Maxi Priest for 'One More Chance' led to a Virgin contract, and the *Pure Pleasure* album. A third single from the LP, 'Nice And Lovely', again failed to repeat the sales of 'Oh Carolina' (which, by that time, had made it onto the soundtrack of Sharon Stone's film, *Sliver*), but it was a fine, light-hearted record in its own right. The album also contained a version of his earlier 'Duppy Or Uglyman' cut, restyled as 'Fraid To Ask'. He returned to the pop charts in 1995 with 'Boombastic', which reached number 2 in the UK following frequent exposure as the soundtrack to an animated television advertisement for jeans. An album followed, produced by the New York team of Robert Livingstone and Shaun 'Sting' Pizzonia for Big Yard Productions, along with Jamaican Tony Kelly as guest producer on two tracks, 'Something Different' and 'How Much More'. Another song, 'Treat Me So Bad', was conducted in alliance with rapper Grand Puba. *Boombastic* quickly went gold in America where Shaggy launched an extensive

tour. He won a Grammy in February 1996 for Best Reggae Album (*Boombastic*). *Midnite Lover* was a lesser album with no hits to increase its profile.
● ALBUMS: *Pure Pleasure* (Virgin 1993)★★★, *Boombastic* (Virgin 1995)★★★★, *Midnite Lover* (Virgin 1997)★★★.

SHARP, DEE

b. Derrick Trought, 1956, London, England. Sharp has the distinction of recording the first ever release for the newly formed Fashion Records, a version of Leo Hall's entry for the 1975 Jamaican Song Festival, 'Let's Dub It Up', with the Investigators. The song topped the reggae chart in the summer of 1980 and led to the equally popular release of 'Follow Your Heart', which also featured a version of the Melodians' classic 'Swing And Dine'. In September 1981 Sharp's career took a change in direction when he joined the Britfunk group Buzzz as the lead vocalist. The line-up featured David Barra (bass guitar), Jenny Evans (vocals), Tesley Francis (keyboards), Dorothy Patterson (vocals) and Tony Scantlebury (drums). The group were experienced reggae musicians, having emerged from Rico's backing band, while Scantlebury had previously been employed as Eddy Grant's drummer. The group signed with RCA Records, who released their debut, 'Sorry My Dear'. The group followed their debut release with a version of Ray Charles's 'Hit The Road Jack', inspired by Big Youth's cover version of the song. The group's third release, 'Obsession', led to an appearance on the BBC Television programme *Ebony*, although only Sharp, Evans and Patterson performed the song. Following the demise of the band, Sharp released a series of solo outings, including 'Magician' and 'Take Your Time', as well as an EP featuring 'Straighten Up And Fly Right', 'That Much I Know' and 'Night And Day'. In the summer of 1983 Fashion released 'Rising To The Top' and 'Give It All You've Got', which re-established Sharp's position as the UK's premier lovers rock singer. His experience in the industry resulted in him becoming a versatile performer, and he is often recruited for a diversity of recording sessions. In 1985, among his many projects, Sharp provided a raunchy rap for Nick Heyward's 'Warning Sign'.

SHERMAN, BIM

b. Jarrett Tomlinson, 1952, Jamaica, West Indies. Sherman's earliest recordings include 'Mighty Ruler' and 'Ever Firm', which appeared on the Love and Ja-Man labels in late 1976/early 1977. Around the same time, a series of singles began appearing on his own Scorpio label. Because of restricted finances, he often used each rhythm track for two different songs, but his writing skills and plaintive vocals ensured that every release sounded fresh. Several Jah Stone DJ versions of his songs were also issued at this time. In 1978, eight of his Scorpio singles, together with 'Mighty Ruler' and 'Ever Firm', were compiled for *Love Forever*, which was released in the UK on the Tribesman label - a classic set that many argue he has never equalled. In 1979 he issued *Lovers Leap* which, while not hitting the heights of its predecessor, proved another consistently strong collection. A year later he was featured on one side of *Bim Sherman Meets Horace Andy And U Black*, a minor but robust and enjoyable set. Shortly after this he settled in the UK, where he met producer Adrian Sherwood. Sherwood subsequently produced *Across The Red Sea* (1982), but it was not the sensation for which followers of both had hoped. Despite the inclusion of several excellent songs, the record lost many of its vocal nuances as Sherman's words were submerged in the mix. In 1984 *Love Forever* was re-released as *Danger*, and he issued the self-produced *Bim Sherman And The Voluntary*, a disappointing work that met with tepid reviews. This was followed by *Haunting Ground*, an uneven set that did boast an excellent Sherwood-produced title track. Even though his voice could be haunting, he was let down by slight songs and uninspired accompaniments, a trend that continued on *Exploitation* and *Too Hot*. Throughout the 80s and early 90s he was a featured vocalist on the highly acclaimed, Sherwood-produced *Singers And Players* series of albums. Fragments of his vocals, together with some complete songs, also appeared in works by Fats Comet, Keith LeBlanc and Gary Clail.

Although remaining one of reggae's pre-eminent roots singers of the 80s and 90s, Bim Sherman was two decades into his recording career before he made a commercial breakthrough in the UK charts. That he did so was largely due to the continued sponsorship of Sherwood, who has always viewed Sherman as a major talent. 'Solid As A Rock' was taken from *Miracle*, an album Sherwood had passed over to Beggars Banquet Records subsidiary Mantra to secure better distribution and promotion for the artist. With a remix by dance producer Steve Osbourne, the single scaled the UK charts and helped to re-energize Sherman's career.

● ALBUMS: *Love Forever* reissued as *Danger* (Tribesman 1978)★★★★, *Lovers Leap* (1979)★★★, with Horace Andy *Bim Sherman Meets Horace Andy And U Black* (Yard International 1980)★★★, *Across The Red Sea* (On-U-Sound 1982)★★★, *Bim Sherman And The Voluntary* (Century 1984)★★, as Bim Sherman And The Allstars *African Rubadub* (RDL 1987)★★★, *Haunting Ground* (RDL/Revolver 1989)★★★, *Exploitation* (RDL/Revolver 1989)★★★, *Too Hot* (Century 1990)★★, *Crazy World* (Century 1992)★★★, with Dub Syndicate *Reality* (Century 1992)★★★, with Dub Syndicate *Lion Heart Dub* (Century 1993)★★★★, with the Discoverers *The Justice League Of Zion* (1994)★★★★, *Miracle* (Mantra 1996)★★★, *It Must Be A Dream* (Mantra 1997)★★★★.

SHERVINGTON, PLUTO

b. Leighton Shervington, August 1950, Kingston, Jamaica, West Indies. In his early twenties Shervington joined a show band called Tomorrow's Children. Fellow performers Ernie Smith and Tinga Stewart had enjoyed commercial success with 'Duppy Or A Gunman' and 'Play De Music', respectively. Both songs were sung in a heavy patois and enjoyed chart status. Inspired by this, Shervington sang the hit 'Ram Goat Liver', and the follow-up, 'Dat', the two of which were paradoxical stories of poverty disguised as comedy tunes, and went over the heads of many listeners. In 1976, when released in the UK, 'Dat' was a Top 5 hit for the newly formed Opal label. Trojan Records realized that they had licensed his earlier hit, 'Ram Goat Liver', and gave Shervington his second UK chart entry, peaking at number 35 two months after the success of 'Dat'. He moved to Miami, Florida, where he began recording and in 1982 returned to the international market for the release of 'Your Honour', which entered the UK

Top 20. His follow-up, 'I Man Bitter', and an album were not commercial successes.
● ALBUMS: *Pluto Again* (KR 1982)★★.

SHERWOOD, ADRIAN

b. *c*.1958. A pioneering force in UK reggae, Sherwood's first attempts to set up labels in the late 70s were disastrous, and cost him a great deal of money in the process. Despite such misadventures, he persevered, and set up the On-U-Sound label to house ex-Pop Group singer Mark Stewart's New Age Steppers project. Over a hundred albums and singles have subsequently been released, including music by Bim Sherman, Dub Syndicate and Mothmen (an embryonic Simply Red). Sherwood styled On-U-Sound after the reggae model of 'house bands' (Revolutionaries, Soul Syndicate, etc.). The label/organization also played out as a sound system, in a similar fashion to its Jamaican counterparts. Among the notable long-term protagonists at On-U-Sound have been Bonjo (African Head Charge), Bim Sherman and Skip McDonald, Doug Wimbush and Keith LeBlanc (Tackhead). However, Sherwood is equally renowned for his production skills, which he learned at first hand from Prince Far-I and Dr Pablo. The Fall, Depeche Mode and Ministry have been among his notable clients. On-U-Sound came to the attention of the public outside reggae circles when self-styled 'white toaster' Gary Clail entered the charts. However, neither this, nor any other individual release, can be described as representative of the rock-reggae-dance fusion that On-U-Sound have fostered. On-U-Sound's eclecticism remains rampant, but as Sherwood himself concedes: 'I'm first and foremost a passionate fan of reggae music'.
● COMPILATIONS: Various Artists *On-U-Sound Present Pay It All Back Volume 4* (On-U-Sound 1993)★★★, *Reggae Archive Volumes 1 & 2* (On-U-Sound)★★★.

SHINEHEAD

b. Edmund Carl Aitken, Kent, England. Although born in the UK, Aitken's family moved to Jamaica when he was two years old, then emigrated to New York in 1976 where he settled permanently. Counting among his influences a diverse array of artists, including the Jackson Five and Otis Redding, together with numerous reggae performers, Shinehead began singing at the age of 19, mixing the Jamaican toasting style with the more urbanized hip-hop that was developing in New York. After studying electrical and computer engineering, his first musical activity came with Downbeat International in 1981, with Brigadier Jerry becoming a formative influence. He quickly developed a reputation for an astonishing range of dancehall skills - mimicking, singing, DJing, selecting, rapping and even whistling to great effect over Downbeat's stock-in-trade Studio One dub plates. It was there that he gained his nickname, by virtue of his distinctive, closely cropped hairstyle. In late 1983 he joined forces with Claude Evans, who ran the African Love sound system-cum-label in Brooklyn. Evans managed to procure a rhythm track the Wailers had reputedly played for Bob Marley, but he had died before using it. In 1984 Shinehead voiced 'Billie Jean'/'Mama Used To Say' over two sides of the rhythm and achieved a massive hit for African Love. The debut album, *Rough And Rugged*, which followed in 1986, showcased his remarkably varied talents with a blend of dancehall, ballads, rap and reggae that yielded further hits in the shape of 'Know How Fi Chat', 'Hello Y'All' and 'Who The Cap Fits'. That same year he guested on Sly And Robbie's popular 'Boops' and was signed to Elektra Records in 1987, but the alliance has proved to be disappointing. The second album, *Unity*, was merely a rearrangement of the first set (some tracks by Run DMC's Jam Master Jay), and contained many of the same tracks, some of which were by then four years old. Increasingly, new material was aimed at the US crossover market, and despite the success of 'Strive' with his fading roots audience in 1990, his fortunes have taken a distinctly downward turn. *Sidewalk University* again assembled the services of assorted pop, rap and dance personnel in a bid for commercial reward, with the single 'Jamaican In New York' selling reasonably well. It is a long way removed from the dazzling quality of his earlier work, although he continues to make combative appearances on sound systems both in the USA and Jamaica.
● ALBUMS: *Rough And Rugged* (African Love Music 1986)★★★★, *Unity* (African Love/Elektra 1988)★★, *The Real Rock* (African

Love/Elektra 1990)★★, *Sidewalk University* (African Love/Elektra 1993)★★, *Troddin'* (Elektra 1994)★★.

SHIRLEY, ROY

b. *c.*1948, Kingston, Jamaica, West Indies. Perhaps one of the most eccentric performers in a business peopled almost exclusively with eccentric performers, Roy Shirley is known to reggae fans worldwide on the strength of a handful of superb releases and some utterly electrifying stage shows. He first recorded for Beverley's in 1964, working in the same territory as luminaries of the ska scene such as Ken Boothe and Joe White. He was also a member of the original Uniques, but his breakthrough came one night in 1966 after watching a Salvation Army band parade down Orange Street. Their beat, Shirley claims, formed the basis of one of the best-known records ever made in Jamaica, and one that many class as the first rocksteady outing - 'Hold Them', produced by Joe Gibbs - which was also his first record. Although the record was a huge hit, Shirley was bitter about the treatment he received from Coxsone Dodd, who 'versioned' the tune with Ken Boothe and renamed it 'Feel Good', the sales seriously damaging those of Shirley's original. Undeterred, Shirley continued his musical career, recording in the rocksteady and reggae styles for Sir JJ, Caltone, Joe Gibbs and most notably, Bunny Lee, whose first big hit was 'Music Field' with Roy Shirley. Another big hit followed in 1971 when Shirley released 'A Sugar' through Randys. He first toured the UK in 1972 with U-Roy and many of the latter's fans admitted that Shirley was a nearly impossible act to follow. Shirley has remained intermittently in the UK ever since, and he set up the All Stars Artistic Federated Union in London in 1976 in order to 'seek promotion and to gain satisfaction for all kinds of artists'. He wanted promising performers to avoid the pitfalls that had dogged his career, and to contribute something to a business that he felt had never paid him his due rewards. He still possesses the same incredibly intense delivery, and he took 1982's Reggae Sunsplash in Jamaica by storm with his outrageous stage act. Despite the setbacks, Shirley remains optimistic that, one day, the tide will turn for him.
● ALBUMS: *Control Them Volume One*

(1995)★★★, *Black Lion Negus Rastafari* (Lion Roots 1996)★★★.

SILK, GARNETT

b. Garnett Smith, *c.*1967, Manchester, Jamaica, West Indies, d. 9 December 1994, Mandeville, Jamaica, West Indies. One of the most significant singer-songwriters to emerge from Jamaica in recent times, Silk began his involvement in music by DJing as Little Bimbo from the tender age of 12. Formative years spent on the Destiny Outernational, Pepper's Disco, Stereophonic and Soul Remembrance sound systems led to his first recording, 'Problem Everywhere', for Delroy 'Callo' Collins in 1987. The following year he moved to Kingston and voiced for Sugar Minott's Youth Promotion label, recording one song, 'No Disrespect'. Next came sessions with the late King Tubby, as well as King Jammy's and Penthouse, before he signed a two-year contract with Steely And Clevie. Despite recording an album with them, only one track, a duet with Chevelle Franklin on 'We Could Be Together', was released during this period. Disillusioned, he returned to the country parish where he grew up, concentrating instead on writing songs, often in the company of his childhood friend, Anthony Rochester. Tony Rebel then introduced him to Courtney Cole, whose Roof International studio was based in Ocho Rios on Jamaica's north coast. From there the hits flowed, with 'I Can See Clearly Now' (a duet with dub poet Yasus Afari) and 'Seven Spanish Angels' proving especially popular. During 1992 he voiced the first of his output for Bobby Digital, who produced his debut album, *It's Growing*, at the end of the year. It was immediately hailed as a masterpiece of contemporary roots music and revealed a lyricist of rare depth and originality. Given his consistent emphasis on cultural themes - typified by 'I Am Vexed', 'The Rod' and the bestselling title song - and a fluid vocal style that imbues all his work with an almost religious intensity, comparisons were inevitably drawn with the late Bob Marley. By mid-1993 he had signed to Atlantic and saw many of his past recordings either reissued or released for the first time. These included further tracks for Roof, Steely And Clevie, Danny Browne, Black Scorpio, Phillip Smart, Top Rank, Jahmento, Star Trail - for whom 'Hello Africa' reached number 1 on the UK reggae charts - and Sly And Robbie. Silk died with his mother when they were trapped in a fire that destroyed her home in Mandeville, Jamaica.

● ALBUMS: *It's Growing* (Blue Mountain/VP 1992)★★★, *Gold* (Charm 1993)★★★, *100% Silk* (VP 1993)★★★.

SILVERTONES

The Silvertones were a vocal trio consisting of Carl Grant, Delroy Denton and Keith Coley. Curiously, although the group did not serve their apprenticeship at Coxsone Dodd's Studio One, they are remembered as Studio One legends. In 1975 they released *Silver Bullets*, which won critical acclaim but failed to make any impression on the charts through inadequate marketing. Four years later, they achieved an enormous hit with 'I Want To Be There'. This was followed by the equally successful releases 'Smile', 'Stop Crying', 'Have A Little Faith' and 'Come Forward', the latter track being credited with the Brentford Rockers, recorded in 1979. The Brentford Rockers featured an all-star line-up including Jackie Mittoo, Pablove Black, Leroy Sibbles, Leroy 'Horsemouth' Wallace, Cleveland and Dalton Brownie, Ernest Ranglin, Roland Alphonso and Johnny Moore. While at Downbeat's they also contributed to *Sir Coxsone's Family Christmas Album Stylee*, performing 'Merry Merry Christmas'.

● ALBUMS: *Silver Bullets* (Trojan 1975)★★★★.

SIMON, TITO

b. Keith Foster, *c.*1948, St. Mary, Jamaica, West Indies. Tito Simon left Jamaica in 1961 to start a new life in the UK. His early involvement in the music industry came in the mid-60s with Dandy Livingstone, recording together as Sugar And Dandy. Their hits included 'Let's Ska' and 'Heaven Knows'. The duo decided to pursue solo careers and Simon quickly became disillusioned with the recording industry. A two-year sabbatical followed, but in 1967 he was enticed back into the industry, supporting top soul performers on their European tours. He also recorded the self-produced 'Suddenly' as Sugar Simone, a soul tune that was an ineffectual attempt at a crossover hit. The b-side of the release, 'King Without A Throne', proved to be the more popular tune within the West Indian community and resulted in a significant hit. In 1972 Simon returned to Jamaica, where he began an association with Clancy Eccles, recording the popular 'Easy Come Easy Go', followed by a string of hits including 'You Can't Be Serious', 'I'll Be True To You' and 'She Aint Nothing But The Real Thing'. In 1973 Simon was featured in a Trojan Records catalogue that was produced to coincide with the West Indian cricket team's summer tour of the UK. In it, he was reported to be optimistic about the forthcoming release of *Build It Up*, which was also the title of his latest single release; the album surfaced as *Just Tito Simon* in 1974. A year later he almost crossed over into the UK pop chart with 'This Monday Morning Feeling', which made a brief appearance on the radio playlists. Trojan added three tracks to his album and re-released the compilation as *This Monday Morning Feeling*. On parting company with Trojan, he joined the Jama group alongside Pat Rhoden and B.B. Seaton, where he recorded 'Running Back For More'. By 1978 his singles 'Please Talk To Me' and 'Things Will Be Better' were worthy hits for Pearl Productions, although the partnership was short-lived. In 1983, recording with the Sus Band, his rendition of 'Can't Stop Loving You' was an indication of his enduring talent. Simon has recorded under a number of aliases, including Lance Hannibal, Jackie Foster, Les Foster and Calva L. Foster, in addition to those already mentioned.

● ALBUMS: *Just Tito Simon* (Horse 1974)★★★.
● COMPILATIONS: *This Monday Morning Feeling* (Trojan 1975)★★★.

SIMPLETON

b. Christopher Harrison, *c.*1975, Kingston, Jamaica, West Indies. He was raised on the outskirts of Kingston in the Papine region of Lower St. Andrews. Harrison was influenced by locally based artists including Brigadier Jerry, Sister Nancy, Chaka Demus, Major Mackerel, Roundhead, Colin Roach and Anthony Malvo. By his own admission, he initially mumbled on the mic at the dance, chatting nervously while he intently studied his feet. Whereas others may have stumbled at this stage, he turned this imperfection into a contrived DJ routine. It has also been wrongly suggested that he did not face the crowd because of his forked teeth, in spite of his performance under the guise of Dracula when appearing on the sound systems. In 1990 Ninjaman enjoyed a hit with 'Heartical Don', and performing as Dracula, Harrison changed the lyrics and the title to 'Simpleton'. Encouraged by the audience response and by the success of Capleton, Harrison adopted Simpleton as his stage name. The change of moniker led to a debut recording session with Colin Fat for the bogle-inspired 'Coca Cola Bottle Shape', which proved an instant hit in the dance and reggae charts worldwide. As is often the case in Jamaica, his success resulted in him being recruited by a number of producers to voice rhythms, including Junior Reid, Steely And Clevie, Bobby Digital, Stone Love and Black Scorpio. In 1993 Simpleton returned to international acclaim with the release of the risqué 'Sperm Rod', produced by Chris Goldfinga, and the popular hits 'Action Speaks Louder Than Words', 'Stay Pon Guard' and 'Need A Little Magic In Your Life'. An encounter with his neighbourhood friend Anthony Malvo resulted in Simpleton's biggest hit to date, 'Quarter To Twelve', which proved to be the top-selling independent reggae single of 1995. As an avid fan of cowboy movies, he illustrated the parallels between Kingston's street violence and film westerns. The success of the tune led to responses from a number of other DJs, including Ninjaman, to which Simpleton replied with 'Nah Watch Nah Clock'. The tune was another smash hit, resulting in the strident 'Sick Under Rastaman Treatment' for Bulby York, 'Pants Buckle' and 'Sweat A Bust' for Must Bust, 'Spot It' for Stingray, 'The Gal Dem' for Robert Livingstone, 'Miss Hottie Hottie' for Jack Scorpio and a combination with Spanner Banner, 'Rock On'.

● ALBUMS: *Coca Cola Bottle Shape* (VP 1991)★★★, *Heaven Me Reach* (World Records 1993)★★★, *Quarter To Twelve* (Greensleeves 1996)★★★★.

SIR LORD COMIC

b. Kingston, Jamaica, West Indies. His initial involvement in the sound systems was as a dancer for the Admiral Deans Sound. In the late 50s, inspired by Count Matchuki's phrases on Coxsone Dodd's Downbeat system, Sir Lord Comic was given an opportunity to talk on the mic. His popularity led to the first DJ record, 'Ska-ing West', which utilized the phrase: 'Adam and Eve went up my sleeve and didn't come down until Christmas Eve'. The phrase has reappeared in later recordings from other DJs, including Dillinger's 'Natty Dread Is Not The Prodigal Son'. Comic's limited recordings include what is regarded as the last great ska tune, 'The Great Wuga Wuga', an advertisement for his sound system. 'Jack Of My Trade' was a vitriolic attack on the up-and-coming DJs, only acknowledging the originators as Count Matchuki, King Stitt and U-Roy. In 1970, with Lee Perry, Comic recorded 'Django Shoots First' aka 'Django Ol' Man River', which appeared on the Trojan Records compilation *Eastwood Rides Again*, and the Jamaican-pressed *Rhythm Shower*, which was eventually released in the UK 15 years later as part of the *Upsetter Box Set*. In the television series *Deep Roots Music*, Comic appeared in the programme about dancehall, where he was interviewed with Count Matchuki.

SISTA REBEKA

b. 1973, London, England. Having relocated to Chapeltown, Leeds, Rebeka embarked on her recording career as a backing vocalist. In 1993 she provided the vocals for a number of dub-plate specials for the Lel Oreness Sound alongside the Leeds-based Jah Movement and Oldham's Dread Lion Studio. During 1995 Rebeka performed on the bill at the renowned Thursday night sessions in north London's Dub Club, where she impressed the lead singer and producer of the Twinkle Brothers, Norman Grant. Intrigued by her vocal styling, he produced her debut, 'Humble Lion', a militant song declaring the majestic power of Ras Tafari. The song, accompanied by the equally popular b-side, 'I Love Jah Jah', was a hit within the roots and culture circuit and was heavily 'rinsed' by the conscientious sound systems. In 1997 she established a credible reputation when she appeared as a soloist at the Leeds West Indian Centre and Manchester's Band On The Wall as part of a showcase featuring Della Grant, E.T. Webster and the Twinkle Brothers. She also featured on a line-up alongside the Lion Roots Massive including Dub Judah, Sister Allison, Tez Fa Zion aka Adhi Prophet and Sister Africa. Her debut, *African Heartbeat*, surfaced in the winter of 1997 to critical acclaim. By 1998 she was recording with Dread Lion for a roots compilation, alongside new material with Norman Grant.

● ALBUMS: *African Heartbeat* (Twinkle 1997)★★★.

SISTER ALLISON

b. Allison Colleen Mason, 5 November 1969, London, England. Mason has worked in radio and as an actress, as well as proving her writing skills both musically and as a poet. In 1990 she began the long haul to stardom performing in talent shows around London. From 1991 she demonstrated her radio DJ skills for Powerjam FM alongside the distinguished Sugar Dread. She also freelanced for the short-lived Rockers FM and BRI FM stations. In her appearances on the Powerjam show she has become recognized as a resolute teacher of black history, and through the programme organizes talent shows for aspiring musicians. In 1993 she joined the harmony group Ebony Hites, where her vocal skills elevated her profile. In 1994 she accepted an acting role playing Vinette in the acclaimed play *Bups 2*. At the same time, as a singer she also recorded the popular 'Fight The Fight', and her debut, *Wailing*, with Norman Grant of the Twinkle Brothers. Her busy schedule also included session work at the Brixton-based Lion Music studios and Barry Isaacs' Reggae On Top, where she featured on Pablo Gad's *Life Without Death*. In 1996 she appeared in two plays, *The Magic Dutch Pot* as Princess Mrs Olusmit, and in the leading role in the celebrated *Miss Run Tings*. She continued to pursue her recording career, working with Mad Professor for *Divas En Roots Volume Three*, the popular 'One Pot', and further sessions with Norman Grant for 'Show I The Way' and 'Sorrow'. In 1997 her diverse career included sessions with Isaacs for 'African Descendants' and with Mad Professor for 'Motivation' and 'Hypocrites', while she appeared on cable television in the situation comedy *Nutty Dreadful*. In addition to her recording and acting commitments she has also earned a reputation as an outstanding live performer, including appearances at various Lion Roots and Twinkle Showcases and as a support to Culture in 1995. She has worked alongside many of the top reggae performers, including Buju Banton, Bunny Wailer, Luciano, Johnny Osbourne, the Mighty Diamonds, Sweetie Irie and the Ruff Cut Band.

● ALBUMS: *Wailing* (Twinkle 1994)★★★, *Ism Skism* (Twinkle 1996)★★★.

SISTER CAROL

b. 1959, Kingston, Jamaica, West Indies. From her upbringing in outright poverty in Denham Town Ghetto, Sister Carol has emerged as a new star of US dancehall. She met her mentor, Brigadier Jerry, at the age of 20, and he inspired her to try the DJ style rather than straight singing. However, she emigrated to Brooklyn, New York, in the late 70s, feeling disaffected by the 'punany' or 'slackness' that had overtaken traditional roots reggae concerns. In America her musical pursuits ran in parallel with a film career, which was initiated when she was spotted duetting with Judy Mowatt on 'Screwface'. This won her a featured role in *Something Wild*, followed by *Married To The Mob*.

● ALBUMS: *Jah Disciples* (RAS 1991)★★★, *Call Mi* (Heartbeat 1995)★★★, *Lyrically Potent* (Hearbeat 1996)★★★, *Potent Dub* (Shanachie 1997)★★★.

SISTER LOVE

Sister Love were formed in south London, England, by Coral Williams and her best friend, Sandra Williams. The two girls enrolled Marcia Henry and approached a collective known as Company X. They arranged a successful audition with Greensleeves Records, who were branching out into lovers rock. The group emerged in the mid-70s and in 1978 topped the UK reggae charts with 'Goodbye Little Man' on the Cool Rockers label. The song was voted as one of the top singles of 1978, beating competition from the crossover hits performed by Janet Kay and Dennis Brown. In 1980 the group released 'Every Little Bit Of My Heart', followed by 'Waiting On You', both of which made a significant impression on the reggae chart. While enjoying their success in the group, Henry elected to pursue a solo career; she was replaced by Sandra Sampson and the group released 'It's Over'. Henry completed sessions as a backing vocalist for Doctor Alimantado on his 1979 release *Kings Bread*, as well as joining with the

Heptones on 'Marcus Garvey School'. In 1981 Henry re-emerged as Ika Black, releasing her solo, self-produced debut, 'Human Life', on her own I&I label. Henry's association with Doctor Alimantado then resulted in her signing to his Keyman label and the release in 1983 of her hit 'Crucial World' and *Special Love*. With the label she also released 'Loving Vibration' and undertook a hectic touring schedule of Europe. While Henry's solo career progressed, Sister Love worked with the Soundoff organization, releasing 'At The Station'. Their success in 1980 led to the outfit being voted the best UK vocal group by the readers of *Black Echoes* in their 1981 reggae awards. In 1984 the group split, which led to Sandra Sampson and Sandra Williams joining Sandra Cross in the Wild Bunch, and they recorded *The Wild Bunch* at Ariwa Sounds the same year. The group toured the USA as part of the Ariwa Posse Tour alongside the truculent DJ Ranking Ann and UK rockers Aquizim.

● ALBUMS: Marcia Henry as Ika Black *Special Love* (Keyman 1983)★★★★.

SISTER NANCY

b. Nancy Russell, Kingston, Jamaica, West Indies. Sister Nancy was one of 15 siblings; her brother Robert, known to her family as Dickie, found fame as Brigadier Jerry. The latter began chanting on Prince Norman's sound system before settling with Jahlove Music. While the Brigadier's reputation as the number one cultural DJ flourished, by her mid-teens, Nancy was occasionally performing on the sound system. Winston Riley was the first producer to take Nancy into the recording studio in 1980 for her debut, 'Papa Dean'. The tune was a success and Nancy's career began in earnest. She performed at Reggae Sunsplash, which was transmitted globally. A notable appearance on *A Dee Jay Explosion* saw Nancy performing 'Chalice A Fe Burn' and 'Boom Chaka Laka'. With Winston Riley in 1982 her debut *One Two* was released, featuring the title track, 'Aint No Stopping Nancy', 'Bam Bam' and 'Only Woman DJ With Degree'. She also recorded a classic rendition of 'King And Queen' with Yellowman. With producer Henry 'Junjo' Lawes, she recorded 'A No Any Man Can Test Sister Nancy', 'Bang Belly' and another Yellowman combination, 'Jah Mek

Us Fe A Purpose'. She continued appearing live in the dancehall where she often performed alongside her brother on the Jahlove Music Sound System. The sound toured internationally to rave reviews, including a celebrated session at Brixton Town Hall, London, where both Jerry and Nancy made their debut performances in the UK.

● ALBUMS: *One Two* (Techniques 1982)★★★, with Yellowman, Purple Man *The Yellow, The Purple And The Nancy* (Greensleeves 1983)★★★★.

SIZZLA

b. Miguel Collins, Jamaica, West Indies. Sizzla served his musical apprenticeship on the Caveman Hi Fi sound system, and in 1995 he released his debut through Zagalou before joining the Firehouse crew. He released a number of singles in Jamaica, notably 'Judgement Morning', 'Lifes Road', 'Blaspheme' and a combination with Shadow Man, 'The Gun'. His achievements earned him a Rockers nomination for Best New Artist. Sizzla quickly established an uncompromising attitude to his songwriting, similar to artists such as Peter Tosh and Mutabaruka. Although he continued their legacy, Sizzla was also able to appeal to a younger audience, empathizing with the struggles and experiences of the Jamaican youth. In 1996 as part of the Firehouse crew, he toured the globe to considerable critical acclaim alongside Luciano and Mikey General. In the middle of his hectic touring schedule, Sizzla recorded 'Ins And Outs' with Louie Culture, and 'Love Amongst My Brethren', 'No Other Like Jah' and 'Did You Ever', produced by Philip 'Fatis' Burrell, with whom he enjoyed an extensive association.

In 1997 Sizzla began working with Bobby Digital; the recording sessions featured Sly Dunbar, Robbie Shakespeare and Dean Fraser, whose saxophone graced the hit 'Black Woman And Child', a song that has since become an anthem. It subsequently featured as the title track of Sizzla's first album with Bobby Digital. He maintained a high profile in the singles market, releasing 'Like Mountain', 'Babylon A Listen' and a combination with Luciano, 'Build A Better World'. Sizzla has been hailed as an integral part of the 90s cultural revolution, particularly with the enlightening *Black Woman And Child*.

● ALBUMS: *Burning Up* (RAS 1995)★★★,
Praise Ye Jah (Xterminator 1997)★★★★, *Black Woman And Child* (Greensleeves 1997)★★★★.

SKA

The generic title for Jamaican music recorded between 1961 and 1967, ska emerged from Jamaican R&B, which itself was largely based on American R&B and doo-wop. The difference was that while the US style smoothed out and became soul, the Jamaican sound, if anything, became wilder and more jerky, in what is commonly assumed to be an exaggeration of the 'jump' beat played on the black radio stations of Miami and New Orleans in the late 50s, and readily heard in Jamaica. Ska was fuelled by the sound systems, the over-amplified mobile discos that were (and still are) Jamaica's preferred method of enjoying music. At first, from the start of the 50s, sound systems used American records. By the late 50s competition had become so fierce between rival systems that finding an exclusive record by an American act had become a preoccupation - the right song could maintain a sound system's pre-eminence over its rivals. Eventually, as the wild beat of the likes of Amos Milburn, Wynonie Harris *et al.* began to fade into the past, sound system owners formed an alliance with indigenous Jamaican singers and musicians, which resulted in a hybrid of doo-wop, R&B and jazz that eventually precipitated ska, the jump-up sound where the jump took precedence over everything else.

The sound system bosses became Jamaica's first record producers, and included Sir Coxsone Dodd, Duke Reid and King Edwards, their names reflecting the showmanship and drive for supremacy of the sound systems. The singers included Delroy Wilson, Jiving Juniors (see Derrick Harriott), Alton (Ellis) and Eddy, Lord Creator, and many more. These artists quickly became Jamaica's first stars. The instrumental outings of the bands, under the leadership of talents such as trombonist Don Drummond, tenor saxman Roland Alphonso, and alto sax player Tommy McCook, if anything, outshone the vocal records, with a frequently freewheeling, heavy-jazz philosophy that many have since tried, but failed, to imitate. By 1964 ska had become popular among mods in England, where it was known as Blue Beat, the name of the fore-most UK licensing label. British acts such as Georgie Fame And The Blue Flames, and The Migil 5 had hits in the ska style, while more authentic Jamaican acts such as Millie, Prince Buster and the Skatalites all gained chart entries. By 1966 ska was beginning to burn out in Jamaica, to be replaced by the more sedate sound of rocksteady. However, ska has remained intermittently popular, demonstrated by several 'ska revivals', the most successful of which was the UK 2-Tone movement in the late 70s. It seems that the beat will never truly exhaust itself. At any given time, somewhere in the world, from Japan to Germany, a would-be Skatalites can be unearthed, making a nightclub jump to the infectious rhythms of this most animated of musics.

● COMPILATIONS: Various Artists: *Ska Authentic* (Studio One)★★★★, *The History Of Ska* (Bamboo 1969)★★★, *Intensified Volumes 1 & 2* (Mango/Island 1979)★★★, *Club Ska '67* (Mango/Island 1980)★★★★.

● VIDEOS: *Ska Explosion 2* (Visionary 1994).

SKATALITES

The Skatalites were formed in June 1964, drawing from the ranks of session musicians then recording in the studios of Kingston, Jamaica. The personnel included Don Drummond (trombone), Roland Alphonso (tenor saxophone), Tommy McCook (tenor saxophone), Johnny 'Dizzy' Moore (trumpet), Lester Sterling (alto saxophone), Jerome 'Jah Jerry' Hines (guitar), Jackie Mittoo (piano), Lloyd Brevett (bass) and Lloyd Knibbs (drums). The band name was a Tommy McCook pun on the Soviet space satellite of 1963. The Skatalites' music, reputedly named after the characteristic 'ska' sound made by the guitar when playing the 'after beat', was a powerful synthesis, combining elements of R&B and swing jazz in arrangements and solos, underpinned by the uniquely Jamaican-stressed 'after beat', as opposed to the 'down beat' of R&B. Many of the musicians had learned music at Alpha Boys' School in Kingston, subsequently honing their talent in the Jamaican swing bands of the 40s and early 50s, and in numerous 'hotel bands' playing for the tourist trade. Most of the musicians thereby developed recognizable individual styles. Their repertoire was drawn from many sources, including adaptations of Latin tunes, movie themes and updated mento, a Jamaican folk song form. Perhaps their most famous and identifiable tune was 'Guns Of Navarone', recorded in 1965 and a big club hit in the UK in the mid-60s. They recorded hundreds of superb instrumentals for various producers, either under the group name or as a band led by the particular musician who had arranged the session. Under the Skatalite name they made important music for Coxsone Dodd and Duke Reid, as well as for Justin and Philip Yap's Top Deck record label. They stayed together for just over two years until August 1965, when a combination of financial, organizational and personal problems caused the break-up of the band after their last gig, a police dance at the Runaway Bay Hotel. Of the main protagonists, Jackie Mittoo and Roland Alphonso were persuaded by Coxsone Dodd to form the Soul Brothers band, who made instrumentals and supplied backing tracks at Studio One until 1967. McCook worked principally for Duke Reid, where he formed the studio band known as the Supersonics, and was musical co-director for Reid's Treasure Isle label with alto saxophonist Herman Marquis. The tragically wayward Don Drummond suffered from severe depression and died on 6 May 1969 in Belle Vue Asylum, Kingston. The Skatalites had backed virtually every singer of note in the studios, at the same time laying the musical foundation for subsequent developments in Jamaican music. They released a reunion album in 1975 - not playing ska, but high-quality instrumental reggae. In 1984 the band played the Jamaican and London 'Sunsplash' concerts to rapturous acclaim. The re-formed group also toured Japan with vocalists Prince Buster and Lord Tanamo in 1989, recording live and in the studio.

● ALBUMS: *Ska Boo-Da-Ba* (Top Deck/Doctor Bird 1965)★★★★, *Ska Authentic* (Studio One 1967)★★★, *The Skatalites* (Treasure Isle 1975)★★★, *Return Of The Big Guns* (Island 1984)★★★, *Live At Reggae Sunsplash* (Synergy 1986)★★★★, *Stretching Out* (ROIR 1987, reissued 1998)★★★, *Celebration Time* (Studio One 1988)★★★.

● COMPILATIONS: *Best Of The Skatalites* (Studio One 1974)★★★, *Scattered Lights* (Top Deck 1984)★★★, *Foundation Ska* (Heartbeat 1997)★★★★.

SLICKERS

Derrick Crooks (b. 1937, Westmoreland, Jamaica, West Indies) initially performed alongside his brother Sidney and Glen Adams as part of the embryonic Pioneers in 1962. The group released their debut, 'Sometime', in 1965 for producer Leslie Kong, before joining Ken Lack's Caltone enterprise. While the Pioneers' career gained momentum, Crooks pursued his recording career alongside an assortment of vocalists. He enrolled other singers and together they performed as the Slickers. The Pioneers and Slickers were often mistaken for one another because of their similar vocal stylings. The Slickers' debut release, 'Nana', produced by Neremiah Reid, was a commercial success in Jamaica and flourished in the burgeoning UK reggae market. By 1969 the group were recording with Leslie Kong, who released the popular 'Run Fatty' and with Joe Gibbs, who released 'Mother Matty', alongside the cautionary 'Man Beware'. In 1970 the Slickers recorded with Byron Lee, who is credited as the producer of the group's distinguished hit, 'Johnny Too Bad'. The tune was featured on the soundtrack to *The Harder They Come* (according to the album's sensationalist liner-notes, one of the writers was reputed to have gone underground while the other was on death row!). The group released sporadic hits through to the mid-70s, including 'Fight Against The Law' and 'St Jago De La Vega'. In 1978, 'Johnny Too Bad' was revitalized by Bunny Wailer and was included on the sadly underrated *Protest*.

SLY AND ROBBIE

Sly Dunbar (b. Lowell Charles Dunbar, 10 May 1952, Kingston, Jamaica, West Indies; drums) and Robbie Shakespeare (b. 27 September 1953, Kingston, Jamaica, West Indies; bass). Dunbar, nicknamed 'Sly' in honour of his fondness for Sly And The Family Stone, was an established figure in Skin Flesh And Bones when he met Shakespeare. They have probably played on more reggae records than the rest of Jamaica's many session musicians put together. The pair began working together as a team in 1975 and they quickly became Jamaica's leading, and most distinctive, rhythm section. They have played on numerous releases, including recordings by U-Roy, Peter Tosh, Bunny Wailer,

Culture and Black Uhuru, while Dunbar also made several solo albums, all of which featured Shakespeare. They have constantly sought to push back the boundaries surrounding the music with their consistently inventive work. Dunbar drummed his first session for Lee Perry as one of the Upsetters; the resulting 'Night Doctor' was a big hit both in Jamaica and the UK. He next moved to Skin Flesh And Bones, whose variations on the reggae-meets-disco/soul sound brought them a great deal of session work and a residency at Kingston's Tit for Tat club. Sly was still searching for more, however, and he moved on to another session group in the mid-70s, the Revolutionaries. This move changed the course of reggae music through the group's work at Joseph 'Joe Joe' Hookim's Channel One Studio and their pioneering rockers sound. It was with the Revolutionaries that he teamed up with bass player Robbie Shakespeare, who had undergone a similar apprenticeship with session bands, notably Bunny Lee's Aggrovators. The two formed a friendship that turned into a musical partnership that was to dominate reggae music throughout the remainder of the 70s, 80s and on into the 90s.

Known simply as Sly And Robbie (and occasionally Drumbar And Basspeare), they not only formed their own label, Taxi, which produced many hit records for scores of well-known artists but also found time to do session work for just about every important name in reggae. They toured extensively as the powerhouse rhythm section for Black Uhuru and, as their fame spread outside of reggae circles, they worked with Grace Jones, Bob Dylan, Ian Dury and Joan Armatrading, among a host of other rock stars. In the early 80s they were among the first to use the burgeoning 'new technology' to musical effect; they demonstrated that it could be used to its full advantage without compromising their musicianship in any way. In a genre controlled by producers and 'this week's star', reggae musicians have rarely been accorded their proper respect, but the accolades heaped on Sly And Robbie have helped to redress the balance. Sly And Robbie's mastery of the digital genre, coupled with their abiding love of and respect for the music's history, has placed them at the forefront of Kingston's producers of

the early 90s. Their 'Murder She Wrote' cut for Chaka Demus And Pliers set the tone for 1992, while 'Tease Me' for the same duo, built around a sample from the Skatalites' 60s hit, 'Ball Of Fire', was another significant UK chart success in 1993 - this was quite remarkable for a team whose successful career had already spanned three decades. They achieved further commercial (if not artistic) success with 1997's celebrity-packed *Friends*, with guest singers including Maxi Priest, Ali Campbell (UB40) and Mick Hucknall (Simply Red) brought in to cover reggae standards. Hucknall's bland cover version of Gregory Isaacs' 'Night Nurse' reached the UK charts the same year.

● ALBUMS: *Disco Dub* (Gorgon 1978)★★, *Gamblers Choice* (Taxi 1980)★★★, *Raiders Of The Lost Dub* (Mango/Island 1981)★★★, *60s, 70s Into The 80s* (Mango/Island 1981)★★★, *Dub Extravaganza* (CSA 1984)★★★, *A Dub Experience* (Island 1985)★★★, *Language Barrier* (Island 1985)★★★, *Electro Reggae* (Island 1986)★★★, *The Sting* (Taxi 1986)★★★, *Rhythm Killers* (4th & Broadway 1987)★★★★, *Dub Rockers Delight* (Blue Moon 1987)★★★, *The Summit* (RAS 1988)★★★, *Silent Assassin* (4th & Broadway 1990)★★★, *Friends* (East West 1997)★★.

Productions include: Various Artists *Present Taxi* (Taxi 1981)★★★★, *Crucial Reggae* (Taxi 1984)★★★, *Taxi Wax* (Taxi 1984)★★★, *Taxi Gang* (Taxi 1984)★★★, *Taxi Connection Live In London* (Taxi 1986)★★★, *Taxi Fare* (Taxi 1987)★★★, *Two Rhythms Clash* (RAS 1990)★★★, *DJ Riot* (Mango/Island 1990)★★★, *Sound Of The 90s* (1990)★★★, *Carib Soul* (1990)★★★, *Present Sound Of Sound* (Musidisc 1994)★★★, *Present Ragga Pon Top* (Musidisc 1994)★★★.

● COMPILATIONS: *Reggae Greats* (Island 1985)★★★, *Hits 1987-90* (Sonic Sounds 1991)★★★★.

SMART, LEROY

b. Jamaica, West Indies. A distinguished vocalist of the hard-working, soulful school, Leroy Smart - the self-styled 'Don' - was orphaned at the age of two and brought up in Kingston's Alpha Catholic Boys School and Home - the first home for many of Jamaica's musical talents. His reputation precedes him as one of Jamaica's most outrageous and colourful characters, and he is held in high esteem by the reggae fraternity, to the point where his name is often discussed not only with reverence but in awe. Consquently, the stories of his struggles in life have assumed far greater importance over the years than his manifest vocal talents. He began recording in the early 70s and made the usual rounds of Kingston producers, first achieving success with Jimmy Radway/Rodway and then with Bunny Lee, Gussie Clarke and Joseph 'Joe Joe' Hookim and many others. His stage shows were truly outrageous and were famed as much for their acrobatic displays as his vocal pyrotechnics, while his agonized, mannered singing defied categorization. He achieved classic status on a number of records throughout the 70s, including 'Pride And Ambition', 'Ballistic Affair', 'God Helps The Man' and 'Mr Smart'/'Happiness Is My Desire'. He continued to record in the 80s and on into the 90s too, hitting again with 'She Just A Draw Card' and 'I Am The Don'. His vocal power and forceful personality have always ensured that he is never far from the forefront of reggae music.

● ALBUMS: *Jah Loves Everyone* (Burning Sounds 1978)★★★, *Dread Hot In Africa* (Burning Sounds 1978)★★★, *Impressions Of* (Burning Sounds 1978)★★★, *She Love It In The Morning* (GG's 1984)★★, *She Just A Draw Card* (Worldwide Success 1985)★★, *Showcase* (Fatman 1985)★★★, *Live Up Roots Children* (Striker Lee 1985)★★★, *Bank Account* (Powerhouse 1985)★★★, *Musical Don* (Skengdon 1988)★★★, *Propaganda* (Burning Sounds 1988)★★★, *Talk About Friends* (1993)★★★.

SMILEY CULTURE

b. David Emmanuel, *c*.1960, London, England. The son of a Jamaican father and South American mother, Smiley gained his nickname at school, where his method of chatting up girls was simply to ask for a smile. He served his apprenticeship with a number of local sounds before hitting the big time with south London's Saxon sound system, the home of a formidable amount of British reggae talent, including Maxi Priest, Tippa Irie and Phillip Papa Levi. His live reputation attracted the attention of record producers and his first recording for Fashion Records, 'Cockney Translation', featuring Smiley slipping effortlessly from Jamaican patois to a south London accent, touched a nerve and sold an unprecedented 40,000 copies. His follow-up, 'Police Officer', again featuring the cockney and 'yardy' voices, did even better and reached the national Top 20 in early 1985. Appearances on BBC Television's *Top Of The Pops* followed - a first for a reggae DJ - and Smiley became a 'star'. A major recording contract with Polydor Records followed. As well as hosting his own television show, *Club Mix*, Smiley also found time for a cameo appearance in the film *Absolute Beginners*, singing Miles Davis's 'So What'. He continued to record, including some interesting collaborations with American hip-hop artists. Smiley is important in that he was among the first English-based reggae artists to challenge the Jamaicans and succeed. The British public also took him to their hearts, while the lyrics of 'Cockney Translation' are now used by teachers and lecturers to illustrate the effects and influence of immigration on the English language.

● ALBUMS: *The Original* (Top Notch 1986)★★★, *Tongue In Cheek* (Polydor 1986)★★★.

SMITH, ERNIE

b. Glenroy Ernest Smith, *c*.1948, Jamaica, West Indies. Smith initially enjoyed notoriety when his single 'Pitta Patta', backed with 'Lichfield Gardens', topped the Jamaican charts in 1973, utilizing Lee Perry's 'musical transplant' rhythm. The song was voted as the best song of the year in Jamaica by *Swing* magazine. The lyrics were also adapted by Lloyd Charmers for his lewd 'Big Eight', marketed as the reggae alternative to Judge Dread's hit. An album followed, with Smith covering 'I Love You To Want Me' and 'Help Me Make It Through The Night', both successfully recorded by John Holt. In 1974 Smith followed the hit with 'Duppy Or A Gunman' and the equally popular 'Key Card', echoing the patois style made popular by Pluto. 'Duppy Or A Gunman' was successfully covered by Inner Circle and interest in the original was regenerated 10 years later with Yellowman. Smith became involved in the Wildflower collective, known as XYZ productions, alongside Lloyd Charmers, where they released a number of chart-topping hits including Ken Boothe's interpretation of 'Everything I Own', which was an international bestseller. In addition to his own recording, Smith was also responsible for Tinga Stewart's Jamaican Song Festival winner, 'Play De Music'. Johnny Nash had recorded the disdained *Celebrate Life* which led the singer on a trip to Jamaica seeking inspiration. The result was Smith's composition 'Tears On My Pillow (I Can't Stand It)' which topped the UK chart in June 1975. By 1976 Smith's style was no longer in vogue, although he continued to enjoy popularity with more mature listeners, releasing a number of middle-of-the-road and gospel-influenced albums. In 1980 he recorded a version of Bob Marley's 'Bend Down Low', produced with Lloyd Charmers. The song was included on an album featuring re-recordings of his greatest hits.

● ALBUMS: *Life Is Just For Living* (Trojan 1974)★★★★, *Ernie* (Federal 1975)★★★, *For The Good Times* (Trojan 1976)★★★, *I'll Sing For Jesus* (Wildflower 1978)★★, *Pure Gold Rock Steady* (Wildflower 1979)★★★, *After 30 Years Life Is Just For Living* (Ernie Smith Music 1997)★★★.

● COMPILATIONS: *Mr Smith's Classics* (KR 1982)★★★★.

SMITH, SLIM

b. Keith Smith, c.1948, Kingston, Jamaica, West Indies, d. 1973. Smith first came to prominence as a member of the Victors Youth Band, who were highly praised at the 1964 Jamaican Festival. He subsequently became a founding member and lead vocalist of the Techniques, who secured a recording contract with Duke Reid's Treasure Isle label. From 1964-65 they recorded several hits, two of which, 'I Am In Love' and 'Little Did You Know', are included on the Techniques' *Classics* compilation. After leaving the group in 1965, he visited Canada where he recorded his first solo album, *Toronto '66*, which almost instantly sank into obscurity. On his return to Jamaica, he commenced recording for Prince Buster and Coxsone Dodd's Studio One label, the main rival to Duke Reid. His Studio One recordings brilliantly highlight his passionate, soulful voice, which had an almost manic edge, and confirm him as one of Jamaica's greatest singers. His hits from this

period include 'I've Got Your Number', 'Hip Hug' and 'Rougher Yet', many of which were later compiled for *Born To Love*. In 1967 he formed a new group, the Uniques, and commenced his association with producer Bunny Lee. They topped the Jamaican hit parade with 'Let Me Go Girl', but after recording one album, *Absolutely The Uniques*, Smith left the group, staying with Lee to concentrate on a solo career. He had a hit almost immediately with 'Everybody Needs Love'. An album of the same name quickly followed, as did many further hits. By 1972 personal problems led to him being detained at Bellevue sanatorium, and the following year he committed suicide. His death stunned Jamaica. Still widely regarded as one of Jamaica's great vocalists, his enduring popularity has thankfuly resulted in the reissue of the bulk of his work.

● ALBUMS: *Toronto '66* (1966)★★, *Everybody Needs Love* (1969, reissued Pama 1989)★★★★, *Just A Dream* (1971, reissued Pama 1989)★★★.

● COMPILATIONS: *The Time Has Come* (Pama 1984)★★★, *Memorial* (Trojan 1985)★★★★, *Dance Hall Connection* (Third World 1986)★★★, *Born To Love (1966-68)* (Studio One 1979)★★★, *20 Super Hits* (Sonic Sounds 1991)★★★, *Rain From The Skies* (Trojan 1992)★★★, *20 Rare Grooves* (Rhino 1994)★★★★.

SMITH, WAYNE

b. 5 December 1965, Waterhouse, Kingston, Jamaica, West Indies. Smith began singing while at school and in church, where he cultivated his unique vocal technique. After achieving his educational qualifications he began an apprenticeship as an electrical engineer. His training centred around the Papine region of St. Andrew's, where many top performers began their musical careers, including Brigadier Jerry, Sister Nancy, Anthony Malvo and Chaka Demus. Smith spent his free time at King Jammy's (then Prince Jammy) sound system, hoping for an opportunity on the microphone. His persistence came to fruition and, inspired by the audience's response, Jammy recorded Smith's debut, 'Aint No Me Without You', followed by the dancehall favourites 'Change My Mind', 'Life Is A Moment In Space' and 'Ism Skism'. Smith was featured in the Channel 4 television reggae documentary *Deep Roots Music*, where he is filmed recording in King Tubby's studio. Like many artists, Smith began working with other producers, including sessions at Channel One, and a series of hits followed including 'Smoker Supa', versions of 'Karma Chameleon' and Dennis Brown's 'No More Will I Roam'. In the mid-80s Smith returned to working with the newly promoted King Jammy, enjoying success with 'Aint No Meaning' and 'Come Along'.

In late 1984 he was directly involved in what is considered by many to be a pivotal phase in the Jamaican recording industry. The occasion of Smith's and Noel Daley's tinkerings with a Casio music box has been well documented, although the unprecedented success of this event proved to be a turning point for both Smith and King Jammy. The resulting song, 'Under Me Sleng Teng', was a massive hit around the world and led to countless versions. From its initial release in 1985 the rhythm continues to provide the basis for a number of reggae hits. Having the distinction of introducing the most covered accentuation in the music's history inevitably led to enormous expectations, which Smith endured with calm assurance. He demonstrated his talent for songwriting and singing, and drew on his formative training for programming on *Sleng Teng* with the tracks 'Icky All Over', 'Love Don't Love Me' and 'Walk Like A Granny'. He continued to produce hits, notably 'Rapid Dem Love' and 'My Sweet Love', before relocating to the USA where he set up his own Sleng Teng label.

● ALBUMS: *Youthman Skanking* (Black Joy 1982)★★★, *Supa Smoker* (Channel One 1983)★★★, with Patrick Andy *Showdown* (Channel One 1984)★★★, *Sleng Teng* (Greensleeves 1985)★★★★, *Computer Mix* (Shanachie 1986)★★★★.

SNOW

b. Darrin O'Brien, 1971, Toronto, Canada. Snow is the most commercially successful white DJ ever; his debut UK single, 'Informer', reached the UK Top 3 in March 1993. Snow was raised in the Allenbury projects of Toronto and became a frequent visitor to reggae blues parties, where he assimilated the styles of Junior Reid, Eek A Mouse, Tenor Saw and Nitty Gritty. Considered a 'problem child', he spent 18 months in prison on a murder charge at the age of 19, before finally being acquitted - an experience that inspired the lyrics of 'Informer'. Rap mixer DJ Prince introduced him to MC Shan in New York, who in turn recommended the East West label. They signed him in late 1992, his debut studio sessions resulting in *12 Inches Of Snow*, released in spring 1993. 'Lonely Monday Morning' subsequently became his first US single. Despite adverse criticism, his gift for mimicry is a keen one, and by virtue of 'Informer', he has already entered reggae's record books.

● ALBUMS: *12 Inches Of Snow* (East West 1993)★★★★, *Murder Love* (East West 1995)★★★, *Justuss* (East West 1997)★★★.

SONS OF JAH

The Sons Of Jah were a vocal trio formed in Trenchtown, Jamaica, in 1976, led by the enigmatic Trevor Bow (b. Kingston, Jamaica, West Indies). Throughout his career he has been assisted by a variety of vocalists, including Derrick Donaldson, Bunny MacKensie and Howard Haughton. The group's debut release, 'Tell Them Jah Son', surfaced in the UK through the inauguration of Michael Campbell and King Sounds' Grove Muzik collective. Bow's long-standing friendship with Bob Marley And The Wailers resulted in recording sessions at Tuff Gong Studios, ably assisted by the drum and bass duo of Carlton 'Carly' Barrett and Aston 'Familyman' Barrett. By 1978 Bow had set up his own Natty Congo label, releasing *Bankrupt Morality* alongside the singles 'Psalm 72', which proved a big hit on night-time radio, and 'Israel Woman'. Although the group were known for performing in the militant roots style, Bow's passion for rocksteady resulted in the recording of a sadly overlooked medley of Techniques songs. Although based in Ladbroke Grove, London, the Sons always recorded in Jamaica as they felt British musicians were unable to reproduce convincingly the Trenchtown sound. His Natty Congo label was intended solely for Sons Of Jah releases, although he released some Errol Dunkley material. Following Bob Marley's death in 1981, Bow made a cameo appearance as a cavalryman alongside Aswad and King Sounds in the video for the posthumous release of 'Buffalo Soldier'. In 1982 the Sons recorded 'Breaking Down The Barriers', which demonstrated the group's crystal-clear harmonies; the rhythm was also used for Ranking Dread's phenomenal 'Shut Mi Mouth', regarded as the DJ's classic. The Sons built a loyal following and the release of 'Johnny Too Late' and 'Marshall Rock' maintained the band's profile in 1983. Following the success of the singles, it was not until 1985 that news of the band's demise surfaced. Undeterred by the events, Bow performed as the Son Of Jah, returning to Tuff Gong to record 'Living Intact', 'Hard Times Love', 'Wise Man Says' and 'Love Is A Treasure', compiled on *Writings On The Wall*.

● ALBUMS: *Bankrupt Morality* (Natty Congo 1978)★★★★, *Burning Black* (Natty Congo 1979)★★★, *Showcase* (Natty Congo 1981)★★★, *Universal Message* (Natty Congo 1982)★★★, *Writings On The Wall* (Natty Congo 1985)★★★.

SOUL SYNDICATE

Yet another of the top session teams that determined the sound and feel of reggae music at any given time in its evolution, the Soul Syndicate were hugely influential in the early to mid-70s. Their work with Winston 'Niney' Holness, Duke Reid, Keith Hudson and many others was brash and exciting and added a different dimension to the roots sound of the period. The core members were the supremely talented Earl 'Chinna' Smith on guitar, Carlton 'Santa' Davis on drums, George 'Fully' Fullwood on bass, Tony Chin on rhythm guitar and Bernard 'Touter' Harvey, who later joined the Wailers, on keyboards. At one stage their featured vocalist was Freddie McGregor. This basic nucleus also recorded for Bunny Lee as the Aggrovators as the decade wore on. Like so many of the musicians that have made reggae music over the years, their names and work remain relatively unknown outside of the genre's cognoscenti, but it is hoped that, one day, their work (and that of so many others) will be given its proper recognition.

● ALBUMS: *Harvest Uptown* (Soul Syndicate 1978)★★★, *Was Is Always* (Epiphany 1979)★★, *Friends And Family* (Epiphany 1996)★★★.

SOUND SYSTEM

It is impossible to overemphasize the importance of sound systems to the development of reggae music, as just about every record producer, singer and DJ from the 50s onwards has been closely involved with them in one way or another. They were the forerunners of today's mobile disco, but the amount and weight of their amplification equipment ensured the sound of the music could be felt as strongly as it was heard. In the 50s, R&B radio stations from southern American cities beamed their music to a responsive Jamaican audience, and the popularity of R&B prompted enterprising locals to start their own sound systems. Operators such as Coxsone Dodd ('Sir Coxsone The Down Beat') and Duke Reid ('The Trojan') became stars in Jamaica on the strength of their sounds - both for the records that they played and for the way in which they presented them. The top outfits would play in competition against each other and the rivalry was frequently violent and bloody. Records were hunted out in the USA where vast amounts of money were spent on the right tunes - the label details would then be scratched out to stop their rivals discovering the identities of these top tunes.

The sound system operators started to make their own R&B-based recordings as the supply of hard R&B records began to dry up in the late 50s, and the black American audiences moved towards a smoother style of music, which failed to spark the interest of the Jamaican audiences. At first, these recordings were intended solely for exclusive use (on acetate disc or dub plate) by the sound that made them, but they proved so popular that the top 'sounds' began to release these records, and ska and the Jamaican recording industry were born. From this point onwards, the development of Jamaican music through ska, rocksteady, reggae, rockers, dub, dance hall and ragga was inextricably linked with sound systems, both as the testing ground for new records, but, more importantly, for singers and DJs to test out the crowd's response as they took their turns at the microphone. Their popularity prompted the proliferation of sound systems in New York, London and Toronto - at first, anywhere with an expatriate Jamaican community - but later, their influence spread in more diverse directions; the importance of Jamaican Sounds to the development of hip-hop and rap in America, for instance, has yet to be fully credited. The Sounds have gone through as many changes in styles and fashion as reggae music and have become a cultural rallying point across the globe. The current fashion is for playing 'specials' - one-off acetate discs recorded exclusively by current big names, extolling the virtues of the particular sound for which the 'special' has been voiced, usually to the tune and rhythm of a popular 'commercial' hit record. DJs' live contributions are kept to a minimum where once they dominated the sound. In many ways, the wheel has turned full circle, but to hear a top sound system playing out either in the warmth of a Kingston open-air dance or crowded together in a small club in London or New York is to understand fully the strength and power of Jamaican music, and to experience its direct and very real influence on its own committed following.

SPANNER BANNER

b. Jamaica, West Indies. The younger brother of Pliers (Chaka Demus And Pliers), Spanner Banner spent several years perfecting his singing and songwriting skills in and around the Kingston studios of Jamaica from 1989 onwards. Possessed of a fragile yet deeply melodic voice, he worked as a DJ on the St. Annes sound system circuit to hone his style before attempting to follow in the footsteps of his brother. His sobriquet was corrupted from the family name Bonner, given a twist in rhyming slang to place him in the same 'toolkit' as Pliers. His co-composition with Chaka Demus And Pliers, 'Tease Me', had already helped to launch their career, but it was 1996 before he recorded his own debut. *Chill*, promoted by a single of the same title, was the first fruit of a major recording contract with Island Records. Five of the tracks were produced by Sly And Robbie, and one by Bobby Digital, among other collaborators. Guest singers included Chaka Demus And Pliers ('Slow Motion'), Tony Rebel ('Universal Love') and Luciano ('What We Need Is Love').
● ALBUMS: *Chill* (Island 1996)★★★, *Lover's Story* (Sweet Angel 1997)★★.

SPENCE, BARRINGTON

Spence's vocal style was frequently compared with that of the Studio One veteran Ken Boothe. In 1975 he recorded 'Come Back My Darling', which was an agreeable example of Boothe's influence on the young singer. His follow-up, 'Darling Dry Your Eyes', benefited from the pro-

duction skills of Prince Tony Robinson, the engineering expertise of a young Errol Thompson and masterful musical backing supplied by Skin Flesh And Bones. While with Robinson, Spence adapted Junior Byles' masterpiece 'Curly Locks' as 'Let Locks Grow'. The single was slammed by the critics for lacking originality; nevertheless, the song proved extremely popular, gaining international notoriety for the performer. Spence's versions of Boothe's 'The Train Is Coming' as 'Train To Rhodesia', and Byles' 'Curly Locks' as 'House Of Dreadlocks', were featured on Big Youth's *Dread Locks Dread*. Spence's sessions with Robinson resulted in *Speak Softly*, which included the hits along with 'Jah For All', 'Living Just A Little' and his own composition, 'Let's Get It On'. Other singles included 'For The Rest Of My Life', 'Living A Little Laughing A Little' and 'Natty Dread Have Wisdom'. The unfair dismissal of Spence as a mere imitator blighted his career and he was unable to fulfil his potential. In 1982 he found success with 'Falling In Love' for Larry Lawrence, and while with Derrick Spence, he had a hit with 'I See A Blackman Cry'. A year later, Spence recorded alongside DJ Joe Sealy for the single 'You Don't Have To Dance', with the New York-based producer Lloyd Barnes.
● ALBUMS: *Speak Softly* (Trojan 1975)★★★.

SPICE, MIKEY

b. Michael Theophilus Johnson, 21 July 1965, Jamaica, West Indies. Spice emerged in 1995 with a myriad of single releases. His popularity spread when he recorded a reggae version of Barry White's 'Practice What You Preach', both a dancehall smash and a number 1 on the reggae chart. Proving he was no one-hit-wonder, the hits kept coming, including 'Signs And Wonders', 'I Wanna Know', 'Lovin' In Your Eyes' 'I'll Be There', 'When You're Lonely', 'Open Your Eyes' and 'Born Again'. In May 1995, his debut, *Happiness*, surfaced, featuring three of the aforementioned hits. The release of *Close The Door* found the singer covering a number of soft soul hits. Nicknamed 'Jamaica's Barry White', he covered 'Can't Get Enough' and 'I'm Gonna Love You Just A Little Bit More' as 'Deeper And Deeper' and 'Just The Way You Are', although the title track was originally a hit for Teddy Pendergrass. Spice's phenomenal popularity continued unabashed in 1996 when 'So Much Things To Say' and a combination tune with Shaggy, 'Shake Your Body', were released. Spice had also recorded with the UK's Saxon sound system operator, Musclehead, who sampled a version of the Wailers' 'Thankyou Lord'. The hit 'Jah Never Fail I' showed that, although regarded as a lovers singer, he could perform equally well as a conscientious roots performer. With Courtney Cole at Roof International, he maintained his lovers profile for 'Acting Like A Stranger'. Spice continues to be regarded as one of the leading exponents of the genre in the late 90s, and has had as many as five hits on the reggae Top 20 in the same week.

● ALBUMS: *Happiness* (X Rated 1995)★★★★, *Close The Door* (Charm 1995)★★, *Born Again* (VP 1996)★★★, *So Much Things To Say* (Big Ship 1996)★★★, *It's All About Time* (Firehouse 1997)★★★.

● COMPILATIONS: *Reggae Max* (Jet Star 1997)★★★.

STARLITES

Earl 'Chinna' Smith, George 'Fully' Fullwood, Carlton 'Santa' Davis and Tony Chin have consistently provided solid backing to many of Jamaica's top performers, including Big Youth, Peter Tosh and also his son Andrew Tosh. The players originally performed as the nucleus of the Soul Syndicate band, which featured a variety of lead vocalists including Freddie McGregor and Stanley Beckford. In 1973, following his departure from the Soul Syndicate, Beckford formed the Starlites, recording with Alvin 'GG' Ranglin. The group released a series of successful local hits in Kingston, including 'Healing In The Barnyard', 'Hold My Hand', 'Mama Dee' and 'You're A Wanted Man'. The singles showcased Beckford's performances in patois, which proved popular among the Jamaican audience. In 1975 the group enjoyed their biggest hit with 'Soldering', popular Jamaican slang for the sexual act. The single was immediately banned by RJR and JBC, which probably enhanced the financial success of the record. The tune was successfully covered by Big Youth on *Dread Locks Dread* as 'Natty Dread She Want'. Unfortunately, the Starlites were unable to repeat the success of the song and by the late 70s, the group had disbanded. In 1980 Beckford resurfaced at the Jamaican Song Festival with the Turbines, who were victorious with 'Come Sing With Me'. A number of local hits, produced with Alvin 'GG' Ranglin, surfaced, including 'Where Have All The Young Girls Gone', 'Balm Yard' and the calypso-influenced 'Carnival'. Beckford restated his position as a song festival performer with a second victory in 1987, when he performed 'Dem Haffe Squirm', which has been followed by a sporadic output.

● ALBUMS: *Soldering* (1995)★★★, as Stanley And The Turbines *Big Bamboo* (Jamaica Gold 1993)★★★.

STEEL PULSE

Probably the UK's most highly regarded roots reggae outfit, Steel Pulse originally formed at Handsworth School, Birmingham, and comprised David Hinds (lead vocals, guitar), Basil Gabbidon (lead guitar, vocals) and Ronnie McQueen (bass). However, it is Hinds who, as songwriter, has always been the engine behind Steel Pulse, from their early days establishing themselves in the Birmingham club scene. Formed in 1975, their debut release, 'Kibudu, Mansetta And Abuku', arrived on the small independent label Dip, and linked the plight of urban black youth with the image of a greater African homeland. They followed it with 'Nyah Love' for Anchor. Surprisingly, they were initially refused live dates in Caribbean venues in the Midlands because of their Rastafarian beliefs. Aligning themselves closely with the Rock Against Racism organization, they chose to tour with sympathetic elements of the punk movement, including the Stranglers, XTC, etc.: 'Punks had a way of enjoying themselves - throw bottles at you, beer, spit at you, that kind of thing'. Eventually they found a more natural home in support slots for Burning Spear, which brought them to the attention of Island Records. Their first release for Island was the 'Ku Klux Klan' single, a considered tilt at the evils of racism, and one often accompanied by a visual parody of the sect on stage. By this time their ranks had swelled to include Selwyn 'Bumbo' Brown (keyboards), Steve 'Grizzly' Nesbitt (drums), Fonso Martin (vocals, percussion) and Michael Riley (vocals). *Handsworth Revolution* was an accomplished long-playing debut and one of the major landmarks in the evolution of British reggae. However, despite moderate commercial and critical success over three albums, the relationship with Island had soured by the advent of *Caught You* (released in the USA as *Reggae Fever*). They switched to Elektra Records, and unveiled their most consistent collection of songs since their debut with *True Democracy*, distinguished by the Garvey-eulogizing 'Rally Around' cut. A further definitive set arrived in *Earth Crisis*. Unfortunately, Elektra chose to take a leaf out of Island's book in trying to coerce Steel Pulse into a more mainstream vein, asking them to emulate the pop-reggae stance of Eddy Grant. *Babylon Bandit* was consequently weakened, but did contain the anthemic 'Not King James Version', which was a powerful indictment on the omission of black people and history from certain versions of the Bible. Their next move was to MCA for *State Of Emergency*, which retained some of the synthesized dance elements of its predecessor. Though it was a significantly happier compromise, it still paled before any of their earlier albums. *Rastafari Centennial* was recorded live at the Elysée Montmartre in Paris, and dedicated to the hundred-year anniversary of the birth of Haile Selassie. It was the first recording since the defection of Fonso Martin, leaving the trio of Hinds, Nesbitt and Selwyn. While they still faced inverted snobbery at the hands of British reggae fans, in America their reputation was growing, and they became the first ever reggae band to appear on the *Tonight* television show. Their profile was raised further when, in 1992, Hinds challenged the New York Taxi and Limousine Commission in the Supreme High Court, asserting that their cab drivers discriminated against black people in general and Rastas in particular.

● ALBUMS: *Handsworth Revolution* (Island 1978)★★★★, *Tribute To The Martyrs* (Island 1979)★★★, *Caught You/Reggae Fever* (Mango/Island 1980)★★★, *True Democracy* (Elektra 1982)★★★, *Earth Crisis* (Elektra 1984)★★★, *Babylon Bandit* (Elektra 1985)★★, *State Of Emergency* (MCA 1988)★★, *Victims* (MCA 1992)★★, *Rastafari Centennial* (MCA 1992)★★★, *Rage And Fury* (Bluemoon 1997)★★★.

● COMPILATIONS: *Reggae Greats* (Mango/Island 1985)★★★★, *Sound System: The Island Anthology* (Island Jamaica 1997)★★★★.

STEELY AND CLEVIE

This Jamaican studio 'band' comprises Wycliffe 'Steely' Johnson and Cleveland 'Clevie' Browne. Every five years or so, Jamaica produces a rhythm section that dominates reggae. In the 70s it was the Barrett Brothers, who drove the Upsetters and Bob Marley's Wailers. The late 70s/early 80s belonged to Sly And Robbie, but by 1986 reggae required a team fully conversant with computerized music: Steely And Clevie fulfilled that role. Wycliffe 'Steely' Johnson first surfaced with Sugar Minott's Youth Promotion organization, playing keyboards on Minott's classic *Ghetto-ology* (1978). After a period with the Generation Gap, he joined the Roots Radics, earning a reputation for hard work and innovation. When the Radics became *the* band for the new dancehall music of the early 80s, it gave Steely a perfect understanding of a minimal, raw-basics kind of reggae. Drummer Cleveland 'Clevie' Browne (pronounced 'Brown-ie') began playing as part of the Browne Bunch in the 70s with brothers Dalton and Danny. During the late 70s he played sessions at Studio One, backing Freddie McGregor, among others. In the early 80s McGregor hired Clevie for his road group, known as the Studio One Band, and on tour, Clevie came into contact with equipment that was not yet *de rigeur* in Jamaican studios; he consequently became interested in drum machines, while his fellow-drummers declared them an abomination. Prior to that, Clevie had recorded tracks with Bob Marley in 1979, when the singer was using a primitive drum machine in the studio. In the mid-80s Clevie's brothers, Danny And Dalton, were the musical pulse of the Bloodfire Posse, the first all-electronic reggae group. By the time 'digital' music arrived, Clevie was ready for it. At some point in the late 70s, Steely And Clevie met during sessions for Augustus Pablo at Lee Perry's Black Ark studio, working on Hugh Mundell's *Africa Must Be Free By 1983*. The pair's relationship was enhanced by their contrasting characters - Clevie the studious, mild musician, and Steely the louder, ragga character. When they took up residence as house band at King Jammy's studio in 1986, they were clearly on the verge of something new and exciting. Jammy's was the engine of mid-80s reggae; from there, Steely And Clevie worked with everyone, cutting 10 singles a week at its peak in 1987 and a stream of albums from various artists such as Cocoa Tea, Dennis Brown, Admiral Bailey and Lieutenant Stitchie. Jammy's produced the best ragga sounds on the island at the time, and although producer King Jammy received the praise, much of the work was done by Steely And Clevie, engineers Bobby Digital and Squingie Francis, and the arranger, Mikey Bennett. They also gigged for most of the other influential producers in Jamaica; hence, they knew virtually everyone when they began their own label - Steely And Clevie - in 1988. They immediately hit with a debut release from Johnny P., making the DJ a star. The formula of brash, unusual beats and strong melodies also worked for Foxy Brown, relaunched Tiger's career, produced hits for Anthony Red Rose, Anthony Malvo and Little Twitch, and revived older acts Dillinger and Johnny Osbourne. Sessions for Gussie Clarke helped to establish his studio as the major technological force in late 80s reggae, and Steely And Clevie cut a series of inimitable 'one rhythm' albums on their own label: *Limousine*, *Bursting Out*, *Real Rock Style* and *Can't Do The Work*. Broader attention followed with work for former Soul II Soul singer Caron Wheeler, Maxi Priest, Aswad and J.C. Lodge. While they have not yet been inclined to sign to a major label, it seems that, despite competition from the Firehouse Crew and Mafia And Fluxy, Steely And Clevie will continue their dominance of the reggae studio for the foreseeable future.

● COMPILATIONS: Various Artists *Bursting Out* (S&C 1988)★★★★, *At The Top* (Black Solidarity 1988)★★★, *Can't Do The Work* (S&C 1989)★★★★, *Limousine* (S&C 989)★★★, *Real Rock Style* (S&C/Jet Star 1989)★★★★, *Godfather* (VP 1990)★★★, *Lion Attack* (VP 1990)★★★, *Poco In The East* (S&C 1990), *More Poco* (VP 1990)★★★, *Girl Talk* (VP 1991)★★★, *Present Soundboy Clash* (Profile 1991)★★★, *Play Studio One Vintage* (Heartbeat 1992)★★★★.

STELIN, TENA

Tena Stelin takes his name from the Amharic language of Ethiopia, which, translated, means 'greetings'. He began his career in the late 80s as

a UK-based vocalist with the Conscious Sounds label and initially enjoyed a roots hit with 'Can't Touch Jah'. Much of the recording for the Conscious Sounds collective's output took place at the Manasseh studio run by sound system operator Nick Manasseh. The UK roots scene enjoys a cult following, with releases appearing on cassette corresponding with African rather than reggae recordings. In 1990 DJ Joey Jay, widely acknowledged as a pioneer of UK roots, began transmitting the sound legally with Nick Manasseh across London when the radio station Kiss FM was granted a broadcasting licence. This resulted in wider exposure for Stelin, along with other notable performers, including Devon Russell and Sound Iration. In 1989 Stelin had recorded 'Give Thanks And Praise' and 'King Of Kings Parts One And Two' with Sound Iration. Stelin's producer, Dougie Wardrop, employed a session band known as Centry who enjoyed several hits, including 'Stepping Time' and 'Thunder Mountain'. The release of *Wicked Invention* was received with rave reviews, though in 1990 the roots revival was still impending. As a bonus for those purchasing the CD and cassette version, *Sound Iration In Dub* were included. Recording at Digital B, Easy Street and The Toy Factory he maintained his profile with producer Morris Johnson.

● ALBUMS: *Wicked Invention* (Conscious Sound 1990)★★, with Centry *Thunder Mountain* (Conscious Sounds 1990)★★★, *Sacred Songs* (Conscious Sounds 1993)★★★, *Take A Look At The World* (Conscious Sound 1994)★★, *Sun And Moon* (Conscious Sound 1994)★★, with Centry *Release The Chains* (Conscious Sounds 1995)★★.

STEPHENS, RICHIE

b. Richard Stephenson, 5 December 1966, Savannah-La-Mar, Jamaica, West Indies. Stephens gained his initial showbusiness experience helping bands to move their equipment when they performed in his home-town. He was soon performing as lead singer for a variety of bands, including Stars Incorporated and the Elements, serenading on the island's hotel circuit. His popularity led to a commission from the Jamaican tourist board to represent the island touring the Caribbean, South America and Europe. In 1985 he returned to Jamaica, where in Montego Bay he recorded his debut, a version of 'So Amazing'. In 1988 he released the self-composed 'Buff Baff' for the Top Rank group in Jamaica, which became a dancehall anthem. He began recording a series of hits for a number of producers and in 1990 he appeared at the annual Sting Concert. Coinciding with his success at Sting he won the accolade of Jamaica's Song Of The Year for the hit 'By Your Side'. His fame led to a worldwide tour alongside Shabba Ranks, and the recording of a song purported to be Stephens' composition, 'Slow And Sexy', alongside R&B star Johnny Gill. His vocal proficiency led to a one-album contract with Motown Records in the USA, and two *Billboard* hits, 'Legacy', with DJ Mad Cobra, and a combination with Patra, 'Body Slam'. His crossover success also led to Stephens performing on Soul II Soul's 1992 Top 5 hit, 'Joy'. In 1993, with his Motown contract ended, he returned to the dancehall, where, with Garnett Silk, they achieved the accolade of Jamaica's Best Dual Combination for their rendition of 'Fight Back'. He has maintained a high profile in the reggae charts and confirmed his independence by setting up his own Pot Of Gold productions. In November 1996 he topped the New York and Jamaican charts simultaneously alongside Bounty Killer for the ragga hit, 'Maniac'.

In 1997 he was acknowledged as Top Singer in the Jamaican Binns Awards. He enjoyed a string of hits through his appropriately titled production house, Charm, including a solo composition and an enlightened warning for pubescent females, 'Slop Dem'. He also recorded in combination with General Degree the contradictory 'Girls Galore', and worked as a producer for 'Bounce Along', performed by Wayne Wonder and Spragga Benz. Although the hits continued he still worked with other producers, notably the U-based Frenchie, who recorded 'Gave You My Heart' and a second combination with General Degree, 'Come Give Me Your Love', which enjoyed crossover success in the summer of 1997. While he secured international recognition, he concurrently maintained his hardcore status with a further combination hit alongside Bounty Killer, 'Get Wise'.

● ALBUMS: *On Broadway* (Blue Mountain 1990)★★★, *Sincerely* (Jammy's 1990)★★, *Richie Stephens* (Motown 1992)★, *Forever* (Charm 1995)★★, *Miracles* (Charm 1996)★★★, *Winner* (Greensleeves 1998)★★★

STEPHENS, TANYA

b. Tanya Stephenson, 1974, Jamaica, West Indies. Tanya Stephens has been hailed as an intimidating rival to the lewd DJ queen Lady Saw. In 1993 Stephens recorded a notable collaboration with Galaxy P, 'One Touch', that proved successful, although her notoriety seemed short-lived. Her initial foray into the recording business was interrupted by a sabbatical after the birth of her first child. With her distinctive style, Stephens soon returned triumphantly to the dancehall and by 1996 her career was in full swing. She won critical acclaim when she appeared at the Sting 95 and Penthouse Showcase. Her success led to the recording of an album for X-Rated and a series of successful singles, including 'Hang Up The 'Phone', 'Man Fi Rule', 'Big Heavy Gal', '1-1-9', 'Nuff Man Flop' and 'Workout'. Her big break came with the haughty 'Yuh Nuh Ready Fi Dis Yet', performed over Dave 'Rude Boy' Kelly's infamous 'Pepper Seed' rhythm. Her notoriety was later enhanced by the reggae chart-topping 'Big Ninja Bike', produced by Harvel Hart and the Annex crew; the double entendres were not subtle, with lines such as: 'Me wanna man wid a big ninja bike fe wi ride from - Me no 'ave di right gear - Bounce me all night 'pon di divan - Give mi de right slam'. This was followed by a surfeit of singles, including 'Goggle' for the Shocking Vibes crew and the racy 'Handle The Ride' for Bobby Digital. Her celebrity status resulted in the eventual release of the X-Rated album, which featured guest vocals from Prezident Brown and Yammie Bolo, and tracks including 'Love How Yu Body Tan', 'Bruck Out' and 'Yuh Na Wicked'.

● ALBUMS: *Too Hype* (VP 1998)★★★★, *Big Things A Gwaan* (Runn 1998)★★.

STEPPER, REGGIE

Stepper is a DJ considered to be among the better examples of the new Jamaican 'chatters'. His album for Tommy 'Pipper' Mason was recorded with the help of rhythms donated by Mixing Lab, Music Works and Penthouse. Stepper arrived at Mason's studio a relative unknown, but emerged as a new dancehall star, going on to work with production team Steely And Clevie.

● ALBUMS: *Kim Bo King* (King Dragon 1990)★★★.

STERLING, KEITH

b. Keith Sterling-Mcleod, January 1952, Kingston, Jamaica, West Indies. Sterling comes from a musical family and his older brothers have all been involved in the Jamaican recording industry. Lester played alto saxophone in the Skatalites, Roy was a trumpeter with Lynn Tait And The Jets and Gladstone also played in the horn section. Keith Sterling's supporting role led to work on the hotel circuit along Jamaica's north coast and his eventual signing to Boris Gardiner's Happening band. He began working as a freelance musician, playing keyboards for Inner Circle, Lloyd Parks' We The People and Jimmy Cliff's Oneness. As a session musician Sterling spent the mid-70s extending his accomplished keyboard skills on a number of hits, notably for Bob Marley And The Wailers, which proved a revelation even to him, as he had previously reported that he had never worked with Marley. He was, however, credited on the significant *Songs Of Freedom* compilation, and surmised that he may have provided overdubs. By the late 70s Sterling joined Word Sound And Power alongside Sly And Robbie, playing on every Peter Tosh album from *Bush Doctor* through to the definitive compilation. In 1984 Sterling began working at the Harry J. studio as an in-house producer, although little of his work from this period has surfaced. In 1988 the second version of Word Sound And Power, aka the Soul Syndicate band, was re-formed to play at a Peter Tosh tribute concert in Burbank, California, USA. The group supported Andrew Tosh, which led to a world tour and a session for the release of *Make Place For The Youth*. Sterling continues to be involved in session work, having played keyboards for most of the top names in reggae.

● ALBUMS: with the Soul Syndicate *Harvest Uptown* (Soul Syndicate 1978)★★★.

STEWART, DELANO

b. Winston Delano Stewart, 5 January 1947, Kingston, Jamaica, West Indies. Stewart began his career recording alongside B.B. Seaton and Maurice Roberts as part of the vocal trio the Gaylads. By the late 60s Stewart left the group to pursue a solo career and embarked on a recording career with Sonia Pottinger, with whom he had worked as part of the Gaylads. In 1969 her production skills strengthened his success as a solo performer when she released 'Got To Come Back', followed by the more successful 'Stay A Little Bit Longer'. Further releases included 'That's Life', which provided the rhythm track for Big Youth's 'Facts Of Life', which paradoxically included a version of 'ABC Rocksteady' on the b-side. Other releases, 'Dance With Me', 'Rocking Sensation' and 'Don't Believe In Him', were included on his debut *Stay A Little Bit Longer*. In the early 70s, Stewart moved to New York and maintained a low profile. By 1975 he returned with the critically acclaimed release 'Spinning Wheel', which faltered owing to lack of promotion.

● ALBUMS: *Stay A Little Bit Longer* (Trojan/High Note 1968)★★★.

STEWART, TINGA

b. Neville Stewart, *c*.1959, Kingston, Jamaica, West Indies. Stewart came to prominence when he won the 1974 Jamaican Song Festival singing 'Play De Music' which became a reggae hit in both Jamaica and the UK. In 1975 Stewart composed 'Hooray Festival', the winning entry for his brother Roman Stewart, and, inspired by these consecutive victories, the Opal label in the UK released Roman's track 'Oh But If I Could Do My Life Again'. Stewart became involved with Lloyd Charmers and Ernie Smith on their Wildflower project, much of whose output later surfaced through Opal. The brothers' success at the Festival resulted in them being branded with an image as 'festival singers', which had an unhelpful effect on their early careers. Stewart continued to release singles through the 80s, including 'Gypsy Rasta', 'Key To Your Heart' and his version of 'Red Red Wine'. He eventually revived his roots credibility when he recorded 'Take Time To Know' with Ninjaman. Their recording is widely acknowledged as being the first combination tune, which led to a multitude of singer and DJ hits. Previously, the DJs had voiced over an old master tape, whereas in combination style, the artists recorded together. He continued recording in combination for 'Knock

Out Batty' with Tinga Love and 'I Wanna Take You Home' with Little Twitch. His revival resulted in a tour of Japan in 1989 as part of the Reggae Sunsplash world tour. On his return he became involved in production work, licensing his output to the RAS label in the USA. He also continued to record his own tracks, including 'Gonna Fall In Love', 'In The Mood', 'Street Dancing' and the rootsy 'Son Of A Slave'.
● ALBUMS: *With The Dancehall DJs* (RAS 1993)★★, *Aware Of Love* (VP 1994)★★, *No Drugs* (Jammys 1988)★★★.

STRICTLY ROOTS

There are many bands around the world who have encroached on the sound of Jamaica. The old adage that a white man cannot play the blues is similarly quoted in regard to reggae. The Blue Riddim band from the USA and Zound System from Japan both played at different Reggae Sunsplash shows, and although both were entertaining, they lacked an authentic feel for the music. On the west coast of America, an audience for reggae was burgeoning, inspired by expatriate Jamaican Tony Moses. Strictly Roots emerged from San Francisco and featured a mixed line-up including representatives from Jamaica to give the group more credibility. The band embraced Rastafari and received an award for a local concert from the Sonoma County Sherrif's Department.

STUDIO ONE

(see Dodd, Coxsone)

SUPERCAT

b. William Maragh, *c.*1966, Kingston, Jamaica, West Indies. Of mixed African and East Indian descent, Supercat began his musical career on the Soul Imperial sound system at the age of seven. In 1981 Winston Riley produced 'Mr Walker', but the road to fame was bought to an abrupt halt when Maragh was incarcerated in the General Penitentiary. On his release, encouraged by fellow performer Early B., Supercat was chanting on the Kilimanjaro sound. The sound system offered the opportunity to perform alongside such notable artists as the Lone Ranger, John Wayne and Jim Kelly. In 1985 the singles 'Ride And Shut Off' and his contribution to the notorious Sleng Teng rhythm,

'Trash And Ready', enhanced Supercat's career. These were followed by his biggest hit, 'Boops', the story of a 'sugar daddy' that started a series of related singles, and also 'Cry Fi De Youth', both of which featured on his debut *Si Boops Deh*. His success continued with the modestly titled 'Don Dada', which was a warning to the up-and-coming DJs of the time, including Shabba Ranks, Ninjaman and Cutty Ranks. In spite of his somewhat aggressive stance on the record, Supercat was invited to perform at the UK One Love concert in 1991. A few weeks before the show, he was in New York when one of the exponents of the Waterhouse style, Nitty Gritty, was shot. Unfortunately, Supercat was in the area when the shooting took place and media speculation pointed to him as the prime suspect; as a result, he did not appear at the show. By 1992, his innocence was proved and he secured a contract with Columbia Records, resulting in the release of 'It Fe Done' in combination with Josey Wales. Supercat also diversified into the hip-hop market when he appeared alongside young stablemates Kris Kross, notably on 'Jump - Supercat Dessork Mix'. While maintaining a career with Columbia, he ventured into production work under the guise of Wild Apache the Don Dada, named after his dancehall hit.

He continued to voice his own recordings, including his version of Fats Domino's 'My Girl Josephine', performed with Jack Radics and featured on the film soundtrack to *Prêt A Porter*. Supercat was unable to match the success of Ini Kamoze, who contributed to the soundtrack of the same film. The song was featured on Supercat's own *The Struggle Continues*, which also included appearances from Sugar Minott and U-Roy for the vintage reggae-styled 'A Class Rub A Dub'.
● ALBUMS: *Si Boops Deh* (Techniques 1985)★★★, *Sweets For My Sweets* (VP 1990)★★★, *Don Dada* (Columbia 1992)★★, with Nicodemus, Junior Demus, Junior Cat *The Good The Bad The Ugly And The Crazy* (Wild Apache 1994)★★★, with Nicodemus, Junior Demus, Junior Cat *Cabin Stabbin* (Wild Apache 1994)★★★, *The Struggle Continues* (Columbia 1995)★★.

SUTHERLAND, NADINE

b. 1968, Kingston, Jamaica, West Indies. She began performing in 1980 and balanced her recording career, which was managed by her parents, with her education. She studied business administration at college and when Bob Marley heard her work, she was recruited to Tuff Gong. Following on from his unsuccessful Wail 'N' Soul venture, a determined Marley put all his energies into the 'Gong' and signed newcomers Sutherland and Dallol along with Rita Marley, Tyrone Taylor and the Melody Makers. Sutherland's live appearances helped to groom her for stardom and she performed outside of Jamaica in 1982 at a memorial concert for Bob Marley, alongside Ziggy Marley And The Melody Makers, the I Threes and the Wailers. Viewed by many as a soft alternative to the ghetto sounds, Sutherland was unable to make an impression in the reggae charts.

In 1986 she toured supporting Bunny Wailer in the USA along with Leroy Sibbles of the Heptones. She found work as a backing vocalist at Gussie Clarke's Music Works studio, and by the late 80s she recorded over Gregory Isaacs' 'Mind You Dis' rhythm on the song 'Mr Hard To Please', featured on the one-rhythm *Music Works Showcase '89*.

During the early 90s she worked with the then top producer in Jamaica, Donovan Germain, at his Penthouse studios. Her 1993 hit with Terror Fabulous, 'Action', was used by the Jamaican Labour Party as their campaign theme (incidentally, without her consent). The same year, she enjoyed a number 1 placing on the reggae chart when Buju Banton's 1992 hit 'Dickie' was re-released featuring Sutherland's vocals as 'Wicked Dickie'. In 1995 East West Records secured the rights to 'Action' and reissued it. With stronger marketing, it reached the *Billboard* Top 40.

● ALBUMS: *Nadine Until* (1985)★★★, *Nadine* (VP 1997)★★★★.

SWEETIE IRIE

b. Derrick Bent, January 1971, London, England. Sweetie Irie began chatting on various sound systems around London. His performance on the Nasty Love sound system brought him to the attention of Angus Gaye of Aswad. The group had recently topped the pop chart with a cover version of 'Don't Turn Around' and hoped to repeat the feat with 'On And On'. Concerned that pop success might alienate the group's reggae fans, Aswad asked Sweetie Irie to DJ on the song for the dancehall mix.

In 1989 he made his first appearance in the UK pop chart. A second UK chart placing followed in 1990 with the group for 'Smile'. The gravel-voiced DJ's future was assured and a contract with Mango led to the release of 'New Talk' with Sweetie's sparring partner, Joe 90. In 1991 with producers Angus Gaye and Tony 'Gad' Robinson, *DJ Of The Future* was released, which included the two hits along with 'Maaga Man', 'She Want It All Night Long' and 'Winery'. 'Call Me', lifted from the album for single release, resulted in Mango having to compensate a telephone subscriber for the cost of changing telephone number - on the track, Sweetie Irie invites the girls to call him on a fictitious set of digits, unaware that it was a genuine number! The success of Scritti Politti's collaboration with ragga DJ Shabba Ranks, for a rendition of the Beatles' 'She's A Woman', inspired Virgin Records and the group to try the formula again. Sweetie Irie performed on a version of 'Take Me In Your Arms And Love Me', which was also remixed by Gussie Prento at Fashion's A Class Studios. The collaboration resulted in his third UK chart placing. The 'One Love' concert in London, with a host of performers including Big Youth, Bob Andy and Alton Ellis, featured a surprise appearance by Sweetie Irie and Joe 90. Their performance was, however, criticized, as the show was designed to promote culture and righteousness, and the two DJs bounced onstage, gyrating in a suggestive manner. His next release, 'The Agony', appeared in 1992. Releases have continued at a steady rate, including a jungle hit with the Rebel MC under the guise of Blackstar, entitled 'Get Wild'.

His 1995 release, 'Last Night', was his first attempt at self-production, and met with an encouraging response, especially in the Far East. At the beginning of 1996 he recorded with lovers rock singer Winsome.

● ALBUMS: *DJ Of The Future* (Mango 1991)★★★.

SYMARIP

Symarip evolved from the UK ska band the Pyramids, who had recorded with the then leader of the Equals, Eddy Grant. The group formed in 1969, consisting of Monty Naismith, Ray Ellis, Michael Thomas, Joshua Roberts and Frank Pitter. On the track 'Skinhead Jamboree', they called for less conflict and documented the essential gear for a 'bovver boy'. The success of 'Skinhead Moonstomp' led to the release in 1970 of an album of the same name, including versions of Roland Alphonso's 'Phoenix City' as 'Phoenix Reggae', Nancy Sinatra's 'These Boots Are Made For Walking', 'Fung Shu' and 'Skinhead Girl'. The single was re-pressed in response to the interest engendered in the skinhead era during the 2-Tone craze.

● ALBUMS: *Skinhead Moonstomp* (Trojan 1970)★★★.

TAITT, LYNN

b. *c*.1946, Jamaica, West Indies. Taitt took up the guitar when he was 14 - before that time, he had been involved in steel-pan music. However, he was soon fronting his own band in Trinidad, who were booked by Byron Lee to play the 1962 Independence celebrations in Jamaica. Taitt decided to stay in Jamaica, working his way through the Sheiks, the Cavaliers and the Comets - all 'live' bands that did not actually make any recordings - although he had recorded with the Skatalites. His next group, Lynn Taitt And The Jets, which included Hux Brown, Headley Bennett, Hopeton Lewis, Gladstone Anderson and Winston Wright, were contracted to Federal Records in 1967. Their recording of 'Take It Easy' was one of the first rocksteady records and went straight to number 1. Many see the rocksteady period in Jamaican music as one of the most creative and musically adventurous, and Lynn Taitt And The Jets were the rocksteady session band at the eye of the storm. They recorded hit after hit for Federal, Wirl, Derrick Harriott, Bunny Lee and Beverley's, Sonia Pottinger and Duke Reid, sometimes performing up to five sessions a day for different producers. Taitt's modesty about his part in this musical evolution was as gentle as his guitar playing, being interested only in 'creating beautiful music'. Some of his recordings with Johnny Nash, such as 'Cupid' and 'Hold Me Tight', even crept into the UK national charts, and he will always be fondly remembered as a musical giant of the rocksteady era.

● ALBUMS: *Rock Steady Greatest Hits* (Merritone)★★★, *I'm In The Mood For Moods* (KM 1997)★★★.

TAMLINS

The Tamlins were a three-part vocal harmony group featuring Derek Lara, brother of Studio One vocalist Jennifer Lara, Carlton Hines and

Sylvanus 'Junior' Moore. They were as respected in Jamaica as the likes of Culture, the Mighty Diamonds and the Gladiators. The trio began recording in the mid-70s, enjoying hits with 'Hurting Me', 'If I Were A Carpenter' and 'Undying Love'. In 1976 the group was signed to the State label, a subsidiary of Polydor Records notable for the UK pop group the Rubettes. The project was produced by Byron Lee and Neville Hinds, and included a reggae cover version of the Ohio Players' 'Skin Tight', which 20 years later inspired Red Dragon's dancehall favourite. By 1978 the group had released numerous singles, notably Donovan Germain's production of 'Testify' and a number of Gussie Clarke's productions, including 'Ting A Ling', 'Season For Girls' and 'Got A Feeling'. In 1979 the Tamlins provided backing vocals on tour with Peter Tosh to promote his album Bush Doctor. His appearance at the Rainbow Theatre in Finsbury Park, London, was released on video and demonstrates the group's talent as back-up vocalists, but sadly omits their opening performance of their own catalogue of hits. Tosh subsequently invited them to provide back-up vocals on the sessions for Mystic Man, Wanted Dread And Alive and a number of tracks for Mama Africa. Following from the group's involvement with Tosh, they returned to Jamaica where Derrick Harriot approached them to perform alongside Joy White as part of a group to be known as Reasons. The combination recorded a medley of Christmas carols as 'Christmas Songbook', but despite media enthusiasm for the project, it faltered. The group returned to Music Works with Gussie Clarke, who produced further hits, including a remake of Desmond Dekker's 'Hey Grandma'. With Sly And Robbie the group covered the Chi-Lites' 'Go Away Dream', 'Stars', 'Smiling Faces' and 'Baltimore'. In 1982 the group recorded sessions for veteran DJ U. Brown, who produced 'Red Rose', originally written by B.B. Seaton. The song enjoyed a revival in the 90s when Sharon Forrester recorded her version with Papa San. In 1994 the Tamlins provided back-up vocals for the Wailers' Jah Message. The band continue to record, notably the hit 'Keep That Light', and in the 90s enjoyed a resurgence in popularity through the Star Trail production team with a remake of 'Baltimore', backed with a version of Lord

Creator's 'Kingston Town'. The vocalists concurrently pursued solo careers; Moore, recording as Ricky Tamlin, enjoyed a hit with 'Call Me' and Hines worked with Te-Track alongside Gussie Clarke. The most successful has been Lara, with the notable hits 'Gun Man' and 'Me No Have It', the albums Motherless Child and, in combination with Beres Hammond, Just A Vibe (later repackaged as Expression).

● ALBUMS: Black Beauty (State 1976)★★, Red Rose (Vista 1983)★★★, I'll Be Waiting (Imp 1989)★★, Love Divine (Heartbeat 1990)★★★★, No Surrender (VP 1994)★★★, with the Mighty Diamonds From The Foundation (Music Works 1996)★★★★.

● COMPILATIONS: Best Of (Channel One 1993)★★★★.

TAN TAN

b. Edward Thornton, c.1934, Jamaica, West Indies. Tan Tan is acknowledged as one of Jamaica's leading trumpeters, having played with a number of notable performers. From humble beginnings playing over a comb wrapped in paper, by the mid-50s Tan Tan was playing trumpet alongside Don Drummond on trombone in the Roy Coulton band, performing at the Glass Bucket and Silver Slipper clubs. The band were also the first combo to play live on Jamaican radio and were later employed to accompany jazz legends on world tours. While touring, Tan Tan decided to settle in Europe and Drummond returned to Jamaica. Tan Tan played in a number of bands in Europe before settling with Georgie Fame And The Blue Flames in 1963. The band enjoyed a string of hits featuring Tan Tan's accomplished trumpet playing, which led to his being invited to perform on the Beatles hit 'Got To Get You Into My Life'. Although Tan Tan remained with Georgie Fame, he was also enrolled to perform alongside Boney M. Despite Tan Tan having been involved on the Jamaican music scene from its earliest years, it was not until he performed with Aswad that he made a significant impression within the reggae community. He played in the band's dextrous horn section, featuring Michael 'Bammi' Rose and Vin Gordon. Classic tunes include 'African Children', 'Love Fire' (which provided the rhythm for Dennis Brown's 'Promised Land'), a version of the Maytals' '54-46 That's My

Number', as well as the dancehall anthems 'Pull Up' and 'Bubbling'. The horn section also provided the musical foundation for other Grove Music performers, including King Sounds and the Sons Of Jah.
● ALBUMS: with Aswad *A New Chapter Of Dub* (Mango/Island 1982)★★★, *Musical Nostalgia For Today* (Macabees 1985)★★★, with Ossie Scott *At Their Best* (Shelley 1996)★★★.

TASSILLI PLAYERS

Tassilli Players worked on an open-house philosophy, with a floating pool of musicians centred around ex-Cosmics and Harare Dread member Dave Hake. Hake came from Coventry, England, where his contemporaries included the 2-Tone ska bands the Specials and Selecter. He later relocated to Manchester where he discovered Coxsone Dodd's Studio One label, which became a major influence on the performer's aspirations. He embarked on a period of self-discovery, including a spell in a Kibbutz, a sojourn with a Bedouin in the Sinai Desert, a hasty retreat from war-torn Israel and a tranquil period of rejuvenation in Ireland. It was the latter visit that inspired the concept of the Tassilli Players. In London he became involved with Zion Train, who produced his series of experimental dub albums. The players also featured on a series of dub compilations, including *Dubhead* and *Lead With The Bass*. In addition to his own Tassilli Players projects, Hake forged a strong relationship with Zion Train and joined Chris 'Forkebeard' Hetter as part of the band's distinctive brass section. The duo were recognized for their contribution to the archetypal *Homegrown Fantasy*, which demonstrated their talents on 'Dance Of Life' and a version of the Gladiators' 'Get Ready'. By 1996 the duo continued to pursue Tassilli projects alongside a continuous touring schedule. The Players were also recruited to provide the captivating horn riff on Morcheeba's reggae-styled 'Friction', featured on the acclaimed *Big Calm*.
● ALBUMS: with Zion Train *Great Sporting Moments In Dub* (Universal Egg/Zion 1993)★★★, *The Wonderful World Of Weed In Dub* (Universal Egg 1997)★★★, *In Outer Space* (Universal Egg 1997)★★★, *At The Cow Shed* (Universal Egg 1997)★★.

TAXI RECORDS
(see Sly And Robbie)

TAYLOR, ROD

b. Jamaica, West Indies. Taylor, known as Rocky T, came to prominence in 1978 with Bertram Brown's Freedom Sounds collective, noted for introducing Prince Allah, Earl Zero, Philip Frazier. Jimmy Dean, Sylvan White and Lloyd Jackson. Taylor recorded his debut, 'Ethiopian Kings', based on Frankie Jones's avowal that many biblical heroes were black men: 'King David - he was a black man - King Solomon he was a black man - King Moses - he was a black man - from Africa yeah - they fight for equal rights and justice'. The song was an instant hit, which led to sessions with Mickey Dread for the equally popular 'His Imperial Majesty', which featured a well-used rhythm, immortalized in dub as 'Saturday Night Style'. In 1979 Taylor began working with a variety of producers, including Prince Far I ('Run Run' and 'No One Can Tell I About Jah'), Prince Hammer ('If Jah Should Come Now'), Ossie Hibbert ('Every Little Thing'), Manzie ('Let Love Abide') and Bertram Brown ('In The Right Way' and 'Don't Give It Up'). His collaboration with Prince Hammer preceded the release of his debut album, featuring the Roots Radics and the debut of Lincoln Scott as the drummer. In 1980 the hits continued with 'Night In September', produced by Papa Kojak, 'Lord Is My Light' for Ganja Farm and 'Soul To Soul' for Tad Dawkins, which lent its title to the celebrated album featuring Barry Brown, Welton Irie and Carlton Livingstone. Further releases included 'Jah Is Calling' and 'Promised Land', backed with the popular 'Wicked Intention' by Barrington Levy.
● ALBUMS: *If Jah Should Come Now* (Little Luke 1980)★★★, *Where Is Your Love Mankind* (Greensleeves 1980)★★.
● COMPILATIONS: with various artists *Ethiopian Kings* (RRR 1981)★★★.

TAYLOR, TYRONE

b. 1957, Negril, Jamaica, West Indies. Taylor recorded his first outing with producer Joe Gibbs when he was only 12 years old. The result, 'Delilah', surfaced in the UK as the b-side to Dennis Walks' hit, 'Having A Party'. Disappointed with the song, Taylor drifted among some of Jamaica's top session men, learning to play a number of instruments. One of his most influential benefactors was Willie Lindo, who encouraged him to persevere with a career in the music business. Taylor went on to record with a number of producers, notably with Jack Ruby and Winston 'Niney' Holness, and was signed to Bob Marley's Tuff Gong enterprise. Taylor's sessions with Holness resulted in two Jamaican hits, 'Just A Feeling' and 'Sufferation', the latter featuring a special King Tubby mix. In 1983 Taylor enjoyed international popularity when he released the semi-autobiographical 'Cottage In Negril', a self-production through his own Love Time production company. The single surfaced at a time when dancehall was at its most popular, and despite his gentler approach, he was able to earn the title of Best Selling Singer Of 1983. At the following year's Sunsplash festival he appeared alongside Bob Andy, with whom his songwriting skills are often compared, Edi Fitzroy and Dennis Brown. His subsequent release, 'Come To Me', was not as successful as its predecessor. Undeterred, MCA, who had enjoyed a UK number 1 hit with Musical Youth, signed Taylor on the strength of 'Cottage In Negril'. The contract led to the release of 'Pledge To The Sun', which failed to generate sufficient enthusiasm for further output. He had recorded an album's worth of material that was not released. A tour of Europe was arranged without any support from the label, and disillusionment from lack of promotion led to his premature departure from the contract. Following this setback, little was heard from Taylor but he bounced back on the roots market, releasing sporadic hits, most notably in 1987 when he released 'Members Only' and 'Be For Real'. By 1993 he had returned to working with his original guiding mentor, Willie Lindo, who produced *The Way To Paradise*, which featured mainly cover versions in Taylor's inimitable style. The following year he teamed up with producer Clive Hunt, returning to Bob Marley's Tuff Gong studio, and released the hit 'Rainy Sunset'.

● ALBUMS: *Sings For Members Only* (Techniques 1989)★★★★, *Jamming In The Hills* (1990)★★★, *The Way To Paradise* (1994)★★.

● COMPILATIONS: *Cottage In Negril* (1989)★★★.

TECHNIQUES

Formed by Winston Riley in 1962 while still at school, the Techniques' original line-up additionally featured fellow vocalists Slim Smith, Franklyn White and Frederick Waite. Together they performed at future Jamaican prime minister Edward Seaga's club, Chocomo Lawn, an important showcase for local talent at the time, appearing alongside Byron Lee, Tommy McCook, Alton Ellis, Marcia Griffiths, and the Sensations, who included Riley's brother Buster. The group were spotted by talent scouts from the British-based Columbia Records, upon which their first single, 'No One', appeared. This was not released in Jamaica, however, and it was not until 1965 when singer Stranger Cole introduced them to producer Duke Reid that they recorded their earliest Jamaican releases, 'Don't Leave Me', 'When You Are Wrong', and the popular 'Little Did You Know', featuring the peerless falsetto vocals of Slim Smith. With the advent of rocksteady in 1967, vocal harmony groups specializing in Chicago soul-style love songs came into their own, and the Techniques, under Reid's aegis, were perfectly placed to capitalize on the trend. Throughout 1967, the hits poured out of Reid's Treasure Isle studio, situated above his Orange Street liquor store. His classic productions on artists such as Alton Ellis, the Paragons, Phylis Dillon, the Melodians, Dobby Dobson, and many others, all backed by Tommy McCook And the Supersonics, briefly toppled Coxsone Dodd's dominance as Jamaica's leading hit-maker.

In 1966 the original group had broken up, Smith leaving to pursue a solo career at Studio One, then later with producer Bunny Lee as part of the Uniques vocal trio, before his tragic end. Franklyn White's whereabouts remain unknown, but Frederick Waite emigrated to the UK where he managed Musical Youth, whose members included several of his offspring, achieving a UK number 1 with 'Pass The Dutchie' in 1982. Smith's place was filled by Pat Kelly, who sang lead on some of their most popular records, including 'You Don't Care', versions of Curtis Mayfield's 'You'll Want Me Back' and 'Queen Majesty', the Temptations' 'I Wish It Would Rain' and 'Run Come Celebrate', 'I'm In The Mood', 'There Comes A Time' and the sublime 'It's You I Love'. Other hits from this period featuring different lead singers include 'My Girl', 'Drink Wine', 'Love Is Not A Gamble' and 'Travelling Man'. The Techniques left Treasure Isle in 1968 with Riley going on to set up his own Techniques label, producing other artists and further sides by the group, whose personnel during this period included Jackie Parris, ex-Termite Lloyd Parks, Morvin Brooks and Bruce Ruffin. Subsequent releases included another version of 'Travelling Man', 'Your Love's A Game' and 'Lonely Man', all featuring Dave Barker (Dave And Ansell Collins) on lead vocals, 'What Am I To Do', with Pat Kelly again as lead vocalist, 'What's It All About', and 'Go Find Yourself A Fool'. Riley went on to become one of the most successful producers of the 80s, achieving massive hits with General Echo, Tenor Saw, Supercat and others. As a group, the Techniques recorded sporadically over the following years.

A re-recording of 'Love Is Not A Gamble', with ex-Paragon Tyrone Evans on lead vocals, appeared as a 12-inch in 1982, followed by an album of the same title, since which time they have remained silent.

● ALBUMS: *Little Did You Know* (Treasure Isle 1965)★★★★.

● COMPILATIONS: *Unforgettable Days* covers 1965-72 (Techniques 1981)★★★★, *I'll Never Fall In Love* (Techniques 1982)★★★, *Classics* (Techniques 1991)★★★★, *Run Come Celebrate - Their Greatest Reggae Hits* (Heartbeat 1993)★★★★.

TENNORS, CLIVE

Clive was an original member of 70s reggae hit-makers the Tennors, who worked for the Studio One and Treasure Isle empires, finding success with tracks such as 'Cleopatra', 'Ride Yu Donkey' and 'Another Scorcher'. Though a solo career was widely mooted, it was not until the late 80s that any evidence of Clive Tennors' work came to light. In 1986 he appeared at a series of club dates in Miami. Following a brace of singles, he released his debut long-player, named after one of the Tennors' most popular tunes, 'Ride Yu Donkey'.

● ALBUMS: *Ride Yu Donkey* (Unicorn 1991)★★★.

TENOR FLY

b. Jonathan Sutter, Brixton, London, England. Tenor Fly began his career with Lloyd Coxsone's International Sound System, working alongside such dignitaries as Jah Screechy and Blacker Dread. In 1989 his debut release, 'Roughneck Fashion', topped the UK reggae chart, and was swiftly followed by the equally successful 'Inner Cities'. His growing reputation led to collaborations with the Ragga Twins (under the guise of Demon Rocker), the highly acclaimed DJ Top Cat, and seasoned vocalist Nerious Joseph. He has also enjoyed crossover success, having three consecutive Top 40 hits with the Rebel MC, 'Tribal Bass', 'Wickedest Sound' and 'Coming On Strong'. In 1994 his satirical interpretation of the Monty Python *Life Of Brian* chant, 'Bright Side Of Life', over a sample of Nina Simone's 'My Baby Just Cares For Me', rewarded him with a UK Top 50 hit. His success was followed by the Big Orange duet, 'Let's Play', reuniting the DJ with Nerious Joseph. In 1996 Tenor Fly toured Japan, appearing alongside Top Cat and Sweetie Irie at the annual Japan Splash Festival. On his return he was invited to perform on the Louchie Lou And Michie One album, *Danger Us*, for the track 'Before The Night Is Over'. In 1997 he embarked on recording sessions for his long-awaited debut, to be released by his advocate Top Cat on the DJ's own Nine Lives label.

TENOR SAW

b. Clive Bright, 1966, Kingston, Jamaica, West Indies, d. August 1988, Houston, Texas, USA. One of the most influential singers of the early digital era, Tenor Saw's eerie, hypnotic wail was imbued with an almost religious fervour. He was raised in the Payne Avenue district of west Kingston, recording his debut, 'Roll Call', in 1984 for George Phang's Powerhouse label after an introduction by Nitty Gritty. During 1985 he sang with Sugar Minott's Youth Promotion sound system and label, recording 'Lots Of Sign' and 'Pumpkin Belly' (also versioned for King Jammy's). 'Run Come Call Me' and 'Fever' were also sizeable hits. None, however, could compare to 'Ring The Alarm', which Tenor Saw voiced magnificently over Winston Riley's 'Stalag' rhythm for the Techniques label. There was no bigger record that year and it continues to be regarded as an anthem in today's dancehalls. 'Golden Hen' for Uptempo continued the sequence of consecutive hits into 1986, when Minott released his debut album, *Fever*. Tenor had already left for Miami and the Skengdon crew, where 'Dancehall Feeling' and the posthumously released 'Bad Boys' was recorded. After a trip to England and the successful 'Never Work On A Sunday' for Donovan Germain, Tenor journeyed to New York in 1987. There he recorded the epic 'Victory Train' with Freddie McGregor's Studio One Band, and further singles for Witty, Robert Livingston ('Come Me Just A Come'), and Jah Life. His duet with General Doggie on 'Chill Out Chill Out', for Digital English, was the most enigmatic of singers' swan-songs. In August 1988 he was killed by a speeding car in Houston, Texas.

● ALBUMS: with Don Angelo *Clash* (Witty 1985)★★★, *Fever* (Blue Mountain 1986)★★★★, with various *Strictly Livestock* (Greensleeves 1986)★★★, with Cocoa Tea *Clash* (Witty 1987)★★★, *Lives On* (1992)★★.

TERROR FABULOUS

b. *c.*1974. Jamaican DJ who became one of the fastest-rising stars of the dancehall scene in the 90s. His skills were learned on local streets in his early teens, before he completed a course in electrical engineering and was introduced to producer Dave Kelly. In tandem they produced a single, 'Dorothy', which brought both to wider fame and recognition. His growing profile saw him signed to East West Records in the UK, for whom his debut album included hit singles 'Action' (with Nadine Sutherland), 'Miss Goody Goody' (with Maxi Priest) and the title track (with Gary Minott).

● ALBUMS: *Yaga Yaga* (East West 1994)★★★, *Glamorous* (New Sound 1994)★★.

THIRD WORLD

Reggae band blending roots and soul, comprising Michael 'Ibo' Cooper (keyboards), Stephen 'Cat' Coore (guitar, cello), Richard Daley (bass), Willie 'Roots' Stewart (drums), Irvin 'Carrot' Jarrett (percussion), William 'Bunny Rugs' Clarke (lead vocals, guitar) and Milton 'Prilly' Hamilton (vocals). Coore and Cooper first played together at the end of the 60s, and the early years of the band saw the line-up in a state of flux. Coore, Cooper and Daley,

plus drummer Carl Barovier (later replaced by Cornell Marshall and Willie Stewart), had all played with Inner Circle, a band that pursued a similar 'uptown reggae' course. By 1975 the line-up had settled to the aforementioned, minus Bunny Rugs, who had been pursuing a soul-reggae direction in a series of solo projects, aided by a uniquely spirited voice. Their mellow, carefully crafted debut, *Third World*, found them signed to Island Records and supporting Bob Marley at his breakthrough concerts at London's Lyceum in the summer of 1975. *96 Degrees In The Shade* found the band and new singer Clarke in fine form, and delivered a huge international hit in the shape of a cover version of the O'Jays/Gamble And Huff song, 'Now That We've Found Love'. The *Journey To Addis* album offered more of the same - a mix of roots and sweet soul. Further hits, 'Cool Meditation' (1979), 'Dancing On The Floor' (1981) and 'Try Jah Love' (1982), the latter two for a new label, CBS Records, kept their name in the public eye. A lone record for Winston 'Niney' Holness in Jamaica accurately summarized their attitude: 'Roots With Quality'. The late 80s saw the band increasingly lauded in the USA, attracting album contributions from Stevie Wonder, Stetsasonic's Daddy O, the Brecker Brothers and Jamal-Ski. Third World still gig regularly, and have the wisdom to continue working occasionally with their original producer, Geoffrey Chung. They remain a name worth watching out for, even if they have not yet set the world alight on record.

● ALBUMS: *Third World* (Island 1976)★★★, *96 Degrees In The Shade* (Island 1977)★★★, *Journey To Addis* (Island 1978)★★★, *Prisoner In The Street* (Island 1980)★★★, *Rock The World* (Columbia 1985)★★★, *Sense Of Purpose* (Columbia 1985)★★★, *You've Got The Power* (Columbia 1987)★★★, *Hold On To Love* (Columbia 1987)★★★, *Serious Business* (Mercury 1989)★★★.

● COMPILATIONS: *Reggae Ambassadors* (Island 1985)★★★★.

● VIDEOS: *Prisoner In The Street* (Channel 5 1989).

THOMAS, JAH

b. Nkrumah Thomas (named after nationalist leader Kwame Nkrumah), *c.*1958, Kingston, Jamaica, West Indies. He began recording in the mid-70s, supported by Alvin 'GG' Ranglin and commencing with 'Midnight Rock'. International success came when the newly formed Greensleeves label, set up by the owners of a record shop in Ealing, released Thomas's debut album in 1978. *Stop You Loafin'* was a popular release and introduced reggae fans to the artwork of Tony McDermott, who has designed many covers for the label. The set was produced at Channel One by Joseph 'Joe Joe' Hookim, and a host of top musicians provided the backing, including Sly Dunbar, Robbie Shakespeare and Ansell Collins. Thomas's success led to a further outing, *Dance Hall Style*, from another specialist record shop, but it was unable to emulate Greensleeves' success. Two albums with similar titles surfaced; the first was a self-production on his own label, Midnight Rock, and the other was produced by Jah Life, resulting in confusion and dwindling record sales for Thomas. Putting aside his DJ career, he decided to concentrate on producing other artists, including Robin Hood, Robert Ffrench and the two Palmers; Triston Palmer enjoyed a massive hit with 'Joker Smoker' and Michael Palmer hit with 'Ghetto Dance'. At Christmas 1985 his production of Michael Palmer's 'Happy Merry Christmas' was released as the b-side to 'Where Is Santa Claus' by Mr And Mrs Yellowman, and proved to be the favoured chant. Thomas continued to enjoy hits as a DJ with 'Shoulder Move', 'Clean Your Teeth', 'Polka Dot' and 'Posse', the latter recorded in combination with Jim Brown.

● ALBUMS: *Stop You Loafin'* (Greensleeves 1978)★★★★, *Dance Hall Style* (Silver Camel 1979)★★★★, *Dance On The Corner* (Midnight Rock 1979)★★★, *Dance Pon De Corner* (Jah Life 1979)★★★, *Black Ash Dub* (Trojan 1980)★★, *Tribute To The Reggae King* (Midnight Rock 1981/Vista 1983)★★, *Shoulder Move* (Midnight Rock 1983)★★, *Nah Fight Over Woman* (Vista 1983)★★★.

THOMAS, NICKY

b. Cecil Nicholas Thomas, 1949, Portland, Jamaica, West Indies, d. 1990. Working as a labourer on the same building site as Albert Griffiths, Clinton Fearon and David Webber, later to become the Gladiators, Nicky Thomas also dreamed of success in the music business.

His break came with the Derrick Harriot-produced 'Run Mr Nigel Run'. He found greater success working with Joel Gibson (later known as Joe Gibbs) in 1969. The collaboration produced a number of hits, including 'God Bless The Children' and 'Mama's Song', along with cover versions of 'Rainy Night In Georgia' and 'If I Had A Hammer'. In the summer of 1970 the release of 'Love Of The Common People' took Thomas into the UK Top 10 and a tour followed. Thomas decided to stay in the UK to promote a compilation, *Love Of The Common People*, which featured tracks recorded with Gibbs in 1969. The release of 'Yesterday Man' almost returned Thomas to the UK chart, after being lifted from his self-produced set, *Tell It Like It Is*. One of the most important tracks, 'BBC', revealed his frustration with the derision reggae suffered at the hands of most Radio 1 presenters. Undeterred by radio indifference, he continued to record in a commercial vein, earning a minor hit with 'Images Of You'. He also released 'Suzanne Beware Of The Devil', produced by Dandy Livingstone. Unfortunately for Thomas, it was the producer's own vocal version that secured a UK Top 20 hit when it was released in 1972 as the b-side to 'What Do You Wanna Make Those Eyes At Me For'. In 1974 he released a cover version of the Kinks' hit, 'Lola', and toured the UK, with backing supplied by a group who later found fame as Misty In Roots. The tour went well, playing to ecstatic crowds, and Thomas proved to be especially popular with the female element in the audiences. He was also featured in the television programme *Aquarius*, recording at Chalk Farm studio, London, and the accompanying interview gave him the chance to express his opinions regarding reggae and the media. In 1983 Paul Young, inspired by Thomas's rendition of 'Love Of The Common People', enjoyed his third Top 10 hit with the song. Trojan Records bowed to public demand for the original version with its release on a 'maxi-single', along with 'Yesterday Man' and the most requested tune at his live shows, 'Have A Little Faith'.

● ALBUMS: *Love Of The Common People* (Trojan 1970)★★★★, *Tell It Like It Is* (Trojan 1971)★★, *Images Of You* (Trojan 1973)★★.

● COMPILATIONS: *Doing The Moon Walk* (Trojan 1991)★★★★.

THOMPSON, CARROLL

b. 1960, Letchworth, Hertfordshire, England. Thompson's voice was nurtured while singing in school and church choirs, but she studied for a career in the pharmaceuticals industry. In the mid-70s she provided backing vocals in a number of UK-based recording studios, following a successful audition to join the disco band Sugar Cane (the group was a further attempt at disco domination by Frank Farian, but was later abandoned). She sang on sessions for UK-based reggae performers, as well as Imagination and soca star Norma White. Thompson subsequently embarked on a solo career and by 1981 she had topped the reggae chart twice, with 'I'm Sorry' and 'Simply In Love', for the Itals. In 1982 she scooped two accolades at the GLR Reggae Awards. She was voted best female performer and 'Hopelessly In Love' was deemed the best song. She maintained a high profile with the release of 'Smiling In The Morning' for Excaliber, 'Your Love' and 'Hopelessly Without You' for S&G, with whom she also worked in a production role. Her prominence led to the release of a single by her harmony singer, Saffrice, 'Dreaming Of Your Love', through S&G. As they were unable to provide Thompson with the necessary promotion, the S&G group initiated an agreement with the Red Bus label to further her career. The releases of 'Just A Little Bit' and 'A Happy Song' were met with animosity from the media and the ballads faltered, resulting in a short-term agreement. Her prolific career continued, however, and in 1983 she secured further awards, including a citation from the *Voice*, and was voted top female vocalist for the second time by GLR listeners. She also recorded duets with Sugar Minott ('Make It With You') and Trevor Walters ('Love Won't Let Us Wait'). Her solo hits include 'Honest I Do', 'Give Me A Chance' and 'You Make It Heaven'. By 1984 her recorded output had dwindled, although the release of 'Baby Be True' secured an acceptable chart placing. Thompson maintained her high profile with commendable performances at both the GLR Reggae Awards and fifth *Black Echoes* Awards ceremonies. In 1985 she worked with the funk group Total Contrast, resulting in the release of 'Apple Of My Eye'. In 1990 she was invited to provide the lead vocals on a joint production with Aswad and Courtney Pine, for the release of a version of Diana Ross's 'I'm Still Waiting', which sat at the lower end of the UK chart. She also entered the UK chart in the same year as a featured vocalist for Movement 98 with 'Joy & Heartbreak' and 'Sunrise'. In 1994 Thompson joined Alton Ellis, Prince Lincoln, Justin Hinds, Dennis Alcapone and Owen Gray in a memorial concert for Gene Rondo.

● ALBUMS: *Hopelessly In Love* (Carib Gems 1981)★★★, *Carroll Thompson* (Carousel 1983)★★.

THOMPSON, ERROL

b. *c.*1952, Kingston, Jamaica, West Indies, d. 1983. Thompson began working for Joel Gibson (later Joe Gibbs), following in the footsteps of Lee Perry, who had ventured into his own Black Ark Recording Studio. Thompson was working alongside Winston 'Niney' Holness at Randy's Studio in North Parade as a recording engineer. With Gibbs as the producer and Thompson as the engineer, they had a run of hits throughout the 70s. Early in the 70s they had hits with Peter Tosh ('Maga Dog'), Dennis Brown ('Money In My Pocket'), Big Youth ('Foreman Vs Frazier') and Delroy Wilson ('Pretty Girl'). The early hits were recorded in a two-track studio at the back of Gibbs' record shop, but the duo's success led to a relocation to North Parade, known as Joe Gibbs Record Globe (the site was used in the film *Rockers*). At the new studio the duo became known as the Mighty Two and Thompson's more prominent role as producer for Joe Gibbs productions was acknowledged by the formation of the Errol T and Belmont labels. By the mid-70s, many artists had had hits produced by the Mighty Two, including Culture ('Two Sevens Clash'), Bobby Melody ('Jah Bring I Joy'), Trinity ('Three Piece Suit'), Ruddy Thomas ('Loving Pauper'), Prince Far I ('Heavy Manners'), Big Youth ('Equal Rights Style') and Dennis Brown ('Money In My Pocket'). Brown's remake entered the UK Top 20 in 1979, but was preceded in 1977 by the number 1 hit 'Up Town Top Ranking' by Althea And Donna, which had 'Calico Suit' credited to the Mighty Two on the b-side. The duo continued to dominate the reggae charts with a number of Dennis Brown albums and a series of dub albums, notably the *African Dub* series. By the late 70s/early 80s the duo worked with Eek A Mouse ('Virgin Girl') and Yellowman ('Which One A Dem A Wear De Ring'). Gibbs left for Miami in the early 80s and in 1983 there were rumours that Thompson had been attacked and killed in Kingston. He had fathered three children by Marcia Griffiths.

● COMPILATIONS: Various Artists *African Dub All-Mighty Chapters 1, 2 & 3* (Joe Gibbs 1975, 1976, Lightnight 1978)★★★★, with Joe Gibbs *The Mighty Two* (Heartbeat 1990)★★★.

THOMPSON, LINVAL

b. *c*.1959, Kingston, Jamaica, West Indies. Thompson was raised in Queens, New York, and at the age of 16 recorded 'No Other Woman'. On returning to Jamaica he began recording with Phil Pratt, although little surfaced on vinyl from these sessions. Having declined an opportunity to record with Bunny Lee following an introduction by his long-time friend Johnny Clarke, he recorded a dub plate with Tippertone. Back in New York, he resumed his studies in engineering but was soon drawn back towards the music business. Owing to the increasing demand for reggae in the USA, Thompson established a fruitful business supplying fresh rhythms to record buyers, and his success led him back to Jamaica. On his return he recorded 'Kung Fu Fighting' with manic producer Lee Perry, which heralded the beginning of a prolific career. Encouraged by the sales of 'Don't Cut Off Your Dreadlocks', produced by Bunny Lee, the album, including the title track, also appeared in the UK. Thompson began to produce his own material and a contract with Trojan Records led to the release of *I Love Marijuana* and its dub version, *Negrea Love Dub*, both of which enjoyed healthy sales. Establishing his reputation as a producer, his services were enrolled by Cornell Campbell, the Wailing Souls, the Viceroys, Tapper Zukie, Barrington Levy, Trinity, Ranking Dread and Roman Stewart. Ranking Dread's set included DJ versions of Thompson's own 'I Love Marijuana' as 'Marijuana In My Soul', and 'Africa Is For Blackman' as 'Africa'. The DJ hit the UK headlines following suggestions that he was a member of the 'Yardies', supposedly a criminal West Indian organization, although the term 'Yardie' simply referred to someone from Jamaica, i.e., 'Back A Yard'. Thompson's sessions with Trinity led to the release of *Rock In The Ghetto* through Trojan, while, lifted from the same set, Greensleeves Records released 'Don't Try To Use Me'. In 1983 the release of *Baby Father* included the classic 'Shouldn't Lift Your Hand', a track that condemned violence against women, with lyrics stating: 'You shouldn't lift your feet to kick the young lady, You shouldn't lift your hand to lick the young girlie'. As further illustration of Thompson's entrepreneurial skills, he formed a partnership with Mikey Scott in the UK for the Strong Like Sampson and Thompson Koos record labels to distribute his output.

● ALBUMS: *Don't Cut Off Your Dreadlocks* (Third World 1976)★★★, *I Love Marijuana* (Trojan 1978)★★★, *I Love Jah* (Burning Sounds 1979)★★★, *If I Follow My Heart* (Burning Sounds 1980)★★, *Look How Me Sexy* (Greensleeves 1982), *Baby Father* (Greensleeves 1983)★★★, *Starlight* (Mango 1989)★★.

THRILLER U

b. Eustace C. Hamilton, *c*.1962, Kingston, Jamaica, West Indies. Thriller U's style is similar to that of Frankie Paul. His 1989 recording of 'It's Over', produced by Hugh 'Redman' James, was a hit and he toured the UK on the strength of it. The song was a lament to an unfaithful lover, over a classic rhythm with an irresistible riff. He released a number of singles, including 'Big Bamboo', 'Private Property', 'Are You Really Ready For Love', 'I'll Prove It To You', 'Where Would I Go' and 'Since You Came Into My Life'. He also recorded with Pan Head ('Run Down The Man'), Flourgon ('Girls Just Wanna Have Fun') and Johnny P ('Young And She Green'). He worked with a number of producers including Ossie Hibbert, Bobby Digital, King Jammy and Donovan Germain. The George Michael ballad 'Careless Whisper', and the Jennifer Rush epic 'The Power Of Love', were both successfully covered by Thriller U, produced by Redman in 1990 and Ossie Hibbert in 1991, respectively. Although often considered as a Jamaican purveyor of lovers rock, he occasionally drifted into the dancehall style, notably on the track 'Sweetest Sound', which was featured on his album with Admiral Tibet, *Two Good To Be True*. In 1991 he recorded one of the many reggae versions of 'I Wanna Sex You Up' with Johnny Nice and Studio One legend

Jennifer Lara. Sly Dunbar and Robbie Shakespeare set up a new project, *Punishers*, and enrolled the services of Thriller U for 'One Day In Your Life'. He continues to release occasional recordings and enjoyed a hit in 1995 with 'The Mind Is Willing'.
● ALBUMS: *Crazy* (Penthouse 1990)★★★★, with Admiral Tibet *Two Good To Be True* (Blue Mountain 1990)★★★, *Hilary* (VP 1991)★★★, *On And On* (VP 1991)★★★, *The Danger* (VP 1992)★★★, *Waiting For You* (Jammys 1992)★★★, *The Best Of Me* (World 1993)★★★, *Drive* (VP 1993)★★.

THUNDER, SHELLY

One of a rash of female DJs (including Lady Patra, etc.), native New Yorker Thunder was at the forefront of a spirited response to the macho belligerence of dancehall exponents such as Shabba Ranks, Cutty Ranks and others. Her first big hit was 1988's 'Kuff', a humorous suggestion that Jamaica's women should give their menfolk a smack around the ears whenever they stepped out of line. Other early singles, 'Small Horse Woman' and 'Man Ah Rush Me', continued in a similar vein. She made her major label debut in 1991, but, despite the assertions of a number of critics, it failed to signal her breakthrough into the mainstream.
● ALBUMS: *Small Horse Woman* (Hawkeye 1986)★★★, *Fresh Out The Pack* (Mango/Island 1989)★★★, *Backbone Of The Nation* (Mango/Island 1991)★★.

TIGER

b. Norman Jackson, 1960, Kingston, Jamaica, West Indies. Tiger is one of the most entertaining of all Jamaican DJs, his voice a crazy growl one moment and something completely different the next. He recorded his singing debut, 'Why Can't You Leave Dreadlocks Alone', in 1978, under the name of Ranking Tiger, following with 'Knock Three Times' and 'Love Line' in 1981. Changing to a DJ style, he established his reputation on the Black Star sound system, before releasing 'Bad Boy Stylee' and 'Mi Lover Mi Lover', all the time working out his own material on a tiny electronic keyboard. 'No Wanga Gut' and 'No Puppy Love' were his first real hits in 1985 and two years later Mango issued Tiger's self-produced debut album. By that time he was a true DJ sensation and embarked upon a remarkable series of songs for producers such as Harry J. ('Sitting In La La'), Kangal, Kings Crown, Ayeola ('Iron Dumpling') and his own Tiger label. He reappeared the following year with a trio of releases for the Paradise label, of which 'Rap Pon Riddim' was his strangest to date. In 1989 he returned to the top with strong tunes for King Jammy, Gussie Clarke, Robert Livingston, Taxi, Steely And Clevie ('Ram Dancehall'), Blacka Dread and Penthouse, recording a duet with US rappers the Fat Boys in 1990 and becoming one of the first ragga DJs to make an impression on the hip-hop scene. His best year to date was 1992: 'When' for Steely And Clevie proved a significant crossover record and helped usher in the new bogle style; Penthouse released the belated *Deadly* album and hits for them ('Crying Fool'), Wild Apache, Exterminator, Shocking Vibes ('Yuh Dead Now') and Tiger's own Hide & Seek label followed. 'Beep Beep Move Over' was voiced in response to the mimicking Zebra. By 1993 Tiger's Chaos production company was signed to Columbia Records, who released *Claws Of The Cat* that year. In December 1993 Tiger was seriously injured in a Kingston motorcycle accident, but made a brave recovery.
● ALBUMS: *Me Name Tiger* (Mango 1987)★★★★, *Meets General Trees Live In Concert* (CSA 1987)★★, *Bam Bam* (RAS 1988)★★★, *Shocking Colour* (Jammys 1989)★★★, *Ram Dancehall* (Steely & Clevie 1990)★★★, *Love Affair* (Rohit 1990)★★, *Touch Is A Move* (Blue Trac 1990)★★★, *Tiger A Tiger* (New Name 1991)★★★, *Ready Fi Dem* (VP 1991)★★, *Deadly* (Penthouse 1992)★★★, *Claws Of The Cat* (Columbia 1993)★★★.

TIME UNLIMITED

Time Unlimited were a Jamaican vocal group assembled in the early 70s by Orville Smith. The line-up featured Smith alongside Junior Delgado, Glasford Manning and Hugh Marshall. In 1973 the group recorded sessions with Lee Perry at the Black Ark, although only 'Reaction' and 'The Twenty Third Psalm' were released. Following the Perry sessions the group recorded with Tommy Cowan and Warrick Lyn's Talent Corporation, as well as the Total Sounds studios, which released 'Give Me Love'. Disenchanted

with their experiences in the recording industry, the quartet disbanded in 1975. The individual members pursued successful careers: Junior Delgado began a prolific career as a soloist; Smith recorded with Dennis Brown the assertive hit 'Won't Give Up'; and Manning joined the underrated vocal group the Jewels, who recorded the classic 'Love And Livity'. Time Unlimited re-emerged as a trio when Smith recruited Hugh Blackwood and Donovan Joseph to complete the line-up. Both performers were considered well qualified for the roles: Blackwood's debut recording, 'Pick Your Choice', had been produced by the veteran DJ Sir Lord Comic, proving a sizeable hit in 1973, while Joseph had worked alongside Gregory Isaacs and the Congos. By 1980 the new line-up recorded 'Living Inna Jamdown', produced by Sly And Robbie. Their negligible releases resulted in periods of obscurity, but in 1982 they returned to the spotlight, working with Earl 'Chinna' Smith and the High Times Band. With Smith the group toured Jamaica promoting their hits 'Nature In Love', 'One Road' and 'Backfire'. The group also inaugurated their own short-lived label, Africa Productions, which collapsed after only two releases. In 1983 they released the memorable '2000 Years' and were also recruited to provide backing vocals for dub poet Mutabaruka's release, 'Johnny Drughead'. The band eventually released their debut, *Devils Angel*, in 1985, featuring the conscientious 'Live Upright' and the analytical 'African Woman'. Although the group's output was considered to be inconsistent, their long-term influence on the industry is widely acknowledged.
● ALBUMS: *Devils Angel* (Live Wire 1985)★★★.

TIPPA IRIE
b. Anthony Henry, 1965, London, England. Raised in a south London community where the sound system business was a way of life, by the age of 13 Henry was performing with local sound systems and learning the art of chatting in rhyme by listening to Jamaican DJs on record. At 15 he was an adept MC with King Tubby's sound system in Brixton (not to be confused with the Jamaican dub maestro). Although British MCs were previously held to be inferior to their Jamaican counterparts, when dancehall took a grip on reggae in the early 80s,

it coincided with the rise of the most talented 'chatters' Britain had ever produced. The live recordings of sound system sessions that swept Jamaica were soon copied in London, and Tippa found himself on three live albums in 1983, *Live At DSYC Volumes 1-3*, recorded at London's Dick Shepherd Youth Centre. They had an enormous impact, showcasing British youngsters who were proving themselves as powerful with a rhyme as their Jamaican counterparts. When Tippa joined Saxon he was alongside the best reggae rappers in Britain, including Phillip Papa Levi, Peter King, Daddy Rusty, Daddy Colonel, Sandy, and later, Smiley Culture, Asher Senator and singer Maxi Priest. It was the most powerful line-up any UK sound had ever assembled. In 1984 Saxon recorded a live album for Greensleeves Records, who picked up Tippa for studio recordings. 'Sleng Teng Finish Already', 'Telephone' and 'It's Good To Have The Feeling You're The Best' all sold well and gained him appearances on television shows such as *Club Mix*. No-one expected 'Hello Darling' to plant Tippa on *Top Of The Pops*, but the cheeky single was a smash hit. However, because it was so unexpected, it took a long time for Tippa's follow-up to arrive, and consequently, 'Heartbeat' merely scraped the charts. A further attempt at chart success came with the appropriately titled 'Panic Panic', with Tippa lost on a dance record. That year's album, *Is It Really Happening To Me?*, summed up the pressure he felt. Tippa chose to return to grass roots, and *Two Sides Of...* in 1987 found him more relaxed on album than previously: this was Tippa, ragga MC, not chart-climber. In 1988, he teamed with Jamaican ragga star Papa San to record *JA To UK MC Clash*, another fine, low-key album, and in 1989 issued *A Me Dis*, which also earned a debut American release on Miles Copeland's IRS label. He eventually left Saxon in the summer of 1989. Meanwhile, the mainstream media kept one eye open for him, and he made several television appearances in 1988, including on BBC Television's current affairs programme *Panorama*, as an anti-crack spokesperson. While he might never recapture the success of 'Hello Darling', Tippa can never be entirely discounted - as long as there is a lyric in his head, he will be working.
● ALBUMS: *Coughing Up Fire* (1984)★★★★, *Is*

It Really Happening To Me? (Greensleeves 1985)★★, *Two Sides Of* (GT's 1987)★★★, with Papa San *JA To UK MC Clash* (Fashion 1988)★★★★, *A Me Dis* (GT's 1989)★★★, *Original Raggamuffin* (Mango/Island 1990)★★★, with Peter Hunningale *A New Decade* (Mango/Island 1991)★★★★, with Hunningale *Done Cook And Currie* (Tribal Base 1992)★★★.

TOOTS AND THE MAYTALS
(see Maytals)

TOP CAT
b. Anthony Codrington, *c*.1973, Manchester, England. Codrington's nickname came from his schooldays, when he was likened to the roguish cartoon cat. Moving to south London resulted in Anthony completing his education in Lewisham, home of the renowned Saxon sound system. His father was influential in inspiring his love of music, which was further fuelled when visiting relatives in Jamaica. In the early 80s he chatted on various sound systems, but was unable to make a living from this and pursued a career outside of music. However, he perpetually performed on the microphone at dances and in 1988 he recorded 'Love Mi Sess', an ode to marijuana that rocketed to the number 1 position in the reggae chart. His success led to a career in music and following the release of *Sensemilla Man*, he embarked on an international promotional tour, making personal appearances on sound systems throughout Europe and America. The Battersea, London-based Fashion label realized Top Cat's potential and a number of tunes were recorded at the A Class studio, including 'Request The Style' and 'Shot A Batty Boy', which failed to attract media attention. Top Cat's 1992 release, 'Over You Body', held the number 1 spot in the reggae chart for nine weeks, ironically on his own 9 Lives label. The label released a number of recordings from Anthony Red Rose, Simpleton, Mike Anthony, Prento Youth and Poison Chang. The follow-up, 'Push Up Your Lighter', was equally successful and, when remixed for the 'junglist posse', topped the chart representing this genre. Accolades from the media were bestowed upon Top Cat and his success continued with the chart-topping 1994 Christmas

hit, 'Wine Up You Body', along with *Nine Lives Of The Cat*. A visit to Jamaica found Top Cat recording with Poison Chang, resulting in the third clash album of Jamaican and English DJs, the two previous ones being Papa San versus Tippa Irie and Johnny Ringo versus Asher Senator. In 1995, 'Sweetest Thing' with its Jackson Five riff, an appearance on BBC Television's *The Vibe*, and a duet with General Levy on 'Girls Dem', maintained his high profile.

● ALBUMS: *Sensemilla Man* (1989)★★★, *Request The Style* (1992)★★, *Nine Lives Of The Cat* (Nine Lives 1995)★★★, with Poison Chang *JA To UK MC Clash Part Three - Top Cat Meets Poison Chang* (Fashion 1995)★★★, with General Levy *Rumble In The Jungle* (Glamma 1995)★★★★, *Cat O' Nine Tails* (Nine Lives 1996)★★★.

TOSH, ANDREW
b. Andrew McIntosh, June 1967, Kingston, Jamaica, West Indies. Andrew was exposed to Wailers music from birth, as his father was the late Peter Tosh and his mother was Shirley Livingstone, sister of Bunny Wailer. Owing to his father's promotional commitments, he spent his formative years with his grandmother. By his early teens he was living with his father, who taught him the basic elements of singing. His first recording session was held at Sonic Sounds in 1985 with DJ Charlie Chaplin producing, resulting in his debut, 'Vanity Love'. He also recorded 'Lick A Shot' with Jimmy Cliff, but the single was not released until the late 80s. In September 1987 Peter Tosh was gunned down in his home and this motivated Andrew to continue his father's work. He began by singing 'Jah Guide' and an emotional 'Equal Rights' at his father's funeral service, in Kingston's National Arena. He then recorded with Winston 'Niney' Holness *The Original Man*, which was released in the UK on the Trojan subsidiary Attack. However, the label had become unfashionable in the reggae market and the cover design did little to help the album. At the Peter Tosh tribute concert in the USA, he formed a partnership with Carlton 'Santa' Davis, George 'Fully' Fullwood, Keith 'Sterling' McLeod and Tony Chin, who had previously backed Peter Tosh as Word Sound And Power. The result of the part-

nership was an album recorded in the USA, *Make Place For The Youth*, which mainly consisted of original material with the exception of a version of Bob Marley's 'Small Axe'. Andrew Tosh was also involved in Bunny Wailer's project to release rediscovered Wailers material, as his voice resembled his father's. In 1994 the Heartbeat label in the USA re-released *Original Man*, complete with dub versions and a vastly improved cover. In the mid-90s he re-recorded his father's hit, 'Legalise It', with the additional line, 'President Clinton smoke it'.

● ALBUMS: *The Original Man* (Observer/Attack 1987)★★★★, *Make Place For The Youth* (Tomatoe 1989)★★★.

TOSH, PETER

b. Winston Hubert McIntosh, 19 October 1944, Westmoreland, Jamaica, West Indies, d. 11 September 1987, Kingston, Jamaica. Of all the reggae singers from the mid-60s, no-one else 'came on strong' like Peter Tosh, who declared it so on his anthem, 'I'm The Toughest'. He provided the bite to Bob Marley's bark in the original Wailers, and it was he who appeared most true to the rude boy image that the group fostered during the ska era. Tosh was the first to emerge from the morass of doo-wop wails and chants that constituted the Wailers' early records, recording as Peter Tosh or Peter Touch and The Wailers on 'Hoot Nanny Hoot', 'Shame And Scandal', and 'Maga Dog', the latter another theme for the singer. He also made records without the Wailers and with Rita Anderson, who later became Rita Marley. The Wailers were a loose band by 1966; Bob Marley went to America to seek work, and Peter and Neville 'Bunny Wailer' Livingstone recorded both together and separately. At one point, Tosh spent a brief period in prison, possibly on charges of possessing marijuana. When he was not working with the Wailers, he recorded solo material ('Maga Dog' again, or 'Leave My Business') with producer Joe Gibbs, retaining his ferocious vocal style. When the Wailers worked with Leslie Kong in 1969, Tosh was at the forefront with 'Soon Come' and 'Stop The Train', but at Lee Perry's Wailers sessions (1970-71) he was often reduced to harmonizing, save for three mighty tracks - '400 Years', an attack on slavery, 'No Sympathy', where Tosh equated rejection in love with the lot of the black ghetto resident, and 'Downpresser', another anti-oppression statement and probably his best record. When the Wailers split from Perry and joined Island Records, the writing was on the wall for Tosh; Island apparently preferred Marley's cooler, more sympathetic style, and despite contributing 'Get Up Stand Up' to *Burnin'*, the band's second album for the label, both Tosh and Bunny Wailer left the group in 1973. Tosh concentrated on work for his own label, Intel Diplo HIM (meaning: Intelligent Diplomat for His Imperial Majesty), and signed to Virgin Records in 1976. The patronage of Mick Jagger at Rolling Stones Records, which he joined in 1978, nearly gave him a chart hit with a cover version of the Temptations' 'Don't Look Back', although reggae fans complained that Jagger's voice was louder than Tosh's in the mix. *Bush Doctor*, his first album for the label, sold well, but *Mystic Man* and *Wanted, Dread & Alive*, did not. He also released three albums with EMI, the last, *No Nuclear War*, being his best since *Legalize It*. The record won the first Grammy Award for best reggae album in March 1988, but by that time, Tosh was dead, shot during a robbery at his home in Kingston in September 1987.

● ALBUMS: *Legalize It* (Virgin 1976)★★★★, *Equal Rights* (Virgin 1977)★★★★, *Bush Doctor* (Rolling Stones 1978)★★★★, *Mystic Man* (Rolling Stones/EMI 1979)★★★, *Wanted, Dread & Alive* (Rolling Stones/Dynamic 1981)★★★, *Mama Africa* (Intel Diplo/EMI 1983)★★★, *Captured Live* (EMI 1984)★★★, *No Nuclear War* (EMI 1987)★★★.

● COMPILATIONS: *The Toughest* (Parlophone 1988)★★★, *The Gold Collection* (EMI 1996)★★★, *Honorary Citizen* (Legacy 1997)★★★.

● VIDEOS: *Live* (PMI 1986), *Downpresser Man* (Hendring Video 1988), *Red X* (1993).

TOYIN

b. Toyin Adekale, 21 December 1963, London, England. Toyin came to prominence performing with the Instigators. She left the band after the release of their debut single and embarked on a solo career. Influenced by Jean Adebambo and Carroll Thompson, she performed as a lovers rock soloist, topping the reggae charts with the

alluring 'It's You'. Demonstrating her independence and determination, she formed the group Pure And Simple, undertaking managerial duties. In addition to recording her own material, she covered Sister Sledge's 'Smile', and 'It's Not Love' for Anthony 'Sir George' Brightly. Toyin was also asked to sing on the British Reggae Artists Famine Appeal for 1985's 'Let's Make Africa Green Again'. Following her involvement in the charitable project, she promoted her brand of lovers rock among leather obsessives in Wales during the May Bank Holiday. The success of the mini-tour led to a lengthy summer entertaining the patrons of a number of UK holiday camps. In the 90s she released the occasional hit, including a particularly riveting combination with Daddy Screw, 'Man With The Agony', produced by her former colleagues from the Instigators, Mafia And Fluxy.
● ALBUMS: *Love And Leather* (Criminal Records 1985)★★.

TRADITION
The north London, England-based reggae band Tradition were formed in 1976, performing as Special Brew. The original line-up featured Chris Henry (bass), Paul Thompson (keyboards), Tony Matthews (drums), Michael Johnson (guitar) and Grace Reed (vocals). Following the departure of Reed and Johnson, the vacant roles were filled by Les McNeil and Paul Dawkins (ex-bass player for Junior English). The group linked up with Venture where they recorded 'Moving On', which has since become their anthem, 'Rastafari', and a version of 'Summertime'. In 1978 the group released the classic 'Why Why' on a then innovative 12-inch discomix single. The song (and its respective dub version), which described some of the hostilities faced by blacks in a predominantly white environment, was a 10-minute opus and was well received. The group had carved a niche and continued to release a series of critically acclaimed hits. The playing skills of the band were utilized by David Tyrone, who employed the group to perform on sessions, including Aurora York's cover versions of 'Don't It Make My Brown Eyes Blue' and 'We Do It', alongside Dennis Pinnock's classic 'Dennis The Menace' and 'Ride On'. A series of live shows enhanced the group's reputation when they supported artists including Alton Ellis, Delroy Wilson, Honey Boy and Culture. Their 1978 release, 'Breezin'', was voted the best single of 1978 in the *Echoes* readers poll. The accomplishments of the group led to a contract with RCA Records in 1978, who released their international debut, 'Born To Love You'. As with the majority of reggae signings to major labels, the contract was short-lived and the band's output was limited to a few releases. In 1979 Shakeel Khan replaced Paul Dawkins, who had left the group and released his solo hit, 'Ebony Eyes'. By 1982 the diminishing line-up released an instrumental single, 'Tribute To A King', and *Spirit Of Ecstasy*, which was essentially a showcase of Paul Thompson's keyboard skills. Les McNeil pursued a solo career with the release of 'Love Mechanic' and enjoyed a massive hit performing as part of Eargasm for 'This A Lovers Rock'. In 1983 David Tyrone set up the Chams label, releasing the band's back catalogue as well as Les McNeil's 'I Gave You Everything' and 'Be Gentle With Me'.
● ALBUMS: *Moving On* (RCA 1978)★★★, *Alternative Routes* (Venture/RCA 1978)★★, *Tradition In Dub* remixed and re-released as *High Risk Dub* (Venture 1979)★★★, *Tell Your Friends About Dub* (RCA 1980)★★★, *Spirit Of Ecstasy - Featuring Paul Thompson* (Solid Groove 1982)★★.

TRINITY
b. Wade Brammer, 1954, Kingston, Jamaica, West Indies. After working as a DJ on several local sound systems, Trinity made his recording debut in March 1976 with 'Set Up Yourself' for Joseph 'Joe Joe' Hookim. Shortly after this, he recorded 'Words Of The Prophet' for Yabby You, who also released his fine debut album, *Shanty Town Determination*. Heavily influenced by Big Youth, he developed a strong and entertaining style of his own. In late 1976 he joined his neighbourhood friend and fellow DJ Dillinger for an excellent single for Hookim, 'Crank Face', and a rather hurriedly recorded album, *Clash*, for UK producer Clement Bushay. In 1977 he had more than 20 singles released, including 'Pumps And Pride' for Winston Riley, 'Smoking Rock' for Tommy Cowan, 'John Saw Them Coming' for Joe Gibbs and 'Peace Conference In A Western Kingston' for Yabby You. His biggest hit that year

was the irresistible 'Three Piece Suit' for Joe Gibbs, highlighting his excellent delivery, witty lyrics and sheer enthusiasm, and an outstanding album of the same name quickly followed. An answer record to this, Althea And Donna's 'Uptown Top Ranking' (1977), became an even bigger hit, eventually topping the UK pop charts. Trinity recorded his response, 'Slim Thing' (1978), but it was a disappointing reply. In 1977 he had another strong album with *Uptown Girl*, produced by Bunny Lee, and the following year he shared an album with Ranking Trevor (*Three Piece Chicken And Chips*), and appeared on the Mighty Diamonds' *Showcase*. Subsequent recordings met with less success, and in the 80s, he commenced a new career as a singer under the name Junior Brammer, with two albums being issued, *Telephone Line* and *Hold Your Corner*.

● ALBUMS: *Shanty Town Determination* (TR International 1976)★★★★, with Dillinger *Clash* (Burning Sounds 1976)★★, *Three Piece Suit* (Joe Gibbs 1977)★★★★, *Uptown Girl* (Magnum 1977)★★★★, with Ranking Trevor *Three Piece Chicken And Chips* (Cha Cha 1978)★★★, with the Mighty Diamonds *Showcase* (Burning Sounds 1978)★★★, *Bad Card* (Joe Gibbs 1979)★★★, *Rock In The Ghetto* (Trojan 1979)★★★, *Full House* (JB Music 1980)★★★, *Side Kicks* (Vista Sounds 1983)★★★, *Teen Jam* (Kingdom 1983)★★★, *Natty Tired To Carry Load* (Burning Sounds 1988)★★★, *Big Big Man* (Lagoon 1993)★★★. As Junior Brammer: *Telephone Line* (John Dread 1987)★★★, *Hold Your Corner* (Live & Learn 1987)★★★.

● COMPILATIONS: *Best Of* (Culture Press 1985)★★★★.

TROJAN RECORDS

The most commercially successful of UK reggae labels, Trojan had almost 30 hit singles placed on the UK national charts between 1969 and 1976. 'The Trojan' was the nickname of Jamaican producer Duke Reid (from the truck that was used to transport his sound system) and the label was originally founded to release his Treasure Isle recordings in Britain, yet it expanded to license and release the work of nearly every major Jamaican producer. Trojan's directors were Chris Blackwell (of Island Records) and Lee Gopthal, whose Pyramid label

had already enjoyed chart success in 1967 with Desmond Dekker's '007'. Early success for Trojan came with Jimmy Cliff's 'Wonderful World, Beautiful People' in 1969 and soon the UK charts were full of singles from artists such as John Holt, Ken Boothe, the Pioneers and Nicky Thomas. Sometimes Trojan would 'sweeten' the Jamaican productions by adding strings at London's Chalk Farm studios, and among the biggest-sellers were the pop-reggae of Bob And Marcia and Greyhound. However, the label's only number 1 was a more rootsy record, 'Double Barrel', by Dave And Ansell Collins (1972). Trojan's Big Shot subsidiary enjoyed strong sales with 'Big Six' and other lewd monologues by Judge Dread, and the compilation collections *Tighten Up Volumes* achieved cult status in the UK. Blackwell left the company to concentrate on releasing progressive rock through his Island label but Gopthal stayed on and expanded the Trojan group. In 1975 Trojan's parent company and distributor, B&C, collapsed. The Trojan catalogue was purchased by Marcel Rodd of Saga Records and the label was thereafter devoted to reissues. This policy was continued into the 90s by Trojan's next owner, Colin Newman of Receiver Records.

● COMPILATIONS: *The Trojan Story* (Trojan 1971)★★★★, *The Trojan Story* (Trojan 1988)★★★★, *20 Reggae Classics Volumes 1, 2, 3 & 4* (Trojan 1988)★★★★, *Tighten Up Box Set Vols 1, 2 & 3* (Trojan 1989)★★★★, *The History Of Trojan Records 1968-71, Volume One* (Trojan 1995)★★★★, *The History Of Trojan Records 1972-1975* (Trojan 1996)★★★★, *Jackpot Of Hits (Explosive Rockesteady)* (Trojan 1997)★★★★.

TUCKER, JUNIOR

b. Leslie Tucker, 1966, Kingston, Jamaica, West Indies. Tucker began his career as a talented child musician. He came from a musical family; his uncle was a vocalist with Count Ossie And The Mystic Revelation Of Rastafari. In 1976 Tucker recorded a version of 'Sideshow' with Earl 'Chinna' Smith, which had been a major hit for Barry Biggs in the same year. In April 1978 the One Love Peace Concert included a performance from Tucker, during which he sang 'Happy', 'Mr Melody' and a cover version of the Jacksons' 'Enjoy Yourself', which was featured on *It's A Small Small World*. The nine-track album also featured the first reggae cover version of Stephen Bishop's 'On And On', which was a hit for Aswad in 1989, and 'Who's Loving You'. Still working with his original producer, Tommy Cowan, in 1980, he enjoyed a big hit with 'Some Guys Have All The Luck'. The 'child star' label persisted, however, and Tucker then took a break from music. In the late 80s he worked with Handel Tucker and Erskine Thompson, and his first release with them, 'Don't Test', demonstrated all the bravado then prevalent in the dancehall and married reggae with opera. The follow-up, 'Sixteen (Into The Night)', was also overlooked, as was his recording featuring DJ Lieutenant Stitchie, 'Are You Ready', and 'Love Is The Strongest Emotion'. In 1991 Tucker recorded a cover version of Curtis Mayfield's 'You Don't Care' with Steely And Clevie. In 1993 he achieved a reggae number 1 hit with 'Love Of A Lifetime', and in the mid-90s he recorded with Richie Stephens, Buccaneer, Papa San, General Degree and Beenie Man. In 1994 he released 'Born To Love You', which was also a hit.

● ALBUMS: *It's A Small Small World* (Top Ranking 1978)★★★★, *Don't Test* (Ten 1990)★★★, *Love Of A Lifetime* (VP 1993)★★★, *Secret Lover* (Main Street 1995)★★★, *True Confession* (VP 1996)★★★.

TUFF, TONY

b. Winston Morris, *c.*1955, Kingston, Jamaica, West Indies. Tuff started his career singing in the vocal group the African Brothers alongside Sugar Minott and Derrick 'Bubble' Howard. The group enjoyed a number of hits in the mid-70s, notably 'Party Night'. They recorded as a group with Rupie Edwards and Coxsone Dodd, but in 1978 the group disintegrated when Dodd favoured Minott as a soloist, and took him on as an apprentice at Studio One. Tuff decided to pursue other careers, but by the early 80s he was back in the recording studio. His first solo outing, 'I'm So Glad', a self-production, appeared on his own Winston label in Jamaica. Encouraged by its success, he worked with Ranking Joe and Sugar Minott for the release of *The Best Of Tony Tuff* and *Presenting Tony Tuff*. His talents were also employed by the Yabby You Grove music connection and he achieved international success with the release of *Tony Tuff*. The songs were produced in the UK by King Sounds and the artwork on the cover was designed by Brinsley Forde of Aswad. When Tuff returned to Jamaica he performed on the sound systems, including Lees Unlimited and Volcano. His appearance on the Volcano Sound System coincided with his work with producer Henry 'Junjo' Lawes, who ran the sound. Tuff enjoyed a number of successful singles, notably 'Water Pumpee' and 'Mix Me Down', which were both smash hits in the dancehalls and on the reggae chart.

● ALBUMS: *Presenting Tony Tuff* (Black Roots 1980)★★★, *Reggae In The City* (1981)★★★, *Love Is Everywhere* (1981)★★★, *Tony Tuff* (Grove Music/Island 1981)★★★★, *The Best Of Tony Tuff* (Vista 1983)★★★, *Come Fe Mash It* (Volcano 1983)★★★, *Render Your Heart* (CSA 1983)★★★, *Ketch A Fire* (Music Master 1984)★★★, with the African Brothers *Collectors Item* (Uptempo 1987)★★, *Hustling* (Scorcher 1991)★★★.

TWINKLE BROTHERS

This group comprised Norman Grant (vocals, drums), Ralston Grant (vocals, rhythm guitar), Eric Barnard (piano), Karl Hyatt (vocals, percussion) and Albert Green (congas, percussion). All the members were born in Falmouth, Jamaica. Formed in 1962 by the Grant brothers, the Twinkles won various local musical awards and talent competitions before recording their earliest side, 'Somebody Please Help Me', in 1966 for producer Leslie Kong. The group went on to record for other producers such as Duke Reid, Lee Perry, Sid Bucknor, Phill Pratt, Ken Chang and Bunny Lee. In the early 70s they went into self-production, financing their sessions through Norman's employment as a solo artist. Their music embraced calypso, soul, pop and soft reggae, which they had performed on Jamaica's north coast hotel circuit. In 1975 an expanded line-up released the celebrated *Rasta Pon Top*, which included Rastafari anthems such as 'Give Rasta Praise', 'It Gwine Dreada', 'Beat Them Jah Jah' and the fiery, assertive title track. Over the next few years a number of Norman Grant productions featuring other artists surfaced, including titles by Alla, the Mystics, Phillip Parkinson and DJs Sir Lee and Ili P, as well as further Twinkle Brothers efforts, 'Jah Army' and a Rasta version of Jim Reeves' 'Distant Drums'. In 1977 the group signed to Virgin Records' newly established Frontline label, a move that saw the release of the highly acclaimed *Love*. This was followed by the patchy *Praise Jah*, and triumphantly, in 1980, by the classic *Countrymen*, which featured premier heavy roots items such as 'Never Get Burn', 'Since I Threw The Comb Away' and 'Jah Kingdom Come'. The group were later dropped by Virgin and more or less ceased to be an entity, with Norman Grant settling in the UK to concentrate on a solo career while retaining the Twinkle Brothers epithet. He continues to issue albums and 12-inch singles on his own Twinkle label, and has built himself a large fanbase, particularly in Europe where he is an in-demand live attraction. Other recordings, notably the excellent vocal/dub *Right Way*, have emerged through London roots doyen and sound system operator Jah Shaka's label.

● ALBUMS: *Rasta Pon Top* (Grounation 1975)★★★, *Love* (Front Line 1977)★★★★, *Praise Jah* (Front Line 1979)★★, *Countrymen* (Front Line 1980)★★★★, *Me No You* (Twinkle 1981)★★★, *Underground* (Twinkle 1982)★★★, *Dub Massacre Parts 1 - 5* (Twinkle 1982-90)★★★, *Burden Bearer* (Twinkle 1983)★★★, *Enter Zion* (Twinkle 1983)★★★, *Live From Reggae Sunsplash* (Twinkle 1984)★★, *Right Way* (1985)★★★★, *Kilimanjaro* (Twinkle 1985)★★★, *Anti-Apartheid* (Twinkle 1985)★★★, *Respect And Honour* (Twinkle 1987)★★★, *Twinkle Love Songs* (Twinkle 1987)★★★, *New Songs For Jah* (Twinkle 1989)★★★, *Rastafari Chant* (Twinkle 1989)★★★, *All Is Well* (Twinkle 1990)★★★, *Free Africa* (Front Line 1990)★★★, *Live In Warsaw* (Twinkle 1990)★★, *Unification* (Twinkle 1990)★★★, *Wind Of Change* (Twinkle 1990)★★★, *Old Cuts* dub album (1991)★★★★, *Don't Forget Africa* (Twinkle 1992)★★★, *Twinkle Love Songs Volume 2* (Twinkle 1992)★★, *Dub With Strings* (Twinkle 1992)★★★, *Babylon Rise Again* (Twinkle 1992)★★★, *Higher Heights (Twinkle Inna Polish Stylee)* (1993)★★★, with Trebunia Family *Comeback Twinkle 2* (Ryszard 1994)★★★.

● COMPILATIONS: *Crucial Cuts* (Virgin 1983)★★★★, *All The Hits From 1970-88* (Twinkle 1988)★★★★.

U-Roy

b. Ewart Beckford, 1942, Kingston, Jamaica, West Indies. U-Roy began as a sound system DJ in 1961, spinning records for the Doctor Dickies set, later known as Dickies Dynamic, in such well-known Jamaican venues as Victoria Pier, Foresters Hall and Emmett Park. His inspiration was the DJ Winston 'Count' Matchuki, who worked for Coxsone Dodd and subsequently on Prince Buster's Voice Of The People sound system. By the mid-60s he was DJ for Sir George The Atomic, based around Maxfield Avenue in Kingston. Around 1967 he began to work with King Tubby as DJ for his Home Town Hi-Fi. From this association developed the whole modern DJ style; Tubby's work at Duke Reid's studio, where he was disc-cutter, led him to discover dub. He found that by dropping out the vocal track and remixing the remaining rhythm tracks, he could create new 'versions' of much-loved tunes. He began to record a series of special acetate recordings, or dub plates, for exclusive use on his sound system. The space left by the absent vocal tracks enabled U-Roy to improvise his own jive-talk raps or toasts when the sound system played dances. The effect in the dancehall was immediate and electrifying. In 1969 U-Roy was invited to play for Dodd's Down Beat sound system, playing the second set behind King Stitt. U-Roy became dissatisfied with playing the latest Coxsone music only after Stitt had first exposed it to dance patrons, and returned to Tubby's. He then began his recording career in earnest, recording two discs for Lee Perry, 'Earth's Rightful Ruler' and 'OK Corral', before moving to producer Keith Hudson, for whom he made the outstanding 'Dynamic Fashion Way'.

U-Roy then began recording for Duke Reid, using as backing tracks Reid's rocksteady hits from 1966-67; their success was unprecedented. His first record for Reid, 'Wake The Town', which used Alton Ellis's 'Girl I've Got A Date' as backing, immediately soared to the top of both Jamaican radio charts. His next two releases, 'Rule The Nation' and 'Wear You To The Ball', soon joined it. These three releases held the top three positions in the Jamaican charts for 12 weeks during early 1970. Other sound system DJs were quick to follow U-Roy, including Dennis Alcapone and Scotty. The radio stations refused to play DJ music in order to give singers a chance, so big was the demand. U-Roy recorded 32 tracks for Reid, in the process versioning almost every rocksteady hit issued on the label and releasing two albums. By 1973 he was recording for other producers, including Alvin 'GG' Ranglin, Bunny Lee, Glen Brown and Lloyd Charmers, as well as issuing self-productions. However, the rise of the next DJ generation, including Big Youth, signalled the partial eclipse of U-Roy. In 1975 he made a series of albums for producer Prince Tony Robinson that were leased to Virgin Records in the UK, wherein the DJ revisited Reid's earlier hits in the then prevalent rockers style. He appeared at the London Lyceum in August 1976, backed by a band featuring Channel One stalwarts Sly Dunbar (bass) and Ansell Collins (organ). He operated his own sound system, Stur-Gav, featuring Ranking Joe and selector Jah Screw. When they left after the sound system was broken up during the turbulent 1980 Jamaican election, it was rebuilt with new DJs Charlie Chaplin and Josey Wales, and Inspector Willie as selector. U-Roy continued to record sporadically throughout the 80s, recording 'Hustling', a single for Gussie Clarke, in 1984, and two excellent albums for DJs-turned-producers Tapper Zukie and Prince Jazzbo, in 1986 and 1987, respectively. In 1991 he played a successful 'revival' concert at the Hammersmith Palais, London. U-Roy is the man who is responsible for putting the DJ on the map, both as a recording artist in Jamaica and as a major indirect influence on the US rappers - as such, his importance is immense.

● ALBUMS: *Version Galore* (Trojan 1971)★★★★, *U-Roy* (Attack/Trojan 1974)★★★★, *Dread Inna Babylon* (Virgin 1975)★★★★, *Natty Rebel* (Virgin 1976)★★★, *Dread In A Africa* (1976)★★★, *U-Roy Meet King Attorney* (1977)★★★, *Rasta Ambassador* (Virgin 1977)★★★, *Jah Son Of Africa* (Front Line 1978)★★★, *With Words Of Wisdom* (Front Line 1979)★★★, *Love Is Not A Gamble* (Stateline 1980)★★★, *Crucial Cuts* (Virgin 1983)★★★, *Line Up And Come* (Tappa 1987)★★★, *Music Addict* (RAS 1987)★★★, as U-Roy And Friends *With A Flick Of My Musical Wrist* 1970-73 recordings (Trojan 1988)★★★★, *True Born African* (Ariwa 1991)★★★, with Josey Wales *Teacher Meets The Student* (Sonic Sounds 1992)★★★, *Original DJ* (Frontline/Virgin 1995)★★★.

● COMPILATIONS: *The Best Of U-Roy* (Live & Love 1977)★★★, *Version Of Wisdom* (Front Line 1990)★★★, *Natty Rebel - Extra Version* (Virgin 1991)★★★, *U-Roy CD Box Set* (Virgin 1991)★★★★, *Super Boss* (Esoldun/Treasure Isle 1992)★★★.

UB40

Named after the form issued to unemployed people in Britain to receive benefit, UB40 are the most long-lasting proponents of crossover reggae in the UK. The multiracial band was formed around the brothers Robin (b. 25 December 1954, Birmingham, England; lead guitar) and Ali Campbell (b. 15 February 1959, Birmingham, England; lead vocals, guitar), the sons of Birmingham folk club singers Lorna and Ian Campbell. Other founder-members included Earl Falconer (b. 23 January 1957, Birmingham, England; bass), Mickey Virtue (b. 19 January 1957, Birmingham, England; keyboards), Brian Travers (b. 7 February 1959; saxophone), Jim Brown (b. 21 November 1957; drums), and Norman Hassan (b. 26 January 1958, Birmingham, England; percussion). Reggae toaster Astro (b. Terence Wilson, 24 June 1957) joined UB40 to record 'Food For Thought' with local producer Bob Lamb (former drummer with Locomotive and the Steve Gibbons band). 'King' (coupled with 'Food For Thought') was a tribute to Martin Luther King. The debut, *Signing Off*, boasted an album sleeve with a 12-inch square replica of the notorious, bright yellow unemployment card. This image attracted a large contingent of disaffected youths as well as proving popular with followers of the 2-Tone/ska scene. The following year, the group formed their own label, DEP International, on which they released 'One In Ten', an impassioned protest about unemployment. *Labour Of Love*, a collection of cover versions, signalled a return to the reggae mainstream and it brought UB40's first number 1 in 'Red Red Wine' (1983). Originally written by Neil Diamond, it had been a big reggae hit for Tony Tribe in 1969. The album contained further hit singles in Jimmy Cliff's 'Many Rivers To Cross' (1983), Eric Donaldson's 'Cherry Oh Baby' (1984) and 'Don't Break My Heart' in 1985. The follow-up, *Geffrey Morgan*, a UK number 3 album, supplied the group with the Top 10 hit 'If It Happens Again'. 'I Got You Babe' (1986) was a different kind of cover version, as Ali Campbell and Chrissie Hynde of the Pretenders duetted on the Sonny And Cher hit. The same team had a further hit in 1988 with a revival of Lorna Bennett's 1969 reggae song 'Breakfast In Bed'. *Rat In Mi Kitchen* included the African liberation anthem 'Sing Our Own Song', with Herb Alpert on trumpet. After performing 'Red Red Wine' at the 1988 Nelson Mandela Concert at Wembley, renewed promotion in the USA resulted in the single reaching the number 1 spot. The group had further singles success with the Chi-lites' 'Homely Girl' (1989) and Lord Creator's 'Kingston Town' (1990), both of which appeared on a second volume of cover versions, *Labour Of Love II* (which has subsequently sold over five million copies worldwide). In 1990, the group had separate Top 10 hits in the UK and USA, as a Campbell/Robert Palmer duet on Bob Dylan's 'I'll Be Your Baby Tonight' charted in Britain, and a revival of the Temptations' 'The Way You Do The Things You Do' was a hit in America. Throughout the 80s, the group toured frequently in Europe and North America and played in Russia in 1986, filming the tour for video release. Following a quiet period they returned in 1993 with a version of 'I Can't Help Falling In Love With You', which reached number 1 in the UK, also fostering the career of new pop-reggae star Bitty McClean. The following year they backed Pato Banton on his worldwide hit cover version of the Equals' 'Baby Come Back'. Litigation took place in 1995 when Debbie Banks, an amateur poet, claimed that their major hit 'Don't Break My Heart' was based upon her lyrics. She won the case and was awarded a substantial amount in back royalties. Campbell released his debut solo album the same year. After an extended sabbatical the band returned in 1997 with another solid collection, *Guns In The Ghetto*. The following year the band backed various chatters, including Beenie Man, Lady Saw, Mad Cobra, Ninja Man and Lieutenant Stitchie, on the excellent *UB40 Present The Dancehall Album*, recorded at Ali Campbell and Brian Travers' Jamaican studio. It was the first instalment in a series that plans to showcase Jamaican reggae both old and new.

● ALBUMS: *Signing Off* (Graduate 1980)★★★, *Present Arms* (DEP 1981)★★★, *Present Arms In Dub* (DEP 1981)★★★, *UB44* (DEP 1982)★★★, *UB40 Live* (DEP 1983)★★★, *Labour Of Love* (DEP 1983)★★★★, *Geffrey Morgan* (DEP 1984)★★★★, *Baggariddim* (DEP 1985)★★★, *Rat In Mi Kitchen* (DEP 1986)★★★, *UB40* (DEP 1988)★★★★, *Labour Of Love II* (DEP 1989)★★★, *Promises And Lies* (DEP 1993)★★★, *Guns In The Ghetto* (Virgin 1997)★★★, with various artists *UB40 Present The Dancehall Album* (Virgin 1998)★★★★.
Solo: Ali Campbell *Big Love* (Virgin 1995)★★★.
● COMPILATIONS: *The Singles Album* (Graduate 1982)★★★, *The UB40 File* double album (Graduate 1985)★★★, *The Best Of UB40, Volume I* (DEP 1987)★★★★, *UB40 Box Set* (Virgin 1991)★★★★, *The Best Of UB40 Volume 2* (DEP 1995)★★.
● VIDEOS: *Labour Of Love* (Virgin Vision 1984), *Best Of UB40* (Virgin Vision 1987), *CCCP The Video Mix* (Virgin Vision 1987), *UB40 Live* (Virgin Vision 1988), *Dance With The Devil* (Virgin Vision 1988), *Labour Of Love II* (Virgin Vision 1990), *A Family Affair Live In Concert* (Virgin Vision 1991), *Live In The New South Africa* (PMI 1995).

UK MCs

By the early 80s, UK reggae fans (DJ fans in particular) felt that they had assimilated enough of Jamaica's musical output, and demanded a voice of their own. Lovers rock in the mid-70s had been a peculiarly English phenomenon, which started as a reaction against the dominant rasta/roots music of the time, and the rise of the UK MCs mirrored it in many ways. The increasing availability of live sound system tapes from Jamaica from the late 70s onwards meant that DJs in the UK were able to study their Jamaican counterparts at work on the set, as opposed to their finished work on record, and for a time, many DJs simply reproduced the lyrics they had heard on tape. The better ones soon realized that this was not good enough, and Saxon Sound were at the forefront of this revolution, with English DJs - now MCs - riding rhythms in a very English way, which had repercussions throughout the reggae world, and on into US rap music too. Phillip Papa Levi was Saxon's top MC, and the first to record, but close behind him were Peter King, the 'fast style' originator, Smiley Culture, Asher Senator, Tippa Irie, Daddy Colonel and Rusty. Saxon Sound were unassailable and many memorable sound system 'battles' were fought at unglamorous venues such as Lewisham Boys Club, as Saxon consistently proved that they were the best. The Midlands also had their own home-grown stars, and Macka B and Pato Banton came to the fore - Macka B, in particular, was incomparable, and not afraid to reveal his musical influences - one of his party turns was set to the melody of 'Hey Big Spender'.

DJs had recorded in the UK previously - Papa Face and Laurel And Hardy had both made strong records that were very popular - but the release of Phillip 'Papa' Levi's 'Mi God, Mi King', in 1984, changed everything when, towards the end of the record, he adopted the UK 'fast style'. Peter King was the originator of this style (he claimed that his girlfriend was unhappy about his constantly practising lyrics, so he performed them in double time in order to finish more quickly!), but Levi was the first to put the style on record. 'Mi God, Mi King' was quickly released in Jamaica where it went straight to number 1 and stayed there - the first English DJ record ever to top the Jamaican charts - and Levi was promptly signed by Island Records. Smiley Culture's Fashion Records release, 'Cockney Translation', stayed at the top of the UK reggae charts for weeks in 1984 and the follow-up, 'Police Officer', went straight into the UK national charts in early 1985. Jamaican and American DJs desperately tried to replicate the UK style, which concentrated on lyrics that actually told a story, often in a humorous way, with repeated punchlines or hooklines. The subjects usually related personal experiences, without having to pretend, as they once had, that they had been raised in western Kingston. From this point, English DJs were no longer

regarded as second best, and many classic records have been made in the UK in the ensuing years. Tippa Irie has made a long-standing commitment to UK reggae music; Macka B has produced some of the genre's most incisive lyrics, such as 'Invasion' and 'Don't Judge Me' - two all-time classics. Levi continues to record without making any apologies or concessions to anyone - his '84 Tion' was a fine account of a second-generation black English upbringing, while Top Cat's version, to an updated 'Lock Jaw' rhythm track, proved one of the most popular records in the UK during the latter part of 1993. With continued success for Top Cat and other new chatters including General Levy, Starkey Banton and Glamma Kid, the UK MC is definitely here to stay.
● COMPILATIONS: Various Artists: *Great British M.C.'s* (Fashion 1985)★★★★, *Coughing Up Fire - Saxon Studio Live* (Greensleeves 1985)★★★.

UK REGGAE
Far too often derided as being a mere derivative of the original Jamaican article, UK Reggae has long since cast off the charges of imitation, and has become a vibrant, exciting reggae form in its own right. Inevitably, early British reggae music was chiefly built on the input of Jamaicans resident in the UK. Ernest Ranglin arrived in Britain in 1963 at the request of Island Records boss Chris Blackwell, and, working as musical director, cut a huge hit for Millie, 'My Boy Lollipop', in 1964. Other British ska efforts, however, were less accomplished, and it was not until 1968-69 that producers such as Clancy Collins and Laurel Aitken began to make British reggae - albeit the work of Caribbean expatriates - worthy of its name. Another early mover in the field was Eddy Grant, who made one classic with the Pyramids, 'Train Tour To Rainbow City', in 1969. Reggae soon became hugely popular in the UK, chiefly thanks to the efforts of two labels, Trojan and Pama Records, both dealing principally with Jamaican-recorded product. By 1970-71, British reggae bands such as the Cimarons and the Undivided could regularly be found on the club circuit, either in their own right or backing visiting Jamaican artists. By 1974 the Cimarons had developed their own style, slightly more subdued than the Jamaican

version, and wholly recognizable as their own; their *On The Rock* set remains underrated to this day. The lovers rock scene, a blend of soul and rub-a-dub rhythms, spawned a multitude of popular, chiefly female acts: 15-16-17, Brown Sugar (featuring future Soul II Soul diva Caron Wheeler), Carroll Thompson and Janet Kay, among them. The mid-70s saw a vast number of new reggae bands and artists emerge in the UK: Steel Pulse, the first UK reggae band to be taken seriously by the rock world; a youthful Aswad, whose 'Warrior Charge' is a stepper's classic; Matumbi, who mixed lovers grooves and roots with ease, resulting in a Top 40 hit, 'Point Of View' in 1979; and Linton Kwesi Johnson, the pioneering dub poet, backed by Matumbi member Dennis Bovell's Dub Band.

Inevitably, studios specializing in reggae emerged in the UK, including London's Mark Angelos and Easy Street, and at the turn of the 80s, two label-owning studio complexes arrived, Ariwa and Fashion Records, the former, under the aegis of producer-owner Neil Fraser (aka Mad Professor), specializing in lovers and dub, the latter tackling an eclectic mix. The 80s saw Aswad rise to chart success with the number 1 'Don't Turn Around', and the emergence of uniquely British-sounding artists such as Smiley Culture and the internationally successful Maxi Priest, whose style crossed lovers rock with dancehall and soul. Meanwhile, Britain's MC culture, built on the success of the likes of Saxon and Jah Tubby's sound systems in the mid-80s, had unleashed a volley of unique DJs, including Tippa Irie, Phillip Papa Levi and Macka B. Jamaican acts such as Barrington Levy, Dennis Brown and Pat Kelly even came to Britain to record, an idea that might have seemed laughable in the 60s. Trojan also had a successor in the shape of Greensleeves Records, a label that could be relied upon for releasing chiefly Jamaican product. By the 90s, British reggae was no longer a meaningful term: the music had proved its worldwide appeal, with its hybrids, such as bhangramuffin, a fusion of Asian and ragga styles, sounding truly 'international'.

UNIQUES

The original line-up of this vocal harmony group consisted of Slim Smith (b. Keith Smith, *c*.1948, Kingston, Jamaica, West Indies, d. 1973), Roy Shirley (b. *c*.1948, Kingston, Jamaica, West Indies) and Franklyn White. The formative years of the Uniques overlap confusingly with the Techniques. In an interview that appeared in the Canada-based magazine *Reggae Quarterly* in the early 80s, Shirley stated that he formed the group with Smith and White, when the latter pair left the Techniques. They made their first recording, 'The Journey', for Ken Lack's Caltone label. Other early ska sides included 'Do Me Good', and 'Evil Love' for J.J. Johnson in 1966, the same year as the Techniques' earliest records, just prior to Smith's sabbatical at Studio One and Shirley's successful resumption of his solo career. White's subsequent whereabouts remain unknown. Towards the end of 1967 Smith left Coxsone and formed the Uniques Mk. 2, teaming up with Martin Riley (aka Jimmy Riley), brother of Technique Winston Riley, and Lloyd Charmers (b. Lloyd Tyrell, 1938, Kingston, Jamaica, West Indies), former member of the Charmers, with whom he had recently enjoyed some success with 'Time After Time' for Prince Buster. He had previously recorded as a solo singer for Coxsone Dodd in 1964. Cornell Campbell was another who featured around this time. The group borrowed some money from one Winston Lowe and recorded their debut, 'Watch This Sound', a version of the Stephen Stills/Buffalo Springfield protest song 'For What It's Worth', and the achingly soulful 'Out Of Love'. These were a success, as were subsequent recordings such as 'People Rock Steady', 'Never Let Me Go', 'Gypsy Woman', 'Let Me Go Girl', 'Speak No Evil', 'Girl Of My Dreams', 'My Woman's Love', 'Love & Devotion', 'Girls Like Dirt', 'The Beatitude' (aka 'Blessed Are The Meek') and the classic 'My Conversation', which producer Bunny Lee gave to Rupie Edwards, who built an entire LP around it. This was the first one-rhythm album, predating the vogue for such discs by several years. These were all produced by Bunny Lee, though some carry a credit for Winston Lowe. They also recorded the wonderful 'Secretly' (1969) for Lloyd Daley, though this seems to have been a one-off. These records were issued in the UK on a variety of Trojan and Pama labels, some acknowledged as the work of the Uniques, some allowing Slim Smith the sole credit. Trojan issued *Absolutely The Uniques* in 1969. The group folded during that same year, the members separating to pursue solo careers, Smith, until his untimely demise, with Bunny Lee, and Charmers moving deeper into production work.

● ALBUMS: *Absolutely The Uniques* (Trojan 1969)★★★★.

● COMPILATIONS: *The Best Of ...* (Trojan 1994)★★★★.

UPSETTERS

This was a collective tag for whatever group reggae producer Lee Perry had in his studio at the time of recording, or for his sporadic live dates. The name was drawn from his massive 1967 Jamaican smash, 'The Upsetter', and had previously been used by saxophonist Roland Alphonso, who in turn drew it from Little Richard's stage band. The Upsetters secured a UK Top 5 hit in 1969 with the hugely influential 'Return Of Django'. Among those who passed through Perry's Upsetters were Glen Adams, Winston Wright, (organ), Aston 'Familyman' Barrett, Boris Gardiner (bass), Carlton Barrett, Lloyd 'Tinleg' Adams, Mikey 'Boo' Richards, Sly Dunbar, Clevie Browne (drums), Hux Brown (guitar) and innumerable others. Perry was dictatorial with his bands, and hence, always achieved a totally different sound from the other producers using the same musicians in the hot-house music business of Jamaica.

● ALBUMS: *The Upsetter* (Trojan 1969)★★★★, *Many Moods Of The Upsetter* (1970)★★★, *Scratch The Upsetter Again* (1970)★★★★.

● COMPILATIONS: *The Upsetter Collection* (Trojan 1981)★★★★, *Upsetters A Go Go* (Heartbeat 1996)★★★.

VERSION

The origins of version lie in the late 60s when producers removed the vocals from the a-side, leaving the rhythm track on the b-side. Version simply means an alternative cut. The exercise made economic sense and the DJs could use the version on the sound systems, generating interest in the song prior to its release. The versions evolved into dub, where the recording engineer would not only drop the vocals, but the rhythm would disappear and reappear, with the occasional echo adding a new dimension to the sound. As recording facilities improved, the mixers began experimenting with sound, and version became dub. The innovator of dub is acknowledged as being King Tubby, who was initially employed to cut versions for Bunny Lee and Lee Perry. By the mid-70s, virtually all Jamaica's producers featured a version on the b-side and now many of today's dub remixes of dance tunes are directly inspired by 'version'. Whole albums surfaced with vocals on one side accompanied by the respective versions on the other. The term version also describes the employment of a number of performers to sing, DJ or play a particular instrument over the same backing track - there are many one-rhythm albums (popularly known as 'version excursions') available from Jamaica, but the first compilation is widely acknowledged to be *Yamahah Skank*, produced by Rupie Edwards, over Slim Smith's 'My Conversation'. The most 'versioned' tune was Wayne Smith's 'Under Me Sleng Teng' (1985), produced by King Jammy (then Prince Jammy) who began his career as an assistant to King Tubby. The tune had over 200 versions and is recognized as the innovator for the digital style that has remained popular throughout the late 80s and 90s. In 1986 Winston Riley resurrected his mid-70s Stalag rhythm and enjoyed a huge hit with 'Ring The Alarm' by Tenor Saw. The tune resurfaced yet again in

1992 when Buju Banton rode the rhythm for 'Ring The Alarm, Quick' in combination with Tenor Saw. Sound system DJs and audiences loved the variety of versions and would mix the various recordings so that one rhythm would feature a host of artists. The studios were quick to respond to the trend and releases appeared featuring a multitudinous array of artists; the ultimate release was the epic 'Can't Stop The Dance' by the Yardcore Collective, whose line-up featured many of the island's top DJs. Version turned full circle in the 90s when enterprising producers cut out the vocals in the guise of a 'P.A. Mix' on their releases. In 1995, King Jammy revived his innovative tune on *Sleng Teng Extravaganza '95*, featuring the modish stars updating the rhythm with their own interpretations.

● COMPILATIONS: *Shalom Dub* (Klik 1975)★★★, *Yamahah Skank* (Success 1976)★★★, *Sleng Teng Extravaganza Volumes 1 & 2* (Jammys 1985)★★★, *Stalag 17,18,19* (Techniques 1987)★★★, *Music Works Showcase 88* (Greensleeves 1988)★★★★, *Music Works Showcase 1989* (Greensleeves 1989)★★★, *Selekta Showcase* (Greensleeves 1990)★★★, *One Man One Vote* (Greensleeves 1991)★★★, *Good Fellas* (Penthouse 1992)★★★, *Sleng Teng Extravaganza '95* (Greensleeves 1995)★★★.

VIBRONICS

From Leicester, England, the mysterious Stevie Vibronics initially appeared on the Egg Experience '97 shows, where his enigmatic stage presence inspired Zion Train to sign the arranger. He initially experimented with music programming at home, producing dub sounds that surfaced on dub plates for sound systems. His major influences came from attending Jah Shaka and Abashanti sessions. With the advent of sequenced music in the 90s, Vibronics created a digital dub sound that resulted in 'Universal Love', a particular favourite with the Abashanti crew. His sessions with Zion Train led to the release of 'Jah Light, Jah Love', which proved popular within the UK roots scene and led to a combination with Jah Free. Jah Free was notorious for his penchant for booming out the basslines, and Vibronics was an ideal partner. The duo performed on a series of dub conferences across Europe, and, inspired by the orig-

inal 'Dub Conference' organizer Winston Edwards, they recorded *Outernational Dub Conference Volume One*. Acclaimed as 'the Roni Size of reggae', Vibronics played his original dubs through his Atari, which he mixed live on stage utilizing his Soundcraft desk.

● ALBUMS: with Jah Free *Outernational Dub Conference Volume One* (Universal Egg 1998)★★★★.

VICEROYS

Formed in Jamaica, West Indies, around 1966, the group was formed by lead vocalist and song-writer Wesley Tinglin (b. *c*.1947, Jamaica, West Indies). They recorded, initially as the Voiceroys, for Coxsone Dodd's Studio One label, with early recordings including 'Love And Unity' (1967), 'Fat Fish' (1968) and 'Ya Ho' (1968). In 1968 they recorded 'Lip And Tongue' and 'Send Requests' for the Morgan's label. In the early 70s they joined Winston Riley as the Inturns, finding success with 'Mission Impossible', and in the mid-70s returned to Studio One to record as the Voiceroys with 'The Struggle' and 'Slogan On The Wall'. In 1978 they adopted the name the Interns, and recorded *Detour* for Phill Pratt, which was largely ignored at the time. Shortly after this, they changed name yet again, to the Viceroys, and the line-up stabilized with Wesley Tinglin being supported by harmony singers Neville Ingram and Norris Reid. Reid had already had a handful of singles released under his own name, and continued to further his solo career while remaining a full-time member of the group. They had a big hit with 'Heart Made Of Stone' (1980), a Sly And Robbie production, and followed it with the self-produced 'Shaddai Children' (1981). In 1982 they recorded *We Must Unite*, on which the combination of their rural, rootsy harmonies with Linval Thompson's heavy-duty production attracted a great deal of attention. They then repeated the formula for *Brethren And Sistren* (1983), which was their biggest-selling record, and *Detour* was re-released later that year in response to public interest in the group. Shortly after this, Norris Reid left the group to concentrate on his solo career with Augustus Pablo, and was replaced by Chris Wayne, who had made a name for himself singing on Sugar Minott's Youth Promotion sound system. The group's *Chancery Lane*

(1984) was recorded for Winston Riley, but was a rather low-key outing that did not enjoy the popularity of their previous albums. They commenced recording a new album, but it was never released, and nothing further has been heard from them. Chris Wayne left the group in 1985 and has since recorded an album for Wackies, *Freedom Street* (1988), and two for Sugar Minott - *Progress* (1989) and *Talk About Love* (1991). Norris Reid has continued to record for Augustus Pablo, and his first album, *Root And Vine*, was issued in 1988.

● ALBUMS: As the Interns *Detour* (1979)★★. As the Viceroys: *We Must Unite* (Trojan 1982)★★★, *Brethren And Sistren* (CSA 1983)★★★, *Chancery Lane* (Greensleeves 1984)★★, *Ya Ho* (Burning Sounds 1985)★★★.

WADE, WAYNE

b. *c*.1960, Kingston, Jamaica, West Indies. Wade began his singing career in the mid-70s and was hailed as the latest prodigy produced by Yabby You through the Grove Music collective. His initial success came in 1976 with 'Black Is Our Colour', released on the newly formed Mango label. The success of the single was followed with an interpretation of the Paragons' 'Happy Go Lucky Girl', which demonstrated his refined vocals. The song was an instant hit, which led to the release of a discomix in 1977 featuring DJ Prince Pompado, with 'I Kissed A Rose' on the b-side. Realizing the potential of covering Paragon hits, Wade recorded 'On The Beach', which was equally popular and also surfaced in discomix style with DJ Ranking Trevor. Wade subsequently interpreted other rocksteady hits, including 'Everybody Bawling', 'I Can't Hide' and 'You Don't Want Me'. In the early 80s he recorded with Dillinger for his Oak Sound productions. Wade appeared alongside the producer and the Tamlins, Al Campbell, and Trinity for the successful 'Five Man Army'. Other releases included 'Kings Of Kings', 'Now I Know' and, with Tommy McCook, 'Riding Forward'. In 1981 Wade enjoyed hits with the Linval Thompson-produced 'Round The World', 'Tell Me What's Going On', 'Poor And Humble' and 'Down In Iran'. By 1983 Wade had settled in the Netherlands where he recorded a version of Lionel Ritchie's 'Lady'. Wade signed a contract with Epic that resulted in a re-release of 'Lady', followed by the less successful 'Try Again'. Wade continued to record but he has yet to recapture the past glories of his work with Yabby You.

● ALBUMS: *Black Is Our Colour* (Grove Music 1978)★★, *Dancing Time* (Grove 1979)★★★, *Evil Woman* (1980)★★★, with Yabby You, Michael Prophet *Prophecy* (WLN 1983)★★★, *Poor And Humble* (1985)★★★, *Respect Due Always* (1986)★★, *Innocent Man* (1990)★★★.

WAILER, BUNNY

b. Neville O'Riley Livingston, 10 April 1947, Kingston, Jamaica, West Indies. Bunny Wailer's relationship with Bob Marley and Peter Tosh, the two other principal members of the Wailers in the 60s and early 70s, stretched back to his childhood, when Marley and Wailer lived under the same roof in Trench Town. As teenagers, Peter, Bob and Bunny would spend their evenings practising harmonies, tutored by Joe Higgs of Higgs And Wilson fame. In the early 60s, as the nascent Jamaican recording industry began to gather strength, the trio formed the Wailers, recruiting other friends such as Junior Braithwaite, Beverley Kelso and Cherry Smith into the fold. Possessed of a high tenor, rather in the style of American soul singers of the Curtis Mayfield school, Bunny's role in the Wailers was principally that of harmony singer. However, on occasions his voice was featured as lead on songs such as 'Dancing Shoes', 'He Who Feels It Knows It' and the beautiful 'Sunday Morning', recorded in the early 60s for the group's first producer, Coxsone Dodd. Bunny spent part of 1967 in prison on charges of marijuana possession. It was this experience that prompted him to write the song 'Battering Down Sentence', which later appeared on his solo debut, *Blackheart Man*. The Wailers spent a couple of years recording for other producers, most notably Leslie Kong and Lee Perry, as well as issuing their own self-produced efforts on their Wail 'N' Soul 'M' and Tuff Gong labels. During this period, Bunny contributed lead vocals on 'This Train', 'Riding High', 'Brain Washing' and 'Dreamland'. In 1972 the Wailers signed to Island Records. With founder Chris Blackwell's understanding of contemporary rock markets, and the emphasis on albums and live shows, the Wailers brought the sound of roots reggae to an international audience with *Catch A Fire* (1973) and *Burnin'* (1973), the latter featuring two fine songs from Bunny, 'Hallelujah Time' and 'Pass It On'. These albums broke the Wailers outside of Jamaica and its expatriate environs in the USA and Europe, establishing a new worldwide respect and focus for reggae music. However, this success had taken its toll on the group. Peter Tosh resented the way in which Marley appeared to be promoted as leader of the group, and Bunny, for largely unspecified reasons, seemed reluctant to take part in the endless globe-betrotting necessary to consolidate their success in Europe and America. By 1974, just prior to the release of *Natty Dread*, both Peter and Bunny left the group to concentrate on their solo careers.

Bunny Wailer inaugurated his own Solomonic label, upon which all his recordings have since appeared in Jamaica. His first solo record, 'Searching For Love', had emerged in limited quantities in the early 70s, concurrently with his involvement with the Wailers. His other Solomonic releases, 'Life Line', 'Bide Up', 'Pass It On' (different to the version on the *Burnin'* album) and 'Arabs Oil Weapon', credited to the Wailers, came out in 1975. A year later Island released *Blackheart Man* to immediate and unanimous acclaim from the world's music press. With tracks such as 'Rastaman', 'Reincarnated Souls', 'Bide Up', 'Fig Tree', 'Amagideon' (sic) and the title track, *Blackheart Man* is still regarded as Bunny's masterpiece. His subsequent albums continued in much the same vein, with varying degrees of success, until he adapted to incorporate aspects of the burgeoning dancehall style, finding success with records such as 'Riding', an adaptation of the Perry-produced 'Riding High' track, 'Crucial', 'Cool Runnings', 'Rock And Groove' and the rootsy 'Rise And Shine'. An album of Wailers cover versions, *Bunny Wailer Sings The Wailers*, garnered further critical plaudits, followed by a similar collection entitled *Tribute To The Hon. Robert Nesta Marley*, in honour of the passing of his old partner. However, as the decade wore on, Wailer, like many of the old-school Rasta artists, seemed increasingly out of step with the digital ragga that had taken over in 1986, and he has since relied mainly on the loyalty of existing fans outside of Jamaica. Recent albums have made little impact upon the reggae scene at a grass-roots level, despite the acclaim heaped upon the lushly packaged *Liberation*, seen by many critics as a return to the roots militancy of previous years.

● ALBUMS: *Blackheart Man* (Island 1976)★★★★, *Protest* (Island 1977)★★, *Struggle* (Island 1978)★★, *In I Fathers House* (Solomonic 1980)★★★, *Bunny Wailer Sings The Wailers* (Island 1981)★★★★, *Tribute To The Hon. Nesta Marley* (Solomonic 1981)★★, *Rock 'n' Groove*

(Solomonic 1981)★★★, *Hook Line & Sinker* (Solomonic 1982)★★★, *Roots Radics Rockers Reggae* (Shanachie 1984)★★★, *Marketplace* (Solomonic 1986)★★, *Bunny Wailer Live* (Solomonic 1986)★★, *Roots Man Skanking* (Shanachie 1987)★★★, *Rule Dancehall* (Solomonic 1987)★★, *Liberation* (Solomonic 1989)★★★, *Gumption* (Solomonic 1991)★★, *Hall Of Fame: A Tribute To Bob Marley's 50th Anniversary* (Solomonic 1996)★★★.
● VIDEOS : *Blackheart Man* (Hendring Video 1990).

WAILERS

(see Marley, Bob)

WAILING SOULS

Originally named the Renegades, the group initially consisted of Lloyd 'Bread' McDonald and George 'Buddy' Haye, with Winston 'Pipe' Matthews as lead vocalist. This line-up recorded backing vocals for an Ernest Ranglin album before breaking up in 1968. Matthews and McDonald then teamed up with Oswald Downer and Norman Davis, recording 'Gold Digger' for Lloyd Daley. Their next move was to Coxsone Dodd at Studio One where, like so many other Jamaican artists, they recorded some of their finest work, often credited to the Classics. However, they became Pipe And The Pipers when they recorded two classic singles, 'Harbour Shark' and 'Back Biter', for Bob Marley's Tuff Gong label in the early 70s. Their vocals had a raw edge, neatly counterpointed by their harmonies, and their early work set the pattern for their entire career. Their vocal prowess, and ability to write songs almost to order, meant that for the next 20 years they were never far from the limelight, recording in whatever musical style was fashionable at the time, and still making fine music of lasting quality. In 1974 Davis and Downes left and Hill rejoined. Joe Higgs also entered the group's ranks for a short time, but left to tour the USA with Jimmy Cliff. Their next producer, Joseph 'Joe Joe' Hookim, put them firmly in the hit parade with a succession of local hits for Channel One, notably 'Things And Time', 'Joy Within Your Heart' and 'Very Well'. In 1976 Garth Dennis (of Black Uhuru) joined the group. Their next move was towards more artistic and financial independence with the formation of their own label, Massive, and their first two releases, 'Bredda Gravalicious' and 'Feel The Spirit', were massive hits in 1977/8. They moved on to Sly And Robbie's Taxi label in the early 80s for two more hit records, 'Old Broom' and 'Sugar Plum Plum'. Their next release for producer Henry 'Junjo' Lawes, 'Fire House Rock', was one of their most popular records. Somehow, they also found time (and energy) to make some beautiful records for Linval Thompson during this artistically and commercially successful period. Throughout the 80s, they continued to make superbly crafted, conscious records, which, although out of step with the times, still sold well to discerning listeners worldwide. They also proved that they could still succeed in the dancehalls, with some tunes for King Jammy towards the end of the decade. The 90s saw them signed to Sony.
● ALBUMS: *The Wailing Souls* (Studio One 1976)★★★, *Wild Suspense* (Massive/Island 1979)★★★, *Fire House Rock* (Greensleeves 1980)★★★, *Wailing* (Jah Guidance 1981)★★★, *Inch Pinchers* (Greensleeves 1983)★★★, *On The Rocks* (Greensleeves 1983)★★★, *Soul & Power* (Studio One 1984)★★★, *Stranded* (Greensleeves 1984)★★★, *Lay It On The Line* (Live & Learn 1986)★★★, *Kingston 14* (Live & Learn 1987)★★★, *Stormy Night* (Rohit 1990)★★★, *All Over The World* (1992)★★★, *Tension* (Big Ship 1997)★★.
● COMPILATIONS: *Best Of* (Empire 1984)★★★, *Very Best Of* (Greensleeves 1987)★★★★.

WALES, JOSEY

b. Joseph Sterling, Kingston, Jamaica, West Indies. Raised in West Kingston, he began DJing in 1977 with the Roots Unlimited sound system, alongside Buru Banton, taking his name from a popular Clint Eastwood movie. The next three and a half years were spent on U-Roy's King Sturgav Hi-Fi where he enjoyed a successful partnership with Charlie Chaplin. By 1982 his gruff, reality-laced lyrics could be heard on live dancehall albums for Bunny Roots' Kris Disk label. He then joined Volcano, which, under the auspices of owner, promoter and producer Henry 'Junjo' Lawes, had become the leading sound system on the island. Lawes produced

Wales' first hit, 'Leggo Mi Hand', later that same year, and work began on a debut album, *The Outlaw Josey Wales*, which confirmed his status as a serious rival to Yellowman when released in 1983. *Two Giant Clash* witnessed them both sharing the same Roots Radics rhythms, but the follow-up set, *No Way Better Than Yard*, in 1984, was produced by Wales himself and Mickey Pep from Cornerstone, with no discernable decrease in quality. Wales took his talents to King Jammy and the hits continued to flow. 'Na Lef Jamaica', 'Water Come A Mi Eye', 'It's Raining', 'Culture A Lick' and 'My Special Prayer' showed that his feel for plain speaking and cultural ghetto truths was undiminished. The following three years reaped several fine albums, including ones for both George Phang (*Undercover Lover*) and Black Solidarity (*Rulin'*). He introduced both Admiral Bailey and Shabba Ranks to the Jammys camp. By 1988 Wales could be heard voicing for Gussie Clarke, Exterminator and even Jimmy Cliff. Relocating to America he briefly recorded for Count Shelly before going into semi-retirement, occasionally guesting on stage shows and sound systems. In 1993 he made a successful come-back, topping the UK reggae charts with 'Hey Girl', a duet with Beres Hammond. Further tunes with Hammond and then for Tapper Zukie, Exterminator, Gussie Clarke, Bobby Digital and King Jammy quickly followed, with Wales often reworking his former lyrics to renewed effect. A good example of this is *Cowboy Style*, which King Jammy released in 1994. In March 1997 Wales was shot and robbed in a Kingston bar. He survived the attack and later that year topped the Jamaican charts with the country reggae release 'Bush Wacked'.

● ALBUMS: *The Outlaw Josey Wales* (Greensleeves 1983)★★★★, with Yellowman *Two Giants Clash* (Greensleeves 1984)★★★★, *No Way Better Than Yard* (Greensleeves 1984)★★★★, *Rulin'* (Black Solidarity 1986)★★★★, *Na Lef Jamaica* (Mango/Island 1986)★★, with Early B *Josey Wales Meets Early B* (Sonic Sounds 1987)★★★, *Ha Fi Say So* (Jammys 1988)★★★, *Undercover Lover* (Powerhouse 1989)★★★★, *Special Prayer* (VP 1990)★★★, *Code Of Conduct* (Powerhouse 1991)★★★, with U-Roy *Teacher Meets The Student* (Sonic Sounds 1992)★★★, *Cowboy Style* (Jammys/ Greensleeves 1994)★★★★.

WALKS, DENNIS

In the late 60s Walks recorded with Joe Gibbs the hit 'Having A Party', although he is best remembered for his work with producer Harry Mudie with whom he released 'Drifter' in 1971. A year later the hits, 'Time Will Tell', coupled with 'Under A Shady Tree', and with I. Roy, 'Heart Don't Leap', maintained his profile. Walks continued recording with Mudie and in 1974 Count Shelley released 'Margaret' with Mudies All Stars, which successfully paralleled its pre-decessor. Both songs were used as the basis for the hits 'Car Pound Drifter' by Bongo Herman and 'Margaret's Dream' by Lennie Hibbert. By 1975 Mudie's output on the Moodisc label was distributed in the UK where Walks reached the reggae Top 10 with 'Sad Sweet Dreamer' and the re-released 'Margaret'. Walks appeared as the support act to Mac And Katie Kissoon at the Empire Ballroom in Leicester Square, London. In the autumn of 1975 the UK-based Cactus label re-released Mudie's productions, including 'Leaving Rome' and revived interest in 'Drifter'. Walks' debut was also used to provide the accentuation for the *Reggae Bible* compilation featuring 11 cuts of the rhythm. In 1982 Walks revived his career when he recorded the chart-busting 'Roast Fish And Cornbread' with DJ Billy Boyo, 'Shut Up Your Face' with Lee Van Cliff, and 'The Lover'. In 1983 further hits surfaced when he teamed up with DJ and producer Jah Thomas for 'Fisherman' and 'Shoulder To Shoulder', both of which demonstrated his fine vocals.

● ALBUMS: *Meet Dennis Walks* (Moodisc 1974)★★★.

WALLACE, LEROY 'HORSEMOUTH'

b. 1950, Rose Town, Kingston, Jamaica, West Indies. Drummer Wallace began his career in 1964 and played with a variety of session groups including the Soul Vendors, the Sound Dimension and the Soul Brothers. These bands were frequently hired by Coxsone Dodd at Studio One and Wallace worked with luminaries such as Lee Perry and Jackie Mittoo. As Mad Roy he was one of Jamaica's early exponents of the new DJ style alongside Dennis Alcapone, U-Roy and King Stitt. In 1975 Wallace recorded, using the name Horsemouth, the track 'Herb Vendor', which was a hit for Larry Lawrence's

Ethnic Fight label. By 1976 Wallace played on sessions including Inner Circle's *Reggae Thing* and demonstrated his writing ability when he penned the closing track, 'This World'. He was also employed to play on sessions for Augustus Pablo, notably on his production of the late Hugh Mundell classic, *Africa Must Be Free By 1983*. The success of Jimmy Cliff in *The Harder They Come* inspired the filming of Theodoros Bafaloukas's *Rockers*. Wallace accepted the lead role and starred alongside Richard 'Dirty Harry' Hall. The film was a who's who of Jamaican reggae, featuring cameo appearances from many of the island's top performers. In spite of the rave reviews, the film lacked the support it deserved and was not widely distributed. The legendary Jamaican One Love Peace Concert featured a personal appearance from Wallace as Jamaica's newest film star. His celebrity status resulted in the studio bosses employing other drummers, but his fee enabled him to concentrate on his own projects. By the early 80s he had set up his own Horsemouth label and released 'Reggae Music' which established his resurgence as a vocalist. To promote the recording and secure a contract for his other sessions, he arrived in the UK in the autumn of 1981 and worked with Tapper Zukie, Errol Dunkley, Prince Far I and Junior Delgado. In 1982, with DJ Ranking Dread, the release of 'If Nanny Was Here' proved a hit in the dancehall.

● ALBUMS: with various artists *Rockers* (Island 1979)★★★★, *The Concept Of I & I Philosophy* (Horsemouth 1982)★★★, *Love And Unity* (Horsemouth 1983)★★★.

● FILMS: *Rockers* (1979).

WASHINGTON, DELROY

b. 1952, Westmoreland, Jamaica, West Indies. Washington arrived in Britain in the early 60s and soon became involved in the UK reggae scene. He worked in tour management and played a variety of instruments on various recording sessions. In 1971 he recorded some unreleased material for CBS Records in a group known as Rebel. Other bands who benefited from his professionalism included the Mayfields and the Classics. He performed as a soloist for Count Shelley who recorded 'Jah Man A Come', a version of the Temptations' 'Papa Was A Rolling Stone' and 'Way To Reason'. In 1972

Washington was enrolled to sing background harmonies with the Wailers for their Island Records debut *Catch A Fire*. Bob Marley's encouragement during the sessions proved an inspiration to Washington throughout his career. Further single releases followed including 'Time Will Stand' and 'Have You Ever Loved Someone'. By 1977 Virgin Records were signing reggae acts and Delroy Washington was one of the first to release material with the label with 'Give All The Praise To Jah'. This firmly established his position in the reggae chart. Musicians involved in the project were the nucleus of Aswad, Angus Gaye and Tony 'Gad' Robinson, alongside other members of the Grove music posse. Washington's live performances were greeted with enthusiasm, although the alliance between punk and reggae at the time occasionally resulted in ugly scenes. He continued to record for Virgin, including sessions in Jamaica with the notable studio engineer Karl Pitterson. Tracks included 'Freedom Fighters', 'Dress Back Satan', 'Jah Wonderful' and 'Brothers In Trouble'. Following his departure from Virgin Washington took a sabbatical, but returned in 1980 as the Delroy Washington Band, who enjoyed a hit with 'Magic' on the newly formed Direction Discs label.

● ALBUMS: *I Sus* (Virgin 1977)★★★, *Rasta* (Virgin 1978)★★.

WAYNE, CHRIS

b. Kingston, Jamaica, West Indies. Wayne was surrounded by music from an early age, being inspired by his Jonestown neighbour Johnny Osbourne, who released hit after hit as part of the Wildcats, and later with the Sensations, prior to his relocation to Canada. Wayne was also influenced by American R&B and by the age of seven he was performing Michael Jackson material. By his teens Wayne was providing backing vocals at Joe Gibbs' studio, which led to a solo career. His initial foray into the business proved disastrous when the tapes of his sessions with Bingi Gene, of Sugar Minott's Youth Promotion organization, were lost *en route* to the pressing plant. Undeterred, Wayne pursued his musical aspirations when he began working with Studio One veterans Wesley Tinglin and the Viceroys. He replaced vocalist Norris Reid, who had left the group to concentrate on solo work with

Augustus Pablo. Wayne performed on the 1984 release *Chancery Lane*, although early pressings did not credit the performer in spite of the fact that he was pictured on the cover. The album featured 'Take Care Of The Youths', 'Life Is Not An Easy Game', 'Push Push' and Wayne's own composition, 'New Clothes'. The group embarked on recording sessions for a follow-up album that did not surface, and in 1985 Wayne left to re-establish his solo career. He returned to Youth Promotion, where, this time, his master tapes safely reached the pressing plant, resulting in 'Aint That Enough' and 'Fan Me Pretty Girl'. Wayne continued to maintain a satisfactory profile within the reggae charts and his contribution to the music is widely acknowledged.

● ALBUMS: *Freedom Street* (Wackies 1988)★★★, *Progress* (Heartbeat 1989)★★★, *Talk About Love* (Heartbeat 1991)★★★.

WEBBER, MERLENE

b. *c*.1952, Jamaica, West Indies. Webber came from a musical family and initially performed alongside her sister Joyce as half of the Webber Sisters, remembered for 'You I Love'. Her brother David was in the original line-up of the Gladiators recording at Studio One, where Merlene also recorded with Coxsone Dodd. It was at the celebrated Brentford Road studio that Merlene and Joyce began their recording career. Merlene was asked to record as a soloist, resulting in 'No Happiness'. Her distinctive vocal style soon appeared on a number of releases in the early 70s, including her version of Tammy Wynette's country hit 'Stand By Your Man', produced by Clancy Eccles. The follow-up, 'Hard Life', offered a change of style and proved especially popular in the dancehall, as it related to ghetto life in Kingston. However, she remained in obscurity until the mid-70s, when, in 1976, she worked with producer Lloyd Campbell, and released her rendition of Cat Stevens' 'The First Cut Is The Deepest', inspired by P.P. Arnold's interpretation of the song. The single proved a success, and her debut album was released. The compilation included a reworking of her cover version of 'Stand By Your Man', but regrettably she was unable to capitalize on the former single's success. By 1980 she released 'Dream Dream' and 'Chanting Is', while her debut com-

pilation was repackaged and re-released. She continues to release sporadic recordings, including 'The Right Track' for the Joe Frazier organization.

● ALBUMS: *Once You Hit The Road* (Jama 1976)★★, *Letter To Mummy And Daddy* (No 1 Rock 1980)★★.

WEBSTER, E.T.

b. Errol Webster, Jamaica, West Indies. Webster, encouraged by his peers, began singing at an early age. In 1967 he successfully auditioned to perform as part of Billy Vernon And The Celestials, the premier touring band in the north of Jamaica. During his association with the band, he made his first international appearance touring California with the group in 1969. After three years of touring he felt confident enough to pursue a career as a solo singer and became one of Jamaica's leading balladeers and cabaret artists. He has since become a household name in Jamaica following a succession of popular hits, notably 'Can We Meet'. In 1987 he released 'Music Is Life' from the debut album of the same name, which, through sponsorship from Desnoes and Geddes, was launched at New Kingston's prestigious Epiphany Club. In 1988 he received an award as best cabaret performer and a year later was honoured by the then prime minister of Jamaica, Michael Manley. His prolific output was accompanied by a hectic touring schedule during which he continued to entertain the tourists on the north coast as well as appearing at the Reggae Sunsplash festival, being acclaimed as the most outstanding performer at the annual beach party. His international reputation led to supporting roles for some of the top R&B/soul acts, including Billy Paul, the Chi-Lites, the Manhattans, Ronnie Dyson and Chuck Jackson. Webster was also the featured act at two Miss Jamaica World Fashion Shows, made US appearances with Heavy D, Papa San, Cocoa Tea, Supercat and Inner Circle, and at the eighth Annual American Awards show in Chicago he was recognized for his outstanding contribution to reggae music. His prolific recording career resulted in an association with Norman Grant who has released all of Webster's recent output, including 'Place Called Home', 'Love Doctor' and the classic 'Mankind'.

● ALBUMS: *Music Is Life* (Sonic 1987)★★★,

Musical Explosion (Sonic 1990)★★★, *Hit A Boom* (Twinkle 1992)★★★, *Changes* (Twinkle 1993)★★★, *Reflections* (Imp 1993)★★, with the Twinkle Brothers *Twinkle Sample Volumes One And Two* (Twinkle 1993)★★★, *Lament Of A Dread* (Twinkle 1994)★★, *Mankind* (Twinkle 1995)★★★.

WELTON IRIE

b. 1961, Jamaica, West Indies. Welton began his career performing as, simply, Welton, chanting on Big John's Stereophonic Sound (later known as Echo Tone Hi Fi) in 1976. He initially emulated his hero Ranking Trevor, sometimes proving indistinguishable. Welton built up a hardcore group of devotees, enabling him to introduce young talent to the sound. One of Welton's protégés was General Echo, who, alongside Big John and Flux, was inexplicably gunned down by police in Kingston. Welton moved to the Gemini sound, notable for allowing King Yellowman to make his debut on the sound system circuit in a clash with Jack Ruby's Hi Power sound. Following his departure to the Virgo sound, Johnny Ringo stepped in and Welton performed alongside the Lone Ranger. Welton and the Lone Ranger began their recording careers as a duo with Coxsone Dodd at Studio One, performing in a style similar to Michigan And Smiley. It was at this time that Welton added Irie to his name following a recommendation from Dodd. The duo recorded a version of 'Joe Frazier' for 'Big Fight' and echoed Bob Marley with 'Chase Them Crazy'. The partnership was short-lived, and in the early 80s Welton released a succession of hits for a variety of producers, including 'The Bomb' over the Baba Boom rhythm and 'Army Life', which inspired Yellowman's preferred interpretation, retitled 'Soldier Take Over'. A session with Sly And Robbie resulted in the number 1 hit 'Ballerina', followed by the equally popular tribute to marijuana, 'Lambs Bread International'. Welton also demonstrated that he was a proponent of black pride with the unyielding 'Black Man Stand Up Pon Foot'. Other songs included 'Parish Connection', 'Dance A Cork', 'A Weh You Fah', 'Serve Me Long', 'Jailhouse Affair', 'How You Keep A Dance' and 'Come Nurse'. By 1983 Welton returned to the Gemini Sound for an international tour along-

side Johnny Ringo and Squiddly Ranking.
● ALBUMS: *It Feels So Good* (Starlight 1982)★★, with others *Junjo Presents Aces International* (Greensleeves 1982)★★★, *A Dee Jay Explosion* (Heartbeat 1982)★★★, *Ghetto Man Corner* (Pantomime 1983)★★★.

WHEELER, CARON

b. *c*.1962, England. Wheeler was raised in Jamaica; her father was a bass player, and her mother a singer with a Jamaican drama company. Wheeler's interest in music began at the age of 12, singing lovers rock with female reggae trio Brown Sugar, who had four number 1 singles in the specialist charts by the time she was 16. She moved on to form backing trio Afrodiziak, whose vocals were utilized live or on sessions with artists such as the Jam. Other backing duties for Elvis Costello, Phil Collins, Neneh Cherry and Aswad followed, and she earned a gold record for her liaison with Erasure in 1988. However, she became frustrated with the record business and effectively retired that year, taking a job in a library. The break refuelled her creative instincts, and when she returned as part of Soul II Soul in 1990 it was to her greatest success so far.

Though never part of the group proper, she won a Grammy for Best Vocal Performance on 'Back To Life', one of the two platinum singles on which she sang (the other being 'Keep On Movin''). She subsequently embarked on her solo career by signing with Orange Tree Productions, eventually securing a contract with RCA. Her distinctive voice was soon utilized not only for the blend of pop, soul and hip-hop that had characterized the music of her former employers, but also for blasting the white domination of the UK record industry. Her alienation was revealed in the title track of her debut album: 'Many moons ago, We were told the streets were paved with gold, So our people came by air and sea, To earn a money they could keep, Then fly back home, Sadly this never came to be, When we learned that we had just been invited, To clean up after the war'. Afterwards, her frustration with Britain saw her move to the USA for a second collection. This diverse set included a collaboration with Jam and Lewis on 'I Adore You', the production of former Soul II Soul man Jazzie B on 'Wonder', and a cover version of Jimi Hendrix's 'And The Wind Cries Mary'.

● ALBUMS: *UK Blak* (RCA 1990)★★★, *Blue (Is The Colour Of Pain)* (RCA 1991)★★★, *Beach Of The War Goddess* (1993)★★★.

WILLIAMS, GINGER

b. 1956, Jamaica, West Indies. Williams accompanied her family in 1962 when they emigrated to the UK. After she completed her education she joined the north London group Green Mango. They played in and around the Tottenham area and although they were a popular act, she felt disenchanted with gigging and in 1972 left the group. A year later she met producer Ronnie Williams, who took her to the studio to record her debut, 'I Can't Resist Your Tenderness', which, on its eventual release in 1974, was an instant hit. The song is an early example of the burgeoning style that was later categorized as lovers rock. The single surfaced on Count Shelly's newly formed Paradise label. Following the birth of her third child, Williams returned to the reggae chart with 'In My Heart There Is A Place'. She was nominated in the 1974 Black Music Poll as Best Newcomer and Female Artist. In 1975 she recorded with Dennis Harris ('Tenderness') and the following year with Bill Campbell ('Oh Baby Come Back'). Williams continued recording with Campbell in 1977, releasing 'I'll Still Love You', 'I'm Just A Girl', and a duet with the producer, 'The Vow'. Williams was unable to repeat the success of her debut, although she has enjoyed isolated hits over the years. Notable releases included 'Love Me Tonight' and 'Strange World'. In 1996 a compilation surfaced hailing Williams as 'the first lady of lovers rock', and included 'As Long As You Love Me' and 'Tenderly'.

● ALBUMS: *B & B Super Hits* (BB 1977)★★★.

● COMPILATIONS: *Greatest Hits* (Jet Star 1996)★★.

WILLIAMS, WILLIE

b. St. Ann's, Jamaica, West Indies. Williams is best known for his huge 'Armagideon Time' hit for Coxsone Dodd in 1979, one of the records that heralded the dancehall era, in which old Studio One rhythms were revitalized and garnished with new lyrics. In this case, the original Sound Dimension instrumental, 'Real Rock', was dusted down for Williams' lyrics. The Clash were sufficiently impressed to try their hand at the song. The rhythm has always been popular and there are still innumerable versions doing the rounds in the mid-90s. Williams started in the music business at the age of 14, recording 'Calling' for Dodd, and going on to run his own sound system, Tripletone, at the end of the decade. In the early 70s he ran his own label, Soul Sounds, producing the likes of Delroy Wilson and the Versatiles. He also sang alongside Freddie McGregor with the Generation Gap. Dodd issued a number of follow-up singles, including 'Addis Adaba' and 'Jah Righteous Plan', though they failed to make as much of an impression. He also recorded for Yabby You, cutting a variation on his big hit entitled 'Armagideon Man', but further success eluded him. However, he has continued to make records, some of which, such as 'Sweet Home' for Black Victory records, were extremely good, but he is still seeking the record that will re-establish his name in the marketplace.

● ALBUMS: *Messenger Man* (Jah Muzik 1980)★★★★, *Armagideon Time* (Studio One 1982)★★★, *Unity* (Blackstar 1987)★★★, *Natty With A Cause* (Jah Shaka 1992)★★★, *See Me* (Jah Shaka 1993)★★★.

WILSON, DELROY

b. 1948, Kingston, Jamaica, West Indies, d. 6 March 1995, Kingston, Jamaica, West Indies. Like Dennis Brown and Freddie McGregor, Delroy Wilson was barely out of short trousers when he recorded his debut single for Coxsone Dodd's Studio One label. His first hit, 'Joe Liges' (1963), was written by Lee Perry, who at the time was working as a talent-spotter, songwriter and singer for Dodd; the track was a lyrical attack on former Dodd employee and now rival, Prince Buster ('One hand wash the other, but you don't remember your brother, Joe Liges, Joe Liges, stop criticise'), set to a rollicking early ska rhythm. The record was so popular that his follow-up, 'Spirit In The Sky', another Perry-penned barb aimed at Buster, was actually credited to Joe Liges when it was released in the UK on the Bluebeat and Black Swan labels. Delroy went on to cut numerous records in the same vein for Dodd, including 'One Two Three', 'I Shall Not Remove', a duet with Slim Smith entiled 'Look Who Is Back Again', and the anti-Buster 'Prince Pharoah', notable for being the only occasion on which Dodd himself is heard on record, admonishing Buster in a coded, spoken outburst.

Wilson's voice broke just in time for the emergence of rocksteady in 1966, and his version of the Tams' 'Dancing Mood' of that year, one of the first rocksteady records, became a monstrous hit, alerting music fans to a new soul-styled crooner to match Alton Ellis. Throughout the rest of the decade, Wilson, still recording mainly for Studio One, increased his popularity with titles such as 'Riding For A Fall', another Tams cover version, 'Once Upon A Time', 'Run Run', 'Won't You Come Home', 'Never Conquer', 'True Believer', 'One One', 'I'm Not A King', 'Rain From The Skies' and 'Feel Good All Over', as well as covering the Temptations' 'Get Ready'. Leaving Studio One in 1969, Wilson sojourned briefly at Bunny Lee's camp, which resulted in a popular reading of the Isley Brothers' 'This Old Heart Of Mine' (1969), before moving to Sonia Pottinger's Tip Top Records, where he cut the excellent 'It Hurts' and a version of the Elgins' 'Put Yourself In My Place' (both 1969). He teamed up once more with Bunny Lee and enjoyed a huge Jamaican hit with the anthemic 'Better Must Come' (1971), which was so popular that it was adopted as a theme song by Michael Manley's PNP to increase their vote among 'sufferers', during that year's election campaign. In 1972 his success continued with 'Cool Operator', again for Lee, and throughout the next few years he maintained his position as one of reggae's best-loved singers, with songs such as 'Mash Up Illiteracy' and 'Pretty Girl' for Joe Gibbs, 'Love' for Gussie Clarke, 'Rascal Man' for Winston Niney' Holness, a cover version of the Four Tops' 'Ask The Lonely' for Harry J., 'It's A Shame' (a version of the Detroit Spinners song for Joseph 'Joe Joe' Hookim), 'Have Some Mercy' for A. Folder, and 'Keep On Running' for Prince Tony. In 1976 his career took a further step forward when he recorded a hugely popular version of Bob Marley's 'I'm Still Waiting' for Lloyd Charmers LTD label, later followed by the well-received Sarge, still regarded by most aficionados as his best set. The misnomered Greatest Hits was also issued by Prince Tony during this period. Further recordings towards the end of the decade, including 'All In This Thing Together', 'Halfway Up The Stairs' and 'Come In Heaven' for Gussie Clarke, did well, but Wilson's career floundered somewhat during the early part of the 80s, apart from a few sporadic sides, including the popular 'Let's Get Married' for London's Fashion Records. The digital age, however, provided a revival of fortunes with the massive 'Don't Put The Blame On Me'/'Stop Acting Strange' for King Jammy in 1987, and 'Ease Up', a cut of the famous 'Rumours' rhythm for Bunny Lee, as well as albums such as Looking For Love for Phil Pratt and Which Way Is Up, produced by Errol 'Flabba' Holt for Blue Mountain, since which time he has once again drifted into semi-retirement. Despite being one of the best singers Jamaica has ever produced, Wilson was rarely able to consolidate the success that came his way; nevertheless, he remained a much-loved and respected, but sorely underused and, outside of reggae circles, underrated performer.

● ALBUMS: I Shall Not Remove (Studio One c.1966)★★★★, Best Of Delroy Wilson aka Original 12 (c.1969)★★★, Good All Over (1969)★★★, Songs For I (1974)★★★, Sarge (1976)★★★★, Looking For Love (1986)★★★★, Which Way Is Up (Blue Mountain 1987)★★★★.
● COMPILATIONS: Greatest Hits (1976)★★★★, Collection (Striker Lee 1985)★★★★.

WINGLESS ANGELS

Wingless Angels were a group of five Nyahbingi Rastafarian drummers who were later joined by Sister Maureen. The five consisted of Justin Hinds, Winston 'Black Skull' Thomas, Bongo Neville, Bongo Locksey and Warren Williamson. Hinds is best remembered for the ska hit, 'Carry Go Bring Come', which he recorded with the Dominoes. He continued recording through to 1984, when he returned to his home-town of Steertown, Jamaica, opting for a rural lifestyle. Black Skull had previously worked with Talking Heads and Bad Brains, prior to savouring the tranquility of the Jamaican countryside. The remaining three members had only performed within the local community; Locksey was a drum-maker and fisherman, Williamson was admired for his skill in carving birds from coconut shells, while Neville was regarded as the keeper of the drums. The group played drum and chant sessions throughout the night, and this inspired local resident, Keith Richards of the Rolling Stones, to find out more about the band. Richards had acquired a villa high above Ocho Rios in 1972 when the band were recording *Goats Head Soup* in Kingston's Dynamic Recording Studio, and he befriended the group and eventually persuaded them to record in his villa. Sister Maureen had joined the band by this time, having been recruited after an impromptu performance with the group in a Steertown bar. At the beginning of the sessions, the assembly also featured the late Bongo Jackie, also known as Iron Lion. Richards' commitment to Jamaican music is widely acknowledged - he had previously recorded with Peter Tosh and Max Romeo. With the Angels, he contributed his subtle, complementary guitar licks over the African trinity of the funde, bass and kette drums. The rock 'n' roll hero known to the band as 'bredda Keith' also recruited Frankie Gavin, a notable Irish violinist, re-emphasizing his belief in the legend of an Afro-Celtic empathy. The sessions resulted in the Angels' debut album, which featured 'Roll Jordan Roll', 'Keyman', 'Bright Soul', 'I Write My Name' and, inspired by Iron Lion's untimely demise, 'Enjoy Yourself.'

● ALBUMS: *Wingless Angels* (Island Jamaica 1997)★★★★.

WONDER, WAYNE

b. Von Wayne Charles, *c.*1972, Kingston, Jamaica, West Indies. Wonder's first reggae recordings appeared in the late 80s, when he was working with producer Lloyd Dennis. 'You Me And She' was followed by 'Night And Day', produced by Soljie. In 1991 the beautifully crafted 'Don't Take It Personal' was also produced by Soljie. Wonder's sweet singing style was soon employed by a number of producers in Jamaica, but his most prolific output came at the Penthouse studio with Donovan Germain and Dave Kelly. In 1991 he released 'I'm Only Human' and 'Baby You And I', both of which enhanced his appeal among women. His cover version of Delroy Wilson's 'I Don't Know Why' as 'Movie Star' was a classic. The song also provided Buju Banton with a hit when he rode the tune for 'Bonafide Love'. Another cover version found Wonder singing over a remake of a King

Jammy's rhythm, 'Run Down The World', for his interpretation of En Vogue's 'Hold On'. A tour of the UK was arranged in 1992 featuring the Penthouse crew, including Wonder alongside Marcia Griffiths, Tony Rebel and Buju Banton. With Tony Rebel, Wonder's sweet vocals graced the enduring 'Smaddy Pickney', a toast over 'I'm Only Human' and 'Cross Over The Bridge'. Buju Banton had secured a contract with the Stateside Mercury label and Wonder provided the singing vocals on 'Searching' and 'Commitment', as well as composing the tunes with Buju. In 1994 he toured again with Buju as part of the Penthouse Showcase. By 1995 Wonder had moved on to recording with other producers and enjoyed combination hits with Don Yute ('Sensi Ride') and Buccaneer ('Trust'). He was also a featured vocalist with King Jammy's when he resurrected the Sleng Teng Rhythm, appearing on the compilation *Sleng Teng Extravaganza '95*.

● ALBUMS: with Sanchez *Penthouse Presents (Volume One & Two)* (Penthouse 1990/91)★★★, *Wayne Wonder* (VP 1991)★★★, *Don't Have To* (Penthouse 1991)★★, *One More Chance* (World 1992)★★★, *All Original Bombshell* (Penthouse 1996)★★★.

● COMPILATIONS: *The Collection* (Pickout 1997)★★★.

WRIGHT, WINSTON

b. 1944, d. 1993. Wright's name is largely unknown outside of the committed reggae fraternity, but the sound of his organ-playing is familiar to anyone who has ever had more than a passing acquaintance with the music. Winston emerged on the Kingston music scene in the mid-60s and began playing sessions in the rock-steady era, initially for Duke Reid, but as his work became better known, he was in constant demand from many other top producers. His mastery of, and feel for, the Hammond organ earned him an integral role in Tommy McCook's Supersonics - Duke Reid's house band. He later hit the UK charts in 1969 as one of Harry J.'s All Stars with 'Liquidator', and also made some of his finest recordings that same year with Clancy Eccles' Dynamites. Throughout the 70s he worked as part of the Dynamic Sounds nucleus of musicians, and from 1975 onwards was a member of Toots And The Maytals' touring band. He still continued his session work for

Kingston's producers when he was at home 'resting', and his contributions to many classic 70s recordings were as uncredited and anonymous as his 60s output. More recently, he returned to Dynamic Sounds where he acted as arranger, mixer and keyboard player. His tragic and untimely death in 1993 robbed the reggae world of one of its greatest unsung talents.

● ALBUMS: with the Dynamites *Fire Corner* (Trojan/Clandisc 1969)★★★★, with the Harry J All Stars *Liquidator* (Trojan 1970)★★★★, with the Dynamites *Herbsman* (Trojan/Clandisc 1970)★★★, *Grass Roots* (Third World 1976)★★★★, *Jump The Fence* (Third World 1976)★★★★.

YABBY YOU

b. Vivian Jackson, 1950, Kingston, Jamaica, West Indies. Yabby acquired his nickname from the drawn-out, chanting refrain on his 1972 debut single, 'Conquering Lion': 'Be You, Yabby Yabby You'. Despite courting controversy in his repudiation of Rastafarian godhead Haile Selassie, in favour of a personalized form of Christianity, his output throughout the 70s and early 80s nonetheless rarely deviated far from the orthodox Rastafarianism typically expressed at the time. As leader of the Prophets (additional personnel at various times included Alrick Forbes, Dada Smith, Bobby Melody and the Ralph Brothers), Yabby recorded a remarkable series of roots reggae classics, including 'Jah Vengeance', 'Run Come Rally', 'Love Thy Neighbours', 'Valley Of Jehosaphat', 'Judgement On The Land', 'Fire In Kingston', 'Chant Down Babylon' and many others, mostly appearing on his own Vivian Jackson and Prophets labels in Jamaica.

With the release of *Ramadam* in 1975, the UK variation of the Jamaican-issued *Conquering Lion* (several tracks were different), Yabby swiftly acquired cult status in the UK, his name becoming synonymous with reggae music of a particularly deep, spiritual nature. The subsequent King Tubby dub albums (*Prophecy Of Dub*, *King Tubby Meets Vivian Jackson*, *Beware Dub*) are rightly regarded as classics. Jackson also gained a reputation as a producer of other artists, including DJs Trinity, Jah Stitch, Dillinger, Prince Pompado, Tapper Zukie and Clint Eastwood, and singers Wayne Wade, Junior Brown, Willie Williams, Patrick Andy, Tony Tuff and Michael Prophet.

In the 80s he retreated from the music business as his health deteriorated, though he made something of a comeback in the early 90s with some new productions and the reappearance of many of his classic singles and albums, re-pressed from the original stampers to cater for the large European collectors' market.

● ALBUMS: *Conquering Lion* aka *Ramadam* (Prophet 1975)★★★★, *King Tubby's Prophecy Of Dub* (Prophet 1976)★★★★, *King Tubby Meets Vivian Jackson* aka *Chant Down Babylon* and *Walls Of Jerusalem* (Prophet 1976)★★★★, *Deliver Me From My Enemies* (Prophet 1977)★★★, *Beware Dub* (Grove Music 1978)★★★, *Jah Jah Way* (Island 1980)★★★, *One Love, One Heart* (Shanachie 1983)★★★, *Fleeing From The City* (Shanachie 1988)★★★.

● COMPILATIONS: *Yabby You Collection* (Greensleeves 1984)★★★, *Jesus Dread 1972 - 1977* (Blood & Fire 1997)★★★.

YARD TAPES

Also known as 'Sound Tapes', yard tapes are simply live recordings of reggae sound systems in action. They first became popular around 1981, as dancehall began to exert a huge influence over the reggae audience. Yard tapes offered an opportunity to hear the top Jamaican sounds in action, with reggae stars performing live over dub plates, often showcasing material that would not be available on record for months, if ever. Although sometimes suffering from poor sound quality, their deficiencies were more than compensated for by the sense of occasion and the sheer excitement of hearing what constituted reggae in its natural habitat: the dancehall. 'Yard' means 'home' in Jamaican slang, i.e., Jamaica. Yard tapes remain a unique, perennially popular, and exclusively reggae phenomenon to this day.

YELLOWMAN

b. Winston Foster, 1959, Kingston, Jamaica, West Indies. Yellowman was the DJing sensation of the early 80s and he achieved this status with a fair amount of talent and inventive and amusing lyrics. He built his early career around the fact that he was an albino and his success has to be viewed within its initial Jamaican context. The albino or 'dundus' is virtually an outcast in Jamaican society and Foster's early years were incredibly difficult. Against all the odds, he used this background to his advantage and, like King Stitt, who had previously traded on his physical deformities, Foster paraded himself in the Kingston dancehalls as 'Yellowman', a DJ with endless lyrics about how sexy, attractive and appealing he was to the opposite sex. Within a matter of months, he went from social pariah to headlining act at Jamaican stage shows and his popularity rocketed; the irony of his act was not lost on his audiences. His records were both witty and relevant - 'Soldier Take Over' being a fine example - and he was the first to release a live album - not of a stage show but recorded live on a sound system - *Live At Aces*, which proved hugely successful and was widely imitated. It captured him at the height of his powers and in full control of his 'fans'; none of the excitement is lost in the transition from dancehall to record. Yellowman's records sold well and he toured the USA and UK to ecstatic crowds - his first sell-out London shows caused traffic jams and road-blocks around the venue. It seemed that he could do no wrong, and even his version of 'I'm Getting Married In The Morning' sold well. He was soon signed to a major contract with CBS Records and was 'King Yellow' to everyone in the reggae business. However, this did not last, and by the mid-80s it had become difficult to sell his records to the fickle reggae market. Nevertheless, by this time he had been adopted by 'pop' audiences all over the world as a novelty act and while he has never become a major star, he is still very popular and his records sell in vast quantities in many countries. He has released more records than a great many other reggae acts - no mean feat in a business dominated by excess. Having become both rich and successful through his DJing work, it is mainly his ability to laugh at himself and encourage others to share the joke that has endeared him to so many.

● ALBUMS: *Them A Mad Over Me* (J&L 1981)★★★, *Mr Yellowman* (Greensleeves 1982)★★★, *Bad Boy Skanking* (Greensleeves 1982)★★★, *Yellowman Has Arrived With Toyan* (Joe Gibbs 1982)★, *Live At Sunsplash* (Sunsplash 1982)★★★, with Purple Man, Sister Nancy *The Yellow, The Purple, And The Nancy* (Greensleeves 1983)★★★★, *Divorced* (Burning Sounds 1983)★★, *Zungguzungguguzungguengg* (Greensleeves 1983)★★, *King Yellowman* (Columbia 1984)★★, *Nobody Move, Nobody Get Hurt* (Greensleeves 1984)★★, with Josey Wales *Two Giants Clash* (Greensleeves 1984)★★★★, with Charlie Chaplin *Slackness Vs Pure Culture*

(Arrival 1984)★★★★, *Galong Galong Galong*
(Greensleeves 1985)★★, *Going To The Chapel*
(Greensleeves 1986)★★, *Rambo* (Moving Target
1986)★★★, *Yellow Like Cheese* (RAS 1987)★★,
Don't Burn It Down (Shanachie/Greensleeves
1987)★★, *Blueberry Hill* (Greensleeves/Rohit
1987)★★★, with General Trees *A Reggae
Calypso Encounter* (Rohit 1987)★★, *King Of The
Dancehall* (Rohit 1988)★★, with Charlie
Chaplin *The Negril Chill* (ROIR 1988)★★★,
Sings The Blues (Rohit 1988)★★, *Rides Again*
(RAS 1988)★★★, *One In A Million* (Shanachie
1988)★★, *Badness* (La/Unicorn 1990)★★★,
Thief (Mixing Lab 1990)★★, *Party* (RAS
1991)★★★, *Reggae On The Move* (RAS
1992)★★, *Live In England* (Greensleeves
1992)★★, *In Bed With Yellowman* (1993)★★,
Freedom Of Speech (Ras 1997)★★★.
● COMPILATIONS: *20 Super Hits* (Sonic Sounds
1990)★★★★.
● VIDEOS: *Raw And Rough (Live At Dollars
Lawn)* (Jetstar 1989).

YVAD

b. Kevin Davy. It was one of Bob Marley's wishes
to help young musicians to achieve their goals,
and at his Tuff Gong Studios a number of performers were supported, including Tyrone
Taylor, Junior Tucker, Diana King, Nadine
Sutherland and one of the more recent artists,
Yvad. His debut single, 'We Need Love', surfaced
through the Tuff Gong label but did not make
any impression on the charts. The RAS label in
Washington, USA, were suitably impressed and
signed the singer for the release of *Young Gifted
And Dread*. He has also enjoyed media exposure
on American television, including video promotion on MTV and Black Entertainment
Television. To promote the album he was
selected to support fellow RAS artists Israel
Vibration on their US tour.
● ALBUMS: *Young Gifted And Dread* (RAS
1996)★★★.

ZAP POW

Zap Pow were formed in the early 70s. The
group consisted of some of the finest musicians
in Jamaica and included Max Edwards (drums,
vocals), Mike Williams (bass, vocals), Dwight
Pinkney (guitar, vocals) and Beres Hammond
(lead vocals); the horn section featured Glen
DaCosta (tenor saxophone), Joe McCormack
(trombone) and David Madden (trumpet,
vocals). In 1971 they recorded their debut,
'Mystic Mood', followed by the popular
'Breaking Down The Barriers', 'Nice Nice Time'
and the internationally successful 'This Is
Reggae Music'. These hits featured on an album
released only in Jamaica, assuring their local
popularity. In 1976 the group recorded 'Jungle
Beat' and 'Sweet Loving Love' at Harry J.'s and
Dynamic studios. *Zap Pow Now* featured
unusual packaging, with the outer sleeve resem-
bling a book of matches, and the album secured
healthy sales within the reggae market and
topped the UK chart. The success inspired
Trojan Records to re-release their debut with the
addition of 'Money', 'Crazy Woman', 'Wild
Honey' and a version of Harold Melvin And The
Bluenotes' 'If You Don't Know Me By Now'. The
label released the latter as a single, which provided a minor hit. By 1980 Hammond had left
the group to pursue a successful solo career.
Pinkney's guitar skills were utilized in
numerous sessions for artists including Roots
Radics, and at Penthouse Studios for producer
Donovan Germain. Edwards pursued a solo
career, almost crossing over into pop territory
with the release of 'Rockers Arena'. Williams
became known as Mikey Zap Pow, enjoying a hit
with 'Sunshine People', and pursued a career in
journalism, with particular emphasis on reggae.
The horn section was featured on many sessions, including some for Bob Marley And The
Wailers. They also toured individually supporting Sly And Robbie's Taxi Gang and Lloyd

Parks' We The People Band. Madden released a solo album, *David ... Going Bananas*, which featured his vocals and trumpet-playing on tracks that included 'Musical Message' and a return to 'Mystic Mood'. The album was followed by *The Reggae Trumpetaa*, while fellow horn player DaCosta released *Mind Blowing Melody*.

● ALBUMS: *Zap Pow Now* (Vulcan 1976)★★★, *Revolution* (Trojan 1976)★★★.

ZEPHANIAH, BENJAMIN

b. Benjamin Obadiah Iqbal Zephaniah, 1958, Handsworth, Birmingham, England. Zephaniah states that he cannot remember a time when he was not creating poetry, inspired primarily by the music and lyricists of Jamaica. His first performance was in a church in 1968, and by the age of 15 he had established a following in his home-town. In 1980 he moved to London, where his first book of poetry, *Pen Rhythm*, was published, and proved so successful that it ran to three editions. Although an eminent writer, it was his notoriety as a dub poet that brought him to prominence. The 1983 release of *Dub Ranting* led to tracks being played at rallies against sus laws, unemployment, homelessness and far-right politics. His campaign to introduce poetry to the masses was boosted by the release of *Rasta*, which prompted media interest and television appearances. The album topped the Yugoslavian pop chart and featured the Wailers, who had not played alongside any performer since the death of Bob Marley. The collaboration featured a tribute to Nelson Mandela, which led to an introductory meeting following the South African president's eventual release from prison. In 1990 he recorded *Us And Dem* and decided to promote the album outside the normal circuit, playing to audiences in Zimbabwe, India, Pakistan, Columbia and South Africa, where the oral tradition is still strong. In 1991 over a 22-day period he performed to an audience on every continent of the globe. In 1996 Zephaniah worked with children in South Africa at the behest of Nelson Mandela and hosted the president's Two Nations Concert at London's Royal Albert Hall. His musical collaborations include work with the Ariwa Sounds posse, Acid Jazz, Bomb The Bass and Sinead O'Connor.

● ALBUMS: *Dub Ranting* (Upright 1983)★★★★, *Rasta* (Upright/Helidon 1987)★★★, *Us And Dem* (Mango/Island 1990)★★★, *Back To Roots* (Acid Jazz 1995)★★, *Hazardous Dub* (Acid Jazz 1996)★★★, *Overstanding* (57 Productions 1996)★★, *Reggae Head* (57 Productions 1997)★★.

ZERO, EARL

b. Earl Anthony Jackson, 1952, Greenwich Town, West Kingston, Jamaica, West Indies. Zero began his recording career with Bunny Lee, who produced his self-penned 'None Shall Escape The Judgement'. The song was given to Johnny Clarke, who had previously enjoyed hits with producer Rupie Edwards. While Clarke's career took off, Zero had to wait until 1975 when, with singer/producer Al Campbell, 'Righteous Works' became a substantial hit. Guided by Tommy Cowan of Talent Corporation, he recorded 'Please Officer' and the legendary 'City Of The Weak Heart'. The song was covered with a slight variation to the lyrics by fellow Talent Corporation recording star Jacob Miller, and was included on the release of his album *Killer Miller*.

By 1976 Zero had joined Bertram Brown's Freedom Sounds for the release of 'Get Happy' and was reunited with Al Campbell for 'Heart Desire'. In the following years, his output remained steady: 'Visions Of Love', 'Pure And Clean', 'Shackles And Chains', 'Jah Guide' and 'Blackbird' earned him cult status. In 1979 he recorded with the Soul Syndicate, featuring Carlton 'Santa' Davis, George 'Fully' Fullwood, Tony Chin and Earl 'Chinna' Smith, who also produced the session. In the UK, 'City Of The Weakheart' was released as 'City Of The Wicked' as a discomix through Greensleeves Records. The songs were featured on *Visions Of Love*, which surfaced in 1980 along with remakes of his earlier recordings, including 'None Shall Escape The Judgement', 'Shackles And Chains', 'I No Lie' and 'Please Officer'.

● ALBUMS: *Visions Of Love* (Epiphany 1980)★★★, *In The Right Way* (Student/Ital 1981)★★, *Only Jah Can Ease The Pressure* (White Label 1990)★★★.

● COMPILATIONS: with various artists *Ethiopian Kings* (RRR 1981)★★★.

ZION TRAIN

UK's Zion Train formed in 1990 and have proved to be innovators in the revolutionary new wave of dub. While many other groups preferred a revivalist stance, the north London-based co-operative have established an enviable reputation. The cross-cultural line-up consists of Molora (vocals, percussion), Neil (DJ, beats, bass), Colin C (melodica), Dave Hake (trumpet, also part of the Tassilli Players) and Chris Hetter (trombone). Influenced by Jah Shaka, Lee Perry and other dub masters, the group's dub/roots dance equation was first unveiled on the sequential singles 'Power One' and 'Power Two'. As well as recording dub sounds, the collective also ran the Bass Odyssey club and their own sound system, produced their own magazine, *The Wobbler*, and released the first promotional dub video, *Get Ready*, and a CD-ROM to accompany *Homegrown Fantasy*, their debut release for China Records. One of their most effective and highly regarded works was the 'Follow Like Wolves' single, a fertile cross between dub and house music, with samples drawn from the Specials' back-catalogue. In a departure from usual reggae practice, they subsequently instigated the (no copyright) Soundpool, allowing free sampling, and thus dispensing with the need for acquisitive lawyers. They have also worked with Junior Reid, Maxi Priest, Studio One veteran Devon Russell and the Dub Syndicate, as well as Indian tabla players and Brazilian drummers. In 1996 the group ventured into the ambient/house/acid dub territory and performed with artists including the Shamen, New Model Army and Gary Clail, and instigated the re-formation of Ruts DC for a collaboration on a live session for BBC Radio. The release of *Grow Together* featured Dave Ruffy, the Ruts' drummer, and an acid revival of the group's 1979 hit 'Babylon's Burning'. That single was followed by 'Rise', with which they achieved their first exposure on national daytime radio. Extensive touring and major festival appearances have secured the band international popularity. They later released 'Stand Up And Fight', featuring Kate Cameron on lead vocals and a 19-minute soulful reggae remix.

● ALBUMS: *Passage To Indica* (Zion 1994)★★★★, *Great Sporting Moments In Dub* (Zion 1994)★★★, *Natural Wonders Of The World* (Universal Egg 1994)★★★, *Siren* (Universal Egg 1995)★★★, *Homegrown Fantasy* (China 1995)★★★, *Grow Together* (China 1996)★★★★, *Single Minded And Alive* (China 1997)★★★.

● COMPILATIONS: *Forward Roots* cassette only (Zion 1993).

ZUKIE, TAPPER

b. David Sinclair, Jamaica, West Indies. Zukie began as a DJ in his early teens, influenced by U-Roy and Dennis Alcapone. In order to curb his youthful tendencies towards trouble, his mother sent him to England in 1973, where producer Bunny Lee organized some live shows and recording sessions under the aegis of the UK-based entrepreneur Larry Lawrence, for whom he cut his debut, 'Jump And Twist'. He also recorded material for Clem Bushay that later emerged as *Man A Warrior*. On his return to Jamaica he again worked for Bunny Lee, though Zukie's ambitions to become as famous as U-Roy led him to record 'Judge I Oh Lord' for Lloydie Slim, and 'Natty Dread Don't Cry' for Lee. Zukie's frustration at Bunny Lee's indifference eventually resulted in an altercation with the producer. The police were called, but their differences were settled when Lee offered him some rhythms on which he could DJ himself. These, and others Zukie obtained from Joseph 'Joe Joe' Hookim, were recorded in a spare hour at King Tubby's studio, and eventually issued as *MPLA* in 1976.

In 1975 he returned to the UK to find that he had gained something of a cult following owing to the belated popularity of *Man A Warrior*. An arrangement with Klik Records saw the release of 'MPLA' as a single, which met with immediate success, and Klik persuaded Zukie to let them release the whole album, which finally established his name in the higher echelons of DJs. Other recordings dating from the same period included a batch of singles for Yabby You, including 'Don't Get Crazy' and 'Natty Dread On The Mountain Top'. While in the UK, he appeared alongside new-wave heroine Patti Smith, who proved to be an admirer of *Man A Warrior*. The album was later reissued on Smith's and partner Lenny Kaye's Mer label, while Smith later contributed sleeve-notes to *Man From Bosrah*. Zukie also produced a number of artists during this period for his own

Stars label, including Junior Ross and The Spear ('Babylon Fall', 'Judgement Time'), Prince Alla ('Bosrah', 'Daniel' and 'Heaven Is My Roof') and one all-time classic for Horace Andy, 'Natty Dread A Weh She Want'. In addition, he released two dub albums, *Escape From Hell* and *Tapper Zukie In Dub*. His protégés, Knowledge, were signed to A&M Records but subsequently dropped. His fortunes improved further with the release of *Peace In The Ghetto* and *Tapper Roots*, as well as popular singles such as 'She Want A Phensic' and his first big Jamaican hit, 'Oh Lord'. Returning to Jamaica, Zukie became active again in his local community. Largely silent during the late 80s, he has returned with a vengeance in the 90s, producing huge hits for stars such as Dennis Brown and Beres Hammond, and opening his own compact disc centre on Eastwood Park Road in Kingston in 1994.

● ALBUMS: *Man A Warrior* (Klik 1975)★★★★, *MPLA* (Klik 1976)★★, *Man From Bosrah* (Stars 1977)★★, *Escape From Hell* (Stars 1977)★★, *Tapper Zukie In Dub* (Stars 1977)★★★, *Peace In The Ghetto* (Stars 1978)★★★★, *Tapper Roots* (Stars/Front Line 1978)★★★, *People Are You Ready?* (Stars 1983)★★★, *Raggamuffin* (World Enterprise 1986)★★★.

RECOMMENDED LISTENING

Abyssinians	*Forward On To Zion*
Abyssinians	*Satta Massa Gana*
Alcapone, Dennis	*Forever Version*
Alcapone, Dennis	*My Voice Is Insured For Half A Million Dollars*
Alphonso, Roland	*Best Of*
Alphonso, Roland	*King Of Sax*
Andy, Bob	*Song Book*
Andy, Horace	*Skylarking*
Banton, Buju	*Inna Heights*
Banton, Buju	*Til Shiloh*
Beenie Man	*Maestro*
Big Youth	*Everyday Skank*
Big Youth	*Dread Locks Dread*
Big Youth	*Natty Cultural Dread*
Big Youth	*Screaming Target*
Black Uhuru	*Showcase*
Black Uhuru	*Sinsemilla*
Black Uhuru	*Vital Selection*
Bounty Killer	*Ghetto Gramma*
Brooks, Cedric 'Im'	*Flash Forward*
Brown, Dennis	*Brown Sugar*
Brown, Dennis	*Just Dennis*
Brown, Dennis	*Love Has Found Its Way*
Brown, Dennis	*Money In My Pocket*
Brown, Dennis	*Visions*
Brown, Dennis	*Wolf And Leopards*
Brown, Glen, And Others	*Boat To Progress*
Brown, Glen, And Others	*Check The Winner*
Brown, Glen, And Others	*Dubble Attack*
Burning Spear	*Hail H.I.M.*
Burning Spear	*Marcus Children* aka *Social Living*
Burning Spear	*Marcus Garvey*
Burning Spear	*Rocking Time*
Burning Spear	*Studio One Presents*
Carlton And His Shoes	*Love Me Forever*
Chin-Loy, Herman	*Aquarius Dub*
Clarendonians	*Best Of*
Congos	*Heart Of The Congos*
Count Ossie & The Mystic Revelation Of Rastafari	*Grounation*

Culture	*Two Sevens Clash*
Daley, Lloyd 'Matador' (Collection)	*Scandal*
Daley, Lloyd 'Matador' (Collection)	*Way Back When*
Dekker, Desmond	*The Original Reggae Hit Sound*
Dekker, Desmond	*This Is Desmond Dekker*
Dillinger	*CB 200*
Dodd, Coxsone (Studio One Collection)	*All Star Top Hits*
Dodd, Coxsone (Studio One Collection)	*Pirates Choice*
Dodd, Coxsone (Studio One Dub)	*Dub Store Special*
Dodd, Coxsone (Studio One Dub)	*Hi Fashion Dub Top Ten*
Dr. Alimantado	*Best Dressed Chicken In Town*
Dread, Mikey	*African Anthem*
Drummond, Don	*Best Of*
Drummond, Don	*Greatest Hits*
Drummond, Don	*Memorial Album*
Eccles, Clancy, And Friends	*Fatty Fatty*
Edwards, Rupie, And Friends	*Yahama Skank* aka *Let There Be Version*
Ellis, Alton	*Mr Soul Of Jamaica*
Ellis, Alton	*Sings Rock And Soul*
Ellis, Alton	*Sunday Coming*
Ellis, Alton	*The Best Of*
Frazer, Dean	*Big Bad Sax*
Gibbon, Leroy	*Four Season Lover*
Gibbs, Joe	*African Dub Almighty Chapters 1, 2 & 3*
Gibbs, Joe, And Friends	*The Reggae Train*
Gladiators	*Trenchtown Mix Up*
Heptones	*Heptones*
Heptones	*On Top*
Hudson, Keith	*Flesh Of My Skin*
Hudson, Keith	*Pick A Dub*
Hudson, Keith	*Rasta Communication*
Hudson, Keith, And Friends	*Studio Kinda Cloudy*
I. Roy	*Hell And Sorrow*
I. Roy	*Presenting I Roy*
Impact All Stars	*Java Java Dub*
Isaacs, Gregory	*Best Of...Vols. 1 & 2*
Isaacs, Gregory	*Cool Ruler*
Isaacs, Gregory	*Extra Classic*
Isaacs, Gregory	*Lovers Rock* (*Lonely Lover* and *More Gregory*)
Isaacs, Gregory	*Soon Forward*
Isaacs, Gregory	*Warning*
Israel Vibration	*The Same Song*
Kamoze, Ini	*Ini Kamoze*
Keith And Tex	*Stop That Train*
Kelly, Pat	*Pat Kelly Sings*
King Tubby	*Creation Of Dub*
Kong, Lelsie (Beverleys Collection)	*King Kong*
Kong, Leslie (Beverleys Collection)	*The Best Of Beverleys*
Locks, Fred	*Black Star Liners*
Macka B	*Sign Of The Times*
Marley, Bob, And The Wailers	*African Herbsman*

Marley, Bob, And The Wailers	*All The Hits*
Marley, Bob, And The Wailers	*Best Of (Studio One)*
Marley, Bob, And The Wailers	*Burnin'*
Marley, Bob, And The Wailers	*Catch A Fire*
Marley, Bob, And The Wailers	*Exodus*
Marley, Bob, And The Wailers	*Live*
Marley, Bob, And The Wailers	*Natty Dread*
Marley, Bob, And The Wailers	*Songs Of Freedom*
Marley, Bob, And The Wailers	*Soul Revolution 1 & 2*
Marley, Bob, And The Wailers	*Survival*
Marley, Bob, And The Wailers	*Upsetter Record Shop Part 2*
Marley, Bob, And The Wailers	*Wailing Wailers*
Maytals	*Do The Reggae*
Maytals	*From The Roots*
McGregor, Freddie	*Bobby Babylon*
McKay, Freddie	*Picture On The Wall*
Mighty Diamonds	*Changes*
Mighty Diamonds	*Right Time/I Need A Roof*
Minott, Sugar	*Back Roots*
Minott, Sugar	*Live Loving*
Minott, Sugar	*Showcase*
Mittoo, Jackie	*Macka Fat*
Mutabaruka	*Check It*
Niney And Friends	*Blood And Fire*
Observer All Stars	*Dubbing With The Observer*
Osbourne, Johnny	*Truths & Rights*
Pablo, Augustus (Rockers Collection)	*Classic Rockers 2*
Pablo, Augustus (Rockers Collection)	*Original Rockers*
Pablo, Augustus	*East Of The River Nile*
Pablo, Augustus	*King Tubby Meets Rockers Uptown*
Pablo, Augustus	*This Is*
Paragons	*On The Beach*
Paul, Frankie	*Sara*
Prince Buster	*Fabulous Greatest Hits*
Prince Jazzbo	*Choice Of Version*
Radway, Jimmy	*Micron Dub*
Ranks, Shabba	*Rapping With The Ladies*
Red Rat	*Oh No It's ...*
Reid, Duke (Treasure Isle Collection)	*Hottest Hits Vols. 1 & 2*
Revolutionaries	*Vital Dub Well Charge*
Royal Rasses	*Humanity*
Royals	*Pick Up The Pieces*
Scientist	*Scientist Meets The Space Invaders*
Sherman, Bim	*Love Forever/Danger*
Sizzla	*Black Woman & Child*
Skatalites	*Ska Authentic*
Smith, Slim	*Early Days*
Techniques	*Classics*
Tella, Sylvia	*Spell*
Tenor Saw	*Fever*
Tetrack	*Let's Get Started*

Trinity Vs Dillinger	*Clash*
Twinkle Brothers	*Countrymen*
U-Roy	*Dread Inna Babylon*
U-Roy	*Version Galore - Sound Of Now*
Uniques	*Early Days*
Upsetter And Friends	*Excaliburman*
Upsetter And Friends	*Open The Gate*
Upsetter And Friends	*Public Jestering*
Upsetter And Friends	*The Upsetter Collection*
Upsetters	*Blackboard Jungle Dub*
Upsetters	*Megaton Dub 2*
Upsetters	*Super Ape*
Various (Ska)	*Intensified*
Various (Ska)	*More Intensified*
Various (Ska)	*Scattered Lights*
Various (Ska)	*Ska Boo Da Ba*
Various (Ska)	*Ska Strictly For You*
Various	*A DeeJay Explosion Inna Dance Hall Style*
Various	*Greensleeves Sampler 1 - 17*
Various	*King Tubby Soundclash*
Various	*Knotty Vision*
Various	*Monkey Business*
Various	*Rebel Music*
Various	*Reggae Hits Vols. 1 - 22*
Various	*Sleng Teng Extravaganza*
Various	*Tougher Than Tough*
Wailer, Bunny	*Blackheart Man*
Wailer, Bunny	*Dub D'sco*
Wailer, Bunny	*Sings The Wailers*
Wailing Souls	*Presenting*
Wailing Souls	*Wild Suspense*
Wilson, Delroy	*Feel Good All Over*
Wilson, Delroy	*Original 12 (The Best Of)*
Yabby You And The Prophets	*Conquering Lion*
Yabby You And The Prophets	*King Tubbys Prophecy Of Dub*
Yellowman	*Galong, Galong, Galong*
Yellowman	*Mr Yellowman*
Zion Train	*Single Minded & Alive*

Compiled from lists drawn up by Harry Hawkes, Paul Cooteur, Lol Bell-Brown and Salsri Nyah.

BIBLIOGRAPHY/SOURCES

BOOKS

General Reference

Black Music In Britain - Essays On The Afro-Asian Contribution To Popular Music, ed. Paul Oliver (Open University Press 1990).

Deep Roots Music, Howard Johnson & Jim Pines (Proteus/Channel Four 1982).
The book to accompany Channel Four's groundbreaking *Deep Roots Music* series.

Jah Music - The Evolution Of The Popular Jamaican Song, Sebastian Clarke (Heinemann Educational Books 1980).
An in-depth analysis of the music and artists following on from reggae's big overground break in the 70s.

The Pop Process, Richard Mabey (Hutchinson Educational 1969).
Mainly concerns pop music but there is some particularly perceptive analysis on the influence of ska on pop music and dance in the UK.

Reggae, A People's Music, Rolston Kallyndyr & Henderson Dalrymple (Carib Arawak Publications 1976).
The first (slim) book ever written about the music.

Reggae Bloodlines - In Search Of The Music & Culture Of Jamaica, Stephen Davis & Peter Simon (Anchor Press Doubleday 1977).
Excellent pictures but the text is often misleading and misrepresentative.

Reggae International, Stephen Davis & Peter Simon (Thames & Hudson 1983).
A much-improved update of *Reggae Bloodlines* with contributions from writers such as Carl Gayle. The presentation is faultless.

Reggae Island - Jamaican Music In The Digital Age, Brian Jahn & Tom Weber (Kingston Publishers Ltd. 1992).
A strictly up-to-date look at the 90s music scene in Jamaica with fine photographs and interviews with most of the current top performers.

Rock File, Charlie Gillett (First Pictorial Presentations New English Library 1972).
Interesting for 'Skins Rule' by Pete Fowler and the confused (and confusing) 'Johnny Cool & The

Isle of Sirens' by one Johnny Copasetic, two early looks at the phenomenon.

Rock File 2, Charlie Gillett (Panther 1974).
Worthy of inclusion for 'Are You Ready For Rude & Rough Reggae' by Carl Gayle.

The Rock Primer, ed. John Collis (Penguin 1980).
Well worthwhile for the 'reggae' section by Nick Kimberley - essential singles and albums.

Biographies

Bob Marley

Inevitably, Bob Marley has had more books written about his career than the rest of reggae's musicians put together (which is hardly his fault) and, because of the very nature of his talent and fame, many are very, very good. How could they fail with the subject matter?

Bob Marley - The Roots Of Reggae, Cathy McKnight & John Tobler (Star 1977).
A slim paperback which makes up in enthusiasm what it lacks in knowledge and background: 'Reggae is power and Marley knows it!'

Bob Marley - Soul Rebel - Natural Mystic, Adrian Boot & Vivien Goldman (Eel Pie/Hutchinson 1981).
Lovely photographs and an interesting text.

Catch A Fire - The Life Of Bob Marley, Timothy White (Elmtree Books 1983). Revised and updated as: *Catch A Fire - The Life Of Bob Marley*, Timothy White (Omnibus Press 1991).
Highly entertaining account concentrating on the early years of Bob Marley's career.

Bob Marley, Stephen Davis (Arthur Baker 1983). Revised and updated as: *Bob Marley - Conquering Lion Of Reggae*, Stephen Davis (Plexus 1993).
A more objective overview of Bob Marley's career.

Bob Marley - Rebel With A Cause, Dennis Morris (DMMP Publications 1986).
Large format picture book. The photographs are beautiful.

Bob Marley - Reggae King Of The World, Malika Lee Whitney & Dermot Hussey (Plexus/Kingston Publishers Ltd 1984).
Large format with superb rare photographs. Written from a Jamaican point of view.

Bob Marley - The Illustrated Discography/Biography, Observer Station (Omnibus Press 1985).
A run-down on some of the vast recorded output of Bob Marley & The Wailers.

Bob Marley In His Own Words, Ian McCann (Omnibus Press 1993).
Exactly what it says - a selection of quotes (painstakingly compiled) from Bob Marley on a wide range of subjects.

Bob Marley: Songs Of Freedom - An Illustrated Song Book, (Hal Leonard/Polygram Music Publishing 1992).

Specialist Publishers

Black Star & Muzik Tree have put together some of the best books ever written about reggae music, researched and written *by* fans of the music *for* fans of the music. Sometimes a little too esoteric for the man in the street, but more often 100% essential.

Rhythm Wise, Ray Hurford (Muzik Tree/Black Star 1989).
Rhythm Wise Two, Jean Scrivener (Black Star 1990).
Rhythm Wise Three, Jean Scrivener (Black Star 1991).
Details of many of the rhythms (or backing tracks) that reggae musicians endlessly recycle and update - the backbone of the music.

More Axe, Ray Hurford, Geoff Sullivan, Dave Hendley & Colin Moore (Muzik Tree/Black Star 1987).

More Axe 7, Ray Hurford, Ian McCann, David Katz, Ardella Jones & Tero Kaski (Muzik Tree/Black Star 1989).
Interviews and articles taken from the long-running 'Small Axe' fanzine.

Reggae Inna Dancehall Style, Tero Kaski & Pekka Vuorinen (Black Star 1984).
Excellent, in-depth look at Volcano Hi Power Sound System and all its major stars. Fascinating enough at the time, but becoming more and more absorbing as time goes by.

King Jammy's, Beth Lesser (Muzik Tree/Black Star 1989).
One of the best reggae books ever - mainly about Jammy's digital revolution of reggae music, but packed full of insight and anecdotes. Essential.

Discographies

Studio One has dominated the Jamaican music scene since its inception and there are two discographies documenting Coxsone Dodd's recorded works.

Downbeat Special - Studio One Album Discography, Rob Chapman (Self-published 1985).
An illustrated discography detailing Studio One's vast long-playing output.

Never Grow Old - Studio One Singles Listing & Rhythm Directory, Rob Chapman (Self-published 1989).
A very brave attempt to make some kind of sense of Studio One's vast recorded output - a little like painting the Forth Bridge but fascinating nevertheless. Second edition revised and updated in 1992.

Reggae Discography, Hermann Moter (Minotaurus Projekt 1983).
A good attempt. Needs to be updated urgently.

Background Reading

The Rastafarians - The Dreadlocks Of Jamaica, Leonard E. Barrett (Heinemann/Sangsters 1977).

Dread - The Rastafarians Of Jamaica, Joseph Owens (Sangsters 1976).

Rastaman - The Rastafarian Movement In England, Ernest Cashmore (Allen & Unwin 1979).

Rastafari & Reggae - A Dictionary Source Book, Rebekah Michelle (Mulvaney/Greenwood Press 1991).

Jamaica - Babylon On A Thin Wire, Adrian Boot & Michael Thomas (Thames & Hudson 1976).

Jah Revenge - Babylon Revisited, Michael Thomas & Adrian Boot (Eel Pie Publishing 1982).

The Harder They Come, Michael Thelwell (Pluto Press 1980).
A 'novelization' of the film of the same name which actually takes on a life of its own.

The Children Of Sisyphus, Orlando Patterson (Houghton Mifflin 1965).
Another novel that fills in many of the gaps in the music's background.

Beats Of The Heart - Popular Music Of The World, Jeremy Marre & Hannah Charlton (Pluto Press 1985).
Some revealing insights on the making of 'Roots Rock Reggae'.

The How To Be Jamaican Handbook - The Jamrite Cultural Dissemination Committee, Kim Robinson, Harclyde Walcott & Trevor Fearon (Jamrite Publications 1987).
Irreverent, hilarious look at Jamaica & Jamaicans.

The Illustrated Encyclopedia Of Black Music, Various authors (Salamander 1982).
One of the first music encyclopedias that actually took reggae music into account, with some very detailed biographies and potted histories.

Sociology/Anthropology

Reggae has been picked over by sociologists for some time now and there are a growing number of books about what the music means (as opposed to the music itself) and its influence on youth subcultures.

Subculture - The Meaning Of Style, Dick Hebdige (New Accents 1979).

Cut 'N' Mix - Culture, Identity & Caribbean Music, Dick Hebdige (Comedia 1987).

Black Culture From JA To UK - The Reggae Trading From JA To UK, Simon Jones (Macmillan 1988).

Noises In The Blood - Orality Gender & The 'Vulgar' Body Of Jamaican Popular Culture, Carolyn Cooper (Warwick University Caribbean Studies/Macmillan 1993).

Resistance Through Rituals - Youth Subcultures In Post-War Britain, ed. Stuart Hall & Tony Jefferson (Hutchinson 1975).

Magazines

Swing Magazine
Pioneering late 60s/early 70s Jamaican magazine with extensive musical coverage.

Blues & Soul Magazine
In the 70s (for a time) carried a reggae feature every issue - initially by Chris Lane and then by Dave Hendley. These offered the first insights into a neglected and ignored musical form. The best of these were collected in *The Best Of Rebel Music* fanzine. The Blues & Soul features were seminal in that they represented the first time that the music was taken seriously in print.

Black Music Magazine
Also in the 70s, this contained some superb articles by Carl Gayle and some in-depth Jamaican reports.

Reggae Quarterly
The only magazine to cover the dancehall phenomenon of the 80s - put together by Beth Lesser & Dave Kingston from Canada.

Black Echoes (now Echoes)
This newspaper's weekly format offers little scope for in-depth analysis, but its review sections and occasional articles are still well worth reading.

Some reggae fanzines have been worthwhile, such as *Pressure Drop* - although it only ran to two issues in the mid-70s, the second issue still stands the test of time. *Small Axe*, the most committed and longest-serving fanzine, is now in temporary retirement after the release of the innovative *Small Axe Files* series. *Boom Shacka Lacka* was issued in direct response to the lack of roots music coverage in the late 80s and, with the current upsurge of interest in said music, now seems somewhat redundant. There have been more over the years but a couple of the most interesting (and visually appealing) have been in Finnish - *Cool Runnings* - and Japanese - *Riddim* and *Reggae Magazine*. I am unqualified to comment further on them.

Roger Dalke's long-running series of UK label discographies make up in hard information what they lack in grammar and punctuation. Lists of catalogue numbers and record titles rarely appeal to anyone other than seriously involved followers of the music. Particularly useful editions include:

Record Selector 15
Record Selector 16
Record Selector 17

FILMS

A number of reggae films have appeared over the years - the first, Horace Ove's *Reggae,* documented the shows at Wembley in 1970, while *The Harder They Come,* starring Jimmy Cliff, was the catalyst - in many instances even more so than the success of Bob Marley - that started the overground interest in the music. *Rockers, Babylon, Country Man* and *Smile Orange* are all well worth investigating and there is now a vast catalogue of live shows and sound systems available on home video.

Television, too, has produced some interesting programmes. *Reggae From The Edinburgh Festival* has never been repeated since it was first shown in the early 70s. *Deep Roots Music* was a brave attempt to convey the essence of the music, and featured some spellbinding footage. It followed in the footsteps of *Roots Rock Reggae*, which, even though it was accused of being a promotional exercise for recent Virgin signings, was also marvellous in parts and went places no film crew had previously imagined. The director of *Roots Rock Reggae*, Jeremy Marre, also made a film on British Reggae for LWT's *Aquarius* series. His experiences (detailed in the *Beats Of The Heart* book) show the obstacles faced by the music and its followers.

VIDEOS

Bob Marley, inevitably, has had many videos made about his life and music:

Bob Marley - Live At Santa Monica
Bob Marley - One Love Peace Concert - The momentous Kingston concert in 1978.
Legend - The Best Of Bob Marley & The Wailers
Caribbean Nights - A documentary on the life of Bob Marley.
Bob Marley & The Wailers Live At The Rainbow 1977
Time Will Tell - A beautiful cinematic biography.

Peter Tosh was the subject of the *Stepping Razor (Red X)* documentary (1993).

One other notable video:

Various Artists: *This Is Ska*.
Recorded live at Kingston's Sombrero Club in the early 60s, featuring Prince Buster, Jimmy Cliff, the Maytals, the Charmers and Stranger Cole.

Harry Hawkes

INDEX